# ANTITRUST ECONOMICS AT A TIME OF UPHEAVAL:
# Recent Competition Policy Cases on Two Continents

John E. Kwoka, Jr., Tommaso M. Valletti
& Lawrence J. White, eds.

Competition Policy International, 2023

To all my family–those who preceded and made my career possible, and those with me now who have supported me unfailingly
**J.E.K.**

To Charitini, Maria, & Costa: everything makes so much sense because of you
**T.V.**

To David & Kelsey: the best-of-all son and daughter-in-law
**L.J.W.**

All rights reserved.
No photocopying: copyright licences do not apply.
The information provided in this publication is general and may not apply in a specific situation. Legal advice should always be sought before taking any legal action based on the information provided. The publisher accepts no responsibility for any acts or omissions contained herein. Enquiries concerning reproduction should be sent to Competition Policy International at the address below.

Copyright © 2023 by Competition Policy International
140 S. Dearborn, Suite 1000 · Chicago, IL 60603, USA
www.competitionpolicyinternational.com
contact@competitionpolicyinternational.com

Printed in the United States of America

First Printing, 2023

ISBN 978-1-950769-30-8 (Paperback)
ISBN 978-1-950769-31-5 (Electronic)

Names: Kwoka, John E., editor. | Valletti, Tommaso M., editor. | White, Lawrence J., editor.
Title: Antitrust economics at a time of upheaval : recent competition policy cases on two continents / John E. Kwoka, Tommaso M. Valletti, [and] Lawrence J. White, editors.
Description: Chicago : Competition Policy International, 2023.
Identifiers: LCCN 2023908962 (print) | ISBN 978-1-950769-30-8 (paperback) | ISBN 978-1-950769-31-5 (ebook)
Subjects: LCSH: Antitrust law--United States--Cases. | Antitrust law—Europe--Cases. | Consolidation and merger of corporations--Case studies. | Price fixing--Case studies. | Competition, Unfair. | Electronic commerce--Law and legislation. | BISAC: LAW / Antitrust. | BUSINESS & ECONOMICS / Mergers & Acquisitions.
Classification: LCC KF1649 .K861 2023 (print) | LCC KF1649 .K861 2023 (ebook) | DDC 343.072/1--dc23.

Cover and book design by Inesfera. www.inesfera.com

# Preface

The past few years have been a time of upheaval for competition policy on both sides of the Atlantic. And with a reinvigoration of antitrust policy has come a reinvigoration of antitrust economics. We – the three editors of this volume – felt that the time was ripe for a chronicling of these changes.

This book took shape during the spring and summer of 2021. There was a great deal of activity that was occurring in the world of competition policy. Partly this reflected a rising tide of antitrust activity in the United States – at the federal level and also at the state level – as well as the greater attention generally to competition policy by the Biden Administration and its appointees; and partly this reflected a generally more aggressive attitude toward competition policy that had been present in the European Union and the United Kingdom for the previous decade or so.

We wanted to bring this heightened trans-Atlantic level of activity to the attention of practitioners, scholars, and students – in both economics and in law. As has been well documented elsewhere, economics has been an important and rising component of antitrust – directly in cases as well as in academic writings – for well over four decades. Since economics was heavily involved in the activity that we wanted to highlight, we felt that a useful vehicle for our purpose would be to have leading antitrust economists who were involved in recent important antitrust cases – in the U.S., the UK, and the EU – write about those cases and the economics arguments that featured in those cases. Further, since all three of us are economists who have been involved with competition policy and antitrust cases for many decades, this inclination came naturally.

The result is this collection of 18 essays about recent major competition policy cases on both sides of the Atlantic. The cases cover the major areas of modern antitrust: mergers of various kinds; monopolistic (restrictive) practices; and anticompetitive agreements. In all instances the basic economic features of these important cases should be accessible to all readers who have an interest in antitrust. For a few chapters, the authors have provided more detail on the relevant economics in an appendix.

We believe that this book should be useful in undergraduate courses in public policy toward business, in business school courses on public policy, and in law school antitrust courses. We also believe that this book can be a valuable supplement in graduate economics courses that cover antitrust. And we have no doubt that antitrust practitioners – lawyers and economists – on both sides of the Atlantic will be interested in the analyses that are described in these chapters.

Further, we hope that these case studies will be useful for scholars: to help them find motivating examples for their research and to reassess whether their frameworks reasonably fit the reality of cases and judicial decisions or need to be adjusted.

We wish to thank Elisa Ramundo, Sam Sadden, and Andrew Leyden of Competition Policy International for their enthusiastic support for this project from the beginning. And we thank the authors of the chapters in this volume, who have provided interesting and important economics insights in their analyses of these important cases.

# Table of Contents

Dedications ..................................................................................................................iii

Preface ......................................................................................................................v

Editors' Bios ............................................................................................................viii

Authors' Bios ............................................................................................................ix

Introduction .............................................................................................................xii

<u>I. MERGERS</u>

**1. Vertical, Horizontal, and Potential Competition: The Proposed Acquisition of Farelogix by Sabre**
By Chris Doyle, Kostis Hatzitaskos, Kate Maxwell Koegel & Aviv Nevo ......................2

**2. Innovation Concerns in European Merger Control: *Dow/DuPont* and *Bayer/Monsanto***
By Daniel Coublucq, David Kovo & Tommaso Valletti ................................................20

**3. Efficiencies, Remedies, and Competition: The *Sprint/T-Mobile* Merger**
By John Asker & Michael L. Katz ..............................................................................45

**4. Upward Pricing Pressure in Supermarket Mergers: The *UK's Asda/Sainsbury* Case**
By Howard Smith ......................................................................................................72

**5. Evaluating a Theory of Harm in a Vertical Merger: *AT&T/Time Warner***
By Dennis W. Carlton, Georgi V. Giozov, Mark A. Israel & Allan L. Shampine ............90

**6. Bidding Analysis and Innovation Concerns in Merger Control: *General Electric/Alstom***
By Daniel Coublucq & Giulio Federico .....................................................................109

**7. Mergers and Monopsony: The *Anthem-Cigna* Merger**
By David Dranove, Dov Rothman & Samuel Weglein ..............................................132

**8. Cross-Market Hospital Mergers: The *Cedars-Sinai/Huntington Memorial* Litigation**
By Gregory S. Vistnes ............................................................................................151

II. MONOPOLY CONDUCT/ABUSE OF DOMINANCE

**9. A Landmark Antitrust Case in Digital Markets:** *Google Search (Shopping)*
By Andrea Amelio ...............................................................................................168

**10. Market Definition for Two-Sided Markets:** *Ohio v. American Express*
By Michael L. Katz...............................................................................................188

**11. Excessive Pricing as an Antitrust Harm: Three UK Cases in Generic Pharmaceuticals**
By Julie Bon & Mike Walker.................................................................................208

**12. Extension of Its Search Monopoly: The EC Case against Google Android**
By Cristina Caffarra & Federico Etro....................................................................230

**13. Targeted Below-Cost Pricing in the Semiconductor Industry: The** *Qualcomm Predation* **Case**
By Liliane Giardino-Karlinger................................................................................253

**14. Advertising, Customer Data, and Competition: The German** *Facebook* **Case**
By Rupprecht Podszun .........................................................................................276

**15. Using and Misusing Microeconomics:** *Federal Trade Commission v. Qualcomm*
By Carl Shapiro & Keith Waehrer.........................................................................294

**16. Platform Price Parity Clauses: The Hotel Booking Industry**
By Thibaud Vergé.................................................................................................315

III. ANTICOMPETITIVE AGREEMENTS

**17. No-Poaching Agreements as Antitrust Violations: Animation Workers Antitrust Litigation**
By Orley Ashenfelter & Ruth Gilgenbach..............................................................338

**18. Can Four Traders Fix the Price of Money? The Euro-US Dollar Antitrust Litigation**
By Edward A. Snyder............................................................................................361

# Editors' Bios

**John Kwoka** is the Neal F. Finnegan Distinguished Professor of Economics at Northeastern University. He recently served as Chief Economic Advisor to the Chair of the Federal Trade Commission. He previously served at the Antitrust Division of the Justice Department, the Federal Communications Commission, and once before at the FTC. Kwoka's recent research has focused on merger and remedies policy and has resulted in two books: *Mergers, Merger Control, and Remedies and Controlling Mergers and Market Power*.

**Tommaso Valletti** is Professor of Economics at Imperial College London, where he currently heads the Department of Economics & Public Policy. He is the Director of the Centre for Economic Policy Research (CEPR) Research and Policy Network on Competition Policy. He is the Editor of the Journal of Competition Law & Economics. He was the Chief Competition Economist of the European Commission (DG COMP) between 2016 and 2019.

**Lawrence J. White** is the Robert Kavesh Professor of Economics at the Stern School of Business, New York University. He is also the General Editor of the Review of Industrial Organization and has been Secretary-Treasurer of the Western Economic Association International. He has taken leave from NYU to serve in the U.S. Government three times: During 1986-1989 he was a Board Member on the Federal Home Loan Bank Board (and, in that capacity, also a board member for Freddie Mac); during 1982-1983 he was the Chief Economist of the Antitrust Division of the U.S. Department of Justice; and in 1978-1979 he was a Senior Staff Economist on the President's Council of Economic Advisers.

# Authors' Bios

**Andrea Amelio** is an economist and is First Counsellor at the European Union Delegation to the UK covering competition policy and energy. Previously, he coordinated the Chief Economist Team's work on antitrust cases and policy and worked on the review of EU competition regulations in the Antitrust Coordination Unit at the European Commission.

**Orley Ashenfelter** is the Joseph Douglas Green 1895 Professor of Economics at Princeton University. He is a member of the National Academy of Sciences and the American Philosophical Society and is a past-President of the American Economic Association.

**John Asker** is a Professor of Economics at UCLA, where he holds the Armen A. Alchian Chair in Economic Theory. He is an Editor of the *Journal of Political Economy*, a Research Associate at the National Bureau of Economic Research, and a Senior Advisor to Cornerstone Research.

**Julie Bon** is Deputy Chief Economic Adviser at the UK Competition and Markets Authority (CMA). Prior to this, Julie was a Director of Economics at the CMA. She holds a Ph.D. in Economics from the European University Institute in Florence, Italy.

**Cristina Caffarra** is an economic consultant with over 25 years' experience. She has led economic analyses and given expert testimony in multiple landmark cases before the European agencies and courts, and contributed with writing and talks to the global debate on the state of competition policy, and the digital economy in particular. She is a co-founder of the Competition Research Policy Network at CEPR.

**Dennis W. Carlton** is the David McDaniel Keller Professor of Economics Emeritus at the Booth School of Business, Research Associate NBER, Senior Managing Director of Compass Lexecon Inc., and the former Deputy Assistant Attorney General for Economic Analysis, Antitrust Division of the U.S. Department of Justice. His research focuses on industrial organization and antitrust, and he has published widely on these topics.

**Daniel Coublucq** is a Ph.D. Economist and works as a Senior Economist at the European Commission. He has worked on several high-profile merger cases, both at the Chief Economist Team of the European Commission's Competition Directorate and in private practice.

**Chris Doyle** is an Economics Director at the UK Competition and Markets Authority. Previously he was a Principal at RBB Economics.

**David Dranove** is the Walter McNerney Professor of Health Management and Professor of Strategy at Northwestern University's Kellogg School of Management. He is the 2022 recipient of the Victor Fuchs Award given by the American Society of Health Economists for lifetime achievement in the field.

**Federico Etro** is Professor of Economics at the University of Florence, Italy, teaching international economics. His research focuses also on industrial organization and macroeconomics, and he is currently the editor of the *Journal of Cultural Economics*. He has been a consultant on high-profile competition cases involving abuse of dominance, collusive conduct, and mergers in the EU and other jurisdictions.

**Giulio Federico** is a Head of Unit at the European Commission, currently working on post-pandemic recovery packages for member states of the European Union. Prior to his current post, he served for over eight years in the Chief Economist Team of the Competition Directorate of the European Commission, coordinating the economic review of complex mergers and of antitrust investigations. He holds a DPhil in Economics from the University of Oxford.

**Liliane Giardino-Karlinger** is an economist at the European Commission, coordinating the Chief Economist Team's work on antitrust cases and policy. Before joining the European Commission, she held several positions as Assistant Professor in economics at universities in Austria and Italy.

**Ruth Gilgenbach** is a partner at Ashenfelter & Ashmore, an economics consulting firm, and lectures in the Economics Department at Rutgers University. Previously, she was an economist in the antitrust division of the Texas Attorney General.

**Georgi Giozov** is an economic consultant with Compass Lexecon, where he serves as a Senior Vice President specializing in applied econometrics and antitrust economics. He holds a B.A. in Economics, *summa cum laude*, from Connecticut College and a Master's degree in Applied Economics from Johns Hopkins University.

**Kostis Hatzitaskos** is a Vice President at Cornerstone Research's Chicago office and co-head of its antitrust and competition practice. He consults with merging parties and government agencies in merger investigations and litigation.

**Mark Israel** is a Senior Managing Director at Compass Lexecon, and a member of the four-person Global Executive Committee that runs the firm worldwide. His work is entirely focused on industrial organization economics, through a combination of expert and consulting work and an active ongoing research agenda focused on antitrust and merger topics.

**Michael L. Katz** is the Sarin Chair Emeritus in Strategy and Leadership in the Haas School of Business and Distinguished Professor Emeritus in the Department of Economics, both at the University of California, Berkeley. He is also a Senior Fellow in the Office of Healthcare Transformation of the Singapore Ministry of Health.

**Kate Maxwell Koegel** is a manager at Cornerstone Research's Chicago office and works on antitrust, competition, and labor matters. As part of her work in the antitrust and competition practice, she consults with merging parties and government agencies in merger investigations and litigation.

**David Kovo** is a Member of the Chief Economist team of DG Competition at the European Commission since 2014. He is also a Visiting Professor of competition economics at the College of Europe since 2019. He has previously held economist positions in the Economic Consulting team of Deloitte LLP in London and in the UK Office of Fair Trading (currently the Competition and Markets Authority).

**Aviv Nevo** is the George A. Weiss and Lydia Bravo Weiss Penn Integrates Knowledge Professor at the University of Pennsylvania with appointments at the Wharton School and Department of Economics. He previously served as the Deputy Assistant Attorney General for Economic Analysis in the U.S. Department of Justice Antitrust Division, and is currently serving as the Director of the Bureau of Economics at the U.S. Federal Trade Commission.

**Rupprecht Podszun** is a law professor at Heinrich Heine University Düsseldorf, Germany, and the director of the University's Institute for Competition Law.

**Dov Rothman** is a managing principal at Analysis Group. He has served on the faculty of Columbia University and has worked as an expert economist on behalf of the U.S. Department of Justice and Federal Trade Commission as well as on matters before them.

**Allan Shampine** is an Executive Vice President at Compass Lexecon.

**Carl Shapiro** is a Distinguished Professor of the Graduate School at the University of California at Berkeley. He twice served as the Deputy Assistant Attorney General for Economics at the Antitrust Division of the U.S. Department of Justice, during 2009-2011 and during 1995-96.

**Howard Smith** is an Associate Professor in the Department of Economics at the University of Oxford. He is a member of the Academic Advisory Group at the Competition and Markets Authority, an associate at the Institute for Fiscal Studies, and a fellow of the Center for Economic Policy Research.

**Edward A. Snyder** is the William S. Beinecke Professor of Economics and Management at Yale School of Management. He conducts research on Industrial Organization topics and teaches *Economic Analysis of High-Tech Industries*.

**Thibaud Vergé** is Vice-President at the Autorité de la Concurrence (Paris) and Professor of Economics at ENSAE Paris (on leave). He holds an engineering degree from Ecole Polytechnique and a Ph.D. from the Toulouse School of Economics.

**Gregory Vistnes** is a Vice President at Charles River Associates and formerly held senior positions at both the Federal Trade Commission and the DOJ's Antitrust Division. One of his specialties is analyzing competition in the healthcare sector.

**Keith Waehrer** has consulted for government agencies and private clients in a wide range of industries. He has held positions in the Antitrust Division of the U.S. Department of Justice and private consulting firms. He is currently a Managing Direct at Secretariat Economists.

**Mike Walker** has been the Chief Economic Advisor at the UK's Competition and Markets Authority since 2013. Prior to that he worked in private practice for CRA.

**Samuel Weglein** is a Managing Principal of Analysis Group, based in Boston. He focuses on competition in healthcare, financial, and technology markets.

# INTRODUCTION

The role of economics in competition policy – or as it is called in the U.S., antitrust policy – has undergone a profound upheaval in recent times. The extended period in which a relatively free-market approach dominated U.S. policy has been challenged in the early 2020s by a more eclectic economic perspective and increasingly replaced by a more activist enforcement policy. European and British enforcement agencies never subscribed so fully to the free market approach; consequently, practice there has always provided an instructive alternative model for competition policy.

This book chronicles what might be described as the first wave of this economic and policy upheaval: 18 important antitrust cases that are at the forefront of this upheaval. Many of these cases would likely not have been brought at all – or not in the same fashion or in the same countries – in past years. Some of these cases have arisen in the U.S. – the original home of antitrust – while other noteworthy cases in this book have been brought in the EU and the UK.

We emphasize that all of the case studies in this book are focused on *economics*: the economic underpinnings of the allegations of the case; the economic framework and evidence that was employed; and the economic logic of the case resolution. Underscoring this perspective, we have sought in each case to have as an author an economist or economists who were involved in the case in some significant way, either in a supervisory role at one of the antitrust agencies, or as an academic or professional consultant to one party (enforcement agency or company) in the case. As a result each author provides an account that is unparalleled in its insight and accuracy – all the while being careful to explain both sides of the economic issues. For these reasons the case studies in this book capture this important moment in competition policy in major jurisdictions.

## FORCES FOR CHANGE

This upheaval in antitrust has been the outgrowth of several major forces. The first and perhaps the most important of these has been many economists' reaction to the "Chicago School" of free-market economics that took hold a half century ago. That earlier school of thought analyzed the purposes and methods of antitrust policy from a strict economics perspective, and thereby ultimately shifted antitrust from a largely legal doctrine to an economic-efficiency-oriented policy. Economics became a tool for understanding the meaning of competition and interpreting business practices and consolidation in light of their efficiency consequences. Mergers were increasingly viewed as pro-competitive, while traditional concerns with, for example, predatory pricing, vertical integration, and conglomerate effects were dismissed or were subject to stringent tests that few claims could satisfy. This approach narrowed the lens through which antitrust viewed competition problems.

Over time that paradigm has been challenged by a new body of academic work on competition that has rebuilt the foundations of some of the pre-Chicago theories. This new work has ensured that the older approaches can meet contemporary standards of "rationality" and logic, and has developed newer theories to be tested empirically and employed in policy determinations where appropriate. Over a considerable period of time, this new economic learning gained credibility and adherents, and moved into the mainstream of competition economics. It has increasingly provided the basis for the analysis of competitive concerns that the Chicago School had dismissed.

A second major force for change has been a growing body of evidence of the effects of this relatively permissive approach toward mergers and monopoly practices. In the U.S. in particular, there has been a documented decline in enforcement against all but the most obviously anticompetitive mergers – those resulting in only two or three firms. And even when mergers were challenged, they were often allowed to proceed after the enforcement agencies imposed "behavioral remedies" that sought to make the merged firm's managers act against their natural interests; it was not surprising that the merged firm would then try (and often succeed) to find ways around these restrictions.

Similarly, evidence mounted that both mergers and monopoly practices by the major tech companies have gone almost entirely unchallenged, and often unexamined. Amazon, Google, Facebook, Apple, and Microsoft have collectively acquired nearly one thousand companies and engaged in a variety of competitively questionable business practices – including self-preferencing, misuse of data, tying, and foreclosing practices. Until recently these had not been challenged in the U.S. and other major antitrust jurisdictions.

In addition, there has been a growing realization that the exercise of monopsony power – market power that is exercised by buyers, as a consequence of a merger or of just a strong buyer position, or an agreement or understanding among buyers (including employers of workers) – could also be a problem in relevant markets. Although antitrust enforcers have always acknowledged that the antitrust laws covered monopsony and have known that – in principle – buyer power could be an area of concern, there was little actual attention to monopsony issues.

Overall, this accommodating enforcement posture has been associated with: increasing concentration in many markets; the largely unchecked rise of dominant companies, particularly in the tech sector; reductions in new-firm startups and entrants into major markets; abnormally high margins and profits; and declines in many measures of competition throughout the economy. While some observers interpret the evidence differently and still approve this hands-off approach, others view this deep-seated faith in the market with concern and have sought to reinvigorate antitrust policy in the U.S.

At the same time, an important third force for change has been the contrasting approach to competition policy that has been pursued in the EU and the UK (as compared with the U.S.). Those jurisdictions never subscribed to the strong efficiency-first standard that characterized U.S. policy from the early 1980s onward – partly because their mandates focused more on protecting the competitive process (which would ultimately benefit consumers) than on the supposed efficiencies of the predicted outcomes As a result, the EU Directorate General for Competition (DG Comp) and the UK Competition and Markets Authority (CMA) have used their different authority and procedures to examine and sometimes challenge practices and mergers that in the U.S. would not have been challenged.

For example, concern over predatory pricing and other predatory practices, vertical mergers, innovation concerns, and portfolio ("conglomerate") effects have all been given closer attention by DG Comp and the CMA. Allegations of predatory conduct and vertical foreclosure are viewed more holistically in these jurisdictions rather than measured against the specific price-cost, recoupment, and foreclosure tests that have been used (and in some cases, required by the courts) in the U.S. And certain tech company practices have been viewed more critically and challenged in Europe – although much as in the U.S., there is debate as to whether the remedies that are often employed against those companies have in fact been effective in preserving or restoring competition.

In the merger area, too, cases have been viewed differently – occasionally to the point of public disagreement between the U.S. and European authorities – but more recently these differences have narrowed. Indeed, all three jurisdictions have issued guidelines that describe their procedures and standards for evaluating mergers, and over time and iterations these guidelines have converged in substance and approach. Reflecting this convergence, the agencies now routinely confer about mergers that are reported to two or more of the agencies. Yet differences remain: again due to differences in what the jurisdictions believe to be antitrust offenses, in the burdens of proof, and (at times) in the objectives themselves.

Because of these forces, there is now much ferment in competition policy worldwide. Reflecting this, all of the major antitrust agencies in these jurisdictions – the FTC and the DOJ in the U.S. from 2021 onward, plus DG Comp in the EU and the CMA in the UK – have made clear by their leadership, statements, and actions their determination to pursue a different approach in the face of ongoing competition concerns. No longer does traditional economic thinking about the virtues of the market eliminate concern over competitive problems; instead, a broader and more modern framework is to be used in making those assessments. And with differences still present among jurisdictions, it is no longer sufficient simply to examine what is happening in any single jurisdiction; at present, major initiatives often originate in the EU or the UK.

## AN OVERVIEW OF THE AREAS COVERED

As was noted above, this book chronicles this upheaval in antitrust policy and the new initiatives that it has spawned. It does so by compiling 18 important antitrust cases of recent years in the major jurisdictions, with key individuals' explaining the economic and policy issues of each case and how these issues were debated and addressed by the relevant enforcement agency or the reviewing court, and finally assessing the merits of that resolution from an economic perspective.[1]

---

[1] We believe that it is important to note that all of the chapter contributors were asked to provide balanced accounts of their cases, rather than advocacy documents.

The case studies in this book fall roughly into the three broad categories that were outlined above: mergers; monopoly practices; and price fixing.[2] Here we briefly introduce the broad topics and highlight their distinctive importance in the antitrust upheaval.

## *Mergers*

As was noted above, mergers have increasingly been evaluated with the use of similar standards and techniques in all jurisdictions. In both the U.S. and the EU, the standard involves a substantial or significant lessening of competition. In virtually all jurisdictions, this is operationalized through the use of public guidelines or guidance.[3] In all jurisdictions, market shares and concentration are relevant, as are the closeness of the firms' products (measured by diversion) and other factors that are well known in economics and from experience to be important in assessing the strength of competition. Specifics vary with the type of mergers: horizontal (between direct competitors); vertical (between firms at different stages of production); or otherwise related.

Included in this case book are important examples of mergers in the U.S., the EU, and the UK that raise new issues or issues that had been long overlooked across these major jurisdictions. Their new treatment is the subject of these case studies.

## *Monopoly Conduct*

Monopoly conduct – or as it is called in most countries, abuse of dominance – encompasses a range of practices by a dominant company to defend or extend its market position against encroachment by a prospective or rising competitor. Specific practices include: predatory pricing and related conduct; foreclosing a rival's access to necessary inputs or to crucial distribution outlets; constructing barriers to entry (including access to inputs or distribution outlets); excessive pricing; or leveraging dominance in one market into another through tying or bundling strategies.

The range of practices is matched by the number of analytical frameworks that are necessary to examine them. Few of these frameworks lend themselves to bright line tests; consequently, economic analyses often encounter difficulties in distinguishing between fairly normal business behavior and truly anticompetitive conduct. This can lead to protracted economic disputes and lengthy legal or administrative proceedings.

Moreover, different jurisdictions view many of these practices quite differently: The U.S. has adopted more specific and stringent tests for finding antitrust violations than have most other jurisdictions. Predatory pricing, for example, has been defined by the U.S. Supreme Court as necessarily requiring pricing below some appropriate measure of cost together with the prospect of recoupment by the alleged predator. The standards in the UK and the EU differ from that of the U.S.: The former standards allow for a more holistic approach to judging the competitive effects – and thereby arguably allow for other economic theories of predation.

---

2 And, again, the concerns about market power in some of the cases extend to the exercise of monopsony power.

3 These are currently undergoing revision in the U.S. and they have recently been updated in the UK.

These issues – and some novel approaches – are apparent in the cases on monopoly practices in this book across the three jurisdictions.

### *Anticompetitive Agreements*

Price-fixing agreements and similar distortions of observed competitive variables – quantities, market shares, advertising, etc. – are almost always per se violations of antitrust in nearly all jurisdictions. The rationale for this strong enforcement approach is that there are almost never any compensating benefits from allowing direct competitors to act collectively. But pricing and other distortions also take many other, generally more subtle forms; and while these latter are more difficult to assess, they are important in practice as well as interesting in economics.

The cases here illustrate some new issues and initiatives by antitrust authorities to prevent anticompetitive pricing distortions – both straightforward efforts by companies but also less direct methods for altering price competition. Along the way, these cases also illustrate how different jurisdictions sometimes view pricing practices quite differently.

## CONCLUSION

In sum, the accounts of the 18 important cases in this book provide a window into modern economic thinking about an array of antitrust issues that have been addressed across two continents. The economic insights that are provided by the authors of these case studies will surely provide a useful guide for a better understanding of antitrust at this time of upheaval.

# I. MERGERS

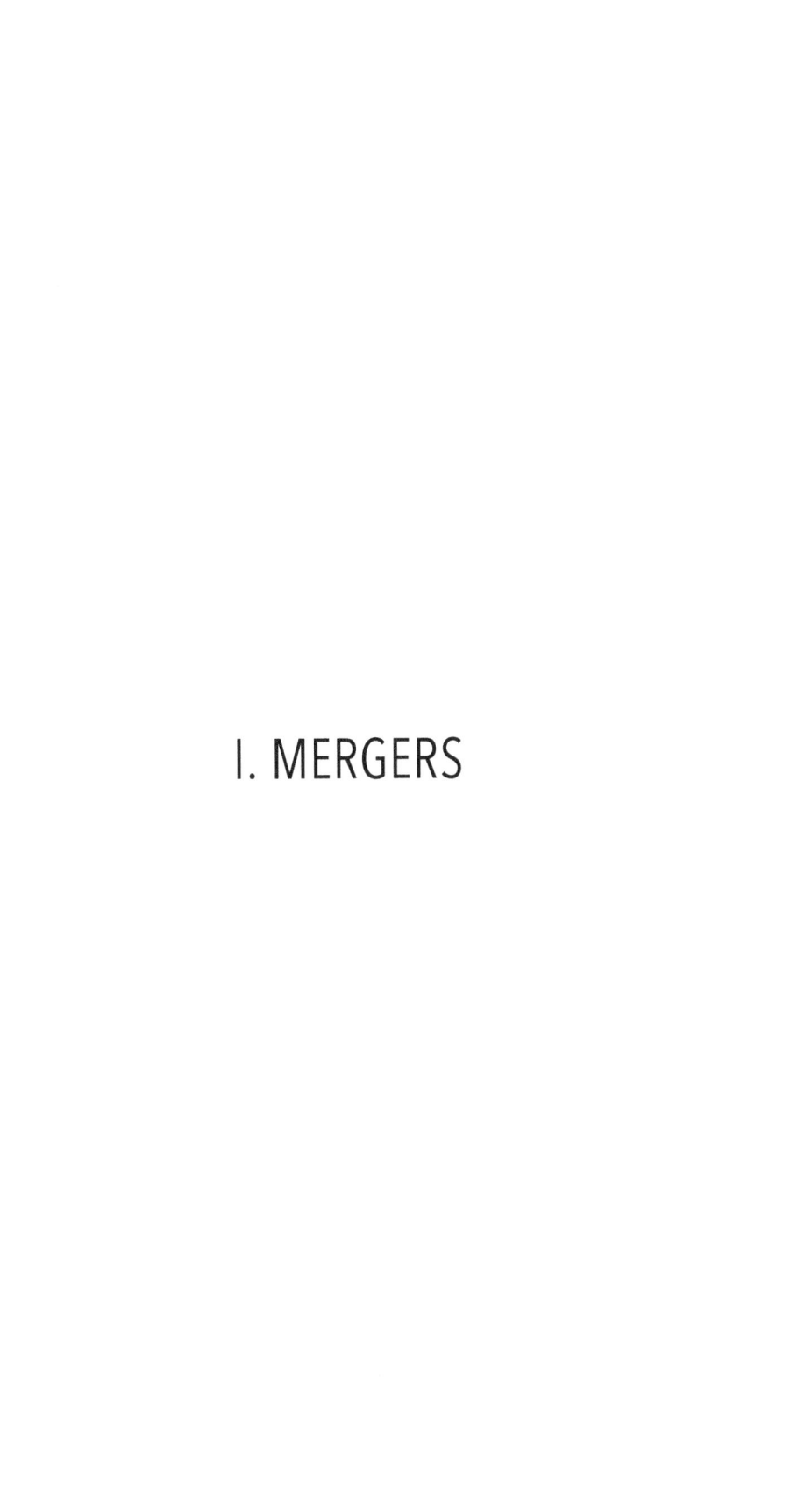

# CHAPTER 1

# Vertical, Horizontal, and Potential Competition: The Proposed Acquisition of Farelogix by Sabre

By Chris Doyle, Kostis Hatzitaskos, Kate Maxwell Koegel & Aviv Nevo[1]

## I. INTRODUCTION

On November 14, 2018, Sabre Corporation announced an agreement to acquire Farelogix, Inc. for $360 million. Sabre is a global distribution system, a company that compiles information from airlines, supplies this information to travel agents who book flights and complete other transactions through its interface. Farelogix is a technology company that sells various technology services to airlines.

The proposed merger was investigated by both the U.S. Department of Justice ("DOJ") and the UK Competition and Markets Authority ("CMA"). The DOJ challenged the merger, which led to a two-week trial in January and February of 2020 in the United States District Court for the District of Delaware (the U.S. Court). The U.S. Court ruled against the DOJ on April 7, 2020.[2] Two days later, the CMA issued its final report: The CMA concluded that the proposed merger would lead to a Substantial Lessening of Competition.[3] The merging parties abandoned their merger shortly thereafter: on May 1, 2020. In this chapter we discuss the economic analysis of the merger across both the DOJ and CMA reviews.

While this proposed merger was relatively small, as measured by the acquisition price, it has many of the characteristics of acquisitions in the modern economy; consequently, there are potentially broad lessons to be learned: For example, in today's digital economy, firms are connected through various complex complementary and rivalrous relationships – often simultaneously. This means that mergers might not be neatly classified into vertical or horizontal. Furthermore, these relationships are

---

[1] Dr Doyle was the Economics Director on the UK Competition and Market Authority's case team. Professor Nevo was the U.S. Department of Justice economic expert for Sabre/Farelogix. Drs. Hatzitaskos and Koegel supported him. The views expressed in this article are solely those of the authors and are not purported to reflect the views of Cornerstone Research, the U.S. Department of Justice, or the CMA. This chapter was written before Nevo joined the U.S. Federal Trade Commission ("FTC"), and the views expressed herein are those of the authors and do not necessarily reflect the views of the FTC or any individual Commissioner.

[2] *See* U.S. District Court for the District of Delaware (2020) for the public decision.

[3] *See* CMA (2020b) for its final report.

fast evolving and are often resistant to the application of traditional antitrust tools – which forces a careful consideration of the nature of competition and innovation within the context of an industry. Indeed, many of the competitive impacts might involve a harm to innovation: This is an area that is well known to be difficult to prove. This means that one might need some faith in interpreting historical evidence, and the application of historical standards of proof might make blocking some mergers a nearly impossible task.

The proposed merger of Sabre and Farelogix provides one example of the challenges with regard to how industries sometimes defy conventional antitrust classifications and require complex economic consideration of the truly relevant market facts. It highlights the difficulties that enforcement agencies are likely to face in bringing cases that involve potential competition and harm to innovation. Our goal – beyond describing the specifics of the case – is to highlight these difficulties and draw broader conclusions.

We organize our discussion as follows: In the next section, we discuss industry background and the basic facts of the case. Next, we discuss the economic arguments that were made by the U.S. and UK agencies against the merger, followed by the arguments that were made by the merging parties in favor of the merger. We then summarize the outcome and subsequent developments. We conclude with some takeaways from the case.

## II. BACKGROUND OF THE INDUSTRY AND CASE

The Sabre-Farelogix proposed merger occurred in a market for services that is essential for the modern travel industry. Although global distribution systems companies ("GDSs") are involved in processing almost all of the airline bookings that are made through travel agencies, these large firms are almost invisible to the end consumer. GDSs are third-party software companies that compile information from many airlines and supply this information to travel agents who book flights and complete other transactions through the GDS interface. GDSs emerged in the 1960s as an intermediary between airlines and travel agents and still play that role today.

Today, travel agencies can be classified into two main forms: traditional travel agencies ("TTAs"); and online travel agencies ("OTAs"). TTAs are mostly business travel agencies, also known as "travel management companies" ("TMCs"), boutique travel agencies, etc., and they still use GDSs to book flights. TMCs in particular are important customers for airlines as they represent business travelers who tend to be relatively price-insensitive. OTAs – such as Expedia and Travelocity – arose alongside TTAs as personal computers and the internet became more ubiquitous, and have given travelers an additional option through which to shop for and book flights. Widespread access to technology also enabled airlines to sell tickets directly to consumers through their own websites, which we will refer to as "airline.com." The resulting system – which is the current state of the industry – is a mix of the "direct channel" (the airlines' websites) along with the "indirect channel" (TTAs and OTAs), almost all of which still maintain connections to the airlines through the GDSs.

The related, yet distinct, services that GDSs offer to airlines and travel agents are typically offered as a bundle: First, in response to a query by a travel agent, a GDS accesses the airlines' databases to construct an "offer" from a specific airline. Next, the GDS aggregates offers across airlines, so that travel agents do not need to query multiple airlines separately. Finally, the GDS offers an interface that delivers these aggregated offers to travel agents; allows the agent to make a booking; and (after an agent makes a booking) the interface allows the agent to adjust the bookings as needed. The DOJ referred to this last step – the facilitation, processing, and modification of bookings – as "booking services," and used it as its proposed antitrust market.[4]

Even as GDSs have grown significantly over the years and digital technology overall greatly improved in the early 21st century, the core GDS offerings – of offer creation, aggregation, and booking services that GDSs offered at the time of the proposed merger – were relatively unchanged by new technology, which was an area of dissatisfaction for airlines.

Sabre is one of three large GDSs providers, with U.S. revenue in 2018 of about $3.9 billion. At the time of the merger, Sabre accounted for over 50 percent of bookings through U.S. travel agencies and an even larger share of the sales through the TMCs that were often used by business travelers at the time of the merger.

In contrast, Farelogix is a much smaller travel technology company that sold various technology services to airlines and was recognized as an industry innovator. In 2018, its revenues were roughly $42 million. This was around 1 percent of Sabre's revenue and a little over 10 percent of the $360 million that Sabre agreed to pay to acquire Farelogix. Despite its small size, Farelogix was a noted innovator in the industry: it developed standards and products that introduced new capabilities to an industry where little had changed over time. The existing GDSs, on the other hand, had a reputation for being slow to adopt new technology.

In an attempt to improve upon the outdated offerings of GDSs, Farelogix engineered and adopted a technology standard: the "New Distribution Capability" ("NDC"). At a high level, the NDC standard used modern software, as compared to some of the legacy software that was used by GDSs. Farelogix made the source code for NDC public and free.

This new technology standard enabled Farelogix to create NDC-compatible applications that allowed it to improve upon current booking services but also to offer merchandising services. The inclusion of merchandising services in airline bookings allows airlines to create offers with a wide range of ancillary services such as: extra luggage allowance; the option to upgrade seats; make in-flight purchases; and add extras, such as airport parking and meal options. As we will discuss below, the NDC technology could in principle be used to replace parts of the GDS bundle of services, and could work together with other services that are provided by the GDS, which is called "GDS pass-through." Alternatively, NDC could be used to generate components that together could create a bundle that would largely replace the GDS, which is called "GDS bypass."

---

4  Clark, Lien & Wilder (2021, p. 657).

Consistent with their history of being resistant to innovation and change, the GDSs were initially slow to adopt the NDC standard and facilitate the distribution of NDC content on their platforms. However, in more recent years they have been investing in this area, in what appears in part to be a response to the threat of airlines' using NDC distribution solutions such as those of Farelogix to bypass the GDSs entirely or to reduce the central role of the GDSs in the industry. As a result, the whole industry was beginning to undergo a lengthy and complex process of far-reaching change.

However, the limitations of the outdated software and technology that were used by GDSs meant at the time of the proposed merger that airlines had a limited ability to distribute personalized offers with ancillary products within the indirect channel – despite growing demand to do so. Airlines especially value this service, as ancillary products present opportunities for high-margin revenue.

Two Farelogix products were the focus of the economic analysis: First, Farelogix offered booking services to airlines through its "Open Connect" ("OC") product. This product allowed airlines either to establish direct relationships with travel agents outside of a GDS or to continue to use the GDS's other services but substitute Farelogix technology for the GDS's booking service functionality: In essence, Farelogix's OC allowed either GDS bypass or GDS pass-through. Whether through GDS bypass or pass-through, Farelogix OC facilitated the disintermediation of the GDS bundle, as it allowed airlines to attempt either to bypass the GDS entirely or to reduce its significance.

Second, Farelogix supplied "FLX M": a merchandising solution that allowed airlines to create offers with a wide range of ancillary services such as extra luggage allowance, the option to upgrade their seat, in-flight purchases, airport parking, or meal options. This was particularly important in the context of an industry shift towards personalization and the sale of ancillaries, which provide new revenue opportunities for airlines. Sabre had its own merchandising solutions – "Dynamic Retailer" and "Ancillary Services" – but these had more limited functionality.

## III. THE ECONOMIC ARGUMENTS AGAINST THE MERGER

The competitive concerns with the merger were centered on two services: distribution and merchandising. In each of these areas, the competitive concerns stemmed from Farelogix's role as an innovator in contrast to the staid GDS offerings.

### A. Competitive Concerns: Distribution

Given this broader industry dynamic, both the DOJ and CMA expressed concern that the proposed merger would lessen competition in "booking services," as the DOJ termed it, or in "distribution solutions," as the CMA referred to it.

Generally, there was the concern that the merger would represent the elimination of a horizontal competitor because Farelogix and Sabre competed directly in booking services. In addition to the "standard" concerns from a loss of a competitor, this elimination carried with it two additional potential outcomes: First, the elimination of Farelogix from the booking services market would harm the bargaining position of airlines *vis-à-vis* the GDSs in an industry that was characterized by long-term contracts and relatively little price competition. Without the potential of using Farelogix, airlines may have faced higher GDS prices. Second, given Farelogix's history of innovation, Sabre's history of low adaption, and the potential for Farelogix's technology to disintermediate the GDSs, there was concern that the acquisition of Farelogix could lead to an overall decrease in innovation in the booking services market.

In arguing that the elimination of Farelogix as an independent company would harm the bargaining position of airlines, the DOJ examined how the prices for the GDS services were determined in the past. Every five to ten years, the GDSs and airlines would negotiate contracts that would determine the pricing for the following period. The DOJ examined how the outcome of these negotiations changed over time, especially as the leverage of airlines changed.[5] The negotiations were not frequent enough and the data were too coarse to allow for a formal econometric analysis. However, the observed outcomes combined with supporting documentary evidence offered a pattern of the airlines utilizing the threat of using Farelogix to obtain more favorable terms from Sabre.

The 2005-2006 round of negotiations was the first in which airlines were able to use the threat of services such as Farelogix to disintermediate the GDSs and reduce their central role in distribution. In particular, Farelogix's Open Connect product allowed airlines either to bypass the GDS by directly connecting with travel agents, or to use Open Connect to offer enhanced content to travel agents while still using the GDS (GDS pass-through). Indeed, with the new presence of Farelogix, the airlines were able to avoid price increases and instead retain the *status quo*.

By the next round of negotiations in 2011-2012, Farelogix was the only firm that offered an alternative for booking services, and the airlines managed – again – to avoid price increases.[6] This outcome suggests that Farelogix provided a meaningful competitive constraint on the GDSs. Without the threat of relying more heavily on Farelogix, the airlines might have been unable to negotiate for lower pricing, or to pressure the GDSs to innovate. Consistent with this observation, the airlines indicated that they were concerned and provided testimony that opposed the merger.

The DOJ argued, based on these past outcomes, the documentary evidence, and testimony by some of the airlines, that the elimination of Farelogix as the only credible alternative in booking services would put the airlines in a worse bargaining position and therefore lead to higher prices and worse terms of trade.

In addition to the harm to bargaining power, the DOJ and CMA were concerned about the central role that Farelogix played in spurring GDS innovation and disruption. The factual record was clear that Farelogix introduced updated standards and technology to an industry that traditionally maintained old data infrastructure and

---

[5] The detailed price data are not part of the public record, but the pattern over time was discussed in open court.

[6] That the airlines used Farelogix as leverage to obtain lower pricing was even acknowledged by the merging parties' expert in a contemporaneous white paper that was discussed at trial (U.S. District Court, 2020).

had little competitive pressure to change. By contrast, the GDS product offering did not change much over time and was based on outdated technology. Farelogix was one of the only industry entities that offered more advanced technology, which as we discussed earlier, gave airlines more flexibility.

Previous technological acquisitions by the existing GDSs had not yielded industry change, and the GDSs showed consistent lack of investment in NDC. Thus, the DOJ and CMA argued that the possibility that Sabre would acquire Farelogix and fail to invest further was consistent with its prior conduct. It was the DOJ and CMA's view that Farelogix – if left independent of the GDSs – would continue to innovate and push the industry forward, which would force the GDSs to invest.

The DOJ's concerns were based on basic economic logic and models and in many ways seemed straightforward. Yet there were no data to conduct any meaningful econometric analysis or to estimate substitution patterns by the end costumers. Indeed, as we discuss below, it was not easy to define and measure the relevant prices. Therefore, the DOJ's case was based on the merging firms' own documents, which often referred to each other as competitors, and on historical outcomes in contract negotiations, some of which happened more than a decade earlier.

As is the case in many mergers that involve concerns with respect to future competition, computing shares was not easy and had to rely on Sabre's pre-merger predictions. This meant that some of the standard analyses in merger cases were difficult to perform. For example, even conducting the "hypothetical monopolist test" was not trivial since Sabre did not offer booking services as a stand-alone product and therefore it was not clear what price to use as the base in this test.

All of the concerns that we have discussed so far are horizontal in nature: The DOJ chose to define a booking services market that focused on the component of the GDS bundle that Farelogix most directly replaced. In that framework, Farelogix and Sabre competed to provide the same service to airlines, and this was competition that would be eliminated as a consequence of the merger.

An alternative way to express the concerns over the merger is to interpret the merger as vertical or "diagonal." (Sweeting & Corus (2021)).[7] Under this view Farelogix could be seen as providing an important input to a self-supply channel for airlines; this self-supply could be considered to be a downstream rival of Sabre – even if Farelogix could be considered to be upstream of Sabre. It is arguably through this channel that Farelogix's services challenged its GDS rivals, by allowing airlines to rely less wholly on GDSs by using elements of Farelogix to enhance the airline.com experience, instead of directly through horizontal competition. The merger would have eliminated this channel and left GDSs as the only option, which would thus increase their bargaining leverage over the airlines.

Whether one approaches the merger as horizontal, vertical, or diagonal, the concern articulated by both agencies was that the merger would lessen competition in

---

[7] A diagonal merger is defined as one where a downstream firm acquires an upstream supplier from which the downstream firm does not purchase inputs but which supplies inputs to one or more of its downstream rivals.

distribution. Evidence from Sabre itself indicated that it competed with Farelogix in some market or manner – albeit difficult to define – in that Sabre recognized Farelogix as a competitive constraint in the past and saw opportunities to raise prices in the future if the merger were to remove that constraint.

## B. Competitive Concerns: Merchandising

In addition to the concerns with respect to distribution, the CMA also investigated in detail the impact of the merger on merchandising; this was not part of the DOJ's case.[8] Interestingly, there was a role reversal over which firm had the higher market share in this segment of the business, which was outside the GDS bundle: Farelogix was widely regarded as offering a best-in-class product, which was used by several of the world's largest airlines. In contrast, Sabre's offering was weak: Its functionality was limited, and a lack of interoperability meant that it could be used only by airlines that were also users of Sabre's other IT solutions. As a result, Sabre had a small share of merchandising.

The CMA was concerned that – while a standalone Sabre would expand to become a strong competitor in merchandising and meet the threat that was posed by Farelogix – the merged firm would abandon these independent development efforts. It was therefore based on a dynamic counterfactual, rather than simply adopting pre-merger conditions, and focused on the loss of innovation by the acquiring firm, rather than the target.

This type of concern – which the CMA has investigated in a number of other cases – has been dubbed by some commentators as a "reverse killer acquisition."[9] These tend to arise when large established companies acquire a leading provider of an emerging product category that increasingly interacts with their existing offering, whether as a complement or through displacing it for certain uses.[10] In such circumstances the incumbent may identify the need to be active in this emerging product segment as a strategic priority in order to support or defend their existing revenues, with a purchase of the leading provider the most straightforward way to achieve this. Given the powerful incentives – which after all have been substantial enough to drive the spending of hundreds of millions of dollars on the merger under investigation – it is far from clear that absent this the incumbent would simply do nothing.

The CMA's case was therefore focused on Sabre's incentives: The CMA argued that Sabre had a strong incentive to improve its merchandising offering in order to protect the substantial revenues from its GDS. The Authority noted that a GDS generates value not only by distributing content but also by performing offer-creation functions: combining price, schedule, and availability content for the airlines. However, with the emergence of new retailing models that were based on the NDC standard, the airlines were increasingly able to undertake the offer-creation function themselves, which potentially relegated the GDS to the role of merely transmitting information. More

---
8  For an extended discussion of the CMA's merchandising concerns, *see* Bon et al. (2021).

9  Caffarra, Crawford & Valletti (2020).

10  Similar issues were also examined in the CMA's investigations into *PayPal/iZettle* and *Amazon/Deliveroo*, *see* CMA (2019) and CMA (2020a).

generally, the CMA believed that Sabre had an incentive to develop a stand-alone merchandising solution that could interoperate with a range of IT systems, which would allow it to expand its customer base beyond the users of its other services.

The evidence that the CMA used to support this view of Sabre's incentives included Sabre's public statements to investors with regard to its rationale for the deal and its internal documents. These made clear that Sabre had an existing "Next Generation Retailing" strategy that included a new and more competitive merchandising solution based on NDC technology. They also showed that one of the synergies of the deal that Sabre identified was saving investment that would otherwise be required to improve its own merchandising product.

In addition to having the incentive, the CMA also argued that Sabre would have had the ability to improve its offering, and therefore that this (counterfactual) expansion would be successful. It highlighted Sabre's considerable industry experience, widespread customer relationships, and ability to offer the enhanced merchandising product alongside its range of related IT solutions. More specifically, it emphasized the fact that Sabre had already been investing in related technology and begun making proposals to airlines, which then demonstrated its own confidence in its innovation efforts. As a result, the CMA argued that Sabre would have been likely to become a significant competitor in merchandising within the next three to five years.

Of course, the fact that Sabre would have been a competitor to Farelogix might not be sufficient to establish that the merger would have been anticompetitive. As in any merger case, there would be less cause for concern if sufficient competitors remain. However, the CMA argued that the merged entity would face only a single major rival in merchandising – Amadeus – so that the transaction would reduce the number of major entities from three to two.

This was based largely on an assessment of rivals' technology (only a limited number offered NDC-compatible merchandising solutions), airlines' views, and some evidence from bidding data. The latter showed that Farelogix had won three times as many bids as any other individual competitor, though given the small number of tenders and wide variation in the scale of contracts, it placed as much weight on understanding the profile of firms' customers. The CMA found that, while Farelogix's customer base included some of the largest airlines in the world, and it had continued to win, negotiate, and renew major contracts, the size of contracts won by rivals were less significant.

## IV. THE ECONOMIC ARGUMENTS IN SUPPORT OF THE MERGER

The merging parties' arguments in support of the merger involved distribution and merchandising – but also Farelogix's broad place in the travel industry. The parties viewed the merger as non-threatening to competition in distribution and asserted that Farelogix's role as an innovator in distribution would be a complement to the existing GDS system. The merging parties further argued that Farelogix's merchandising system would allow Sabre to add services in a pro-competitive manner.

## A. Arguments for the Merger: Distribution

To address the concerns raised on distribution, the merging parties countered with various arguments that there would be no substantial lessening of competition. One of their primary conceits was that the merging parties were not actually in competition with one another at all.

In the U.S. litigation, the merging parties took issue with the DOJ's proposed market: First, they argued that "booking services" do not exist as a separate product. Executives from the merging parties testified that they do not use the term, that Sabre has never charged a separate fee for booking services, and that separating these services from other GDS services was an artificial construct that was created by the DOJ. Instead, they argued that they see the GDS as a monolithic bundle that simultaneously provides several services to both airlines and travel agents.

Second, the merging parties argued that if Farelogix offered booking services and the GDS did not, then the merging parties simply did not compete with one another. Sabre offered services to – and had customer relationships with – both airlines and travel agents, and therefore it was a two-sided platform. By contrast, Farelogix was merely a technology provider to airlines, with no direct relationship with travel agents and therefore was not a two-sided platform.[11] In support of this reasoning, the parties presented evidence that travel agents were not concerned about the competitive consequences of the merger.

Third, the parties argued that Farelogix, as a technological product, should be thought of as a complement rather than a substitute to the GDS. As a complement, the merger would help Sabre improve its GDS offering and enhance rather than lessen competition. As such, they claimed that the merger was (in essence) a vertical merger and that it was therefore pro-competitive.[12] The merging parties argued that the industry would not – even with Farelogix present – shift to a GDS bypass system and that the industry was already using a pass-through system to incorporate more technology into the GDS offerings.

## B. Arguments for the Merger: Merchandising

In relation to merchandising, the parties emphasized Sabre's weak position at the time.[13] As was noted above, its functionality was limited, and there was a lack

---

[11] This economic argument also supported a legal argument that related to the U.S. Supreme Court's opinion in *Amex* that two-sided platforms can compete only with other two-sided platforms. This interpretation of *Amex* is subject to legal debate, and some commentators have argued that this interpretation is inconsistent with sensible economics. *See, e.g.,* Ewalt (2020); see also the chapter in this book by Michael Katz on the *Amex* case.

[12] This argument was aided, somewhat, by the first draft of the U.S. Vertical Merger Guidelines, which were issued a few days before the trial, and seemed to argue that significant efficiencies could be expected in vertical mergers. The final 2020 Vertical Guidelines that were issued by the FTC and DOJ retreated somewhat from this view, and the agencies are currently (as of October 2022) revising these Guidelines even further.

[13] Further details of the parties' arguments to the CMA in favor of the merger are available in their submissions, which can be found on the CMA case page: *See* https://www.gov.uk/cma-cases/sabre-farelogix-merger-inquiry.

of interoperability that meant it could only be used by airlines who were also users of Sabre's other IT applications. As a result, Sabre did not have a high share of the merchandising market.

Although this was a point of common ground between the merging parties and competition authorities, the merging parties placed substantial weight on it. They submitted that, given this context, the theory of harm that the CMA advanced was improper and unduly speculative in nature and would require overwhelming evidence for the CMA to show that a substantial lessening of competition was a likely outcome. They argued that the three-to-five-year counterfactual period was longer than the two-to-three years that was typically considered, and that it rested on a series of highly speculative assumptions. They argued that, given the dynamic nature of the market, no more than a short-to-medium timeframe is appropriate to assess the impact of the transaction.

The merging parties also argued that Sabre would not be able to develop a credible product in the time period in question. Some of the points that they submitted remain confidential, but one of these was that greater investment would not necessarily translate into a workable product. They noted that, despite investing significant resources, Sabre had over the past years failed to develop a competitive merchandising product.[14]

Finally, the merging parties submitted that, in any event, there would remain many other effective providers of merchandising. They pointed to a range of firms that were active in the industry and argued that many of these were technologically superior to Sabre. To support this point, the parties placed substantial emphasis on recent quantitative bidding data. They submitted that this showed that the parties are not each other's closest competitors, and that several rivals frequently bid against them and exert the greatest competitive constraint.

Going beyond the static constraint from rivals, the merging parties placed significant emphasis on the dynamic constraint that competitors would impose. They claimed that the CMA's analysis was asymmetric and inconsistent in its treatment of the potential for innovation and expansion by Sabre, on the one hand, and by rivals on the other. They argued that these firms also had an incentive to invest and expand their offerings, and as a result that the CMA had failed to show that Sabre would innovate at a faster pace than its rivals.

## C. Arguments for the Merger: Farelogix's Place in the Industry

The merging parties further argued that even if Sabre and Farelogix were to be seen as competing, Farelogix was a weak competitor that would not constrain Sabre in the future. While the DOJ and CMA argued that Farelogix was a company with great potential to grow and disrupt the industry, the merging parties painted Farelogix as an aging startup whose time of innovation had passed.

First, they argued that the fundamental weakness as a tool for GDS bypass of Farelogix's Open Connect was that it did not support comparison shopping. Unlike a GDS, a travel agent could not turn to a single solution to search all airlines simultane-

---

14 *See* Sabre's Response to Provisional Findings, para. 4.4.

ously; instead, travel agents would have to maintain connections to each airline separately and determine how to aggregate the results of separate queries. Consistent with this, the merging parties pointed to the low adoption of Open Connect and to travel agent testimony that indicated that they had no desire to switch away from the GDS.

Second, Farelogix was not a new firm. Despite a reputation for being innovative, it was still small after almost 20 years in the industry and had a track record of missing its growth forecasts. The merging parties argued that any theories of harm that relied on Farelogix's growing its presence were speculative.

Third, and relatedly, they argued that even if more flights were booked through Open Connect in the future, these bookings should not be attributed to Farelogix when considering market share. For example, even though Sabre's own valuation of Farelogix conducted as part of the due diligence for the merger predicted that Farelogix's Open Connect would grow, the merging parties argued that the growth would represent GDS pass-through and so those bookings should be attributed to the GDS – not Farelogix.

More generally, the merging parties argued that Farelogix's time as an innovator in distribution was over. They argued that Farelogix had failed to establish itself and that the future was GDS pass-through, wherein Farelogix would at best represent a complementary component of the GDS – not a replacement. They argued that several other firms now also offered that same component, and GDSs were working towards building it themselves. Because Sabre in particular had not made sufficient progress, bringing Farelogix in-house to Sabre would result in efficiencies.

Overall, the two sides did not merely disagree on details and questions of degree. They presented fundamentally different views of the products and the marketplace. In arguing their views, the two sides both relied heavily upon documentary evidence and broader economic theory – for example, the nature of the market and data limited the ability of either side to provide detailed pricing analysis. The ability to then evaluate the arguments put forward by the merging parties was heavily reliant upon the ability to appropriately weigh and consider sometimes contradictory documents.

## V. THE OUTCOME AND SUBSEQUENT DEVELOPMENTS

As was noted earlier, the CMA ultimately blocked the merger as anticompetitive. However, the U.S. District Court was the first to rule, two days earlier, and found against the DOJ. At a high level, the decision seems to have been based on two key findings.

First, the District Court noted that Sabre was a two-sided platform while Farelogix was not; and hence as a matter of law and the U.S. Supreme Court's decision in *Amex*, the two could not be in the same market.[15] The Court stated "[t]he first dispositive flaw in the government's case is that, as a matter of antitrust law, Sabre, which is a two-sided platform…does not compete with Farelogix, which…is a one-sided platform." While this may be true in law, it is not necessarily true in economic practice.

---

15 U.S. District Court (2020, p. 69).

As we discuss below, the Court also found that Farelogix applied pricing pressure to Sabre, which is definitional to the economic concept of competition and implies that the two do compete in *some* relevant antitrust market.

Second, stressing that the plaintiff had the burden of proof, the rejected the DOJ's claims, even though the court noted that in a multitude of ways it was persuaded more by the DOJ than by the merging parties. This view is best summarized in the following quote from the decision (U.S. District Court 2020, pp. 91 – 92):

> The Court recognizes that the outcome here may strike some, including the litigants, as somewhat odd. On several points that received a great deal of attention at trial – whether Farelogix is a valuable company enjoying relative success in the market, whether Sabre and Farelogix compete, whether Sabre understands GDS bypass is a threat, whether Sabre stands to lose revenue even from the expansion of GDS passthrough, and Sabre's motivation for its proposed acquisition of Farelogix – the Court is more persuaded by DOJ than by Defendants. This is largely due to the surprising lack of credibility on these points of certain defense witnesses, including Sabre CEO Menke, Sabre deal leader Boyle, and Farelogix CEO Davidson. Despite these findings and conclusions, however, Defendants have won this case. This is because the burden of proof was on DOJ, not Defendants. Defendants opted to tell the Court a story that is not adequately supported by the facts, but it was their choice whether to do so, and their failing does not determine the outcome of this case. Instead, it is DOJ which, under the law, has the obligation to prove its contention that the Sabre-Farelogix transaction will harm competition in a relevant product and geographic market. DOJ failed.

It seems that the court accepted both the DOJ's evidence and general theories, but felt that the DOJ – and its expert – had not provided sufficient evidence to meet the burden of proof that was required to block the merger. For example, on the topic of harm to innovation, the court derided the DOJ's evidence as merely vague theories. However, it is not clear what additional evidence the court would have liked to see for the DOJ to meet its burden that the transaction will harm competition. As we noted earlier, the available data did not allow for a detailed econometric analysis and the economic theories underlying the DOJ case were fairly basic (and the court seemed to accept them). Even computing market shares, and showing that the merger surpassed certain thresholds, was not easy given the available data and the fact that the case was mostly about potential competition and future innovation.

This issue of the burden of proof seemed to weigh especially heavily on the District Court given its reading of the *Amex* decision. The District Court seemed to struggle with the idea that *Amex* suggests that as a matter of law a two-sided platform does not compete with a firm that only serves one side of the market, but at the same time there was evidence (summarized by the court in the above quote) that the two competed.

This separation, between a somewhat strange reading of the law and clear facts, makes the decision at times difficult to follow from an economic perspective. For example, the District Court was not convinced by the DOJ's market definition, yet the court found that Sabre and Farelogix competed.[16] From an economic perspective, one would think that this would indicate that the two competed in *some* relevant antitrust market – even if that market was not "booking services." Indeed, the Horizontal Merger Guidelines note that direct evidence of competitive effects can inform market definition.[17] Nonetheless, the District Court did not find the market definition evidence it was presented persuasive.

The U.S. District Court's decision on competitive effects was equally two-sided: It found that the merging parties competed, that historically Sabre had resisted change while Farelogix was an innovator, and that "the evidence suggests that Sabre will have the incentive to raise prices, reduce availability of [Farelogix's distribution product], and stifle innovation. Nevertheless, DOJ has not persuaded the Court that Sabre will likely act consistent with its history or these incentives and actually harm competition."[18]

In contrast to this, in the UK, the CMA found that the merger would give rise to a loss of competition in distribution. In reaching this finding, there was a notable difference in its approach (as compared to the U.S. case), with limited emphasis on market definition or legal precedent and instead a focus on direct evidence of competitive effects.

In reaching this finding, the CMA recognized that the evidence was to some extent mixed. Consistent with the U.S. court's findings, the CMA accepted that Farelogix had a limited position and a low growth rate, and that it was likely that GDS bypass technology (such as Farelogix's) would remain relatively small as the market moved towards GDS pass-through.

However, in a key difference to the U.S. District Court, the CMA found that this was precisely because Farelogix was driving incumbents to innovate in response to the threat that it posed, as was shown by the key evidence in Sabre's internal documents. It also found that the diminished incentive if Farelogix was not present would not be replaced by rivals, as none of these were comparable to Farelogix, which had a strong reputation and track record of successfully delivering to large airlines.

The CMA therefore found that the lost competition from Farelogix would reduce the pressure on Sabre to continue innovating. In evaluating the importance of this, the CMA was of the view that it was appropriate to be particularly cautious about any loss of competition – even from a smaller competitor – in a relatively concentrated service such as distribution. It also noted that the implementation of the new technology was actually still nascent and had much further to evolve in the future, and the CMA emphasized the continuing importance of innovation efforts.

Finally, the CMA was dismissive of the parties' efficiency claims in relation to

---

16 U.S. District Court (2020, p. 31): "Notwithstanding Defendants' repeated denials at trial…a preponderance of the evidence shows that Sabre and Farelogix do view each other as competitors, although only in a limited fashion."

17 U.S. DOJ and FTC (2010).

18 U.S. District Court (2020, pp. 87-88).

distribution. This was on the basis of the limited evidence that the parties had put forward to demonstrate that: these efficiencies could be expected to emerge; they would be merger-specific; and they would be timely and sufficient to prevent a loss of competition from arising.

The CMA also found that there would be a loss of competition in merchandising, and this was actually the main focus of its concerns. In particular, the CMA found that, in the absence of the merger, Sabre would undertake a major organic innovation and expansion effort in merchandising.

The main point of consideration on merchandising ultimately proved to be the potential expansion of rivals. The CMA agreed with the parties that it was essential to assess this in detail, so as to avoid an asymmetric approach that considered only the expansion of the merging parties. This proved somewhat challenging given the diverse range of providers that were active in the travel technology area and the wide range of offerings and business models that they employed.

However, after a fairly extensive evidence-gathering effort that included speaking to these potential rivals about their expansion plans and reviewing their internal documents, the CMA concluded that they would continue to provide only a limited constraint. For example, one rival was facing significant financial challenges after a series of accounting irregularities were identified, leading to the suspension of its trading on the Irish Stock Exchange and the loss of a major customer. Others had broad aspirations to grow, but reported this was "not a top strategic priority," that they were focused on other products, that they would likely face a number of difficulties, and had future product roadmaps that the CMA interpreted as demonstrating more modest ambitions than Sabre.

Following the decisions of the U.S. District Court and UK CMA, there were a number of notable subsequent developments:

- Shortly following the UK decision, Sabre abandoned the merger.
- Less than three months later, Farelogix was purchased by Accelya, another leading provider of travel technology applications – albeit one that didn't give rise to competition concerns as it offered products focused on distinctly different activities such as commercial planning, back-office settlement, and data analytics.
- Despite abandoning the merger, Sabre pursued an appeal of the CMA decision to the UK's specialist court: The Competition Appeal Tribunal. However, Sabre then dropped its grounds of appeal against the CMA's substantive decision and pursued only a challenge on the legal issue of the CMA's jurisdiction, which it lost.[19]
- The DOJ appealed the U.S. District Court decision. Since the merger was abandoned, the appellate court vacated the U.S. District Court decision as moot. However, the appellate court noted that its decision to vacate "should not be construed as detracting from the persuasive force of the District Court's opinion, should courts and litigants find its reasoning persuasive."

---

19 Competition Appeal Tribunal (2021).

Thus the U.S. District Court's treatment of competition between multi-sided platforms and one-sided platforms is not precedent but might influence future cases.[20]

- Finally, and most notably, the airline industry was hit particularly hard by the COVID-19 pandemic. This makes it difficult – at least in the short term – to evaluate subsequent market developments and assess whether competition has evolved as was predicted during the merger challenge proceedings.

## VI. CONCLUSION AND REFLECTIONS ON THE CASE

The case clearly raises a question as to why such different outcomes were reached in the U.S. and UK. There is likely no single answer to this, but one notable difference is that the UK has an administrative system: The CMA therefore reaches its own decisions, instead of having to take cases to court.[21]

Nonetheless, CMA case teams also face a high degree of independent scrutiny, as while the decision to begin an in-depth investigation is taken by CMA staff, final CMA decisions are taken by an external panel, who operate in a quasi-judicial capacity independent of the CMA staff and Board.[22] The CMA panel includes experienced economists and senior business figures in addition to lawyers, and it is possible that this broader expertise helps contribute to a focus on the facts of the case, rather than legal precedent, and an openness to more complex economic ideas.

In any event, in relation to distribution, there was a close alignment in how the U.S. and UK agencies assessed the case – even if the ultimate outcomes varied.

As we noted in the Introduction, this case has many of the characteristics of acquisitions in the digital economy, and as such there are potentially broad lessons to be learned. Specifically, this case highlights many of the difficulties that arise when enforcement agencies challenge mergers – and potentially conduct – in the digital economy. Clearly one must be careful in attempting to draw wide-reaching lessons from a single case, but we offer the following reflections.

First, it is difficult to bring challenges in dynamic industries. There can be considerable uncertainty, and disagreement, as to the future in industries where firms, products, and business models are evolving rapidly. There is also often less scope to rely on traditional quantitative tools, such as assessments of switching or bidding or demand estimation, as these can be inherently backwards-looking. However, the challenges in quantifying harm in these cases do not mean that they do not raise competition issues. Courts, enforcers, and regulators need to take care not to get caught in a "CSI effect," where they set a burden of proof that is unattainable in these industries.

Second, complex industries may not neatly fit the horizontal versus vertical classification that is traditionally used in merger analysis; *both* horizontal and vertical effects might be present in a given merger. Both horizontal and vertical concerns can

---

20 *See* Koenig (2020).
21 *See* Hatzitaskos, Howells & Nevo (2021) for a further discussion.
22 For further details on the operation of the CMA panel, *see* Coleman (2022) and Feasey (2020).

be about marginal changes to incentives, such as pricing; but both could give rise to more complex considerations, such as product entry or exit and fundamental redesigns and repositioning that are based on different inputs: Even if in the current state of the industry a merger might be classified as either vertical or horizontal, this might change in the future. Here too the decision maker needs to take care not to get caught up in unhelpful "labeling" and instead should focus on the substance of the effect of the merger on competition. For example, while the DOJ and CMA both formulated their concern as horizontal, the DOJ focused on defining a relevant market and calculating market shares as part of seeking a presumption of harm under U.S. law. For this merger, it was the market for booking services. The DOJ considered bookings that were made through Open Connect to be Farelogix's market share of booking services. This share appeared to be small, but it understated the importance of Farelogix to the industry, for the reasons that were discussed above. The DOJ further argued that bookings that were made directly through "airline.com" belonged outside the proposed market, because airlines could not reasonably recoup enough business from airline.com to overcome a price increase that affected TTA and OTA and therefore a hypothetical monopolist could impose such an increase.[23]

The CMA, however, did not set out a precise market definition because it did not seek a presumption of harm. Instead the CMA defined a broader market for all distribution solutions, encompassing a range of channels and technologies, and it considered the interplay between these in more detail in its competitive assessment.

Third, and very much related, is the observation that relying on legal precedent and market definition can become a distraction from the facts of the case. This clearly was an issue for the U.S. District Court that felt that as a matter law a two-sided platform could not be in the same market as a one-sided firm. This was despite its finding that Farelogix and Sabre competed in the past and that airlines – also not a two-sided platform – belonged in the distribution market (through the distribution from their websites) and therefore compete with Sabre. There is clearly a logical inconsistency here.[24] This is an example how from an economic perspective, these more traditional and legalistic approaches may be particularly unsuitable for dynamic cases, which may require a bespoke assessment of competitive effects.

Fourth, merging parties and competition authorities must consider the importance of reverse-killer acquisition concerns in dynamic markets. The UK's investigation of this theory of harm in merchandising was an important point of difference between the two cases, as this was ultimately the focus of many of its concerns. In fact, some commentators have argued that reverse-killer acquisitions are actually likely to be much more common than the more well-known killer acquisitions.[25]

Finally, there may be legitimate efficiency claims in dynamic cases, but these must be carefully scrutinized by agencies, assessed within the appropriate framework, and

---

23 *See* the discussion of the hypothetical monopolist test in the Merger Guidelines (2010).

24 Clark, Lien & Wilder (2021) point out that the market for GDSs does not resemble a textbook two-sided market, limiting the appropriate application of *Amex* (Clark, Lien & Wilder, 2021).

25 Caffarra, Crawford & Valletti (2020).

held to proper evidentiary standards. Moreover, while a common efficiency argument is that the acquirer's scale and resources will enable the challenger to grow rapidly, the speed with which Farelogix was purchased by another major industry player shows that these benefits may often not be merger-specific, and thus raises a question of why only a powerful incumbent would be able to provide them.

## REFERENCES

Bon, Julie, San Sau Fung, Alan Reilly, Terry Ridout, Robert Ryan & Mike Walker (2021). "Recent Developments at the CMA: 2020–2021." *Review of Industrial Organization* 59: 665–692.

Caffarra, Cristina, Greg Crawford & Tommaso Valletti (2020). "'How tech rolls': Potential competition and 'reverse' killer acquisitions." *VoxEU*.

Clark, Brian, Jeffrey S. Lien & Jeffrey M. Wilder (2021). "The Year in Review: Economics at the Antitrust Division, 2020–2021." *Review of Industrial Organization* 59:651–663.

Competition Appeal Tribunal (2021). "Sabre Corporation v. Competition and Markets Authority." *Judgment* Case No: 1345/4/12/20.

CMA (2019). "Completed acquisition by PayPal Holdings, Inc. of iZettle AB." Final report.

CMA (2020a). "Anticipated acquisition by Amazon of a minority shareholding and certain rights in Deliveroo." Final report.

CMA (2020b). "Anticipated acquisition by Sabre Corporation of Farelogix Inc." Final report.

Coleman, Martin (2022). "Speech to the Law Society, 2022," *speech delivered to The Law Society's Competition Section*.

Ewalt, Andrew (2020). "Two Sides to Every Story: Growing Tensions Between Legal Rules and Economic Realities for Platform Industries." *Competition Policy International*.

Feasey, Richard (2020). "The role of the CMA panel in decision making: Merger enforcement and reform," *speech delivered to the Law Council of Australia's Competition and Consumer (ACCC) Annual Conference*.

Hatzitaskos, Kostis, Brad Howells & Aviv Nevo (2021). "A tale of two sides: Sabre/Farelogix in the United States and the UK." *Journal of European Competition Law & Practice*.

Koenig, Bryan (2020). "3rd Circ.'s Sabre Ruling Hints at 'Persuasive' Merger Defense." *Law360*.

Latham, Oliver, Isabel Tecu & Nitika Bagaria (2020). "Beyond Killer Acquisitions: Are There More Common Potential Competition Issues in Tech Deals and How Can These be Assessed?" *CPI Antitrust Chronicle*.

Sabre (2020). "Response to Provisional Findings."

Sweeting, Andrew & Sinan Corus (2021). "Economic issues in merger analysis for platforms: Recent trends and case studies." *Competition Law Insight*.

U.S. Department of Justice and Federal Trade Commission (2010). "Horizontal Merger Guidelines."

U.S. District Court for the District of Delaware (2020). "Opinion." *United States of America v. Sabre Corp., Sabre GLBL Inc., Farelogix Inc., and Sandler Capital Partners V, L.P.*

## CHAPTER 2

# Innovation Concerns in European Merger Control: *Dow/DuPont* and *Bayer/Monsanto*

*By Daniel Coublucq, David Kovo & Tommaso Valletti*[1]

## I. INTRODUCTION

The agrochemical and biotech industry has been the object of several waves of consolidation over time. The number of integrated Research and Development ("R&D") companies decreased from more than 40 firms in 1960 to only six companies in 2008 (BASF, Bayer, Dow, DuPont, Monsanto, and Syngenta; *see* Figure 1). By "integrated" players, we refer to companies with all the necessary capabilities to support all stages of the innovation and commercialization process: discovery, development, registrations and regulatory obligations, and commercialization on a global basis.

The latest wave of consolidation started with the proposed mergers between Dow and DuPont (which was approved by the European Commission on March 27, 2017), ChemChina and Syngenta (which was approved on April 5, 2017), and Bayer and Monsanto (which was approved on March 21, 2018).

This chapter discusses the latest and most important mergers in this large industry consolidation. It examines not only standard pricing effects, but also the difficult and novel issues related to how a merger affects innovation competition. While the economics underpinning unilateral price effects from a merger are now well-established, the economics behind the effect of a merger on innovation competition are more complex and these transactions offered an opportunity to further our understanding of these effects – which are becoming increasingly important in several other cases.

Dow and DuPont were U.S.-based companies, with a turnover of USD 48 billion and USD 24 billion, respectively, in 2016. While the two companies were active in the production of a broad range of products, the Commission's investigation focused on crop protection – and in particular on herbicides, insecticides, and fungicides.

---

[1] The authors worked for the European Commission in these cases. The views expressed in the text are those of the authors and cannot be regarded as stating an official position of the European Commission. This article relies on a number of previous academic and policy articles by the authors. These are listed in the References Section and include the following: Bertuzzi et al. (2017), Bertuzzi et al. (2018), Buehler et al. (2017), Federico et al. (2017), Federico et al. (2018), Kokkoris & Valletti (2020). The authors wish to thank Giulio Federico, John Kwoka, and Larry White for very helpful comments and suggestions.

Bayer was a German company that was active in pharmaceuticals, consumer health, agriculture, and animal health. Monsanto was a U.S. agriculture company that produced seeds for broad acre crops,[2] fruits, and vegetables. It also produced plant biotechnology traits and supplied crop protection products. Monsanto was perhaps most known for its glyphosate herbicide – which is sold under the "Roundup" brand – and the development of genetically modified ("GM") crops. Monsanto was the leading seed supplier worldwide, while Bayer was a leading firm in crop protection. The Commission's investigation focused mostly on the overlaps in vegetable and broad acre crop seeds and GM and non-GM traits.

**Figure 1. Consolidation in the crop protection industry since 1960**

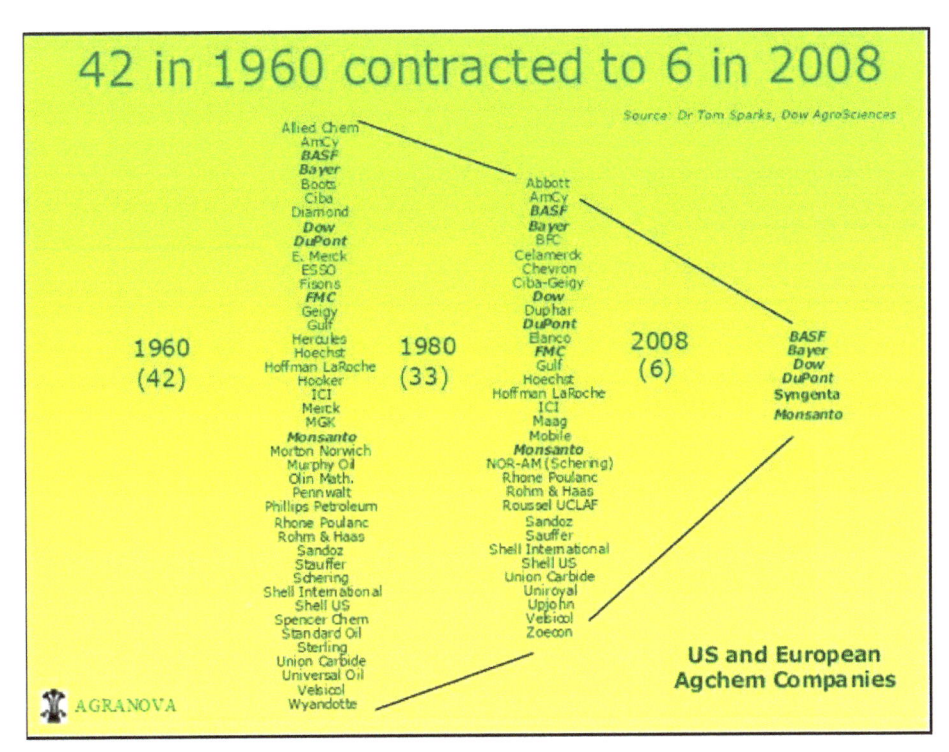

**Source:** Authors' adaptation of Figure 10 of the European Commission decision for Case M.7932 – *Dow/DuPont*.

In line with its case practice, the Commission assesses transactions that take place in the same industry according to the so-called "priority rule": The Commission assessed the first transaction to be notified (*Dow/DuPont*) without regard to the subsequently notified acquisition of Monsanto by Bayer. The latter was, in turn,

---

[2] Broad acre crop farming is a term that is used to describe farms or industries that are engaged in the production of crops that require the use of extensive parcels of land. These include grains, oilseeds, and other crops, such as: maize, soy, wheat, rice, barley, peas, sorghum, hemp, and sunflower.

analyzed in light of the market structure that was created after the *Dow/DuPont* merger.[3]

*Dow/DuPont* was notified on June 22, 2016, and was subject to an in-depth investigation. The transaction was approved conditionally on March 27, 2017, subject to an extensive remedy to address the competition concerns that were raised. *Bayer/Monsanto* was notified on June 30, 2017, and it was also subject to an in-depth investigation. The transaction was approved conditionally on March 21, 2018, subject to an extensive remedy as well.

In *Dow/DuPont*, the Commission's concerns related to the reduction of price competition in several markets for crop protection products and a reduction in innovation competition. Innovation – both to improve existing products and to develop new active ingredients – was a central dimension of competition between companies in the crop protection industry, where Dow and DuPont were two important companies among the limited number of companies that were active globally through the entire R&D process. In order to address the competition concerns, the Parties divested the relevant DuPont crop protection business in the markets where DuPont and Dow overlapped. They also divested the entirety of DuPont's global R&D organization. The divestment package was sold to FMC, a U.S.-headquartered global chemical company that is active in the agricultural business.

In *Bayer/Monsanto*, the Commission's concerns related to the reduction of price and innovation competition in a significant number of markets where the Parties' activities overlapped: notably for the development of seeds and traits, and herbicides. In addition, the merger would have strengthened Monsanto's dominant position in certain markets where Bayer was an important challenger. In order to address the competition concerns, the Parties divested Bayer's business and assets in the overlapping crop protection, seeds, and traits markets where competition concerns were raised. Bayer also divested its global R&D organization for seeds and traits, as well as Bayer's R&D project to develop a challenger product for Monsanto's glyphosate herbicide and corresponding herbicide-tolerant seeds. The divestment package was sold to BASF, an EU-headquartered global chemical company. BASF was considered as a suitable purchaser since it had no or limited activities in the areas where competition concerns were raised.

## II. BACKGROUND OF THE CASE AND THE ISSUES

As introduced above, for both *Dow/DuPont* and *Bayer/Monsanto*, the analysis of innovation competition and innovation concerns played a prominent role in the Commission's assessment.

---

[3] Between the two mergers, the Commission also analyzed the acquisition of Syngenta by ChemChina. The acquisition was approved in 2017, conditional on the divestiture of parts of the crop protection business of ChemChina in the EU. ChemChina was active in the crop protection industry in Europe through its wholly owned Israel-based subsidiary Adama: the world's largest producer of generic crop protection products. While Syngenta produced crop protection products that were based on active ingredients that it developed itself, Adama produced only generics that were based on active ingredients that were developed by third parties and for which the patent had expired. Thus, the concerns with the transaction related mainly to product market competition and not to innovation competition. *See* European Commission Decision in Case M.7962 – *ChemChina/Syngenta* (2017).

By innovation we mean all R&D activities targeted at improving current products (or their production processes) as well as discovering and developing new products. By innovation concerns we mean the possibility that, following the transaction, the merging parties would (1) discontinue, delay, or redirect current or prospective innovation efforts in areas where their activities and assets overlap or (2) raise the price of their innovative products (compared to the counterfactual) once these are introduced into the market.

The **innovation activities that were of concern in the two mergers** focused on two main areas: crop protection and biotech. *Dow/DuPont* mainly concerned innovation in the area of crop protection, while *Bayer/Monsanto* mainly involved biotech innovation for the development of new traits.

Crop protection products are chemical products that target weeds (herbicides), insects (insecticides), and diseases (fungicides) affecting a particular crop. Innovation in crop protection is not only key to improving a crop yield, but also to develop safer products for humans and the environment. The essential component of a formulated product is the active ingredient ("AI").

Biotech instead consists of applying science to develop new crops with certain characteristics. These plant characteristics are called "traits." For instance, traits relate to the size of the plant, its resistance to certain pests, resilience to drought, etc.

Seeds are critical inputs for farmers, who need seed varieties that are adapted to the soil and climate where the crop is cultivated.

Historically, specific plant characteristics have been achieved via natural breeding. Biotechnologies have allowed the development of traits in laboratories, which are then introgressed into plant varieties. Such lab-based development can be either GM or non-GM; this depends on the biotechnology that is used to bring the trait into the seed.

Once these traits are introgressed into plant varieties – into a seed – the seeds are then commercialized by seed companies. Certain firms are vertically integrated, in the sense that they both develop traits (which they may license to other seed companies, in addition to the captive use in their own seeds) and commercialize seeds.

These industries are characterized by **high barriers to entry and expansion** in R&D, as well as commercialization (*e.g.*, the regulatory approval of a developed product). Absent appropriate regulatory interventions, these barriers make any loss of competition from a merger particularly hard to mitigate by the market itself.

First, substantial R&D costs must be incurred over many years before the first sales and profits are achieved. Discovering and developing a new AIs in crop protection takes approximately 10 years and an investment of around USD 280 million. This involves complex R&D organizations and specific assets, to support not only the discovery of a new AI but also significant further optimization of the molecules and formulations, as well as the necessary field tests and studies that are required to obtain the approval of the new AI in different world regions. Developing a new trait with biotechnologies takes approximately 10 years from early discovery to regulatory approval and marketing commercial varieties that incorporate the trait, at a total cost of approximately USD 100-200 million.

Second, global testing, breeding, and marketing capabilities are required to operate effectively and compete on a worldwide scale. Moreover, global regulatory know-how and capabilities are required to overcome strict regulatory barriers.

Third, intellectual property rights ("IPRs") and patents favor the more established firms. Related to this, the Commission found that there were significant links across the five main firms (*i.e.*, Bayer, Dow, DuPont, Monsanto, and Syngenta) – common shareholdings,[4] and licensing and cross-licensing agreements – which further increased the *de facto* concentration in the industry.

## A. Overview of the Innovation Concerns

The Commission's innovation concerns centered on the possibility that, following the transaction:

- First, the merging parties would limit future price competition between their forthcoming and their existing products, or between their forthcoming products.
- Second, the merged entity would discontinue, delay, or redirect the innovation efforts that were related to overlapping lines of research that targeted similar applications.
- Third, the transaction would remove more broadly one of very few global integrated competitors with innovation capabilities in certain markets.

These innovation concerns were not entirely new – especially for markets and industries in which the merging parties have strong innovation capabilities and track records, face few rivals with such capabilities and are protected by significant barriers to entry in R&D.

Indeed, innovation-related concerns had already featured in previous European Commission decisions in sectors such as pharmaceuticals,[5] engineering,[6] and financial services.[7]

At the same time, the analysis of innovation competition in *Dow/DuPont* and *Bayer/Monsanto* represented significant steps forward in terms of prominence of the innovation-related analyses and also in terms of the novel aspects of these cases.

First, in previous cases that involved innovation competition, the concerns were mainly related to late pipeline products, and to a lesser extent to earlier stages of the

---

[4] In *Dow/DuPont* and *Bayer/Monsanto*, the Commission found that the crop protection, seeds, and traits industries are characterized by significant common shareholdings. The Commission noted that all concentration measures – such as market shares or the Herfindahl-Hirschman index ("HHI") – that are used as a proxy of market power, are based on the assumption that firms are fully independent one from the other. Therefore, in the presence of common shareholdings, standard concentration measures, such as market shares or the HHI, are likely to underestimate the level of concentration of the market structure and, thus, the market power of the merging parties. See Section 4.4 of the European Commission Decision in Case M.8084 – *Bayer/Monsanto* (2018) and Section 1.5.5 of the European Commission Decision in Case M.7932 – *Dow/DuPont* (2017).

[5] European Commission Decision in Case M.7275 - *GSK/Novartis Oncology*.

[6] European Commission Decision in Case M.7278 - *General Electric/Alstom*.

[7] European Commission Decision in Case M.6166 - *Deutsche Borse/NYSE*.

R&D process. For instance, in *General Electric/Alstom*[8] the Commission's concerns focused on the overlap in the very large gas turbines that each merging party had in its pipeline. Similarly, in *GSK/Novartis Oncology*,[9] the Commission's concerns focused on the overlap in innovative cancer treatments, as there were only three firms with an existing product or a product in advanced development (Phase III) for skin cancer and ovarian cancer.

The historic focus on overlaps between products in the final development stage, rather than also overlaps in research and early development stage, was probably related to the increased complexity in the analysis of competition between merging parties as one moves from the former to the latter. These difficulties may relate to the ability to identify overlaps between the merging parties' activities and assets at an early stage, as well as possibly a view among certain practitioners that the further the R&D effort is from reaching the market, the higher the uncertainty that harm from a merger may materialize.

Second, *Dow/DuPont* and *Bayer/Monsanto* triggered significant new developments in the economic literature that addressed the effect of mergers on innovation competition. While the earlier economic literature on innovation had relevance to the context, it became apparent that one could not apply those results in a merger case. Specifically, this earlier literature focused on the effects on innovation from varying some proxy for the intensity of competition among all firms in the market. None of these papers examined specifically the impact on innovation from merger-induced unilateral effects.[10]

Recent contributions in the economics literature do precisely this. They shy away from more general (but also generic) characterizations and ask instead the more specific question of what happens in an industry before and after a merger – when innovation is an important parameter of competition. The main insight is that there is an effect on innovation competition that is very much like the diversion effect that is at the heart of the analysis of unilateral effects on price competition.[11] If additional investment in R&D by a firm, say, reduces the expected profits of a rival (and *vice versa*), because it drives customers away, then a merger between these two firms internalizes this negative externality, which leads to less investment in R&D. This is not the only effect – though it is an important one.

---

8 European Commission Decision in Case M.7278 - *General Electric/Alstom*.

9 European Commission Decision in Case M.7275 - *GSK/Novartis Oncology*.

10 For instance, the theoretical framework of the "inverted U" developed that was developed by Aghion et al. (2005) when considering changes in the intensity of competition, basically varies some uniform conduct parameter that is common industry-wide. While this could be relevant, for instance, in the case of coordinated effects, this is not the typical starting point in a merger assessment. In a merger, a fundamental channel comes from the unilateral effects of the merging parties, as opposed to the outsiders to the merger. Therefore, it is difficult to distil the merger implications from Aghion et al. (2005), which instead should be read more as a contribution that is informative for thinking, for instance, about the strength of IPRs, or the effects of globalization. Similarly, Aghion et al. (2001) proxy competition by a symmetric change in an industry-wide parameter of product differentiation. *See also* Vives (2008) and Lopez & Vives (2018) for approaches along these lines.

11 Farrell & Shapiro (2010).

**The innovation theory of harm.** The economic analysis of the case is contained in Annex 4 of the *Dow/DuPont* Decision. While there is no explicit model there, the analysis is based on contemporaneous work of Federico et al. (2017, 2018).[12] Federico et al. (2017) consider a model where innovation is *ex novo*, and all firms can eventually produce substitute products if they are successful. Federico et al. (2018) extend this framework to a setting where firms start with baseline existing differentiated products that can be improved by innovating. In both contributions, innovation is probabilistic: by spending more a firm can improve the probability of achieving a successful innovation. Firms play a two-stage game: Price competition follows an initial stage where innovation is chosen. The difference between the expected profits that a firm will realize in the second stage if it innovates and the expected profits that it will get if it does not, drives the marginal gains from R&D in the first stage.

Federico et al. (2017, 2018) show that the overall impact from a merger on innovation will arise from two effects: First, there is an "innovation externality" (or business-stealing effect). In their models, an increase in R&D expenditures by one firm always reduces the expected profits of its rivals. This negative externality would be internalized following a merger, which leads unambiguously to a reduction in post-merger R&D efforts, all else equal.

Second, merged firms will be able to coordinate the prices of the portfolio of the goods that they sell. Federico et al. (2018) call this the "price coordination" effect. If the merger increases pre-innovation profits in the product market by more than it increases post-innovation profits, price coordination introduces a downward pressure on the merging firms' incentive to innovate. If the converse is true, it exerts an upward pressure.

Thus, in theory, this effect could go either way as far as innovation is concerned. Federico et al. (2018) use demand functions such that this price coordination channel effect is always positive, so that – again in theory – it could be a proper countervailing force to the innovation externality; this positive price coordination effect after a merger is assumed at the outset in Federico et al. (2017). The model has complexities, and Federico et al. (2018) resort to numerical parameterization: for the parameter ranges that they consider, they find that the innovation externality prevails and outweighs the price coordination channel. R&D investment by the rivals increases, but never enough to compensate the loss arising from the merged parties.

Finally, they show that the innovation result can be reversed if there are sufficiently high merger-related efficiency gains. In particular, they consider improvements in the effectiveness of innovation and reductions in R&D costs. As for consumer surplus, since the merger always comes with higher future prices, these efficiency gains have to be strong to reverse the result.

## B. The Innovation Theory of Harm: An Example

This section exemplifies the economics underpinning unilateral effects from a merger on innovation competition, illustrating the main economic forces described

---
12 *See also* Motta & Tarantino (2021) and Gilbert (2019).

above. We consider a simplified setting with two firms only: Firm 1 and firm 2. Each firm can devote resources to increase the probability of obtaining an innovative product. More specifically, to obtain a probability of success that is denoted by $p$, a firm must spend $p^2/2$. The quadratic cost specification captures the decreasing returns to innovation: The increasing marginal cost of innovating; we ensure that probabilities cannot exceed 1.

The payoffs for these firms are summarized in Table 1. If a firm is not successful, it earns zero. If it is the only successful innovator, it earns a profit (gross of R&D costs) that is normalized to 1. If two firms are jointly successful in their R&D efforts, and they compete against each other, they earn $d$ each. We do not model competition explicitly; but one can assume that, in the normal case where products are substitutes, it must be $0 < d < 1/2$. The extreme case $d = 0$ corresponds to a situation of pure Bertrand competition between identical products. For the benefit of the discussion, we also consider the case where $1/2 < d < 1$, so that products are quite differentiated and/or investments are complementary, and total industry profits ($2d$) increase when both firms are successful innovators.[13]

For the merger case, the merged entity will have two plants at its disposal: the former firms 1 and 2. We denote the total profit that is earned by the merged entity in case both plants are successful in their independent research efforts by $m$. The plausible case where the investments result in substitute products is $m = 1$. We also consider the case where there can be differentiation or complementarities: when $1 < m < 2$.

**Table 1. Gross Payoffs of Firms 1 & 2**

| Firm 2<br>Firm 1 | Successful | Unsuccessful |
|---|---|---|
| Successful | Duopoly: d, d<br>Merger: m | Duopoly: 1, 0<br>Merger: 1 |
| Unsuccessful | Duopoly: 0, 1<br>Merger: 1 | Duopoly: 0, 0<br>Merger: 0 |

The market structure that is induced by a merger matters only in the top left corner. In the other cases either there is no product, or there is an uncontested monopoly both with or without a merger. We consider first the case of duopoly competition: The case prior to a merger. The payoff of firm 1 is

$$\pi_1 = 1 \bullet p_1(1 - p_2) + d \bullet p_1 p_2 + (1 - p_1) \bullet 0 - \frac{p_1^2}{2},$$

and a similar expression also holds true for firm 2 simply by reversing the subscripts.

---

[13] This is the case that is considered by Bourreau et al. (2021) when they introduce a "demand expansion effect."

The first-order condition becomes[14]

$$\frac{\partial \pi_1}{\partial p_1} = 1 - (1-d)p_2 - p_1 = 0 .$$

In a symmetric equilibrium where $p_1 = p_2$ we have that, in a duopoly, each firm's probability of success is

$$p^D \equiv p_1 = p_2 = \frac{1}{2-d},$$

which is always between 0 and 1 because of the restriction $0 < d < 1$.

Let us turn to the case of a merger to monopoly: Imagine that the two firms merge their research facilities and form a new firm that we denote as $M$. The new entity will then maximize

$$\pi_M = 1 \bullet \left[ p_1(1-p_2) + p_2(1-p_1) \right] + m \bullet p_1 p_2 - \frac{p_1^2}{2} - \frac{p_2^2}{2} .$$

The first-order condition becomes[15]

$$\frac{\partial \pi_M}{\partial p_1} = 1 - (2-m)p_2 - p_1 = 0 ,$$

and a similar expression also holds for the other research lab. In a symmetric equilibrium where $p_1 = p_2$ we have that, after a merger to monopoly, each lab's probability of success is

$$p^M \equiv p_1 = p_2 = \frac{1}{3-m} .$$

which is again between 0 and 1, as $1 < m < 2$.

**Effect of the Merger on Innovation.** The comparison between the two first-order conditions in the two cases indicates what changes after a merger, as compared to duopoly competition. On the one hand, if both research efforts are successful (with probability $p_1 p_2$), the merged entity will earn $m$ instead of $d$: This is the price coordination effect. On the other hand, the merged entity also anticipates that, if it innovates with a plant (*e.g.*, plant 1 with probability $p_1$) it will cannibalize some of the profits that it would have received from the other plant (*e.g.*, plant 2) in the event that this is also successful (in the monopoly first-order condition, there is an extra negative term that is equal to $-p_2 \bullet 1$). This is the business stealing (or innovation externality) effect.

When we compare the relevant expressions, we find that the probability of a successful innovation (and hence R&D spend) will be *lower* after the merger when the

---

14 The second-order condition is satisfied.

15 The second-order conditions are satisfied. In our example, it is never optimal for the merged entity to shut down completely one of the two plants. Hence the criticism of Denicoló & Polo (2018) does not apply.

following condition applies:

$$p^D > p^M \leftrightarrow d > m - 1 .$$

Some immediate conclusions can be drawn from this stylized analysis.

Let us start from the case where the innovative products would be perfect substitutes for each other: $m = 1$. Then the condition simplifies to $d > 0$. Hence, we obtain a first result: *It is never possible that a merger to monopoly increases total investments.*

If instead the merger generates synergies, or the innovative products are differentiated, then it is possible that the merger is beneficial for investments: This would happen when $m > d + 1$. It is not sufficient that synergies (or differentiation) exist, but they also have to be sufficiently strong. If these synergies (or differentiation) come from investment complementarities, it is also likely that they would exist under duopoly competition (unless the synergies/complementarities are uniquely merger-specific). In this case, it follows that also $d$ is high in a duopoly; hence $m$ has to be particularly high. In other words, *complementarities are a necessary but not sufficient condition for a merger to have a positive effect on investments.*

**Effect of the Merger on Consumer Surplus.** The ultimate effect to be assessed is not limited to innovation. Instead one has to evaluate what happens to consumer surplus after a merger. Table 2 summarizes consumer surplus in each of the possible states.

Table 2. Consumer Surplus in the Various Scenarios

| Firm 2<br>Firm 1 | Successful | Unsuccessful |
|---|---|---|
| Successful | Duopoly: $CS^d$<br>Merger: $CS^{m2}$ | Duopoly: $CS^m$<br>Merger: $CS^m$ |
| Unsuccessful | Duopoly: $CS^m$<br>Merger: $CS^m$ | Duopoly: 0<br>Merger: 0 |

$CS^m$ indicates consumer surplus when only one firm is successful (and therefore it will be an uncontested monopolist); $CS^d$ denotes consumer surplus when there are two successful innovators that compete against each other; and $CS^{m2}$ indicates consumer surplus when there are two successful innovators and the market is monopolized. Without any innovation, consumer surplus is normalized to zero. The ranking of these variables is: $CS^m \leq CS^{m2} < CS^d$. The last inequality is strict, as consumers must benefit (in the absence of merger-specific efficiencies) from competition between two competing firms, as compared to a monopoly, when the firms offer the same set of products. Instead, the first inequality may not be strict. If the two innovations are perfect substitutes ($m = 1$), then it will also be $CS^m = CS^{m2}$.

Prior to the merger, expected consumer surplus is

$$CS^D = p^{D^2} CS^d + 2p^D(1 - p^D) CS^m .$$

After the merger, expected consumer surplus is

$$CS^M = p^{M^2}CS^{m2} + 2p^M(1-p^M)CS^m .$$

We cannot venture into a general analysis here, as we have put little structure on consumer preferences. Still, we can make some simple but important observations. We take the benchmark case where innovations are perfect substitutes ($m = 1$):

First, note that from the previous analysis $p^D > p^M \leftrightarrow d > 0$, which always holds for any $d > 0$. Second, exploiting the fact that $CS^m = CS^{m2}$, we can write:

$$CS^D - CS^M = p^{D^2}CS^d - p^{M^2}CS^m + [2p^D(1-p^D) - 2p^M(1-p^M)]CS^m .$$

The difference between the first two terms $[p^{D^2}CS^d - p^{M^2}CS^m]$ is positive, as both $p^D > p^M$ and $CS^d > CS^m$. As for the last term, the sign depends on $[2p^D(1-p^D) - 2p^M(1-p^M)]$. As long as the probabilities of success are below 50 percent (which is standard in cases with highly uncertain innovations), then $p^D > p^M$ ensures that this bracketed term is positive. Consumers then lose twice: Because there are (on average) fewer innovations overall; and also because, for innovations that would have occurred simultaneously, the consumers do not benefit from future price competition.

The comparison becomes even more evident if we consider the case of perfect competition in a duopoly, when $d$ approaches 0. In this case the two probabilities $p^D$ and $p^M$ converge to each other. The last term vanishes, and we are left with:

$$CS^D - CS^M = p^{D^2}\left(CS^d - CS^m\right) > 0 .$$

In this extreme case, the merger has no effect on innovation. Still, consumers are worse off because they do not get any benefit from *ex post* competition. The main implication is that there are two effects that one has to consider when analyzing the effect of a merger on consumers: Whether the merger has any *impact on innovation*; and, additionally, the *impact on future prices that are typically higher after a merger*.

**The Role of Efficiencies.** Without claiming generality, one can still use this framework to obtain at least a sense of the magnitude of the efficiencies that would be needed in order for a merger to have a positive effect on consumers. Suppose that the innovations are pure substitutes for each other. Additionally, imagine that competition in a duopoly is described by tough Bertrand competition, so that $d = 0$. Finally, assume that there are merger-specific cost synergies that increase *ex post* profits (so that they would stimulate innovation) but do not feed into cheaper prices for consumers. Hence it is also $CS^m = CS^{m2}$. In particular, let us assume that (fixed) cost savings are about 10 percent of *ex post* profits, so that $m = 1.1$ (these are arguably quite large efficiency gains). Then, under all these assumptions, it is:

$$p^D = 0.5 < p^M \approx 0.53 .$$

In other words, the *ex post* efficiency gains for the merged monopolist are sufficient to spur additional innovation effort compared to a duopoly. Is this enough for consumers to be better off? Simple calculations show that

$$CS^M - CS^D \approx 0.276 CS^m - 0.25 CS^d \ .$$

Can this expression be positive? It depends on the shape of the demand function, but it is not very likely. For instance, it is well-known that, with a linear demand and constant marginal cost of production, consumer surplus with competition is four times larger than consumer surplus with monopoly, in which case:

$$CS^M - CS^D \approx 0.276 CS^m - 0.25 CS^d = -0.724 CS^m < 0 \ ,$$

so that consumers are still worse off after a merger, because the increase in the probability of innovation does not compensate for the fact that they gain little from it.

The importance of this analysis is straightforward: When considering the effect of a merger on consumers, one has to take into account both the impact on innovation and the impact on future prices. The condition for a merger to have a positive effect on consumers is more stringent than the condition to have a positive effect on innovation. This is because – whatever the innovation levels – the merger suppresses future price competition, to the detriment of consumers. We conclude that *the conditions to find a positive impact of a merger on consumers (rather than innovation alone) become more stringent.*

## III. THE COMMISSION'S CASE AND ECONOMIC ANALYSIS

### A. Market Definition

In *Dow/DuPont*, the Commission defined the relevant product market by crop and by pest, since farmers buy crop protection products to address a particular pest (weeds, insects, or fungi) for a particular crop (*e.g.*, corn, cotton, etc.). The assessment of product market competition was related to the degree of overlaps between existing products and forthcoming products; the latter are products that are in the development stage, with a high probability of coming to the market.

In order to assess innovation competition, which is related to the earlier stage of the R&D process, the Commission took a wider approach in term of market definition by considering: (i) whether the Parties had overlapping lines of research for new AIs: lines of research that target the same innovation spaces;[16] and (ii) whether the Parties had unique capabilities to innovate in certain innovation spaces.

In *Bayer/Monsanto*, the Commission defined product markets based on the crop dimension for vegetables seeds and also broad acre seeds. In the EU, the Parties' activities overlapped for 16 vegetable crops – *e.g.*, tomatoes, cucumbers – and there was further product market competition for very granular segments (such as cherry tomatoes) at a national level. For broad acre seeds, the Parties' activities overlapped for the commercialization of oilseed rape seeds and the licensing of cotton seeds.

---

[16] A line of research includes the set of scientists, patents, assets, and equipment that are dedicated to a given research target – an innovation space – whose output is an AI.

For traits, the Commission found that the licensing of traits was a market upstream of seed breeding and commercialization, and defined the relevant product markets by functionality and crop for single traits (for example, herbicide tolerance traits for soybean) and for stacks (or combinations) of traits (for example, a stack of two traits for cotton – one that provides tolerance to a certain herbicide and one that provides resistance to a certain class of insects). The markets for the licensing of traits and trait stacks were found to be global in scope.

## B. Structure of the Assessment

The **first part of the assessment** focused on the impact of the merger on actual and potential price competition in the product market.

The Commission identified competition concerns that were based on overlaps between existing-to-existing products, forthcoming-to-forthcoming products in development stages, and forthcoming-to-existing products.

In *Dow/Dupont*, these concerns were particularly pronounced for selective herbicides[17] and insecticides.

Depending on the specific market analyzed, the Commission found that the transaction would have created or strengthened a dominant position or in any event would have eliminated an important competitive constraint (as the Parties were important and close competitors within a limited number of alternatives for herbicides against specific weeds for cereals in most EEA countries).[18] In particular, among the few remaining R&D-integrated players, Dow and DuPont were both specialized in broadleaf herbicides for cereals; although this was the less the case for Bayer and BASF, Syngenta was specialized in herbicides for grass weeds, and Monsanto in non-selective herbicides. The Commission found competition concerns in 28 herbicides markets in the EEA including, for example, oilseed rape herbicides, sunflower herbicides, and rice herbicides.

For insecticides, the Parties' products were targeting similar insects (for example, Lepidoptera, a key chewing insect) for the same crops (*e.g.*, specific fruits and vegetables), while Bayer's and Syngenta's portfolio consisted largely of older products under regulatory pressure, and BASF had a minimal presence in insecticides. The Commission found competition concerns in approximately 40 insecticides markets in the EEA. For example, in fruit crops, vegetable crops, corn, and cotton.

For *Bayer/Monsanto*, the Parties overlapped in 16 vegetable crops (such as tomatoes and cucumbers) and in a very large number of segments (such as cherry tomatoes for glasshouses). In its assessment, the Commission considered approximately

---

17 Selective herbicides are herbicides that are designed to eliminate only specific weeds, while leaving intact the crop on which they are applied. Non-selective herbicides kill many types of plants, including cultivated crops, and are therefore either applied between the harvest of one crop and the sowing of the next, or are applied to (genetically-modified) crops that are resistant to that specific non-selective herbicide.

18 Under European Union competition law, either of these findings (elimination of an important competitive constraint, and creation or strengthening of a dominant position) is sufficient to raise an antitrust objection to a proposed merger.

1800 segment/country combinations, and competition concerns were raised[19] in approximately 200 segment/country combinations, that represented a significant part of Bayer's vegetable seeds activities. With regard to broad acre crops, the Commission found that the proposed merger would have led to competition concerns for: (i) the commercialization of oil seed rape seeds in France, Ireland, Estonia, and the UK; and (ii) the licensing of cotton seeds in Europe.

The **second part of the assessment** focused on the impact of the merger on innovation competition.

Innovation in both crop protection and traits for seeds takes place in narrow (that is, specific and reasonably defined) innovation spaces. From the early stages of an R&D project, companies define their targets by considering specific crop/pest combinations for crop protection in the *Dow/DuPont* merger case and specific type of traits/crops for traits in the *Bayer/Monsanto* merger case. The Commission found that not all R&D organizations were active in every innovation space.

In both mergers, the Parties had overlapping lines of research in the discovery stage. In *Dow/DuPont*, these concerns related mostly to overlapping lines of research on new active ingredients for selective herbicides and insecticides that targeted similar crops and pests. Moreover, the Parties had actual lines of research with similar discovery targets in herbicides, insecticides, and fungicides. Overall, the investigation showed that closeness in innovation was persistent, and the merging parties were close innovation competitors for past innovations and for current innovations.

For *Bayer/Monsanto*, the Commission found that the Parties' lines of research overlapped in several innovation areas: Weed control for canola, cotton, soybean, and non-GM wheat; insect control for cotton; cross-crop weed control; and cross-crop insect control.

More broadly, in both cases the Commission found that the merging parties were among the very few global integrated companies with R&D capabilities in crop protection and biotech. The Commission's assessment can be summarized as follows.

First, innovation in the crop protection and biotech industry is not random, and each global R&D firm focuses more prominently on certain areas, while leaving unaddressed other areas. Therefore, it was possible to identify a number of innovation spaces and research targets on which each merging party focused pre-merger.

The Commission identified various types of overlaps that affected innovation competition: From overlaps at the same level of the R&D process (discovery-to-discovery overlaps) to overlaps between activities at different level of the R&D process (*e.g.*, discovery-to-pipeline or even discovery-to-product overlaps).

Second, the Commission found that the crop protection and biotech sectors were already very concentrated, and not all global integrated competitors were active in each of the overlapping innovation spaces. Therefore, at the level of individual innovation spaces concentration was often substantially higher than at the level of the industry overall. The Commission collected this information by analyzing internal

---

19 Depending on the relevant market, the basis for the concerns was the creation or strengthening of a dominant position or the elimination of an important competitive constraint due to the importance and closeness of competition between Bayer and Monsanto.

documents of the Parties with respect to their R&D targets and research projects, and by sending requests for information to all of the global integrated R&D companies asking them to indicate for each innovation space whether they had an active R&D project or a pipeline product in development.

Third, in several innovation spaces with overlapping lines of research targets and lines of research, the merging parties were important innovators and with similar lines of research, as was indicated by their corresponding patents shares (t), internal documents of the Parties, and the Commission's patent analysis, which indicated that the merging parties owned some of the best-quality patents targeting similar applications.

Fourth, the Commission's concerns were confirmed by evidence from internal documents that envisioned a significant decrease of R&D capabilities post-merger or at least discontinuation, delay, or reorientation of the parties' overlapping lines of research and pipeline products.

Finally, the Commission considered if any loss of innovation competition between the merging parties could be offset in principle by **efficiencies** that would increase the ability or incentives of the merging parties to engage in R&D.

A possible efficiency relates to the notion of appropriability: The ability by an innovator to prevent knowledge spillovers to other firms (so as to avoid imitation by rivals). However, in the agrochemical and biotech industries IPRs are robust and the risk of imitation by a competitor is low. Most of the innovation in these industries materializes in terms of new products that are patent protected for a long time (20 years) and that enjoy significant sales with high margins during the patent period and often also post-patent expiry. As a result, firms are typically able to appropriate the reward from their own innovation efforts.

Other potential efficiencies relate to the possibility that the merger would combine complementary innovation assets or would generate cost-related synergies that would increase the productivity of R&D. None of these claims were formally made or substantiated by the parties in the two mergers.

## C. Quantitative Evidence Based on Patents for the Merging Parties as Important and Close Innovation Competitors

As discussed above, the assessment of innovation competition is related to the earlier stage of the R&D. In both *Dow/DuPont* and *Bayer/Monsanto*, in order to capture this earlier stage of the R&D (*i.e.*, the discovery stage), the Commission conducted an analysis of patents to assess the key elements of an innovation theory of harm: (i) the importance of the merging parties as innovators; (ii) the degree of concentration in research; (iii) the combined share of patents for the merging parties; and (iv) the closeness of competition between the merging parties in term of innovation efforts. While the patent analyses in both cases share the same principles, the implementation in each case differed in some respects due to the type of data that were available. More details are presented in the technical annexes of the Decisions.[20]

**Description of patent data available**. The Commission collected patent data that were used in the normal course of business by the merging parties. In addition

---

20 *See* Annex 1 of the European Commission Decision in Case M.7932 – *Dow/DuPont* (2017) and Annex 1 of the European Commission Decision in Case M.8084 – *Bayer/Monsanto* (2018).

to the patents of the merging parties, the data collected included as well the patents from other innovators. In order to assess innovation competition, the Commission considered the patents that corresponded to the discovery stage of the R&D process – corresponding to the "research" stage of the R&D process.

**Patent data and closeness of competition in innovation efforts.** While the patent data that were collected in *Bayer/Monsanto* included granular information on the crops and types of traits (*e.g.*, weed control for canola) and was directly related to the innovation spaces – lines of research or research targets – the patent data that were collected in *Dow/DuPont* were less granular and included information only on the type of crop protections that were targeted: Herbicides, insecticides, or fungicides. While the patent data that were available allowed an assessment of the importance of the merging parties as innovators in both cases (*see* below for more details), the assessment of the closeness of competition was different.

In *Bayer/Monsanto*, given the granularity of the data that were available (at the level of innovation spaces), the patent shares – *e.g.*, in weed control for Canola – were also directly relevant to assess the closeness of competition between the merging parties.

In *Dow/DuPont*, since it was possible to calculate patent shares only at an aggregated level – for herbicides in general, insecticides, or fungicides – the Commission identified in a first stage the best-quality patents of the merging parties, and in a second stage collected internal documents on research projects that were based on these best-quality patents. The review of these internal documents brought additional evidence in the assessment of the closeness of competition for the innovation efforts of the merging parties.

**Measurement of patent quality.** The Commission evaluated the quality of the patents of the merging parties and of their competitors. It is a standard in the economic literature to use a forward-citation analysis, consisting of calculating for each patent the number of citations that are accumulated from subsequent patents.[21] This methodology was also recognized by a Court proceeding in the U.S.[22]

In both cases, the forward-citation analysis showed that patent quality was very heterogenous, where most patents were never or rarely cited, and therefore with little technical quality and economic significance, while a few patents account for most of the citations; *see* Figure 2 for an illustration in the *Dow/DuPont* case. Given the significant heterogeneity in patent quality, the firms' technological strength would not be well reflected with simple patent counts per firm, and a citation-based index was more appropriate to calculate patent shares.

**Internal citations.** Citations of a given patent come from subsequent patents: They are either owned by the same firm that holds the cited patent ("internal citations" or "self-citations") or owned by different firms ("external citations"). One methodological point that was raised in both cases is whether internal citations should be given the same weight as external citations in the forward-citations indices of the firms' technological strength.

---

[21] *See* Tratjenberg (1990), Griliches (1990), Jaffe et al. (1993), Aghion et al. (2005), Hall et al. (2005), Cohen (2010), Ernst & Omland (2011), and Bloom et al. (2013).

[22] *Comcast Cable v. Sprint Communications*, Civil Action No. 12-859, District Court for the Eastern District of Pennsylvania, November 21, 2016.

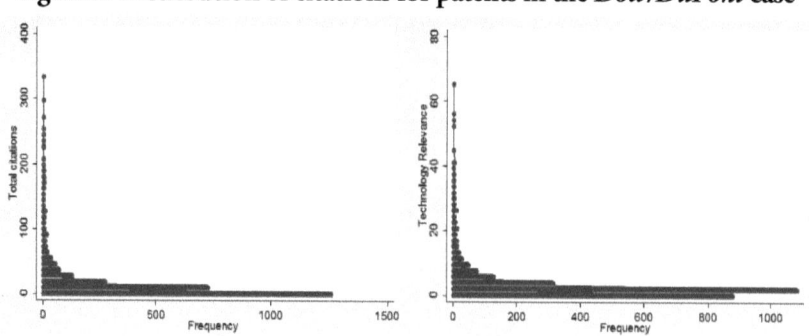

**Figure 2. Distribution of citations for patents in the *Dow/DuPont* case**

**Source:** Annex 1 of the European Commission decision for Case M.7932 – *Dow/DuPont*, Figure 4.

The economic literature provides mixed findings in that regard. In particular, while it recognizes the importance of internal citations – for example, to capture continuous innovation effort in a certain area – it also shows that the relevance of internal citations declines with the size of the patent portfolio that is owned by the firm (Hall et al., 2005). In particular, internal citations can increase automatically with the size of the patent portfolio, regardless of whether these internal citations are indicative of patent quality.

The Commission adopted two different approaches in *Dow/DuPont* and *Bayer/Monsanto*.

In *Dow/DuPont*, the Commission put more weight on external citations – on the basis of case-specific facts. Indeed, one of the merging parties had a very different patent strategy than the strategies of its competitors, which resulted in a much smaller patent portfolio with significantly higher (average) quality than the portfolios of its competitors. Moreover, one non-merging party had a patent portfolio of a much greater size than its competitors. The inclusion of internal citations (*i.e.*, using total citations) would have underestimated the strength of this merging party and would have risked overestimating the strength of this specific competitor, irrespective of the quality of their respective patent portfolios.

In *Bayer/Monsanto*, the analysis of (biotech) patent data revealed that a (conglomerate) firm that was active in several industries had also a large share of internal citations, coming mainly from industries other than biotech. Moreover, since the purpose of the patent analysis was to assess the importance of the innovators within the biotech industry, it also made sense for the purpose of the merger assessment to consider only citations that came from subsequent patents in the biotech industry. The approach taken was therefore to consider only cited and citing patents from the biotech industry.

The approach that was taken in *Bayer/Monsanto* has the merit of still including internal citations in the analysis, while limiting its distorting effect due to internal citations that come from sectors other than the sector of interest for the merger assessment (which can be particularly distortive for large conglomerate firms with many internal citations across industries).

**Quantile approach versus non-linear weights applied to total citations.** In *Dow/DuPont*, various samples of (cited) patents were considered: (i) all patents; (ii) the patents with quality above the median quality (referred to as the "top50 sample"); and (iii) patents with quality above the 75th percentile (referred to as the "top25 sample"). Another sample of patents (the top 10 percent) was also considered: Patents above the 90th percentile in terms of quality (this sample of patents included some innovations that were related to "blockbuster" products – the most successful products in term of sales). Such an approach, which does not consider the entire sample of patents, finds support in the economic literature, in particular Hall et al. (2005).[23]

Alternatively, the literature also indicates that non-linear weights could be applied to citations to measure the value of a patent portfolio.[24] Tratjenberg (1990) suggests applying two non-linear weights to the full sample of patents: (i) a 1.1 exponential non-linear weight applied to the number of citations; and (ii) a 1.3 exponential non-linear weight applied to the number of citations, which gives more importance to the highly cited patents and therefore to breakthrough innovations. In the patent analysis, the results that were obtained by applying a 1.1 (respectively 1.3) non-linear weight to the number of citations over the entire sample of patents were very similar to the results that were obtained with a simple average of the number of citations over the top 50 percent sample (respectively top 25 percent sample) of patents.

In *Bayer/Monsanto*, the Commission applied directly the 1.1 and 1.3 non-linear weights to the total number of citations over the entire sample of patents.

**Control for the age of patents.** It is well-established in the economic literature that older patents mechanically receive more citations. In other words, the quality (as judged by citations) of "young" patents tends to be underestimated.

In *Dow/DuPont*, the Commission used a relevance metric – which was provided by PatentSight[25] – that adjusted the number of citations received by the age of the cited patents. In *Bayer/Monsanto*, the Commission took a different approach due to data limitations; it was not possible to use the same metric due to the restriction that applied to citing the patents of the Biotech industry. As an alternative, to mitigate the issue, the analysis was based on patents from the same cohort, *i.e.*, focusing only on biotech patents that were published after 2011.

**Overview of results.** In *Dow/DuPont*, the patent analysis indicated that both merging parties were important innovators; they owned some of the best-quality pat-

---

23 Hall et al. (2005) show that for firms with fewer than the median number of citations per patents, it makes no difference how far below the median they fall (which also includes patents with zero citations), while firms with more than the median number of citations per patent exhibit a very significant increase in market value. *See also* Coad & Rao (2008), who find that innovativeness appears to have a small or no influence on firm growth for the median firm.

24 Tratjenberg (1990) finds that the value of an innovation for customers is more skewed than what could be inferred from a count of citations, and therefore that a non-linear weight should be applied to citations to measure the value of an innovation. *See also* Harhoff et al. (2003).

25 The metric is called "Technology Relevance" and is based on the number of worldwide citations that are received from later patents, adjusted for age, patent office practices, and technology fields. PatentSight is a service company that was used by the merging parties. *See* https://www.patentsight.com/. *See also* Ernst & Omland (2011) for a description of the methodology that is used by PatentSight.

ents, especially in herbicides and insecticides. Moreover, for one merging party in particular, the patent analysis revealed that, while having the smallest patent portfolio, its patents were on average of a significantly higher quality than those of its competitors.

The merging parties accounted for a significant combined patent share, in the range of 50-60 percent for insecticides based on external citations (40-50 percent based on total citations), and 40-50 percent for selective herbicides based on external citations (30-40 percent based on total citations). The patent shares were also used to calculate concentration indexes, which showed a highly concentrated patenting field.

In *Bayer/Monsanto*, the analysis of patent data also indicated that the merging parties were important and close innovators, with significant combined patent shares in several innovation spaces, such as: Canola/weed control (90-100 percent combined patent share); cotton/insect control (80-90 percent); cotton/weed control (70-80 percent); insect control for cross-crops (40-50 percent); and weed control for cross-crops (50-60 percent).

## IV. THE MERGING PARTIES' ARGUMENTS

In the course of the two merger proceedings, the Parties presented a number of arguments to contest the Commission's concerns related to innovation competition.

**First**, in both cases, the Parties argued that they were neither important nor close competitors. The Commission rejected these concerns by relying on: (1) its analysis of overlaps in the relevant segments; (2) its patent analysis; and (3) evidence from internal documents (*see* previous Section for details on these legs of the Commission's assessment).

**Second**, in *Dow/DuPont* the Parties argued that the expected higher profits after the merger (as a result of the loss of product market competition between the parties) would lead to more investment. Therefore, any price effects that would be expected from the merger should be balanced against an allegedly positive effect of the merger on innovation.

The Commission noted that while less-intense competition in the product market increases the profits from innovating (the profits from the post-innovation outcome), which tends to increase innovation incentives, less intense competition in the product market also increases the profits from not innovating (the profits from the pre-innovation outcome), which tends to decrease innovation incentives.

Therefore, less intense competition in the product market has an ambiguous effect on the incentives to innovate. The recent economic literature that was cited above that analyses the effect of mergers on competition in innovation and competition in the product market finds that less competition typically reduces market-wide innovation – in particular in concentrated markets (absent efficiencies). This is because, absent efficiencies, the reduction of innovation incentives from innovation rivalry tends to dominate over any potential increase in innovation incentives from the reduction in product market competition that stems from the price coordination (*see* model above for an illustration of the innovation theory of harm).

Moreover, even if the effects of a merger on future product market competition increased the innovation incentives to the point of neutralizing the adverse impact on innovation incentives due to the innovation externality, consumers would still be harmed by the loss of future product competition (that is, the higher prices induced by the conventional price-related unilateral effects of the merger).

**Third**, in *Dow/DuPont* and *Bayer/Monsanto* the Parties argued that the success of the ongoing projects that underlay the overlaps that were identified by the Commission at the discovery stage were still highly uncertain (say, a 20 percent probability of success), and it was impossible at that stage to identify with sufficient precision the target application of the resulting product.

For several reasons, the Commission rejected these concerns: In the first place, even if there is uncertainty as to the outcome of the innovation process, a merger between firms with competing lines of research is likely to affect the incentives to invest in R&D. If the two companies expect that their products, if successful, would steal revenues from each other, they would have an incentive to either delay, reorient or discontinue lines of research or pipelines at the discovery stage. In particular, in both cases, the Commission found evidence that the Parties would have cut back on the investment to develop innovative products with significant reduction in their R&D capabilities, and would likely have reduced incentives to continue with ongoing innovation efforts that were targeting the same applications.

In any event, even absent any delay, reorientation, or discontinuation of one of the two lines of research, consumers would suffer from higher prices on the resulting products – once these are developed and brought to market by the merged entity.

In the second place, with regard to the target application of the resulting product, the Commission considered that the respective research targets were clear enough to generate an expectation that revenues could be cannibalized across the two lines of research. While the process of innovation is inherently uncertain, a good "innovation case" should feature innovation activities that are reasonably well identified in terms of overlap.

**Fourth**, in *Bayer/Monsanto* the Parties presented a theoretical economic model that in their view showed that most of the consumer harm from a merger that involves both price competition and innovation competition comes from the price effects, while a smaller share of the harm to consumers would come from the reduction in innovation competition. On this basis, the Parties claimed that only in extreme cases can the Commission raise a standalone concern that is related to reduction in innovation competition.

The Commission rejected this claim based on a number of arguments. In the first place, the Parties' distinction between harm that is related to innovation competition and harm that is related to price competition was arbitrary. The Parties assumed that the harm that is related to the loss of innovation competition applied only to the reduction of product variety due to reductions in innovation efforts. They instead considered future price effects only as a reduction in price competition.

In the second place, the ultimate objective of merger control was to devise a remedy that would eliminate any of the expected consumer harm – regardless of the label that is associated with that harm (whether it is a loss of innovation competition or a loss of future price competition). This competitive harm could be remedied only by divesting the ongoing overlapping lines of research and, if needed, the R&D assets that would be necessary to continue those projects and generate in the future further projects in the same innovation space.

**Fifth**, in *Bayer/Monsanto* the Parties claimed that even if they were working on overlapping lines of research, after the merger they would keep developing both lines, so that there would be no innovation-related harm for consumers. The merging parties' arguments were based on the fact that the two projects were often differentiated and it would make sense for the merged entity to keep both.

The Commission rejected the argument because even if it were true that both projects would be developed by the merged entity, there would still be harm for consumers related to the loss of future price competition. Moreover, the claims appeared to be inconsistent with the large cut in R&D projects and capabilities that were predicted from internal documents.

## V. THE OUTCOME, AND SUBSEQUENT DEVELOPMENTS

In both cases the merging parties had to make significant concessions in order to secure a clearance of their transaction. The rationale that underpinned the innovation-related **remedies** was not only to eliminate the Commission's concerns in relation to the ongoing R&D projects, but also to ensure that the third-party that acquired the divested assets would have the capabilities to preserve the viability and competitiveness of the divested current products on a lasting basis throughout their lifecycle, and to act further as a global integrated R&D competitor on a lasting basis.

The remedies in *Dow/DuPont* involved the sale of a large part of DuPont's herbicide and insecticide businesses to FMC. The divested business included AIs as well as all tangible and intangible assets that underpinned the divested products (including the facilities where the products are manufactured) and relevant personnel. To mitigate the innovation-related concerns, the remedy included DuPont's R&D organization (pipeline projects as well as R&D facilities and employees).[26] Up to that point, FMC was a generic player with some development activities in crop protection, but the Commission considered that the divested assets enabled FMC to become an integrated R&D company in the areas where competition concerns had to be remedied.[27]

In *Bayer/Monsanto* instead, the remedy consisted of the sale of Bayer's business in seeds and traits to BASF. The divested assets were worth more than EUR 7 billion – one of the largest divestitures in the history of EU merger control. The assets included, first, Bayer's global vegetable seed business and its global broad acre crop seed and trait business, subject to limited reverse carve-outs. Both divestitures included the

---

26 The commitments included also all the transition services and supply agreements deemed necessary by the Commission to eliminate the concerns identified.

27 In relation to the approval of the buyer of divested assets in the context of merger proceedings, under EU competition law, the Commission's role is to examine whether the buyer proposed by the merging parties is suitable in terms of ability and incentive to replace the competitive constraint lost due to the merger.

R&D centers of the respective businesses.[28] Second, to address the competition concerns that related to crop protection products, Bayer committed to divest its global glufosinate ammonium business, its assets that related to current and pipeline glyphosate products in the EEA, and three non-selective herbicide lines of research.

In parallel investigations in the U.S., for both *Dow/DuPont*[29] and *Bayer/Monsanto*,[30] the Department of Justice also raised antitrust concerns related to product market competition (higher prices, lower quality, and fewer choice) as well as innovation competition. Both proposed mergers were approved subject to assets divestitures.

While an *ex post* evaluation of a remedy in terms of innovation is difficult to carry out and could be the subject of another paper, some elements point toward a success of the divestment packages. First, following the remedy package in the *Dow/DuPont* merger, FMC was awarded the Agrow Award for the best R&D pipeline in both 2018 and 2020. Moreover, public information indicates that FMC is making progress on several discovery pipelines and development pipelines: for herbicides, insecticides, and fungicides; in fruits and vegetables; and in rice, cereals, corn, and soy.[31]

Second, following the remedy package in *Bayer/Monsanto*, BASF has currently several solutions in seeds and traits for broad acre crops, such as for canola and oilseed rape varieties, soybean seeds, and cotton seeds. Some of these traits and seeds that are currently being developed by BASF apply to both Europe and North America.

## VI. CONCLUSION AND REFLECTIONS ON THE CASES

An important point of these cases has been to re-focus attention on the unilateral effects in innovation rivalry that may result from a merger. This is very much in line with the intuition that was developed in the 2010 U.S. Guidelines, which put an early focus on contestability and innovation diversion as a primary competition concern. *E.g.*, para. 6.4 notes that a problem "is most likely to occur if at least one of the merging firms is engaging in efforts to introduce new products that would capture substantial revenues from the other merging firm."

While this insight has not been pursued in very many instances in U.S. case practice, we hope that these EC case studies provide a useful *roadmap* and a set of *limiting principles* that can be used to assess when innovation concerns arise in the context of a merger:

- Innovation must be an important parameter of competition. Conversely, if firms spend very little on R&D, an innovation angle will not be relevant.
- There should be a limited number of significant innovators in certain innova-

---

[28] To ensure that the businesses remained competitive and viable, Bayer also included its seed activities in areas where there were no competition concerns, such as in wheat and soybean.

[29] https://www.justice.gov/opa/pr/justice-department-requires-divestiture-certain-herbicides-insecticides-and-plastics#:~:text=The%20Department%20of%20Justice%20announced,valued%2-0at%20about%20%24130%20billion.

[30] https://www.justice.gov/opa/pr/justice-department-secures-largest-merger-divestiture-ever-preserve-competition-threatened.

[31] *See, e.g.*, https://www.fmc.com/en/innovation/research-development.

tion spaces. For instance, in both *Dow/DuPont* and *Bayer/Monsanto* the firms in question had very specific targeted markets, so that there could be a mapping between R&D and expected future markets and profits. In other sectors, instead, the ultimate uses for discoveries may be not so clear, so that there may be many more competitors that could eventually be considered as potential threats.
- Related to the previous point, the concepts of closeness and overlaps in capabilities of firms to innovate are applicable. A merger will be more of a concern if it puts together two close competitors that have similar capabilities. It is essential here to understand where such capabilities of the firms come from – whether, for instance, from specific scientists and scientific areas, or from general purpose technologies that could be employed by rivals too. Also, the analysis of current (static) product or pipeline overlaps is not sufficient to capture fully the reduction of competition that arises from a merger.
- The possibility of entry is important: Concerns are higher when there are fewer prospects for future entry in the event that the market is monopolized (for instance, because of the time lags for regulatory approvals). Here the recent history of the industry should be important to show patterns of entry and exit.
- A key aspect of an examination of innovation is the extent of its appropriability: The extent to which, when a firm innovates, it is able to retain the gains from such innovation. Can this firm get a patent? Or can it easily license to other users? If the answer is yes – if the industry is subject to an efficient regime of IPRs – then the merger concerns, *ceteris paribus*, are higher. If instead the industry is subject to uninternalized involuntary spillovers – if the benefits of innovation will accrue also to rivals without direct benefits to the innovator – the converse will be true.
- A different way of expressing the previous point is to examine the nature of innovation: If innovators, protected by IPRs, produce substitute products, this is when we would expect the negative innovation externality to be at play. If instead innovation brings demand expanding effects for rivals or other complementarities that cannot be achieved by other contractual arrangements, then a merger could be beneficial to innovation and to consumers.

## REFERENCES

Aghion, P., C. Harris, P. Howitt & J. Vickers (2001). "Competition, imitation and growth with step-by-step innovation," Review of Economic Studies, 68, 467-492.

Aghion, P., N. Bloom, R. Blundell, R. Griffith & P. Howitt (2005). "Competition and innovation: an inverted-U relationship," Quarterly Journal of Economics, 120(2), 701–728.

Bertuzzi et al (2017). "Dow/DuPont: protecting product and innovation competition," European Commission Competition Merger Brief, Issue 2/2017.

Bertuzzi et al (2018). "Bayer/Monsanto - protecting innovation and product competition in seeds, traits and pesticides," European Commission Competition Merger Brief, Issue 2/2018.

Bloom, N., M. Schankerman & J. Van Reenen (2013). "Identifying technology spillovers and product market rivalry," Econometrica, 81(4), 1347–1393.

Buehler, B., D. Coublucq, C. Hariton, G. Langus & T. Valletti (2017). "Recent Developments at DG Competition: 2016/2017," Review of Industrial Organization, 51, 397–422.

Bourreau, M., B. Jullien & Y. Lefouili (2021). "Mergers and Demand-Enhancing Innovation," CEPR Discussion Paper.

Coad, A. & R. Rao (2008). "Innovation and firm growth in high-tech sectors: A quantile regression approach," Research Policy, 37(4), 633–648.

Cohen, W. M. (2010). "Fifty years of empirical studies of innovative activity and performance," in B. H. Hall & N. Rosenberg (Eds.), Handbook of economics of innovation (pp. 129–213). Amsterdam: Elsevier.

Denicoló, V. & M. Polo (2018). "Duplicative research, mergers and innovation," Economics Letters, 166, 56-59.

Ernst, H. & N. Omland (2011). "The patent asset index: A new approach to benchmark patent portfolios," World Patent Information, 33(1), 34–41.

European Commission Decision in Case M.6166 - *Deutsche Borse/NYSE*.

European Commission Decision in Case M.7275 - *GSK/Novartis Oncology*.

European Commission Decision in Case M.7278 - *General Electric/Alstom*.

European Commission Decision in Case M.7932 - *Dow/DuPont* (2017).

European Commission Decision in Case M.7962 - *ChemChina/Syngenta* (2017).

European Commission Decision in Case M.8084 - *Bayer/Monsanto* (2018).

Farrell, J. & C. Shapiro (2010). "Antitrust Evaluation of Horizontal Mergers: An Economic Alternative to Market Definition," B. E. Journal of Theoretical Economics 10, Article 9.

Federico, G., G. Langus & T. Valletti (2017). "A simple model of mergers and innovation," Economics Letters, 157: 136-140.

Federico, G., G. Langus & T. Valletti (2018). "Horizontal mergers and product innovation," International Journal of Industrial Organization, 59: 1-23 (2018).

Gilbert, R. (2019). "Competition, Mergers, and R&D Diversity," Review of Industrial Organization.

Griliches, Z. (1990). "Patent statistics as economic indicators: A survey," Journal of Economic Literature, 28(4), 1661–1707.

Hall, B., A. Jaffe & M. Tratjenberg (2005). "Market value and patent citations," RAND Journal of Economics, 36(1), 16–38.

Harhoff, D., F. M. Scherer & K. Vopel (2003). "Exploring the tail of patented invention value," in O. Granstrand (Ed.), Economics, law and intellectual property. Boston: Springer.

Jaffe, A., M. Tratjenberg & R. Henderson (1993). "Geographic localization of knowledge spillovers as evidenced by patent citations," The Quarterly Journal of Economics, 108(3), 577–598.

Kokkoris, I. & T. Valletti (2020). "Innovation Considerations in Merger Control," Journal of Competition Law & Economics, 16(2), 220-261.

Lopez, A. & X. Vives (2018). "Overlapping Ownership, R&D Spillovers, and Antitrust Policy," Journal of Political Economy.

Motta, M. & E. Tarantino (2021). "The effect of horizontal mergers, when firms compete in prices and investments," International Journal of Industrial Organization, Volume 78.

Tratjenberg, M. (1990). "A penny for your quotes: Patent citations and the value of innovations," The Rand Journal of Economics, 21(1), 172–187.

Vives, X. (2008). "Innovation and Competitive Pressure," Journal of Industrial Economics 61: 419– 69.

# CHAPTER 3
# Efficiencies, Remedies, and Competition: The *Sprint/T-Mobile* Merger

*By John Asker & Michael L. Katz*[1]

## I. INTRODUCTION

On April 29, 2018, the then third-largest mobile wireless service provider in the United States – T-Mobile – proposed acquiring the fourth-largest provider: Sprint. T-Mobile and Sprint offered mobile wireless voice and data services to residential and business customers in the United States, Puerto Rico, and the U.S. Virgin Islands. The proposed transaction would combine the firms' customer bases and assets (notably spectrum licenses and cell site leases) in a single entity: New T-Mobile.

Because it was a telecommunications merger that involved the transfer of spectrum licenses, the transaction was subject to review by antitrust agencies and public utilities regulators at both the state and federal levels. Subject to various conditions that were reached through negotiation and settlement, the proposed merger received approval from the U.S. Department of Justice ("DOJ"), the Federal Communications Commission ("FCC"), and several state attorneys general. However, in June 2019 the attorneys general for 13 states and the District of Columbia filed suit in federal district court to block the transaction.

The district court held a two-week trial in December 2019, with a day of closing arguments the following January; the court ruled in favor of the defendants in February 2020. The transaction closed on April 1, 2020.[2]

The settlements, trial, and subsequent court opinion touched on issues that involved the appropriate approach and standards for merger review by courts:

- *The Role of the Structural Presumption.* At trial, the plaintiffs relied on the "structural presumption" that a merger harms competition if it significantly increases concentration in an already concentrated market. The defendants challenged the theoretical and empirical bases for the numerical thresholds used in applying the presumption. However, subject to some reservations, the court found

---

[1] In this matter, John Asker was retained as a consultant and potential testifying expert by Sprint and Softbank (Sprint's majority shareholder), and Michael Katz was retained as a consultant and testifying expert by T-Mobile. No confidential information is disclosed in this chapter.

[2] The closing required the approval of the transaction by the California Public Utilities Commission and a Tunney Act review of the settlement with the DOJ by another federal district court. These delayed the closing until April 1.

the plaintiff's application of the structural presumption was sufficient to meet their initial burden.
- *Predicting Coordinated Effects.* Critics of the merger, including the State plaintiffs, argued that the merger posed a substantial risk of facilitating coordination among New T-Mobile, AT&T, and Verizon Wireless. It generally is difficult to quantify coordinated effects, and in recent decades merger enforcement has given more weight to unilateral effects. Formal economic analysis ended up playing little role at trial, and the court rejected the prediction that New T-Mobile would settle for its current market share and coordinate with rivals after substantially increasing its capacity through the merger.
- *Treatment of Efficiencies.* Sprint and T-Mobile argued that their proposed merger would generate substantial efficiencies that would benefit consumers. The role of efficiencies in merger analysis has been subject to ongoing debate.[3] Some courts treat efficiencies as a "defense" against a finding that a merger harms competition. By contrast, under a consumer welfare standard, as the trial court recognized, consideration of merger efficiencies is central to the determination of whether the merger is pro- or anticompetitive. Regardless of the view taken, efficiencies are rarely, if ever, considered by the courts to be sufficient to offset otherwise substantial competitive harms. In the present matter, however, the court found that the efficiencies were substantial, and the efficiencies appear to have played an important role in the court's conclusion that the proposed merger would benefit consumers.
- *Weakened Competitor Defense.* The merging parties argued that Sprint was in decline and hence its acquisition by T-Mobile would not eliminate a vigorous, independent, competitor. Although some courts have been receptive to weakened competitor or "flailing firm" defenses, others have treated them with considerable skepticism.[4] In the present case, the parties succeeded in convincing the court that Sprint's current market share overstated the firm's future competitive strength.
- *Litigating the Fix.* Mergers that might be anticompetitive as proposed are frequently approved by the federal antitrust agencies subject to divestitures or other remedies that are expected to cure (or fix) the potential problems that would otherwise follow from the merger. However, even if an agency rejects a potential remedy, the merging parties may be able to commit to it unilaterally and force the agency to challenge the modified transaction. This is known as "litigating the fix."[5]

There is ongoing debate about whether allowing parties to litigate the fix is sound antitrust policy. Salop (2013) has shown that allowing parties to litigate the fix gives

---

[3] For a brief but insightful review, *see* Baker (2009). *See also*, United States District Court Southern District of New York, *State of New York et al. v. Deutsche Telekom AG, et al.*, Decision and Order, filed February 11, 2020 (hereinafter *Opinion*), pp. 57-59.

[4] *See* Kazmerzak & Widnell (2020).

[5] *See* Gelfand & Brannon (2016) for a discussion.

the agencies less pre-trial bargaining power to negotiate what they consider to be appropriate fixes. Questions have also been raised about whether proposing fixes after announcing the initial transaction wastes agency resources or undermines the agencies' abilities to develop sound trial strategies.[6] In the present case, the merging parties committed to the fix through settlements with the DOJ and FCC. The trial court credited the fix with a procompetitive impact despite the plaintiffs' (the state attorneys general) claims that it was inadequate.

- *Role of Sophisticated Economics.* The role of economics in merger review was highlighted by the differences in the sophistication and complexity of analyses that were presented in different forums. The analyses submitted to the DOJ and FCC were much more sophisticated than those that were presented to the trial court, and the court's opinion seemed to dismiss expert analysis. However, the core of the opinion was consistent with the application of standard and well-accepted economic frameworks. Moreover, the more sophisticated analyses that were presented to the DOJ and FCC played a role in shaping the settlements with those agencies, which in turn influenced the court.

## II. INDUSTRY BACKGROUND AND MERGER RATIONALE

Prior to the merger, the U.S. wireless industry comprised four nationwide, facilities-based providers: Verizon, AT&T, T-Mobile, and Sprint. These "mobile network operators" ("MNOs") collectively provided service to the vast majority of mobile wireless users. AT&T and Verizon each had nearly 100 million wireless subscribers, while T-Mobile had 70-80 million, and Sprint had approximately 40 million.[7] In addition to the four largest providers, there were several, much smaller, regional network operators. Mobile wireless services were also offered by "mobile virtual network operators" ("MVNOs") – firms that did not own their own wireless networks and instead purchased wholesale wireless services from facilities-based providers and resold these services to end users under the MVNOs' brand names.

Maintaining a cellular network requires investment, particularly as new technologies are introduced. The four national MNOs had persistent differences in their levels of network investment. From 2015 to 2019, Verizon averaged $10.5 billion per year in wireless capital expenditures, and AT&T $10.2 billion. By contrast, T-Mobile averaged $5.1 billion, and Sprint averaged $3.3 billion.[8]

The electromagnetic spectrum holdings of the MNOs also varied. At a high level, there were three "flavors" of spectrum that were available to carriers at the time of the transaction: low-, mid-, and high-frequency bands. Generally, as the frequency of the

---

[6] *See, for example*, U.S. Department of Justice and U.S. Federal Trade Commission, Request for Information on Merger Enforcement, January 18, 2022, Question 8.a.

[7] *Opinion*, pp. 21 and 23.

[8] These numbers are based on FCC (2020, Fig II.A.26).

spectrum increases, capacity increases but propagation degrades. That is, more data can be carried, but the signal does not carry as far and can have trouble penetrating buildings and other physical barriers.[9] At the time that the merger was proposed, AT&T, T-Mobile, and Verizon all had substantial low-band spectrum holdings, which allowed them to offer broad coverage. T-Mobile's spectrum holdings were relatively concentrated in low-band spectrum, which contributed to congestion problems on its network. By contrast, Sprint held no low-band spectrum and a substantial amount of higher-frequency mid-band spectrum, which meant that it was poorly positioned to provide broad coverage but was well-positioned to provide high capacity where it did offer coverage.

The differences in investment histories and spectrum holdings were reflected in network quality levels. The merging parties demonstrated the differences in network quality with the use of the Nielsen Mobile Performance ("NMP") dataset, which follows the experiences of roughly 45,000 wireless consumers.[10] For each network, two metrics of quality were calculated at a highly localized level:[11] speed, which was measured in megabits per second ("Mbps"); and coverage, which was measured as the percentage of time on 4G LTE coverage. Because network quality varied across locations and different consumers used their phones in different locations, it was useful to examine individual-specific network-quality metrics. For each consumer and network pair in the sample, average speed, worst speed, average coverage, and worst coverage were calculated. The worst speed (or coverage) measure corresponded to the speed (or coverage) that was the network's worst of any of the local areas that the consumer visited.

The NMP data confirmed industry views of network quality: For most consumers, Sprint's network offered poor coverage but good speeds, while T-Mobile's offered good coverage but poor speeds. The data also showed that AT&T and Verizon both tended to offer higher-quality services than either Sprint or T-Mobile. These findings also aligned with consumer perceptions.

The merging parties argued that these data were critical to understanding the effects of the proposed merger and that: (a) absent the merger, neither Sprint nor T-Mobile had sufficient network quality to put strong competitive pressure on AT&T and Verizon; and (b) even in the absence of any detailed modeling, New T-Mobile could reasonably be expected to offer greater speed than could T-Mobile alone and greater coverage than could Sprint alone, which would allow New T-Mobile to be a more effective competitor than either standalone firm.

The merging parties offered various visualizations that pointed to the potential competitive benefit of increased network quality. For instance, Figure 1 compares the

---

9 For a brief, user-friendly introduction to spectrum characteristics, *see* https://www.nasa.gov/directorates/heo/scan/spectrum/overview/index.html, accessed August 4, 2022.

10 Nielsen, "Mobile Performance," *available at* http://www.nielsen.com/us/en/solutions/capabilities/nielsen- mobile-performance.html, accessed October 25, 2018.

11 A local area was defined by layering a grid of hexagons over the U.S. The basic hexagonal unit was approximately 2/3 of a mile across. In less densely populated areas these basic hexagonal units were combined.

number of Verizon customers in California that would experience speeds that were more than 10 percent slower were they to switch to T-Mobile with and without a contemplated 10 percent increase in network speed due to the merger. Visualization such as Figure 1, together with statements from the parties' engineers that New T-Mobile would surpass AT&T and Verizon in delivered speed, were used to explain that the contemplated network improvements would make New T-Mobile a competitive option for a much larger set of consumers than would be the case for either of T-Mobile or Sprint on a standalone basis.

**Figure 1: Californian Verizon consumers that would experience a 10% speed drop if they were to switch to T-Mobile.**

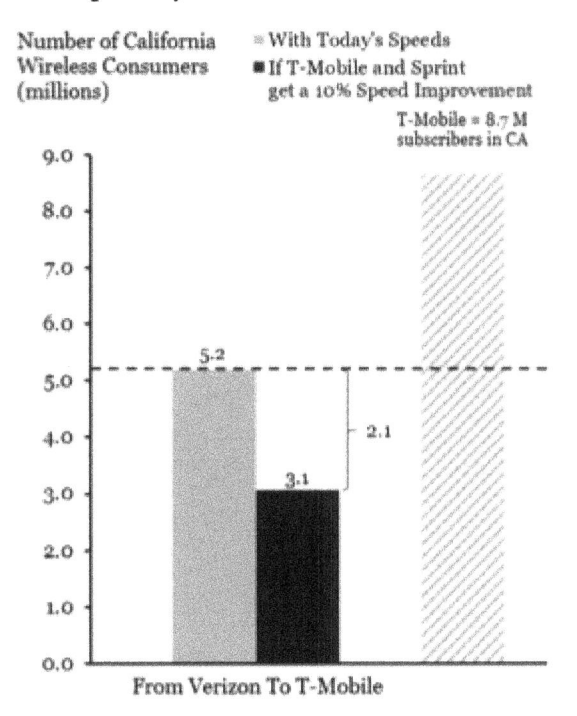

**Source:** Rebuttal Testimony of Timothy F. Bresnahan (Public Version), January 29, 2019 C.P.U.C. Docket Number A.18-07-011 and A.18-07-012.[12]

## III. AGENCY REVIEW

As was noted above, the transaction was subject to review by antitrust agencies and public utilities regulators at both the state and federal levels. In what follows, we focus on the competition issues that were raised by state and federal antitrust agencies as well as by the FCC; the FCC reviewed the proposed merger under a "public inter-

---

12 *Available at* https://www.tellusventure.com/downloads/cpuc/tmobile_sprint/joint_applicants_bresnahan_rebuttal_testimony_tmobile_sprint_29jan2019.pdf, accessed 5 May 2022.

est" standard that has been interpreted as incorporating traditional antitrust considerations as well as broader, unspecified concerns.[13]

Agency staff raised high-level concerns about the effects of the merger. Although they raised questions about the merging parties' analyses of those effects, agency staff did not share any analyses of their own with the merging parties. Hence, the discussion below focuses on the analyses that the parties put before the reviewing agencies, as well as comments that the FCC published in its order approving the merger subject to conditions. The FCC and DOJ reviews operated in tandem, and the agencies appeared to cooperate closely. Hence, to the extent that the discussion below tends to draw on the FCC record, which contains more public material regarding the agency's thinking, it should be read as reflecting the interaction between the parties and both federal agencies.[14]

## A. Agency Concerns Regarding Coordinated and Unilateral Effects

DOJ and FCC staff were concerned that, by eliminating Sprint as an independent competitor, the proposed merger would make it easier for the remaining three national MNOs to coordinate to reduce the intensity of competition and/or would give New T-Mobile unilateral incentives to increase its prices. Both agencies characterized the pre-merger industry structure as one in which AT&T and Verizon competed in a premium industry segment, while Sprint and T-Mobile competed for more value-conscious consumers.

Because of the difficulties in quantifying coordinated effects, arguments about the likely effects of mergers on coordination often center of how the merger affects industry mavericks.[15] This merger was no different. Staff raised the concern that, absent the merger, Sprint and/or T-Mobile would continue to be industry mavericks but, post-merger, the combined firm would be part of a cozy triopoly. By contrast, T-Mobile argued that, as the result of substantial merger efficiencies, New T-Mobile would be a super maverick – one willing and able to place competitive pressure on AT&T and Verizon to an extent that neither standalone T-Mobile nor Sprint ever could.

In addition, Sprint and T-Mobile argued that, because consumers tend to stick with their wireless service providers and it is costly to acquire new customers rapidly, New T-Mobile would have incentives to engage in penetration pricing in order to build up its customer base in anticipation of having lower costs in the future. They also argued that, based on a checklist of factors that mirrored those of Stigler (1964), collusion was unlikely. Specifically, the parties argued that relatively low level of price transparency, substantial product differentiation, the existence of market asymme-

---

[13] For example, the merging parties identified potentially substantial merger benefits that would accrue to consumers of fixed broadband services. Such out-of-market benefits are generally ignored as a matter of antitrust law but could be considered under the FCC's public-interest standard.

[14] Interaction with the state regulators, and in particular the California Public Utility Commission, also largely reflected interaction between the parties and the FCC interaction, at least in terms of economic substance.

[15] *See* Baker (2002) for a discussion of mavericks and coordinated effects.

tries, and the relatively low frequency with which consumers make purchasing decision all contributed to a conclusion that coordination was unlikely. As we discuss below, however, the academic literature at present provides little basis to quantify the degree to which a proposed merger will increase the likelihood of successful coordination under various conditions.

The DOJ remained concerned that, absent the divestitures to which the parties were committed (*see* below), "[t]he merger would also leave the market vulnerable to increased coordination among the remaining three carriers."[16] Although the DOJ did not provide an explanation of its reasoning, the reduction in the number of national MNOs and the more-symmetrical market positions of the remaining firms very likely were key factors.[17] In its final order, the FCC considered all of these arguments and found "that the record does not support a conclusion that post-transaction coordination is likely."[18] The FCC also found that the divestitures would further mitigate any coordination risk.[19]

Although "coordinated effects" received considerable attention, the DOJ's and FCC's principal theory that was relevant to the assessment of the proposed merger's potential competitive harms (or benefits) was that of "unilateral effects," which arise when a merger lessens competition even if the non-merging suppliers in the industry continue to act in their unchanged self-interests.[20]

Whether it is profitable for a firm to raise the price of one of its products depends, in part, on how much it will lose sales to its rivals as the price rises – the incentive to raise price is smaller when the volume of lost sales is larger. To see how a merger can affect the profitability of raising price, consider two firms – $A$ and $B$ – that are contemplating merging. When the firms are independent of one another and firm $A$ contemplates increasing its price, any sales that it would lose to firm $B$ reduce $A$'s incentive to increase its price. Once the two firms have merged, however, the merged firm does not consider sales that shift from $A$ to $B$ to be lost, which increases the firm's incentive to raise its price as long as those sales earn a positive margin.

A merger's effects on unilateral pricing incentives also depends on how the merger affects marginal costs. To the extent that merger efficiencies result in a firm that has lower marginal costs of output than would either firm on a standalone basis, the transaction creates incentives for the merged firm to reduce its prices. Changes in costs can also affect a firm's choice of product quality: By reducing the marginal costs of increasing quality, merger efficiencies can generate incentives for the post-merger firm to provide higher quality services than would either firm as an independent entity.

---

16 DOJ (2019.c.).

17 The text of the complaint is only 8.5 pages long. (*Id.*).

18 Federal Communications Commission (2019), *Memorandum opinion and order, declaratory ruling, and order of proposed modification*, FCC-19-103A1. Adopted October 16, 2019, (hereinafter *FCC Final Order*), ¶ 188.

19 *Id.* The DOJ (2019.b.), in its competitive impact statement, also pointed to the divestitures as mitigating coordination risk.

20 For a general description of unilateral effects, *see Horizontal Merger Guidelines*, §§ 1 and 6.

In theory, the unilateral effects of a merger can be positive or negative; a factual inquiry is required to determine the net effect of a merger. With regard to the potential for generating competitive harms, a key empirical question was the degree to which Sprint and T-Mobile were close competitors of one another. This closeness is typically measured by "diversion ratios."[21] Both the DOJ and FCC were particularly concerned about the loss of head-to-head competition between Sprint and T-Mobile to serve value-conscious consumers, especially buyers of pre-paid services, such as those that were offered by Sprint's Boost brand and T-Mobile's Metro by T-Mobile brand. With regard to the potential for generating competitive benefits, there were two broad issues: One was the extent to which the proposed merger would reduce the marginal costs of additional output and/or quality. A second issue was the value to consumers of any quality improvements that the proposed merger might generate.

Sprint and T-Mobile presented extensive evidence to the agencies with regard to both merger efficiencies and the nature of consumer demand; the latter was relevant for assessing both how close Sprint and T-Mobile were as competitors and for assessing the value of increased quality.

## B. The Merging Parties' Efficiencies Modeling

DOJ and FCC staff initially expressed skepticism with regard to the potential for the proposed merger to generate substantial efficiencies. Consequently, the parties engaged in extensive efficiency modeling. The DOJ never disclosed whether it engaged in independent modeling of the merger's potential efficiencies, although the FCC reported that it conducted various sensitivity analyses with respect to the parties' modeling.

The vast majority of the marginal cost savings that were projected to be realized due to the merger were from the integration of the Sprint and T-Mobile radio access networks. When an MNO's traffic significantly increases, the firm must increase capacity in order to prevent users' network experiences from degrading below acceptable levels. MNOs have a range of options to increase capacity, and an MNO will generally try to implement the most cost-effective solutions first. As the MNO exhausts its most attractive capacity solutions, it must turn to options that generally are more expensive means of solving congestion. The proposed merger was projected to reduce network marginal costs by increasing the network capacity that can be provided using lower-cost capacity-expansion options – thus avoiding the need to use higher-cost options.

The extent of marginal costs savings was projected with the use two stages of modeling: First, the "Network Build Model" was used to generate projections of network investment and performance under various scenarios. For any given spectrum inventory, baseline network, and traffic forecast, the Network Build Model determined the incremental cell sites and equipment beyond the baseline network that were necessary to accommodate the traffic while satisfying the relevant network performance planning

---

21 The diversion ratio between two products measures the "fraction of unit sales lost by the first product due to an increase in its price that would be diverted to the second product." (*Horizontal Merger Guidelines*, § 6.1.).

criteria. Once the outputs of the Network Build Model were in hand, it was conceptually straightforward to use those results in the second stage to calculate how total costs varied with the level of traffic that was served on each of the standalone Sprint, standalone T-Mobile, and New T-Mobile networks. The resulting changes were the respective networks' marginal costs of additional traffic.

The Network Build Model was based on T-Mobile's ordinary-course-of-business network model and was developed by T-Mobile in consultation with Sprint to evaluate the merger. One reason for adhering as closely to existing models as possible was to avoid claims that the modeling as rigged to favor the merger – a claim that had strongly undermined AT&T's arguments before the DOJ and FCC when AT&T unsuccessfully attempted to obtain antitrust clearance for its proposed acquisition of T-Mobile in 2011.[22] It was necessary to extend the existing T-Mobile network modeling to incorporate the deployment of emerging 5G technology, as well as to cover the networks of Sprint and the proposed merged firm. Sprint did not have a comparable model of its own: Network coverage, rather than congestion, was Sprint's primary concern.

There were several sources of the proposed merger's cost savings:
- *Benefits of Resource Pooling in the Presence of Load Diversity.* As standalone companies, either the Sprint or the T-Mobile network could become congested at a time and place when the other network was not congested. By pooling network resources, the "excess" capacity on one network could be used to offset the congestion on the other, which would reduce the need to make costly incremental network investments to handle increases in network traffic.
- *Cell-Site Level Economies of Scale Deploying Spectrum.* The merged firm would be able to deploy Sprint and T-Mobile's combined spectrum holdings at every New T-Mobile site. Critically, the costs of deploying spectrum at a site typically rise less than proportionately with the amount of spectrum that is deployed.
- *Benefits of a Diverse Spectrum Portfolio.* New T-Mobile planned to combine Sprint's and T-Mobile's spectrum portfolios, which were complementary in that they were weighted toward different bands with different propagation characteristics. When deployed by a single company, each spectrum band could be used for the type of traffic for which it was best suited, which increased the capacity that could be realized from a given spectrum portfolio.
- *Enhanced Spectral Efficiency due to More Rapid 5G Deployment.* The proposed transaction would accelerate the migration of customers to 5G, which had a higher degree of spectral efficiency than do the radio technologies that were currently widely deployed. Two factors promoted the acceleration: First, because of various engineering complementarities,

---

[22] For a discussion of flaws that FCC staff identified in the model used by the AT&T to defend its proposed acquisition of T-Mobile, see DeGraba & Rosston (2018).

New T-Mobile would be able to maintain the necessary transitional LTE capability using less than the sum of the spectrum that Sprint and T-Mobile would have had to use as standalone companies. Second, New T-Mobile would have additional scale that would make it more attractive for manufacturers to accelerate the roll out of access devices – *e.g.*, smartphones – that functioned on New T-Mobile's 5G network.

- *Roaming Efficiencies.* Because of its substantial network-coverage limitations, Sprint had roaming agreements with other carriers to provide coverage outside of Sprint's network's footprint. Post-merger, New T-Mobile would provide most of the network services that, had Sprint remained a separate company, would have been provided under roaming agreements. New T-Mobile's marginal costs were projected to be far below the traffic-sensitive roaming fees Sprint was paying.

The DOJ offered no assessment of merger efficiencies other than the conclusion that, absent the required divestitures, the efficiencies were insufficient to fully offset the loss of Sprint as an independent competitor. For its part, the FCC found that the parties' "models yield verifiable quantifications of marginal cost benefits, but with some uncertainty as to certain modeling choices and inputs."[23] For example, the size of the projected savings was sensitive to the projected growth in traffic volume, as well as to assumptions of the deployment of new network technologies. FCC staff undertook various sensitivity analyses and predicted "substantial marginal cost savings" in all of the scenarios considered.[24]

## C. The Merging Parties' Demand Analyses

The merging parties also presented a detailed econometric demand model that estimated substitution patterns and supported a merger simulation. Specifically, the merging parties used the Nielsen NMP data, described above, to estimate a model of how consumers select a wireless brand given where, when, and how they use their phone. This demand model adopted a discrete-choice framework and was estimated as a standard conditional logit model of brand choice. As described in the Technical Appendix, the utility specification that was used to estimate demand did not include price, and the effect of price enters through the location-specific brand fixed effects.

The demand model supplied two things: First, it provided a quantitative measure of consumers' response to quality changes. Consumers were found to put a high value on network quality.[25] The quantitative findings were corroborated by testimony from executives regarding the importance of network quality as well as by the high levels of annual network investment made to maintain quality.

Second, the demand model provided diversion ratios, which measured the extent of substitution between firms in the event of a price change. Diversion ratios varied

---

23 *FCC Final Order*, Appendix F, ¶ 92.
24 *FCC Final Order*, ¶ 161.
25 Specific quantifications of the value of quality are not publicly available.

across firms. Of those consumers who would leave AT&T in the event of a price increase, 40 percent were estimated to switch to Verizon. Of those consumers who would leave T-Mobile in the event of a price increase, 35 percent would go to Verizon, while 28 percent would go to AT&T, 12 percent to Sprint, and 12 percent to regional carriers and MVNOs.[26]

The primary challenge to the demand model related to the accuracy of the diversion ratios. The estimates were critiqued by FCC staff, as well as by economists who were retained by DISH, for resembling share-proportional diversion.[27] A vigorous written and oral exchange occurred among economists working for the merging parties, the FCC, and DISH, as to whether the estimated diversion ratios represented an empirical finding or an artifact of modeling choices.[28] Ultimately, the FCC cited various concerns regarding the structure of the model, the reliability of the NMP data, and the possible impact of omitted variables as reasons to dismiss the empirical finding of nearly share-proportional diversion ratios.[29]

This exchange occurred against a broader discussion as to whether porting data, which tracks switching (churn) from one firm to another on a weekly or monthly basis was more indicative of substitution patterns than that arising from the formal econometric modeling. As noted by Chen & Schwartz (2016), "It is widely recognized, of course, that churn and diversion ratios can differ depending on the specific reasons for churn…"[30] The difficulty in mapping porting data (which reflect changes in any factors that influence consumer purchase decisions) to diversion (which reflects the impact of a single firm's price change) was readily apparent in this matter given that extensive switching between any two firms was present in both directions within the same time period.

The FCC acknowledged the limitations of switching data but, nonetheless, concluded that "…porting data, while not perfect, is the most reliable diversion proxy available in this record."[31] As a result, the *FCC Final Order* did not rely on the demand modeling. DOJ staff also engaged with the demand modeling but never disclosed whether, or to what extent, it shaped their final thinking on the transaction.

---

26 T-Mobile, in this instance, refers to T-Mobile's prepaid brands. Table 1, in the technical appendix, shows the full set of estimated diversion ratios.

27 *FCC Final Order*, ¶ 127. DISH has not shared with us its reasons for intervening, but it is notable that the agreements ultimately reached between the merging parties and the FCC and DOJ to obtain approval to merge have greatly facilitated DISH's entry as a mobile network operator.

28 The back-and-forth addressed questions that related to: whether, as a theoretical matter, the model could generate diversion ratios that were substantially different from share ratios; whether in the data at hand the differences from share-based diversion were substantial; and whether alternative data rebutted the results, among other issues.

29 *FCC Final Order*, ¶¶ 128-129.

30 Chen & Schwartz (2016).

31 *FCC Final Order*, ¶ 128.

## D. The Merging Parties' Merger Simulation

A variety of merger simulations were offered by the parties. These simulations combined a Bertrand-Nash pricing model with estimates of pre-merger marginal costs and several different estimates of diversion ratios, namely estimates based on: (a) the demand model; (b) two industry surveys of switching behavior; and (c) internal T-Mobile estimates of additions and deactivations. These simulations quantified the impact of the transaction on consumer surplus under various scenarios that captured different marginal cost reductions and quality improvements. The parties argued that consumers would benefit from the merger even if conditions were not imposed by the FCC or DOJ.

The FCC staff adopted the simulation framework, and modified it in several ways. Most notably, they assumed diversion ratios based on porting data. Based on the simulations and the overall record, the FCC concluded that, in certain areas (*e.g.*, rural) and customer segments (*e.g.*, quality-conscious consumers), the increases in network quality and capacity would outweigh the upward pricing pressures created by the loss of competition between Sprint and T-Mobile, so that consumers would benefit from the merger even in the absence of conditions.[32] However, the FCC was concerned that price-conscious consumers in densely populated areas might suffer because the FCC concluded that the parties' prepaid brands, Boost Mobile and Metro, were particularly close competitors.[33]

## E. Settlements

The DOJ, FCC, and Attorneys General of several states reached settlements with the merging parties. The DOJ remained concerned about both coordinated and unilateral effects, and it filed a complaint in federal district court along with a proposed final judgment (consent decree) that contained remedies that the DOJ concluded were sufficient to address its concerns.[34] As noted above, the FCC recognized that the proposed merger would generate benefits for some consumers even absent settlement conditions, but the agency was concerned with potential adverse competitive effects to serve price-conscious consumers in urban areas.[35] The FCC concluded that – with the settlement conditions and commitments in place – the merger did not threaten harm to competition and was in the public interest.

Most fundamentally, the DOJ and FCC settlements were intended to allow DISH – which was not a mobile wireless services provider but had amassed a considerable portfolio of spectrum licenses that were suitable for providing such services – to enter the market as a nationwide, facilities-based provider that would replace the competition that would be lost from the elimination of Sprint. The merging parties agreed to make a range of resources available to DISH to support its entry efforts,

---

32 *FCC Final Order*, ¶¶ 10, 11.
33 *FCC Final Order*, ¶¶ 9, 11.
34 DOJ (2019.a).
35 *FCC Final Order*, ¶¶ 8-11 and 20.

including: the Boost Mobile prepaid brand and associated customer base (which was owned by Sprint); Sprint's 800 MHz spectrum licenses; wholesale capacity that would be supplied to DISH while DISH built out its own radio access network; and the option to obtain the merging parties' decommissioned cell sites and retail locations. The merging parties also agreed that they would not interfere with DISH's efforts to deploy a nationwide 5G network.

The settlements also included commitments by the merging parties with respect to their post-merger competitive conduct. Specifically:

- *Wholesale Commitments*: New T-Mobile would abide by the terms of all of the merging parties' existing wholesale supply agreements with MVNOs and extend those terms for the seven-year duration of the Proposed Final Judgment and would engage in good-faith negotiations to amend the terms of its MVNO agreement with Altice – a company that offered broadband access, cable television, and mobile data services – to include access to the New T-Mobile network;
- *Retail Price Commitments*: New T-Mobile would not raise retail prices above the levels that prevailed in February 2019 for a period of three years from that date, and Sprint customers would be able to keep their current Sprint rate plan or switch to a better New T-Mobile plan; and
- *Network Build Commitments*: New T-Mobile would meet a series of specific performance targets for the deployment of a 5G network.

In addition, DISH made network build commitments to the FCC, including a commitment to build a nationwide 5G broadband network by June 2023, as well as interim coverage commitments.

Critics of the settlement argued that it was largely a conduct remedy rather than a structural one. Further, some argued, "[t]he extreme dependency of Dish on the good graces of New T-Mobile creates abundant opportunities for the merged firm to engage in strategic pricing, slowdown of provision, alteration of terms or quality of the assets and services, and so forth" and that the settlement "has all the hallmarks of a detailed, regulatory, and interventionist remedy of the sort previously and properly criticized by the DOJ."[36] Skepticism was also expressed as to whether Dish would ever build out a competitive national network and, even if it did, whether the delay in realizing any competitive benefits from the creation this new network would be too great to offset any competitive harms arising from the merger.

## IV. THE STATE LITIGATION

The attorneys general for several states and the District of Columbia also found the settlement conditions to be insufficient and filed a complaint in federal district court that asserted that the proposed merger would violate Section 7 of the Clayton

---

36 *State of New York v. Deutsche Telecom AG*, Brief of Amici Curiae Nicholas Economides, John Kwoka, Thomas Philippon, Robert Seamans, Hal Singer, Marshall Steinbaum, and Lawrence J. White in Support of Plaintiffs, 01/13/20, available as NET Institute Working Paper 20-01.

Act by harming competition in the markets – at the national level and in many local areas – for retail mobile wireless telecommunications services.

The court applied a standard, three-stage process to assess these claims: First, the plaintiffs were required to establish a *prima facie* case of harm to competition that showed that the proposed merger would lead to high concentration in one or more relevant markets. If the plaintiffs met their initial burden, then the defendants (T-Mobile and Sprint) would present evidence in the second stage to rebut the *prima facie* case by demonstrating that the market-share analysis was not indicative of actual competitive effects. If the defendants succeeded in the second stage, the burden would shift back to the plaintiffs in a final stage in which to provide additional evidence that the merger would harm competition. Although the burden of production shifted between the parties, the ultimate burden of persuasion was always with the plaintiffs.

In order to focus on the economic logic, the summary of the parties' arguments and the court's decision below are organized by economic issue, rather than the district court's three-phase framework.

## A. Concentrations Measures and their Implications

The plaintiffs relied on the "structural presumption" that a merger harms competition if it significantly increases concentration in an already concentrated market. The three most significant points of contention between the parties were: (a) whether local markets were an appropriate frame for analysis; (b) how MVNOs should be treated in calculating concentration in the relevant market; and (c) the validity of standard concentration thresholds.

With regard to geographic market definition, the plaintiffs argued that there was a national relevant market as well as local relevant markets that corresponded to "Cellular Market Areas."[37] The defendants agreed that a national market existed but challenged the usefulness of the narrower geographic markets because: prices were largely determined at the national level; most advertising was nationwide; and network investment policies – *e.g.*, network performance targets – were set at the national level. The court concluded that there were sufficiently important decisions that were taken at the local level that both national and local relevant markets were appropriate. The court also relied on the FCC's and DOJ's having reached a similar conclusion in analyzing MNO mergers.

The parties also disagreed on how MVNOs should be treated when calculating market shares and concentration metrics. Although the court framed the issue as one of market delineation, it really was one of attribution and the appropriate calculation of shares. The plaintiffs argued that an MVNO's share should be attributed to the MNO(s) that provided the wholesale services to the MVNO be-

---

37 "Cellular Market Areas" (CMAs) are standard geographic areas used by the FCC for administrative convenience in the licensing of Cellular systems. CMAs comprise Metropolitan Statistical Areas (MSAs) and Rural Service Areas (RSAs). CMAs and the counties they comprise are listed in "Common Carrier Public Mobile Services Information, Cellular MSA/RSA Markets and Counties," Public Notice, Rep. No. CL-92-40, 7 FCC Rcd 742 (1992)." See 47 CFR § 22.909

cause wholesale fees constituted such a high percentage of an MVNO's costs (and the selling MNO had the ability to affect that price) and the MVNO had only a limited ability to differentiate itself. The defendants argued that MVNOs – particularly those that were operated by cable television/broadband providers – had the ability to differentiate themselves through bundling with other services, and these companies were often willing to sell service at very low incremental prices as additions to service bundles.

The court sided with the plaintiffs and ruled that MVNOs were not independent competitors and that their revenues should be allocated to the underlying wholesale providers when calculating market shares. However, the court also stated that "MVNOs do undoubtedly compete with MNOs in some ways and should not be altogether excluded from broader consideration."[38] The Court further stated that the treatment of MVNOs and DISH's impending entry (in part as an MVNO) "may ultimately reduce the persuasive force of market share statistics in the final analysis."[39]

The final issue with regard to the plaintiffs' application of the structural presumption concerned the validity of the concentration thresholds that underlay the presumption. The court examined two thresholds to determine whether the proposed merger would presumptively harm competition:

- whether the resulting firm would have a market share greater than 30 percent, which was the approach of *Philadelphia National Bank*, 374 U.S. 321 (1963); and
- whether the merger would increase the Herfindahl-Hirschman Index (HHI) by more than 200 points and result in an HHI of greater than 2,500, which followed the U.S. Department of Justice and Federal Trade Commission 2010 *Horizontal Merger Guidelines*.

There is little or no theoretical or empirical basis for the use of either the 30-percent-share or the 2,500-HHI concentration thresholds, while thresholds that are based on the *change* in concentration have firmer theoretical footing.[40] As pointed out by the defendants, the plaintiffs made no attempt at trial to use economic theory or data to show that the generic thresholds were appropriate given the specifics of the markets at issue in the case. The court noted that this fact further reduced its confidence in the informativeness of the concentration analysis.

The court concluded that the plaintiffs had met their initial burden – the merger was presumptively anticompetitive if either the market-share or the HHI threshold was applied – but also indicated that it had limited confidence in the presumption as applied to the present case. This conclusion set up the next step under the three-stage pro-

---

38 *Opinion*, p. 45.

39 *Opinion*, p. 46.

40 *See* Willig (1991) for an early attempt at providing a theoretical basis for having concentration thresholds that are based on both the level and change in concentration. For a more recent contribution to the debate, *see* Nocke & Whinston (2022). For a summary of the inconclusive state of empirical work on merger retrospectives, *see* Asker & Nocke (2021). Kwoka (2017) offers a different view.

cess applied by the Court, *i.e.*, that "[d]efendants may … rebut evidence of high market concentration by producing evidence that 'show[s] that the market-share statistics [give] an inaccurate account of the acquisition['s] probable effects on competition.'"[41]

The defendants argued that market-share statistics did indeed give an inaccurate account and that the proposed merger would strengthen – not weaken – competition. The plaintiffs responded by offering analyses beyond concentration figures to project competitive effects and by challenging various elements of the defendants' rebuttal case.

## B. A More Sophisticated Examination of Competitive Effects

The plaintiffs emphasized unilateral effects at trial. This may have been due to the difficulty that economists have in quantifying the extent to which a merger would increase the likelihood of coordination. For example, economic theory identifies several factors as potentially affecting the ability of firms to coordinate successfully, including the number of firms that would have to coordinate for it to be successful, the degree to which pricing is observable to rivals, whether customer orders are large and infrequent, and whether a firm can gain competitive advantage by secretly investing in innovations that are difficult for rivals to match quickly after the innovation has been launched in the market. However, the academic literature at present provides little basis to conclude whether a merger that is undertaken in the presence of some combination of factors results in a (say) 20-, 50-, or 80-percent increase in the likelihood of coordination.[42]

Nevertheless, in their pre-trial reports, economic experts for the two sides engaged on several issues with regard to coordinated effects. The plaintiffs organized much of their discussion around an elegant distillation of the incentive of an individual firm to defect from coordination that arises in a simple, repeated-game model. A firm contemplating whether to deviate from coordination would compare the *gains* from deviating – the amount by which the profit it earns deviating until caught exceeds its coordination profit – with the *losses* it would suffer – the amount by which its coordination profits would have exceeded the profits it will earn while being punished for deviating. The flow gains and losses have to be weighted to account for the length of time that the firm would deviate before being punished, the length of the punishment period, and the firm's rate-of-time preference. All of these considerations are captured by δ, the discount factor. If the punishment lasts $T$ periods, then the firm will disrupt coordination if and only if

$$\frac{\delta(1-\delta^T)}{(1-\delta)} < \frac{deviation\ profit - coordination\ profit}{coordination\ profit - punnishment\ profit},$$

where the right-hand side of the equation is the "disruption index." The higher is the disruption index, the greater is the range of values of δ for which the firm will find

---

[41] *Opinion*, p. 55, citation omitted.

[42] *See* Asker & Nocke (2021) for a discussion of theoretical and empirical work on coordinated effects. For a different interpretation of existing studies, *see* Kwoka (2017).

it profitable to disrupt coordination by being a maverick. A finding that the merger would decrease the disruption index was interpreted to mean that the merger would make it less likely that a firm would act as a maverick. The disruption index was used to give economic structure to a discussion of factors that indicated whether the transaction would make coordination significantly more likely.

In a pre-trial expert report, the defendants used their merger simulation to quantify the disruption index and in the process argued that: (1) the plaintiffs had failed to articulate clearly either the conduct over which the suppliers allegedly would coordinate or the degree to which they would do so, which meant that the plaintiffs had failed to provide a valid basis for calculating the coordination profit; and (2) under reasonable assumptions (such as those that are often made in the repeated game/collusion literature), the post-merger disruption index was either higher than the pre-merger index or was inconsistent with coordination given any plausible discount rate.

Perhaps because of the difficulties of quantifying coordinated effects, at trial the plaintiffs primarily relied on: (a) business documents that the plaintiffs interpreted as showing that the defendants believed post-merger coordination was likely, and (b) the testimony of lay witnesses to assert that Sprint and T-Mobile were mavericks. The court did not find the documents to be probative, and the court agreed with the defendants that the fact that two out of the four industry leaders were allegedly mavericks suggested that collusion was hard to sustain in this industry. Moreover, the court determined that, given its spectrum holdings, recent investment and hiring decisions, and commitments to the DOJ and FCC, DISH was more likely to be an influential maverick in the future than was Sprint,[43] which suffered from "demonstrably poor network quality and numerous financial constraints."[44] Ultimately, the court concluded that New T-Mobile would use its increased capacity to compete more aggressively rather than engage in coordination.

At trial, the plaintiffs' lead economic expert focused on unilateral effects. The arguments at trial were based on upward pricing pressure analyses. Neither party introduced a full-blown merger simulation model at trial. Although there were disagreements between the plaintiffs' and the defendants' experts at trial with regard to the projected magnitude of unilateral effects in the absence of efficiencies, these disagreements were of relatively little significance with respect to assessing the merger.

The big issue was the magnitude of the efficiencies: At trial, the defendants' economic expert demonstrated that plugging the defendants' estimates of the merger's marginal cost savings into the formula that was used by the plaintiffs' economic expert to calculate pricing pressure yielded a prediction that prices would fall substantially.

## C. Merger Efficiencies

There has been disagreement among the courts with regard to the role of efficiencies in merger analysis. Some courts have treated efficiencies as a "defense"

---

43 *Opinion*, pp. 108-109, and 126.

44 *Opinion*, p. 84. Indeed, the court stated that it was "not persuaded… that Sprint possesses the financial and operational means to survive in the near term as a national wireless carrier." (*Id.* p. 163.).

against a finding that a merger harms competition. From an economic perspective, this approach makes little sense: An efficiencies analysis helps to determine whether a transaction makes competition stronger or weaker. The court in the present matter recognized that the consideration of efficiencies is a key component of the assessment of competitive effects.

Under the approach that is summarized in the *Horizontal Merger Guidelines* (§10) and widely adopted by courts, "[c]ognizable efficiencies are merger-specific efficiencies that have been verified and do not arise from anticompetitive reductions in output or service." The plaintiffs argued that the efficiencies that were identified by the defendants were neither merger-specific nor verifiable.

The plaintiffs challenged the merger specificity by arguing that there were several other means of achieving the projected benefits of the proposed merger, including: the acquisition of additional spectrum through federal license auctions or secondary markets; investments in additional cell sites to allow greater frequency reuse; the implementation of a technology known as "Dynamic Spectrum Sharing" ("DSS"), which increases the efficiency of spectrum use by allowing a network to allocate a spectrum band to LTE or 5G on a real-time basis; or having either Sprint or T-Mobile instead merge with DISH. Sprint and T-Mobile executives testified that all of these alternatives were inadequate and had highly uncertain benefits. The Court found that the claimed efficiencies were merger-specific on the grounds that:[45]

> …it may be that Defendants are not entirely incapable of improving their networks and services through means other [than] the Proposed Merger. But none of those alternatives appear reasonably practical, especially in the short term, and neither company as a standalone can achieve the level of efficiencies promised by the Proposed Merger.

The plaintiffs also attacked the verifiability of the projected efficiencies. As was discussed above, the defendants addressed verifiability in large part by relying on detailed efficiency modeling – the Network Build Model – that utilized ordinary-course-of-business principles and techniques.

The plaintiffs attacked the Network Build Model as something that had been created for purposes of litigation, rather than an existing model that was used in the ordinary course of business. Specifically, the Network Build Model differed from T-Mobile's ordinary-course models in that it also modeled Sprint and was more forward-looking, including the modeling of 5G. The court observed that these extensions covered factors that someone conducting an efficiencies-modeling exercise would naturally want to take into account, and the court found that the litigation model "hewed as closely to ordinary business principles as could be reasonably expected under the circumstances."[46]

The plaintiffs also argued that T-Mobile's efficiencies modeling unreasonably restricted the standalone firms' abilities to acquire additional spectrum or adopt new

---

45 *Opinion*, p. 71.

46 *Opinion*, p. 77.

technologies – specifically DSS. One of plaintiffs' economic experts presented sensitivity analyses purporting to show that efficiencies were much smaller than shown by defendants' modeling.

Sprint and T-Mobile executives testified that the plaintiffs' alternative assumptions regarding the availability and usability of additional spectrum were unrealistic because they accounted neither for associated sharing obligations and power limits, nor the geographic scopes of the licenses, nor the time necessary to put "available" spectrum actually into use. Defendant witnesses also testified that plaintiffs failed to properly account for certain spectrum efficiency losses ("overhead") associated with DSS as well as limitations on where it can be applied. Under cross examination, the plaintiffs' engineering expert testified that he had identified possibilities but was offering no prediction of what would actually happen with regard to spectrum purchases or technology deployment.

The sensitivity analyses presented by plaintiff's economic expert witness were internally inconsistent because they relied on parameter values that violated certain financial constraints faced by T-Mobile while at the same time using other parameter values that were generated by those constraints. Plaintiff's expert also failed to account for the costs of deploying additional spectrum, thus underestimating standalone T-Mobile's network marginal costs.

T-Mobile bolstered support for its efficiencies projections by pointing out that many of the network efficiencies that were generated by its 2013 acquisition of Metro PCS were similar in character and implementation to those that were anticipated from the proposed merger with Sprint, and many of the MetroPCS efficiencies were achieved ahead of schedule and exceeded the pre-merger projected total value. These facts gave the court much greater confidence in T-Mobile's efficiency projections for its proposed acquisition of Sprint.[47]

Engineering modeling predicted that New T-Mobile would have higher speeds than either standalone company, but economic modeling was necessary to translate higher speeds into consumer benefits that could be measured in dollars. The defendants' economic expert projected benefits primarily by extrapolating the results of an existing empirical study of fixed-line broadband internet access.[48] One of the plaintiffs' economic experts testified that any estimates of the consumer benefits of the greater network speeds the proposed merger would generate were unreliable because, at present, consumers had no uses for services with those speeds. The court rejected this argument for neglecting the likely innovation in applications; the court commented on the expert's argument that "The same may have been said about airplane speeds and pilotless flying machines in 1920."[49]

Ultimately, the court found "that Defendants' proposed efficiencies are cognizable and increase the likelihood that the Proposed Merger would enhance competition

---

47 *Opinion*, pp. 82-83.
48 Specifically, Nevo et al. (2016).
49 *Opinion*, p. 79.

in the relevant markets to the benefit of all consumers."[50] In a nod to some of the concerns that had been raised by the plaintiffs – as well as the unsettled legal treatment of efficiencies in merger review – the court was careful to note that efficiencies were just one of several factors on which its overall finding with regard to the proposed merger's legality.[51]

## D. Sprint as a Weakened Competitor

The defendants also argued that, if it remained as a standalone company, Sprint would continue to decline in competitive significance. Specifically, the defendants characterized a downward spiral in which Sprint had a lower-quality network than its rivals, which would lead to higher "churn" – customer loss – and a poor reputation with consumers, which would lead to poor financial performance, which in turn would undermine Sprint's ability to invest in its network.

The plaintiffs asserted that there were several means for Sprint to become a strong competitor as a standalone company, including: greater network investment; improvements in deployed technology; future low-band spectrum acquisitions; entering commercial partnerships to address coverage gaps; or merging with DISH or an MVNO. The Court rejected these arguments as either speculative or unrealistic.

The plaintiffs also tried to use the proposed merger's break-up provisions as an argument against the deal. The plaintiffs noted that the substantial payment and spectrum transfer that T-Mobile received from AT&T as a break-up fee for their unsuccessful merger attempt had allowed T-Mobile to become a much stronger competitor. The plaintiffs argued that the break-up fee for the proposed Sprint-T-Mobile merger – coupled with a roaming agreement that T-Mobile had entered into with Sprint as an inducement to pursue the deal – could have a similar effect on Sprint if the proposed merger were enjoined.

This argument did not appear to sway the trial court. If courts were to accept such arguments, then parties that propose to merge in the future would have incentives to design their break-up agreements in ways that minimize the competitive strength of the party that would receive the break-up payment.

## E. Litigating the Fix

The plaintiffs argued that the conditions of the settlements with the DOJ and FCC were inadequate to ensure that the proposed merger would not harm competition. The defendants argued that the conditions were unnecessary but eliminated any residual concerns that one might have.

The plaintiffs criticized several of the settlement conditions as being behavioral rather than structural. Although there are valid concerns with respect to the long-term effectiveness of behavioral remedies, the defendants pointed out that the behavioral remedies were intended only as temporary measures in support of the overall remedy

---

50 *Opinion*, p. 83.
51 *Opinion*, p. 83.

(including asset divestitures) that were designed to facilitate a structural change to the industry by allowing DISH to become a new facilities-based carrier.

The plaintiffs argued that the settlement was unlikely to prevent harm to competition because DISH's entry would neither be sufficiently timely nor likely to replace the competition that was lost due to T-Mobile's acquisition of Sprint, and that there was a substantial risk that DISH would fail to honor its entry commitments.[52] The court, however, concluded that DISH would build its promised network and would replace the competition that was lost by Sprint's acquisition—especially given the court's finding that Sprint was very likely to continue to decline in competitive significance. The court also took comfort in the fact that the DOJ and the FCC both had approved the proposed merger conditional on the terms of DISH's entry.

## V. IS THERE A ROLE FOR SOPHISTICATED ECONOMICS IN MERGER REVIEW?

As a final matter, the Court's opinion drew attention for apparently downplaying the role of expert witnesses and analytical modeling. Specifically, the Court described the parties as offering "competing crystal balls" and stated that:[53]

> ...the parties' costly and conflicting engineering, economic, and scholarly business models, along with the incompatible visions of the competitive future their experts' shades-of-gray forecasts portray, essentially cancel each other out as helpful evidence the Court could comfortably endorse as decidedly affirming one side rather than the other.

The Court emphasized that it found "especially relevant and compelling… the plausibility and persuasiveness of particular witnesses' trial presentations" based in part on its assessment of "their credibility and demeanor on the witness stand."[54] In summary, the Court concluded that executives of the merged entity intended to continue and amplify T-Mobile's "UnCarrier" strategy rather than reduce the company's aggressiveness.

Nevertheless, economics does appear to have played a role: First, there was vigorous engagement on the economic modeling in the regulatory investigations that were conducted by the FCC and DOJ. This likely contributed to – and shaped the terms of – the settlements with those agencies. Second, the sequence of reports and rebuttal reports between experts in pre-trial expert discovery contained a wealth of detailed economics. This exchange likely shaped the evidence that was presented to the court. For example, as was described above, there was extensive pre-trial expert exchanges on coordinated effects that led to streamlined presentations at trial. Third, the econo-

---

52 In arguing for a standard under which DISH would have to fully replace Sprint as a competitor, the plaintiffs effectively gave no weight to the merger's efficiencies.

53 *Opinion*, pp. 4-5.

54 *Opinion*, pp. 7-8.

mists who were retained by both sides worked closely with counsel in shaping the overall narratives that were presented to the court.

Our assessment is that each of these elements likely shaped the court's final opinion. The court recognized the impacts of the FCC and DOJ settlements on the likelihood of a pro-competitive outcome that would arise from the merger. In the absence of the rigorous economic debate between the two sides during expert discovery, one side might have attempted to present at trial economic evidence that appeared to be dispositive but actually was subject to sound rebuttal. Last, despite dismissing much of the expert evidence, the underlying logic of the court's opinion is structured in a way that mirrors the structure that was adopted by the economic experts on both sides; we suspect that this is no accident.

## VI. A PREMATURE RETROSPECTIVE

The period between the consummation of the merger and the writing of this chapter (late 2022) provides a window with which to examine post-merger outcomes. At the time of writing, T-Mobile is widely acknowledged to have the best spectrum portfolio, and its network capacity and speed have increased dramatically as a result of the merger and subsequent investments in its network. In its opinion, the court predicted that "New T-Mobile would likely make use of [its asymmetric capacity] advantage by cutting prices to take market share from its biggest competitors."[55] Leading industry analyst Craig Moffett's July 2022 statement that "The combination of a single telecom operator [T-Mobile] having both the industry's best network and its lowest prices is unprecedented, and we believe paves the way to significant share gains…"[56] suggests that the court was correct.

Figure 2 shows two measures of prices between January 2016 and August 2022. The heavy solid line is the Bureau of Labor Statistics ("BLS") Producer Price Index for Wireless Telecommunications Carriers ("Wireless PPI") expressed in constant 2016 dollars (that is, adjusted for inflation based on the Consumer Price Index for all Urban Consumers). The Wireless PPI is a measure of average revenue per subscriber for the industry.[57] The lighter solid line is the Consumer Price Index for Wireless Telecommunications Services ("Wireless CPI") similarly adjusted for inflation. The Wireless CPI is a measure of the prices available to consumers seeking to sign up for service with a carrier as the sampling date.[58]

The merger closed on April 1, 2020. Three months later, the Wireless CPI jumped up 3.6 percent (in nominal terms). The Wireless PPI exhibited a much

---

55 *Opinion*, p. 137.

56 https://www.nexttv.com/news/moffettnathanson-sees-cables-q2-broadband-growth-slipping-as-wireless-momentum-continues, accessed October 3, 2022.

57 *See* https://www.bls.gov/ppi/factsheets/producer-price-index-for-wireless-telecommunications-carriers-naics-517312.htm, accessed September 21, 2022. This URL also discusses sampling, quality adjustments and other measurement details.

58 *See* https://www.bls.gov/cpi/factsheets/telecommunications.htm, accessed September 21, 2022. This URL also discusses sampling, quality adjustments, and other measurement details.

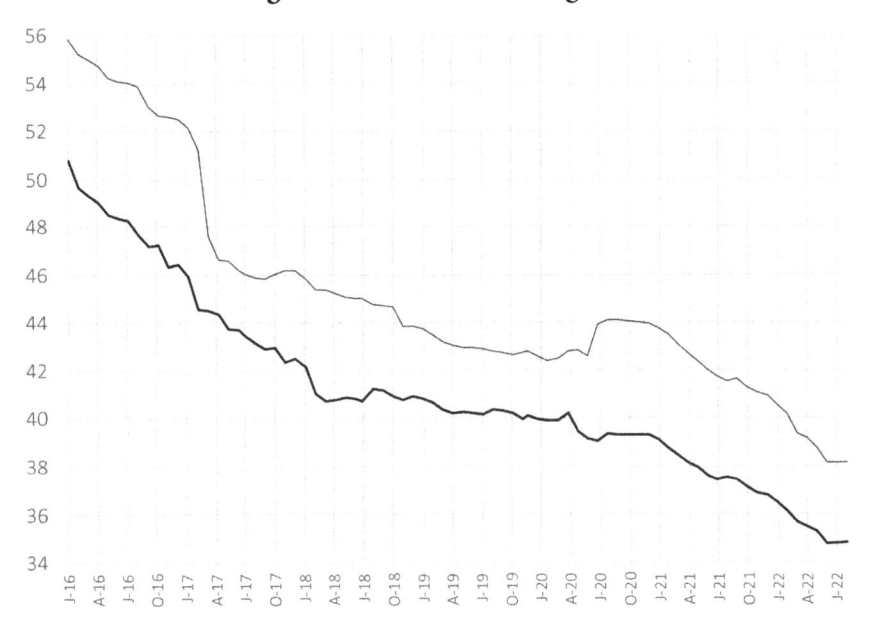

**Figure 2: Pre- and Post-Merger Prices**

Notes: The heavy line plots the PPI data for Wireless telecommunications carriers as constructed by the BLS (series id PCU517312517312), after adjusting for changes in the aggregate CPI level (using series id CUUR0000SA0) since January 2016. The lighter solid line plots the CPI data for Wireless telephone service as constructed by the BLS (series id CUUR0000SEED03) and similarly adjusted by the aggregate CPI.

smaller increase, which might be expected given that it reflects prices paid under existing, possibly long-term contracts. Given the abrupt price increases followed by the return to the earlier downward trends in both indexes, we conjecture that this increase is the result of removing Sprint pricing plans from the data used to calculate the price indexes, as opposed to price increases by the remaining service providers. Moreover, to the extent that Sprint had been offering lower-quality services than were the other major wireless providers, the BLS data overstate the change in quality-adjusted prices paid by consumers. The BLS also does not adjust for the benefits of some quality changes (such as the introduction of 5G), which likely means that these indexes further understate the decrease in quality-adjusted real prices.[59] However, absent a baseline for comparison, these data to do not tell us whether prices would have fallen faster or slower if the merger had not been consummated.

The DISH remedy was controversial, with the plaintiffs in the litigation asserting that DISH was unlikely to become a serious competitor. Under the terms of its com-

---

59 Similarly, it is unclear from BLS documentation how the CPI and PPI incorporate device subsidies. A recent increase in device subsidies corresponds to a decrease in the overall cost of mobile data services. (*See* https://www.counterpointresearch.com/cable-players-capture-nearly-one-third-us-postpaid-phone-net-additions-q2-2022/, accessed August 4, 2022.).

mitments to the FCC, Dish was required to have built out a 5G network that covered 20 percent of the U.S. population by June 14, 2022.[60] Dish met this requirement and has announced that it is launching a new postpaid brand, Boost Infinite. That said, Dish's subscriber base, as at 2Q 2022 was reported at 7.87 million, which is 1.1 million less than the number of subscribers originally inherited from Boost.[61] Other MVNOs, particularly those associated with leading cable companies, have fared better. Contrary to predictions by the state plaintiffs, Comcast's and Charter's MVNOs offer lower prices than do the three national MNOs, and cable company MVNOs accounted for almost one-third of postpaid phone net additions in the second quarter of 2022.[62]

## TECHNICAL APPENDIX

This appendix provides addition information with regard to the merging parties' demand model, which was estimated as a standard conditional logit model of brand choice with the use of individual-level data on carrier choice and usage (which was provided by the NMP data that were discussed in the main text).

Formally, each person was indexed by $I$, of data use intensity type $t$, living in location $l$, assigned a utility level $u_{itlb}$ to brand $b$. The utility level was specified as:

$$u_{itlb} = \alpha_{lb} + \alpha_{tb} + \beta_t x_{ib} + \gamma_b C_i + \epsilon_{ib},$$

where $x_{ib}$ is a list of the network quality metrics, subscripted by $i$ and $b$ to reflect that an individual $i$'s experienced quality for brand $b$ depends on where and when she uses her phone; $\alpha_{lb}$ and $\alpha_{tb}$ capture brand preferences that depend on the individual's location of residence and whether she is a light, medium, or heavy data use type;[63] $\gamma_b$ captures brand preferences that may depend on consumer demographics that are given by $C_i$;[64] $\epsilon_{ib}$ is a stochastic term that is distributed type-I extreme value that reflects the determinates of choice that are not included in the model; and $\beta_t$ are the preference coefficients that govern how much individuals of data use type $t$ (light, medium, or heavy) value each network quality product characteristic.[65] The parameter $\beta_t$ also var-

---

60 See https://www.rcrwireless.com/20220615/5g/dish-wireless-buildout-reaches-20-of-u-s-population, accessed September 21, 2022.

61 See https://www.fiercewireless.com/wireless/dish-drops-another-210k-wireless-subs-2q, accessed September 21, 2022.

62 Matthew Orf, "Cable Players Capture Nearly One-third of US Postpaid Phone Net Additions in Q2 2022," Counterpoint Research, *available at* https://www.counterpointresearch.com/cable-players-capture-nearly-one-third-us-postpaid-phone-net-additions-q2-2022/, accessed October 3, 2022.

63 Light data users were users that on average utilized less than 30 megabytes of data per day. Medium data users utilized on average between 30 and 100 megabytes of data per day. Heavy data users utilized on average more than 100 megabytes per day. Across the four national carriers, 15-23 percent of users were light, and 30-38 percent were medium.

64 The precise configuration of consumer demographics is not publicly available.

65 As was noted in Section II, these individual-specific network quality product characteristics were average speed and worst speed, and average coverage and worst coverage, and depended on how and where each consumer in the sample used her phone.

ies by whether individual $i$ was a light, medium, or heavy data user.

The estimated parameters are $\alpha_{lb}$, $\alpha_{tb}$, $\beta_t$, and $\gamma_b$. The NMP data were used to measure $x_{ib}$, and both census and NMP data were used to measure $C_i$.[66]

In the demand model, consumers choose from one of seven brands and an outside option. The seven brands that were modeled directly – including measuring the network quality that they offer – were AT&T, Sprint, T-Mobile, Verizon, Cricket, Boost/Virgin, and MetroPCS. The outside option in the model – whose network quality was not measured – represents options such as US Cellular, Tracfone, Xfinity, Google, and other MVNOs.

The utility specification that was used to estimate demand did not include price. Instead, the effect of price enters through the location-specific brand fixed effects: . Note that because there was only one national price for each carrier (no plan-specific information was available in the data), the price coefficient could not be separately identified from location-brand fixed effects in the conditional logit regression. The price coefficient was recovered via calibration that used price – which is proxied by the average monthly revenue per user – by carrier, information on margins and the Bertrand-Nash equilibrium conditions (*see* the section on the merger simulation in the main text above). When calibrating the price coefficient the location-specific brand fixed effects were separated into a price effect – $\delta p_b$ – and the remaining location-brand fixed effect, $\xi_{lb}$: $u_{itlb} = \xi_{lb} + \delta p_b + \alpha_{tb} + \beta_t x_{ib} + \gamma_b C_i + \varepsilon_{ib}$.

The diversion ratios that were generated by the demand model are reported in Table 1.

**Table 1: Diversion Ratios**

| | | | | Diversion To: | | | | |
|---|---|---|---|---|---|---|---|---|
| Diversion From: | AT&T | Verizon | Sprint | T-Mobile | Boost/Virgin | MetroPCS | Cricket | Regional Carriers and MVNOs |
| AT&T | - | 40.0% | 11.0% | 19.1% | 3.8% | 5.4% | 3.6% | 17.1% |
| Verizon | 33.8% | - | 12.4% | 20.4% | 4.2% | 5.5% | 3.5% | 20.3% |
| Sprint | 24.6% | 32.6% | - | 19.2% | 4.0% | 5.2% | 2.5% | 12.1% |
| T-Mobile | 27.5% | 34.8% | 12.4% | - | 4.0% | 6.9% | 2.7% | 11.7% |
| Boost/Virgin | 22.0% | 28.4% | 10.3% | 16.0% | - | 5.9% | 2.8% | 14.5% |
| MetroPCS | 22.7% | 27.6% | 9.9% | 20.4% | 4.4% | - | 2.8% | 12.3% |
| Cricket | 25.9% | 29.5% | 8.2% | 13.5% | 3.5% | 4.7% | - | 14.6% |
| Regional Carriers and MVNOs | 27.5% | 38.7% | 8.7% | 13.0% | 4.1% | 4.7% | 3.3% | - |

**Source**: Rebuttal Testimony of Timothy F. Bresnahan (Public Version), January 29, 2019 C.P.U.C. Docket Number A.18-07-011 and A.18-07-012. *Available at* https://www.tellusventure.com/downloads/cpuc/tmobile_sprint/joint_applicants_bresnahan_rebuttal_testimony_tmobile_sprint_29jan2019.pdf, accessed May 5, 2022.

---

66 This choice model was estimated directly with the use of maximum likelihood.

# REFERENCES

Asker, John & Volker Nocke (2021). "Collusion, Mergers and other Antitrust Issues." In *Handbook of Industrial Organization, Volume 5*. Edited by Katherine Ho, Ali Hortasçu & Alessandro Lizzeri, 177-279. Elsevier.

Baker, Jonathan (2002). "Mavericks, Mergers, and Exclusion: Proving Coordinated Competitive Effects under the Antitrust Laws." *NYU Law Review* 77: 135-203.

Baker, Jonathan (2009). "Efficiencies and High Concentration: Heinz Proposes to Acquire Beech-Nut (2001)." In *The Antitrust Revolution: Economics, Competition, and Policy (5th edition)*. Edited by John E. Kwoka, Jr. & Lawrence J. White, 157-177. Oxford: Oxford University Press.

Chen, Yongmin & Marius Schwartz (2016). "Churn Versus Diversion in Antitrust: An Illustrative Model." *Economica* 83: 564-583.

DeGraba, Patrick & Gregory L. Rosston (2018). "The Proposed Merger of AT&T and T-Mobile: Rethinking Possible (2011)." In *The Antitrust Revolution: Economics, Competition, and Policy (7th edition)*. Edited by John E. Kwoka, Jr. & Lawrence J. White, 123-146. Oxford: Oxford University Press.

Federal Communications Commission (2020). *2020 Communications Marketplace Report*. Adopted December 31, 2020.

Gelfand, David & Leah Brannon (2016). "A Primer on Litigating the Fix." *Antitrust* 30(1): 10-14.

Kazmerzak, Karen & Nicholas Widnell (2020). "The Distressed Business Standard in Times of Crisis." *Antitrust* 34(3): 22-27.

Kwoka, John (2017). "The Structural Presumption and the Safe Harbor in Merger Review: False Positives or Unwarranted Concerns." *Antitrust Law Journal* 81(3): 837-872.

Nevo, Aviv, John L. Turner & Jonathan W. Williams (2016). "Usage-Based Pricing and Demand for Residential Broadband." *Econometrica* 84(2): 411-443

Nocke, Volker & Michael Whinston (2022). "Concentration Thresholds for Horizontal Mergers." *American Economic Review* 112(6): 1915-48.

Steven C. Salop (2013). "Merger Settlement and Enforcement Policy for Optimal Deterrence and Maximum Welfare," *Fordham Law Review* 81(5): 2647-2682

Stigler, George (1964). "A Theory of Oligopoly." *Journal of Political Economy* 72(1): 44-61.

U.S. Department of Justice (2019.a). *United States of America et al. v. Deutsche Telekom et al.*, [Proposed] Final Judgment, United States District Court for the District of Columbia, filed July 26, 2019.

U.S. Department of Justice (2019.b). *United States of America et al. v. Deutsche Telekom et al.*, Competitive Impact Statement, United States District Court for the District of Columbia, filed July 30, 2019.

U.S. Department of Justice (2019.c). *United States of America et al. v. Deutsche Telekom et al.*, Fifth Amended Complaint, United States District Court for the District of Columbia, filed November 27, 2019.

U.S. Department of Justice and the Federal Trade Commission (2010). *Horizontal Merger Guidelines*.

# CHAPTER 4
# Upward Pricing Pressure in Supermarket Mergers: The UK's *Asda/Sainsbury* Case

By Howard Smith[1]

## I. INTRODUCTION

The supermarket industry is the UK's most high-profile industry in terms of its share of household budgets. Almost every household in the country is a regular customer of this industry. The average household spends 11 percent of its budget at firms in the supermarket industry. For the poorest 20 percent this figure is over 14 percent.[2]

Supermarkets were the focus of a large amount of antitrust interest in the 2000s. At this time there was a public perception that UK grocery prices tended to be higher than other comparable EU countries and the U.S.[3] There were numerous inquiries, which established a framework that was used by the Competition Commission ("CC") for thinking about supermarket competition. These inquiries included two "market inquiries" into the sector – wide-ranging investigations which looked in general at the state of competition in the sector (*see* CC (2000, 2008)) – and a number of merger inquiries.

In one of the key merger inquiries, the CC blocked all potential mergers between the top-three firms and the fourth. This was the *Safeway* case of 2003 (*see* CC (2003)). After this, there appeared to be a consensus that mergers between the largest four supermarkets would be unsuccessful with the competition authorities. Certainly, no such mergers were proposed for another 15 years.

In 2018, Asda (which was owned by Wal-Mart Stores Inc.), and Sainsbury decided to challenge this apparent consensus. They were the second- and third- largest of the supermarket firms. Why did they think that they had a chance of their merger being approved, when the *Safeway* case had suggested that mergers of top-four firms are unacceptable? Perhaps it was because over the 15 years since 2003 the UK grocery market had experienced the expansion of new firms such as the discounters – *i.e.*, Aldi and Lidl – and changes in the way that people shop for groceries, such as online shopping.

---

1 Howard Smith advised the CMA in the *Asda/Sainsbury* case. Any views expressed here are his own and not those of the CMA. I am grateful to the editors, and to Ivan Olszak, Rob Ryan, and John Thanassoulis, for comments on an earlier draft. Any errors are my own.

2 *See* paragraph 15 of CMA (2019).

3 *See* Introduction to CC (2000).

Or perhaps it was because the UK competition authorities had, since 2003, taken up new tools for assessing mergers, based on a relatively new indicator of competitive harm, namely, the Gross Upward Pricing Pressure Index ("GUPPI"). A great advantage of the use of GUPPI – not shared by the old approach used in the *Safeway* case, which was based on market shares – was that it was flexible enough to take account of the changes to the industry since 2003. In the old approach, the competition authority would have had to decide whether the discounters, online shopping firms, etc., were part of the relevant market. In the new approach such binary judgements were unnecessary.

Despite these changes, the Competition and Markets Authority ("CMA"), the CC's successor since 2013, blocked the merger. The parties raised many objections to this decision. They did not object to the principle of using GUPPI indicators. Their objection was to the CMA's way of doing so. The Authority calculated a GUPPI indicator for each store operated by the merging parties. It then adopted a decision rule: if the GUPPI for any store was above a "threshold" value then the merger was classed as being likely to cause harm to consumers at the store. The parties argued that: (i) the GUPPI is a theoretical predictor of price changes, and the CMA did not provide any direct evidence that a GUPPI exceeding the threshold causes price rises; (ii) the modelling method the CMA used for estimating store-level GUPPI indicators was imprecise, and could result in false positives from the decision rule; and (iii) the CMA's choice of GUPPI threshold was too low and much lower than in other recent merger cases.

The case therefore raised several questions about the application of GUPPI to retail mergers. It also raised broader questions about UK merger policy in the future: Given that the GUPPI threshold in this case is much lower than most recent merger cases, can the case be seen as a tightening of UK merger policy? This question is interesting in light of recent commentary that emphasizes the desirability of such a tightening-up (*see, for example*, Baker (2018), Philippon (2019) and Berry et al. (2019)).

This chapter discusses the *Asda/Sainsbury* case. We focus on the main business activity of the two firms: in-store grocery retailing that is sold from supermarkets. We do not cover other aspects of the case, such as petrol retailing, convenience store retailing, and online retailing.[4] We also focus on the use of GUPPI at the level of the individual store – which can be seen as the centerpiece of the investigation – rather than on the CMA's assessment at what they call a "national" level, where national refers to effects across the stores in the UK as a whole.[5]

In Section II we discuss the UK competition authorities' framework for thinking about retail competition, and its application to the key *Safeway* case of 2003. In Section III we discuss changes since *Safeway* to the grocery market. In Section IV we

---

4 The CMA defined a *convenience* store as having a sales area that is less than 280m$^2$ and a *supermarket* store as having a sales area that is above this threshold.

5 As we discuss in Section II, the CMA's framework allowed for firms to compete in some variables at a national level and others at a store level. However, the Authority's framework emphasized that national competitive effects should be seen as derived from the aggregation of local effects, so that the local analysis can be seen as the centerpiece of the analysis.

discuss the GUPPI indicator and its application to retail mergers. In Section V we discuss the CMA's use of GUPPI in *Asda/Sainsbury*. In Section VI we discuss the areas of disagreement between the parties and the CMA. In Section VII we conclude with some reflections on the case.

## II. BACKGROUND: THE CMA'S ANALYTICAL FRAMEWORK AND THE LANDMARK *SAFEWAY* CASE

In the years 2000-2008, there was an abundance of UK supermarket inquiries: two market inquiries and a number of merger inquiries. During this time the UK competition authorities developed a framework for analyzing the supermarket industry, which the CMA subsequently has developed further.

We can summarize this framework as follows.[6] The relevant market in product space is the supermarket store: stores are judged to be in the same product market depending on the firm that runs the store (which determines its positioning in quality/price space) and the size of the store (which determines the range of products in the store). The geographic market is a local area given by a drive-time around each store.

The dominant form of grocery shopping is the weekly one-stop shopping trip; two stores are good substitutes for this type of shopping only if the stores are large enough, are operated by firms that cater to one-stop shoppers in terms of product range, and are close enough to each other in terms of drive-time.

Supermarket firms compete in multiple variables: price, quality, product range, and service. The CMA uses the acronym "PQRS" to refer to these. Firms set some of these store-by-store (say, product range) and some nationally at a chain-wide level (say, prices or quality).[7,8] Even when firms set a variable nationally, however, the effect of changing the variable on overall firm profits is determined by the aggregation of store-level effects. Consequently, the analysis should generally start locally at a store level and build up.[9]

In a specific merger case the CMA must decide if the merger is likely to result in a "substantial lessening of competition" ("SLC") at any of the stores that belong to the parties. To apply its framework the CMA uses a two-step approach:

1. In the first step, the Authority identifies the stores where there is the *potential* for a SLC, under the CMA's theories of harm, and filters out those where there is no such potential. This involves examining the drive-times

---

6 The CMA's approach to retail mergers is set out in its *Retail Mergers Commentary*. See CMA (2017a).

7 Ever since about 2000 most UK supermarket firms tend to set national rather than store-by-store prices. *See* CC (2008) for a discussion.

8 Hereafter for convenience we will mostly refer to prices when discussing the GUPPI analysis. However, the CMA interpret the GUPPI as indicating the competitive effect of a merger on any of the PQRS variables.

9 The store-level choice modelling framework in Smith (2004) was used in the first market inquiry into the sector: *see* CC (2000). Since then UK authorities have used an approach founded at store-level when studying the industry.

between the parties' stores, alongside other store characteristics such as size and product offering.
2. In the second step, for each store that is identified in stage 1, the CMA determines whether a SLC is likely to arise because of the merger. This can be done by alternative means: *e.g.*, a simple count of the number of competitors the store faces (as in *Safeway*); or pricing pressure indices calculated for each store (as in *Asda/Sainsbury*). Then, depending on how many stores with a SLC this this exercise finds, the CMA decides whether the merger should be blocked or some other remedy is found, such as divestiture of the problematic stores.

For present purposes, it is worth reviewing the key *Safeway* case. Safeway was the fourth-largest firm, and the CC ruled in 2003 that none of its three larger rivals – Tesco, Asda, and Sainsbury – could buy it. This indicated in effect that mergers among the big four supermarket firms were unacceptable.

The CC used the two-step approach that we mentioned above. In Step 1 the CC identified the stores with the potential for a SLC; and in Step 2 the CC examined the effect of the merger on the number of independent firms – *e.g.*, Sainsbury, Tesco, etc. – competing in each store's local area.[10] The CC had a rule: If the merger reduced the number of competitors from *four to three*, then it would lead to a SLC.

When this exercise was implemented, the CC found many local areas with SLCs, for any merger of Safeway with its three larger competitors. The number of areas with SLCs was high enough in each case that divestiture of individual stores was not an option, and, consequently, these three mergers were all ruled out. Safeway was instead allowed to merge with a smaller rival, namely Morrisons. This case put down a very effective "marker": No merger between the top four firms was proposed for another 15 years.

## III. CHANGES IN THE GROCERY MARKET: DISCOUNTERS, ONLINE SHOPPING, AND SHOPPING FREQUENCY

Why did Asda and Sainsbury think that their merger could get approval 15 years after the *Safeway* case? In this section we discuss one potential reason: changes in the grocery market.

Table 1 provides information on the structure of the supermarket industry in 2018. The table classifies the main firms into a number of types. The "Big Four" are the top four firms by sales.[11] They operate many large supermarket stores that are suitable for one-stop shoppers. The "Discounters" (Aldi and Lidl) sell a more limited range of products in smaller stores at low prices. The "Convenience" firms

---

10 For these counts the CC excluded the discounters such as Aldi and Lidl. They were judged to be outside the market definition.

11 Before 2003, when Morrisons acquired Safeway, there were five firms of this type, and the term "Big Five" would have been appropriate.

sell from small stores in neighborhood locations. The "Online" firms – which are a recent addition to the list – deliver products directly to consumers' homes.

The table reports the number of stores that each firm had in 2018. Together Asda and Sainsbury operated over 2,000 stores. The reported numbers include smaller stores – "convenience stores" – and larger stores – "supermarkets" – even though the former are not in the CMA's definition of the product market. Some of the Big Four including Sainsbury operated convenience stores as well as supermarkets.

The table also reports industry revenue shares from the market research company Kantar.[12] For each firm these revenue shares aggregate over online and in-store shopping and include revenue from both supermarkets and convenience stores. They should not be treated as shares of an antitrust market. The figures do however help us see changes between 2003 and 2018 the industry revenue shares. Both years are given in Table 1. The joint industry revenue share of the top four firms – reported as "C4" in the table – did not change greatly between 2003 and 2018, which suggests that the industry has not changed greatly. There were however three changes to the industry in this period which the parties and the CMA agreed were potentially important.[13]

## A. Industry Change 1: The Rise of the Discounters

Whereas in 2003 the discounters – *i.e.*, Aldi and Lidl – were fringe firms with only a 3.1 percent joint industry share, by 2018 they had grown to a 13 percent share. This growth continued: Table 1 shows that by 2022 their joint share had grown to 16.1 percent. There were a few factors that underlay this trend: In the early days their growth was accelerated during the recession that followed 2008, when price-sensitive consumers were keen to buy groceries at lower prices. More recently, their growth has been a consequence of a decision to rebrand: larger stores, a wider product range, and higher quality.

## B. Industry Change 2: The Rise of Online Shopping

Online shopping rose from a 0 percent to a 6 percent share of industry revenue between 2003 and 2018.[14] Most of this was supplied by the Big Four. Ocado was the only online-only firm in 2018; and, as Table 1 shows, its share was only 1 percent of industry revenue in 2018.

---

12 Industry revenue shares from Kantar are for Great Britain and are available from https://www.kantarworldpanel.com/en/grocery-market-share/great-britain. The 2018 and 2022 figures are for January 28 and August 7 respectively. The 2003 figures are taken from https://www.fooddeserts.org/images/supshare.htm which does not provide information for the supermarket types in the final two rows of the table.

13 *See* Chapter 4 of CMA (2019) for a more detailed discussion of these trends.

14 *See* Chapter 4 of CMA (2019).

## Table 1: Industry Revenue Shares of the Main Firms.

|  | Type | # Stores | Industry Revenue Share (%) |  |  |
|---|---|---|---|---|---|
|  |  | 2018 | 2003 | 2018 | 2022 |
| Tesco | Big Four | 3,400 | 27.0 | 27.9 | 26.9 |
| Sainsbury | Big Four | 1,428 | 16.2 | 16.2 | 14.8 |
| Safeway | Big Four |  | 9.2 |  |  |
| Asda | Big Four | 676 | 16.2 | 15.5 | 13.9 |
| Morrison | Big Four | 500 | 6.0 | 10.7 | 9.3 |
| Aldi | Discounter | 800 | 1.7 | 7.0 | 9.1 |
| Lidl | Discounter | 700 | 1.4 | 5.0 | 7.0 |
| Co-op | Convenience | 2,500 | 5.2 | 5.8 | 6.5 |
| Somerfield | Convenience |  | 6.2 |  |  |
| Waitrose | Premium | 300 | 3.2 | 5.2 | 4.6 |
| Iceland | Frozen Food | 900 | 2.3 | 2.3 | 2.3 |
| Ocado | Online |  |  | 1.1 | 1.8 |
| Other outlets |  |  |  | 1.6 | 2.0 |
| Symbols/independents |  |  |  | 1.6 | 1.6 |
| C4 |  |  | 68.6 | 70.3 | 64.9 |
| HHI |  |  |  | 1541.9 |  |
| **Pro forma HHI post hypothetical *Asda/Sainsbury* merger** |  |  |  | 2044.1 |  |
| Change in HHI from the hypothetical merger |  |  |  | 502.2 |  |

Notes: Revenue shares are from Kantar and are for Great Britain. They include online as well as in-store shopping. Store numbers are from Figure 3.1 of CMA (2019) and include convenience stores (<280m$^2$) and supermarkets (>280m$^2$). The Big Four were the Big Five before Safeway was taken over by Morrisons in 2003. Symbols are independent retailers that are members of a larger group with joint marketing and buying initiatives.

## C. Industry Change 3: A Decline in the Importance of One-stop Shopping

The third way in which the market had changed was that consumers were shopping more frequently, buying smaller bundles per store visit, and consequently making greater use of convenience stores and discounters. This had the potential to expose the main supermarkets to greater competition.

## D. The Asda/Sainsbury Merger in HHI Terms

Table 1 also reports the Herfindahl–Hirschman concentration index ("HHI") that we get from the industry shares in 2018, and the change in HHI if the *Asda/Sainsbury* merger had taken place. These HHI figures would flag the merger as having competitive concerns, by application of the thresholds for HHI and changes in HHI given in the U.S. Merger Guidelines. Of course, this exercise has many caveats: As we have already noted, the industry revenue shares are unlikely to be a good measure of the shares of a properly-defined antitrust market; the exercise does not account for sub-national variation; and market shares (even when properly defined) have an ambiguous relationship with market power, particularly when products are differentiated. For all these reasons, and others, upward-pricing pressure methods like the GUPPI were introduced.

## IV. THE USE OF GUPPI IN UK RETAIL MERGER ASSESSMENT

The GUPPI is one of the most commonly used indices in the upward pricing pressure ("UPP") approach to measuring the competitive harm from a merger. The general idea of the UPP approach is that when setting prices, or setting other instruments of competition such as product quality, each party to a prospective merger imposes an externality on the other party. Post-merger, however, merging firms will account for this externality and compete less strongly. UPP indicators measure the size of the externality.

To fix ideas, consider a differentiated products Bertrand oligopoly model, with prices that satisfy a Nash equilibrium, where the stores represent the differentiated products. Let there be an imaginary Sainsbury store $S$ which competes in a local market with other stores including an Asda store $A$. We assume that: consumers are one-stop shoppers who buy a fixed bundle of groceries; the costs and prices are for a unit of this bundle; the firm sets the price of the bundle at the bundle level; and the consumer never considers splitting the bundle across two stores. The Sainsbury store sets price $P_S$ for the bundle, which has a marginal cost $C_S$.

Prior to the merger the first-order condition for store $S$ is given by

$$P_S + \left[\frac{\partial Q_S}{\partial P_S}\right]^{-1} Q_S = C_S \qquad (1)$$

where $Q_S$ is the total quantity that is sold by store $S$. This equation is the standard condition for optimal pricing in the Bertrand oligopoly model: The left-hand-side is marginal revenue and the right-hand-side is marginal cost.

After the merger first order condition for store $S$ takes the form

$$P_S + \left[\frac{\partial Q_S}{\partial P_S}\right]^{-1} Q_S = C_S - \left[\frac{\partial Q_S}{\partial P_S}\right]^{-1} \left[\frac{\partial Q_A}{\partial P_S}\right] (P_A - C_A). \qquad (2)$$

The right-hand side has an extra term, relative to the previous equation: the externality on store $A$ that store $S$ accounts for post-merger. The externality is the value of sales that are diverted to store $A$ from store $S$ after the price increase. The derivative $\partial Q_A / \partial P_S$ is positive, since the two stores are substitutes, which implies that the externality on store $A$ from a price increase at store $S$ is positive.

The externality in equation (2) is the product of two terms. The first is the *diversion ratio* from store $S$ to store $A$ – a measure of the closeness of substitution between the two stores. This is given by the number of consumers that switch from $S$ to $A$, the event of a marginal price increase at $S$, as a fraction of all consumers who switch away, defined formally as follows:

$$D_{S \to A} = - \left[ \frac{\partial Q_S}{\partial P_S} \right]^{-1} \left[ \frac{\partial Q_A}{\partial P_S} \right]. \tag{3}$$

The second term is the profits per unit at the store $A$ given by the markup: $(P_A - C_A)$. Multiplying these two pieces of information gives the externality: the value to $A$ of the switching customers. This externality is referred to as the Upward Pricing Pressure – $UPP_{S \to A}$ – at store $S$ from the merger with store $A$:

$$UPP_{S \to A} = D_{S \to A} \times (P_A - C_A). \tag{4}$$

In order to provide a unit-free measure of the externality we divide the UPP by price which gives the GUPPI indicator:

$$GUPPI_{S \to A} = D_{S \to A} \times M_A \times \frac{P_A}{P_S}. \tag{5}$$

There are three components on the right-hand side of this equation: The first $D_{S \to A}$ is the diversion ratio as defined above. The second $M_A = (P_A - C_A)/P_A$ is the profit margin at $A$. The third $P_A/P_S$ is the ratio of $A$'s and $S$'s prices.

The framework makes it easy for the competition authority to incorporate efficiencies from the merger into the analysis, assuming that there is a reliable estimate of efficiencies. To see this, note that the UPP term in the first order condition (2) is added to the marginal cost $C_S$. Hence, if the merger reduces marginal cost $C_S$ by more than the UPP, it does not have a net upward effect on prices. Or, equivalently, if the reduction in marginal cost $C_S$ expressed as a fraction of price $P_A$ is greater than the GUPPI indicator.

The UPP and GUPPI indicators have important limitations. They only measure the impact of the merger on the unilateral pricing incentives of the merging partners (at the pre-merger prices) and do not measure how much equilibrium prices change as a result of the merger. As we noted in the previous paragraph, we can interpret the UPP term as a new marginal cost that the firms consider after the merger. How much of a cost change is passed through to equilibrium prices depends on the shape of the demand curve and how rivals respond to the price change, none of which is included in the UPP analysis.

Three issues of practical implementation have been at the fore in UK retail merger cases. First, how should the competition authority calculate the diversion ratio when there are many stores? The diversion ratios in the GUPPI are often estimated with the use of a consumer survey. In the case of retail mergers, these ask those consumers exiting store $S$ which alternative store they would use if $S$ were unavailable. This method is practical only when the number of stores is small. In a major merger there could be many hundreds of stores – Table 1 shows that Sainsbury and Asda together have over 2000 stores – and the cost of conducting a survey in each store would be very high.

The second issue is how to use the GUPPI to determine if there is a SLC. The GUPPI measure can be used in a number of alternative ways: It can be used in a non-deterministic way alongside many other pieces of qualitative and quantitative evidence. Alternatively, it can be used in a deterministic *final decision rule*: If the GUPPI for store $S$ exceeds a specific threshold, then the store is classified as having a SLC.

The third issue arises in cases where a final decision rule is used: To what level should the GUPPI threshold be set? If a marginal cost efficiency is expected from the merger, then the competition authority may adjust the threshold upwards by the appropriate amount. The competition authority might also take into account: the rate at which it expects pricing pressure to be passed through to consumers; the presence of measurement errors in GUPPI; and recent precedents in merger cases.

## V. THE CMA'S FINDINGS

The CMA began its analysis by identifying the theories of harm through which there could be a SLC from the merger, and then gathering evidence with respect to each theory. The Authority had many theories of harm. We focus on those that related to unilateral effects at the store-level.

The CMA used the two-step procedure that was discussed in section II: In Step 1 the CMA identified stores where a SLC is possible, because both parties to the merger are in close proximity (*i.e.*, within a 15 minute drive time); this resulted in a high percentage of the parties' stores being identified (77 percent of Sainsbury stores and 85 percent of Asda's). In Step 2 the CMA calculated a GUPPI for each of the stores identified in Step 1.

In light of the large number of stores that were identified in Step 1, the CMA used a decision rule approach in Step 2: The GUPPI for each store was compared to a threshold set by the CMA, as the final decider for whether there was an SLC at that store. This avoided the time-consuming process of making an "in the round" judgement for each store based on both the GUPPI score and other information.

The practical calculation of the GUPPI indicators required three pieces of information for each store: a profit margin, relative prices, and a diversion ratio. The most difficult of these was the diversion ratio. To obtain a diversion ratio for each store, the CMA could in principle survey consumers at all the stores identified in Step 1, to find out their second-choice store in the event of a price increase. However, this would be very expensive in practice. So, instead, the CMA surveyed consumers at, and calculated diversion ratios for, a sample of the stores, and used these data in an econometric model to predict diversion ratios for all the stores.

The model was referred to by the CMA as the Weighted Share of Shops ("WSS"). It is worth writing it down, which requires some further notation. Consider the diversion ratio $D_{k \to j}$ for centroid store $k$ and competitor store $j$. Let centroid store $k$ have owner $F(k)$ – which could be Asda or Sainsbury – and the set $J(k)$ of competitors. The CMA assumed that $J(k)$ consisted of all supermarket-sized stores that were up to a 15-minute drive-time away from $k$. The competitor store $j$ has owner $F(j)$. Let the drive-time between the stores be denoted $x_{kj}$.

Let $p_{F(k)F(j)}(x_{kj})$ be a weight, to be estimated using diversion ratios from the sampled stores, that indicates the competitive importance to centroid store $k$ owned by firm $F(k)$ of a competitor store $j$ owned by firm $F(j)$ and at a drive-time of $x_{kj}$ from $k$. Let $p_O$ be the probability that the shopper diverts to an option other than a store in $J$: e.g., online, a convenience store, or a store that is more than 15 minutes' drive-time away.

The CMA calculated the diversion ratio from store $k$ to store $j$ as follows:

$$D_{k \to j} = (1 - p_O) \frac{p_{F(k)F(j)}(x_{kj})}{\Sigma_{j^* \in J(k)} p_{F(k)F(j^*)}(x_{kj^*})}. \quad (6)$$

In this expression $(1 - p_O)$ is the probability that the consumer diverts to a store in $J(k)$. The fraction gives the share of such shoppers that divert to store $j$.

To obtain the weights $p_{F(k)F(j)}(x_{kj})$ the CMA estimated a regression model of the following form:

$$p_{kj} = p_{F(k)F(j)}(x_{kj}) + e_{kj} \quad (7)$$

for the 100 centroid stores in the sample and all their competitors. The left-hand-side variable $p_{kj}$ is the observed diversion ratio from store $j$ to store $k$ from the CMA's consumer survey; $p_{F(k)F(j)}(\cdot)$ is a flexible function; and $e_{kj}$ is an econometric error. The equation was estimated separately for each centroid-store firm (Asda and Sainsbury) and for each competitor firm (Tesco, Lidl, etc.).

Figure 1 provides an example of the data and estimated function for one of these regressions: the case where the centroid store $k$ is a Sainsbury and the competitor store $j$ is a Tesco.

On the vertical axis is the observed diversion ratio $p_{kj}$ and on the horizontal axis is the drive-time $x_{kj}$. Each dot in the figure is an observation for a centroid Sainsbury and a competing Tesco. We can see that the number of observations in this regression is not particularly large: it is limited by the number of Sainsbury stores that are sampled (50).

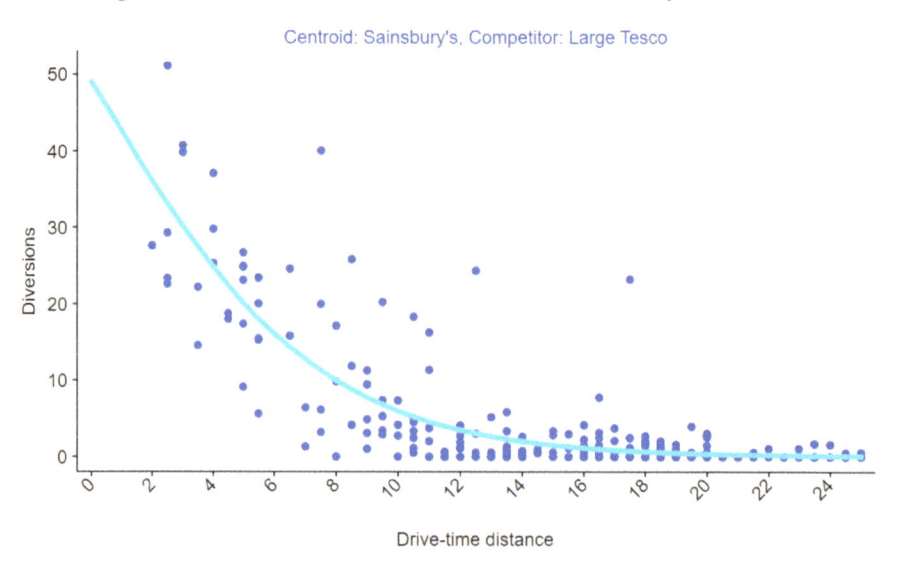

**Figure 1: Estimated diversion ratio from Sainsbury to a Tesco**

Centroid: Sainsbury's, Competitor: Large Tesco

[Scatter plot with y-axis "Diversions" ranging 0 to 50, x-axis "Drive-time distance" ranging 0 to 24]

**Source:** Figure 8.3 of CMA (2018b).

The estimated functions $p_{F(k)F(j)}(\cdot)$ from all these regressions were then used in equation (6) to predict the diversion ratios for all the stores for which a GUPPI is required: both for those that were in the sample and for those that are not.

The expression for the diversion ratio in equation (6) is in principle quite flexible: The set of rivals $J(k)$ varies from one centroid store $k$ to another, and the weights $p_{F(k)F(j)}(x_{kj})$ depend on the owner of the centroid store, the owner of the competitor store, and the drive-time between the stores.

It is interesting to note that the standard multinomial logit model is a special case of the WSS model. To see this concretely, assume that the weights in equation (6) are given by:

$$p_{F(k)F(j)}(x_{kj}) = exp\left(f_{F(k)F(j)}(x_{kj})\right) \qquad (8)$$

where $f_{F(k)F(j)}(x_{kj})$ is a function to be estimated. Then equation (6) is the standard multinomial logit choice probability expression. A feature of this specification is that the function $f_{F(k)F(j)}(x_{kj})$ can be estimated using standard maximum likelihood methods at individual consumer level with the consumer survey that the CMA carried out. The use of this standard model would bring a couple of advantages: (i) its estimated diversion ratios are unbiased under the maintained assumptions of the model and (ii) the statistical precision of the model estimates should be satisfactory given that the unit of observation is the individual consumer, and the CMA had a large sample of consumers. These properties are valuable given that, as we discuss below, the parties argued that the CMA's estimates were biased and imprecise. The CMA did not discuss the option of using a logit model in their report, however it seems worth considering in future retail mergers where the WSS approach is taken.[15]

## A. Margins and the GUPPI Figures

The GUPPI also required margins. Here the CMA relied upon accounting data supplied by the parties. A starting point would be to use the difference between revenues and the cost of buying the goods from suppliers. This is readily available from company accounts, but is likely to be an upper bound to the true variable margin because it does not include variable aspects of other costs such as distribution and labor costs.

The parties conducted their own econometric analysis to come up with a figure for how much of these costs are variable. The CMA accepted the parties' estimates while stating that it suspected that the cost estimates were too high and the consequent margins were too low (resulting, if so, in a GUPPI that was too low).

## B. The CMA's Choice of GUPPI Threshold and the CMA's Decision

To activate the store-level decision rule, which classified each store as to whether it would have an SLC from the merger, a GUPPI threshold must be set. To do this the CMA began with an assessment of the marginal cost reduction from the merger. The CMA concluded that the appropriate figure to use was 1.25 percent of each retailer's price. With this efficiency gain in hand, the logic of the model is that a GUPPI of 1.25 percent or less would imply no upward pricing pressure from the merger. Hence, 1.25 percent represents a lower bound to the threshold that the CMA could set.

The CMA decided to set the threshold at 2.75 percent. The Authority expressed the belief that this threshold allowed a sufficient margin above the lower bound of 1.25 percent to be satisfied that an SLC would probably follow from the merger. In making what was only a small upward adjustment to the GUPPI threshold relative to the lower bound of 1.25 percent, the CMA attached importance to the fact that groceries were an important part of household budgets and its high confidence in the accuracy of the GUPPI estimates.

Applying its decision rule using this threshold, the CMA found SLCs in 45 percent of Sainsbury stores and 57 percent of Asda stores identified in Stage 1. The CMA considered the possibility of store divestitures as an alternative remedy, but ruled this out because of the high percentage of stores with SLCs. The CMA therefore blocked the merger.

---

15 The logit approach has the further advantage that it allows the consumer's location easily to be incorporated into the analysis, which is likely to further improve accuracy of the diversion ratio estimates; to do this the survey would have to ask consumers either their home location or the distance/drive-time from their home to the store they have chosen. A criticism of the logit model, when estimated using first-choice data, is that the diversion ratios are determined by market shares rather than coming from observed substation patterns. However, this criticism does not apply in this setting, because the CMA in effect have first and second choice data for each consumer, and the model is being used to estimate substitution probabilities (*i.e.*, second choice probabilities) directly from the data.

## VI. THE PARTIES' RESPONSE AND THE CMA'S COUNTER-RESPONSE

The parties raised a number of objections to the CMA analysis. We focus on four that relate to the CMA's use of GUPPI at the store level.[16]

### A. Objection 1: No Evidence that a Positive GUPPI Causes Price Changes

The GUPPI is in essence a theoretical predictor of price changes, and it does not constitute direct evidence in support of the view that the GUPPI causes actual price rises. An example of the type of evidence the parties were seeking would be an analysis of how firms actually react at store level in terms of real decisions – *e.g.*, changes to prices, promotions, store budgets for refurbishment, etc. – in response to an observed change in market conditions near a store, such as the entry of a rival. The parties suggested that this kind of evidence is particularly important when GUPPIs are used as a decisional rule rather than as one of many pieces of information.[17] The parties provided evidence of the sort that they considered valuable: data, from their own records, of how they adjusted budgets – *e.g.*, for store refitting – in response to changes in local concentration. They argued that this evidence suggested that their stores did not react at all to entry by a competitor store whose significance was equivalent to a store from the other merging party with a GUPPI similar to the CMA's threshold.

In reply, the CMA reviewed the evidence the parties put forward and argued that it had methodological flaws. After adjusting the methods for these flaws, the CMA found that the evidence supported the CMA's choice of threshold.[18] The CMA added that it was entirely plausible that a small but positive GUPPI would have real implications for prices or other variables: after all, the parties in this industry were sophisticated firms who adjust prices optimally, and fixed costs to price adjustment are not large enough to impede the effects of GUPPI.[19]

### B. Objection 2: The CMA's Estimates of Store-level Diversion Ratios Were Biased and Imprecise

The CMA's diversion ratio estimates were obtained as was discussed in Section V: The CMA estimated a model from a sample of stores and used this model to predict diversion ratios in all stores including those not in the sample. The parties suspected that these estimates had two statistical problems: they were very imprecise and biased upwards. If either suspicion was correct, there would be the potential for many false positives: finding SLCs for stores where there were actually none.

---

16 The objections are discussed in *Parties' Response to the Provisional Findings Report*, available at https://www.gov.uk/cma-cases/j-sainsbury-plc-asda-group-ltd-merger-inquiry.

17 GUPPI was used as a decisional rule in the *Ladbrokes/Coral* case (*see* CMA (2016)), and in this case the CMA had indeed sought the kind of evidence that the parties were calling for in *Asda/Sainsbury*.

18 *See* CMA (2019) paragraph 8.301.

19 *See* CMA (2019) paragraphs 8.285-8.286.

To investigate these suspicions, the parties conducted a within-sample fit exercise: For the stores that were in the sample, the parties compared the diversion ratios predicted by the CMA's model with the diversion ratios from the data, which they took to be the true values. On the question of precision, the parties claimed that these prediction errors were large. On the question of bias, the parties claimed that the CMA's model tended to over-predict diversion ratios when the true diversion ratio was low. The parties argued that their exercise confirmed their suspicions of imprecision and bias.

These problems, they argued, called for a conservative approach to the GUPPI. Perhaps it should not be used in a final decision rule? Or, if it is used in a decision rule, perhaps the threshold for the rule should be set at a higher level so as to reduce the risk of false positives? Going further, they argued that the size of this adjustment should be separately itemized and set on a formal basis.

In response, the CMA argued that it did adjust the GUPPI threshold upwards to account for the effect of uncertainty in the GUPPI estimates. But they rejected the idea that they should identify the extent of this factor separately from other factors that affected the threshold. The CMA also disagreed with the parties' claim that the adjustment should be based on a statistical confidence interval standard; this, they argued, would set a higher standard for quantitative evidence than for qualitative evidence.[20] On the question of upward bias in diversion ratio estimates, the CMA again disputed the parties' claim.[21]

## C. Objection 3: The CMA's Assessment of Substantiality Was Not Well Founded

For the CMA the test of whether the lessening of competition was "substantial" amounted to whether, on the balance of probabilities, the pricing pressure that was indicated by the GUPPI threshold would translate into harm to consumers. The CMA argued that "in assessing what may constitute 'substantial' [...] we have had regard to the fact that groceries are a non-discretionary expenditure that accounts for a significant share of household spend, proportionally more so for low-income households."[22] In practice this meant that the set a relatively low GUPPI threshold because of these features of the industry.

The parties objected to this by arguing that this test had no legal foundation: They noted that the Enterprise Act 2002, which sets out merger law in the UK, did not specify a different test for markets that are an important share of household budgets, or which cater to a non-discretionary type of expenditure. It is, however, the job of the CMA to interpret the legislation and the meaning of substantiality: they were not persuaded by the parties' objection, and did not adjust their approach.

---

20 *See* CMA (2019) paragraph 8.294.

21 The discussion of this point was quite technical and hinged on whether it was acceptable in this context for the expected value of the error in equation (7) to be positive when the dependent variable is low. *See* CMA (2019) paragraph 8.243-8.244 and Appendix E for a detailed discussion.

22 *See* CMA (2019) paragraph 8.283.

## D. Objection 4: The CMA's GUPPI Threshold of 2.75 Percent is Too Low Relative to Precedents

This objection was central to the case. As a starting point for thinking about the appropriate choice of GUPPI threshold, we note that CMA could not set anything lower than 1.25 percent, as this was the marginal cost reduction (expressed as a percentage of price) that the CMA expected from the merger. The threshold set by the CMA would have to be adjusted upwards from this level. The size of its upward adjustment was influenced by two main factors: (i) the fact that grocery shopping was non-discretionary and important in consumer budgets, which would suggest a relatively low upward adjustment, and (ii) the level of uncertainty in the store-level GUPPI estimates, which the CMA did not consider to be high. The CMA set the upward adjustment at 1.5 percent resulting in a GUPPI threshold of 2.75 percent.

The parties were expecting a much higher GUPPI threshold. It was not wholly unreasonable that they were surprised. Consider the following quotation from the CMA's report on the 2017 *Tesco/Booker* merger inquiry.[23]

> "In the past, for some (but not all) horizontal mergers, the CMA has taken the approach that a GUPPI of less than 5% indicates that concerns could be ruled out. Typically, this has been followed by closer examination of markets where the GUPPI was 5% or higher. In other cases, the CMA has signalled that a higher threshold may be appropriate." CMA (2017b), paragraph 9.46.

This paragraph suggests at the very least that in horizontal mergers a 5 percent threshold is quite common – and that a higher threshold might be reasonable – as a safe harbor. It seems logical moreover that a threshold for the purpose of a decision rule, as used in *Asda/Sainsbury*, might be higher than that for the purpose of a safe harbor. The quoted paragraph did not bind the hands of the CMA in setting future thresholds. But it did summarize, in the CMA's own words, recent precedents.

The parties could find no domestic or international precedent for such a low GUPPI threshold.[24] The parties pointed in particular to two recent UK precedents: First, *Tesco/Booker*, which was a vertical merger between the UK's largest supermarket and the UK's largest wholesaler. In this case the CMA used a screening approach (rather than the decision rule approach used in *Asda/Sainsbury*) and set a safe harbor threshold of 5 percent: stores with a GUPPI below this were unlikely to be problematic. This made the *Asda/Sainsbury* threshold incoherent, the parties claimed: a store with a GUPPI of, say, 3 percent would be classified as giving rise to an SLC in *Asda/Sainsbury* but would be put in a safe harbor in *Tesco/Booker*. The second precedent was *Ladbrokes/Coral*: This case – similar to *Asda/Safeway* – used a decision rule approach.

---

23 The quotation is paragraph 9.46 of CMA (2017b); *see also* footnote 250 in CMA (2017b) for case references that support the quoted text.

24 The parties pointed out that the CMA's GUPPI threshold seemed to lower than the practice in the EU, which had not used such a low threshold.

That case set a threshold of 10 percent. The parties used these two precedents to argue that a reasonable GUPPI threshold for *Asda/Sainsbury* should be at least as high as the 5 percent that was used in *Tesco/Booker* and potentially as high as the 10 percent that was used in *Ladbrokes/Coral*.

The CMA, in reply, argued that precedents are in general of limited importance in a big merger inquiry such as *Asda/Sainsbury*: The threshold should be assessed afresh for each case. They pointed out that the CMA's merger guidance does not provide any concrete GUPPI threshold figure, whether for a decision rule or for a safe harbor.

The CMA disputed the relevance of either of the two cases that the parties had used. Neither were horizontal merger cases for the supermarket industry.[25] If recent cases are to be referenced, the CMA argued, it would be better to use a horizontal merger case within the same industry. The most recent such case was *Somerfield/Morrison* in 2005. This was a horizontal merger case for supermarket firms, and one of the first to use an upward pricing pressure indicator. Although the indicator that was used in *Somerfield/Morrison* was not GUPPI – it instead used the "indicative price rise" ("IPR") indicator – it is possible to "translate" from IPR thresholds to GUPPI thresholds. The threshold in *Somerfield/Morrison* translated to a GUPPI threshold of 3.2 percent: This was not much higher than the 2.75 percent that was used by the CMA in *Asda/Sainsbury*.[26] The CMA concluded that its GUPPI threshold was not out of line with precedent, with respect to mergers in the supermarket industry.

## VII. REFLECTIONS ON THE CASE

At a broad-brush level, the *Asda/Sainsbury* merger always looked questionable. Precedent was against it: The most recent case that examined mergers between the Big Four – the *Safeway* case of 2003 – ruled them out. The simplest possible HHI-based test – using the industry revenue shares in Table 1 – put it above standard thresholds in the U.S. merger guidelines for flagging a detrimental merger.

The CMA's decision to block the merger was a reaffirmation of the view of the UK's competition authorities – which emerged after many inquiries in the early 2000s – that the supermarket industry was concentrated enough. The industry had not changed enough since then to overturn this.

There were many important questions that were raised by the parties about the appropriate use of GUPPI in retail cases and more broadly: Did the CMA's modelling method result in unacceptably noisy estimates of the GUPPI in individual stores? Should the GUPPI threshold take explicit account of these errors?

The question that became central in this case, however, was whether the CMA's choice of a threshold was too low. The parties thought so, and they were not alone: Third-party economists that commented on the case seemed to agree.[27]

---

25 *Ladbrokes/Coral* was a betting shop merger, and *Tesco/Booker* was a vertical merger case (which had used vertical GUPPI rather than the horizontal GUPPI in *Asda/Sainsbury*).

26 *See* CMA (2019) paragraph 8.264.

27 *See, for example,* Forbes & Hughes (2019).

Overall, it seems clear that the CMA did set a relatively low GUPPI threshold in this case, much lower than some recent merger cases that used a GUPPI approach. Moreover, this threshold was low by international standards. But it is also true that the Authority's threshold was similar to the implied GUPPI threshold in the most recent case of a major horizontal merger in the supermarket industry: *Somerfield/Morrison*. This case is arguably the most relevant comparison, because it is in the same industry.

What this appears to tell us is that in practice the CMA can vary the GUPPI threshold that it uses quite widely from one merger case to another, particularly when the cases are in different industries. It also suggests that there are important industry-specific factors that can drive the level of the GUPPI threshold in a merger case. As we noted at the outset, one such industry-specific factor stands out where supermarkets are concerned: the importance of the industry to consumers. There is no other industry that occupies a greater share of consumer budgets – particularly for the lowest-income consumers. And as the CMA emphasized, much of this grocery spending is likely to be non-discretionary. This has not changed since the early 2000s. The CMA took this factor into account, and behaved in a manner that was consistent with previous supermarket merger cases – GUPPI or no GUPPI.

Does the low GUPPI threshold, then, represent a tightening of UK merger policy? From the argument in the previous paragraph – the low GUPPI was a consequence of industry-specific factors – it seems not: As the CMA stressed throughout its report, the Authority takes a case-by-case approach to the choice of a GUPPI threshold, and previous GUPPI threshold choices do not bind the CMA in the future.

## REFERENCES

Baker, J. (2019). *The Antitrust Paradigm: Restoring a Competitive Economy*, Harvard University Press.

Farrell, J. & C. Shapiro (2010). "Antitrust Evaluation of Horizontal Mergers: An Economic Alternative to Market Definition," *The B.E. Journal of Theoretical Economics Policies and Perspectives*, Vol 10, No. 1.

Berry, S., M. Gaynor & F. Scott Morton (2019). "Do Increasing Markups Matter? Lessons from Empirical Industrial Organization," *Journal of Economic Perspectives* Vol 33. No. 3.

Salop, S. & S. Moresi (2009). "Updating the Merger Guidelines: Comments," *available at* http://www.ftc.gov/os/comments/horizontalmergerguides/545095- 00032.pdf.

Competition Commission (2000). *Supermarkets: A Report on the Supply of Groceries from Multiple Stores in the United Kingdom*, (London, U.K.: The Stationery Office).

Competition Commission (2003). *Safeway plc and Asda Group Limited (owned by Wal-Mart Stores Inc.); Wm Morrison Supermarkets PLC; J Sainsbury plc; and Tesco plc: A report on the mergers in contemplation*, (London, U.K.: The Stationery Office).

Competition Commission (2005). *Somerfield plc and Wm Morrison Supermarkets plc: A report on the acquisition by Somerfield plc of 115 stores from Wm Morrison Supermarkets plc*, (London, U.K.: The Stationery Office).

Competition Commission (2008). *The supply of groceries in the UK: market investigation,* (London, U.K.: The Stationery Office).

Competition and Markets Authority (2016). *Ladbrokes and Coral: A report on the anticipated merger between Ladbrokes plc and certain businesses of Gala Coral Group Limited,* (London, U.K.: The Stationery Office).

Competition and Markets Authority (2017a). *Retail Mergers Commentary,* (London, U.K.: The Stationery Office).

Competition and Markets Authority (2017b). *Tesco and Booker: A report on the anticipated acquisition by Tesco PLC of Booker Group plc,* (London, U.K.: The Stationery Office).

Competition and Markets Authority (2019). *Anticipated merger between J Sainsbury PLC and Asda Group Ltd,* (London, U.K.: The Stationery Office).

Competition and Markets Authority (2021). *Merger Guidelines,* (London, U.K.: The Stationery Office).

Forbes, B. & M. Hughes (2020). *Economic Evidence in Retailer Mergers After Sainsbury's/Asda: Death by GUPPI? Available at* https://www.alixpartners.com/media/13831/mc20_chapter-3_alixpartners.pdf.

Miller, N. & G. Sheu (2021). "Quantitative Methods for Evaluating the Unilateral Effects of Mergers," *Review of Industrial Organization*, Vol. 58, No. 1, 143-177.

Philippon, T. (2019). *The Great Reversal: How America Gave Up on Free Markets*, Harvard University Press.

Smith, H. (2004). "Supermarket Choice and Supermarket Competition in Market Equilibrium" *The Review of Economic Studies*, Volume 71, Issue 1.

Thomassen, Ø., H. Smith, S. Seiler & P. Schiraldi (2017). "Multi-category competition and market power: A model of supermarket pricing," *American Economic Review* 107(8).

Valletti, T. & H. Zenger (2021). "Mergers with Differentiated Products: Where Do We Stand?" *Review of Industrial Organization* 58:179–212.

## CHAPTER 5
# Evaluating a Theory of Harm in a Vertical Merger: *AT&T/Time Warner*

*By Dennis W. Carlton, Georgi V. Giozov, Mark A. Israel & Allan L. Shampine*[1]

## I. INTRODUCTION

This case study focuses on the theory of harm that was presented by the government in the 2018 *AT&T/Time Warner* merger, which was challenged by the U.S. Department of Justice ("DOJ"), litigated, and permitted to proceed by the court. The same theory of harm and remedy appeared in the *Comcast/NBCU* merger. Analysis of that merger's outcome was thus prominently featured in the *AT&T/Time Warner* trial and is also discussed here for the same reason.[2]

The *AT&T/Time Warner* case was the first vertical merger case litigated to conclusion by the DOJ in the last forty years,[3] and, because it was litigated, the record contains specific detailed predictions that we can evaluate. By contrast, there is less information available about the *Comcast/NBCU* case.

As noted, the FCC and DOJ applied a similar vertical model in *Comcast/NBCU* as the DOJ applied in *AT&T/Time Warner*.[4] However, the *Comcast/NBCU* merger was allowed to proceed with remedies under a government monitored consent decree. The government declined to offer the same remedies in *AT&T/Time Warner*; but the merging parties unilaterally instituted a similar remedy to the antitrust concerns, as a private contract between AT&T and current and future customers of Warner Media's Turner networks that would not require enforcement by the government. The remedy was thus inextricably linked to the analysis of the transaction. Indeed, the obvious question is whether the remedies were effective in either case – and, more generally, whether the mergers, with remedies, were harmful to competition and consumers.

---

1  The authors worked on behalf of AT&T in the *AT&T/Time Warner* matter, and Prof. Carlton testified on behalf of AT&T at trial. Dr. Israel also worked on behalf of Comcast in the *Comcast/NBCU* matter, which is referenced in our discussion of the *AT&T* case. The authors thank Thomas Hazlett, Ken Heyer, Daniel O'Brien, Sam Peltzman, Clifford Winston, and an anonymous referee for helpful comments.

2  For further discussion, *see* Carlton, Israel & Shampine (2019); Shapiro (2021); and Carlton, Giozov, Israel & Shampine (2022).

3  *See, e.g.,* Reardon & Sorrentino (2019).

4  *See, e.g.*, Rogerson (2019) and Carlton Redacted (2018a, Section V.D.).

## II. THE PROPOSED MERGER AND MARKET STRUCTURE

The proposed merger involved AT&T acquiring Time Warner for roughly $85 billion. Although the companies operated a range of businesses, the focus of the competitive analysis was on the pay-TV ecosystem, which the government characterized as operating at three levels: video content creation (*e.g.*, movie and television production studios), video content aggregation (*e.g.*, basic and premium cable networks), and video content distribution (*e.g.*, satellite video providers and cable companies). As described below, the transaction was a vertical one, involving firms at different levels of this vertical chain.

AT&T operated at the video content distribution level of the chain. In particular, at the time of the transaction, AT&T was a telecommunications provider that, through its DIRECTV and U-verse businesses, served over 25 million pay-TV customers. Pay-TV providers are referred to as multi-channel video programming distributors ("MVPDs"). MVPDs included direct broadcast satellite providers (*e.g.*, DIRECTV and DISH), cable companies (*e.g.*, Comcast and Cox), telecommunications companies (*e.g.*, Verizon), as well as video distributors operating over the Internet (virtual MVPDs, or "vMVPDs"). AT&T also provided wireless and wireline telecommunications services, but those were not at issue.

Time Warner operated at the video content aggregation and the video content creation levels of the vertical chain. In particular, Time Warner was a video content aggregator that, through its Turner Broadcasting Systems business, licensed a variety of basic cable networks, including the cable networks TNT, TBS, and CNN. It also licensed its premium cable network, HBO, but that network was not at issue in the case. Time Warner created video content such as movies and TV shows, but the trial was not focused on video content creation, but instead was focused on the licensing of Turner's basic cable networks (that is the video content aggregation level of the chain).

Overall, the case was about the vertical relationship between Time Warner (Turner) as a video content aggregator (through its basic cable networks) and AT&T (DIRECTV/U-verse) as a distributor of cable network programming.

## III. ANTITRUST APPROACH TO VERTICAL AND HORIZONTAL MERGERS

Traditionally, antitrust enforcers and regulators have been less concerned about vertical mergers than about horizontal mergers. Both horizontal and vertical mergers can, in some circumstances, harm competition; but the concerns in the two types of cases are different. A key concern in a horizontal merger is that, post-merger, the two divisions of the combined firm (which were previously separate firms) will internalize the harm that more aggressive competition has on the other and will thereby soften competition, which will lead to higher prices. In a vertical merger, there can be a concern that the vertically integrated firm will leverage market power that one division of the combined firm possesses to create or increase market power for the other division.[5]

Vertical integration can both: (i) produce benefits (*e.g.*, the elimination of double marginalization, or EDM, which is a specific illustration of the "Cournot complements" result that mergers of complements create downward pricing pressure); and (ii) raise concerns about raising rivals' costs (which can create upward pricing pressure). The benefits to competition work through the internalization of incentives: When two firms, each of which has some ability to set prices above marginal costs, offer complementary products – such as video content and video distribution – reducing prices or making investments to improve one of the complementary products can benefit *both* firms, and consumers as well.

For example, if one firm produces distinctive cars and the other customized engines, then as the engine becomes better, the overall car becomes better. Both the car manufacturer and the engine manufacturer make more sales. When they are separate, however, neither firm receives all of the benefits from lower prices or increased investments; instead, some of the benefits spill over to the other firm. A vertical merger brings the benefits to both firms under one roof, which, *ceteris paribus*, increases the incentives to reduce prices or make investments, since the combined firm internalizes the full set of benefits when making pricing and investment decisions.

The possible harm to competition from a vertical merger may be less obvious than the harm from a horizontal merger, but it can occur in some settings. If the merged/integrated firm increases the upstream price of the input that it sells to its downstream rivals, the integrated firm will make less money from selling the input to those rivals than was the case pre-merger (since it was presumably setting the price pre-merger to maximize its profits from the sale on the input); but there is an offsetting benefit since the sales of the integrated firm's downstream product can increase because it now faces weaker (higher-cost) downstream competitors: In essence, the sales of the input by the upstream firm to a rival of the downstream firm create an externality that affects the downstream firm. With vertical integration, the (integrated upstream) input seller internalizes this externality, and that can create an incentive for the upstream entity to increase the price of that input to rival downstream firms, which results in upward pressure on downstream prices.

Given that there are (at least) two offsetting effects of a vertical merger, one needs to use some economic model to predict the net effect of the interactions of these two effects. We now turn to the model used by the government.

## IV. THE GOVERNMENT'S MODEL IN *AT&T/TIME WARNER* AND *COMCAST/NBCU*

In this section we explain the government's model, discuss disputed assumptions that underlie the theory and parameter values, and review the various predictions based on different assumptions.

---

[5] There can be other concerns with vertical mergers, but this concern was the one raised for this case.

## A. Theory

The government's model consists of two parts: an upstream bargaining model that determines the price of the input to rival distributors; and a downstream merger simulation that determines the prices of the retail products given the outcome of the bargaining model.[6] For the bargaining model, the basic premise is that a content creator negotiates with each distributor over the price of the content, holding all other entities' prices constant. The parties split the joint profits from reaching a deal (the "gains from trade") based on their relative bargaining strengths in a bargaining game that was first described by John Nash (a "Nash bargaining model").

The outcome of the negotiation depends importantly on the "threat points": What happens to each party if they fail to reach an agreement. In the case of a television network and a video distributor such as a cable company, the model assumes that failure to reach an agreement means that the cable company does not broadcast the network: a "blackout."

For the *AT&T* case, the content at issue was the Turner (Time Warner) networks (cable only), while the distributors at issue were multichannel video programming distributors ("MVPDs") such as direct broadcast satellite ("DBS") companies and cable companies. For the *Comcast* case, the content at issue was the NBC Universal networks (both cable and broadcast), while the distributors at issue were also MVPDs such as DBS companies and cable companies.[7]

The government's upstream bargaining model focuses on the change in pricing incentives that arise when a content provider merges vertically with one of the distributors of its content. According to the model, due to the merger, if the parties fail to reach an agreement, the content provider's threat point improves from the pre-merger situation because the distributor, lacking the content, will lose some subscribers who will move to the vertically integrated content provider's distribution arm. Thus, unlike in the pre-merger situation, the "pain" suffered by the content provider from not striking a deal with certain distributors is lower. Under the model, this improvement in the content provider's threat point will, all else equal, result in the licensing distributor's paying a higher price for the content.[8] In the upstream bargaining model, the model does not explicitly take into account that any increase in the input price will affect downstream prices.

The predicted content price increase in the government model is roughly the bargaining split times the incremental profit to the vertically integrated distributor if the rival distributor did not carry the content. Another way to think of this content price increase is that after integration, the economic (opportunity) cost of selling to a downstream rival distributor now increases to reflect the fact that a sale of content to a downstream rival deprives the vertically integrated firm of some of its own potential

---

6 *See* Shapiro Redacted (2018, pp. 39-58). For a discussion of the model in the related *Comcast/NBCU* matter, *see* Rogerson (2014, pp. 534-575).

7 The government did not apply its model to HBO, which is sold as a stand-alone product, and did not claim that there would be price increases or the withholding of HBO.

8 *See, e.g.,* Shapiro Redacted (2018, Figures 8 and 9).

downstream sales. As a result, the price that the vertically integrated firm charges the downstream rival has upward pricing pressure.

Consequently, in the *AT&T* case, the concern was that (the post-merger, integrated) AT&T would increase the price of, say, TNT content to Comcast, to reflect the opportunity cost to AT&T's own distribution subsidiary – DIRECTV – from AT&T's (upstream) licensing the content to Comcast, which can take sales away from DIRECTV.

Hence, the key parameter values for determining the size of the predicted content price increase are: the bargaining split (what fraction of the gains from trade the content provider gets, as determined by the relative bargaining strengths of the upstream content provider and the downstream distributor); the departure rate (what fraction of subscribers the distributor will lose if it does not carry the content); the diversion rate (what fraction of the lost subscribers will go to the vertically integrated downstream distributor); and the profit margins from a sale upstream and downstream at the vertically integrated distributor (which affect the potential gains and losses to the merged firm if a rival distributor does not carry the content).

The second stage of the overall model consists of inserting the price changes for content that is predicted by the bargaining model into a merger simulation and solving for the equilibrium prices that would be set by the various MVPDs. Benefits from the elimination of double marginalization ("EDM") are reflected at this stage. (Here there was no dispute as to the presence of EDM, only as to its magnitude, but in other cases there may be disputes about whether, for example, pre-merger contracting practices have already solved for double marginalization.) Because the model incorporates both the possibility of increased content costs of other MVPDs (potentially pushing retail prices upwards) and the possibility of lowered content costs of the vertically integrated MVPD (potentially pushing retail prices downwards), the direction of the merger's effect on average retail prices, and on consumer welfare, is ambiguous as a matter of economic theory, but instead depends on the specific modeling assumptions and parameter values.

The government and the merging parties agreed that although the mechanism for harm is the increase in content prices to rivals, it is the overall retail pricing to consumers that matters: One needs to take into account the desirable effects of creating efficiencies from vertical integration alongside the harmful effects from raising rivals' costs, so as to determine the merger's all-in effect.

## B. The Base Government Price Predictions in Comcast/NBCU and AT&T/Time Warner

The focus in this section is on the predictions in *AT&T/Time Warner*. The *Comcast/NBCU* predictions were not made public, but, for the sake of context, we note that Rogerson (2014) has estimated that the government predictions for content price increases – on the assumption that no remedy had been put in place – would have been at least 9 percent and might have been as high as 45 percent.[9]

---

9 Rogerson (2014, pp. 546-550, 555).

For the *AT&T/Time Warner* merger, the government estimated that prices to rival MVPDs per subscriber per month for the Turner networks would increase by an average of $0.76, or 16.2 percent compared to what they would otherwise have been.[10] The merger simulation was applied per MVPD and region; but overall the government predicted that DIRECTV's average retail prices would fall by $0.26, and the other MVPDs' prices would rise between $0.22 and $0.60, for an overall average retail price increase of about $0.27 per subscriber per month.[11] The government reported that average MVPD subscriber bills ranged from $120 to $160 per month.[12] The increase of $0.27 is roughly 0.19 percent of $140 (the mid-point of $120 and $160), and while these bills may include other bundled services, there was no dispute that $0.27 was a tiny increase relative to subscriber payments for MVPD services.[13]

Thus, the prediction was that DIRECTV retail prices would be about $0.26 lower, but that overall average MVPD retail price would be about $0.27 higher. The government argued that while a $0.27 price increase may appear to be small, it would affect enough consumers to total roughly $24 million per month.[14] As will be discussed below, these predictions were presented as a basis for challenging the merger; but these predictions did not take into account the remedy that was unilaterally adopted by AT&T.

## C. The Model's Assumptions and Predictions of Content and Retail Prices

As noted above, the key parameter value assumptions that feed into the bargaining model are the bargaining split, the departure rate, the diversion rate, and the profit margins on the upstream and downstream subsidiaries of the merged firm. There was dispute in both merger cases about those assumptions and hence about the price predictions made by the model. However, in *Comcast/NBCU*, the details are not public.[15]

For *AT&T/Time Warner*, with respect to profit margins, the government expert used AT&T (DIRECTV) margins from early 2016 and predicted that those would remain constant going forward. The AT&T expert (Carlton) used more recent, and smaller, margins; he observed that AT&T's margins had declined each year since 2012 and that third-party analysts predicted that these margins would continue to decline.[16]

With respect to the diversion rate, the government expert assumed diversion that was proportional to then-current subscriber shares. The government expert

---

10 Shapiro Redacted (2018, Figure 13).

11 Shapiro Redacted (2018, Figure 15).

12 Shapiro Redacted (2018, pp. 21-22).

13 Carlton Redacted (2018b, ¶ 5).

14 Shapiro Redacted (2018; Figure 15). Note that this is a prediction that holds all else constant; consequently, it ought to be measured relative to trend. Both content and retail prices had been trending higher prior to the merger.

15 Rogerson (2014, pp. 543-553).

16 Carlton Redacted (2018b, ¶¶ 45-46).

assumed that the "outside good" – cord cutting – would have a roughly 10 percent share, based on the same survey that was relied upon for the departure rate (discussed further below). The AT&T expert used the subscriber share for cord-cutters in the government's subscriber share data source (20 percent), and noted that the source predicted that cord-cutting would grow rapidly in importance.[17]

With respect to the bargaining split, the government expert assumed a 50 percent split and claimed that this split was supported by estimates of the various parties' weighted average cost of capital, whose ratios the government took as a proxy for bargaining strength.[18] The AT&T expert did not put forward a specific alternative figure for bargaining weights but noted that the government's predictions of net consumer harm were not robust to changes in that assumed value for bargaining strength.[19]

With respect to the departure rate, the government expert assumed a departure rate of 9.4 percent;[20] this was based primarily on a survey by a consulting firm (Altman Vilandrie & Co.) on behalf of Charter Communications (which was an MVPD that opposed the proposed merger). The government expert claimed that this was also consistent with an econometric analysis of the Viacom/Suddenlink blackout, which both experts agreed was a relevant benchmark.[21]

With respect to the survey, the merging parties presented testimony that the survey was flawed; also, the departure figure for Turner (and no other network) had been increased at the last minute by the consulting firm at the urging of Charter in the shadow of the litigation.[22] Had the original unchanged figure been used, the government's model would predict retail price reductions, not increases.[23]

As to the Viacom/Suddenlink blackout, the AT&T expert pointed out that the government expert's estimates were contradicted by Suddenlink's own public statements to investors that the impact of the blackout on departures had been only about 2.0-2.5 percent. Furthermore, the AT&T expert argued that the government expert's econometric analysis had failed to account for the fact that the entire industry expe-

---

17 Carlton (2018c, p. 2448). Shapiro Redacted (2018, n. 241). Carlton Redacted (2018b, ¶ 69). Leon (2018, pp. 137-141). The court noted that the survey firm relied upon by the government expert had altered the actual survey results in the shadow of the litigation and without explanation reduced the reported cord-cutting estimate by 40 percent, which cast doubt on its credibility.

18 Shapiro Redacted (2018, p. 42).

19 More specifically, the AT&T expert noted that the government expert relied upon a document that claimed that MVPDs were paying more to Turner than the content was worth: that MVPDs would actually be better off not carrying the Turner networks. That fact called into question the credibility of the document; but if true, the implication would be that Turner networks were receiving all or almost all of the gains from trade. If the government had assumed that Turner received 71 percent or more of the gains from trade (holding other assumptions constant), the government's model would predict net consumer benefits. Carlton Redacted (2018b, Section VI.E.).

20 Shapiro Redacted (2018, p. 128).

21 Shapiro Redacted (2018, Section 8.1).

22 Leon (2018, pp. 122-129).

23 Leon (2018, p. 129); Carlton Redacted (2018b, ¶ 65).

rienced a downturn in subscribership at that time. Accounting for that downturn reduced the government expert's econometric estimate to 4.8 percent.[24] This reduced econometric estimate was also supported by third-party analyses.[25] The AT&T expert also pointed out that MVPDs had long-term contracts in place such that Turner could not raise prices to them until the contracts next came up for renewal. That fact could be incorporated into the pricing predictions.

Collectively, the model prediction under the alternative assumptions was a $0.48 **decrease** in retail prices, as compared to the government base prediction of a $0.27 increase.[26]

The court ultimately agreed with the analysis of AT&T and its economic expert concluding that "the evidence is insufficient to support the inputs and assumptions incorporated into [the government expert's] bargaining model." In doing so the court credited AT&T's economic expert's opinion on the appropriate input values for the bargaining model.[27]

## D. The Relevance of Predictions in Light of Remedies and Industry Structure

If we set aside the debate about the assumed input values, there is a more fundamental question about whether the government's model captures enough of the salient details of the industry and the transaction such that its predictions are even relevant to post-merger outcomes.

In particular, the model did not account for the merging parties' contractual arbitration commitment in any way. In *Comcast/NBCU*, the government imposed a consent decree with a remedy to address the vertical concerns. The key element of the consent decree was an agreement to engage in binding "baseball-style" arbitration[28] where, if the distributor invoked arbitration, the content provider could not withhold the content during the arbitration proceeding: In essence, the content provider could not unilaterally impose a blackout; instead, the distributor was guaranteed to be able to retain access to the programming at prices that would be determined by the arbitrator pursuant to the baseball-style final offer arbitration – even if the distributor rejected all proposed terms from the content provider.

In *AT&T/Time Warner*, the government refused to agree to the same remedy (the government having indicated at the time that it sought to move away from what it characterized as behavioral merger remedies). However, the parties made a unilateral binding contractual commitment to baseball-style arbitration that also provided that the distributor could continue to air the content after demanding arbitration.

---

[24] Carlton Redacted (2018b, ¶¶ 56-57); Leon (2018, pp. 129-131).

[25] Carlton Redacted (2018b, ¶¶ 59); Leon (2018, pp. 129-130).

[26] Carlton Redacted (2018b, ¶ 72).

[27] Leon (2018, pp. 118-149).

[28] Baseball-style arbitration means that each party submits a final offer and the arbitrator must choose one of the two offers (rather than any compromise between them).

Again, the distributor was guaranteed to be able to retain access to the programming even if the distributor rejected all proposed terms from the content provider.

While the government raised possible concerns over the limitations of baseball-style arbitration, the judge who presided over the *AT&T/Time Warner* trial was also presiding over the *Comcast/NBCU* consent decree and had been told for years by the government that the arbitration commitment was effective for *Comcast/NBCU*. Although the government was clear that it no longer wished to engage in remedies of this type, neither the government nor its expert ever provided a clear explanation as to why the arbitration commitment should be any less effective in *AT&T/Time Warner* than the government had been telling the judge it had been in *Comcast/NBCU*.[29] Furthermore, the government expert clearly stated that his model, and its predictions, did not account for the arbitration commitment.[30,31]

In addition, the AT&T expert argued that there were a range of other core features of the industry that had not been correctly modeled. For example, while Nash-in-Nash is a well-known bargaining model, it is not clear that it is applicable in the video industry. These questions have been hotly debated in the broader academic community as well. For example, 37 antitrust scholars in an *amicus* filing stated that the "simple Nash bargaining model … addresses one-shot, bilateral negotiation, while actual bargaining between video content providers and distributors is repeated and multilateral." However, a separate brief supported aspects of the government's appeal with respect to the government's model.[32]

More generally, debate about the model fell primarily into four categories, with the debate generally focused on how much impact various simplifying assumptions were likely to have on the model's predictions: First, the simple Nash bargaining model assumes a one-shot game; but in this industry, for example, negotiations play out over time and reputation effects may matter. Second, the simple Nash bargaining model assumes a bilateral negotiation that is uninfluenced by the terms of other negotiations; but "most-favored-nation" ("MFN") clauses (where a distributor is guaranteed rates that will remain at least as favorable as rates to other specified distributors through the

---

29 *See, e.g.*, Shapiro (2021, p. 32): "Judge Leon himself had been supervising that consent decree since 2011. DOJ had repeatedly told Judge Leon that binding arbitration was an effective remedy in the Comcast/NBCU merger."

30 *See, e.g.*, Shapiro (2021, pp. 32-33): "At trial, AT&T argued that Turner's offer of binding arbitration would prevent Turner from increasing prices to rival MVPDs. … My analysis addressed the merger between AT&T and Time Warner as originally proposed, not as it was modified in response to the DOJ complaint. … The appeals court accurately observed that my quantification of harm to consumer[s] 'failed to take into account Turner Broadcasting System's post-litigation irrevocable offers of no-blackout arbitration agreements, which a government expert acknowledged would require a new model.'"

31 *See also* Katz (2018, pp. 2643-2757) for further discussion of the arbitration commitment and the government model.

32 37 Economists, Antitrust Scholars, and Former Government Antitrust Officials (2018, p. 15); Carlton Redacted (2018b, ¶ 35); 27 Antitrust Scholars (2018). The Court referred to the government expert's model as a "Rube Goldberg" contraption. The AT&T expert noted that, although that would be one description of the government's complicated model, in fairness to the government expert, economists often have such models, and there are such models in the literature. Carlton (2018c).

life of the contract) are common in the industry, so that the outcome of one negotiation explicitly affects other negotiations, which violates the Nash assumption.

Third, the model assumes away a wide range of real-world responses to a boycott, including, in particular, the ability of MVPDs to reduce their retail prices in response to losing content, so as to retain subscribers (whether through an overall price decrease or through targeted promotional efforts). Fourth, the full model – including bargaining and merger simulation – "essentially ignored equilibrium feedback effects [between the two parts of the model]… Since the equilibrium feedback effects can be complex it is difficult to say how the Department of Justice's estimate of the consumer harm generated by the merger would have changed had it used the fully correct procedure."[33]

The government expert claimed that there was some "limited support" for the model's predictions based on a redacted FCC analysis of DIRECTV and Fox that was conducted in 2010. However, the details of that analysis were not public and were not part of the discovery in *AT&T/Time Warner*, and the government expert did not do any analysis himself of that transaction. The AT&T expert did analyze that transaction and found no evidence of a price increase that was associated with vertical integration.[34]

## V. AVAILABLE EVIDENCE ON POST-MERGER OUTCOMES

### A. The Comcast/NBCU Experience

The government expectation in *Comcast/NBCU* was presumably that the arbitration remedy would work, and so neither content nor retail prices would rise as a result of the merger.[35] If that expectation was incorrect, and the theory of harm was correct, one might expect to see higher content prices and higher retail prices as a result of the merger. If we do not observe higher content and retail prices, it could be that the remedy was effective, or the theory of harm was incorrect, or both. The available evidence indicates that NBCU content prices were not elevated as a result of the merger, which is consistent with the presence of an effective remedy, and/or a flaw in the underlying model that predicted harm.

The first piece of evidence on NBCU content prices is simply the government's own assertions as to the effectiveness of its remedy. While the consent decree was in effect, Judge Leon, who presided over the *AT&T/Time Warner* trial, also presided over the consent decree in *Comcast/NBCU*. DOJ had for years told Judge Leon that the consent decree with *Comcast/NBCU* – including the arbitration commitment – had been effective.[36]

---

33 Rogerson (2020, p. 428). *See also* Shapiro (2021, p. 27): "Rogerson (2020) correctly notes that the approach that I took 'was not fully correct' in the sense that I calculated RRC and EDM based on pre-merger prices rather than equilibrium prices."

34 Carlton Redacted (2018b, ¶ 24).

35 Again, relative to pre-existing trends and other non-merger related industry changes.

36 Shapiro (2021, pp. 32-33).

The only other extant empirical retrospective on the *Comcast/NBCU* merger of which the authors are aware – Ford (2017, p.1) – found "no systematic increase in the prices for Comcast's networks following the merger. ... The evidence suggests either that there was no net positive effect on incentives to raise prices above competitive levels following the vertical merger, or else that the behavioral remedies placed on the Comcast-NBCU merger have been effective."[37]

In the *AT&T/Time Warner* trial, the AT&T expert reported results on the *Comcast/NBCU* price effects, based on a variety of econometric analyses using data from SNL Kagan (a standard industry source that reports estimates of average affiliate fees) as well as confidential data from DIRECTV, DISH, and Charter that were produced during discovery.[38] The government identified DIRECTV and DISH as Comcast's primary competitors, and hence the MVPDs that were most likely for Comcast to target with increased NBCU rates.

The AT&T expert showed that there was no evidence of any statistically significant increases in NBCU rates that were related to vertical integration with Comcast with the use of any of the available data sets. To the contrary, the point estimates that were obtained from difference-in-difference analyses (estimated over the 2010-2017 period, or 2010-2015 for Charter) as well as cross-sectional analyses (estimated from 2017 cross-sectional data, or 2015 for Charter) were typically negative – which indicated lower prices that were due to the merger. And the only statistically significant results were negative.[39]

In sum, the econometric evidence on NBCU's content prices (affiliate fees) as of the time of the *AT&T/Time Warner* trial (2018) – seven years after NBCU's vertical integration with Comcast – indicated that there was no statistically detectable increase in NBCU's networks' affiliate fees, and the government presented no econometric evidence or claims to the contrary.

The *Comcast/NBCU* consent decree expired on September 1, 2018.[40] However, the DOJ notified Comcast that it would continue to monitor Comcast even absent a formal consent decree structure, which calls into question how much change in regulatory oversight actually occurred.[41]

Nonetheless, we can examine publicly available data from SNL Kagan to determine if there are any obvious discontinuities in NBCU rates since the consent decree ended. Given the existence of overlapping long-term contracts, any changes in average rates, such as those estimated by SNL Kagan, would be expected to appear gradually over the course of five years or so. Based on SNL Kagan data, average NBCU

---

37 Ford (2017, p.1). This paper was written after the government complaint in AT&T was filed in light of the relevance of the Comcast/NBCU experience to the government's claims.

38 The SNL Kagan data are publicly available and copyrighted by S&P Global Market Intelligence and its affiliates, as applicable. (The provider does not guarantee the accuracy or adequacy of its content and shall not be held liable for any damages or losses in connection with any use of the content.).

39 Carlton Redacted (2018a, Section V.C and Appendix C); Carlton (2018c, pp. 2471-2475).

40 *Id.*

41 Chmielewski (2018).

rates increased in 2018 but stayed relatively flat in 2019 and 2020. That timing is inconsistent with a hypothesis that rates increased substantially because of expiration of the consent decree given that most, if not all, of the 2018 rate increases reflected in the SNL Kagan estimates were set pursuant to contracts that were signed during the consent decree period.[42] Econometric analysis confirms that intuition.[43]

## B. *The AT&T/Time Warner Experience Post-Merger*

We begin by noting that AT&T has now spun off DIRECTV and WarnerMedia. The fact that AT&T has sold the assets off at a loss suggests that AT&T's hopes for financial success were wrong. Nevertheless, it is exactly the correct economic outcome for the government to allow mergers to go forward – absent competitive concerns – and let the parties enjoy the fruits of success or consequences of failure.

We now turn to a discussion of parameter values, before discussing content prices and retail prices.

### 1. *Evidence on Model-Assumed Parameter Values*

To begin, we note that the assumed parameter values for modeling the *AT&T/Time Warner* merger were intended to be forward-looking. In particular, there were long-term contracts in place at the time of the merger that would have prevented any predicted price increases, so the model's price predictions were only relevant years into the future and would depend upon the assumed parameter values in those future years.[44] Thus, it is highly relevant whether the parameter values that were assumed at the time of trial have, in fact, been born out over time.

For departure rates in the event of a blackout, we are unaware of any new evidence one way or the other. There have been no blackouts of the Turner networks – temporary or otherwise – since the merger. That is not surprising given the guarantee of continued carriage in the arbitration commitment.

For margins, the financial data that were relied upon by the government and the parties in the trial are not publicly available. However, it is clear that DIRECTV's financial state has deteriorated, and AT&T has spun off DIRECTV.[45] This means that the lower margins that were used by the AT&T expert were likely the more relevant ones to use – in contrast to those used by the government's expert.

---

42 Multi-year agreements typically specify prices by year, and those prices are typically rising over time, often in a non-linear fashion.

43 Carlton, Giozov, Israel & Shampine (2022).

44 *See, e.g.,* Shapiro (2021, pp. 15-17): "Turner would have the ability to set higher prices for these MVPDs only over time, as their contracts expired and were renegotiated. … The Appeals Court likewise stated: 'Whatever errors the district court may have made in evaluating the inputs for Professor Shapiro's quantitative model, the model did not take into account long-term contracts, which would constrain Turner Broadcasting's ability to raise content prices for distributors.'" In essence, ignoring contracts that protect from harms is problematic, especially so if the efficiencies (and consumer benefits) result immediately but the harms arise only in the future because of contractual protections.

45 *See, e.g.,* Blumenthal (2021).

With respect to diversion, the government relied upon subscriber shares, and the data source that was used by the government and the merging parties – SNL Kagan – is publicly available, so we can observe how matters have developed. The government expert assumed that satellite MVPD shares would remain constant and that cord-cutting would actually decline. The AT&T expert disputed those assumed parameter values but used only a higher estimate of cord-cutting without assuming further increases in the future. We examine first the MVPD shares that ignore cord-cutting; we then examine how cord-cutting has developed.

First, if we ignore cord-cutting, subscribership to satellite providers such as DIRECTV has declined faster than for cable providers, resulting in the MVPD shares of satellite providers like DIRECTV shrinking from roughly 34 percent in 2017 to roughly 27 percent in 2021.[46]

Second, cord-cutting has exploded. The actual figures for cord-cutting have exceeded SNL Kagan's predictions in every year since the merger, and SNL Kagan now estimates that in 2021, 48.1 percent of television households no longer subscribe to MVPDs: Roughly *half* of U.S. households have become cord-cutters.[47] By comparison, in 2015 roughly 83 percent of television households had MVPD service and 17 percent did not.[48]

In summary, the AT&T expert's key forward-looking parameter values for the model appear to have been more accurate than the government expert's. Using the more recent data for the key parameter values to run the model would produce estimates of even greater declines in retail prices (relative to trend) than were presented by the AT&T expert at trial.

### 2. *Evidence on Content Prices*

As was noted earlier, the model as implemented by the government expert always predicts a content price increase from the vertical merger (although it could be *de minimis*). However, while public data from SNL Kagan do suggest a change in trend post-merger, the change is *downwards*, not upwards; *see* Figure 1, which shows the sum of Turner network rates (as reported by SNL Kagan) by year. Rates have actually fallen in 2020, not increased. Nor can this decline be explained by an industry-wide change. Figure 2 plots the sum of Turner network rates, indexed to 100 in 2014, against rates for other basic cable networks (excluding NBCU networks, given its change in integration and regulatory status, which was described above). There is no corresponding industry-wide decline: Turner rates declined against the industry in 2020, according to SNL Kagan.

Arbitrations under the commitment are not public, so it is not a matter of public record whether exercised arbitrations impacted the rates, but the arbitration commitment could create downward pricing pressure on content prices whether exercised or not.

---

46 SNL Kagan, U.S. Multichannel Industry Benchmarks.
47 SNL Kagan, U.S. Multichannel Industry Benchmarks.
48 *Id.*

## Figure 1

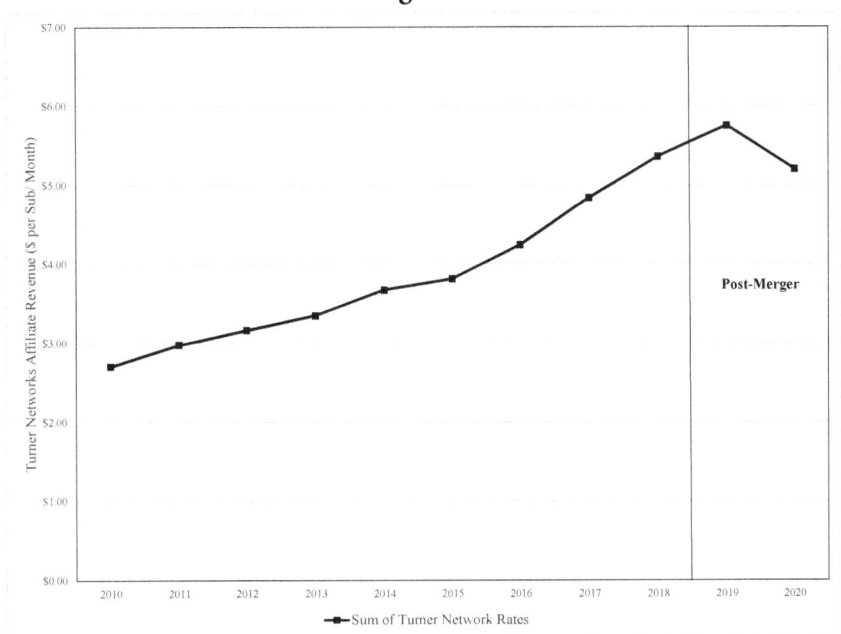

**Source:** SNL Kagan data.

## Figure 2

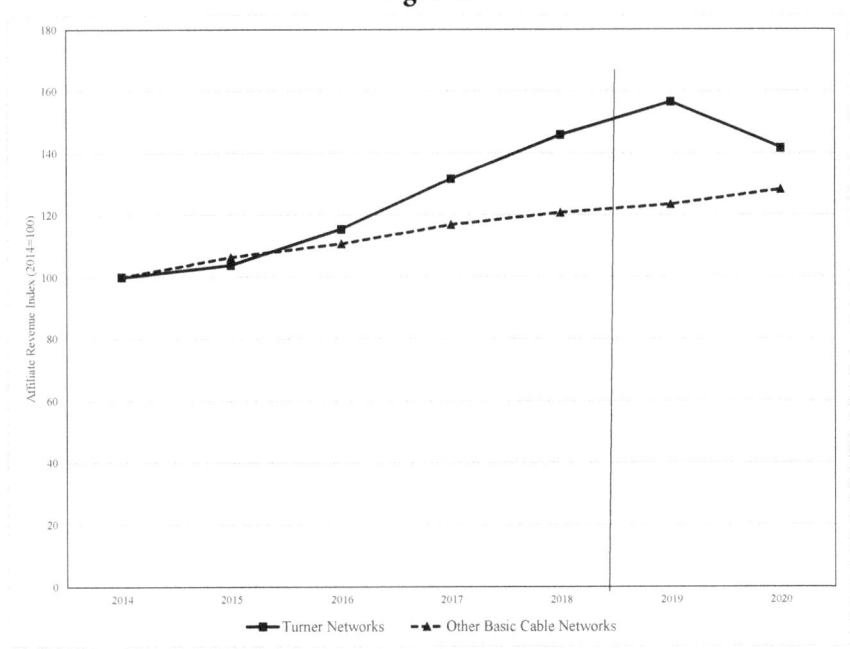

**Source:** SNL Kagan data.

## 3. *Evidence on Retail Prices*

Given that there are no content price increases relative to trend in the post-merger period, the model's predictions about increased retail prices are irrelevant, as those predictions are premised on content prices increasing: Any retail price increases cannot be due to the government's theory of harm because that theory was premised on content price increases (relative to trend) that would drive retail price increases. Nonetheless, we examine retail prices next.

Some commenters have written that retail price increases at DIRECTV and in wireless pricing shortly after the merger are evidence that the government's predictions of harm were correct.[49] As noted above, however, even if the government's theory of harm were correct, the government model did *not* predict retail price increases at DIRECTV, *nor* did it predict retail price increases for AT&T's wireless services. Indeed, the government's theory of harm was entirely unrelated to wireless; and, with regard to video, the government model predicted price *decreases* at DIRECTV itself, and only prices for other MVPDs were predicted to increase slightly.

Some commenters have also suggested that increases in DIRECTV retail prices post-merger have shown harm to competition and that the government's predictions of lower retail prices at DIRECTV were incorrect (*e.g.*, Khan 2020, pp. 1674-1675.) However, these commenters fail to recognize the pre-existing overall upward trend in content and retail prices pre-merger (although the government expert made a point of documenting those trends) and therefore any post-merger changes in price must be measured relative to those trends to avoid confounding the continuation of pre-existing industry trends with merger effects. (That is, the model predicts the effect of the merger at a point in time, holding all other factors at their current levels. The model is not making a prediction that pre-existing trends in prices cease, but rather that whatever those trends are, the price level is elevated by the predicted amount.)

Hence, just seeing that prices have risen post-merger, without controlling for the pre-existing trend or any other marketplace changes, cannot isolate the effect of the merger (it is effectively an invalid merger retrospective); and thus it is uninformative as to the effects of the merger or the validity of the model's predictions.

## VI. LESSONS FOR THE ANALYSIS OF VERTICAL MERGERS

In light of the discussion above, what conclusions can we draw with respect to vertical merger cases generally and the government's model specifically? First, the theory of vertical harm cannot and should not be dismissed out of hand as being inconsistent with economic theory. The theory itself is sound if applied in the right circumstances and supported with appropriate empirical evidence: The issue is whether it is empiri-

---

49 *See, e.g.*, Thomsen (2018), Baker (2020, pp. 10-11), and Khan (2020, p. 1674.) Other commenters have pointed to a multi-year blackout of HBO on DISH as evidence that the government theory of harm was correct. *See, e.g.*, Khan (2020, pp. 1673-1674.) But in fact, the government never predicted that HBO, or any of the Turner networks for that matter, would be withheld from any distributor as a result of the merger.

cally relevant to the specific industry that is under analysis. However, applying that theory appropriately to a particular industry can be difficult; and if done in a faulty way, that application will produce incorrect results – as occurred here.

In general, it can be difficult to specify a model that accurately reflects the complex nature of real-world negotiations and industry facts, as is evident from the experience in *AT&T/Time Warner*. All models involve simplification; but a key lesson from this retrospective is that when using complex models, verification of the reliability of that model in making predictions is desirable – if that is possible. If that verification is not possible, then it may be difficult to have any confidence in a model's predictions of harm.

Empirical evidence from prior transactions can be of great importance, especially if that evidence is in tension with a model's predictions in the case under analysis. The fact that a remedy appears to have been effective both when implemented as a government consent decree and as a unilaterally imposed and self-enforcing contractual remedy in particular is of great interest. The government stated at the time of the *AT&T/Time Warner* merger that it did not wish to enter into a remedy that it would have to monitor on an ongoing basis.

However, as was discussed above, the unilaterally imposed arbitration commitment by AT&T was not a remedy to be administered by the government, but instead was a contractual arrangement that directly changed the bargaining process and is privately enforced just like any other private contract. The government was not required to monitor or enforce it. The merging parties made a legally binding commitment to distributors that were negotiating for content; and that contractual commitment is enforceable by the distributors through the judiciary without any action by the government.

Although the government dismissed contractual commitments in the *AT&T/Time Warner* trial as a "behavioral remedy" that requires on-going monitoring and thus would be likely to be less effective than "structural remedies," in our view that characterization is misleading. The arbitration mechanism operates by changing the incentives that are faced by the merging party in negotiations, relative to the incentives that it would face absent the contractual commitment. As such, it could be properly considered to be a "structural remedy," which, once imposed, requires only that firms operate in their own self-interest. In contrast, a "behavioral remedy" requires ongoing government monitoring because it typically requires firms to act in ways that are counter to their self-interest.

This is not just a semantic debate about how to label the remedy: Regardless of what label one uses to describe it, a contractual commitment such as the one in the *AT&T/Time Warner* case alters the parties' incentives post-merger, can prevent the harms that were claimed by the government, and is self-enforcing: It requires no government monitoring or regulation.[50]

In sum, the retrospective analysis here indicates the government model was incorrect in predicting harm from the *AT&T/Time Warner* merger. That does not mean

---

50 *See, e.g.,* Carlton Redacted (2018a, ¶ 94). Of course, the contractual commitment can fail to achieve its goal; but just as with other contractual provisions, that will depend on the circumstances.

that all vertical cases are wrong, nor should it discourage analysis of vertical mergers. But it does mean that marketplace and transaction details matter a great deal, and overconfidence in economic models that do not capture key theoretical or empirical details is dangerous and can lead to interference with business decisions that raise no competition concerns.

## TECHNICAL APPENDIX[51]

The government expert's model is based on a Nash bargaining solution for content prices, which involves maximizing the product of the gains from trade for the two parties. More specifically, if $n_1$ and $n_2$ are the negotiated payoffs in a proposed bargain and $t_1$ and $t_2$ are the "threat points," or the payoffs if no agreement is reached, then the Nash bargaining solution is the pair $n_1$, $n_2$ that satisfies:

$$\text{choose } p_1 \text{ to } \max(n_1 - t_1)(n_2 - t_2),$$

where $n_1$ and $n_2$ are functions of content price $p_1$ holding all other prices constant, and $t_1$ and $t_2$ are functions of all other prices.

The Nash bargaining solution with symmetric bargaining strength is an even split of the gains from trade, which was also used by the government expert in his implementation of the model. However, he does allow for unequal bargaining power when applying the model to the case. More specifically, when applied to the case of a video content aggregator (*e.g.*, Turner) $u$ and a video content distributor ("MVPD") $d$, with bargaining strengths α and (1-α), respectively, then the following equality must hold:

$$(1 - \alpha)(\pi_u - \pi_u^{-i}) = \alpha(\pi_i - \pi_i^{-i}),$$

where $\pi_u$ is the video content aggregator's profits when it sells content to all video content distributors; $\pi_u^{-i}$ is its profits selling content to all distributors except distributor $i$ in this negotiation; $\pi_i$ is the profit of the distributor $i$ in the negotiation if it carries the content; and $\pi_i^{-i}$ is its profit without the content.

As was noted by the government's expert, this can be solved to yield the pre-merger content price $w_i$ (expressed in per-subscriber per-month terms):

$$w_i = \alpha\left[(p_i - c_i)\frac{\Delta_i^{-i}}{D_i} + \frac{\delta_i D_i^{-i}}{D_i}\right] - (1 - \alpha)\left[a_u - c_u + \frac{\sum_{j \neq i}(w_j + a_u - c_u)\Delta_j^{-i}}{D_i}\right],$$

where the first square bracket multiplied by $D_i$ (the number of subscribers at distributor $i$) is the distributor $i$'s gains from trade without transfers and the second square bracket multiplied by $D_i$ is video content aggregator $u$'s gains from trade without transfers.

The other terms are as follows: $D_i^{-i}$ is the present discounted value of the number of subscribers if the content is permanently foregone; $c_u$ is the content aggregator's

---

51 Adapted from Shapiro Redacted (2018, Appendix G).

direct cost (per-subscriber per-month), and $c_i$ is the distributor's direct cost; $a_u$ is the content aggregator's advertising revenue (also per-subscriber per-month); $p_i$ is the distributor's price per subscriber; $\Delta_i^{-i}$ is the number of subscribers that the distributor loses if it no longer carries the content; and $\delta_i$ is the price response of the distributor when no longer carrying the content.

Post-merger, the only change is that there is an additional element to the content aggregator's gains from trade due to internalizing the effects of a permanent blackout on distributor $i$ by the newly vertically integrated content aggregator-plus-distributor $d$. The change in $w$ can then be found simply by subtracting the two equations. Most of the terms fall out, as they are held constant, which leaves only the new internalized element, multiplied by the bargaining share of the vertically integrated content aggregator/distributor. The predicted change in content price is then equal to

$$\Delta w_i \equiv w_i^* - w_i = (1 - \alpha)(p_d - c_d - w_d)\frac{\left|\Delta_d^{-i}\right|}{D_i},$$

where: $p_d$, $c_d$, and $w_d$ are the vertically integrated aggregator/distributor $d$'s price, direct cost, and content cost, respectively; and the final term is the gain in subscribers to the vertically integrated aggregator/distributor $d$ if distributor $i$ does not carry the content.

The final term can also be expressed as a departure rate times a diversion rate, or the constant annual subscriber loss rate such that it has the same present discounted value of firm $i$'s subscriber loss rate ($\bar{L}$) multiplied by the diversion rate $\gamma_{id}$ (the fraction of lost subscribers from $i$ that go to the vertically integrated distributor $d$). That yields:

$$\Delta w_i \equiv w_i^* - w_i = (1 - \alpha)(p_d - c_d - w_d)\bar{L}\gamma_{id}.$$

These, then, are the four assumptions that were discussed earlier: the bargaining split; the margin of integrated content aggregator/distributor $d$; the departure rate; and the diversion rate.

## REFERENCES

27 Antitrust Scholars (2018). Brief as Amici Curiae in Support of Neither Party, August 13, 2018, https://joeharrington5201922.github.io/pdf/Amicus%20Brief_AT&T%20Time%20Warner.pdf.

37 Economists, Antitrust Scholars, and Former Government Antitrust Officials (2018). Brief Amici Curiae of Support of appellees and Supporting Affirmance, September 26, 2018, https://www.criterioneconomics.com/docs/att-economists-amicus-brief.pdf.

*United States of America v. AT&T Inc., et al.* 2018, February 2, 2018.

Baker, Jonathan (2020). Introduction to John Kwoka, Controlling Mergers and Market Power, Competition Policy International.

Blumenthal, Eli (2021). "DirecTV completes spinoff from AT&T, will turn AT&T TV into DirecTV Stream," CNET, August 2, 2021, https://www.cnet.com/tech/services-and-software/directv-completes-spinoff-from-at-t-will-turn-at-t-tv-into-directv-stream/.

Carlton, Dennis W. (2018a). Expert Report (Redacted), February 2, 2018.

Carlton, Dennis W. (2018b). Rebuttal Expert Report (Redacted), February 26, 2018.

Carlton, Dennis W. (2018c). Trial Testimony of Dennis W. Carlton, April 12, 2018.

Carlton, Dennis; Israel, Mark & Shampine, Allan (2019). "Lessons from AT&T/Time Warner, Competition Policy International—Antitrust Chronicle, July 2019.

Carlton, Dennis; Giozov, Georgi; Israel, Mark & Shampine, Allan (2022). "A Retrospective Analysis of the AT&T/Time Warner Merger," Journal of Law and Economics.

Chmielewski, Dawn (2018). "DOJ Notifies Comcast It Will Continue To Keep An Eye On The Company – Report," Deadline, August 30, 2018, https://deadline.com/2018/08/doj-comcast-scrutiny-continue-post-consent-decree-nbcu-1202455013/.

Ford, George (2017). "A Retrospective Analysis of Vertical Mergers in Multichannel Video Programming Distribution Markets: The Comcast-NBCU Merger," Phoenix Center Policy Bulletin No. 43, December 2017.

Katz, Michael (2018). Trial Testimony, April 16, 2018.

Khan, Lina (2020). "Book Review: The End of Antitrust History Revisited," 133 Harvard Law Review.

Leon, Judge (2018). Memorandum Opinion, *United States of America v. AT&T Inc., et al.*, June 12, 2018.

Reardon, Marguerite and Sorrentino, Mike (2019). "Justice Department won't appeal AT&T-Time Warner decision," CNET, February 26, 2019, https://www.cnet.com/news/justice-department-loses-appeal-to-bust-up-at-t-time-warner-merger/.

Shapiro, Carl (2018). Expert Report (Redacted), *United States of America v. AT&T Inc., et al.*, February 2, 2018.

Shapiro, Carl (2021). "Vertical Mergers and Input Foreclosure: Lessons from the AT&T/Time Warner Case," Review of Industrial Organization, July 19, 2021.

Thomsen, Jacqueline (2018). "AT&T customers see price increases following Time Warner merger," The Hill, July 3, 2018, https://thehill.com/policy/technology/technology/395318-att-customers-see-price-increases-following-time-warner-merger.

Rogerson, William (2014). "A Vertical Merger in the Video Programming and Distribution Industry: Comcast-NBCU," in The Antitrust Revolution, 6th Edition, ed. by John Kwoka, Jr. and Lawrence White, Oxford University Press, 534-575.

Rogerson, William (2020). "Modelling and predicting the competitive effects of vertical mergers: The bargaining leverage over rivals effect," 53 Canadian Journal of Economics 2.

CHAPTER 6

# Bidding Analysis and Innovation Concerns in Merger Control: *General Electric/Alstom*

*By Daniel Coublucq & Giulio Federico*[1]

## I. INTRODUCTION

In September 2015, the European Commission cleared the acquisition of the thermal power, renewable power, and grid businesses of Alstom Société Anonyme ("Alstom") by General Electric Company ("General Electric") subject to conditions.[2]

The European Commission found the merger to be unproblematic with regard to a number of the activities of Alstom (*e.g.*, its renewables, coal-fired and nuclear-related businesses). However, the merger created significant horizontal overlaps in the gas-related part of Alstom's thermal power activities. This was mainly related to the supply of "Heavy Duty Gas Turbines" ("HDGTs"), where the global market leader GE would have acquired the third-largest competitor both in the European Economic Area ("EEA") and at worldwide level (excluding China). Competition concerns focused in particular on the Large and Very Large segments of the HDGT market. The conditions that were offered by GE to secure clearance of the merger consisted of the divestment of significant parts of Alstom's HDGT business to the fifth-largest turbine firm in the world, Ansaldo, seeking to replicate the role of Alstom in the market.

---

1 The authors were part of the European Commission team reviewing this merger. This article relies on a number of previous academic and policy articles by the authors. These are listed in the References section: in particular, A. Claici et al. (2016); and D. Coublucq et al. (2016). The authors wish to thank Thomas Deisenhofer, Dragan Jovanovic, Massimo Motta, and Joao Vareda for insightful discussions during the assessment of the merger. The authors also wish to thank John Kwoka, Massimo Motta, Tommaso Valletti, and Laurence J. White for helpful comments on a previous draft of the paper. The views that are expressed in the text are purely those of the authors and cannot in any circumstances be regarded as stating an official position of the European Commission. The authors are writing in their own capacity, and they are not representing the opinion or interests of the Institution.

2 European Commission Decision in case M.7278 *GE/ALSTOM*, September 8, 2015, non-confidential version available at: https://ec.europa.eu/competition/mergers/cases/decisions/m7278_6857_3.pdf (hereafter, the "Commission Decision"). The merger was announced in April 2014 and was notified to the Commission on January 19, 2015.

The competition review of the *GE/Alstom* merger in Europe was notable for the extensive analysis of data from past tenders for HDGTs, together with an in-depth assessment of the relevant auction framework. The case was also noteworthy for a detailed assessment of innovation concerns.

In terms of the economic review of bidding data, the merger provides a detailed case study of the relevant auction theory and of the type of empirical analysis that can be undertaken in a competition matter. The case illustrates the usefulness of studying the institutional settings in which tenders are organized – and in particular the information that is available to bidders – in order to apply the most suitable auction framework to the conceptual and empirical analysis of competitive effects, and to reach an internally consistent prediction about the effects of a merger. The relative merits of a sealed-bid first-price environment and of a descending-price framework were contrasted in detail in this case, to characterize the likely impact of the merger. The analysis revealed that a sealed-bid first-price framework was more suited to examine the effect of the merger, making the merger assessment similar to that applicable to an "ordinary" case of price competition with differentiated products. This finding had direct implications for the type of empirical analysis to be carried out.

## II. BACKGROUND OF THE CASE

The Commission found that the merger, as initially notified, created significant horizontal overlaps in the supply of HDGTs for power plants.[3]

For a power plant to generate electricity, a natural energy source or fuel provides energy to a machine (sometimes called the "prime mover") that generates mechanical energy and is then connected to a generator that converts the mechanical energy into electrical energy. In a gas-fired power plant, the prime mover is a gas turbine ("GT"). HDGTs are GTs with a power output above 90 Mega Watts ("MW").

Product and geographic market definition in this case was a function of a number of technological characteristics including the frequency for power generation and the output of HDGTs. In large parts of the world, including the EEA, the frequency for power generation is 50 Hz, while in the Americas and some parts of Asia and the Middle East the frequency is 60 Hz.[4] HDGTs are initially designed and developed to run at a specific frequency and cannot be geared to run at both 50 Hz and 60 Hz. Moreover, in the EEA and in the 50 Hz worldwide market, most of the HDGTs sold were "Large" HDGTs: with an output between 200 and 320 MW. The Commission's investigation (and in particular its bidding

---

3 At the time of the merger, gas-fired power plants were expected to play an important role in the European energy mix in the future: first as a flexible complement to renewable energies, and second in phasing out the more polluting coal-fired power plants (for a detailed discussion, *see* Section 8.2.2 of the Commission's Decision).

4 The electrical output of a generator must be maintained at a fixed frequency, 50 Hz or 60 Hz, to match the output of the electrical grid. For example, the frequency is 60 Hz in the U.S. and 50 Hz in Europe.

analysis) focused on the markets for the supply of Large HDGTs that operate at a 50 Hz frequency.[5]

The HDGT industry is R&D- and capital-intensive, with only four full-technology "Original Equipment Manufacturers" ("OEMs") at the time of the merger: the two market leaders (GE, Siemens), followed by Alstom and Mitsubishi Hitachi Power Systems ("MHPS").[6] Alstom was a global competitor that was positioned as the third- or fourth-largest seller, depending on the relevant market. It was competing on par with GE and Siemens in the EEA and was also a significant challenger to GE and Siemens in the 50 Hz market outside the EEA – in particular in the Large and Very Large segments. In the 50Hz market for Large HDGTs, in terms of market structure, GE and Siemens had won a share of 30-40 percent of tenders each during the period preceding the merger (2009-2014), followed by Alstom and MHPS (10-20 percent each). Post-transaction the merged entity would have therefore reached a market share of around 50 percent within the EEA and also at a worldwide level excluding China.

Besides the analysis of market shares, the Commission found that Alstom and GE were close competitors, *inter alia*, because both firms: (i) had a large portfolio of 50 Hz HDGTs that addressed the same segments; (ii) had a worldwide market presence covering the same regions for 50 Hz HDGTs; (iii) had a 50 Hz HDGTs offering that was regarded as comparably reliable by customers and based on proven technology; (iv) were innovative players with extensive R&D capabilities for 50 Hz HDGTs; and (v) were largely targeting the same profile of customers with preferences for operational flexibility (as is shown by the ability to ramp production and maintain efficient operation even at less than full load). Operational flexibility was particularly valuable for customers in the EEA, where gas turbines often worked as back-up sources for generation for intermittent renewable sources, and hence had to operate flexibly. By contrast, the evidence suggested that MHPS was a more distant competitor since it focused more on 60 Hz regions and within 50 Hz it had a focus on the Asian market. Furthermore, MHPS's HDGTs appeared to be most suited for operations where flexibility was not required (base load) – unlike the offerings of Alstom, Siemens, or GE.

As it is set out below, the analysis of the merger found that innovation was an important feature of the industry and that the merger also raised innovation concerns. The market for HDGTs is characterized by a high degree of innovation to upgrade and improve existing products continuously, and to meet the needs of customers in an evolving power generation market. The introduction of a new product is a costly and lengthy procedure that requires significant R&D and capital expenditure investment and several years of development and validation. Reputation and track record are very important in this industry. It takes several decades to develop the technology, know-

---

5 Tenders that took place in China and Iran, while using a 50 Hz frequency, were excluded from the analysis carried out by the European Commission due to specific market access barriers that lead to markedly different competitive conditions compared to the rest of the world. For the sake of clarity, in the following, reference to tenders for 50 Hz include all countries that use a 50 Hz frequency except for China and Iran.

6 A fifth company – Ansaldo – was active in the market. However, its competitiveness and technological strength were found to be weaker as compared to the other four companies.

how, and reputation to compete effectively in the market for 50 Hz HDGTs. At the time of the transaction, significant innovation efforts were focused on the introduction of Very Large HDGTs. Three of the market players (GE, Siemens, and MHPS) already had a Very Large offering in the market, while Alstom was investing heavily in its own Very Large gas turbine (the GT36), and was about to launch it at the time of the announcement of its acquisition by GE. The competitive interaction between GE's Very Large HDGT and Alstom's new Very Large turbine was one of the key issues considered as part of the innovation analysis of the merger.

## III. THE COMMISSION'S CASE AND ECONOMIC ANALYSIS

### A. Unilateral Effects in Bidding Markets

The analysis of unilateral effects in this case centered on the analysis of evidence and data from past tenders for HDGTs. HDGTs are typically supplied through lengthy and complex tenders, organized in multiple stages where bidders make technical and economic offers to the buyer. Rival bidders are differentiated in terms of the technical characteristics of their HDGTs, which affects not only the cost of supply in any particular tender, but also the value that the buyer can obtain from the HDGT (given that this is a function of how the HDGT is likely to operate in the power market, and of the profits that it is likely to earn over its lifetime). Bidder participation in these tenders is typically costly, due to the need to prepare extensive and tailor-made proposals to buyers. Therefore, not all potential bidders participate in each tender, and bidder participation reflects the expected fit between the needs of the buyer and the characteristics of the seller.

In its review of the merger, the Commission conducted a qualitative review of the main features of tenders for HDGTs, and a more formal empirical analysis of data on the outcomes of past tenders for Large HDGTs.[7] To properly frame the empirical analysis and also to assess the arguments that were made by the merging parties, the Commission first reviewed in some depth the nature of unilateral effects in bidding markets, and the relevance of the applicable auction environment.

Procurement auctions can be distinguished in two broad categories: those where bidders have relatively imperfect information about some key competitive parameters when making their final offer to a customer (defined below for convenience as *sealed-bid first-price auctions*); and those where bidders have reliable information on the characteristics of rival bidders and on demand by final customers (defined for simplicity below as *descending-price auctions*, since they can be approximated by an open outcry procurement auction where the price that competing sellers are willing to offer to win a contract is visible to all bidders, and the prices decrease over time until only one seller remains in the auction).[8] In the case at hand, the merging

---

[7] For an extensive description of the Commission's bidding analysis, see Annex I of the Commission's Decision.

[8] For a detailed discussion of these two cases, see Klemperer (2004).

parties had argued that tenders for HDGTs were best analyzed as descending-price auctions.

Even though under some conditions, the outcome of sealed-bid first-price auctions and descending-price auctions can be expected to be similar (according to the "revenue equivalence theorem"), the Commission's analysis sought to establish which of the two auction environments was most relevant for the case at hand, for reasons that are discussed below (*see* sub-section on "*Implications for Merger Assessment*").[9]

### 1. *Unilateral Effects in Sealed-bid First-price Auctions*

In a sealed-bid first-price auction design bidders are paid-as-bid – they are paid their final bid if successful – and make private offers to the buyer (which may be updated over time, if there are multiple bidding rounds). In this setting bidders typically make their offers under conditions of imperfect information as to the offers that are being made by rival bidders and the value that is placed by the buyer on each bid (in a situation with differentiated products).[10]

This implies that when placing their offer(s), each bidder faces a standard trade-off between the probability of their bid being successful and the profit that the bidder will earn if its bid is successful. A higher bid (in the procurement auction setting) will reduce the probability of being the winner, but it will increase the profit that is associated with a successful bid. The equilibrium bid will optimize this trade-off. This mechanism is analogous to the one at work in ordinary markets with differentiated products where pricing optimizes the trade-off between the quantities that are sold and the profit margins on each unit that is sold.[11]

The incentives to increase bids in a first-price procurement auction following a horizontal merger are therefore very similar to those that are at work in markets with differentiated products. The primary difference is that the diversion of sales between competing firms should be understood in terms of the expected sales – the probability of winning the tender – rather than actual sales: Each firm knows that if it bids less aggressively, its probability of winning the tender will decrease, and the probability of winning the tender that is enjoyed by each of its competitors in that tender will increase.

In this setting it is therefore possible to apply the standard intuitions from the analysis of "upwards pricing pressure," and rely on diversion ratios and margins to guide the assessment of expected price effects. In a sealed-bid first-price setting, the diversion ratio between Firm A and Firm B is determined by the fraction of the reduc-

---

[9] The discussion below is based on the basic private value model, where each bidder knows how much they value winning the tender, but that information is private to them. This was the best approximation of the tenders in the case at hand.

[10] As Klemperer (2007) puts it "bidding is closer to sealed-bidding if bidders are differentiated and the criteria for evaluating bids are not fully transparent, so that bidders would not necessarily know whose bids would win even if they were fully informed about others' offers."

[11] For a more in-depth discussion of this analogy, *see* Klemperer (2007).

tion in Firm A's winning probability that is captured by Firm B (and *vice versa* for the diversion ratio from Firm B to Firm A). A merger between Firm A and Firm B will induce each firm to bid less aggressively since a higher bid by Firm A will increase the probability of winning of Firm B, and thus increase its profits (in proportion to its pre-merger margin). Similarly, less aggressive bidding by Firm B, will make it more likely that Firm A will win the tender, and thus increase its profits. The incentives to increase prices are thus determined by the level of diversion between the merging firms (evaluated in terms of winning probabilities) and by the level of pre-merger margins. As in standard markets with price competition with differentiated products, a merger does not need to bring together the two closest competitors – those with the highest diversion ratio – to generate significant price effects – especially if margins are high.[12]

The effects of mergers in sealed-bid auctions with imperfect information are likely to affect a relatively broad class of buyers, rather than being targeted at customers for whom the merging parties are the two preferred bidders.[13] This is because bidding incentives will change for all tenders where the merging parties consider that the winning probability of one of the merging firms would be affected by the bid of the other merging firm (and *vice versa*).[14] This therefore includes also tenders in which the two merging firms are not the two bidders who happen to be offering the highest expected surplus to the buyer (this follows from the fact that the merging parties are not able to identify these tenders ex ante and adjust their bidding behavior only for those tenders). The qualitative evidence on tenders for HDGTs suggested that the first-price auction framework was the most suited to analyze the impact of the merger between GE and Alstom (see the discussion below in the section on qualitative evidence). However, in order to engage with the arguments that were made by the merging parties and to determine the most appropriate auction framework, the Commission also analyzed the nature of merger effects in the alternative paradigm that is provided by descending-price auctions.

### 2. *Unilateral Effects in Descending-price Auctions*

In a standard open-outcry auction where rival bidders compete to purchase a product, the price that is paid by the winning bidder is determined by the willingness to pay of the runner-up bidder: The price that is paid by the winner equals the

---

12 *See* the U.S. Horizontal Merger Guidelines (2010) at p. 21 ("A merger may produce significant unilateral effects for a given product even though many more sales are diverted to products sold by non-merging firms than to products previously sold by the merger partner").

13 This feature of a bidding market is noted in the U.S. Horizontal Merger Guidelines (2010): "when the merging sellers are likely to know which buyers they are best and second best placed to serve, any anticompetitive unilateral effects are apt to be targeted at those buyers; when sellers are less well informed, such effects are more apt to be spread over a broader class of buyers" (page 22).

14 In the case of product suppression of one of the products of the two merging parties, unilateral effects would affect all tenders where the bid of the suppressed product had an impact on the probability of winning of other bidders.

bid of the second-highest bidder (plus a small increment), and all bidders (in an open-outcry context) face incentives to reveal truthfully their willingness to pay. This outcome can be approximated in an ascending price setting, where bidders can observe the offers that are made by rivals and adjust their bids accordingly over time until all bidders but one drops out. The winning bidder therefore purchases the object at a price that is equal to the willingness to pay of the last bidder to drop out of the auction: The runner-up.

In a procurement setting (such as the one relevant for this merger), rival bidders compete to supply a product, and the result described above would apply in a *descending-price* design: where the price that each seller is willing to offer to the buyer drops until only one seller is willing to offer its product, and all other sellers are offering their product at cost. In the situation where bidders differ in their cost of supplying the product and in the value that they offer to the buyer, and bidders have reliable information on the cost of supply of all rival bidders and on the value placed by the buyer on each offer, then the winning bidder will offer a price that allows the buyer to obtain a utility equal to the "surplus" – the difference between the value to the customer and the cost of supply – that is generated by the second-place bidder.[15] This means that the winning bidder is able to extract as profits the difference in surplus that it creates relative to the second-place bidder: The surplus that is offered by the second-place bidder is effectively the outside option for the buyer.[16] In this environment, all bidders except the winner face incentives to offer their product at cost, and therefore earn an expected margin that is close to zero.

In this setting, the constraint on the winning bidder is represented by the second-place bidder, and all other competitors are irrelevant to the final outcome. Following a merger, only tenders where the merging parties were respectively the winner and the runner-up would experience a price increase (if the products of both of the merging parties continue to be offered after the merger). This price increase equals the difference in the surplus between with the second- and third-ranked bidders. One way to approximate this price effect[17] is to consider the winning margins of the second-ranked bidder in *other* tenders where this bidder is the winner, and the

---

15 In the simple case where the value offered to the buyer is uniform and suppliers differ only in their cost of production, the winning bid equals the cost of supply of the second-place bidder (minus a small decrement) as in the standard Bertrand equilibrium with homogenous goods and asymmetric costs. In this case, the buyer obtains as utility the surplus offered by the second-place bidder.

16 For the sake of exposition, consider only two firms 1 and 2 with costs $c1 \leq c2$ that generate value for the customer of v1 and v2, respectively, where for simplicity it is assumed that v1>v2. In a descending price framework, firm 2 ends up bidding at its cost – $b2=c2$ – and firm 1 wins the tender by offering a bid that makes the customer indifferent between the two offers. This implies a winning bid of $b1=(v1−v2)+c2$, and a profit of $(v1−v2)+(c2−c1)$. The profit of the winning bidder is therefore the difference in the (net) surplus that is generated by the two competing bidders (that is: $(v1 − c1) − (v2 − c2)$). For a discussion, *see* Miller (2014).

17 This approximation is exact if the underlying distribution of surpluses to the buyer from winning the tender is uniform. This is the case if both the cost of production and the value offered to the buyer by each bidder is uniformly distributed.

third-ranked bidder is the runner-up.[18] More generally, if the margins of the winning bidders are similar across all auctions, they can be used as a rough guide for the magnitude of price effects from a merger.

Finally, if one of the products of the merging parties is suppressed after the merger, unilateral effects should be expected in all tenders where the suppressed product was either the winner *or* the runner-up (thus affecting a wider set of tenders).

## B. Implications for the Competitive Assessment of Mergers in Bidding Markets

Auction theory suggests that under some conditions, a reduction in the number of bidders from n to n – 1 has the same impact on expected prices (*i.e.*, average prices across all tenders) under a first-price auction and descending-price auction; this result is known as the "Revenue Equivalence Theorem."[19] The difference in the auction format manifests itself in the distribution of price effects across tenders, but not in the expected price: in a descending-price auction, price effects are sharper but more concentrated (as they affect only tenders where the merging parties would have been the winner and runner-up), while in a first-price auction the price effects are more modest but are also more diffuse (affecting all tenders where each of the merging parties faced a positive probability of winning).

To illustrate this result, for the purpose of writing this article we have performed a simple Monte Carlo simulation of 10,000 auctions under the assumption that the value offered by each bidder is the same, but the cost of each bidder varies in each auction and is uniformly distributed between 0 and 1 (this assumption is made to proxy the fact the expected surplus offered by each bidder varies in each auction). The simulation indicates that a merger from 5 to 4 symmetric bidders – the suppression of one of the five bidders – would affect all auctions under a first-price auction framework, but only 40 percent of auctions under the descending-price auction: those where the suppressed product was either the winner or the runner-up. However, the average price effects in the affected auctions are significantly larger in the descending price format: a 50 percent price increase, as compared with a slightly below 20 percent under a first-price auction. The average price effect across all auctions are the same: in line with the Revenue Equivalence Theorem.

This indifference result predicted by auction theory does not imply however that in the context of a merger review one should safely abstract from the format and institutional setting of the tenders in the specific market at hand. An understanding of the relevant auction format remains useful to frame and guide the empirical

---

18 *See* Shapiro (2010): "Merging firms often claim that certain non-merging firms can and will offer an equally good alternative to customers. Customer evidence can be especially valuable in assessing this claim. There can be some tension between this claim and the presence of significant supplier differentiation. We may test this claim with evidence from procurement events in which the merging firms competed as finalists against these non-merging firms. If they really do offer very close substitutes, one would expect to see relatively low margins in those bidding situations."

19 This result applies most directly in a case where a merger leads to the suppression of one of the two products of the merging parties (which is an assumption that applies to the case at hand).

analysis (especially when not all data is readily available). For example, it can help determine how much weight should be placed on the available data on the identity of runner-up bidders (relative to simpler, and often more reliable and readily available, data on participation rates), and guide the empirical analysis of the types of tenders that are likely to be most affected by the merger. Moreover, the conditions under which the Revenue Equivalence Theorem apply are relatively strict and may therefore not always apply (making it necessary to determine and apply the most relevant auction format).

Finally, while it may be tempting to apply the relatively simple conceptual framework provided by descending-price auctions in the context of merger review (by looking only at cases where the merging parties are the winner and runner-up), the Revenue Equivalence Theorem makes it clear that when doing so one must apply the corresponding assumptions on likely price effects for those tenders, in order to reach an internally consistent prediction about the effects of a merger. In particular, the Revenue Equivalence Theorem suggests that it is wrong in the context of a merger review to combine the predictions of merger effects that are derived from the two different auction formats, by assuming, for instance, relatively moderate price effects (such as those that are typically associated with mergers in first-price auctions or in ordinary markets with differentiated products from a UPP analysis)[20] while at the same time assuming that these price effects will apply to only a relatively few bids (*e.g.*, those where the merging parties are the winner and runner-up, as in a descending-price auction). A combination of assumptions of this kind would directly contradict the result of the Revenue Equivalence Theorem, and underestimate the overall price effects of a merger.

For these reasons, the Commission's investigation sought to determine the most appropriate auction framework to analyze tenders for HDGTs to guide the empirical analysis of merger effects. The conceptual review of merger effects across the two main auction paradigms undertaken in this case was also useful to properly consider the claim made by the merging parties that the tenders should have been analyzed as descending-price auctions, and derive consistent implications for likely merger effects under this assumption.

The evidence in this case, as anticipated above, clearly indicated that a sealed-bid first-price environment was more appropriate to analyze the impact of the merger than a descending-price format. The analysis of the merger also illustrated the fact that, despite its apparent simplicity, a descending-price auction framework has demanding informational requirements which were not met in this case, and are likely to be difficult to meet in other real-world examples of bidding markets. This in turn suggests that bidding markets are often likely to be best analyzed as "ordinary" markets with differentiated products (as predicted by the sealed-bid first-price framework).[21]

---

20 Note that in a UPP framework price effects tend to be well below the level of margins, while in a second price ascending auctions price effects are of a similar order of magnitude as profit margins (as discussed above).

21 This is in line with the arguments made by Klemperer (2007).

## C. Qualitative Evidence on Tender Process

As part of its review of the merger, the Commission performed an in-depth assessment of the bidding data. In order to do so, it first determined which of the two auction frameworks described above better characterized the way in which tenders for HDGTs were organized.

The qualitative review indicated that first-price auctions were more appropriate to describe tenders for HDGTs than descending-price auctions, contrary to the arguments made by the merging parties. In particular, the evidence indicated that:

- Bidders had limited information on the characteristics of rival bids and on the customer valuation of each offer. This information was not in the public domain and it was not revealed by customers during the tendering process;
- Information on the second-ranked bidder was frequently not available – even after the tender had been awarded; and when it was available, it appeared to be subjective – with different firms often having different perceptions as to the identity of the runner-up bidder. Evidence from competitors and from customers showed that the evidence as to the identity of the runner-up bidder provided by the merging parties was not reliable and was subject to significant errors;
- Formal or informal shortlisting down to two final bidders during the course of an auction – before a best and final offer – was not the norm. Instead, all stages of the bidding process – including the "firm bid" stage where sellers make their first legally binding bid – were important to determine the competitive outcome of a bid; and
- GE's "losing" margins – the expected profit margins for unsuccessful bids, in the event that the bid would have been accepted – were not close to zero, and not significantly lower than its winning margins. This directly contradicted the predictions from a descending-price auction framework.

As a result of this qualitative evidence, the Commission focused its core empirical analysis of the tender data on measures of closeness and competitive interactions that are more suited for first-price auctions. Nonetheless, when considering the arguments made by the merging parties, the Commission also analyzed the alternative scenario that the tenders should be looked at as descending-price auctions (see sub-section "*The Commission's Assessment of the Merging Parties' Arguments*").

## D. Quantitative Evidence in GE/Alstom

To assess the intensity of competition between the merging parties and the extent of the potential unilateral effects from the merger, the Commission collected tender data from the merging parties and carried out a number of statistical analyses. The analysis focused on tenders for Large HDGTs, which was the largest segment in the global 50 Hz market.

Table 1 illustrates the share of tenders that were won by the merging parties, Siemens, MHPS, and Ansaldo. The main results from this analysis were as follows:

- The merged entity won 40-50 percent of the tenders for the period 2009-2014, with an increase over time;

- Ansaldo won a limited number of tenders; and
- The share of the competitive tenders[22] that were won by Alstom was increasing materially (compared to the share of all tenders), while the share of competitive tenders that were won by MHPS was decreasing (notably driven by a number of non-competitive tenders in Japan). The European Commission considered market shares for competitive tenders as the more relevant metrics since these are the tenders that are the most likely to be affected by a loss of competition between the merging parties.

Table 1. Shares of tenders (all tenders versus competitive tenders)

| Shares of all tenders (where a Large HDGT won) | | | |
|---|---|---|---|
| | 2009-2014 | 2011-2014 | 2009-2014 |
| | Worldwide (without China) | | EEA |
| GE | 30-40% | 40-50% | 30-40% |
| Alstom | 10-20% | 10-20% | 10-20% |
| **Combined** | **40-50%** | **50-60%** | **50-60%** |
| Siemens | 30-40% | 20-30% | 30-40% |
| MHPS | 10-20% | 10-20% | 10-20% |
| Ansaldo | 0-5% | 0-5% | 0-5% |
| Shares of competitive tenders (where a Large HDGT won) | | | |
| | 2009-2014 | 2011-2014 | 2009-2014 |
| | Worldwide (without China) | | EEA |
| GE | 30-40% | 40-50% | 30-40% |
| Alstom | 10-20% | 10-20% | 10-20% |
| **Combined** | **40-50%** | **50-60%** | **40-50%** |
| Siemens | 40-50% | 30-40% | 40-50% |
| MHPS | 5-10% | 5-10% | 5-10% |
| Ansaldo | 0-5% | 5-10% | 0-5% |

**Source:** Extracts from the European Commission Decision for Case M.7278 – *GE/Alstom*, Annex I, Table 4 and Table 5. The published version of the Decision includes figures in ranges only; exact figures are confidential.

Second, the Commission conducted a frequency analysis to analyze how often the merging parties competed against one another in tenders. Since bid submission is costly, only those OEMs that meet a given tender specification and expect to have a reasonable chance of winning would be expected to submit a binding offer. This is particularly

---

22 Competitive tenders are tenders with at least two participants. By contrast, non-competitive tenders are tenders where only one firm participated.

relevant for the smaller suppliers such as Alstom, MHPS, and Ansaldo that were more selective than GE or Siemens in their tender participations. Tender participation was therefore indicative of their expected "product fit" for a given customer, and therefore informative about competitive conditions and the degree of closeness across OEMs.

The frequency analysis indicated that Alstom was the second bidder that GE met most often in tenders – both in terms of firm participation and shortlists. Alstom was behind Siemens, but significantly ahead of MHPS and Ansaldo; see the top panel of Table 2. The frequency analysis also indicated a concentrated market structure, with a significant number of tenders where GE and Alstom directly competed with only one other participant; see bottom panel of Table 2: There was a high proportion of (post-merger) "3-to-2" tenders.

Overall, the participation analysis showed that: (i) after Siemens, Alstom was the firm that participated the most often against GE; (ii) MHPS and Ansaldo had more limited competitive interactions with GE than Alstom; (iii) GE and Alstom competed against each other in a significant number of competitive tenders (roughly half), which were the tenders that were the most likely to suffer from a loss of competition between the merging parties; and (iv) the tenders where the merging parties competed against each other had a concentrated market structure, with a significant proportion of tenders (at least 40-50 percent) with three participants or fewer. This evidence was indicative that the merging parties were close competitors and that the merger would result in a significant loss of competition.

Table 2. Frequency/participation analysis in *GE/Alstom*

| Participation rates for tenders for Large HDGTs in which GE bids | | | |
|---|---|---|---|
| | 2009-2014 | 2011-2014 | 2009-2014 |
| | Worldwide (without China) | | EEA |
| Alstom | 50-60% | 60-70% | 60-70% |
| Siemens | 80-90% | 80-90% | 90-100% |
| MHPS | 40-50% | 50-60% | 20-30% |
| Ansaldo | 20-30% | 30-40% | 30-40% |
| Number of participants in tenders for Large HDGTs where GE and Alstom competed | | | |
| | 2009-2014 | 2011-2014 | 2009-2014 |
| | Worldwide (without China) | | EEA |
| 2 participants | 5-10% | 0-5% | 0-5% |
| 3 participants | 40-50% | 40-50% | 50-60% |
| 4 participants | 40-50% | 40-50% | 40-50% |
| 5 participants | 5-10% | 10-20% | 10-20% |

**Source:** Extracts from the European Commission Decision for Case M.7278 – *GE/Alstom*, Annex I, Table 12 and Table 19.

Third, a win-loss analysis allowed to assess how often the merging parties lost to each other relative to losing to other competitors. While the information on participations discussed above is a necessary step to assess the extent of competition between the merging parties, participations should also be interpreted in light of wins: A firm with frequent participations, but which is infrequently the winner, may not represent a significant competitive force. Conversely, a firm with a significant number of participations and with a commensurate number of wins is likely to exercise a significant competitive constraint on its rivals.

The win-loss analysis indicated that GE had lost to Alstom in a significant number of tenders when Alstom submitted a firm bid: fewer percentage losses than to Siemens, but significantly more than to MHPS and Ansaldo (*see* Table 3, where Alstom accounted for 20-30 percent of GE's losses for the period 2009-2014, increasing to 30-40 percent for the more recent period in 2011-2014, twice as large as MHPS), and that Alstom achieved a significant win rate when it met GE. This evidence indicated that Alstom – by accounting for a significant share of GE's losses – was likely to affect GE's probability of winning tenders.

Moreover, the win-loss analysis indicated that GE accounted for a significant proportion of the tenders that were lost by Alstom: in the range of 20-40 percent, depending on the time period considered (*see* Table 3), and 50-60 percent for customers in Europe. This indicated in particular a significant competitive constraint of GE on Alstom for customers in Europe.

### Table 3. Shares of losses for GE and Alstom

| 2009-2014, Worldwide (without China) | | | | | |
|---|---|---|---|---|---|
| Losing OEM/ Winning OEM | GE | Alstom | Siemens | MHPS | Ansaldo |
| GE | - | 20-30% | 60-70% | 10-20% | 0-5% |
| Alstom | 20-30% | - | 40-50% | 10-20% | 5-10% |
| 2011-2014, Worldwide (without China) | | | | | |
| Losing OEM/ Winning OEM | GE | Alstom | Siemens | MHPS | Ansaldo |
| GE | - | 30-40% | 50-60% | 10-20% | 5-10% |
| Alstom | 30-40% | - | 40-50% | 5-10% | 5-10% |
| 2009-2014, EEA | | | | | |
| Losing OEM/ Winning OEM | GE | Alstom | Siemens | MHPS | Ansaldo |
| GE | - | 20-30% | 70-80% | 10-20% | 0-5% |
| Alstom | 50-60% | - | 30-40% | 10-20% | 0-5% |

**Source:** Extracts from the European Commission decision for Case M.7278 – *GE/Alstom*, Annex I, Table 40.

In order to supplement further the descriptive analyses of the competitive interactions between the different OEMs, a regression analysis was also used to further analyze the bidding data. The regression analysis provided additional and complementary evidence on the findings of the descriptive analyses above:

- A (probit[23]) regression analysis of the probability that GE would win a tender provided additional evidence on the (identity of) specific OEMs that were associated with a lower probability of GE to win. A simple descriptive analysis showed that GE's win rate was in the range of 60-70 percent for tenders where Alstom did not participate, while this win rate was only in the range of 20-30 percent for tenders where Alstom participated. However, factors other than Alstom's participation may have affected the probability of GE to win tenders, such as participation by other OEMs and characteristics of specific tenders. The (probit) regression analysis allowed to test whether GE's probability of winning a tender remained negatively correlated with Alstom's participation once other tenders' characteristics were taken into account. This analysis showed that – even after controlling for factors other than Alstom's participation that might affect GE's probability of winning (such as GE's cost of providing the product that was demanded by customers, the participations of other competitors with Siemens, MHPS, and Ansaldo) – Alstom's participation remained associated with a lower winning probability for GE.[24]

- As regards margins, a simple descriptive analysis showed that GE's margins were significantly lower in tenders where Alstom participated. In order to further test the negative correlation between GE's margins and Alstom's participation in tenders, another regression analysis (based on the same controls as in the probit analysis above) showed that GE's margins were still significantly lower in tenders where Alstom participated.

- In addition, the analysis considered the evolution of GE's margins over time, when comparing tenders where Alstom did not participate and tenders where Alstom participated. While the margins of GE were roughly constant between the initial stage and the final stage of the bidding process for tenders where Alstom did not participate, the margins of GE were decreasing from the initial to the final stage for tenders where Alstom participated. This analysis suggested that even if one controls for tender characteristics that were not related to Alstom's presence, Alstom's participation was associated with lower margins during the course of the tender process. Even if one were to consider conservatively that Alstom had no impact on the margins that were associated with bids at the initial stage of the bidding process (and that any difference at the

---

23 A probit analysis examines the relationship between a binary response variable (*i.e.,* whether GE has won or lost a tender) and other variables potentially affecting the winning probability of GE.

24 It was not possible to carry out a similar econometric analysis of Alstom's probability of winning tenders given that GE was almost always present in tenders where Alstom participated. The necessary statistical variations in GE's participations was therefore not present in the data to perform this econometric analysis.

stage was entirely due to tender characteristics), the presence of Alstom was still associated with a further reduction of margins during the course of the tendering process. This analysis addressed potential endogeneity concerns on bidder participation in tenders.

Last, a supplementary regression analysis showed that GE's margins were significantly lower when the number of participants in tenders increased. This result had two important implications:

- First, it was indicative of a significant price effect even in tenders that had three participants and four participants (including Alstom) pre-merger;
- Second, within the framework of a descending-price auction (which was proposed by the merging parties to assess the merger), where only the winner and runner-up bidder matter to determine the competitive outcome of tenders, the number of participants should not typically be strongly associated with smaller GE margins. Under this framework, GE's margins should depend mainly on the constraint from the runner-up bidder and should not depend on the number of other participants. However, this was contradicted by the data, which indicated that GE's margins decreased with the number of participants. This analysis therefore casts doubt on the descending-price auction model.

Overall, the quantitative analyses that were conducted indicated that Alstom was a close competitor to GE and exerted a significant competitive constraint on GE. The higher prices and margins that were charged by GE in tenders where Alstom was not present – combined with the large number of tenders where GE and Alstom competed against each other – supported the finding that merger would lead to significant competitive harm to consumers. The empirical analysis suggested that GE's prices for HDGTs were higher by 5-10 percent for HDGTs when Alstom was not participating in tenders.

## *E. Innovation Concerns*

The second central element of the Commission's concerns with the merger is that it would have eliminated an important innovator, in a concentrated innovation market with high barriers to entry. The Commission's innovation theory of harm in this case was based on two legs: (a) a specific "product-to-pipeline" concern in the Very Large segment; and (b) a more general concern about the loss of a competitor with significant "R&D capabilities."[25]

In relation to the former, at the time of the merger, General Electric had already started to commercialize its Very Large turbine, while Alstom had a product in late development (the "GT36"). The technical features of the GT36 were similar to those of GE's own product – notably in terms of operational flexibility. This implied that – absent the merger – the merging parties would be close competitors in this segment. The

---

25 For a taxonomy of innovation cases, and a survey of similar recent cases in the U.S. and the EU, *see* the discussion in Federico et al. (2020).

Commission found evidence that indicated that after the merger, GE would have halted the development and commercialization of the GT36. This would have reduced competition in the Very Large segment (compared to the relevant counterfactual), and would have directly harmed innovation. More generally, Alstom had invested significant R&D resources in the GT36 project, and it was an example of Alstom's ability to develop machines at the technology frontier, by building upon its experience with older turbines.

The second element of the Commission's innovation concerns extended beyond the specific overlap that would result by the likely introduction of the GT36, and related more generally to Alstom's role as an important innovator in a market characterized by high barriers to entry and a limited number of credible innovators.

The evidence from the Commission's investigation indicated that Alstom's HDGT technology was one of the most advanced, flexible, and cleanest available, and was particularly well-suited to meet European customers' requirements for operational flexibility. Alstom's HDGT offerings were characterized by its unique "sequential combustion" technology, which allowed its turbines to offer best-in-class performance in flexibility: in particular, in terms of maintaining high efficiency levels at output level below full capacity ("part-load"), and being able to significantly turn down the output of the turbine when needed. Alstom was generally a strong competitor in terms of R&D investments, R&D headcount, and facilities, on par with the two market leaders: GE and Siemens.

An issue that proved to be particularly important in the context of the design of the divestiture required to clear the merger was the importance of having access to an installed base of existing turbines to be an effective innovator in the market. The evidence showed that access to long-term servicing contracts to their installed base allows OEMs to test innovative solutions with existing plants ("front-runner" units), in order to validate and further improve new developments. After testing in "front-runner" units, upgrades can then be applied to other plans, providing additional sources of revenue and increasing the resources for innovation. Access to a large installed base is also a valuable source of information: The access allows OEMs to monitor how the market is evolving and to identify new market requirements, and enabling them to observe the performance of the upgraded units to verify that the product improvement was successful, and to demonstrate commercial validation of new upgrades. Access to significant installed bases therefore generated positive indirect network effects in favor of incumbent firms with a long track record in the industry. Alstom's long track record in the HDGT market and access to a large installed base of existing turbines in the market was therefore an important element in its ability and incentives to innovate. While its installed base was smaller than those of GE and Siemens, it was well ahead of those of MHPS and Ansaldo.

Finally, the Commission's investigation revealed that GE would likely have discontinued the most advanced parts of the Alstom HDGT product offering – and the related R&D that included the support for the Large and Very Large segments, as well as forward-looking R&D efforts to develop further the Alstom technology. In addition, as a result of the discontinuation, GE would no longer have the same ability and incentives as Alstom to develop and sell significant performance upgrades to Alstom's installed base of gas turbines. These effects would have harmed both innovation and future competition in the HDGT market, and thus would exacerbate the static harm to competition in the Large segment that was indicated by the bidding analysis.

## IV. THE MERGING PARTIES' ARGUMENTS

The merging parties presented several arguments to suggest that the transaction would not lead to competitive harm, including arguments on: (a) market definition and the role of MHPS; (b) the analysis of bidding data; (c) countervailing efficiencies; and (d) innovation concerns and the counterfactual.[26]

### A. Market Definition and the Role of MHPS

The merging parties disputed the geographic market definition that was used by the Commission; they argued in particular that the tenders for 50 Hz HDGTs in China were relevant for the competitive assessment, since these tenders involved the same product offerings as in the rest of the 50 Hz market. Including tenders taking place in China would have significantly diluted the market share of Alstom, and increased the one of MHPS. The parties also disputed the characterization of MHPS as a distant competitor to the merging parties, in light of its successful track record in the 50 Hz HDGT market, and its increasing participation rates in recent tenders in the EEA (including a recent tender which the parties claimed had been awarded to MHPS). According to the parties, MHPS's participation rate would increase further post-merger, as it would seek to reposition its offer in order to benefit from the effect of the merger.

### B. Bidding Analysis

In their submissions to the Commission, the merging parties argued that tenders for HDGTs were best characterized by auctions where rival bidders have access to reliable information on the presence and nature of competing offers, and where the outcome is best characterized by a descending-price auction. In this environment, the most relevant constraint on the winning bidder is the runner-up, and the winning margin reflects the comparative advantage of the winner relative to other bidders (*see* the section above for a discussion of anti-competitive effects in a descending-price auction framework). The merging parties also argued that focusing on participation rates was misleading, as tenders were characterized by several rounds of bidding, including a shortlisting phase with a more limited number of bidders. While this was indeed the case for several tenders (approximately 40 percent of cases), the data nonetheless indicated that GE, Alstom, and Siemens were the firms shortlisted most often.

The merging parties also argued that the number of bidders where one of the merging parties won the tender and the other was the runner-up was relatively limited (as a share of the overall number of tenders analyzed by the Commission). Moreover, any price effects in those tenders would also be constrained by the presence of a third

---

[26] For a summary of some of the arguments made by the merging parties (notably on the bidding analysis), *see* the RBB Competition Brief "Estimating post-merger price effects in bidding markets: lessons from GE/Alstom" (June 2016).

strong bidder (typically Siemens), and would therefore be relatively moderate. This argument was considered by the Commission in its alternative analysis of merger effects based on a second-price environment (*see* below).

## C. Efficiencies

Under the EU merger control regime, verifiable and merger-specific efficiencies may counter the adverse effects of a merger, provided that they are passed on to consumers in a timely manner. The merging parties argued that merger-specific efficiencies would be sufficient to countervail the relatively limited harm from the loss of competition for Large HDGTs. The efficiencies would result from: better utilization of facilities; economies of scale in sourcing; the integration by GE of manufacturing services (such as spare parts and repair) that were offered by Alstom; and the application of best practices across the two firms. These efficiencies would apply both to new products and to the servicing of existing products (with the latter accounting for the bulk of the efficiencies). The merging parties quantified the efficiencies resulting from the merger, and argued that they would be larger than the harm that might be due to the loss of direct competition in the Large segment – even if a conservative pass-through rate were assumed.

## D. Innovation Concerns and the Counterfactual

Finally, the parties argued that Alstom's weak financial conditions would have constrained its ability to compete and to innovate going forward. The evidence supporting this claim included Alstom's declining income from operations and negative free cash flow,[27] and high leverage due to a relatively high net debt (at the group level, that is by including all divisions in the company), and an alleged lack of scale and cost competitiveness in the gas turbine business, combined with the prospects for declining demand for gas turbines. While the parties fell short of arguing a formal "failing firm defense" case, they submitted that in the counterfactual absent the merger, the competitive constraint that may have been posed by Alstom would have declined, reducing both the static and dynamic loss of competition from the merger. In particular, the parties mentioned a widening gap between the need to accelerate R&D spending and the ability to do so in view of Alstom's broad product portfolio for its overall thermal power division (encompassing its gas business with HDGTs) requiring R&D on the one hand, and smaller volumes and lower revenues than competitors on the other hand. The parties also pointed to the structural deficiencies of Alstom's gas business, including a lack of offering in North America, a lack of scale, limited cost competitiveness, and an over-exposure to declining European markets.

## E. The Commission's Assessment of the Merging Parties' Arguments

The Commission rejected the main arguments that were put forward by the merging parties to suggest that competition concerns for Large and Very Large HDGTs could be dismissed.

---

27 Free cash flow is broadly speaking the cash left after the company pays for its operating expenses and capital expenditures.

In terms of market definition and the role of MHPS, the fact that non-merging parties other than Siemens participated less than Alstom in tenders that involved GE was indicative of a weaker competitive constraint exercised by these firms. The Commission considered that a potential repositioning by MHPS post-merger was also unlikely to offset potential anti-competitive effects from the merger and replace Alstom in its competitive role in the market in Europe – in particular due to the different characteristics of MHPS' HDGTs and of Alstom's HDGTs.

Moreover, as was discussed above in the section on quantitative evidence, the regression analysis showed that GE's margins were decreasing when the number of bidders increased in tenders. In particular, GE's margins were significantly smaller in tenders with four participants as compared to tenders with three participants. This indicated that, even in tenders with four participants pre-merger – including GE, Siemens, Alstom, and MHPS – anticompetitive effects were likely to be present post-merger: Even if one were to assume conservatively that MHPS would increase its participation post-merger in tenders where pre-merger only GE, Siemens, and Alstom were participating – and thus potentially mitigate the anticompetitive effects of the merger – tenders with four participants pre-merger would still suffer from significant competitive harm.

With regard to the relevance of tenders in China, competitive conditions there were significantly different from the rest of the World and Europe – in particular due to the requirement to have a local partner – and therefore should be excluded from the assessment of the competitive effect of the merger: In particular in relation to European consumers. This conclusion was supported by the fact that the prices in tender markets are individually negotiated with each customer, which allows suppliers to engage in extensive price discrimination. The existence of price discrimination typically supports the definition of a narrower relevant market and means that the price effects of a merger may be targeted at a particular subset of customers.[28]

In relation to the analysis of tender data, for reasons that were set out above, the parties' argument that tenders for HDGTs should be best assessed in the framework of a descending-price auction and that the runner-up data indicated limited competitive concerns was rejected. The Commission instead relied primarily on a first-price auction paradigm to analyze the effects of the transaction. This revealed significant competitive concerns in the Large segment.

In addition, as a further robustness check, an alternative scenario where the tenders would be best characterized as descending-price auctions was also considered. This analysis took as a starting point the runner-up data that were provided by the merging parties and third parties (including competitors and customers). When considering this alternative scenario, the likelihood that certain Alstom HDGTs models would be discontinued post-merger was also taken into account – in line with the evidence from market investigation. This assumption significantly expanded the set of tenders that would be adversely affected by the transaction, to include

---

[28] For a discussion of this point, *see* Shapiro (2010) and the Horizontal Merger Guidelines (Section 3, "Targeted Customers and Price Discrimination").

all tenders where Alstom was *either* the winner or runner-up, independently of the ranking of GE.

For the affected tenders, evidence on the winning margins of the relevant runner-up bidder in *other* tenders where that firm won against the third ranked-bidder allowed to approximate possible price effects from the merger (following the principles that were set out above in the section on price effects in descending-price auctions).[29] On the basis of this methodology, the resulting price effects in the affected tenders were significantly above those that were assumed by the merging parties in their submissions.

Overall, the estimated harm to consumers under the alternative framework of a descending-price auction remained significant, and of a similar order of magnitude to that which was obtained under the assumption of a first-price auction, roughly in line with the predictions from auction theory.

The Commission also considered the efficiencies that were put forward by the merging parties, and accepted that some of the claims would be verifiable, merger-specific, and likely to be passed on to consumers. This related in particular to the efficiencies from more efficient sourcing (effectively an elimination of double marginalization) and from the integration of Alstom's manufacturing assets into the broader business of GE, leading to lower costs of production for several elements of a gas turbine. However, these efficiencies were not enough to outweigh the level of consumer harm under the two alternative auction scenarios (first-price and descending-price), and hence did not alter the conclusion that the merger would lead to competition concerns in the Large HDGT segment.

Finally, in relation to the parties' argument with regard to the counterfactual, the Commission considered that the relevant comparison scenario for evaluating the effects of the transaction should be the pre-merger operational and financial performance of Alstom's gas business and Alstom's best estimates of the future performance of its gas business in the absence of the merger (as captured in its pre-merger, forward-looking projections). In addition, the Commission took into account events that could reasonably be expected to affect Alstom's gas business and that would still have occurred in the absence of the merger, but also the possible alternative steps that Alstom could reasonably take to maintain or strengthen the competitiveness of its gas business – other than the planned merger.

On the basis of the assessment of the financial situation of Alstom at the overall level of the company and in particular of its specific gas business, and the fact that in addition Alstom had planned pre-merger some restructuring measures to improve its financial standing, the Commission concluded that Alstom's financial situation would not have appreciably limited Alstom's ability to compete in HDGT markets absent the merger.

---

29 The Commission also considered a sensitivity where GE's winning margin against Siemens was adjusted downward to account for the fact that these margins may reveal a certain attachment to GE that would not necessarily apply to tenders where GE was the runner-up and Alstom was the winner.

## V. THE OUTCOME, AND SUBSEQUENT DEVELOPMENTS

After an in-depth investigation of the merger, the Commission concluded that the acquisition of Alstom by GE would significantly reduce competition: in particular for Large and Very Large HDGTs.

The *GE/Alstom* merger was ultimately approved subject to the divestiture of key elements of Alstom's HDGT business to a smaller competitor: Ansaldo, the weakest of the five OEMs. The remedy was designed to replicate Alstom's role in the market as an independent firm, and thereby to maintain competition in the short to medium run – in terms of price competition and product variety – and also in the long run: in terms of the ability and incentives of the remedy taker to continue to upgrade and innovate its products.

The divestiture included a complex set of assets: the technology for Large (GT26) and Very Large (GT36) turbines; existing upgrades and pipeline technology for future upgrades; a significant number of Alstom R&D engineers; two test facilities; and several of the long-term servicing agreements for GT26 turbines that had been sold by Alstom in recent years. The design of the remedy was forward-looking: It focused on new technology and R&D capabilities and personnel.

The servicing contracts for a number of the GT26 turbines that had been sold in recent years by Alstom was a key part of the divested business. HDGTs are typically sold together with an initial service agreement that covers a 12- to 15-year period during which the OEM is virtually the monopoly supplier of services to the purchaser of the HDGT. The access to this installed base was considered important for the competitiveness of the purchaser since it provided the remedy-taker with: (i) credibility as a fully-fledged supplier; (ii) a commercial route to the market; (iii) the ability and incentives to innovate (*see* the discussion in the section above on innovation concerns); (iv) economies of scale (*e.g.*, in securing spare parts); and (v) steady cash flows. Thus, the inclusion of the servicing contracts for some HDGTs of Alstom's installed base was considered important for an effective and viable remedy.

While an *ex post* assessment of the remedy is difficult to carry out – *e.g.*, it would require the collection of tender data from GE, Siemens, MHPS, and Ansaldo – public information indicates that Ansaldo has successfully developed Alstom's divested technologies in relation to the Large and Very Large segments.[30]

On the other hand, GE wrote-off a significant part of the value of its power business division in 2017/2018 – mostly due to the under-performing power generation industry compared to what was expected during the acquisition of Alstom in 2015.[31] This suggests that GE may have overpaid for the asset and did not realize some of its anticipated synergies. In the same period, Siemens also announced a restructuring

---

30 *See, for example*, www.ansaldoenergia.com/Pages/GT26, and www.ansaldoenergia.com/business-lines/new-units/gas-turbines/gt36. Ansaldo announced the agreement to supply two Very Large (GT36) gas turbines to Edison in Italy in March and November 2019.

31 *See, for example*, https://www.ge.com/sites/default/files/GE-USQ_Transcript_2017-11-13.pdf.

plan for its Power and Gas Division for similar reasons.[32] While these developments do not have a direct bearing on the competitive impact of the merger in the relevant market for Large and Very Large gas turbines, they provide indirect support for the counterfactual arguments that were put forward by the merging parties during the assessment of the merger – including the risk that was posed by a declining demand for gas turbines. Yet, even this *ex post* evidence would seem to fall short of meeting the legal standard for a "failing firm defense."

## VI. CONCLUSION

The competition review of the *GE/Alstom* merger in Europe was notable for the extensive analysis of bidding data that was undertaken by the European Commission, together with a thorough assessment of the relevant auction framework. The case was also noteworthy for a detailed assessment of innovation concerns.

The case provides a good example of the application of auction theory to the evaluation of mergers, and in particular of the relative merits of applying a sealed-bid first-price auction framework as opposed to a descending price model. This distinction matters because the nature and shape of merger effects differ across the two environments: While the number of tenders that are affected by a merger is generally lower in a descending-price auction framework (as the merger would affect only the tenders where the merging parties are winner and runner-up) compared to a sealed-bid framework (where the merger would affect all tenders where the merging parties competed against each other), the price effects on the affected bids are generally sharper in a descending-auction framework. This implies that combining the predictions of merger effects that are derived from the different auction formats – an assumption of relatively modest price effects on the basis of a sealed-bid framework, but also a relatively limited number of tenders that would be affected on the basis of predictions from a descending-price auction framework – would tend to under-estimate the competitive concerns from a merger.

The Commission's extensive empirical analysis of bidding data in this case illustrates the battery of quantitative techniques that can be applied to tender data, and the type of empirical work that can be applied – depending on the relevant auction framework. In the specific case of *GE/Alstom*, the empirical work suggested that a 4-to-3 merger in bidding markets can have significant effects on pricing – even when the merger does not bring together the two closest competitors.

Finally, the *GE/Alstom* merger review also provides a good case study of innovation concerns: on the basis of a specific "pipeline-to-product" overlap, but also in terms of overlapping R&D capabilities. In this sense, the case was a precursor of the kind of innovation concerns that were studied by the Commission in subsequent mergers in the agrochemical sector (*see* the separate chapter in this book, by Coublucq et al.).

---

[32] *See, for example*, https://www.powermag.com/siemens-will-consolidate-power-divisions-cut-6900-jobs/ and https://www.powermag.com/siemens-will-cut-another-2700-jobs-ge-announces-cuts-in-switzerland/.

# REFERENCES

Claici, A., D. Coublucq, G. Federico, M. Motta & L. Sauri (2016). Recent Developments at DG Competition: 2015/2016. *Review of Industrial Organization*. Vol 49.

Coublucq, D., L. Serritti & J. Vareda (2016). General Electric/Alstom: our heavy duty. *European Commission Competition Merger Brief 1/2016, Article 1*.

Coublucq, D., D. Kovo & T. Valletti (2023). *Chapter on Dow/DuPont and Bayer/Monsanto in this volume*.

Federico, G., F. Scott Morton & C. Shapiro (2020). Antitrust and Innovation: Welcoming and Protecting Disruption. In: J. Lerner and S. Stern (eds.), *Innovation Policy and the Economy*, Volume 20, National Bureau of Economic Research.

Horizontal Merger Guidelines (2010), U.S. Department of Justice and the Federal Trade Commission (August 19, 2010).

Klemperer, P. (2004). *Auctions: Theory and Practice*. Princeton University Press.

Klemperer, P. (2007). Bidding markets. *Journal of Competition Law & Economics*, 3 (1), 1–47.

Miller, N. (2014). Modelling the effects of mergers in procurement. *International Journal of Industrial Organization*. Vol 37.

RBB Competition Brief "Estimating post-merger price effects in bidding markets: lessons from GE/Alstom" (June 2016).

Shapiro, C. (2010). The 2010 Horizontal Merger Guidelines: From Hedgehog to Fox in Forty Years. *Antitrust Law Journal*, Vol. 77.

**CHAPTER 7**

# Mergers and Monopsony: The *Anthem-Cigna* Merger

*By David Dranove, Dov Rothman & Samuel Weglein*[1]

## I. INTRODUCTION

In July 2015, two of the largest health insurers in the United States – Anthem and Cigna – announced their intention to merge.[2] This closely followed the announcement of the intended merger between two other large insurers, Aetna and Humana – *see, e.g.*, Bayot, et al. (2019). The U.S. Department of Justice, eleven states, and the District of Columbia challenged the deal, which resulted in a trial before Judge Amy Barrett Jackson of the U.S. District Court for the District of Columbia.

In many ways, this was a "bread-and-butter" merger case. Both sides devoted considerable resources to the "structural presumption" in the 2010 Horizontal Merger Guidelines ("HMG"), specifically whether the insurers' market shares and the overall market concentration exceeded established thresholds and would therefore be presumptively anticompetitive. They also developed competing models to predict the effects of the merger on insurance premiums.

The testifying economists raised two additional issues that arguably transcended market share and market structure matters: The first was whether the merger could have harmful dynamic effects by reducing the pace of innovation in insurance design. The second was whether the merged entity would have additional bargaining power *vis-à-vis* healthcare providers. Both parties acknowledged that the merged entity could pass on some of the resulting savings from the latter effect to enrollees. The government argued that this was an anticompetitive restriction of competition in the upstream market. Anthem countered that this was an "efficiency" that would lead to lower premiums.

After a lengthy trial that lasted nearly two months, Judge Jackson ruled against the merger. Her decision focused on the structural presumption and the documentary record and did not adjudicate between the competing models.[3] She noted that this

---

[1] Prof. Dranove served as U.S. Department of Justice's economic expert in this matter. Dr. Rothman and Dr. Weglein supported Prof. Dranove's work.

[2] Complaint, *U.S. v. Anthem & Cigna*, United States District Court for the District of Columbia, July 21, 2016 at par. 16.

[3] Memorandum Opinion, *United States of America, et al. v. Anthem, Inc., et al.*, United States District Court for the District of Columbia, February 21, 2017.

seemed to be a "four to three" merger in the market for health insurance sold to large national employers and that reducing the number of national carriers from four to three is significant. Anthem appealed and several months later, a three-judge panel of the Second Circuit upheld Judge Jackson's decision by a 2-1 majority. In his dissent, then Appellate Court Judge Brett Kavanagh asked the district court to revisit the question of whether upstream savings constitute an antitrust harm or a potential efficiency.

In the remainder of this chapter, we discuss the factual background of the case, the key economic issues raised at trial, and the verdict. Although the outcome largely hinged on structural analyses of market shares and market structure, the case presented subtle economic issues that pertained to the relationship between sell-side and buy-side market power, and the impact of the merger on innovation. We discuss both issues at length and suggest avenues for future research that might inform similar merger cases in the future.

## II. BACKGROUND OF THE CASE AND ISSUES

### A. Factual Background

At the time of their decision to merge in 2015, Anthem and Cigna were the second- and third-largest commercial health insurance carriers in the United States.[4] Anthem was the largest licensee of the Blue Cross Blue Shield Association. It held an exclusive license to use the Blue Cross and/or Blue Shield brands in parts of 14 states[5] and was the largest or second largest commercial insurer in all 14 states (AMA 2016). In 2015, Anthem had 38.6 million members,[6] and it earned $79.2 billion in total revenues and $2.6 billion in net income.[7]

Unlike Anthem, Cigna operated in all 50 states. In 2015, Cigna had approximately 15 million members and earned $38 billion in total revenues and $2.3 billion in adjusted income.[8] Cigna had been growing and prior to the announcement of the merger its CEO David Cordani had predicted that the company would double in size over the next seven or eight years.[9]

---

4 *See United States v. Anthem, Inc.*, 236 F. Supp. 3d 171, 178 (D.D.C.), *aff'd*, 855 F.3d 345 (D.C. Cir.), *cert. dismissed*, 137 U.S. 2250 (2017).

5 Anthem was one of 36 licensees of the Blue Cross and Blue Shield Association ("BCBSA"). As licensees of the BCBSA, Anthem and the other licensees were granted the right to sell commercial health insurance under the "Blue Brand" in "exclusive service areas." As the result of a subsequent settlement in unrelated litigation (*In Re: Blue Cross Blue Shield Antitrust Litigation* MDL 2406, Case 2:13-cv-20000-RDP, Settlement Agreement, 10/30/2020), Blue-licensed plans now have limited ability to compete under the Blue Brand outside of their exclusive service areas.

6 Anthem 2015 10-K, p. 3.

7 Anthem 2015 10-K, pp. 43 and 48.

8 "Cigna Fact Sheet 2015," Cigna Corporation, http://www.cigna.com/assets/docs/about-cigna/cigna-facts-brochure.pdf, p. 4.

9 "Q1 2015 Cigna Corp Earnings Call – Final FD (Fair Disclosure) Wire April 30, 2015 Thursday," p. 18.

The U.S. Department of Justice, eleven states, and the District of Columbia (collectively, the government) challenged the merger in July 2016 on the ground that it would violate Section 7 of the Clayton Act.

## B. Summary of Key Issues

The government alleged that the transaction would harm competition in multiple markets, including:[10]

- the sale of commercial health insurance services to national account customers in Anthem's 14 territories;[11]
- the sale of commercial health insurance services to national account customers in the United States;
- the sale of commercial health insurance services to large customer groups in 35 local markets (core-based statistical areas, or "CBSAs") within the 14 Anthem territories; and
- the purchase of commercial health services in those same 35 local markets.

The government also alleged that the transaction would result in a loss of innovation in insurance services.

Key contested issues at the trial included:

- whether the government's markets were properly defined;
- whether the transaction was likely to result in national account customers and large group customers paying higher prices for commercial health insurance services;
- whether the lower payments that healthcare providers would receive post-merger for their services from Anthem and Cigna should be treated as an anticompetitive harm in the upstream markets for the purchase of commercial healthcare services or as efficiencies in downstream markets for the sale of commercial health insurance services; and
- whether the transaction would decrease or increase innovation.

The court divided the trial into two sections, with direct testimony, cross-examinations, and final arguments for both. The first section focused on the market for "national accounts." The second focused on local insurance markets. In both sections, the government and Anthem discussed sell-side (downstream) and buy-side (upstream) markets and presented evidence on competitive effects. The government also presented evidence on innovation in the first section, which it did not repeat in the second. As Judge Jackson's decision largely turned on the testimony from the first half of the trial on national accounts, we will focus our discussion there.

---

10 Complaint at 5, *United States v. Anthem, Inc.*, 236 F. Supp. 3d 171 (D.D.C.) (No. 1:16-cv-1493), *aff'd*, 855 F.3d 345 (D.C. Cir.), *cert. dismissed*, 137 U.S. 2250 (2017).

11 The Anthem territories are territories in which Anthem is a BCBSA licensee.

## C. Market Definition and Market Structure

National accounts customers are very large employers with facilities in several states. While all major insurers recognize national accounts as a distinct market segment, there is no standard definition of a national account employer. The government offered a range of closely related definitions, such as those employers with more than 3,000 employees and facilities in more than one state.

The government described how each national accounts employer secures health insurance by submitting a request for proposals and choosing the insurer whose proposal offers the best overall value. This meant that the prices that are paid by national accounts customers are determined individually and that arbitrage is impossible. An important implication is that national accounts could be targeted by a hypothetical monopolist of the sale of commercial health insurance services.[12]

The government further argued that a hypothetical monopolist that could sell to national accounts in the Anthem territories likely would impose at least a small but significant non-transitory increase in price (a "SSNIP"). This is because the only options for national accounts customers in the Anthem states would be to forgo the provision of health insurance to their employees, to move headquarters to a non-Anthem state, or to build their own network of providers and adjudicate the claims of their covered lives themselves. The government argued that none of these were realistic and concluded that the sale of commercial health insurance to national accounts customers headquartered in the 14 Anthem states is a relevant market.[13]

Anthem argued that the definition of national accounts as a targeted group of customers was unreasonable because it excluded smaller or purely local large group employers; that the product market was too broad because it included both "administrative services only" insurance plans that performed administrative functions and managed networks but did not bear financial risk, as well fully-insured products; and that competitive conditions differed across the 14 states in the Anthem territories.

The government acknowledged that national accounts employers and local employers often purchase insurance from the same sellers. The government also agreed that competitive conditions varied across the 14 states. The government argued that these were not important for consideration of competitive effects, because large firms procure health insurance through a proposal process, and prices are therefore individualized.

In essence, this is a price discrimination market, where each and every large firm – local or national – may experience unique merger effects. As there are literally thou-

---

[12] In essence, national accounts could not defeat the monopolist's price increase by buying commercial health insurance services from a reseller, what the Horizontal Merger Guidelines describe as a form of arbitrage. The Guidelines note that arbitrage is often inherently impossible for many services.

[13] The Government also defined the sale of commercial health insurance to national account customers in the United States to be a relevant market. Anthem argued that shares based on sales to national accounts in the United States would not provide accurate predictions of merger effects. Because Judge Jackson concluded that the merger would lessen competition in the Anthem territories market, she did not address the alleged national market.

sands of large firms headquartered in the 14 Anthem states, an individualized analysis of the harm that might befall each firm was not possible.

The government also argued that national accounts employers have unique needs – primarily "one stop shopping" for national provider networks – that distinguished them from local firms. The government concluded that it was appropriate to treat national accounts as a price discrimination market and estimates of market shares and competitive effects may be thought of as the average effect that would be felt across all 14 states.

With this market definition in hand, the government's sell-side case was fairly straightforward: The government began by pointing to qualitative evidence of head-to-head competition and quantitative evidence of employers' switching between Anthem and Cigna. The government used the switching data to compute diversion ratios, which it then used to color its interpretation of market share data and as inputs into merger simulations. Anthem challenged both the data and methods that were used to compute diversion ratios, raising the possibility that the government did not capture sales from many smaller insurers. Their objections failed to diminish the qualitative argument that Anthem and Cigna were close competitors.

The government then used both public data and information that was obtained through subpoenas of commercial insurers to estimate market shares and market structure in the national accounts market in the 14 Anthem states. The government lacked enrollment data from many small "administrative services only"[14] ("ASO") insurers and used several methods to compute market shares to try to account for this. The government found that Anthem's share of the national accounts market in the 14 states exceeded 40 percent. While Cigna's share was closer to 10 percent, the merger would have caused the Herfindahl-Hirschman Index ("HHI") to increase by more than 500 points, with both the level and change in HHI exceeding the threshold for the structural presumption.[15]

Anthem argued that missing data from small ASO insurers caused the government to overstate Anthem's and Cigna's market shares and the HHI. The government countered that the omitted ASO insurers had a minimal presence, at best, in the national accounts market. Even making what it deemed a generous allowance for the shares of missing ASO insurers, the government concluded that the merger still met the threshold for the structural presumption. Anthem did not offer its own market definition or independently report market shares or the HHI.

The government also defined the sale of commercial health insurance services to "large group" employers – in a CBSA – to be a market.[16] The government argued that

---

14 These are insurance companies that provide the administrative services for large employers that choose to self-insure (in terms of assuming the financial flows and risks of the health insurance that they provide to their employees).

15 Plaintiffs Proposed Findings of Fact, Phase I [Redacted], December 20, 2016, pp. 45-46.

16 For commercial health insurance, "large group" employers are defined as employers with fifty or 100 employers, depending on the state. *See* Plaintiffs Proposed Findings of Fact, Phase II [Redacted], January 17, 2017, p. 2.

a firm that was the only seller of commercial health insurance services to large group employers in a given CBSA would likely impose at least a SSNIP. This is because the only recourse for a large group employer in a given CBSA would be to forgo the provision of health insurance to its employees that resided in the CBSA or to relocate out of the CBSA. Using similar data and methods to those described above, the government alleged that the merger would meet the structural presumption in 35 CBSAs. Anthem raised similar objections.

In addition, the government defined the *purchase* of healthcare services by commercial health insurers in a CBSA to be a market. The government argued that a firm that was the only present and future purchaser of commercial healthcare services in a CBSA would likely be able to impose at least a small but significant and non-transitory *reduction* in the price ("SSNRP") that would be paid to healthcare providers: Hospitals and physicians. The government argued that healthcare providers would likely be forced to accept SSNRPs because they would have no reasonable substitutes to serving commercially insured patients and because the vast majority of healthcare providers would not relocate to a different CBSA in response to a SSNRP. Anthem did not vigorously challenge this definition.

## D. Static Price Effects

Both sides provided estimates of how the merger would affect healthcare insurance prices. The government argued that the sale of insurance to national accounts employers can be likened to an auction: Insurers submit bids in response to "requests for proposals" ("RFPs"), and each employer chooses the bid that offers the highest value net of price. The government then simulated the effects of the merger on prices with an auction model that was developed by Miller (2014).

The Miller model is based on a standard "second-price auction," in which the highest bidder (or, if bidding to sell a product, the lowest bidder) wins the auction but pays (receives) the second highest (lowest) bid price. While this might seem unusual, the outcomes of many types of auctions can resemble the outcomes of second-price auctions. Second-price auctions are easier to model, so economists often base more sophisticated analyses on the second-price auction. The Miller model uses information about market shares and profit margins to infer the degrees of vertical and horizontal differentiation among sellers, which can, in turn, be used to simulate merger effects. Vertical differentiation of insurers includes any features that are equally preferred by all customers, such as lower provider fees. Horizontal differentiation includes any features that are preferred more by some customers than others – such as the locations of providers in insurer networks.

An important feature of second-price auctions – which is captured in the Miller model – is that a merger affects the final price only if the merging parties – in this case Anthem and Cigna – would have been the top bidders. This is because the second-best bid disciplines the best bid, but the merging parties would not bid against each other post-merger, which means that what was previously the third-best bid becomes the second-best bid. Based on results from the Miller model, the government could infer how often Anthem and Cigna disciplined each other's bids and the resulting impact on the winning bid price if the two merged. The government estimated that the merger would cause total insurance spending by national accounts employers in the 14 states to increase by at least $200m per year.

Anthem adjusted the Miller model in two key ways: First, Anthem argued that the merger would result in lower provider prices for its enrollees. Anthem highlighted three mechanisms through which it would achieve these savings: It could exercise an "affiliate clause" that would enable it to apply its negotiated rates to Cigna customers; its greater size would enable it to negotiate lower rates with providers; and it would engage in "re-branding" efforts to induce Cigna customers to migrate to Anthem products, which would enable them to access Anthem's lower rates.

Anthem then treated the estimated reductions in provider prices as efficiencies that improved the vertical position of the combined Anthem-Cigna. This would lead them to reduce their bid prices. To calculate the vertical improvement, Anthem used what it called a "best of best" model to compute the savings in provider prices. It compared what Anthem and Cigna paid each provider for specific services and assumed that, post-merger, it would pay the lower of the two. Anthem computed that this would result in $2.4 billion in "efficiencies" that it would pass through to consumers.

The government disputed Anthem's claims. The government argued that the cost savings (the reductions in payments to providers) were not merger-specific; the magnitude of the cost savings was speculative and not verifiable; and the cost savings were not actual efficiencies.

With respect to merger specificity, the government argued that Cigna's customers could already get access to Anthem's lower rates by purchasing from Anthem. With respect to the magnitude of the cost savings, the government challenged Anthem's calculations and argued that alternative analyses that were put forward by Anthem implied considerably smaller cost savings. With respect to whether the claimed cost savings were actual efficiencies, the government argued that the claimed medical cost savings did not arise from more efficient delivery of care, but instead would effectively be the result of an anticompetitive reduction in output, an argument that we discuss in more detail below.

Anthem further adjusted the Miller model by arguing that after an auction was completed and an employer had chosen an insurer, each employer would enter into a subsequent negotiation with the winning bidder, which would lead to a substantial reduction in the bid price. This would effectively cut insurer profit margins in half and translate into a much smaller estimated merger effect.

The government countered that any subsequent negotiations were little more than "pencil sharpening" that did not materially affect the bid price. Moreover, if subsequent negotiations did substantially affect the bid price, this would invalidate the Miller model, which assumes no further price negotiations. This debate centered on fine points of dynamic game theory and may have led Judge Jackson to be skeptical of both the government's and Anthem's estimates.

## E. Dynamic Innovation Effects

The Horizontal Merger Guidelines caution that "the agencies may consider whether a merger is likely to diminish innovation competition by encouraging the merged firm to curtail its innovative efforts below the level that would prevail in the absence of the merger."[17] Here, the government argued that given the size of the healthcare sector, any impact of the merger on innovation could be decisive.

The government presented evidence that Cigna was a leader in introducing new insurance products and services. These innovations included:

- Wellness programs: Cigna used data analytics to identify enrollees at risk for chronic illnesses and encouraged these individuals – through outreach and financial incentives – to participate in programs that would help manage their conditions. The government argued that Cigna was recognized as an industry leader in wellness programs.
- Collaborative Accountable Care ("CAC"): Cigna partnered with select physician groups to integrate patient data, perform intensive data analytics, and jointly develop treatment plans – especially for patients with chronic diseases. Cigna often paid to upgrade electronic records in physician offices and embedded Cigna-employed nurses within physician practices to serve as care coordinators, which facilitated communication between doctors and Cigna. Cigna provided physicians with practice performance reports and paid bonuses to high performers. Salmon et al. (2012), in the prominent health policy journal *Health Affairs* described the "promising early results" of Cigna's CACs.
- Contracting with providers who agreed to create Accountable Care Organizations ("ACOs"), which accept some financial risk in exchange for reducing the overall costs of their patient populations. In particular, Cigna (and other insurers) would assign enrollees to provider-sponsored ACOs, which typically were large hospital systems or multispecialty group practices. Cigna would compare the annual costs of care for these assigned populations to expected costs, where the latter are based on patient demographics and medical history. If actual costs were less than expected costs, Cigna would share the savings with the ACO. If actual costs exceeded expected costs, Cigna would claw back some of the excess payments. While Cigna did not invent ACOs, the government argued that it was a leader in working with providers who wished to offer their own ACOs but lacked the requisite medical underwriting and data processing capabilities.
- Joint ventures that featured profit- and loss-sharing arrangements between Cigna and a given provider and often featured narrow networks.
- Flexible funding: In addition to full insurance and self-insurance products, Cigna also offered funding options that combined elements of both. This enabled smaller companies – which can typically find self-insurance to be too risky – to migrate from fully-insured plans to self-insured plans as they grow.

---

17 2010 HMG, Section 6.3.

The government claimed that the introduction of innovative insurance design features was a deliberate strategy that was adopted by Cigna to compete with larger carriers such as Anthem that could rely on their size to secure lower input costs. Using a framework that was introduced by Shapiro (2012), which describes the strategic factors that influence the innovative output of firms, the government argued that the merger would reduce the flow of new innovations. We provide more details on the framework and the government's analysis below.

Anthem offered no rebuttal testimony to the government's argument, except to state that Anthem had rapidly adopted many innovations. The government responded that Anthem had been a second-mover and had not introduced any particular innovation to the market.

## F. District Court Ruling

Judge Jackson ruled that the evidence demonstrated that large national employers have a unique set of characteristics and needs and that the industry as a whole recognizes national accounts as a distinct market. Judge Jackson also ruled that the 14 states in the Anthem territories constituted a relevant geographic market because the acquisition would have a direct and immediate effect on competition in Anthem's exclusive territory. She ruled that the merger would substantially lessen competition in the national accounts market in the 14 states; she referred to this as a "four to three" merger. Judge Jackson also ruled that the evidence showed that the proposed acquisition would have an anticompetitive effect on the sale of health insurance to large groups in at least one of the 35 CBSAs that the government identified.

Judge Jackson did not accept Anthem's efficiencies arguments; she ruled that the claimed efficiencies were not cognizable. She found that the claimed efficiencies were not merger-specific because they were not coming about from anything that either party could not achieve on its own. She also questioned the verifiability of the magnitude of the claimed cost savings and the time frame in which they would be realized. In addition, she questioned whether cost savings were actually efficiencies resulting from the merged firm doing something better or at a lower cost.

Finally, Judge Jackson found that some customers chose the Cigna product because of its innovative approach to information and clinical management, and she concluded that the merger "would diminish the opportunity for the firms' ideas to be tested and refined, when this is just the sort of innovation the antitrust rules are supposed to foster."

Judge Jackson did not rule on the upstream case: Whether the post-merger lower prices that would be paid to healthcare providers would be a violation of Section 7 of the Clayton Act as well.

## G. Appellate Court Ruling

In its appeal, Anthem primarily challenged Judge Jackson's findings on its efficiencies defense. In a 2-1 ruling, the appellate court found that Judge Jackson had permissibly concluded that the claimed efficiencies were neither verifiable nor merger-specific. It did not issue a ruling on the cognizability of such efficiencies – but the appellate court did note that "whether the type of redistributional savings claimed [by Anthem] are cognizable ... under Section 7 ... [would] pose potentially substantial additional obstacles to this merger."[18]

## III. MORE ON THE BUY-SIDE CASE

Both parties acknowledged that Anthem had used its size to obtain discounts from healthcare providers that often exceeded discounts that were negotiated by smaller insurers. Both parties also argued that the proposed merger would increase Anthem's buy-side market power and that the increased buy-side market power would result in Anthem's paying healthcare providers lower reimbursement rates.

The government argued that the increased buy-side market power and associated harm to providers were sufficient to block the merger. The government also argued that the harm to providers would translate into additional harm to consumers. Anthem disputed that the increased buy-side market power was sufficient to block the merger and argued that lower reimbursement rates that were paid to providers should be viewed as merger efficiencies that would benefit consumers.

### A. Concepts

The government's case was grounded in the economics of monopsony. The analysis of monopsony is similar to the better-known analysis of monopoly:[19] A monopolist faces downward sloping demand; and if it wishes to increase sales, it must reduce the price on all of its sales. As a result, the marginal revenue from one additional sale is below the selling price, and the monopolist sells less than the socially optimal level of output at a price that is above the competitive output price. A monopsonist faces an upward sloping supply of inputs. If it wishes to purchase more inputs, it must increase the input price that it offers. As a result, the effective cost of purchasing one additional input exceeds the input price because it includes the cost of increasing the input price for all other units. As a result, the monopsonist purchases less than the socially optimal level of inputs at an input price below the competitive input price level. It then produces less than the socially optimal level of output and sells it at a corresponding higher price (if it has market power on the selling side as well).[20]

In Figure 1, S is the upward sloping supply of inputs that a monopsonist faces and MC is the marginal cost of purchasing an additional input, which is also upward sloping to reflect that the monopsonist must increase the input price it offers to purchase more inputs. MRP is the marginal revenue product – effectively, the additional revenue generated by purchasing an additional input. The MRP is downward sloping

---

18 Opinion at 17, *United States of America et al, Appellees v. Anthem, Inc., Appellant and Cigna Corp.*, Appellant; 855 F.3d 345 (D.C. Cir.).

19 In both cases, we assume there is no price discrimination.

20 If the monopsonist produces a homogeneous product and sells that product in a perfectly competitive market, the decreased output that accompanies the monopsonist's (profitable) decreased purchase of inputs need not lead to an increase in the output price.

to reflect that the monopsonist must reduce output price to sell an additional unit of output. The monopsonist purchases the quantity of inputs such that the marginal cost and marginal revenue product of purchasing an additional input are equal, denoted by point A. This is less than the socially optimal level of inputs, denoted by point B.

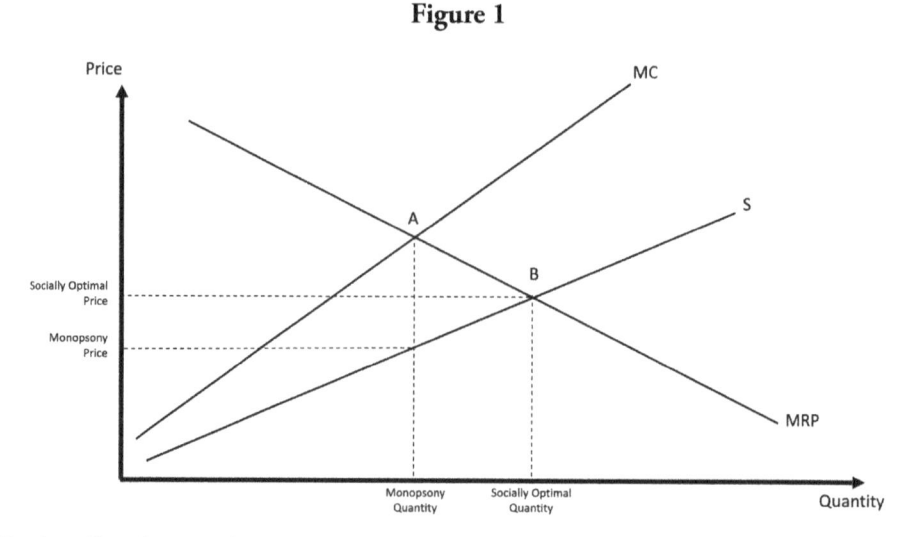

**Figure 1**

## B. Application to Commercial Healthcare Insurers

Commercial health insurers offer rate schedules on a "take-it-or-leave-it" ("TIOLI") basis to many physicians in solo practice and smaller physician groups, which then decide whether to accept the offered rates and participate in the insurers' networks.[21] Commercial insurers negotiate rates with larger physician groups, as well as with most hospitals and hospital systems. A large purchaser may secure lower rates whether through schedules or negotiations. As the economics of schedules and negotiations are somewhat different, we discuss each in turn.

With respect to rate schedules, the offered rates have countervailing effects on the insurer's business downstream. On the one hand, setting lower rates that are paid to providers can result in lower medical costs, which would tend to allow the insurer to offer higher value to employers downstream, and thereby attract more subscribers. On the other hand, lower rates can result in responses by physicians that tend to reduce the value that the insurer can offer to employers, and thereby result in the insurer's losing subscribers. Such responses by physicians may include, for example: not joining the insurer's network; or reducing hours, staffing, and/or time spent per patient. In principle, an insurer sets its reimbursement rates such that the marginal benefit to the insurer of a small, uniform rate decrease is equal to the consequent increase in the insurer's medical costs.

The rate schedule that an insurer chooses will depend on the degree of competition from competing insurers. The more competitive is the purchasing market, the

---

21 They may also offer rate schedules to smaller hospitals, or hospitals that admit relatively few of their patients.

greater will be the pressure on the insurer to keep its reimbursement rates high. Conversely, when an insurer faces less competition, physicians have fewer alternatives, which potentially translates into lower rates that are offered to physicians.

A merger of two insurers may increase the merged insurer's buy-side market power by increasing the importance of the merged insurer to physicians. Post-merger, if a physician does not accept the merged insurer's rates, it will need to replace the profit it would have earned from treating the merged insurer's enrollees. A physician would tend to be willing to accept a lower rate from the merged insurer because the merger narrows the alternative sources of revenue that are available to the physician.

The government argued that the merger of Anthem and Cigna would increase their buy-side market power over solo physicians and smaller physician groups by increasing the merged company's importance to them. An implication is that participating in Anthem's network would likely have been more important to solo physicians and smaller physician groups post-merger, which means that solo physicians and smaller physician groups would likely have been willing to accept lower rates from Anthem post-merger.

As for negotiated rates, the government argued that the merger would increase the combined insurers' leverage over providers. To solidify the reason for this, suppose that prior to the merger, negotiations between a given hospital and Anthem were to break down, so that the hospital was not in Anthem's network. Some of Anthem's customers – those who highly value in-network access to that hospital – would switch to a rival insurer such as Cigna. This switching gives the hospital some leverage over Anthem. Post-merger, the hospital would no longer have the prospect of recapturing business from switching between Anthem and Cigna post-merger. The merged insurers would thus gain additional bargaining leverage over the hospital and the ability to negotiate lower reimbursement rates.

Anthem tacitly agreed with this analysis. Indeed, Anthem's efficiency defense was predicated on the idea that its size enabled it to obtain lower prices from healthcare providers. One way that the government differed with Anthem, which we have already discussed, was whether the resulting fee reductions would be passed on to consumers. Another is whether the fee reductions might adversely affect quality.

## C. Quality of Care

In a standard model, the monopsonist reduces the quantity of the input that it purchases so as to drive down the price of that input; a reduction in the quantity that is purchased and a reduction in the price that is paid are referred to jointly as a monopsony effect. A variant of this framework applies to the case of solo physicians and small physician groups who receive TIOLI rate offers from Anthem. To the extent that Anthem's lowered rate schedule post-merger induced some of these physicians to withdraw from the market, as through early retirement, the quantity of health care that would be available to consumers would tend to be diminished.

This standard framework does not readily apply to the case of hospitals whose rates are negotiated. Anthem argued that a reduction in negotiated provider rates post-merger would lead to an expansion in the quantity of healthcare that would be obtained by consumers. In response, the government argued that Anthem's argument did not apply to healthcare markets because the "quantity" of medical procedures in unit terms is the wrong metric. The relevant metric of output in healthcare markets relates to patient health, which is the ultimate objective of healthcare.

The government's expert offered the following example: Suppose that a health insurer with significant buy-side market power uses that power to drive down the rates that it pays to providers, which induces physicians to spend less time per patient and hospitals to defer investment in cutting-edge diagnostic equipment. This makes adverse health conditions less likely to be identified and treated early, which would result in poorer health outcomes for patients and would necessitate more (or more expensive) medical procedures.

The lower provider rates would thus result in an increase in the quantity of medical care that is needed to attain a given level of health. But it would be a mistake to conclude that the exercise of buy-side market power has improved patient outcomes in this example. The mistake would be to conflate an increase in utilization with an increase in patient welfare. In this example, the reduction in provider rates caused a decrease in the quality of care, which then caused an increase in the quantity of care that is needed as a consequence of a worsening in health outcomes.

### D. Competition to Enter into Collaborative Partnerships with Providers

One of the ways in which health insurers compete is through value-based initiatives, including collaborative partnerships with providers. These programs typically involve significant coordination between the insurer and the provider to set up: the tracking and reporting of data against a set of agreed-upon metrics; consultation between the insurer and the provider with regard to insights gleaned and best practices; and accommodation of a consulting (and in some cases embedded) care coordinator within the physician's practice. As such, these collaborations can require significant investments of resources from both the insurer and provider. Moreover, the level of resources that are required only increases as these relationships progress towards profit-and-loss sharing arrangements.

Because many providers cannot realistically enter into collaborative initiatives with all insurers, insurers compete to be a provider's "preferred partner" in ACO-type arrangements, and they compete to be the exclusive partner in vertically integrated, joint-venture-type arrangements. Providers benefit from this competition because it pushes insurers to be more responsive and focused on tailoring the collaboration initiatives to their specific needs. The government argued that Anthem and Cigna compete with each other to collaborate with providers and the merger would eliminate this competition, which would result in additional harm to providers.

## IV. CAN MORE BUY-SIDE MARKET POWER OFFSET THE NEGATIVE CONSEQUENCES OF MORE SELL-SIDE MARKET POWER?

A firm that is situated in the middle of a supply chain that purchases inputs from "upstream" suppliers and that sells outputs to "downstream" customers can have both buy-side and sell-side market power. And such buy-side and sell-side market power can be reinforcing. A monopsonist purchases less than the competitive level of an input, which means that it sells less than the competitive level of an output. And a firm with sell-side market power produces less than the competitive level of an output, which means that it purchases less than the competitive level of an input.

A merger of two firms that creates or enhances buy- and sell-side market power may therefore result in a reduction in output that causes both downstream and upstream harm: higher prices downstream, and lower prices upstream. Along these lines, the government argued that the Anthem and Cigna merger would enable them to decrease reimbursement rates to providers while increasing premiums to employers, which would thereby result in both upstream and downstream harm.

Anthem did not dispute that the proposed merger would enable the merged firm to reduce reimbursement rates that would be paid to providers; but it did dispute that the lower reimbursement rates that would be paid to providers would translate into downstream harm. Anthem's position was grounded in the economics of Nash bargaining, which assumes that buyers and sellers negotiate "lump sum" payments for fixed quantities, with the implication that an increase in "bargaining leverage" can result in a buyer's negotiating a lower payment for a given quantity. Anthem argued that the proposed merger would increase Anthem's bargaining leverage *vis-à-vis* providers, which would enable the merged firm to reduce reimbursement rates to providers without reducing the quantity that would be supplied by providers.

Anthem's basic theory was that a negotiated reimbursement rate will reflect an insurer's importance to a provider and that an insurer whose network accounts for a greater share of a provider's patient volume will tend to negotiate lower rates.[22] Anthem further argued that because an insurer with increased bargaining leverage can negotiate lower reimbursement rates with providers without reducing the quantity that is supplied by the providers, the lower reimbursement rates are effectively cost efficiencies to the insurer because they enable the insurers to produce a given quantity of insurance services at a lower cost. Anthem took the position that enough of the lower reimbursement rates that would be paid to providers from increased bargaining leverage would be passed through to employers so as to offset any increase in sell-side market power that would result from the merger.

In effect, Anthem proposed to "rob Peter to pay Paul." From Anthem's perspective, "Peter" was a medical provider with market power whose rates exceeded competitive rates. Anthem used the fact that commercial rates often vastly exceeded the rates that were paid by Medicare to justify the claim. "Paul" was an employer that paid for health insurance for its employees. This made the exercise of purchasing power a win-win from an efficiency and social welfare perspective.

Given the government's and Anthem's different positions, the pivotal economic question was whether an insurer with more buy-side market power can reduce the reimbursement rates that it pays providers without resulting in a reduction in supply

---

22 The government also argued that the proposed merger would increase Anthem's bargaining leverage *vis-à-vis* providers.

from providers. If a reduction in reimbursement rates would result in a reduction in supply from providers, then the lower reimbursement rates could translate into additional downstream harm to employers through a quantity distortion. If there is no quantity distortion, then it might be appropriate to rob Peter and pay Paul; and the lower reimbursement rates that are paid to providers could offset some or all of the sell-side market power that would result from the merger.

Neither Judge Jackson nor the appellate court ultimately issued a ruling on this issue.

## V. MORE ON THE INNOVATION CASE

Broadly, an innovation can be the development of a new product that is superior to or at least sufficiently distinct from existing products ("product innovation") or the development or adoption of a production process that significantly reduces costs ("process innovation").[23] In commercial health insurance, offering a superior wellness program, or partnering with a provider to create a narrow network plan, are examples of product innovations. Altering incentives or providing more information to providers with the aim of reducing costs and/or improving the quality of care are examples of a process innovation.

There have been many notable innovations in health insurance. Starting in the 1930s, "health maintenance organizations" ("HMOs") such as Kaiser experimented with ways to "reverse the economic" incentives for overtreatment that are present in fee-for-service reimbursement arrangements (Luft 1978). Many HMOs owned their own hospitals, employed their own physicians, and required patients to receive care from these providers. Starting in the 1970s, indemnity insurers implemented a range of innovations, including mandatory surgical second opinion programs and a prospective payment system for hospitals.[24] Insurers continue to experiment with payment reforms, including bundled payments, shared savings, and pay-for-performance.[25] Other innovations include data-driven disease management programs, the development of narrow provider networks to encourage the use of low-price providers, and online portals that assist enrollees in choosing among in-network providers.

A key question is whether the merger would affect innovation, Insurers compete to offer customers the highest value net of price. The government argued that

---

23 See, e.g., Tirole (1988), p. 389 ("It is also usual to distinguish between product innovations and process innovations. Product innovations create new goods and services; process innovations reduce the cost of producing existing products. Of course, it is not always possible to draw a clear line between the two types of innovation. One firm's new product may lead to a new process for another firm. Also, a product innovation can generally be regarded as a process innovation—imagine that the new product existed prior to the innovation, and that the innovation simply reduced its production cost.").

24 Prospective payment was first introduced by Medicare, which itself has been instrumental in insurance innovation.

25 Under bundled payments, the insurer pays a fixed fee for a bundle of related services, such as all inpatient, outpatient, physician, and therapy services associated with joint replacement surgery. In shared-savings programs, providers receive a bonus if they hold total treatment costs below a benchmark. In pay for performance, providers receive a bonus if they meet certain efficiency or quality standards.

Anthem and Cigna had staked out different, inherently incompatible, approaches to value creation. Anthem relied on lower provider rates, and a principal argument used by Anthem to defend the merger was that it would pass on its lower rates to Cigna enrollees. Cigna relied on being more innovative.

Anthem's and Cigna's different approaches to value creation made sense from an economic and a strategy perspective. Anthem's size and ties to the BCBSA gave it an advantage in negotiating provider rates. If Anthem observed other insurers introducing successful innovations, it could afford to be a late adopter. To compete with Anthem, Cigna, which lacked comparable scale, had to offer a competitive value proposition despite a discount disadvantage. This gave Cigna a stronger incentive to be an early and frequent innovator. The question at trial was whether the merger would affect either the pace or adoption of innovation.

There is no general economic theory that a merger necessarily promotes or retards innovation. Incentives and ability matter for innovation, and a merger can affect both. There is considerable empirical evidence that greater competition spurs innovation in a wide variety of markets.[26] However, it is difficult to predict the effect of a merger on innovation without knowing the specific market context.[27] At trial, the government discussed the relevant economic theory and argued that, in this specific context, the merger would likely retard innovation.

Competition is likely to affect incentives to innovate.[28] A firm that will make substantial sales even if it does not innovate has muted incentives to innovate. In contrast, a firm that will struggle to make sales unless it innovates has stronger incentives to innovate. This is known as the "*contestability* principle."[29] The more that innovation will allow firms to win business away from rivals, the more motivated they will be to innovate to reap the associated profits.

In commercial health insurance, an insurer that has a substantial advantage over rivals due to the large discounts that it has negotiated with healthcare providers may have substantial market share even if it lags in innovation, because it can pass some of those discounts through to employers in the form of lower prices. An insurer with small discounts must find other ways to offer value to employers. Moreover, the larger

---

26 *See, e.g.*, Michael Porter, "Competition and Antitrust: Towards a Productivity-Based Approach to Evaluating Mergers and Joint Ventures," *Antitrust Bulletin* 46 (2000): 4, p. 922; Wesley M. Cohen, "Fifty Years of Empirical Studies of Innovative Activity and Performance," in *Handbook of the Economics of Innovation*, http://dx.doi.org/10.1016/S0169-7218(10)01004-X, p. 137; Thomas J. Holmes & James A. Schmitz, Jr., "Competition and Productivity: A Review of Evidence," *Annual Review of Economics*, 2 (2010), doi:10.1146/annurev.economics.102308.124407, p. 631.

27 *See, e.g.*, Carl Shapiro, "Did Arrow Hit the Bull's Eye?" in *The Rate and Direction of Inventive Activity Revisited*, ed. Josh Lerner & Scott Stern, (Chicago: University of Chicago Press, 2012).

28 *See, e.g.*, Richard Gilbert, "Looking for Mr. Schumpeter: Where are We in the Competition-Innovation Debate?" in *Innovation Policy and the Economy*, Volume 6, ed. Adam B. Jaffe, Josh Lerner & Scott Stern, (Cambridge: MIT Press, 2006); Jonathan Baker, "Beyond Schumpeter vs. Arrow: How Antitrust Fosters Innovation," *Antitrust Law Journal*, 74 (2007): 3, pp. 601–602; Carl Shapiro, "Did Arrow Hit the Bull's Eye?" pp. 362, 366, 368, and 401.

29 Shapiro (2012, p. 364): "The Contestability principle focuses on the extent to which a firm can gain profitable sales from its rivals by offering greater value to customers."

insurer can afford to observe its rivals' innovations, adopting later on those that seem most promising. Owing to its preexisting cost advantage, it is unlikely to lose very many enrollees due to this second-mover strategy, even if its copycat innovations are less effective than those of the first-movers.

A merger can affect the contestability of a market and therefore affect incentives to innovate. Suppose that some of the incremental profits that Firm C earns from innovation come at the expense of Firm A, as Firm C wins customers away from Firm A through its more innovative, higher-quality product. If Firms A and C merge, this "innovation diversion" is internalized. The diversion of sales from A to the more innovative C, which is a component of C's gains from innovating pre-merger, no longer count as a gain to the merged firm. The merger thus reduces the merged firm's incentive to innovate. The higher is the innovation diversion between the two merging firms, the larger will be the reduction in the merged firm's incentive to innovate.[30]

Other factors may affect both the incentive and the ability to innovate. Firms are less likely to make the investments necessary to innovate if they believe that their ideas will be easily and quickly copied by others.[31] *Appropriability* – the ability to retain value for oneself – is high in cases where, for example, copying an innovation is difficult and/or costly. The incentive to innovate is stronger, the more appropriable are the benefits. If a firm anticipates that the response to its innovation will be sufficiently quick and effective, this concern might deter its innovative efforts.

A merger may enable the merged firm to appropriate a greater fraction of the benefits that result from its innovations by removing a competitor who might otherwise copy the innovation. Conversely, in industries where the benefits of innovations are appropriable, a merger may have little or no effect on appropriability and thus would not increase the incentive to innovate.

Additionally, the combination of complementary assets within a firm can create synergies that enhance the ability to innovate.[32] A merger may increase the merged firm's ability to innovate by combining complementary capabilities from the merging firms.

Taken together, the theoretical effect of a merger on innovation is ambiguous; the effect depends on contestability, appropriability, and synergies in the specific market of interest. The government argued that the facts on the ground – evidenced by Cigna's leadership in numerous innovations – showed that contestability was more important than appropriability. Cigna may have been smaller than Anthem, but it had more than sufficient scale to justify investments in innovations.

Anthem argued that even if Cigna was innovative, the merged firm could leverage its size to spread further the adoption of the best of Cigna's innovations. Thus, the

---

30 *See, e.g.*, Joseph Farrell & Carl Shapiro, "Antitrust Evaluation of Horizontal Mergers: An Economic Alternative to Market Definition," *The B.E. Journal of Theoretical Economics*, 10 (2010): 1, pp. 33–34.

31 Shapiro (2012, p. 364) calls this the "appropriability principle": "The appropriability principle focuses on the extent to which a successful innovator can capture the social benefits resulting from its innovation."

32 Shapiro (2012) calls this the "synergy principle."

merger would effectively increase appropriability. Anthem could, for example, offer Cigna's wellness programs to a much larger patient population and implement CACs in more locations with more provider groups.

The government countered that (in the absence of the merger) Anthem could develop its own wellness programs and CACs, continuing to follow its second-mover strategy. The government further argued that Anthem's reliance on low provider rates would work against some innovations – such as CACs and joint ventures to create narrow network plans – that require partnerships with providers. If Anthem acquired Cigna and reduced the rates that it paid to providers under Cigna contracts – by far the biggest source of "efficiencies" that were cited by Anthem – the pace of innovation could significantly slow.

## VI. SUBSEQUENT DEVELOPMENTS

Perhaps the high point of the trial came when Cigna CEO David Cordani gave testimony that seemed to bolster the government claim that merger implementation would be complex and might not yield efficiencies. Anyone who inferred that there might be animosity brewing between Anthem and Cigna was justified when, just a few months after the conclusion of the trial, Cigna sued Anthem to collect a $1.85 billion breakup fee: Cigna argued that Anthem pursued a flawed legal strategy. Anthem countersued for $16 billion, blaming Cigna's leaders for the merger's failure. Both suits were eventually dismissed in 2020.

In the meantime, Cigna wasted no time growing its own business, closing a $67 billion acquisition for pharmacy benefits management company Express Scripts in 2018. As of September 2022, it is still unclear as to whether this merger has generated new efficiencies.

## VII. CONCLUSION

Anthem remains the largest Blue-branded health insurer and the second-largest health insurer, after United Healthcare. Anthem has not made any major acquisitions and may face a new competitive environment in the wake of the recent settlement of class action claims against the Blue Cross Blue Shield Association and its affiliates.[33] The settlement loosens territorial exclusivity, allowing the entry of a second Blue-branded plan in each Blue territory. Not only does this mean that Anthem may face competition from other Blues in its home 14 territories, it also means that Anthem may attempt to enter new markets. It is unclear whether the new rules will facilitate meaningful new competition in either the national accounts market or the various local markets.

Annual health care spending in the United States currently exceeds $3 trillion. A merger of two health insurance heavyweights would be a big deal: literally and figuratively. In retrospect, the direct static merger effect that was predicted by both parties

---

[33] Settlement Agreement, *In Re: Blue Cross Blue Shield Antitrust Litigation MDL 2406*, October 30, 2020.

– essentially +/- $1 billion per year – seems relatively inconsequential. The government correctly noted that the impact of the merger on innovation could have a vastly greater impact on the health economy. Both sides argued that any upstream impact on providers – whether through prices or quality – could also be profound, with the government's argument again emphasizing dynamic effects on supply and quality.

To put it slightly differently: Health spending in the United States increases every year by more than $100 billion. Even if the merger did result in $1 billion in static savings per year, as Anthem predicted, this would be wiped out by three days of healthcare inflation. Static savings may not be sufficient. It is for this reason that health policy analysts have long sought to "bend the cost curve": generate prolonged spending reductions. In antitrust parlance, this suggests a focus on dynamic effects.

While Judge Jackson's opinion spoke to innovation, her decision largely rested on the simple idea that a four-to-three merger would have harmful static effects. Judge Kavanagh's appellate dissent sought greater consideration of the upstream market – though again largely focusing on static effects on prices.

We do not mean to suggest that it is not worth fighting antitrust battles over $1 billion per year. We do believe, however, that future courts that weigh healthcare consolidation should give greater consideration to dynamics. Let us not lose sight of the forest for the trees.

## REFERENCES

American Medical Association (2016). "Competition in Health Insurance: A Comprehensive Study of U.S. Markets."

Bayot, Denrick, Kostis Hatzitaskos, Brad T. Howells & Aviv Nevo (2016). "The Aetna-Humana Proposed Merger," in *The Antitrust Revolution: Economics, Competition, and Policy* 7th Edition, edited by John E Kwoka, Jr. and Lawrence J. White (pp. 22-44). Oxford University Press.

Luft, Harold S. (1978). "How do health-maintenance organizations achieve their 'savings'?" *The New England Journal of Medicine* 298, no. 24: 1336-1343.

Miller, Nathan H. (2014). "Modeling the effects of mergers in procurement," *International Journal of Industrial Organization*, 37: 201-208.

Salmon, Richard B., Mark I. Sanderson, Barbara A. Walters, Karen Kennedy, Robert C. Flores & Alan M. Muney (2012). "A collaborative accountable care model in three practices showed promising early results on costs and quality of care." *Health Affairs* 31(11): 2379-2387.

Shapiro, Carl (2012). "Did Arrow Hit the Bull's Eye?" in *The Rate & Direction of Inventive Activity Revisited*, Ed., Joshua Lerner and Scott Stern (361-404). Chicago: University of Chicago Press.

Tirole, Jean (1988). *The Theory of Industrial Organization*. Boston: MIT Press.

**CHAPTER 8**

# Cross-Market Hospital Mergers: The *Cedars-Sinai/Huntington Memorial* Litigation

*By Gregory S. Vistnes*[1]

## I. INTRODUCTION

In 2020, two hospital systems in the Los Angeles region – Cedars-Sinai Health System ("CSHS") and Huntington Memorial ("HM") – announced an affiliation agreement that, among other things, would allow the two systems to negotiate contract terms jointly with their health plan customers. The California Attorney General ("CAAG"; also the "State") had regulatory oversight over this affiliation. Based on its review, the CAAG concluded that there was a risk that the affiliation would lead to an increase in hospital prices.

The CAAG's concerns with the Cedars-Sinai/Huntington ("CSHS/HM") affiliation were not the ones that typically drive government investigations and interventions.[2] The typical concern with a hospital merger is that the merging hospitals compete in the same relevant market, and that the merger will eliminate this important direct competition. The CAAG's concerns in *CSHS/HM* were very different: The CAAG and the economic expert that it retained to assess the potential competitive effects of affiliation clearly acknowledged that the affiliation would not significantly reduce direct competition.[3] Instead, the CAAG alleged that the affiliation of the two hospital systems – each of which already had substantial market power *but which were acknowledged as competing in distinct markets* – might create incentives for the merged hospital to increase price. Thus, the affiliation posed a risk of harm because of what are often referred to as "cross-market" effects.

The CAAG did not seek to block the affiliation; but, as a precondition for it to proceed, the CAAG required a cap on future price increases at HM and restrictions to prevent the affiliating hospitals (the "Parties") from forcing Payors (*e.g.*, health insur-

---

[1] The views expressed in this paper are those of the author and do not necessarily reflect the views of Charles River Associates ("CRA") or any individual who is associated with CRA.

[2] Because the competitive effects of the affiliation would be similar to a merger, I use the terms affiliation and merger interchangeably in this chapter.

[3] This author was the economic expert who was retained by the CAAG to analyze competitive issues.

ers, such as Blue Cross or Aetna) to contract with all of their hospitals.[4] The Parties challenged those findings and the State's proposed regulatory conditions in court. That litigation was ultimately settled: The affiliation was allowed to proceed; but the Parties agreed to price caps, conduct restraints, and an outside monitor.

The CAAG's decision to seek regulatory relief in *CSHS/HM* because of cross-market merger concerns is noteworthy in at least two regards: First, *CSHS/HM* highlights a recent resurgence of interest by government – particularly antitrust – agencies in the question of whether and when cross-market mergers might reduce competition. Until recently, concerns about such effects – which were variously characterized in the past as conglomerate effects (*e.g.*, Proctor & Gamble's attempt to acquire Clorox in 1957) or portfolio power effects (*e.g.*, General Electric's attempt to acquire Honeywell in 2000) – have been largely dismissed in the U.S. as lacking economic merit and not providing a basis for legitimate competitive concerns.[5]

Recent theory and empirical research that focuses on general acute care hospitals, however, has breathed new life into the question of whether cross-market concerns provide a valid basis for competitive concerns. And while *CSHS/HM* represents the only recent litigation (to date) that alleges cross-market merger effects, state and federal government agencies (as well as academics and policymakers) are expressing concerns about such effects – not only with respect to general acute care hospitals but also in other industries.[6] Thus, rather than viewing *CSHS/HM* as an outlier in government enforcement, *CSHS/HM* – and the issues that it raises – may represent a vanguard of increased future government investigations and enforcement activity. Accordingly, a critical discussion of the issues that were presented in *CSHS/HM* is instructive in terms of how and whether such investigations should proceed.

The factual record and how it played into decisions to intervene in *CSHS/HM* is also noteworthy. This chapter discusses how theory helps identify a set of necessary conditions for harm, as well as a set of possible proxies for those necessary conditions. The extent to which conditions were satisfied in *CHHS/HM* was a market-specific, factual question that the Parties contested in their litigation with the State. Those necessary conditions for harm, however, are not *sufficient* conditions for harm. Thus, it remains an open question of whether and when harm may be *sufficiently likely* to warrant government intervention, even when those necessary conditions for harm are met. That question is not unique to *CSHS/HM* and will likely arise as well in future cross-market cases.

---

4 A complete set of the State's public findings – including a (redacted) copy of the author's report (Vistnes Report, 2020) – is *available at* https://oag.ca.gov/sites/all/files/agweb/pdfs/charities/non-profithosp/ag-decision-huntington-121020.pdf.

5 *See* Vistnes & Sarafidis (2013) for a discussion of the history of cross-market merger concerns, and Varanani (2020) for a discussion of the evolution of those views in the U.S. versus the European Union. More generally, *see* Bork (1978) and the 2001 speech by then Deputy Assistant Attorney General William Kolasky with regard to conglomerate mergers, "Conglomerate Mergers and Range Effects: It's a Long Way from Chicago to Brussels," *available at* https://www.justice.gov/atr/speech/conglomerate-mergers-and-range-effects-its-long-way-chicago-brussels.

6 *See* Vistnes (2023) for a discussion of the different forums in which these concerns are being voiced, and Fulton et al. (2022) for a discussion of how cross-market hospital systems are becoming increasingly prevalent.

## II. THE CSHS/HM AFFILIATION

CSHS is a four-hospital system in Southern California. CSHS's flagship hospital is Cedars-Sinai Medical Center ("CSMC") in west Los Angeles: an 889-bed teaching hospital that offers some of the most complex and sophisticated medical services available. CSHS also includes other locations in the general Los Angeles region: Cedar-Sinai Marina del Rey; Torrance Memorial Medical Center; and Providence Cedars-Sinai Tarzana Medical Center.

HM is a 378-bed hospital that is located in Pasadena: approximately 20 miles (and a 31-minute drive) from the flagship CSMC location. While smaller than CSMC, HM is larger than many other nearby hospitals. And while not offering the full range of the most complex hospital services, HM offers a broader range of those services than do many of the nearby hospitals. Thus, HM is typically viewed as larger – and offering more sophisticated services – than is true of other nearby community hospitals.

CSHS and HM entered into an affiliation agreement in July 2020. Under this affiliation, CSHS and HM would jointly negotiate price and related contract terms. Thus, for the purposes of analyzing potential competitive effects, I treat the affiliation as a merger.

## III. THE BASIS FOR CROSS-MARKET CONCERNS

Three principal mechanisms through which cross-market effects might arise have been identified:[7] Traditional Tying ("TT") theories; the Common Linked Employer ("CLE") theory; and the Change in Control ("CiC") theory. Subsequent empirical research has then provided a basis to believe that the price effects predicted by theory are, at least in some cases, manifesting themselves in reality.

### A. Cross-market Theories

#### 1. *Traditional Tying ("TT") Theories*

A significant body of economic literature discusses "traditional" tying and bundling theories; *see, e.g.,* Whinston (1990), Carlton & Waldman (2002), Nalebuff (2005), Riordan & Salop (1995), Krattenmaker & Salop (1986) and Gowrisankaran et al. (2015). These TT theories typically assume substantial market power in the "tying" market, but significant competition in the other "tied" market. TT theories then typically focus on how a firm can leverage its market power in the tying market to reduce competition in the tied market: often by disadvantaging rivals' ability to compete in the tied market. In other variants of TT theories, economists have examined

---

[7] Other possible causes or mechanisms for cross-market price effects have also been identified, including multi-market contact; increased post-merger quality leading to higher prices; and increased prices for specialized services for which the geographic market is so large that the merging hospitals compete in the same market. *See* Vistnes & Sarafidis (2013) and Vistnes (2023) for a more detailed discussion of all these theories.

how bundling across markets can affect firms' relative bargaining strength (*see, e.g.,* Nalebuff, 2005) or their ability to extract surplus from consumers, thus leading to higher prices without necessarily disadvantaging rivals; *see, e.g.,* Schmalensee (1981).

TT theories also consider "regulatory evasion" in which a firm with market power in one market is unable to exercise that market power fully (due to regulation or other price constraints). By acquiring a firm in a second competitive market, the firm may be able to "shift" its desired price increase from the first market to the second market, thus "evading" the regulation (or other price constraint) that kept prices low in the first market.[8]

### 2. *The Common Linked Employer ("CLE") Theory*

Unlike TT theories that focus on how a merged firm might use market power in one market to affect competition in a second more competitive market, the CLE theory – which is often referred to as the Common Customer theory – asks whether, in the extreme case, two hospitals that are *already monopolists* in their own markets can further increase their market power and thus increase price by merging. More generally, the CLE theory asks whether two hospitals – both of which already have substantial market power (but not necessarily monopoly power) – can further increase their market power by merging.

The intuition that underlies the CLE is as follows (see Vistnes & Sarafides, 2013; Dafny, Ho & Lee, 2019; and Vistnes, 2023): First, assume that there are several distinct geographic markets, with individuals' generally unwilling to travel between those markets for hospital care. Assume, however, that employers (who offer health insurance to their employees) have employees in each of those markets,[9] and those employers want to offer all of their employees a common health plan that provides good hospital coverage regardless of the market in which the employee lives. It follows that, when choosing among competing Payors' health insurance products, an employer will care about whether a Payor's hospital network is adequate in each of the markets – even though the individual employees only care about the hospitals in the single market in which she lives. In this way, the CLE theory assumes an *employer-related* "linkage" across what are – from an individual patient perspective – distinct markets.

Now consider a merger that involves one hospital from each of those distinct markets and assume that each one of those merging hospitals has substantial market power in its own market. Thus, pre-merger, any one of those merging hospitals would create a "hole" in a Payor's hospital network – prevent the Payor from offering acceptable hospital coverage in that market – if the Payor fails to contract with that hospital. And since employers will find a Payor's plan less attractive if it has a hole, a hospital's ability to threaten the Payor's network with a hole allows the hospital to negotiate a higher price from the Payor.

---

[8] *See, for example,* Brennan (1990). This potential for applicability of this theory in the context of cross-market hospital mergers has been noted by Vistnes & Sarafidis (2013), Brand & Rosenbaum (2019), and Dafny, Ho & Lee (2019).

[9] This employer might be a multi-site employer (*e.g.*, a supermarket chain) or a single-site employer with employees living (and commuting from) a relatively large geographic region.

Under these assumptions, the more holes in a Payor's hospital network, the less attractive that Payor's plan will be to the employer. But from the employer's perspective, the *location* of a hole may matter less than the *number* of holes: For example, for an employer with employees throughout Florida, a hole in the Miami network may be equally attractive (or unattractive) as a plan with a hole in the Palm Beach network or the Orlando network.[10] Any one of those three plans – each with one hole – would, however, be more attractive than a plan with two holes in any market and less attractive than a plan with no holes.

This provides the driving intuition of the CLE theory: Pre-merger, a hospital can threaten to create only a single hole in a Payor's hospital network, while post-merger the merged hospital can threaten to create two (or more) holes.[11] If a health plan is significantly worse off with two holes than with a single hole, the cross-market merger increases the hospital's bargaining power – which can result in higher prices.[12]

Simply showing that a health plan is worse off with two holes than with one hole, however, is not sufficient for a cross-market merger to increase price: Cross-market mergers increase price under the CLE theory only if the harm from two holes is *much* worse than the harm from a single hole. Specifically, a "concavity condition" needs to hold: Each incremental hole causes more harm than was caused by the previous hole.[13] Thus, concavity might exist if a Payor's plan becomes a little more unattractive if it incurs a single hole, but much less attractive with two holes, and virtually unmarketable if it has three holes.

But concavity cannot simply be assumed: It may be just as likely that a "convexity condition" holds, in which the incremental harm from additional holes is decreasing.[14] For example, assume that none of a Payor's competitors have any holes in the plans that they offer. As long as the Payor has no holes in its own plan, the Payor may be able to compete effectively. Assume, however, that with a single hole, a Payor's plan

---

10 An employer that seeks hospital coverage for all employees might still consider a Payor with holes in its network because the employer may offer its employees a choice of health plans, and one of those other health plans may provide coverage where the first plan has a hole.

11 This intuition makes clear why each of the merging hospitals needs to have substantial market power: Absent market power, the loss of that hospital would not create an important hole in the Payor's network.

12 While in principle increased prices due to a change in bargaining power might not affect output, in this context higher hospital prices are likely to cause a Payor reaction (*e.g.*, increased efforts to steer patients) that will result affect output.

13 Another way of thinking of concavity, or increasing incremental harm, is that the total is greater than the sum of the parts: If the harm from losing either hospital is $10, concavity holds if the harm from losing both hospitals is greater than $20.

14 There is also a third possible possibility: linearity. Linearity holds when the harm from an incremental hole is neither increasing nor decreasing. Linearity typically exists when there are no linkages across markets; and, consequently, when linearity holds, cross-market mergers will not affect price under the CLE theory. Thus, linearity can be thought of as the baseline assumption underlying the traditional analysis showing that cross-market mergers are unlikely to affect competition. *See* Vistnes & Sarafidis (2013).

becomes almost unmarketable. In that case, the incremental harm from a second hole is minimal: The already-unmarketable plan can't become much more unmarketable. In that case, convexity holds, and a cross-market merger would create incentives to *reduce* price.[15]

### 3. *The Change in Control ("CiC") Theory*

The Change in Control CIC theory is a simple one: Hospitals with low prices are sometimes acquired by hospitals that prefer higher prices. A new owner might prefer a higher price for a variety of reasons. A different perspective provides one potential reason: The acquired hospital may have been setting prices that were "too low" from a market perspective.[16] Alternatively, the acquiring hospital may different objectives, different expectations about the future, different information, or different tolerances for reputational effects from increasing prices. Any of those differences mean that the "optimal price" for the acquired and the acquiring hospitals may differ, and thus a change in ownership may result in price changes.[17]

Notably, the CiC theory is a one of *price* effects, but effects that are not due to a reduction in competition: CiC-related price increases can occur with any change in hospital ownership, regardless of whether the new owner also owns other hospitals in the same or different markets. Higher prices can also result from changes in control even *absent* changes in ownership. This might be the case, for example, if a hospital replaces its CEO or CFO – especially if the new CEO's compensation is more directly tied to the hospital's financial success than was the case for the former CEO.

---

15 Very generally, convexity results in a type of "Cournot complementarity effect" that creates incentives for a post-merger price reduction. *See* Vistnes & Sarafidis (2013) and Dafny, Ho & Lee (2019). *See also* Vita et al. (2022) for a discussion of convexity in a within-market context if the merging hospitals are complements from a Payor's perspective.

16 The idea that a new owner might increase price because the former owner failed to exploit its market power fully, or because it set the "wrong" price, is hardly new. Such an argument was made (but given little weight by the courts or the FTC) to help explain the substantial post-merger price increase that was highlighted by the FTC in its 2004 challenge to the already-consummated Evanston, IL hospital merger. *See In the Matter of Evanston Northwestern Healthcare Corporation*, Docket No. 9315, Opinion of the Commission, 2007, *available at* www.ftc.gov/sites/default/files/documents/cases/2007/08/070806opinion.pdf). Similar arguments were made to explain the dramatic price increase (approximately 1,300 percent) for the drug NeoProfen following Ovation Pharmaceutical's acquisition of that drug from Merck; this was an acquisition that did not involve a reduction in direct competition. *See* https://www.ftc.gov/news-events/news/press-releases/2008/12/ftc-sues-ovation-pharmaceuticals-illegally-acquiring-drug-used-treat-premature-babies-life and https://www.ftc.gov/-system/files/documents/public_statements/418091/081216ovationroschstmt.pdf.

17 This raises the important questions of whether any such price effects should be thought of as "harm" rather than a natural market price adjustment, and under what if any conditions a price increase, even if not attributable to a change in competition, might cause harm and be deemed actionable under state or federal law.

## B. Empirical Research Provides Some Confirmation of Cross-market Price Effects

Brand & Rosenbaum (2019) provide an excellent summary of the empirical literature on cross-market hospital mergers, concluding that "the empirical analyses in this literature provide credible evidence that prices have increased following [cross-market] mergers." The two principal empirical studies regarding cross-market effects concern GAC hospitals.[18] Dafny, Ho & Lee (2019) compare price changes over time between merging hospitals and non-merging hospitals and find that price increases at hospitals involved in a cross-market merger were, on average, 7 to 10 percent higher than at the control group of hospitals that were not involved in a merger. Lewis & Pflum (2017) compare prices at stand-alone hospitals acquired by out-of-market systems to prices at standalone hospitals that were not acquired or exposed to any merger and find cross-market price increases as large as 17 percent.[19]

# IV. CONDITIONS THAT INCREASE THE RISK OF CROSS-MARKET HARM

Unlike unilateral effects theory – which provides a rich set of tools that can be used to predict the extent to which horizontal mergers will reduce competition – cross-market theory provides limited guidance with regard to which particular cross-market mergers are likely to cause significant harm. Theory suggests, however, certain conditions that are associated with the CLE and CiC theories that, if satisfied, increase the risk of harm.[20] These conditions, which are identified in Table 1, are discussed below.[21]

Under the CiC theory, prices can increase if pricing strategies differ between the new and the old owners. A set of "Plus Factors" can be identified that provide possible insight into whether the acquired and acquiring hospitals have different pricing strategies. These Plus Factors include the following:

---

[18] Schmidt (2018) and Melnick & Keeler (2007) also examine merger-related hospital prices, but their findings are less informative about cross-market effects.

[19] Vistnes (2023), however, notes that this supporting empirical literature is very limited in scope and that the two principal studies are at least partially inconsistent with each other and the extent to which they provide support for any particular cross-market theory of harm. Thus, the empirical research should be viewed as important and informative, but absent additional research, not yet compelling.

[20] This focus on the CLE and CiC theories, but not TT theories, reflects the fact that there already exists a large economic literature (as well as a legal literature and relevant court rulings) with regard to TT theories and the conditions under which TT theories predict harm. Just as important, however, those TT theories typically assume that the merged parties have substantial market power in one market but face much greater competition in the other market. As will be discussed below, the evidence (while disputed by the parties) indicated that both CSMC and HM had substantial market power, which thus reduced the likelihood of effects under TT theories. Instead, concerns in *CSHS/HM* focused more on the CLE and CiC theories.

[21] Many of these conditions have been identified elsewhere. For a more detailed discussion of why these conditions are important under the CLE and CiC theories, see Vistnes Report (2020), Varanini (2020), King et al. (2022), and Vistnes (2023).

**Table 1: Conditions That Increase the Risk of Harm under the CiC and CLE Theories**

| | |
|---|---|
| **Change in Control (CiC) Theory** | **History of Cross-Market Price Effects**<br><br>**Outlier Pricing** |
| **Common Linked Employer (CLE) Theory** | **Prevalence of Common Linked Employers**<br>*Proxy: Proximate Geographic Markets*<br>*Proxy: Within State Merger*<br><br>**Market Power in both newly-linked Markets**<br>*Proxy: High market shares*<br>*Proxy: High pre-merger prices*<br><br>**Concavity**<br>*Proxy: Payor Concerns consistent with concavity*<br>*Proxy: Small hospital system size* |

*CiC-Related Plus Factors in CSHS/HM*

- **A history of cross-market price effects**. It can be informative to ask whether the merging hospitals were previously involved in cross-market mergers, and if so, whether those mergers resulted in price increases. A history of such price increases is consistent either with the acquiring hospital either preferring high prices or acquiring other hospitals that have low prices. Thus, a history of cross-market price effects can constitute a CiC-related Plus Factor.
- **Evidence of "outlier pricing."** Evidence that the acquiring hospital sets unusually high prices, or that the acquired hospital sets unusually low prices, means that any post-merger changes in the acquired hospital's price to make it comparable to the acquired hospital would result in a post-merger price increase. Thus, outlier pricing can constitute a CiC-related Plus Factor.

## A. Necessary Conditions for CLE-related Harm

Harm under the CLE theory is contingent on satisfying three necessary conditions: the prevalence of common linked employers;[22] substantial market power

---

22 The likelihood or magnitude of a cross-market effect depends not just on the existence, but also on the *prevalence,* of common linked employers: Unless the hospital can price-discriminate between employers, a merger-related increase in the hospital's bargaining power *vis-à-vis common linked employers* will have little or no effect on price if there is no change in the hospital's bargaining power *vis-à-vis other employers*, and those other employers constrain prices.

at the hospitals across which there are common linked customers; and concavity.[23]

**Prevalence of Common Linked Employers.** Although a fact-based inquiry may be more precise, there exist at least two proxies for the prevalence of common linked employers:[24] One proxy is based on the belief that employers are more likely to have employees in multiple markets when those markets are relatively close to each other. Thus, geographic proximity can be a useful proxy for the prevalence of common linked employers.[25] A second, albeit less precise, proxy – but still based on the assumption that common linked employers are more likely when the merging hospitals are geographically proximate – is whether the merger involves hospitals in the same state.[26]

**Substantial market power at both of the merging parties.** The CLE theory assumes that both of the merging hospitals have substantial market power. In general, assessing a hospital's market power can involve a variety of inquiries, including: consideration of product and geographic differentiation; defining markets and calculating market shares; estimating patient choice models and likely diversion patterns; calculating hospitals' "willingness to pay" ("WTP");[27] and assessing Payors views and history regarding their hospital choices. Accordingly, assessing market power is a fact-intensive, market-specific inquiry.

Table 1 identifies two proxies for market power. One of these – high market shares – is a generally accepted proxy for market power. A second proxy – while appropriately controversial in its reliability – is supra-competitive prices (or profits).[28]

---

23 These conditions, along with certain proxies for those conditions, were referred to as "Plus Factors" in the Vistnes Report (2020). In retrospect, that term was poorly chosen in the context of the CLE theory: Unlike coordinated effects analysis where the Plus Factor term is often used, and where satisfaction of those Plus Factors is neither a necessary nor sufficient condition for harm, the conditions that are discussed in the context of the CLE theory are *necessary* conditions for harm.

24 These two proxies are motivated by a methodology used in the empirical literature to distinguish between within-market and cross-market mergers. The empirical finding (Dafny, Ho & Lee (2019)) that cross-market effects depend on distance, however, is consistent with the assumption that the prevalence of common linked employers is related to distance.

25 The empirical papers that have studied cross-market price effects variously define "proximate" markets as at least 20 miles (Schmitt (2018)) or 45 miles (Lewis & Pflum (2017)), or a 30-minutes' drive time (Dafny, Ho & Lee (2019)), from each other, with Dafny, Ho & Lee providing weak empirical evidence that "nearby markets" begin to turn to "distant markets" at approximately 90-minutes' drive time.

26 This proxy can be very imperfect: Some within-state mergers may involve very distant markets (*e.g.*, San Diego and San Francisco; Dallas and San Antonio, TX; or Miami and Pensacola, FL), while other cross-state mergers may involve nearby markets (*e.g.*, Washington, DC and Alexandria, VA; Philadelphia, PA and Wilmington, DE; or New York City and Newark, NJ). Thus, the Same State proxy seems inferior to the almost-as-easy to use Proximity proxy.

27 WTP models use patient choice data to estimate the relative attractiveness of hospitals to patients based on a variety of characteristics such as: hospital and patient location; hospital size and teaching status; and patient characteristics, such as age and medical needs. A high WTP for a hospital is then indicative of greater hospital market power. *See* Town & Vistnes (2001) and Capps, Dranove & Satterthwaite (2003).

28 Care must be taken to control for factors other than market power that may explain high pre-merger prices: *e.g.*, high costs that are due to: a hospital's teaching status; a complex case mix; or high quality.

**Evidence of Concavity.** Assessing concavity for an individual employer is difficult. Assessing concavity for a Payor that aggregates across the different preferences of various multi-market employers is even more difficult. Thus, of the three necessary conditions for the CLE theory, concavity is likely the most difficult to assess.

Absent a means to measure directly the presence of concavity, proxies can be useful. Payor Concerns is one such proxy. A Payor needs to do more, however, than simply cite concerns with a proposed merger, so as to satisfy this proxy. Instead, a Payor should ideally confirm that the loss of one of the merging hospitals increases the importance of keeping the other merging hospital in its network.

Hospital System Size provides another possible proxy for concavity: A hospital system that includes several hospitals with substantial market power may already be able to threaten significant harm if it threatens to pull out of a plan's network. Accordingly, adding one more hospital through a merger may have little impact on the incremental harm that the merged system can threaten. Thus, cross-market mergers that involve systems that already include multiple hospitals with substantial market power may be more likely to exhibit *convexity* rather than concavity. In contrast, increasing the size of a hospital system may have a much bigger impact on the hospital system's bargaining position when that hospital system is small. Thus, concavity may be more likely with small – or single-hospital – systems.

## V. THE LITIGATED ISSUES IN *CSHS/HM*

The CAAG's economic expert concluded that each of the conditions (including the associated proxies) that are identified in Table 1 were satisfied.[29] Based in part on that finding, the CAAG concluded that the risk of harm was sufficient to require the Parties to accept, for a period of 10 years, two forms of regulatory relief: a price cap; and conduct relief (an "unbundling requirement") that required the Parties to use separate, firewalled contracting teams at CSHS and HM.[30]

The Parties filed suit contesting the CAAG's conclusion that cross-market concerns provided a basis for requiring relief.[31] In addition to arguing that the State's proposed relief would jeopardize the hospitals' ability to provide access to care and to reduce costs, and that it would disadvantage the hospitals relative to other hospitals in the region, the Parties made two sets of economic arguments:[32]

---

29 As discussed below, the CAAG's economic expert did not consider the Small Hospital System Size proxy that is identified in Table 1, but the evidence that was cited in the litigation shows that this proxy was satisfied.

30 The CAAG also required mandatory "baseball-style/final offer" arbitration if Payors claimed that the Parties required conditions that they would not have imposed absent the affiliation. *See* https://oag.ca.gov/news/press-releases/attorney-general-becerra-conditionally-approves-affiliation-agreement-between and https://oag.ca.gov/sites/all/files/agweb/pdfs/charities/nonprofithosp/ag-decision-huntington-121020.pdf?.

31 *See* https://sourceonhealthcare.org/wp-content/uploads/2023/01/2021-03-30-Verified-Petition-and-Complaint-2.pdf. Amici briefs by several healthcare scholars (on behalf of the CAAG) and the American Hospital Association (on behalf of the Parties) were also filed.

32 The Parties also argued that the State's intervention exceeded its legal authority. A discussion of those arguments is outside the scope of this chapter; *but see* the State's response: Opposition to Petition for Writ of Mandate, *PHA v. CDJ*, Superior Court.

The Parties' first set of arguments were market-specific: that cross-market theories were not applicable because the necessary conditions under those theories were not satisfied. In particular, Parties argued that *CSHS/HM* was not a cross-market merger because CSMC and HM were direct competitors in the *same* market. The Parties further argued that within that market, neither hospital had substantial market power.

The Parties' second set of arguments addressed the broader questions of whether policy intervention was warranted, and what form any such intervention should take – even if the necessary conditions for cross-market concerns were met. Specifically, the Parties argued that cross-market concerns did not justify the State's proposed relief: that the State's concerns were speculative; that the State failed properly to balance (or even consider) the costs and benefits of the proposed relief; and that the State's regulatory relief was excessive.

The fact-specific nature of the Parties' first set of arguments, while important in *CSHS/HM*, limits the relevance of the specifics of those arguments to future cross-market cases. The Parties' second set of arguments, however, will likely be relevant in future cross-market cases and thus merits particular attention.

## A. Market-specific Arguments in CSHS/HM

**Market Definition: Do CSMC and HM compete in the same relevant market, or are they in different relevant markets?** While the CAAG claimed that CSMC and HM were in distinct (albeit proximate) geographic markets, the Parties argued that they were in the same market, thus rendering cross-market theories of harm irrelevant. This debate was largely fact-specific.

Evidence that indicated that the hospitals were in different markets included evidence that: Payors did not view the hospitals as good alternatives; travel times and distances between the hospitals were significant; and CSMC and HM drew their patients from very different geographies. The economic expert also estimated a patient-choice model that showed limited diversion between the affiliating hospitals, which thus indicated limited competition between the two and was consistent with their location in separate, distinct markets.

In contrast, the Parties argued that the affiliating hospitals were not in separate markets. The Parties' principal argument here was that – based on at least some of the methodologies that were used to identify cross-market mergers in the two empirical papers that had studied cross-market effects – the hospitals were sufficiently close so that those papers would have treated them as competing in the same market.

**Market Power: Do CSMC and HM both have substantial market power?** Substantial market power at both hospitals is a necessary condition under the CLE (although not the CiC) theory. Thus, in arguing that both of the affiliating hospitals did not have substantial market power, the Parties sought to prove the irrelevance of the CLE theory to the CSHS/HM affiliation.

Assessing market power depends on the facts of the particular market. The CAAG's economic expert concluded that both CSMC and HM had substantial market power. This conclusion was based on: Payor interviews in which they identified the importance of including both of those hospitals in their provider networks; an analysis that showed that in many zip codes, the two hospitals had very high patient shares; and a WTP analysis that showed that the two hospitals had among the highest WTPs of all the hospitals in the Los Angeles region. The economic expert also found evidence that CSMC and HM prices were high, which was consistent with the market power proxy that related to high pre-merger prices.

The Parties contested this evidence. After defining two alternative (but almost entirely different) geographic markets as either CSMC's or HM's primary service area ("PSA"),[33] the Parties calculated their post-affiliation market share as less than 30 percent.[34] This, they claimed, fell below a federal antitrust safety zone and thus presumably showed a lack of market power.[35] The Parties also proposed an alternative methodology for calculating WTP that showed that CSMC and HM were not unique in having high WTPs – which the Parties interpreted as evidence that CSMC and HM did not have substantial market power. The Parties also showed that in at least some cases, certain Payors (including Kaiser) offered hospital networks that excluded both CSMC and HM, which was indicative of a lack of substantial market power on the two hospitals' part.

**The other conditions identified in Table 1.** The CAAG's economic expert concluded that the other conditions in Table 1 were also met, although those arguments were largely unaddressed by the Parties.[36]

With respect to the prevalence of common linked employers, the expert noted that Payor interviews and data analysis indicated that many employers drew their employee from a broad region. More relevant to future cross-market cases is how the concavity question was addressed. The CAAG's economic expert indicated that several Payors expressed concerns consistent with concavity. Additionally, while not discussed in the expert's report, the Hospital System Size proxy was satisfied, with the expert's analysis showing that both of the affiliating systems included only a single hospital with substantial market power. Whether such evidence is sufficient to show concavity may, however, will likely be the subject of further debate in future cross-market cases.

---

33 A PSA constitutes a region that accounts for 75 percent of a hospital's patients.

34 This analysis, as well as many of the Parties' other analyses, included Kaiser patients. The legitimacy of including Kaiser patients was another point of contention: Kaiser is a vertically integrated closed system in which Kaiser patients can use only Kaiser hospitals, and Kaiser hospitals cannot be used by non-Kaiser Payors or their enrollees.

35 The Parties were presumably referencing the 2011 "Statement of Antitrust Enforcement Policy Regarding Accountable Care Organizations Participating in the Medicare Shared Savings Programs" that, while recently withdrawn, was in effect at the time of the litigation. The safety zone that was defined in that Statement, however, did not appear to cover this affiliation, nor did the Parties calculate market shares in the manner that was outlined in that Statement. *See* https://www.justice.gov/sites/default/files/atr/legacy/2011/10/20/276458.pdf for details.

36 To the extent that the Parties successfully demonstrated that the hospitals were in the same market, or did not have substantial market power, addressing these other conditions relevant to the CLE theory was unnecessary: Showing the failure of a single necessary condition is presumably sufficient to show that the CLE theory fails to apply.

## B. CSHS/HM Arguments Likely to Arise in Future Cross-market Cases

Even if the necessary conditions for harm under the CLE and CiC theories were satisfied, the Parties argued that satisfying those necessary conditions did not provide a sufficient basis to justify the CAAG's proposed intervention. Because these arguments are less market-specific, they will likely continue to arise in other cross-market cases.

**Was the CAAG's proposed relief excessive?** As a precondition for allowing the affiliation to proceed, the CAAG required – for a period of 10 years – a price cap and conduct relief that involved an "unbundling requirement" that required the Parties to use separate, firewalled contracting teams at CSHS and HM.

The Parties argued that the price cap was unnecessary given the unbundling requirement. In support of this, they cited the CAAG's economic expert's observation that the unbundling requirement could potentially prevent harm under the CLE (and TT) theories – thus potentially rendering the price cap regulation redundant.

The Vistnes Report (2020) noted, however, that the price cap regulation would be redundant only if the unbundling requirement was entirely effective. If, however, the hospitals could subtly force Payors to accept a bundled package, then harm under the CLE theory or through regulatory evasion remained possible. The CAAG's expert further noted that, because the unbundling requirement provided *no* protection under the CiC theory, the price cap provided incremental relief relative to just the unbundling requirement. Thus, the CAAG argued that the price cap was not redundant, but rather an important safeguard to the proposed relief.

**Were the CAAG's concerns overly speculative?** While noting that the conditions that are identified in Table 1 were satisfied, the CAAG's economist expert acknowledged that the extent of harm from the affiliation was unclear, stating, "while posing a real risk of [harm], the likelihood, and likely magnitude, of cross-market effects is unclear." The Parties emphasized this acknowledgement and argued that concerns about cross-market harm were sufficiently speculative to render the State's intervention inappropriate.

The issue of when the likelihood of harm is sufficiently likely to warrant relief raises what will likely remain an important question in future cross-market mergers – particularly with respect to the CLE theory: To what extent is satisfaction of the *necessary* conditions for harm a *sufficient* basis to conclude that harm sufficient to warrant intervention is likely, and what types of additional evidence will usefully determine when (or if) that sufficiency criteria is met?

In considering the question of when satisfaction of certain conditions provides a sufficient basis for government intervention, however, the *CSHS/HM* litigation may differ in an important respect relative to other cross-market cases. Unlike the federal antitrust laws (*e.g.*, Section 7 of the Clayton Act) that may govern other future cases, the statute that governs the CAAG for matters such as *CSHS/HM* considers more than just antitrust issues: In particular, the CAAG is required to consider also the transaction's potential impact on the accessibility and availability of healthcare services in a public interest context.[37]

The CAAG's expanded set of concerns potentially distinguishes the *CSHS/HM* matter from future cross-merger cases. First, by expanding its set of concerns beyond just competition issues, the CAAG sidestepped the question of whether the CiC theory provides a legitimate basis for challenging a merger based on the antitrust laws that would likely govern the federal antitrust agencies. Second, the expanded scope of concerns that governed the CAAG may lower the threshold level at which concerns are sufficient to warrant intervention: In particular, even if the likelihood of harm is deemed less than what might warrant intervention under federal antitrust statutes, intervention under the statutes that govern the CAAG's actions may nevertheless be warranted.

Whether the State's intervention was warranted in *CSHS/HM* depends on the level of risk that the State is prepared to accept before intervening and whether the benefits of that intervention likely offset the possible costs of intervention. In *CSHS/HM*, the State concluded that its authority – and its mandate to protect consumers from higher prices and impact on access and accessibility – warranted intervention despite the uncertainty over the likelihood and magnitude of cross-market effects. That debate over likely costs and benefits, however, is an important one and may be different in future cross-market cases – depending on market facts and the legal authority under which the cases are brought.[38]

**Would a cost/benefit analysis justify the CAAG's proposed relief?** The Parties argued that the expected harm against which the relief would protect was not properly balanced against the likely benefits that would be lost as a result of that relief.[39] More generally, the Parties argued that the likely benefits of the transaction were simply not considered, much less properly balanced. And, based on the Parties' claim that harm was unlikely or speculative, they argued that a cost-benefit analysis would not justify the State's proposed relief.

## VI. THE SETTLEMENT AGREEMENT

Prior to trial, the State and the Parties entered into a settlement agreement that allowed the affiliation to proceed with certain restrictions.[40]

---

[37] California law (Corporations Code section 5914-5920 et seq., and California Code of Regulations, Title 11, Section 999.5) state that any transaction that involves the sale or transfer of control of a nonprofit hospital must secure the approval of the state Attorney General, with the statutory charge of the Attorney General to determine whether the transaction may impact the accessibility and availability of healthcare services, including to substantially lessen competition or create a monopoly.

[38] *See* Vistnes (2023) and Varanini (2020) for a discussion of: how great and how likely the expected harm should be to warrant intervention; the different factors that may be relevant when assessing harm; and how that requisite level of risk may differ according to the legal statute(s) under which the government seeks relief.

[39] More generally, the Parties argued that the likely benefits of the transaction were simply not considered, much less properly balanced.

[40] The decision to settle rather than litigate meant that a full airing of the strengths and weaknesses of the State's cross-market allegations was never made, nor were the courts given an opportunity to opine on those arguments.

Although the settlement was similar to the CAAG's originally proposed preconditions, it differed regarding several details.[41] It continued to include a price cap on HM, but for a shorter period of time (five rather than 10 years); and, rather than pegging the cap to an index of hospital costs, the cap was simplified to limit price increases at HM to no more than 4.8 percent per year.

The settlement also included several conduct-related provisions that sought (for 10 years) to: prevent all-or-nothing contracts; prevent implicit or explicit financial penalties for health plans that want to contract with only a subset of CSHS/HM hospitals; prevent CSHS/HM from interfering with Payors' use of narrow or tiered networks; and ensure firewalled contracting teams at CSHS/HM when requested by Payors.[42] These conduct provisions serve the same basic purpose as the CAAG's originally proposed Unbundling Provision: to prevent regulatory evasion, and to limit CLE concerns by limiting the hospitals' ability to bundle their hospitals and threaten Payors with the additional holes in their network.

## VII. SUMMARY

The *CSHS/HM* litigation may be the first of many hospital investigations, regulatory actions and court challenges that are based on cross-market concerns, and it raises several issues that are likely to be front-and-center in future cases. Those issues include a debate over: (i) whether the necessary conditions for harm under those theories are met; (ii) whether those necessary conditions are sufficient to create a risk of harm; (iii) whether any likely harm may be sufficient to warrant intervention; and (iv) if so, how that intervention should be crafted.

## REFERENCES

Bork, R. The Antitrust Paradox, Basic Books, Inc. (1978).

Brand, K. & Rosenbaum, T. "A Review of the Economic Literature on Cross-Market Health Care Mergers," *Antitrust Law Journal*, 2019, pp. 533 - 549.

Brennan, T. "Cross-Subsidization and Cost Misallocation by Regulated Monopolists," *Journal of Regulatory Economics*, 1990, pp. 37-51.

Capps, C., Dranove, D. & Satterthwaite, M. "Competition and Market Power in Option Demand Markets," *Rand Journal of Economics*, Winter 2003, pp. 737-763.

Carlton, D. & Waldman, D. "The Strategic Use of Tying to Preserve and Create Market Power in Evolving Industries," *Rand Journal of Economics*, 2002, pp. 194-220.

Dafny, L., Ho, K. & Lee, R. "The Price Effects of Cross-Market Mergers: Theory and Evidence from the Hospital Industry," *Rand Journal of Economics*, Summer 2019, pp. 286-325.

---

41 *Available at* https://oag.ca.gov/system/files/media/nhft-huntington-ag-decision-071921.pdf.

42 The agreement also included a provision under which the State could ask the court to extend the term of these conditions for three additional years.

Fulton, B., Arnold, D. King, J., Montague, A., Greaney, T. & Scheffler, R. "The Rise of Cross-Market Hospital Systems and Their Market Power in the US," *Health Affairs*, 41, No. 11, 2022, pp. 1652 – 1660.

Gowrisankaran, G., Nevo, A. & Town, R.,"Mergers When Prices Are Negotiated: Evidence from the Hospital Industry," *American Economic Review*, 105(1), 2015, pp. 172-203.

King, J., Montague, A., Arnold, D. & Greaney, T. "Antitrust's Healthcare Conundrum: Cross-Market Mergers and the Rise of System Power," *UC Hastings Research Paper*, 2022.

Krattenmaker, T. & Salop, S. "Anticompetitive Exclusion: Raising Rivals' Costs to Achieve Power over Price," *The Yale Law Journal*, 1986, pp. 209-293.

Lewis, M. & Pflum, K. "Hospital Systems and Bargaining Power: Evidence from Out-of-Market Acquisitions," *Rand Journal of Economics*, Fall 2017, pp. 579 – 610.

Nalebuff, B. "Exclusionary Bundling," *Antitrust Bulletin*, 2005, pp. 321-370.

Riordan, M. & Salop, S. "Evaluating Vertical Mergers: A Post-Chicago Approach," *Antitrust Law Journal*, Winter 1995, pp. 513-568.

Schmitt, M. "Multimarket Contact in the Hospital Industry," *American Economic Journal: Economic Policy*, 2018, pp. 361-87.

Schmalensee, R. "Monopolistic Two-Part Pricing Arrangements," *Bell Journal of Economics*, Autumn 1981, pp. 445-466.

Town, R. & Vistnes, G. "Hospital Competition in HMO Networks: An Empirical Analysis of Hospital Pricing Behavior," *Journal of Health Economics*, 2001, pp. 595-609.

Varanini, E. "Addressing the Red Queen Problem: A Proposal for Pursuing Antitrust Challenges to Cross-Market Mergers in Health Care Systems," *Antitrust Law Journal*, 2020, pp. 509-526.

Vistnes, G. "Hospitals, Mergers, and Two-Stage Competition." *Antitrust Law Journal*, January 2000, pp. 671-692.

Vistnes, G. & Sarafidis, Y. "Cross-Market Hospital Mergers: A Holistic Approach," *Antitrust Law Journal*, 2013, pp. 253-293.

Vistnes, G. "Competitive Effects Analysis of the Proposed Cedars-Sinai Health System/Huntington Memorial Hospital Affiliation," December 4, 2020, *available at* https://oag.ca.gov/sites/all/files/agweb/pdfs/charities/nonprofithosp/ag-decision-huntington-121020.pdf?.

Vistnes, G., "Cross-Market Hospital Mergers: Assessing Likely Harm and Implications for Government Action," accepted pending revision, *Antitrust Law Journal*, 2023.

Vita, M., Brand, K., Larson-Koester, M., Petek, N., Taragin, C., Violette, W. & Wood, D. "Economics at the FTC: Estimating Harm from Deception and Analyzing Mergers," *Review of Industrial Organization* (61), November 2022, pp. 405-438.

Whinston, M. "Tying, Foreclosure, and Exclusion," *American Economic Review*, 1990, pp. 837-859.

# II. MONOPOLY CONDUCT/ABUSE OF DOMINANCE

**CHAPTER 9**

# A Landmark Antitrust Case in Digital Markets: *Google Search (Shopping)*

*By Andrea Amelio*[1]

## I. INTRODUCTION

The *Google Search (Shopping)* case was one of the first enforcement actions of a competition authority in digital markets that targeted a Big Tech company. Since this case, many cases of the European Commission (the "Commission") and other competition authorities[2] against Big Tech have followed, including Amazon,[3] Facebook,[4] Apple,[5] and other cases against Google.[6]

The *Google Search (Shopping)* case involved the most important, globally known, and emblematic firm that operates on the internet with a global reach. It dealt with Google's strategic decisions to modify the terms and conditions of access and appearance of rival comparison-shopping companies on its search result page and to enter the market for comparison-shopping services with its new service.

The case has confronted the European General Court with important legal and economic questions. It was the first attempt to adapt the well-known leveraging theory of harm to the complex and dynamic world of the internet and to the new two-sided platform business models. In 2010 when proceedings against Google were initiated, the mainstream economic doctrine about two-sided platforms was promoting a liberal approach and was not very supportive of an antitrust intervention. It is worth recalling that in 2013, the U.S. Federal Trade Commission decided not to bring charges against Google following a similar investigation (Gil-

---

1 The author was involved in the case as a civil servant employed by the European Commission. The information and views set out in this article are those of the author and do not necessarily reflect the official opinion of the European Commission."

2 Among others, see also the U.S. Justice Department suing Monopolist Google For Violating Antitrust Laws in October 2020, https://www.justice.gov/opa/pr/justice-department-sues-monopolist-google-violating-antitrust-laws.

3 *See* EU Commission, *Amazon*, Case AT.40462.

4 *See* EU Commission, *Facebook - Facebook Marketplace*.

5 *See* EU Commission, *Apple - App Store Practices*, Case AT 40716, EU Commission, *Apple - App Store Practices (music streaming)*, Case AT 40437 and EU Commission, *Apple - App Store Practices (e-books/audiobooks)*, Case AT 40652.

6 *See* EU Commission, *Google Android* AT.40099 and *Google Search (AdSense)* AT.40411.

bert 2019). A *laissez-faire* approach for these markets was vocally defended with arguments that interfering in such an environment could have slowed the pace of innovation.

The *Google Search (Shopping)* case thus significantly challenged the common wisdom at the time and was instrumental for a more critical approach towards digital markets. The decision that was adopted by the Commission in 2017 reflected this difficult context; and as a result, the Commission – as was often recognized by the General Court in its judgement – developed a theory of harm that required, for each single element, legal and economic analysis that was supported by a mix of qualitative and quantitative evidence.

The difficulty and complexity of this case and the challenging exchange with a well-resourced company such as Google on many points of economics and law and on factual interpretation of the evidence were also shown by the convoluted evolution of the proceedings. The abandonment of a commitment route, and instead an embrace of a prohibition route, was an important move after several rounds of discussions with Google as to proposed commitments.

This case – notably its length and the difficulties in the remedy discussion – has also been instrumental in starting the current important debate with regard to the regulation of digital markets.[7] The knowledge of the functioning of digital markets that this case has elicited is remarkable, and it has significantly informed the subsequent debate. The endorsement of this case by the General Court gave further support to this approach. The current decision to regulate digital market – as embodied in the recent adoption of the Digital Markets Act – is thus closely connected to this landmark case by the Commission.

This chapter is structured as follows: It will shed some light on the background of the *Google Search (Shopping)* case and the relevant proceedings. It will then summarize the main facts and the legal and economic reasoning that was undertaken by the Commission in its decision, the arguments that were put forward by Google, and the assessment of the General Court in its judgment.

## II. BACKGROUND OF THE CASE

On June 27, 2017, the Commission adopted Decision C(2017) 4444 that Google abused its dominant position in 13 national markets for general search services in the European Economic Area ("EEA") in breach of Article 102 TFEU and Article 54 of the EEA Agreement.

Google was a platform that offered free-of-charge online products and services together with online advertising from which Google generated its revenues. The flagship of Google's products was its online search service, which was powered by its secret algorithm. Google allowed users to search for information on the internet by

---

[7] *See* the report "Unlocking digital competition" that was written by the Digital Competition Expert Panel chaired by Professor Jason Furman in 2019 and the Special Advisers' Report "Digital policy for the digital era" that was written by Jacques Crémer, Yves-Alexandre de Montjoye & Heike Schweitzer.

introducing a query. Google would then respond by producing a page with results. The results page was designed by Google, and it was a collection of links that were normally of three different types: generic results; advertising results; and specialized results.

Each category resulted from a different underlying procedure: Generic search results (also called "blue links") were a set of links that were generated by the Page Rank algorithm, which ranked all of the pages that were contained in Google's database according to certain criteria, which were free of charge for the owner of those pages.

Alongside, in response to a query, Google also produced AdWords results: These were links to advertisement pages that were generated by Google's auction-based online search advertising platform: AdWords. They were not limited to specific categories but were subject to a ranking mechanism that involved real-time auctions that were based not only on quality parameters but also on bids. These results were normally placed above (top of the first page) or below (bottom of the first page) the generic search results, and Google received remuneration from the owner of the advertisement when a user clicked on the link on a pay per click basis.

In response to a query, according to specific rules, Google also provided specialized results: These were links that displayed pictures and dynamic information and were regulated by agreements between Google and the linked website owners. They were generally based on a paid inclusion and were designed to be displayed prominently at the top of the page; the owner of the website was charged on a pay-per-click basis when a user clicked on the link. This was a relatively recent innovation that Google had developed for different services, products, or information, such as finance, flights, etc. Google Shopping was one of them.

Specifically, Google Shopping was designed to return product offers from a set of merchant websites that enabled users to make comparisons. It evolved over time. Google launched the first version of its comparison-shopping service in December 2002 in the U.S. (October 2004 in the United Kingdom, and November 2004 in Germany) as a standalone platform under the brand name "Froogle." Merchants did not have to pay to be listed in Froogle as it was monetized by advertisements.

Froogle was not a successful service, as was recognized by Google. Google thus undertook a transformation of the service. In 2007, it was renamed as Google Product Universal; and importantly Google started to include results of these services directly in its main search results in a dedicated box, which was normally referred to as "Universal," "One Box," or "Shopping Unit."

In May 2012 for the U.S. market and subsequently for EEA markets, Google renamed the service Google Shopping and started a paid inclusion model, in which merchants paid Google when their products were clicked on in Google Shopping and users went directly to the page of Google's merchant partners where they could (if desired) perform the purchase.

# Figure 1. Example of general search page with Google Shopping as reported in the Commission decision.

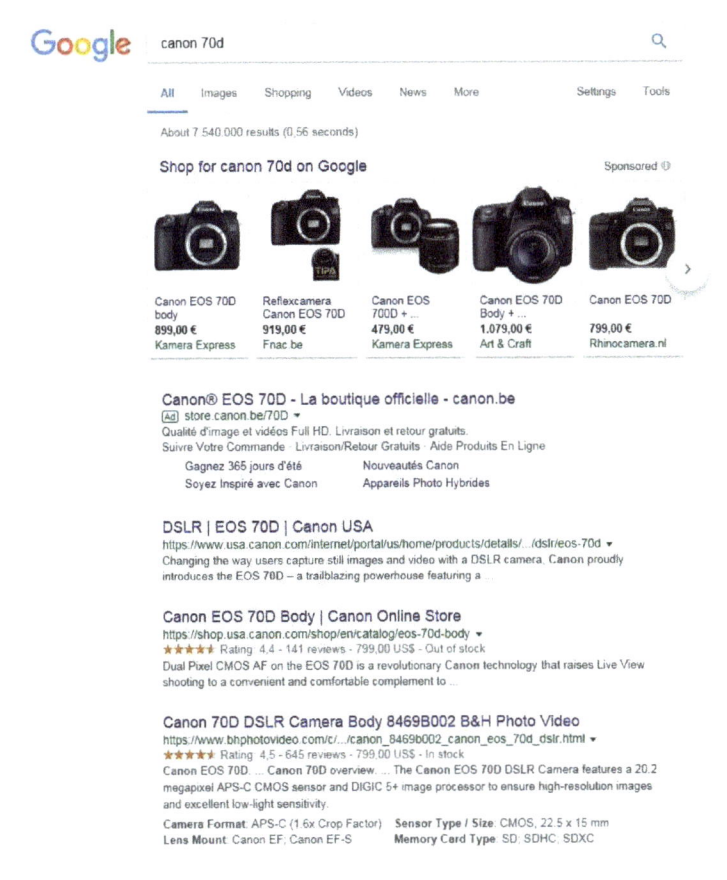

*Source:* the Commission decision.

Meanwhile Google undertook changes to its dedicated algorithms that would identify and automatically demote websites that did not comply with its Webmaster Guidelines. In 2011, in particular, Google introduced the Panda algorithm that had the alleged effects of making competing comparison-shopping websites more prone to be demoted.

The combination of these strategic decisions in the way that Google presented and ranked results over several years led to the general search results page that is depicted in Figure 1 and was the core of this case.

## III. THE PROCEEDINGS OF THE CASE

The *Google Shopping* case gave rise to a complicated and convoluted procedure: The case spanned two Competition Commissioners: Joaquín Almunia and Margrethe Vestager. It lasted seven years from the opening of proceedings to the Commission's decision, and it took another three years to reach the judgement of the General Court. At the time of writing, the case is still not concluded: Google has appealed the General Court's judgement to the EU Court of Justice.

The *Google Shopping* case resulted from several complaints that were lodged with the European Commission in and after 2009. Complaints kept coming in to the Commission until 2014, and were also directed to National Competition Authorities. Many comparison-shopping services were directly involved in these complaints.[8]

On November 30, 2010, the Commission initiated proceedings against Google and formally opened an investigation. The investigation lasted more than two years. On March 13, 2013, the Commission took the preliminary view that Google had abused its dominant position. After three iterations, the third set of commitments that were offered in response by Google was accepted by the Commission; and between May 27 and August 11, 2014, the Commission sent letters to the complainants informing them of its intention to reject their complaints in light of the remedy package that Google had offered.

Nineteen complainants replied negatively, and the Commission in September informed Google that it was not in a position to accept those commitments. This was at the end of Commissioner Almunia's mandate.

The arrival of Commissioner Vestager marked the turning point when on April 15, 2015, the Commission decided to revert to an infringement decision. This turn was a crucial moment for the case, which was also underscored by Google's claims during the General Court proceedings that the Commission failed to explain its decision and did not give Google the opportunity to modify its third set of commitments.[9]

Following this decision, the Commission adopted a supplementary statement of objections on July 14, 2016 and a letter of fact on February 28, 2017. Decision C(2017) 4444 was eventually adopted on June 27, 2017. Google appealed the decision; and on November 10, 2021, the General Court upheld the Commission's decision, including a fine of €2.42 billion. On January 20, 2022, Google appealed the General Court's judgement to the EU Court of Justice.

---

[8] A non-exhaustive list of complainants included: Infederation Ltd. ("Foundem"), Ciao GmbH ("Ciao"), eJustice.fr ("eJustice"), Verband freier Telefonbuchverleger ("VfT"), Bundesverband Deutscher Zeitungsverleger ("BDZV"), the Verband Deutscher Zeitschriftenverleger ("VDZ"), Euro-Cities AG ("Euro-Cities"), Hot Maps Medien GmbH ("Hot Maps"), Mr. Sessolo ("nntp.it"), Elf B.V. ("Elf"), Microsoft Corporation ("Microsoft"), Twenga SA ("Twenga"), La Asociación de Editores de Diarios Españoles ("AEDE"), Yelp Inc. ("Yelp"), Streetmap EU Ltd ("Streetmap"), Expedia Inc. ("Expedia"), Odigeo Group ("Odigeo"), TripAdvisor Inc. ("TripAdvisor"), Nextag Inc. ("Nextag"), Guenstiger.de GmbH ("Guenstiger"), Visual Meta GmbH ("Visual Meta"), Initiative for a Competitive Online Marketplace ("ICOMP"), Bureau Européen des Unions des Consommateurs AISBL ("BEUC"), Open Internet Project ("OIP"), Deutsche Telekom AG ("Deutsche Telekom"), and HolidayCheck AG ("HolidayCheck").

[9] Case C(2017) 4444, section 4.4.

# IV. THE MAIN FINDINGS AND ISSUES OF THE CASE

## A. Market Definition

The Commission's decision concluded that the relevant product markets were the market for online general search services and the market for online comparison-shopping services – both of which are national in scope.[10]

With regard to the market for online general search services, the decision was based on three main findings: First, the Commission concluded that such a service is an economic activity even if it was offered free of charge to users. This type of service was monetized by selling ads to advertisers that also knew the search users' data that were collected when the users agreed to the terms and conditions of online general search services.

Second, from a demand side perspective, limited substitutability was found between general search services and other internet services. Specialized search services mostly provided commercial offerings only, whereas general search services provided all types of online service. Thus, specialized search services did not offer the same breadth of results as was offered by generalized search services.

Third, from a supply-side perspective, the decision indicated limited substitutability as it pointed to the existence of important barriers for other online services to compete in the short term with existing providers of general search services without incurring significant costs or risks. These barriers were mainly direct – the greater the number of queries, the greater the relevance, and the greater the number of users – and indirect: positive feedbacks between users and advertisers. Network effects, significant economies of scale, a brand effect, and limited multi-homing also contributed to barriers. Other important evidence was that many competing services had exited the market, and only Microsoft was able to pursue that business in any meaningful way with its search engine Bing. However, Bing's market share never exceeded 10 percent in any EEA country.

Google disagreed with this finding: It essentially argued that there was a portion of overlapping results across the general search service and the specialized search services. However, the General Court supported the conclusion of the Commission.

With regard to the market for online comparison-shopping services, the Commission based its decision on four main findings: First, from a demand perspective, it found that each specialized search service dealt with queries that focused on a specific subject matter and provided answers on that subject matter alone, so that there was no substitutability between the different specialized search services.

Second, the demand side differentiation meant that there was limited substitutability from a supply perspective. The decision found that the content of databases,

---

[10] Note that an assessment was done as to whether these markets should have been distinguished according to whether internet users use them on computers or on other devices such as tablets or smartphones. The Commission concluded that there was no supporting evidence to differentiate markets further and thus there were only product markets for online general search and for online comparison-shopping services.

the nature and sphere of activity of the operators of websites to which a specialized search service might direct users, and the contractual relationships with those operators were so varied – depending on the type of specialized search that was involved – that it would have been difficult for the provider of a specialized search service to offer, in the short term and without incurring significant additional costs, a different type of specialized search service and therefore to compete in that respect.

Third, general advertising services on the general results pages were different from online comparison-shopping services for reasons that related to the development and functioning of the services: Users did not look for advertising, whereas users did look for shopping suggestions.

Fourth, services that were offered by online direct sellers and merchant platforms were also deemed not sufficient substitutes. Direct sellers offered only their products, whereas merchant platforms included services and obligations that were linked to the actual sale of a product, which thus satisfied different users' needs.

Google strongly disagreed with the conclusion of the Commission. In particular, the assessment of the substitution between merchant platforms and comparison-shopping services was heavily challenged. Google argued that Amazon and eBay marketplaces were strong competitors; Google provided quantitative studies and internal document quotes. In response to this criticism, the Commission provided an articulated assessment of these differences and likely impact. More details will be given below.

The General Court supported the conclusion of the Commission: With regard to the geographical scope of these markets, the observed national partitioning of these services – determined by the different European languages – was the main evidence that was used to reach the above-mentioned conclusion. This evidence was complemented by the presence of search engines that operated nationally. Google did not contest this conclusion, and the General Court supported the Commission's conclusion.

## B. *Google's Dominant Position*

The Commission's decision concluded that, since 2008, Google held a dominant position in the market for general search services in every EEA country except the Czech Republic – where Google had held such a position since 2011. The decision identified the following fundamental sources of Google's dominance in the market for general search: the importance of scale; indirect network effects; and brand effects.

Scale was a crucial factor: Search engines needed to churn large volumes of queries quickly in order to update and refine the relevance of results. The larger the number of queries that were submitted and results that were clicked on, the faster the search engine learned to detect a change in users' behavior, to adapt and to improve the relevance of the results. This held for both free ("blue link") results and for paid search ads.

The importance of scale was amplified by the fact that queries did not all have the same frequencies of usage. As the decision explained, there were common queries ("head" queries) and uncommon queries ("tail" queries). Tail queries made it more difficult for a smaller, rival search engine to provide relevant results. The poor performance for the tail queries negatively affected the user experience, and this reduced traffic for a smaller search engine in general. The decision acknowledged and endorsed the fact that a sufficiently large amount of data was a necessary input for the ability to compete in these markets.

Indirect network effects in the context of two-sided platforms were also an important element: Both general search services and comparison-shopping services were provided by two-sided platforms. The Commission's decision relied on the economic intuition that had been developed in the literature that there were positive feedback effects between the advertisers on one side of the platform and the users of search services on the other side. In line with this economic literature, the decision found that the higher the number of users, the higher was the value for advertisers to post (and to bid for) their ads on the page that contained the results of a search. Similarly, this dynamic was also present in the market for comparison-shopping services, where the two groups of platform customers were potential online consumers and online retailers.

Limited switching was also argued. Based on a survey, the decision found that overall, users were loyal to the Google search engine and that they did not tend to multi-home.

The finding of dominance was also corroborated by the usual analysis of market shares. The decision found that Google had very high and stable market shares by volume, which had almost always exceeded 80 percent since 2008 – except in the Czech Republic, where Google nevertheless became the market leader in January 2011 with a market share that exceeded 70 percent.

Google contested the finding of dominance by relying on two main arguments: It contested the findings with respect to the existence and importance of economies of scale; Google argued that it was not the number of queries received that determined the relevance of the results but instead the quality of the underlying "recipe" of Google's algorithm itself. The support for this statement relied on anecdotal evidence. Google also contested the absence of multi-homing: Google argued that the definition of multi-homing that was used in the Commission's survey was overly restrictive and thus artificially created low percentages of multi-homing. Google provided more studies; but according to the Commission, these studies did not prove the existence of significant multi-homing.

The General Court supported the conclusion of the Commission. It is worth highlighting that during the Court proceedings, Google did not dispute these findings.

## C. *Google's Abuse of Dominance*

The Commission's decision concluded that at different times – dating back as far as January 2008 – Google had abused its dominant position in 13 national markets for general search services within the EEA. It abused its dominant position by strengthening its (already dominant) position in the market for general search services and by extending its dominant position to the neighboring market of comparison-shopping services by distorting competition. It did so by decreasing traffic from its general results pages to competing comparison-shopping services and increasing traffic to its own comparison-shopping service.

The abuse was thus based on a leveraging theory of harm. Google used its dominance in the market for general search services to give its comparison-shopping service an artificial advantage and excluded competing comparison-shopping services, which led to anticompetitive foreclosure.[11] The combination of Google's market power in the general services and the self-preferencing was thus the backbone of the abuse.

To demonstrate Google's foreclosure of competitors, the decision considered a combination of internal documents and factual and empirical evidence. Six key arguments were developed.

First, the decision explained Google's strategic decision to degrade the relative positioning and display of competing comparison-shopping services. Competing comparison-shopping services appeared in the generic results, in the form of blue links. Google Shopping results were instead displayed with richer graphical features, which included images and dynamic information. Competing comparison-shopping services were prone to be demoted within the ranking of generic results due to the application of "adjustment" algorithms – notably the "Panda" algorithm, on account of the characteristics of the comparison-shopping services and their lack of original content. Google Shopping was not subject to these adjustments – despite sharing the same characteristics of its rivals – and was shown at the top of the page.

Second, an analysis of internet users' behavior showed that generic results generated significant traffic to websites when they were ranked within the first three to five results on the first general results page ("above the fold"). Internet users paid little or no attention to subsequent results, which often did not directly appear on the screen, and the first 10 results received approximately 95 percent of internet users' clicks. Another study showed that irrespective of its relevance, the position of a given link in the generic results had a major impact on the click-through rate of that link. There were thus indications that users were behaving with limited rationality in their search for the best results and generally suffered from limited information with respect to the underlying quality of the proposed results.

Third, the decision showed that the introduction of specific algorithmic changes – in particular the launch of the "Panda" algorithm – led to the demotions of competitors' ranking.[12] The Sistrix Visibility Index[13] indicated a substantial decrease in competitors' visibility and therefore a deterioration of display after the introduction of the Panda algorithm. The decision provided graphs that supported the above-mentioned conclusions where the sharp decrease of the visibility index that followed the roll-out of Panda could be observed (*see* the decision, for example, at p. 83).

---

11 This approach was similar to that of the Commission's Guidance Paper, where anticompetitive foreclosure was defined as "a situation where effective access of actual or potential competition to supplies or markets is hampered or eliminated as a result of the conduct of the dominant undertaking whereby the dominant undertaking is likely to be in a position to increase prices to the detriment of consumers." European Commission. (2009), para. 9. Guidance on the Commission's enforcement priorities in applying Article 82 of the EC Treaty to abusive exclusionary conduct by dominant undertakings. (pp. 7–20), OJ C 45, 24.2.2009. *Available at* https://eur-lex.europa.eu/legal-conte nt/EN/TXT/PDF/?uri=CELEX:52009XC0224(01)&from=EN.

12 The introduction of the "Panda" algorithm to the Google search ranking algorithm meant that websites with "non-original" content were ranked lower.

13 The weekly Visibility Index of Sistrix measures the changes in the Google Search ranking of individual sites, based on a large number of keywords. The keywords are chosen in such a way so that they reflect the average search behavior for each country

The decision also presented evidence that this reduction in visibility and ranking reduced traffic. Data on clicks by search result rank and positioning showed that there was a link between visibility, the lay-out of Google's general search results pages and click-through behavior. Results that were displayed higher and in a more visible format attracted significantly more clicks than those that were displayed lower or beyond the first page.

Fourth, the evolution of the visibility index of competitors initially showed a similar trend to the volume of Google's generic search traffic that was received by competitors. All of the graphs that were computed for eight EU countries showed a trend break in the traffic (clicks) to competing shopping comparison services when Panda was introduced. For all EU countries, a stable increase turned into a stable decrease, although the extent of this break varied across countries. Figure 2 is an example of this evidence.

**Figure 2 Evolution of generic search traffic from Google's general search results pages to competing comparison shopping services in United Kingdom.**

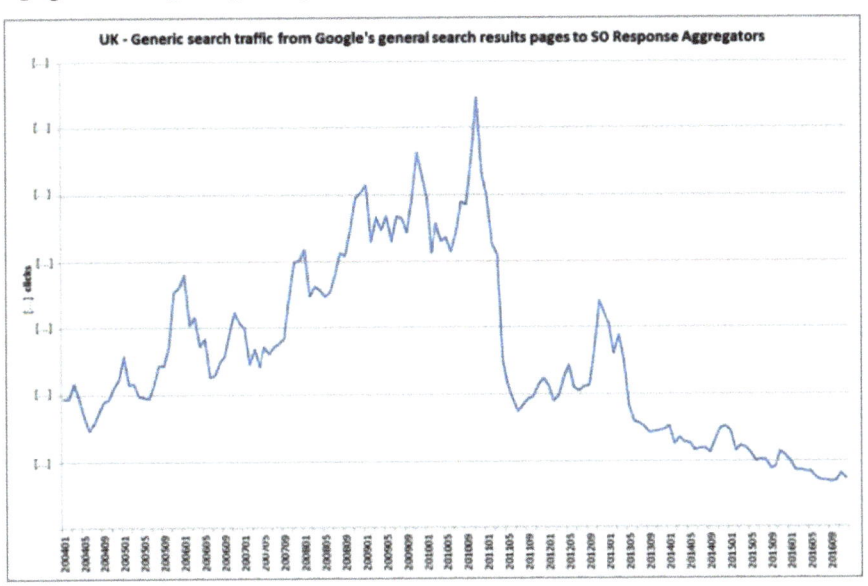

**Source:** the Commission decision.

The decision corroborated this evidence with internal documents that indicated that comparison-shopping services suffered short-term and long-term traffic decreases due to the introduction of systematic demotions.[14]

Fifth, the decision also relied on the results of an experiment that was conducted by Google. In this so-called "ablation" experiment (which was a difference in differences exercise), Google removed its own Shopping Unit from its general result pages for a randomly selected group of users. Comparing the click-through rate of this selected group to the click-through rate of the unchanged display allowed an estimation of the causal effect of the more prominent placement of the Shopping Unit with respect to competitors' traffic.

---

14 Case AT.39740—*Google Search (Shopping)* Article 7 Regulation (EC) 1/2003, page 140, recital 490.

Although Google argued that there were no effects, an adjustment to the analysis that allowed the Commission to correct for the demotions[15] revealed a significant effect on competitors' volume of traffic. The decision illustrated this impact on both the generic and text ad (AdWords) traffic of competitors. The Shopping Unit's effect on text ad traffic (AdWords) suggested that competitors found it difficult to replace lost free generic search traffic with paid text ad traffic.

Sixth, in the same period of time, based on the same two metrics – visibility and clicks – Google's comparison-shopping service experienced a sharp increase in its traffic on a lasting basis.

Based on these six arguments, the Commission's decision concluded that Google's conduct promoted Google's comparison-shopping service – which was not a successful service prior to the conduct – and excluded rivals.

While the decision did not openly discuss Google's incentive to foreclose, from an economic perspective, the structure of Google's business model contained an inherent monetization problem: The strategic decision (and commitment) of Google to distribute free general search services was a core element for Google's incentive to foreclose in adjacent markets, such as the comparison-shopping services market. Only clicks on Google's ads or Google's comparison-shopping service triggered a payment to Google; clicks on the general search results did not. The free Google general search results generated traffic for a wide range of businesses that offered paid products and services. However, Google could not directly monetize this traffic. This feature of the general search services market made the classical Chicago School critique not applicable.

The Chicago School critique argued that a dominant company should have no incentive to foreclose competitors from adjacent markets because the dominant company could make as much profit (if not more) by appropriately pricing its dominant product/service and extracting all the value because of the "one monopoly profit" theory. Google's strategic decision not to price general search services put Google in a situation where the only way for Google to appropriate the value that was created by users' clicks that led to rival comparison-shopping platforms was to appropriate the clicks of those users by directing them instead to its own comparison-shopping service. Sending users to competing comparison-shopping services would amount to a net profit loss and, over time, to an increasing risk of users bypassing Google and going directly to the competing comparison-shopping services.

Google disagreed with the findings and assessment of the decision and raised five main lines of defense: First, Google argued that its conduct was in line with competition on the merits; second, it did not discriminate in favor of its shopping services *vis-à-vis* competitors' services; third it challenged the quantitative findings of the Commission's decision; fourth, it questioned the decision's treatment of merchants' platforms; and fifth it contested the legal basis of the decision.

---

15 The Commission eliminated from the exercise the effect of the demotions that were making the comparison-shopping invisible to the users. Therefore, the Commission restricted the analysis to those instances where comparison-shopping services were ranked in the top positions of the Google search results page.

Google explained that it was entitled to use all "normal" methods to compete to win business – including its right to increase the quality of its technologies and its specialized search services.

According to Google, the decision simply mischaracterized normal competition on the merits. Google grouped product results and product ads to improve the quality of its general search service. By showing these "designs" on its general results pages and developing the innovative technologies that supported them, Google competed on the merits in the market for general search services. Furthermore, as exits of competitors were observed by the Commission, Google argued that not every exclusionary effect is necessarily detrimental to competition, since competition on the merits may lead to the disappearance or marginalization of competitors that are less efficient.[16]

Google continued its defense by stating that it never favored nor discriminated in favor of its own comparison-shopping service. Google explained that it treated its shopping service and generic results (including the Shopping Unit comparisons) differently for legitimate technical reasons. Google thus argued that it was not treating similar situations differently but different situations differently. Therefore, these were not instances of discrimination. Furthermore, the differences in treatment did not provide any undeserved placement on Google's general results pages. Google's shopping service "earned" its place on the results page, and the Commission's decision overlooked the way in which Google had enabled a consistent ranking system according to common relevant standards.

The General Court, however, did not accept Google's arguments and concluded that Google's behavior could be considered a departure from competition on the merits. The Court relied on four main points in its judgement.

First, the Court concluded that favoring and its effects were convincingly demonstrated. It supported the Commission's arguments: that Google's general search engine was an important source of traffic for comparison-shopping services; that the absence of this traffic determined a loss of traffic that led eventually to the exit of competing comparison-shopping services; and that this traffic was not effectively replaceable.

Second, the Court pointed to a "certain form of abnormality" with regard to Google's behavior. The Court reached the conclusion that this favoring was not economically rational. It underlined that the rationale and value of a general search engine lay in its capacity to be open to results from external sources and to display these multiple and diverse sources to enrich and enhance its credibility to customers – and, in turn, to be able to generate advertising income on the advertising side. The fact that Google had stopped this by giving greater prominence only to its service was regarded by the Court as a form of abnormality.

Third, the Court also noted Google's "change of behaviour": The deviation from competition on the merits of the conduct was all the more obvious as it followed a change of conduct by Google. The Court thus endorsed a historical perspective: The Court observed that Google changed its practices after experiencing the failure of its

---

16 Google quoted judgments of 27 March 2012, *Post Danmark* (C-209/10, EU:C:2012:172, paragraph 22), and of 6 September 2017, *Intel v. Commission* (C-413/14 P, EU:C:2017:632, paragraph 134).

dedicated comparison-shopping service (Froogle) and wanted to grant more visibility (and thus traffic) to its grouped products results. Consequently, comparison-shopping services were no longer treated in the same way.

Fourth, the Court concluded that the existence of a common relevant standard that applied to comparison-shopping services – including Google's – was ineffective and unfounded. By examining the difference in treatment that was described in the Commission's decision, the Court supported the findings that a differentiated treatment was applied based on the origin of the results – Google's own comparison-shopping service versus competitors' services – rather than one type of results against the other. The Court went further and concluded that there was no relevance standard, let alone a common standard, as Google could not effectively make comparisons. Google did not have the information to do so, and the Court referred to Google's statement that explained that Google did not know anything about the quality of the results as it was not crawling the website but was simply relying on the feed that was provided by the competitors and that did not provide comparable information.

Google also contested the finding that the practice decreased traffic from Google's general results pages to competing comparison-shopping services and consequently that it increased traffic from Google's general results pages to its own comparison-shopping service. Google argued that although the Commission's decision contained many graphs – *see* for instance Figure 4 – the Commission failed to prove the existence of a causal link between the promotion of its own comparison-shopping service and the reduction of traffic (which Google did not contest) from Google's general results pages to competing comparison-shopping services.

**Figure 3 Traffic from Google's general search results pages to Google's comparison shopping service compared to total traffic to a sample of competing comparison shopping services in United Kingdom.**

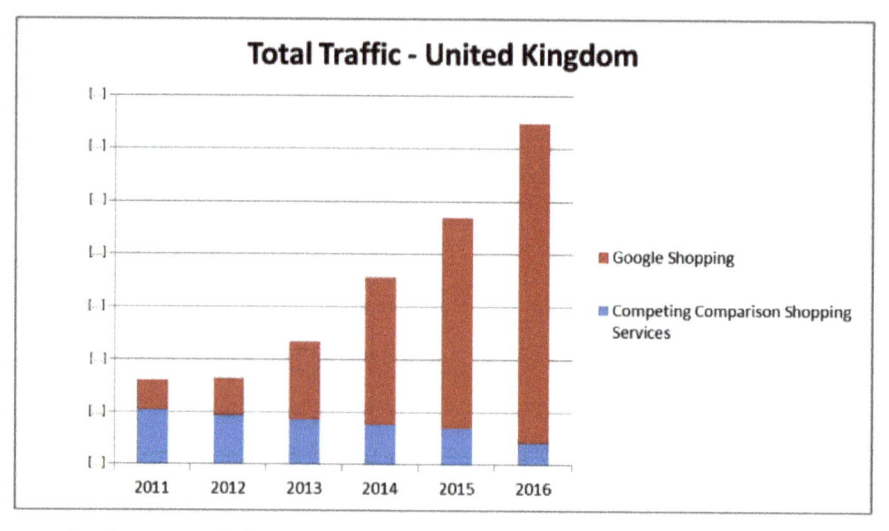

**Source:** the Commission's decision.

Google argued that the counterfactual scenario that included both the promotion of Google comparison-shopping services and the introduction of adjustment algorithms (such as the Panda algorithm that is responsible for the demotion of rival comparison-shopping services) was wrong. The right counterfactual analysis should have examined the scenario where Google refrained from positioning its shopping results at the top of the search result page but kept the installation of the adjustment algorithm. In fact, Google strongly affirmed that adjustment algorithms had to be considered part of the normal functioning of its search engine in order to keep the quality of its search results.

For these reasons, Google concluded that all of the evidence that was collected in the Commission's decision was not applicable as the evidence considered only the effect of the Panda adjustment algorithm and not the promotion of Google's service. By using its proposed counterfactual, Google argued that all of the experiments – including its own ablation experiment – unanimously pointed to no decrease of traffic to competing comparison-shopping services as a result of the introduction of Google shopping service in the search result page. Instead, Google argued that the stagnation of the comparison-shopping services was due to a broad switch of consumers' preferences – as was illustrated by the growing popularity of merchant platforms, such as Amazon and e-Bay. They were effective alternatives for comparison-shopping searches by directing and enabling users to shop online; and as a result, their traffic continued to grow. As was discussed above in the market definition section, this was in stark contrast with the decision, which concluded that merchant platforms were not competing for the same users and were thus in different product markets.

Based on these conclusions, Google stated that, since its practice did not lead to a decrease in traffic to competing comparison-shopping services, any increase in traffic to its own comparison-shopping service could not have been at their expense and exclusionary but instead was the reflection of consumer preferences.

The General Court rejected all of Google's arguments based on four considerations: First, the Court took the view that the analysis of effects needed to include the two strategic decisions of the introduction of a specific adjustment algorithm for generic results (which was responsible for the demotion of competing comparison-shopping services) and the promotion of Google's comparison-shopping service. Google's ablation exercise as presented by Google was thus rejected as it used the wrong counterfactual.

Second, the Court took into account the statements from nine groups that operated comparison-shopping services that indicated that they all suffered significant decreases in traffic from Google's general results pages starting from mid-2007. The Court analyzed the four sources of evidence that were used in the decision: Sistrix Visibility Index (weekly visibility statistics of comparison-shopping services); the raw traffic data that Google provided in the context of the ablation experiment; the traffic data of 361 competing comparison-shopping services that Google produced; and the traffic data for countries where triggering rates were particularly high.

All four sources pointed to significant decreases, and the Court stated that Google did not put forward anything in its submissions to challenge this evidence.

Third, the Court rejected Google's argument that these decreases were due to a change in consumer preferences toward merchant platforms, as Google did not substantiate these claims. On the contrary, the Court concluded that the high visibility and improved display – images, price, and merchant information for Google's comparison-shopping service relative to a blue link to rival services, which was often poorly placed – led consumers to click more on Google's services, which generated the discrepancy in traffic.

Fourth, the Court noted that Google's comparison-shopping service was initially unsuccessful and losing traffic at a rate of approximately 20 percent per year. The Court then observed that – according to specific computations that were undertaken by the Commission with the use of Google's data – Google's comparison-shopping service rose from approximately 5 million to approximately 30 million clicks per month with Product Universal and from approximately 30 million to approximately 120 million clicks per month with Shopping Unit.

Finally, Google also argued that the decision failed to use the correct legal basis. Implicitly, the Commission imposed on Google an obligation to grant access to competitors to proprietary services. The decision thus implicitly identified the conduct as a "refusal to supply" but failed to verify the indispensability criteria as requested in the judgement of November 26, 1998 *Bronner* (C-7/97, EU:C:1998:569) for these types of conduct.

The Court again rejected Google's argument and concluded that the Commission was not required to establish that the conditions that were set out in the judgement of November 26, 1998 *Bronner* (C-7/97, EU:C:1998:569) needed to be satisfied in order to find an infringement in the present case. The Court first noted that the decision in essence dealt with conditions of supply of Google's general search services by accusing Google of not giving equal positioning and display to competitors. Second, the Court found that the decision dealt with issues of access to Google's general search results – notably by acknowledging that Google's general results service had characteristics akin to an essential facility and that the Commission *de facto* concluded that there were no actual or potential viable substitutes.

Despite this premise, the Court concluded that, although related, the practice at issue could be distinguished from a refusal to supply. The Court pointed to the lack of an express refusal to supply: an explicit request and a consequential refusal. It noted that many practices could amount to an implicit refusal to supply as they tend to make access to a market more difficult; nonetheless the judgement of November 26, 1998 *Bronner* (C-7/97, EU:C:1998:569) should not be applied to all of those practices, as the scope of Article 102 TFEU should not have been limited in practice to dealing with indispensable goods. In this regard, the Court pointed to margin squeezes and to non-discrimination cases as examples of practices that raise issues of access but for which it was not necessary to demonstrate the condition of indispensability.

## D. The Anticompetitive Effects

The Commission's decision concluded that the anticompetitive effects were felt in the 13 corresponding national markets for specialized comparison-shopping search services and in those national markets for general search services. The countries concerned were: Belgium, the Czech Republic, Denmark, Germany, Spain, France, Italy, the Netherlands, Austria, Poland, Sweden, the United Kingdom, and Norway. These effects were the negative consequences for competition and for users. The consumers could potentially suffer from an increase in advertising costs and thus eventually the possibility of higher product prices. Consumers' choices would have been reduced, which would make it more difficult for them to reach the most relevant shopping opportunities, and more concentrated markets would have harmed the pace of innovation.

Google disagreed with those conclusions and put forward two arguments: The decision speculated about anticompetitive effects; and the role of merchant platforms was not duly considered in the analysis of effects.

According to Google, there was no evidence that the negative effects that were identified by the decision actually came to pass. Since the conduct spanned many years, its anticompetitive effects ought to have been visible if that conduct had genuinely been harmful to competition. Google contested that no tangible effects were identified. On the contrary, Google argued that the overall number of visits to comparison-shopping services increased and that there was ample material in the file that showed that Google was not able to increase prices or to restrain innovation and that competition in the markets for comparison-shopping services was robust, with internet users' having a wide range of choice.

Google also contended that the decision ignored the competitive pressure of merchant platforms. Merchant platforms' competitive pressure was so strong that no effect could have been found; but this was ignored as the Commission's decision incorrectly determined the product market definition and thereby excluded them. To demonstrate that merchant platforms and comparison-shopping service providers were active in the same market for comparison-shopping services, Google argued that both categories provided – free of charge – the same product search functionality, including price information, to internet users. The services that were offered were therefore substitutable, which was sufficient for both types of provider to impose a competitive constraint on each other, even though merchant platforms provide additional services.

Google submitted three surveys and cited several independent studies that showed that most internet users who wished to purchase a product started their search on a merchant platform and completed their purchase only after comparing products. Merchant platforms were not only a shop but – similar to comparison-shopping services – they also brought together the offers of many shops and allowed users to compare the prices of a single product or model free of charge. Google relied also on internal documents in which Google considered Amazon and eBay to be leaders in the market for comparison-shopping services and, in particular, viewed Amazon as a benchmark and its main competitor, which drove Google's own innovation efforts.

The General Court rejected both arguments and supported the views of the Commission. In doing so, the Court recalled the evidence that the Commission put forward in its decision with regard to the evolution of traffic on Google and the rival comparison-shopping services. The Court concluded that the evidence provided was enough to generate potential anticompetitive effects: The competitive structure of the markets would have been severely affected, competing comparison-shopping services would have exited the market, and the prospects of success of Google's comparison-shopping service would have been artificially enhanced by Google's dominant position on the markets for general search services and by the conduct at issue.

The Court also rejected that merchant platforms were exercising competitive pressure. The Court concluded that merchant platforms served a different purpose, and it noted that the search (and thus comparison) functionality of comparison-shopping services appeared to differ and be better in so far as the functionality relied on a much larger database of offers that translated into a better ability to compare offers and prices in the entire market. The Court based its conclusions on statements of the comparison-shopping services that considered merchant platforms to be business partners and not competitors. This involved comparison-shopping services' bringing to the attention of all internet users – usually in the form of advertising – the offers of merchant platforms; this was a situation (the Court noted) that would be unlikely to arise if both categories of firms were in direct competition with each other.

The Court also noted that comparison-shopping services tended to list offers of large online retailers who wanted to keep control over the marketing and selling of their product. Merchant platforms instead tended to list offers from small and medium-sized retailers that relied on the merchant platforms' marketing and purchasing facilities.

In line with the Commission's decision, the Court thus concluded that there were two different demands and thus that comparison-shopping services and merchant platforms were serving different purposes on the seller side. The conclusion that the services of merchant platforms were not part of the product market of comparison-shopping services allowed the Court to conclude that the competitive pressure of merchant platforms was irrelevant.

Notwithstanding this conclusion, the Court also made use of an analysis that was produced in the Commission's decision that showed that the share of comparison-shopping services in a larger product market – that also included merchant platforms – would have still been significant. The Court thus stated that Article 102 TFEU was still applicable even if an abuse affected only one category of the dominant company's competitors in a given (broader) market.

## E. The Fine and Remedies

The Commission's decision imposed a cease and desist order from this discrimination/favoritism practice or similar conduct that would have the same object or effect. It made clear that although Google could comply with that order in different ways, certain principles had to be respected – regardless of whether or not Google decided to retain Shopping Units or other groups of comparison-shopping search results on its general results pages. Those principles included, in essence, the principle of non-discrimination between Google's comparison-shopping service and competing comparison-shopping services. The decision also imposed a fine of €2.4 billion on Google, which took into account the duration and the gravity of Google's conduct.

Google introduced an arms-length auction remedy that enabled rival comparison-shopping services to bid for access to the Google Shopping Unit at the top of the result page for the placement of product ads, on equal terms, in direct competition with Google. Google's comparison-shopping service would also operate as a separate entity and needed to be profitable on its own.

As stated in the decision, the remedy was subject to monitoring by the Commission, assisted by external technical experts. The remedy that Google proposed, and was accepted by the Commission, generated many comments and discussions as to its legality and effectiveness. On the one hand, there were commentators who argued that such a remedy was compatible with the case law and the auction mechanism was an entirely appropriate and lawful way to ensure that Google was appropriately remunerated for its valuable input, to which significant opportunity costs were attached, and for the innovative advertising technologies that reflected years of investment. On the other hand, other commentators and stakeholders argued that the remedy was not working (*see, e.g.*, Marsden, 2020).

A coalition of 135 companies and 30 trade associations that offered specialized online services – that included travel, accommodation, and jobs – wrote an open letter to the Commission to urge immediate action against Google considering that the *Shopping* decision did not lead to Google's changing anything meaningful.[17] These companied studied the effectiveness of the remedy; and by analyzing 10.5 billion clicks, they found that less than 1 percent of traffic was currently being directed to rival comparison-shopping sites.[18]

The Commission has so far indicated that it took note of the concerns in relation to Google's compliance, which were raised by a number of complainants. The Commission reported that the take-up of the compliance mechanism by competitors of Google Shopping – who could not have displayed their offers in the Shopping Unit before the decision of June 2017 – had substantially increased. In June 2018, only one-third of Shopping Unit results included at least one competitor, and around 6 percent of clicks in the Unit went to competitors. In November 2019, 81 percent of Shopping Unit results included at least one offer of a competitor, and 45.9 percent of clicks went to these competitors.[19]

## V. CONCLUSION

The complexity and variety of the legal and economic arguments that were debated in the *Google Search (Shopping)* case can now be fully appreciated. Despite the fact that the General Court upheld almost all points of the European Commission decision, this case kept generating important debates among commentators.

From the legal angle, the case raised a fundamental question as to the scope of the *Bronner* line of case law and its applicability. Digital markets often involve terms and conditions

---

17  *See* https://www.enpa.eu/policy-issues/joint-industry-letter-against-googles-self-preferencing.

18  *See* https://www.hausfeld.com/en-us/what-we-think/competition-bulletin/antitrust-remedies-in-digital-markets-lessons-for-enforcement-authorities-from-non-compliance-with-eu-google-decisions/ and https://papers.ssrn.com/sol3/papers.cfm?abstract_id=3700748.

19  *See* https://www.europarl.europa.eu/doceo/document/E-9-2019-003869-ASW_EN.html.

of access to proprietary infrastructure. It has been argued that the decision of the Court not to rely on *Bronner* might have significant repercussions for the future assessments of digital cases (*see, e.g.*, Ahlborn et al., 2022). Furthermore, the Court often discussed the principle of non-discrimination, and it gave some guidance. However, commentators argue that the boundaries of this line of case law remain unclear (*see, e.g.,* Hornkohl, 2022).

The judgement also discussed the use of the "as efficient competitor" test and elaborated on its limitations and the opportunity and relevance to conduct such a test. This also led to important debates as to the role of this test in proving an abuse (*see, e.g.*, Gaudin & Mantzari, 2022).

Finally, the Court discussed the role of the counterfactual, its limitations, and the implications for the finding of actual and potential effects. It has been argued that a certain interpretation of the pronouncement of the Court could thus have important effects on the approach to the analysis of effects (*see, e.g.*, Di Giovanni Bezzi, 2022).

Many other comments involve the points of economics and law that this case triggered; *see, for example*, Bostoen (2022), Bougette (2022), and Lindeboom (2022). This simply underlines the importance that this case has had and will have in the years to come.

## REFERENCES

Ahlborn, Christian, Gerwin Van Gerven & William Leslie. "Bronner revisited: Google Shopping and the Resurrection of Discrimination Under Article 102 TFEU," Journal of European Competition Law & Practice, Volume 13, Issue 2, March 2022, pp. 87–98.

Bougette, Patrice, Axel Gautier & Frédéric Marty. "Business Models and Incentives: For an Effects-Based Approach of Self-Preferencing?," Journal of European Competition Law & Practice, Volume 13, Issue 2, March 2022, pp. 136–143.

Bostoen, Friso. "The General Court's Google Shopping Judgment Finetuning the Legal Qualifications and Tests for Platform Abuse," Journal of European Competition Law & Practice, Volume 13, Issue 2, March 2022, pp. 75–86.

Di Giovanni Bezzi, Raffaele. "Anticompetitive Effects and Allocation of the Burden of Proof in Article 102 Cases: Lessons from the Google Shopping Case," Journal of European Competition Law & Practice, Volume 13, Issue 2, March 2022, Pages 112–124.

Gaudin, Germain & Despoina Mantzari. "Google Shopping and the As-Efficient-Competitor Test: Taking Stock and Looking Ahead," Journal of European Competition Law & Practice, Volume 13, Issue 2, March 2022, pp. 125–135.

Gilbert, Richard J. "The U.S. Federal Trade Commission Investigation of Google Search (2013)," in The Antitrust Revolution, John E. Kwoka, Jr. and Lawrence J. White (eds), Oxford University Press, 7th edn., 2019, pp. 489-513.

Hornkohl, Lena. "Article 102 TFEU, Equal Treatment and Discrimination after Google Shopping," Journal of European Competition Law & Practice, Volume 13, Issue 2, March 2022, pp. 99–111.

Lindeboom, Justin. "Rules, Discretion, and Reasoning According to Law: A Dynamic-Positivist Perspective on Google Shopping," Journal of European Competition Law & Practice, Volume 13, Issue 2, March 2022, pp. 63–74.

Marsden, Philip. "Google Shopping for the Empress's New Clothes –When a Remedy Isn't a Remedy (and How to Fix it)," Journal of European Competition Law & Practice, Volume 11, Issue 10, December 2020, pp. 553–560.

# CHAPTER 10
# MARKET DEFINITION FOR TWO-SIDED MARKETS: *OHIO v. AMERICAN EXPRESS*

*By Michael L. Katz*[1]

## I. INTRODUCTION

Section 1 of the Sherman Act prohibits agreements "in restraint of trade" without defining what constitutes a restraint of trade. This imprecision has allowed courts to adapt their interpretation of the statute as new business practices have developed and economic thinking has evolved. But this flexibility comes at a cost: It provides scope for the courts to misinterpret or misapply economics unless Congress acts to correct the courts' mistakes.

*Ohio v. American Express Co.* is a prime example:[2] While claiming to apply modern platform economics, the Supreme Court took an approach that was contrary to the fundamental principles of that field. And, as of November 2022, there is no evidence that Congress will act to correct it.

When making a purchase, a customer chooses which payment mechanism to use from among those that are accepted by the merchant. If the customer chooses an Amex charge card, the merchant must pay a fee to American Express for providing payment services. American Express provides benefits to cardholders, such as financial rewards that are tied to card usage, that are intended to steer consumers to use Amex cards. Because American Express often charges merchants higher fees than do other payment networks, some merchants would like to steer Amex cardholders to use alternative payment mechanisms.

Subject to limited exceptions, American Express's "no-steering rules" ("NSRs") prevent merchants from accepting its cards unless the merchants agree not to promote or encourage the use of credit or charge cards that are branded and issued on competing networks – Discover, MasterCard, and Visa – by offering the merchants' customers discounts or informing customers of the merchants' preference for alterna-

---

1  The author was retained by the U.S. Department of Justice as an expert in *U.S. v. American Express* and *U.S. v. Visa et al.* No confidential information is disclosed in this chapter. This chapter draws heavily on the author's previous writings, and he acknowledges the substantial contributions of Douglas Melamed and Jonathan Sallet.

2  *United States v. Am. Express Co.*, 88 F. Supp. 3d 143 (E.D.N.Y. 2015), *rev'd*, 838 F.3d 179 (2d Cir. 2016), *aff'd sub nom. Ohio v. Am. Express Co.*, 138 S. Ct. 2274 (2018). Katz & Melamed (2020) provide an extensive critique of *Ohio*'s failure to promote the sound evolution of antitrust law.

tive brands of credit and charge cards.[3] For example, the NSRs forbid merchants from making statements such as "you are welcome to use any credit or charge card that you would like, but we want to let you know that American Express charges us more than do other credit and charge card networks."

In 2010, MasterCard and Visa had similar rules, and in October of that year the U.S. Department of Justice and several states sued those companies and American Express. The suit alleged that these companies' NSRs violated the Sherman Act by excluding rivals and harming price competition.[4]

The underlying theory of harm was straightforward: If a credit or charge card network raises the fees that it charges merchants, economically rational merchants will have incentives to steer their customers away from that network and toward rival credit and charge card networks. If merchant steering is allowed, the prospect of losing transaction volume due to steering serves as a disincentive to raise prices. If merchant steering is prohibited, however, a network does not face the prospect of losing business in this way, and the incentive to raise prices is greater than it otherwise would be. In short, NSRs directly harm price competition among credit and charge card networks on an industry-wide basis making networks' firm-specific demand curves less elastic.

Prior to trial, MasterCard and Visa entered into consent decrees to settle the cases against them. American Express went to trial and argued both that its share was too low to allow it to possess market power and that the NSRs had pro-competitive benefits. The plaintiffs prevailed at trial, but American Express successfully appealed. Several of the state plaintiffs then appealed to the Supreme Court, which affirmed the judgment of the Court of Appeals and held that the plaintiffs had failed to prove that American Express's NSRs "have an anticompetitive effect."

There have long been major cases that have challenged the conduct of multi-sided platforms.[5] However, this was the first case to be litigated following the tremendous development of platform economics over the past two decades – much of which was triggered by competition authorities' interest in the payment-card industry in the 1990s. Although both appellate court opinions claimed to apply modern platform economics, both committed a fundamental error that pervades their thinking: They reasoned as if there is a single product with a single price that is purchased by a single decision maker when, in fact, there are two decision-makers on the two sides of the platform that face different prices and generally have differing interests. This way of

---

3 A credit-card user can run a balance on a revolving credit line, while a charge-card user traditionally had to pay his or her account in full after a set period, usually about one month. Most cards issued on American Express are charge cards. American Express also offers credit cards and has some programs that allow cardholders to have revolving credit on their charge cards.

4 Complaint for Equitable Relief for Violation of Section 1 of the Sherman Act, 15 U.S.C. § 1, *United States and Plaintiff States v. Am. Express Co., et al.* (hereinafter, *Complaint*), filed October 4, 2010.

5 Examples include *United States v. Florist's Telegraph Delivery Ass'n*, 1956 Trade Cas. (CCH) ¶ 68,367 (E.D. Mich.) (florist-by-wire association serving florist shops receiving orders and florist shops fulfilling orders), and *United States v. Microsoft Corp.*, 253 F.3d 34, 46 (D.C. Cir. 2001) (operating system serving applications developers and PC users).

thinking blinded the appellate courts to the fact that – by blocking steering that might otherwise induce customers to internalize the merchants' preferences with respect to card use – the NSRs might increase industry output while harming competition and reducing consumer welfare.

Unfortunately, by misapplying platform economics, *Ohio*'s precedents are obstacles to sound antitrust enforcement in large sectors of the modern economy.

## II. INDUSTRY BACKGROUND

Figure 1 provides a high-level schematic of how the general-purpose (as opposed to merchant-specific) credit and charge card industry functions. As is shown, a consumer obtains a credit or charge card from a card-issuing bank and can use this card to make purchases at merchants that accept that brand of card. To accept cards, a merchant must have a relationship with an "acquiring bank." Card issuers and acquirers interact with each other through a network, which provides core services that allow issuers and acquirers to verify that the consumer is entitled to use the card to make the desired purchase (authorization) and to ensure that payments flow to the appropriate parties (settlement).

**Figure 1: Industry Structure**

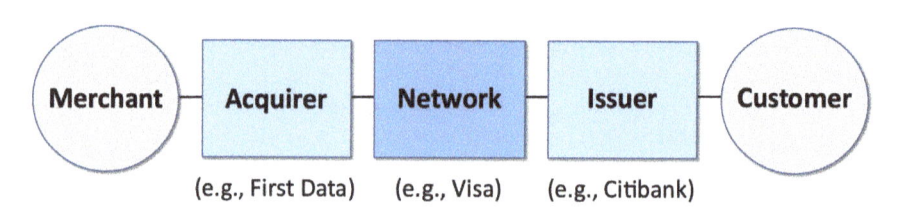

As is shown in Figure 2, American Express was (and is) vertically integrated into all three stages of the vertical chain and also made use of third-party acquirers and issuers.

**Figure 2: American Express Operates at Multiple Stages**

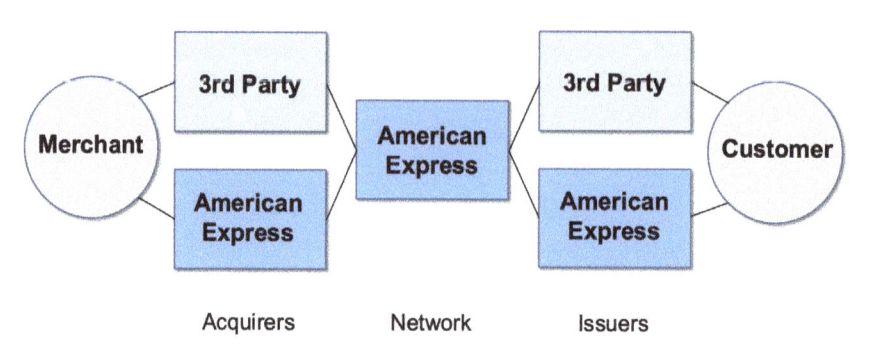

When a consumer makes a purchase at a merchant using a card, the merchant receives less than the purchase amount from the acquirer. The difference is the "merchant discount," which covers the acquirer's profits and costs – including any fees that are paid to the card network and to third-party card issuers. Even when the acquirer and card network are distinct firms, the network's fees are the principal determinant of the merchant discount, and it is a useful shorthand to describe the network as setting the merchant discount and treating merchants as the network's customers.

Merchants and their customers jointly consume payment services, and a transaction takes place only if the two parties utilize the same payment network. Critically, a merchant chooses which payment types and brands to accept, but its customers choose which payment method to use for any given transaction. The principal reason merchants accept credit and charge cards is consumer "insistence": Customers may shop elsewhere if they cannot use their preferred brand of card.

Credit and charge card networks are subject to cross-platform network effects: A consumer finds that holding a network's credit or charge card is more valuable when the number of merchants that accept that card is larger; and a merchant may find that accepting a network's cards is more valuable when the number of consumers who carry that card is greater.

## III. THE FEDERAL DISTRICT COURT OPINION

In summer 2014, a bench trial was held in the Eastern District of New York to determine whether American Express's NSRs violated Section 1 of the Sherman Act. The Court applied the rule of reason with the use of a three-step burden-shifting framework: (1) The plaintiffs had the initial burden to demonstrate that the NSRs had an "adverse effect on competition as a whole in the relevant market;"[6] (2) if the plaintiffs succeeded, the burden would shift to the defendants "to offer evidence of the pro-competitive effects of their agreement;"[7] and (3) if the defendants offered such evidence, then the burden would shift back to the plaintiffs to prove that any "'legitimate competitive benefits' proffered by Defendants could have been achieved through less restrictive means."[8]

### A. Market Definition

The plaintiffs argued that the merchant and issuer sides of credit and charge card platforms could appropriately be analyzed as two, closely interrelated network services markets. Specifically, the plaintiffs argued that the relevant market was for the provision of general-purpose card network services to merchants" in the United States. The rationale for considering the provision of network services to merchants and issuers separately was that "Questions of market power and harm are distinct for the two separate customer groups" and that benefits that

---

[6] *United States v. Am. Express Co.*, 88 F. Supp. 3d 143 (E.D.N.Y. 2015) (hereinafter *District Opinion*), p. 168, quoting *Geneva Pharmaceuticals Technology Corp. v. Barr Laboratories Inc.*, 386 F.3d 485, 506-507 (emphasis removed by the District Court).

[7] *District Opinion*, p. 169, quoting *Geneva Pharmaceuticals*, 386 F.3d 485, 507.

[8] *Id.*

are received by issuers "would not offset the anticompetitive harm imposed" on merchants.[9]

American Express argued that, because a credit or charge card transaction could take place only if both the cardholder and merchant agreed, the appropriate mode of analysis was instead to consider a single market for "transactions" that encompassed both sides simultaneously.

The District Court concluded that collapsing the two sides to a single market would obscure differences on the two sides[10] and that there were[11]

> …at least two separate, yet deeply interrelated, markets: a market for card issuance, in which Amex and Discover compete with thousands of Visa- and MasterCard-issuing banks; and a network services market, in which Visa, MasterCard, Amex, and Discover compete to sell acceptance services.

The District Court appeared to collapse network competition to serve issuers into its consideration of the market for card issuance.[12]

A second issue with regard to market definition was whether debit card network services were close enough substitutes to be included in the relevant market. The plaintiffs' economic expert applied the "hypothetical monopolist test" ("HMT") and used pricing and margin data to calculate a threshold volume of business that would have to be lost in order to render unprofitable a "small but significant non-transitory increase in price" ("SSNIP") above the competitive level. Notably, the SSNIP was calculated in terms of both the merchant discount *and* the two-sided price of network services: The sum of the prices that were charged by a network to users on both of its two sides. Specifically, the HMT showed that it would be profitable for a hypothetical credit and charge card monopolist to raise merchant discounts from current levels while holding the levels of rewards and other cardholder benefits constant. As the Court observed, one of American Express's economic experts testified that this was one way to account for the two-sided nature of the product at issue.[13] Moreover, it was shown that the current merchant discounts were at least as high as competitive levels.[14]

The plaintiffs offered several types of evidence that indicated that debit was not a sufficiently close substitute to merit inclusion in the relevant market. One was the lack of significant reaction by merchants, credit and charge card networks, and cardholders when federal regulation dramatically lowered debit merchant discounts and debit two-sided prices.

American Express argued that data showed that cardholders increasingly viewed debit and credit cards as substitutes. The plaintiffs' expert challenged this interpreta-

---

9  *Complaint*, ¶ 40.

10  *District Opinion*, p. 173.

11  *District Opinion*, p. 151.

12  *District Opinion*, n. 11.

13  *District Opinion*, p. 177.

14  *District Opinion*, p. 196.

tion because the data did not provide evidence that cardholders switched between credit and debit card use in response to price changes.

The District Court determined that debit cards were not in the relevant market. The Court found the plaintiffs' analysis of price changes persuasive and American Express's analysis of card-usage patterns unpersuasive. The Court also observed that: There were significant differences in credit and debit functionality; merchants did not consider credit and debit card acceptance services to be interchangeable; and the credit and charge card networks themselves did not perceive debit as a constraint on their merchant discount rates. Finally, the Court noted that American Express's experience in profitably raising prices through "Value Recapture."[15]

A third market-definition issue concerned the plaintiffs' argument that a separate market for the network services that were offered to merchants in the travel and entertainment ("T&E") sector should be defined. Because credit and charge card networks could identify different merchant types and could prevent arbitrage among them, the networks could – and did – charge different rates to different merchants. For example, an airline might pay a discount rate more than twice that paid by a supermarket. American Express argued that there were no data that reliably demonstrated that prices and margins were correlated across segments. The Court agreed that this was a reason to reject T&E as a distinct submarket.[16]

Using general purpose credit and charge volume in the United States as the metric, the Court found that American Express had a market share of 26.4 percent in 2013, while Visa, MasterCard, and Discover had shares of 45 percent, 23.3 percent, and 5.3 percent, respectively.[17]

## B. Market Power

As a matter of legal process, a plaintiff may establish that a defendant has market power indirectly – by demonstrating that the defendant has a high share in a relevant market – or directly: by showing that there has been actual harm to competition, which implies that the defendant had sufficient market power for its conduct to harm competition.

The District Court relied on both indirect and direct evidence to conclude that:[18]

> American Express possesses sufficient market power in the network services market to harm competition, as evidenced by its significant market share, the market's highly concentrated nature and high barriers to entry, and the insistence of Defendants' cardholder base on using their American Express cards.... The record demonstrates, in fact, that Defendants have the power to repeatedly and profitably raise their merchant prices without worrying about significant merchant attrition.

---

15 *District Opinion*, pp. 178-79. Value Recapture will be further discussed below.
16 *District Opinion*, pp. 186-87.
17 *District Opinion*, p. 188.
18 *District Opinion*, p. 151.

Recall that "insistence" refers to situations in which a consumer would take his or her business elsewhere if a merchant did not accept Amex cards. As Figure 3 illustrates, because merchant discounts were often small relative to the margins that merchants earned on incremental product sales, a merchant would find it unprofitable to refuse Amex cards even if American Express charged a much higher discount rate than its rivals (a one-percentage-point differential could represent a percentage differential of over 30 percent) and only five percent of Amex cardholders were insistent.

**Figure 3: The Effects of Cardholder Insistence**

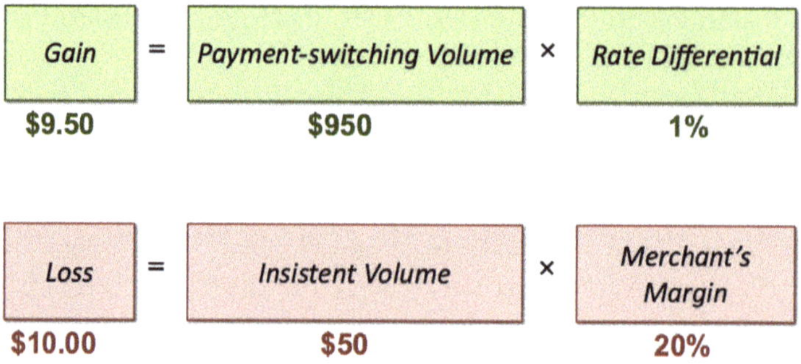

| Gain | = | Payment-switching Volume | × | Rate Differential |
|---|---|---|---|---|
| $9.50 | | $950 | | 1% |

| Loss | = | Insistent Volume | × | Merchant's Margin |
|---|---|---|---|---|
| $10.00 | | $50 | | 20% |

American Express argued that its market share was too low to allow it to possess market power. However, the arithmetic of insistence shows that even a payment network with a "small" overall market share could have substantial market power. Alternatively, one could argue that a payment network has a 100-percent share of its insistent cardholders.

American Express also asserted that insistence reflects superior quality as opposed to the possession of market power. However, a profitable monopoly always offers products that buyers find to be more attractive than alternatives – that's what allows the firm to maintain a higher price without losing all of its sales. Second, superior quality can be a source of market power. There is nothing paradoxical about this fact: Possession of market power due to the provision of a superior product is not, in itself, a violation of American antitrust laws; harming competition is.

The price increases that were cited by the Court in the quotation above provided direct evidence of American Express's market power. Under its Value Recapture pricing initiative, American Express recognized that it had unexploited market power and increased its fees to a large set of merchants. The plaintiffs presented evidence that merchant attrition was insignificant and that American Express found the fee increases to be profitable. The plaintiffs also noted that there was no evidence of accompanying changes in cardholder benefits or any indication that the fees were not already at competitive levels before being increased. The absence of merchant attrition meant that there were no significant cross-platform feedback effects: The increased merchant prices did not directly or indirectly create incentives for cardholders to substitute away from American Express.

Based on this evidence, the Court concluded that the Value Recapture price increases represented increases in the two-sided price starting from levels that were already at or above competitive levels, and were profitable to American Express.[19]

## C. Harm to Competition

The District Court observed that:[20]

> As a general matter, steering is both pro-competitive and ubiquitous. Merchants routinely attempt to influence customers' purchasing decisions, whether by placing a particular brand of cereal at eye level rather than on a bottom shelf, discounting last year's fashion inventory, or offering promotions such as "buy one, get one free."

The Court found that:[21]

> ...Plaintiffs have proven that American Express's [NSRs] have caused actual anticompetitive effects on interbrand competition. By preventing merchants from steering additional charge volume to their least expensive network, for example, the [NSRs] short-circuit the ordinary price-setting mechanism in the network services market by removing the competitive "reward" for networks offering merchants a lower price for acceptance services.

The Court also credited testimony by Discover executives that, by preventing merchants from steering customers to a lower-cost network, the NSRs made it unprofitable for a network to pursue a business strategy that relied on reducing merchant fees in order to generate greater card usage. These executives also testified that Discover would have simultaneously provided high levels of benefits to cardholders, and the record showed that Discover had a history of innovation with respect to cardholder benefits. The District Court found that NSRs had harmed innovation and led to higher merchant discounts and higher two-sided prices.[22]

## D. Pro-competitive Benefits

The burden fell on American Express to show that its conduct had pro-competitive effects. American Express claimed that the NSRs were needed to prevent merchants and/or competing credit and charge networks from free-riding on its investments in providing certain benefits to cardholders and merchants. For example, American Express argued that merchants would free-ride on its rewards program because consumers would be lured to Amex-accepting merchants by the prospect of earning rewards. This argument fails because a cardholder must actually use an Amex card to earn the rewards. Thus, the only way for a merchant to induce a cardholder

---

19 *District Opinion*, p. 196.
20 *District Opinion*, p. 150.
21 *District Opinion*, pp. 151-52.
22 *District Opinion*, pp. 208 and 217-18.

to use a different card is to offer the cardholder a more desirable alternative. In other words, the merchant competes for the rewards rather than free-rides on them.

American Express also claimed that accepting its cards served as a form of merchant credentialing or certification that would benefit merchants even if they steered customers to other card brands. But there were many alternative sources of consumer information, and industry surveys showed that MasterCard and Visa had more powerful credentialing effects. Last, in the case of benefits that American Express provided directly to merchants – *e.g.*, certain analytical services – American Express could explicitly charge merchants for those services.

The District Court recognized that, in principle, the prevention of free-riding could be a legitimate, pro-competitive justification for vertical restraints. But the Court found that, as a factual matter, American Express had not demonstrated that its free-riding claims were justified.[23]

American Express also claimed that its high-cardholder-benefits business model would not be viable absent the NSRs. American Express's CEO even testified that American Express would cease to exist without the NSRs, although other company witnesses were less extreme.[24] The plaintiffs countered that economically rational merchants take both any non-price benefits that they receive and their customers' preferences into account when making payment decisions and, hence, there was no reason to believe that the market would be biased against American Express if its business model actually created more joint value for merchants and cardholders. The District Court found that the defendants' "dire prediction of how business will be impacted by removal of the [NSRs]… is not supported by the evidentiary record."[25]

In closing its discussion of pro-competitive justifications, the District Court noted that it was unsettled as a legal matter within the jurisdiction of the Court of Appeals for the Second Circuit whether benefits on the cardholder side of the platforms could be balanced against harms on the merchant side given the Court's finding that they were two separate markets.[26] However, the Court went on to note that:[27]

> even if such cross-market balancing is appropriate under the rule of reason in a two-sided context, here Defendants have failed to establish that the NDPs are reasonably necessary to robust competition on the *cardholder* side of the [credit and charge card] platform, or that any such gains offset the harm done in the network services market. [Emphasis added.]

---

23 *District Opinion*, pp. 234-38.
24 *District Opinion*, p. 231.
25 *District Opinion*, p. 230.
26 *District Opinion*, p. 229.
27 *District Opinion*, pp. 229-30.

## IV. THE COURT OF APPEALS OPINION

American Express appealed, and three judges in the Court of Appeals for the Second Circuit were empaneled to review the District Court's findings of fact for clear error and its conclusions of law *de novo*.

The Court of Appeals opined that the District Court's reliance on a relevant market for network services to merchants – rather than one incorporating network services to both merchants and issuers/cardholders – was "fatal to its conclusion that Amex violated § 1"[28] because "[s]eparating the two markets here–analyzing the effect of Amex's vertical restraints on the market for [merchant] network services while ignoring their effect on the market for general purpose cards–ignores the two markets' interdependence."[29] However, although the District Court separated the two markets, it recognized that "these markets are inextricably linked with one another" and that one must "appreciate[e] and account[] for the effects that flow from such a relationship."[30]

The Court of Appeals rejected the District Court's application of the Hypothetical Monopolist Test because, *in theory*, even a low level of merchant attrition triggered by an increase in the merchant discount might lead to sufficient cardholder attrition to render a SSNIP unprofitable.[31] However, the District Court explicitly stated that the test was applied in a way that "allow[ed] for the possibility that the SSNIP might result in cross-platform feedback effects,"[32] and the District Court found that, *in fact*, American Express itself had concluded that any such feedback effects had been sufficiently low that it was profitable for the network to raise prices starting from what the District Court found were prices that were already at least as high as the competitive level. These findings implied that a hypothetical credit and charge card network monopolist would also find a SSNIP profitable.

The Court of Appeals observed that the plaintiffs had an "initial burden under the rule-of-reason analysis to show anticompetitive effects on the relevant market 'as a whole'"[33] and asserted that "[b]ecause the [NSRs] affect competition for cardholders as well as merchants, the Plaintiffs' initial burden was to show that the [NSRs] made all Amex consumers on both sides of the platform… worse off overall."[34]

---

28 *United States v. Am. Express Co.*, 838 F.3d 179, 196 (2d Cir. 2016) (hereinafter, *Circuit Opinion*).

29 *Circuit Opinion*, p. 198. See also p. 200.

30 *District Opinion*, p. 173.

31 *Circuit Opinion*, pp. 199-200.

32 *District Opinion*, p. 177.

33 *Circuit Opinion*, pp. 204-05, citing *K.M.B. Warehouse v. Walker Mfg. Co.*, 61 F.3d 123, 127 (1995).

34 *Circuit Opinion*, p. 204. *See also, id.*, pp. 204-05.

However, the precedent on which the Court of Appeals relied stated that:[35]

> To prevail on a § 1 claim, a plaintiff must also show more than just an adverse effect on competition among different sellers of the same product ("intrabrand" competition)... Because the focus of our inquiry is the relevant market as a whole, restriction of intrabrand competition must be balanced against any increases in interbrand competition. [Citations omitted.]

The Court of Appeals concluded that user welfare on both sides of the platform had to be considered because there was a single market that encompassed both sides but nothing in the cited case states how broadly the relevant market must be defined.

The Court of Appeals opined that harm to competition could be shown only by establishing that the conduct reduced output or quality, or elevated prices above the competitive level. It further asserted that separating the merchant- and cardholder-side "markets allows legitimate competitive activities in the market for general purposes to be penalized no matter how output-expanding such activities may be."[36]

The Court of Appeals' criticism might be apt if it were applied to a one-sided analysis that found that prices were higher as a result of the NSRs and used that fact to infer that output was less than it otherwise would have been; in theory, a higher price that is charged to the merchant side of a platform might correspond to an increase in output (whether measured on either side) and might also increase cardholder welfare by more than it decreased merchant welfare.

Indeed, the Court of Appeals accused the District Court of committing such an error:[37]

[t]he District Court erred in concluding that "increases in *merchant* pricing are properly viewed as changes to the net price charged across Amex's integrated platform," *Am. Express Co.*, 88 F. Supp. 3d at 196 (emphasis added), because merchant pricing is only one half of the pertinent equation.

However, the Court of Appeals' selective quotation mischaracterizes the District Court's findings. In fact, the District Court did consider both sides of the equation and explained that:[38]

> *Because these Value Recapture initiatives were not paired with offsetting adjustments on the cardholder side of the platform*, the resulting increases in merchant pricing are properly viewed as changes to the net price charged across Amex's integrated platform. [Emphasis added.]

Elsewhere, the Court of Appeals dismissed the District Court's findings regarding prices by asserting that it was impossible to determine that prices were above competitive levels without having reliable margin data, which the District Court found to

---

35 The *Circuit Opinion*, p. 195, cited *K.M.B.* p. 127. The quotation in the text is from *K.M.B.*, pp. 127-28.
36 *Circuit Opinion*, p. 198.
37 *Circuit Opinion*, p. 202.
38 *District Opinion*, p. 196.

be lacking.[39] But, as discussed above, the District Court determined that prices were elevated above competitive levels without having to determine the precise underlying margins.

Returning to industry output, the Court of Appeals noted industry output had risen over the decades that American Express's – and for much of the time Master-Card's and Visa's – no-steering policies were in place.[40] At best, a discussion of industry output trends over a period during which the policies were always in effect is irrelevant and a diversion. At worst, the Appeals Court's consideration of industry output trends could be interpreted as indicating that the Court believed that the trends could establish whether the NSRs harm competition – which trends alone cannot.

Under an industry-output standard, what matters is whether output grew faster or slower than it would have in the absence of the NSRs. In this regard, recall that the District Court made the factual finding that credit networks' *two-sided* prices were higher than they otherwise would have been, which under the Court of Appeal's single-product view of the world implies that output was lower than it otherwise would have been. The Court of Appeals ignored this implication.

The Court of Appeals also suspended its insistence that only the two-sided price was relevant and concluded that – because American Express had to charge low quality-adjusted prices to cardholders to induce them to be insistent – insistence could not be a source of market power.[41] This conclusion was invalid because a price structure with low prices on one side of the platform did not imply that the two-sided price was low. The Court of Appeals effectively ignored the merchant side of the market and the fact that the NSRs prevented merchants from coordinating with their customers to utilize the credit card brand that maximized their joint benefits – with the consequence that American Express might well be able to increase cardholder insistence by enough with a $1 increase in rewards to be able to profitably raise the price to merchants by, say, $2. In fact, the District Court found that American Express did not pass 100 percent of increased merchant fees on to cardholders.

In concluding that American Express lacked market power, the Court of Appeals also adopted American Express's argument that this was implied by the fact that many small merchants did not accept Amex cards.[42] Among other problems, this argument ignored the fact that a hallmark of a "textbook" monopoly is that it restricts output.

Ultimately, the Court of Appeals found the NSRs to be pro-competitive. "The [NSRs] protect [American Express's rewards] program and … prestige."[43] The Court of Appeals cited no evidence that the NSRs were necessary to prevent free-riding, and it ignored the District Court's findings of fact with regard to the lack of pro-competitive benefits. The Court appears to have confused protecting a competitor with protecting competition.

---

39 *Circuit Opinion*, p. 205, citing *District Opinion*, n. 30.
40 *Circuit Opinion*, p. 206.
41 *Circuit Opinion*, pp. 202-03.
42 *Circuit Opinion*, p. 203.
43 *Circuit Opinion*, p. 204.

## V. THE SUPREME COURT OPINION

Eleven of the plaintiff states filed a petition for certiorari (review) in the Supreme Court. Although the Department of Justice argued against it, the Court granted certiorari. The issue in the case was whether the plaintiffs had carried their burden under the first step in the rule of reason of proving that the NSRs had "an anticompetitive effect."[44] The majority of justices found that the plaintiffs had not done so, and the Court affirmed the judgment of the Court of Appeals.[45]

### A. Market Definition

Notwithstanding economists' and the courts' long recognition that market definition is not always necessary to demonstrate harm to competition, the Supreme Court ruled that: (a) A relevant market must be defined when assessing vertical restraints; and (b) that market must be a single, two-sided one when assessing the conduct of a "transaction platform."

The Supreme Court attempted to rationalize the first ruling by asserting that "[v]ertical restraints often pose no risk to competition unless the entity imposing them has market power, which cannot be evaluated unless the Court first defines the relevant market."[46] As a matter of economics, the claim that one cannot evaluate whether a firm possesses market power without defining a relevant market is false.[47]

Moreover, the Court's implicit distinction between horizontal and vertical restraints provided little justification for ignoring direct evidence that the specific vertical restraints at issue in litigation harmed competition. First, the effects of both horizontal and vertical restraints can depend on the degree of market power that is possessed by the firm that is engaged in the conduct. Second, conditional on the fact that the conduct is being challenged in litigation, it is not evident that restraints before a court are less likely to be harmful when they are vertical rather than horizontal. Third, even if one believed that vertical restraints were less likely to harm competition than horizontal restraints, that would not imply that the failure to produce *indirect* evidence of market power that relies on market definition should trump *direct* evidence of harm such as that cited in the District Court's opinion.

The Supreme Court found that a platform that facilitates transactions between users on its different sides must be assessed within the context of a single, two-sided relevant market based on several claims: First, "[b]ecause they cannot make a sale unless both sides of the platform simultaneously agree to use their services, two-sided

---

44 Because plaintiff states were the appellants, the case at the Supreme Court level became identified as *Ohio v. Am. Express Co.*, 138 S. Ct. 2274 (2018) (hereinafter *U.S. Opinion*).

45 Justice Breyer wrote a scathing dissent that raised several of the points that will be discussed below.

46 *U.S. Opinion*, n. 7, citation omitted.

47 Breshnahan (1989) surveys econometric techniques for estimating market power and none relies on market definition. *See also* Baker (2007, p. 131). Moreover, direct evidence of harm to competition implies that the firm had sufficient market power for its conduct to harm competition.

transaction platforms exhibit more pronounced indirect network effects and interconnected pricing and demand."[48] Second, transaction platforms are "better understood as 'suppl[ying] only one product'—transactions."[49] Third, "[e]valuating both sides of a two-sided transaction platform is also necessary to accurately assess competition," both because "[o]nly other two-sided platforms can compete with a two-sided platform for transactions"[50] and because a platform can facilitate a transaction between users on two different sides of the marketplace only if they both participate on that platform.[51]

The presence of network effects and the need to consider both sides to understand competition are reasons to look at both sides – but this can be done without defining a single, two-sided market. Indeed, that was the District Court's approach.

If correct, the claim that transaction platforms compete only with other transaction platforms might provide a partial rationale for utilizing a single, two-sided relevant market rather than two closely related relevant markets. But that claim is false. As Wright & Yun (2019) have observed, many platforms – including transaction platforms – face competitive alternatives that are not present on both sides. For example, in addition to other ride-sharing platforms, a ride-sharing platform might compete with various modes of transportation (*e.g.*, taxis, public transportation, private automobiles, and walking) on the passenger side of the platform and other occupations (*e.g.*, driving for other ride-sharing platforms, driving for delivery services, and certain classes of non-driving jobs) on the driver side.[52]

Not only did the Supreme Court – and Court of Appeals – make unsound arguments in favor of the single-market approach, the courts failed to recognize strong arguments against this approach.[53]

Relevant markets frequently also serve as the basis for calculating market shares, which are used as proxies for market power. When only a single, two-sided market is defined, a transaction platform will have a single market share. However, there are often significant differences between the competitive conditions on the two sides of a

---

48  *U.S. Opinion*, p. 2286.

49  138 S. Ct. 2274 at 2286 quoting Klein et al. (2006, p. 580). It is not clear that American Express sells "transactions" to merchants, rather than "acceptance services." The key distinction is that, rather than purchasing individual card transactions from American Express, a merchant purchases the right (and the obligation) to hold itself out to the public as accepting all American Express transactions that are proposed by cardholders.

50  *U.S. Opinion*, p. 2287, citing Filistrucchi et al. (2014, p. 301).

51  *U.S. Opinion*, p. 2287.

52  This error in *Ohio* has already led at least one court to rely on an incorrect view of competition: When the proposed merger of Sabre and Farelogix was challenged, the trial court found – and all parties agreed – that Sabre and Farelogix were competitors with one another. Nevertheless, the court held that, "as a matter of antitrust law," Sabre and Farelogix were *not* competitors because the former was a two-sided platform facilitating transactions between airlines and travel agencies, but the latter sold only to airlines and thus was not a two-sided platform. (*United States v. Sabre Corp.*, C.A. No. 19-1548-LPS, 2020 WL 1855433, at *32 (D. Del., April 7, 2020).) *See* the chapter in this volume on this case by Doyle et al.

53  For a more complete discussion, *see* Franck & Peitz (2019) and Katz & Sallet (2018).

transaction platform. As was just noted, the competitors may be different. Differences in competitive conditions on the two sides can also arise from differences in product differentiation, vertical integration, user sophistication, and market institutions (*e.g.*, a cardholder makes choices transaction-by-transaction, while a merchant must either accept all of a network's transactions or none).

Differences in the extent of user multihoming on the two sides can also lead to differences in competitive conditions. One of the foundational articles on platform economics observed that, for transaction-platform industries in which users multi-home on one side and single-home on the other,[54] it does not make sense to speak of the competitiveness of "the market." There are two markets: the market for single-homing agents which is, to a greater or lesser extent, competitive, and a market for multi-homing agents where each platform holds a local monopoly.

Even if the competitors have been correctly identified, a single market share cannot possibly capture the differences in competitive conditions on the two sides, which reduces the reliability of market definition and concentration analysis.

Another way to see the problematic nature of the Supreme Court's approach is that relevant markets are defined as collections of products that are sufficiently close substitutes for one another; and, as the dissenting opinion in *Ohio* observed, the services that are offered by credit and charge card networks to merchants are not substitutes for the services that are offered to cardholders.[55] Some commentators rejected this criticism by analogizing merchant network services and cardholder network services to left and right shoes: Shoes are perfect complements, not substitutes, and are sensibly considered to be a single product.

However, this analogy is inapt, and the reason why illustrates the fundamental error that the appellate courts committed: A shoe buyer cares about only the *total* price that is paid for the pair. By contrast, given that a credit card transaction takes place, the merchant cares about only the merchant discount, while the consumer cares about only the associated rewards; neither party is interested in the two-sided (total) price. This is precisely why two-sided platforms should not be viewed as offering a single product at a single, two-sided price.[56]

## B. Assessing Harm to Competition

The Supreme Court implicitly adopted a standard that a vertical restraint that weakens competition is not illegal unless it eliminates competition entirely. Specifically, the Court observed that the "antisteering provisions do not prevent Visa, MasterCard, or Discover from competing against Amex by offering lower merchant fees

---

54 Armstrong (2006, p. 680).

55 *Ohio v. Am. Express Co.*, 138 S. Ct., p. 2296 (Breyer, J., dissenting).

56 The Supreme Court quoted Filistrucchi et al.'s (2014, p. 297) observation that "a two-sided market [is] different from markets for complementary products" for this reason. But rather than understanding that this point undermined the Court's market definition, the Court took it to mean that treating the services offered to the two sides of credit and charge card platforms as a single product was appropriate because "merchant services and cardholder services are not complements." (*U.S. Opinion*, n. 8.).

or promoting their broader merchant acceptance."[57] Although correct, this observation does not imply that competition was unharmed. A key finding of the District Court was that American Express's NSRs harmed competition by diminishing the effectiveness of rival networks' potential reductions of merchant fees or improvements in the services that they might offer to merchants. Although, even in the presence of the NSRs, rival networks could attempt to compete in the ways that the Supreme Court identified, the networks' incentives to do so and the strength of the resulting competitive pressures were both severely attenuated.

In addition to applying a standard that failed to protect competition, the Supreme Court mischaracterized the District Court's factual findings with respect to competition. Specifically, the Supreme Court opinion claimed that:[58]

> fierce competition between networks has constrained Amex's ability to raise these fees and has, at times, forced Amex to lower them. For instance, when Amex raised its merchant prices between 2005 and 2010 [through Value Recapture], some merchants chose to leave its network. 88 F. Supp. 3d, at 197. And when its remaining merchants complained, Amex stopped raising its merchant prices. *Id.*, at 198.

But, in fact, the District Court explicitly found to the contrary in the passage that was cited above:[59]

> Value Recapture was ultimately ended in 2010 by American Express due to merchant dissatisfaction with the price increases given the economic climate at the time and *not*, it would appear, *due to any competitive pressures imposed by Amex's competitors* in the GPCC network services market. [Emphasis added; citations omitted.]

As did the Court of Appeals, the Supreme Court held that harm to competition could be inferred based on prices if and only if the plaintiffs proved that the defendants' conduct elevated the platform's two-sided price above the competitive level.[60]

The Supreme Court opinion ignored the District Court's factual finding that this condition was satisfied and instead focused on the evidence that was offered by the plaintiffs to show that American Express had increased its transaction prices over time. The Supreme Court dismissed this evidence on the grounds that it was necessary to show that output had been restricted[61] and that "rising prices are equally consistent with growing product demand" absent separate evidence that output is falling.[62] However, the relevant measures are not price and output time trends; the

---

57 *U.S. Opinion*, p. 2290.

58 *U.S. Opinion*, p. 2289.

59 *District Opinion*, p. 198.

60 *U.S. Opinion*, p. 2288.

61 *U.S. Opinion*, p. 2288.

62 *U.S. Opinion*, pp. 2288-89, and *Circuit Opinion*, pp. 31-32, both citing *Brooke Grp. Ltd. v. Brown & Williamson Tobacco Corp.*, 509 U.S. 209, 237 (1993).

relevant measures are how prices and output compare to what they would have been absent the conduct. Under the Supreme Court's (incorrect) view that the two-sided price is a sufficient statistic for market outcomes, the District Court's finding that the NSRs allowed American Express profitably to raise its two-side prices above competitive levels would imply a lower level of output than otherwise, regardless of whether demand was shifting over time.

Although both appellate courts faulted the District Court for not considering the alleged benefits of the NSRs that accrued to cardholders, neither appellate court engaged with the District Court's findings that indicated that the NSRs harmed cardholders as well as merchants: First, by making rival networks' entry more difficult, the NSRs harmed network competition – with adverse consequences for both sides of the industry. Second, the NSRs weakened competition to serve cardholders because there was consequently no need for American Express to try to counter merchant steering. Indeed, an American Express executive testified that, absent the NSRs, American Express might invest *more* in cardholder rewards.[63]

Even if the fees that were charged to cardholders fell while the merchant discount and the two-sided net price rose, there were strong reasons to expect platform users to be harmed overall: They were collectively paying more for transactions than they otherwise would, and the NSRs prevented merchant-cardholder coordination that might otherwise have allowed the two categories of users to come closer to utilizing the brands of cards that maximized joint user benefits.

The Supreme Court followed the Court of Appeals in focusing on changes in output over time as an indicator of competitive effects even though it is invalid.[64] Even holding aside the courts' incorrect focus on time trends rather than the other-things-being-equal differences due to the conduct at issue, the Court's output test is seriously flawed when applied to transaction platforms: In a platform market, the interests of the users on the two sides of the platform typically are not fully aligned, and a platform may be able to exploit this fact to increase its profits in ways that increase output but harm competition and the platform's users.[65]

For example, the NSRs create incentives for credit and charge card networks to adopt price structures that entail charging higher prices to merchants and lower prices to cardholders than would otherwise be the case. Because cardholders make the marginal decisions as to how much to use their credit and charge cards, this change in the price structure could increase the use of credit and charge cards even if networks' two-sided prices increase as well. Moreover, the conduct could increase output relative to the hypothetical in which the conduct does not occur while simultaneously reducing merchants' and cardholders' joint economic welfare.[66]

---

63 *District Opinion*, p. 238.

64 *U.S. Opinion*, p. 2289. The Court also credited American Express's business model for these positive trends but cited no evidence in support of this empirical claim. *Id.*, p. 2290.

65 Edelman & Wright (2015) and Schwartz & Vincent (2006) demonstrate that restraints such as the NSRs can lead to excessive use of a platform.

66 For additional discussion of this point and an example that illustrates it, *see* Katz (2019).

## C. Pro-competitive Benefits

Although the Supreme Court found that the plaintiffs had failed to meet their initial burden, the Court also addressed pro-competitive benefits:[67]

> [The NSRs] actually stem negative externalities in the credit-card market and promote interbrand competition. When merchants steer cardholders away from Amex at the point of sale, it undermines the cardholder's expectation of "welcome acceptance"—the promise of a frictionless transaction. 88 F. Supp. 3d, at 156. A lack of welcome acceptance at one merchant makes a cardholder less likely to use Amex at all other merchants. This externality endangers the viability of the entire Amex network.

The cited portion of the District Court's opinion summarizes a claim that was made by American Express. However, the District Court found that the record did not support American Express's claim; the District Court noted that the defendants had "presented no expert testimony, financial analysis, or other direct evidence establishing that without its [NSRs] it will, in fact, be unable to adapt its business to a more competitive market and will instead cease to be an effective competitor...."[68] The Supreme Court neither addressed the District Court's findings nor cited evidence to support its contrary conclusions.

## VI. A QUESTION OF BALANCE

Although neither appellate court cited it, one reason they may have insisted on utilizing a single, two-sided market is to allow them to balance the effects on merchant and cardholder welfare against one another without having to overturn precedent; some courts interpret the law as disallowing cross-market welfare balancing.[69]

As a matter of sound analysis, however, the issues of market definition and the scope of consumer-welfare balancing are distinct and separable. For example, Crane (2015) concludes that concern with complexity is the strongest justification for avoiding cross-market balancing when assessing mergers. Defining two markets to be one does nothing to reduce the complexity of balancing effects across them.[70]

Moreover, the Supreme Court's insistence on collapsing the analysis of pricing to the consideration of a single, two-sided price mechanistically imposes a specific form of balancing: Any change in the price that is charged to users on one side of the market is balanced one-for-one against changes in the price that is charged to users on the other side – regardless of the nature of the conduct. This approach has two fundamental deficiencies.

First, it is only loosely tethered to consumer welfare. Katz (2019) demonstrates that, due to the presence of network effects and the fact that merchants do not make

---

67 *U.S. Opinion*, 2289, citation omitted.

68 *District Opinion*, p. 231.

69 *See* Werden (2017).

70 Salop et al. (2022) propose defining separate markets on the two sides of a platform while allowing certain forms of balancing.

marginal choices with respect to individual transactions – instead a merchant must choose either to accept all transactions branded on a given network or reject all such transactions – a pair of one-sided price changes that leave the two-sided price unchanged could have significant effects on the total consumer surplus enjoyed by merchants and cardholders. Moreover, conduct can simultaneously reduce the two-sided price *and* aggregate consumer welfare.

Second, the approach taken in *Ohio* balances gains and losses without assessing how those gains and losses are generated. Suppose, for example, that two ride-sharing platforms collude to suppress the payments that are made to drivers and, as a result of the lower payments, charge lower prices to riders. Under *Ohio*'s approach to balancing, showing that the ride-sharing platforms had successfully suppressed payments to drivers would be insufficient to meet even the plaintiff's initial burden of showing harm to competition: The plaintiff would also need to account for any resulting reduction in the price of rides, which might be difficult in practice. This view is manifestly at odds with the *per se* treatment of price fixing. In addition, some have argued that a core rationale for antitrust enforcement is that competitive markets produce fair outcomes.[71] If so, then it would be unfair to allow conduct that harms the competitive process even if some consumers gain more than other consumers lose.

Now, suppose that, by merging, two ride-sharing platforms were able to allocate drivers more efficiently and thus reduce the demand for – and the per-ride payments to – drivers. Under the Supreme Court's whole-market view, the reduction in the payments to drivers should be weighed against any reduction in the prices that are charged to riders. This implies that – holding the price that is charged to riders constant – merger efficiencies with respect to drivers would count as merger *harms*.

In short, the *Ohio* approach to balancing – like much of the opinion – is fundamentally unsound.

# REFERENCES

Armstrong, Mark (2006). "Competition in two-sided markets," *RAND Journal of Economics*, 37(3): 668–691.

Baker, Jonathan B. (2007). "Market definition: An analytical overview." *Antitrust Law Journal*, 74(1): 129 -173.

Bresnahan, Timothy F. (1989). "Empirical studies of industries with market power" in *The Handbook of Industrial Organization*, 2, R. Schmalensee and R.D. Willig (eds.), Amsterdam: Elsevier (1989): 1011-1057.

Crane, Daniel A. (2015). "Balancing Effects Across Markets," *Antitrust Law Journal*, 80(2): 397–412.

Edelman, Benjamin & Julian Wright (2015). "Price Coherence and Excessive Intermediation," *Quarterly Journal of Economics*, 130(3): 1283-1328.

---

71 *See* Scherer (1990) for an interesting history of economists' early views regarding fairness as a rationale for antitrust enforcement.

Filistrucchi, Lapo, Damien Geradin, Eric van Damme & Pauline Affeldt (2014). "Market Definition in Two-Sided Markets: Theory and Practice," *Journal of Competition Law & Economics*, 10(2): 293-339.

Franck, Jens-Uwe & Martin Peitz (2019). *Market Definition and Market Power in the Platform Economy*, report, Center on Regulation in Europe.

Katz, Michael L. (2019). "Platform economics and antitrust enforcement: A little knowledge is a dangerous thing," *Journal of Economics & Management Strategy*, 28(1): 138-152.

Katz, Michael L. & A. Douglas Melamed (2020). "Competition Law as Common Law: American Express and the Evolution of Antitrust," *University of Pennsylvania Law Review*, 168(7): 2061-2106.

Katz, Michael L. & Jonathan Sallet (2018). "Multisided Platforms and Antitrust Enforcement, *Yale Law Journal*, 127(7): 2142-2175.

Klein, Benjamin, Andres V. Lerner, Kevin M. Murphy & Lacey L. Plache (2006). "Competition in two-sided markets: The antitrust economics of payment card interchange fees," *Antitrust Law Journal*, 73(3): 571–626.

Salop, Steven C., Daniel Francis, Lauren Sillman & Michaela Spero Amadeus (2022). "Rebuilding Platform Antitrust: Moving on from Ohio v. American Express," unpublished manuscript, Georgetown University Law Center, *available at* https://scholarship.law.georgetown.edu/facpub/2414/, site accessed July 22, 2022.

Scherer, Frederic M. (1990). "Efficiency, fairness, and the early contributions of economists to the antitrust debate," *Washburn Law Journal*, 29(2): 243-255.

Schwartz, Marius & Daniel R. Vincent, D. (2006). "The no surcharge rule and card user rebates: Vertical control by a payment network," *Review of Network Economics*, 5(1): 72–102.

Werden, Gregory J. (2017). "Cross-market Balancing of Competitive Effects: What Is the Law, and What Should It Be," *Journal of Corporate Law,* 43(1): 119-41.

Wright, Joshua D. & John M. Yun (2019). "Ohio v. American Express: Implications for Non-Transaction Multisided Platforms," *CPI Antitrust Chronicle*, June.

**CHAPTER 11**

# Excessive Pricing as an Antitrust Harm: Three UK Cases in Generic Pharmaceuticals

*By Julie Bon & Mike Walker*[1]

## I. INTRODUCTION

Historically there have been few excessive pricing cases in Europe and even fewer that are pure excessive pricing cases with no exclusionary behavior attached. This has changed recently with a number of excessive pricing cases in pharmaceuticals in the UK. This is not a purely UK phenomenon, as there have also been excessive pricing cases in Italy and at the European Commission level (and in other jurisdictions, such as South Africa).[2]

In this chapter we outline the reasons why there have been relatively few cases historically and acknowledge the strength of these arguments, but then explain the compelling logic of the three recent UK cases. We then discuss some of the interesting areas of economic dispute that have arisen.

This chapter covers three UK cases that were investigated by the Competition and Markets Authority ("CMA"): *Phenytoin*,[3] *Liothyronine*,[4] and *Hydrocortisone*.[5] These three excessive pricing cases involved generic pharmaceuticals that had long been off-patent, in small niche markets with high barriers to entry, such that the incumbent supplier of the drug could enjoy a monopoly position for a long period before attracting entry. They also have important differences: *Phenytoin* is a pure excessive pricing case (no exclusionary behavior) involving no genuinely competitive entry; prices have been reduced only by CMA intervention. *Liothyronine* is also a pure excessive pricing

---

[1] Both authors participated in the CMA's investigations and decisions in these cases. The views in this paper are ours and do not necessarily mirror those of the CMA.

[2] *See* AGCM decision A480 "Price increase of Aspen's drugs (measure No. 26185)" of October 14, 2016; European Commission decision in case AT.40394 – Aspen (February 10, 2021); and Competition Tribunal (RSA) case CR003Apr20 "Babelegi Workwear" of June 1, 2020.

[3] CMA decision CE/9742-13 (December 7, 2016) "Unfair pricing in respect of the supply of phenytoin sodium capsules in the UK."

[4] CMA decision 50395 (July 29, 2021) "Excessive and unfair pricing with respect to the supply of liothyronine tablets in the UK."

[5] CMA decision 50277 (July 15, 2021) "Hydrocortisone tablets Excessive and unfair pricing and Anti-competitive agreements."

case, but here prices have been reduced somewhat from their peak by entry. However, prices remain significantly above costs. *Hydrocortisone* is not a pure excessive pricing case: it also involves exclusionary behavior. However, the alleged exclusionary behavior took place after prices had increased significantly, and the exclusion took place in order to protect those higher prices. It is also the only one of the three cases in which entry has pushed prices down to a range that is close to their original level.[6]

## II. THE LIMITED ECONOMICS LITERATURE ON EXCESSIVE PRICING

Economics 101 implies that excessive pricing is the purest antitrust offense because it is a pure exercise of market power by a firm. First-year economics students are taught that monopolies – as compared with an otherwise similar competitive industry – are bad because they: (i) sell a smaller amount of output; (ii) maintain higher prices; (iii) benefit the owners to the detriment of consumers; and (iv) create deadweight loss to society. So why have competition authorities traditionally shied away from such cases?

There are three broad reasons. The first is a belief that excessive prices tend to be self-correcting. Prices that are substantially above costs will encourage entry in the absence of barriers to entry. The second is that the alternative remedy is one that competition authorities do not like: price regulation. Competition authorities worry that unless there is a way in which they can remove the firm's market power by directly encouraging competition (*e.g.*, by removing barriers to entry) the authorities will have to regulate prices directly. Competition authorities do not like this because it is difficult and is not their core competence. While it is the core expertise of industry-specific regulators, even they find it very difficult.

The third is a concern that competition authority intervention may well make the situation worse. There are typically two dimensions to this argument. One, that capping prices would make entry less likely and so support long-term monopoly when an alternative approach would have led to entry and to long-term competition. Two, that a competition authority would incorrectly identify market power. For instance, it might decide that prices above marginal costs are a sign of market power when in reality they are a return to risky investment that is needed to encourage innovation. Any intervention that improves static efficiency at the cost of damaging dynamic efficiency is likely to be bad for consumer welfare in the long run.

The economics literature on excess pricing within a competition policy context is sparse. What there is, however, is largely in agreement with the above three reasons for avoiding excessive pricing cases.[7] There is general agreement that excessive pricing cases should be initiated only in the presence of very high barriers to entry. If barriers to entry are low enough so that high prices attract new entry that then pushes prices back down within a reasonable period, then excessive pricing cases should be avoided.

---

6 As of the time of writing (September 2022), *Liothyronine* and *Hydrocortisone* are under appeal.

7 *See, inter alia*: De Streel, A. & Motta, M. (2007); Fletcher, A. & Jardine, A. (2008); Evans, D. & Padilla, J. (2004); Jenny, F. (2018); Röller, L. (2008).

There is also general agreement that competition authorities should not intervene in dynamic markets, as the intervention risks undermining investment incentives and damaging long run innovation. Evans & Padilla (2004), in a paper that was funded by Microsoft, argue that this concern is enough to mean that there should be no enforcement against excessive prices. They argue that there is no benchmark for an excessive price that is both objective and efficient (in the sense of not causing consumer harm over the long run). They argue that the cost of Type I errors (false positives) will be high as they will disincentivize innovation, while the cost of Type II errors (false negatives) will be low: The static harm from excessive prices will never outweigh the dynamic harm from intervention.

There is general agreement that using the comparison of prices to costs in finding an excessive price is difficult. On the cost side, these difficulties relate to: (i) the relevance of a price-marginal cost comparison in markets with high sunk costs (*e.g.*, pharmaceuticals, tech); (ii) concerns with respect to the allocation of shared and common costs to particular products; (iii) concerns as to what constitutes a reasonable rate of return; and (iv) concerns with respect to the use of the price-cost relationship at a single point in time as a proxy for the price-cost relationship over the lifetime of the product. The difficulties on the demand side include concerns with respect to price structures in multi-sided markets (*e.g.*, tech markets).

Various authors (*e.g.*, Jenny, 2018; Motta & de Streel, 2007; Röller, 2008) argue that competition authorities should avoid becoming price regulators and so should avoid imposing price-regulation remedies. There is universal agreement that remedies that mitigate the market power of the dominant firm are much to be preferred over remedies that merely seek to mitigate the effect of the market power. Röller, for instance, argues that structural remedies such as removing relevant entry barriers or opening markets should be preferred to behavioral remedies such as price regulation.

Many of the authors argue that excessive pricing cases should be brought only against super-dominant firms – essentially, genuine monopolists – that have not earned that position of super-dominance through successful competition on the merits. The authors have in mind in particular previously state-owned entities that have been gifted their market power through privatization.

Based on the arguments above, Motta & de Streel (2007) argue that excessive pricing cases should be pursued only in exceptional circumstances. They provide four conditions that they argue are necessary for an excessive pricing case:

1. There must be high and persistent barriers to entry that protect a monopoly (or near-monopoly) market position;
2. This monopoly position should be a result of exclusive or special rights (*e.g.*, a former regulated monopoly provider), meaning the monopolist did not earn its monopoly position through competitive success;
3. There must be no way to remove the barriers to entry; if the barriers can be removed within a reasonable time frame, that would be the first best solution; and
4. There must be no sector-specific regulator that is able to impose regulated prices.

The three cases that we discuss below all fall within these conditions for an excessive pricing case.

## III. EXCESSIVE PRICING AS AN ABUSE

Some jurisdictions do not prohibit exploitative abuses as such – notably the U.S., where excessive pricing is not recognized as a possible antitrust infringement.[8] In the EU, Article 102 (a) of the Treaty for the Functioning of the European Union ("TFEU") prohibits conduct by a dominant company, which consists in "directly or indirectly imposing unfair purchase or selling prices or other unfair trading conditions." A price which is unfairly high can therefore constitute an abuse of dominance under EU law. Given that most EU Member States' competition laws are borrowed from the TFEU, these jurisdictions apply similar regimes to the European Union regarding exploitative excessive prices. This includes the UK, where excessive pricing may constitute an abuse of a dominant position under Chapter II of the Competition Act.

Setting out the full legal tests to prove an excessive pricing case is beyond the scope of this chapter, and indeed the competency of its authors. However, in broad terms, in order to establish that a firm has infringed UK or EU competition law through excessive pricing, the competition authority needs to establish:

- that the firm in question has a dominant position in the relevant market in which it operates;
- that the prices charged are excessive relative to an appropriate competitive benchmark – usually, the costs of the dominant firm; and
- that such pricing is unfair in itself or compared to competing products.

It is worth noting that the latter condition – establishing that a price is unfair in itself – usually will imply considering whether demand side conditions might warrant prices in excess of costs and assessing the "economic value" of the product, a concept which we come back to later in this chapter.

More generally, the interpretation of these conditions can give rise to much debate. In particular, in all three cases we present, there were extensive debates with the Parties around the choice of a competitive benchmark against which to assess whether the prices were excessive, as we set out later in this chapter.

## IV. BASIC FACTS OF THE CASES

In this section, we first briefly explain the standard lifecycle of drugs, as this is important background to understand the pricing of drugs and the role of competition in the supply of off-patent drugs. We then present the basic facts of each of the three

---

[8] Excessive prices are not pursued as a competition offense under U.S. federal law because the focus when scrutinizing unilateral conduct in the U.S. is on obtaining a monopoly by anti-competitive means (*monopolization*), not on the exploitation of a monopoly. However, a significant number (about 30) of U.S. states do have laws against "price gouging." *See* https://www.ncsl.org/research/financial-services-and-commerce/price-gouging-state-statutes.aspx for a list of these states.

cases. The Parties' arguments, and the CMA's views on these arguments, are addressed in Section 5.

## A. The Drug Lifecycle and Regulation

Most drugs follow a relatively long lifecycle that has three distinct stages:
- First, the pre-launch stage, which covers the development of new and innovative drugs launched by an originator (*i.e.*, a company that carries out research into new pharmaceuticals). This stage is typically characterized by substantial investments in research and development, with no guarantee of commercial success.
- Second, the market exclusivity stage. This covers the initial launch and sale of new and innovative drugs, which typically will benefit from patent protection – generally for up to 20 years. Originators obtain time-limited exclusivity, in order to recoup the costs of R&D, which is necessary in order to incentivize such innovation.
- Third, the post-exclusivity stage, which starts following patent expiry and loss of exclusivity, as a result of which other pharmaceutical companies can enter the market with generic versions of an originator drug. This is the stage at which price competition is expected to take place. Empirical research in the sector shows that competition from generic drugs typically results in very significant price reductions. For instance, a study by Oxera for the British Generic Manufacturers Association found that prices charged by generic suppliers for a sample of products were on average 60 percent lower than the originator's branded price before the loss of exclusivity, falling to 80-90 percent lower four years after generic entry.[9]

In the UK, drug prices will typically be subject to some form of price regulation in the second stage. However, once a drug becomes generic in the post-exclusivity stage, prices are generally unregulated on the assumption that competition between generic suppliers in the third stage of the drug lifecycle will keep prices low.

Each of the three cases below concerned a drug that was long off patent and hence in the third stage of the drug lifecycle, but where the normal mechanism for keeping prices down – generic entry – was compromised because of high barriers to entry.

## B. Phenytoin[10]

Phenytoin sodium is an anti-epileptic drug. Originally synthesized in 1908 and first commercialized in 1938, it has long been off-patent and superseded by newer drugs with superior clinical characteristics for the treatment of epilepsy. Phenytoin

---

9 Oxera (2019).

10 All the numbers, figures, and charts that are included in this chapter can be found in the non-confidential versions of the three decisions.

sodium is now considered as a treatment for epilepsy only if no other treatments are effective and tolerated by the patient, and only for certain types of epilepsy: it is a "third-line" treatment. It is sold in two different versions: capsules and tablets (which are not interchangeable). The infringement focused on the supply of capsules.

An important feature of phenytoin sodium – which is highly relevant to the case – is that the effectiveness of the drug is very sensitive to the exact formulation. A very small change in the level of the drug can tip a patient from managing the condition to serious adverse side effects (some of which are life changing). For these reasons, clinical guidance recommends that patients who are stabilized on a particular manufacturer's phenytoin sodium should be maintained on that product and should not be switched to another manufacturer's product. This means not just that patients should not be switched to a different delivery mechanism (*e.g.*, from capsules to tablets), but that they should not even be switched to a different manufacturer of capsules.

The result is that the buyers of phenytoin capsules – the public health system – are effectively captive as prescribing physicians do not have the option of switching patients to another drug or another supplier in response to a supplier that increases the price of phenytoin sodium capsules. This clearly limits the scope for competition to keep prices close to costs in this market. Given the barriers to switching existing patients away from a particular manufacturer's drug, and the fact that there are very few if any new patients who use phenytoin due to its inferior properties, there is little (if any) scope for competition through the entry of other generic manufacturers to provide a check on prices.

Prior to September 2012 Pfizer was the sole supplier of phenytoin sodium capsules in the UK, and sold these under the brand name *Epanutin*. *Epanutin* was first marketed in 1938 and was acquired by Pfizer in 2000, by which time it was long off-patent. Pfizer sold Epanutin under the UK price regulation system for branded drugs: the pharmaceutical pricing regulation scheme ("PPRS").[11] This scheme imposes a profit cap on the sales of branded medicines. The PPRS scheme prevented Pfizer from exercising significant market power, despite Pfizer being the sole supplier of capsules. In order to be able to increase prices, Pfizer needed to de-brand *Epanutin* capsules so as to remove them from the PPRS scheme. In September 2012 Pfizer took *Epanutin* out of the PPRS and turned it into a generic drug. This meant that there was no longer any price or profit regulation of the drug.

However, Pfizer was concerned about the reputational risks that might attach to increasing the price of phenytoin sodium capsules significantly. As part of this de-branding, Pfizer changed its distribution model. Instead of distributing *Epanutin* itself, Pfizer signed an exclusive distribution agreement for phenytoin capsules with Flynn, a specialist pharmaceuticals distributor. By selling the marketing authoriza-

---

11 The PPRS was a voluntary agreement between the Department of Health and the Association of the British Pharmaceutical Industry that applied to manufacturers and suppliers of branded medicines to the National Health Service. The PPRS regulated profits rather than prices.

tion for phenytoin sodium capsules to Flynn for a nominal fee, and distributing through Flynn, the CMA found that Pfizer hoped to avoid this reputational risk by no longer being the firm that sets the price of the product for pharmacies (although, of course, it continued to set the wholesale price at which it sold the product to Flynn).

After de-branding, Pfizer and Flynn increased prices considerably. Prices that were charged to the pharmacy sector for the most popular version of the capsules – 100mg, which accounted for over 70 percent of sales – went from £2.21 for a pack of 84 capsules pre-September 2012 to more than £51 overnight. This was a price increase of more than 2,000 percent. This price increase fed directly through to the Drug Tariff price[12] and hence the price paid by the National Health Service ("NHS")[13] (and hence by taxpayers).

**Figure 1: 100mg phenytoin sodium capsule Drug Tariff price (price per pack of 84 capsules)**

**Source:** Figure 3.5 of CMA's 2016 Decision

Pfizer and Flynn then "shared the rents" from this price increase through the price that Pfizer charged Flynn for supplying the capsules, which was also very substantially in excess of the price that Pfizer had charged the pharmacy sector prior to de-branding. Pfizer increased its prices from £2.21 to over £31. Flynn then added its own mark-up.

---

12 The Drug Tariff price is the price that pharmacies are reimbursed for dispensing a product. It is effectively a mark-up over the list price that is set by suppliers, with the mark-up designed to cover the dispensing costs of the pharmacy.

13 In the UK, prescription drugs are not usually paid for by the patient directly, but by the NHS, which is ultimately funded by taxpayer money.

In response to this dramatic price increase, NRIM entered the market in April 2013, although only with a 100mg product. It quickly captured a market share of between 10 and 20 percent, and Pfizer/Flynn lowered their prices somewhat in May 2014 (*see* Figure 1). The price increase relative to the pre-September 2012 price was still over 2,000 percent. In November 2013 the MHRA[14] issued guidance that patients should not be switched between alternative suppliers of phenytoin capsules. The result was that the existing market shares between Pfizer/Flynn and NRIM became permanent as there was no scope for switching patients. It is notable that NRIM abandoned its development of the other capsule strengths (25mg, 50mg, and 300mg) for this reason. It is also noteworthy that the large price increases did not result in any significant reduction in sales[15] and were maintained for a period of over four years, until CMA intervention led to price reductions.

## C. CMA Intervention

The CMA issued its first infringement decision with respect to Pfizer and Flynn in December 2016. The CMA found that Pfizer and Flynn each held a dominant position in their respective markets for the manufacture and supply of phenytoin sodium capsules, and that each abused their dominant position by imposing unfair prices for phenytoin capsules for a period of over four years.[16] The CMA found that on 100mg capsules Pfizer was making an excess of 705 percent – charging a price that was more than eight times its unit costs[17] plus a reasonable rate of return – and Flynn was making an excess of 31 percent. A 31 percent excess over costs that were already in excess of 705 percent implies that Flynn's margin was more than double Pfizer's costs. Given that the CMA found that Flynn did very little except process orders (it did not, for instance, ever take receipt or ship the product[18]), the CMA decided this was excessive pricing. The CMA imposed a penalty of £84.2 million on Pfizer and £5.2 million on Flynn.

Pfizer and Flynn appealed the decision to the UK's specialist competition law court: The Competition Appeals Tribunal ("CAT"). The CAT agreed with the CMA in relation to its findings on market definition and dominance. However, it referred the analysis of the abuse back to the CMA for further consideration because it did not think that the CMA had done enough work to show that Pfizer/Flynn's prices were excessive. In particular, the CAT was concerned that the CMA had not adequately

---

14 The Medicines and Healthcare products Regulatory Agency is responsible for ensuring that medicines and medical devices in the UK work and are acceptably safe.

15 The usage of phenytoin sodium has been declining because it is now a third-line treatment. There appears to have been no effect on volumes of the price increases. The downward trend in usage after the price increases was the same as before the price increases. *See* paragraph 3.44(d) of the CMA decision.

16 This was done under Chapter 2 of the UK Competition Act 1998 and Article 102 of the EC Treaty, which prohibits dominant firms from abusing of their position. Excessive pricing is dealt with under the unfair pricing provision of Chapter 2 and Article 102.

17 These unit costs included both variable and fixed costs.

18 *See* Table 3.2 of the 2016 Decision.

considered whether the prices of phenytoin sodium tablets were a good comparator that suggested that the capsule prices were not excessive.[19]

After additional work on this issue, the CMA issued its second infringement decision in July 2022: The CMA imposed a revised penalty of £63.3 million on Pfizer and £6.7 million on Flynn. As of August 2022, there is no public version of this second decision. Our discussion below is therefore based only on the original published decision.

## D. Liothyronine

Liothyronine is a treatment against hypothyroidism. With strong adverse side effects and disputed efficacy, it has long been displaced by levothyroxine – which is a more effective and cheaper drug – in the treatment of hypothyroidism. However, there remains a subset of patients who do not respond adequately to levothyroxine and are treated with liothyronine. As such, liothyronine is a niche drug: Its volumes over the period were less than 0.5 percent of those of levothyroxine.[20]

Liothyronine tablets were originally developed in the UK in the mid-1950s and sold under the brand name "Tertroxin." The Advanz Pharma Corp. acquired Tertroxin in the early 90s, at which point it was long off-patent. In a very similar pattern to phenytoin, Advanz was limited in its ability to exercise market power as sole supplier of liothyronine because it was sold as a branded product and hence regulated under the PPRS scheme.

In 2007, Advanz devised what it called a "price optimization strategy," The explicit aim of this strategy was to identify long off-patent drugs, where Advanz faced limited or no competition and benefited from high barriers to entry. By de-branding these drugs, Advanz would remove them from price regulation and would therefore be able to exercise its market power.

Liothyronine fitted these characteristics: it was long off-patent; Advanz was the sole supplier of liothyronine in the UK; and barriers to entry were high. Liothyronine is particularly difficult to manufacture due to the low amount of active substance in the product and the sensitivity of liothyronine to minor changes in processing technology. These manufacturing difficulties – combined with the small and declining size of the market – make the process of entry particularly lengthy, expensive, and risky, as compared to other generic medicines.

Advanz began applying its price optimization strategy to liothyronine in October 2007: Advanz removed the Tertroxin brand, re-launched liothyronine as a generic product, and began to implement a series of price increases. Unlike in the case of phenytoin, Advanz did not increase prices in a single jump. Instead, it imple-

---

[19] Paragraph 4 of the CAT's judgement states that "The CMA did not correctly apply the legal test for finding that prices were unfair; it did not appropriately consider what was the right economic value for the product at issue; and it did not take sufficient account of the situation of other, comparable, products, in particular of the phenytoin sodium tablet." CAT judgement in Case Nos. 1275-1276/1/12/17: *Flynn Pharma v. CMA* and *Pfizer v. CMA* (June 17, 2018).

[20] See Table 3.3 of the CMA decision.

mented a series of price increases over a period of 10 years. Prices of liothyronine tablets increased from around £4 per pack of 28 tablets in 2007 to around £250 in 2017: A price increase of over 6000 percent since 2007. *See* Figure 2.

**Figure 2: Advanz's monthly average sales prices ("ASP") for liothyronine tablet packs (January 2007 – July 2017)**

**Source:** Figure 1.1 of the CMA decision.

The price increases were such that, eventually, they attracted new entrants. Despite the high entry costs and small market size, there will be a point where prices are so high that entry becomes attractive. However, given the complexities in manufacturing, the delay between the consideration of entry and actual entry was long, which allowed Advanz to continue to increase prices for a considerable period of time. The first successful entrant (Morningside) first considered entering in 2012 when liothyronine tablets had reached a price of £45 per pack, but only actually entered in 2017, by which point prices had reached £250 per pack. It is quite clear that the prospect of entry was not constraining Advanz's behavior.

Prices have fallen since entry occurred. However, at the time that the CMA issued its decision, prices remained substantially above unit costs plus a reasonable rate of return, and were still on a downward trend. Figure 3 shows the evolution of liothyronine reimbursement prices since entry has occurred.

**Figure 3: NHS reimbursement prices of liothyronine tablet packs since entry**[21]

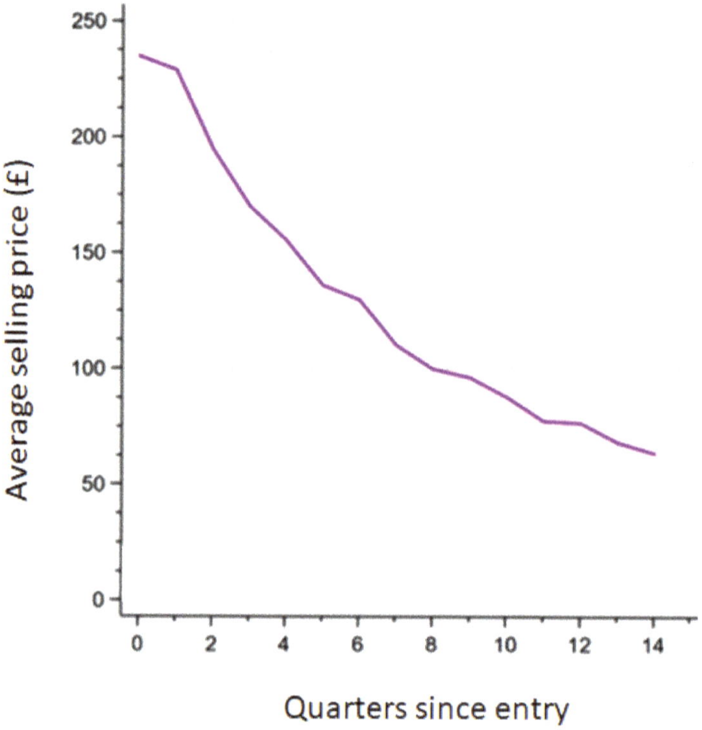

*Source:* Figure 5.10 of CMA decision

### E. CMA intervention

In July 2021, the CMA issued an infringement decision against Advanz and its two previous owners (Cinven and Hg Capital, which are both private equity firms) during the period of the infringement. The CMA found that from 2009 until 2017 – the point at which entry occurred – Advanz held a dominant position in the market for the supply of liothyronine tablets and abused this position by charging excessive prices for supplying liothyronine tablets. As Table 1 shows, the prices that were charged by Advanz were dramatically higher than costs: In 2009, average selling prices were 900 percent in excess of Advanz's unit costs plus a reasonable return. This rose to over 2000 percent excess by the end of the infringement period.

---

[21] Note that prices in Figure 3 are not directly comparable to those in Figure 2. Figure 2 shows Advanz's average selling prices (*i.e.*, manufacturer level prices) whereas Figure 3 shows NHS reimbursement prices (*i.e.*, the price that the NHS reimburses to pharmacies for dispensing liothyronine).

## Table 1: Comparison of Liothyronine average selling prices ("ASP") with costs, per pack

|  | 2009 | 2010 | 2011 | 2012 | 2013 | 2014 | 2015 | 2016 | 2017 |
|---|---|---|---|---|---|---|---|---|---|
| Liothyronine Tablets ASP (£) | 20.80 | 25.66 | 37.73 | 45.52 | 61.84 | 94.63 | 146.42 | 229.23 | 247.77 |
| Cost Plus (£) | 2.08 | 2.10 | 3.12 | 2.75 | 3.99 | 5.11 | 5.63 | 9.87 | 9.78 |
| Differential between ASP and Cost Plus (£) | 18.72 | 23.56 | 34.61 | 42.77 | 57.85 | 89.52 | 140.79 | 219.36 | 237.99 |
| Differential (%) | 900% | 1119% | 1110% | 1554% | 1449% | 1751% | 2501% | 2222% | 2434% |

**Notes**: *Average Selling Prices are annual averages; except for the 2017 figure which is the average to July 2017.*

Cost Plus is calculated as the unit cost per pack (including both fixed and variable costs), plus a reasonable rate of return.

**Source:** Table 1.1 of CMA decision.

The CMA imposed a total fine of just over £100m on Advanz and its owners.

## F. Hydrocortisone[22]

This case concerned hydrocortisone tablets. These were first sold in the UK in 1955 under the brand name Hydrocortone. They went off-patent in the 1970s. Hydrocortisone is a lifesaving drug that is used by tens of thousands of patients in the UK to treat illnesses relating to adrenal insufficiency (*e.g.*, Addison's disease). In April 2008 Auden/Actavis bought the licenses for hydrocortisone tablets for £200,000. It then immediately de-branded the product and, thus, took it out of the price regulation of the PPRS scheme. It then proceeded to increase the price steadily for the next nearly eight years. This is shown in Figure 3. During this period there were no innovations or cost increases to justify the price rises.

As is shown in Figure 4, the price of a pack of 30 tablets of 10mg hydrocortisone rose from less than £1 to £72 by early 2016. The yearly expenditure by the NHS on the drug rose from £0.5m in 2007 to £80m in 2016. The CMA calculated Auden/Actavis' costs at between £2.17 and £4.45 over the period.[23] It also estimated that the total revenue that was earned in excess of costs over the period was more than £260m.[24]

---

22 CMA "Hydrocortisone tablets: excessive and unfair pricing and anti-competitive agreements" (Case 50277, July 15, 2021).
23 Table 5.3 of the CMA decision.
24 Table 5.4 of the CMA decision.

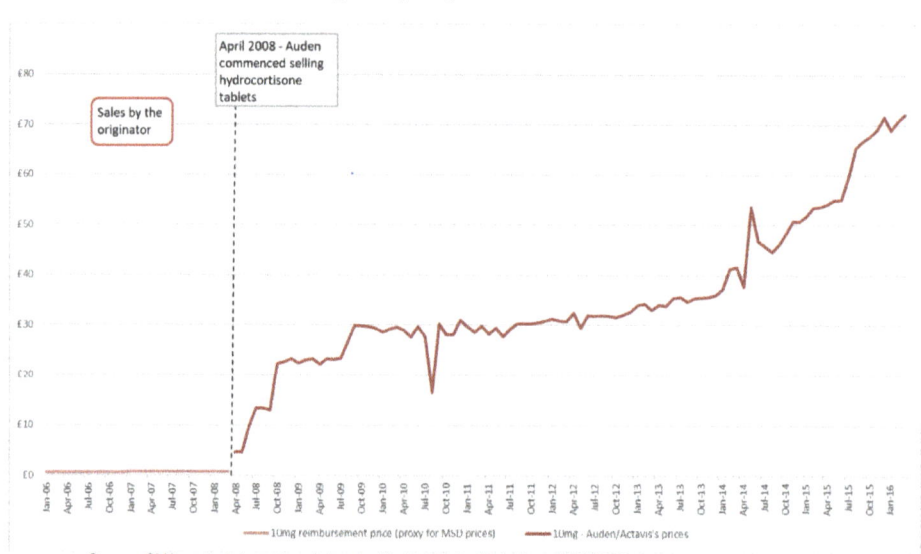

EXCESSIVE PRICING AS AN ANTITRUST HARM: THREE UK CASES IN GENERIC PHARMACEUTICALS

**Figure 4: 10mg hydrocortisone tablet prices between January 2006 and March 2016, price per pack of 30 tablets**[25]

[Chart showing 10mg hydrocortisone tablet prices from Jan-06 to Jan-16, with annotations "Sales by the originator" and "April 2008 - Auden commenced selling hydrocortisone tablets". Price rises from near £0 to approximately £70+ over the period. Legend: 10mg reimbursement price (proxy for MSD prices); 10mg - Auden/Actavis's prices.]

Source: CMA analysis based on data submitted by Auden/Actavis and NHS BSA data.

**Source:** Figure 1.1 of CMA decision.

Successful 10mg entry did not take place until October 2015 and then more substantively from March 2016 onwards. The result was that prices fell from late 2015.[26] As is shown in Figure 5, by early 2021, Auden (now owned by Actavis) had reduced its prices back below £4 per pack.

As with both phenytoin and liothyronine, the increase in prices did not lead to a significant reduction in volumes sold. Volumes rose at about 4 percent per year over the period 2003 to 2020 – with no change to this trend when prices rose, but also no change when they fell.[27]

The *Hydrocortisone* case differs from the other two discussed above in that it is not a "pure" excessive pricing case. The CMA found that there was also an agreement between Auden and two potential entrants – Waymade Plc and AMCo – whereby Auden effectively paid the two potential entrants not to enter. This agreement began

---

25 There is also a 20mg product in addition to the 10mg product. We focus on the 10mg product as this accounts for more than 95 percent of the market. The pattern of price rises was similar for both product doses.

26 There is a slight wrinkle here that we ignore for the purpose of this chapter: Due to a regulatory quirk, the entrants were able to be formally licensed to produce hydrocortisone only for children – not for adults. (This type of limitation is described as a "skinny" label rather than "full" label product). In practice, the drug is the same, and many pharmacies were happy to supply skinny label products to fulfill adult prescriptions. As Figure 5 shows, the degree of differentiation was not enough to stop the entry from having a significant competitive impact and leading to much lower prices.

27 *See* Figure 3.12 of the CMA decision.

220          ANTITRUST ECONOMICS AT A TIME OF UPHEAVAL

in October 2012 and was effectively a "pay for delay" agreement. We do not discuss this further in

**Figure 5: Auden/Actavis's and competitors' 10mg hydrocortisone prices per pack of 30 tablets (April 2008 to April 2021)**

Source: Figure 4.1 of the decision

this paper, beyond noting that it was key to ensuring that entry in response to the excessive 10mg prices did not happen until several years later in October 2015.

In its Decision in July 2021, the CMA imposed fines on Auden, Waymade, and AMCo. Auden was fined £155.2m for the excessive pricing offense and £66m for the "pay for delay" agreement. Waymade and AMCo were fined, respectively, £2.5m and £42.8m for the agreement.

## V. COMMENTARY ON THE THREE CASES

As we set out above, in one sense, these are not difficult or controversial cases. They fall squarely within the exceptions category under the Motta & de Streel conditions. In all three cases, the price increases were very large, and the prices were substantially above the unit costs of the dominant firms. The existence of market power was difficult to argue against. All of the cases involved monopolist providers of a niche drug that were protected by very high barriers to entry. In the case of phenytoin, these are now effectively insurmountable.[28] In the case of liothyronine, entry took more than eight years, and prices remain substantially above their original level. In the case of hydrocortisone, entry took seven years, although prices have now – more than ten years after the start of the price increases – returned to close to their original level.

In all cases, demand was highly inelastic, such that the high prices did not reduce demand. In each case this was because of a lack of substitution options for captive patients. Volumes of phenytoin sodium capsules have been declining, but this is a long-term trend that is due to the product being a third-line treatment, not due to price increases. Liothyronine tablet volumes have remained stable despite NHS reimbursement prices' increasing from an average price of about £11 per pack in 2008 to nearly £250 per pack in 2016.[29] Hydrocortisone tablet volumes have increased steadily regardless of either price increases or price reductions.

In each case the drug was long off-patent when it was de-branded, and the firm that did the de-branding had done nothing to earn the monopoly position of the drugs beyond buying them. The purpose of generic drugs is to lead to lower prices once drugs go off-patent. However, in all three of these cases, the purpose of de-branding by the relevant firms was in order to raise prices substantially.

On one understanding of the institutional set-up, there was no existing regulatory authority that was able to stop the exercise of market power. Our view is that this is the correct view, but we discuss this further below.

However, all three cases have gone to appeal, so there must be some degree of controversy. Below we discuss the arguments that have been put forward by the various Parties as to why the pricing patterns outlined above do not constitute excessive pricing. We focus on the economic arguments, not on the legal or accounting arguments.

## A. What is the Benchmark Price at which Prices Become Excessive?

A key issue in all excessive pricing cases is the question of at what point do prices become "excessive." This requires a benchmark "non-excessive" price against which to compare the actual prices. The standard approach is to use the costs of the dominant firm as the benchmark and then compare its actual prices to its costs. The measurement of costs will normally include the costs directly incurred in supplying the product, and an appropriate apportionment of the indirect costs that are reasonably attributable to the product. In other words, the cost benchmark will include variable and fixed costs, as well as common costs. If actual prices are very significantly above the dominant firm's costs, then its prices would be potentially excessive. There is no clear guidance in economics as to how much above costs should be considered excessive. However, in these cases, that was not a central question because the differences between costs and prices were so large: thousands of percent in each case, even though

---

28 As was explained above, although entry did occur in 2014, this did not have a substantial impact on prices or market shares.

29 NHS reimbursement prices are the prices at which the NHS reimburses pharmacies for prescriptions; the prices would usually be in excess of the prices at which pharmacies purchase the drug – in this case, Advanz's average selling price – so as to allow pharmacies to earn a margin on their activity.

these drugs were long off patent and so the high prices were therefore not justified as a reward for past R&D.

Instead, the focus of the Parties' arguments was on alternative benchmarks. We discuss the three main benchmarks below (although the first two shade into each other):

- the price that incentivizes new entry;
- the price after entry, at which point there is competition between firms; and
- the price for the product, or for a similar product, that is accepted by the regulator.

## 1. *The Price that Incentivizes Entry*

The Parties argued that a price that is below the price that incentivizes entry cannot be excessive. The logic is that a competitive price can be achieved only after there are several competing suppliers in the market – and this can be achieved only after entry has been incentivized.

The essence of the Parties' argument is that a price that is below the level that is consistent with competitive interaction between firms cannot be considered excessive because it is – "by definition" – below the competitive price. It would, the Parties argued, be bizarre for a competition authority to find that prices are excessive at a level below that which incentivized entry, since this would amount to stating that only a monopolist could survive in the market. On its face, this appears to be an attractive argument. What might be wrong with it?

The easiest way to see the problem with this argument is to consider it in light of barriers to entry and the costs of entry. The higher are the barriers to entry, the higher will be the price that is required to incentivize entry. And the higher are the costs of entry, the higher will prices need to be to allow entry to be successful. But this leads to the perverse outcome that, the higher are the barriers to entry and the greater are the costs of entry, the higher are the prices that the dominant firm should be allowed to charge. At the extreme, if barriers to entry are insurmountable, so there cannot be entry or competitive interaction between firms, then the dominant firm would be allowed to charge as high a price as it liked.

We think this outcome is exactly wrong, as it allows firms to exploit the market power that is derived from high barriers to entry. Competition law is explicitly designed to prevent firms from being able to exploit market power. There are of course situations where the ability to exploit temporarily some degree of market power will be necessary in order to reward investment in innovation and so intervention will not be warranted. Indeed, in the second stage of a drugs life, patent protection allows originators sole supply in order to recoup their investment in R&D. However, this was not the case here: The drugs were long off-patent, and the firms selling these drugs had done nothing to earn the monopoly position of the drugs beyond acquiring the rights to sell the drug.

## 2. *The Price After Entry, at which Point There is Competition*

A closely related argument that was proposed by the Parties was that the price under actual competition between firms should be considered as the competitive benchmark. At its simplest, the argument is: If there is competition between firms, then that price must be a competitive price, so any price below that cannot be considered excessive. This implies that the prices that prevailed after entry in each of the three cases should be considered to be a non-excessive benchmark.

The naïve version of this argument clearly cannot work. It would imply that at the moment of entry, all prices below the prevailing price should be considered non-excessive. Allied to the entry-incentivizing argument above, it would effectively remove excessive pricing as an abuse. If entry has not occurred, the price could not be excessive. At the point at which entry has occurred, that price also could not be excessive.

A more plausible version of the argument is that there will be a point after entry when an effectively competitive equilibrium is reached. However, we still need some metric to identify this point. The path of prices after entry differs significantly among the three cases. In *Phenytoin*, there was an initial reduction in prices after entry, but the MHRA guidance in November 2013 ended any possibility of price competition between Pfizer/Flynn and NRIM. Consequently, there was no sense in which the price that prevailed after the entry of NRIM could be considered as a benchmark for effective competition. *Hydrocortisone* provides the opposite experience: After the entry of several firms in late 2015 and early 2016, prices declined to the point at which they are now close to the prices before Auden/Actavis started to increase them and are close to the underlying unit costs of production.[30] *Liothyronine* lies between these two cases and highlights the essential difficulty of this benchmark. Prices peaked at about £250 per pack in the first half of 2017, prior to the entry of two new firms. As was shown in Figure 2, prices have now fallen to somewhere between £60 and £70 per pack. Should this be considered the non-excessive benchmark, since it is the price under competition three-and-a-half years after entry? The Parties would argue yes.

But this may be the wrong conclusion. Prices are continuing to fall, so the current prices do not appear to represent the long-run equilibrium. Prices remain substantially above even the most generous estimate of costs[31] and more than 15 times above their original level. It is hardly a surprise if three firms' competing leads to soft pricing. One of the benefits of competition is that it drives prices close to costs. This does not appear to have happened with liothyronine tablets, which is consistent with competition not being fully effective in this market.

In *Liothyronine* the Parties submitted a Cournot model of competition and argued that the model provided a good indicator of where prices would be under effective competition. The model predicted prices of £126 per pack for a three-firm market, with prices falling to a little over £60 per pack for a seven-firm market.[32]

There are at least two serious problems with this analysis: First, the results were at odds with reality. Prices at the time of the decision (July 2021) were already below £70

---

30 Table 5.3 of the decision provides details.

31 Table 5.3 of the CMA decision shows that under the assumptions that are most generous to the Parties, the highest estimated costs are just over £12 per pack in 2016. The most generous average cost estimate over the whole period is £7.35.

32 *See* para. 5.338 of the CMA decision.

per pack in a three-firm market. Second, the assumption of Cournot competition is odd. The whole point of generics is that prices are typically bid down to close to marginal costs. Given the very low elasticity of demand for the products, Cournot competition is always going to lead to substantial mark-ups over marginal costs. This market is much better modelled as Bertrand competition without capacity constraints. This is a market with no product differentiation, no barriers to switching, and importantly no capacity constraints, and so the main variable over which suppliers compete is price. Bertrand competition would predict prices being driven down towards marginal costs.

### 3. *The Price for the Product, or for a Similar Product, that is Accepted by the Regulator*

The Parties in *Phenytoin* and *Liothyronine* argued that there is a regulator in this industry that has the power to regulate prices: The Department of Health ("DH"). In line with Motta & de Streel (2007), the Parties argued that the presence of a price regulator means that a competition authority ought not to intervene. Price increases in generic drugs have to be notified to the DH. The Parties argued that since the DH did not refuse to accept the price increases, this amounts to tacit acceptance of the price increases by a price regulator. If the price regulator accepts the prices, why should a competition authority get involved?

Another variant of this argument was raised in *Phenytoin*. The manufacturing processes for phenytoin sodium capsules and phenytoin sodium tablets is very similar. The Parties argued that this means that the price of tablets could potentially be used as a benchmark for the prices of capsules if there were reasons to believe that the price of tablets was reasonable. Since the price of tablets at the time had been agreed between the manufacturer – Teva – and the DH, the Parties argued that the price of tablets should be considered as non-excessive and hence a good comparator.[33] Pfizer/Flynn argued that they had in fact used the price of tablets as a comparator and had set the price of capsules at a lower level than the price of tablets.[34]

There is a legal argument as to exactly what powers the DH had. However, we want to focus on the relative bargaining positions of the suppliers and the DH. In all three cases, there was a monopoly supplier of a product that was selling to a health authority that required the supply of the product for patients. It seems to us that the bargaining

---

33 It is true that the DH and Teva had recently come to an agreement over the pricing of phenytoin sodium tablets. However, this was in the context of Teva's being a monopoly supplier of a product for which patients did not have an alternative: As with capsules, patients could not be switched. The DH therefore had to ensure that it came to an agreement with Teva with respect to prices as it could not afford for the product not to be supplied. Teva was a monopoly supplier that had recently increased its prices substantially, and it was in light of this that the DH had come to an agreement with Teva over prices. Over the period 2005 to 2007, the drug tariff price of tablets had risen from £1.70 to £113.62. After discussions with DH, Teva agreed to reduce the price to £30. This was still more than 15 times the original price.

34 There was a separate argument about the value of phenytoin sodium tablets as a comparator after entry occurred in 2009 and 2012. We do not discuss this here, beyond noting that tablets faced very similar issues with respect to competition on the demand side as capsules, with clinical guidance recommending that patients who are stabilized on a particular manufacturer's product should not be switched to another manufacturer.

power in these cases rested with the supplier, not with the buyer. Indeed, the fact that the supplier was able to increase prices in each case so substantially without any volume reaction from the buyer is indicative of where the market power lay in these cases. Arguments about whether the regulator had the ability to resist the exercise of market power seem moot in a world in which the various suppliers clearly did exercise market power.

In these circumstances, it seems reasonable for a competition authority to step in to ensure lower prices. Indeed, in *Phenytoin*, it was a complaint from the DH in September 2012 about excessive prices that started the investigation.

It is worth noting that the idea that the monopoly supplier of an essential drug might have bargaining power underpinned the Italian competition authority's excessive pricing case against Aspen.[35] In this case, Aspen explicitly threatened to exit the Italian market if the Italian health authority did not accept an increase in the price of the relevant drugs. While the health authority did accept the price increases, the Italian competition authority nonetheless found Aspen guilty of excessive pricing and insisted that Aspen reduce its prices. The competition authority successfully defended the case on appeal.

## B. Are Higher Prices a Price Worth Paying for a Competitive Market?

In all three cases, the effect of higher prices has been to, eventually, encourage entry. Thus, NRIM entered the phenytoin sodium capsules market; Morningside (August 2017) and Teva (September 2017) entered the liothyronine market; numerous firms entered the hydrocortisone market.[36] Is this a good thing? Is there an argument (as was made by various Parties) that higher prices are a price worth paying if it leads to firms entering the market and hence to competition?

The Parties argued that, under the CMA's cost benchmark – which in each case was below the price that prompted entry – no entry would have ever occurred, which would thus have maintained a situation of monopoly forever. They argued that this is surely less desirable, in the long run, than a competitive market and hence that it is worth allowing higher prices in order to generate competition.

The first point to make here is that what the Parties refer to as "competition" is not really what competition is about. When the Parties refer to a "competitive market," they mean a market with several firms. What they do not focus on, but which is much more important, is whether the market outcome is an outcome that benefits consumers with prices close to costs. While competitive interaction between firms is in most cases the best way to generate good outcomes for consumers – by incentivizing low prices, innovation, and so on – there are some cases where *de facto* regulation (or self-regulation) will be preferable. This is where the barriers to entry are so high that competitive interaction becomes too expensive, particularly if the scope for competition on parameters other than price is limited or absent.

---

35 *Op. Cit.*

36 Alissa (October 2015), Resolution Chemicals (March 2016), Bristol Laboratories (March 2016), AMCo (Aesica) (May 2016), Teva (February 2017), Genesis Pharmaceuticals (November 2017), and Renata (February 2019).

This was the case here. All of the drugs were long off-patent, and there was very little prospect of quality improvement or innovation. The only thing that matters for consumer welfare is therefore price. *Hydrocortisone* and *Liothyronine* both illustrate this point.

In *Hydrocortisone*, prices are now back at, or close to, their original levels. Does this mean that the higher prices in the interim should just be considered the cost that was required to get the benefit of competition? Even if we are willing to accept that, it is better to have prices that are close to costs as a result of competition – rather than prices that are close to costs due to regulation (which is not an uncontroversial position) – we are still left with more than 10 years of higher prices. NHS expenditure on hydrocortisone tablets over the period 2008 to 2010 was about £550m.[37] This should be compared to expenditure on hydrocortisone tablets of about £0.5m in 2007. This is a high cost of waiting for competition.

*Liothyronine* provides an even starker picture: NHS spending on the drug rose from £600,000 in the year before the infringement started to more than £30m in the last full year of the infringement. Given that prices are still substantially above their pre-infringement level, NHS expenditure remains close to £8m per year. Again, (imperfect) competition seems quite expensive in this market.

## C. Economic Value

The seminal excessive pricing case in Europe is the *United Brands* case.[38] This refers to "a price which is excessive because it has no reasonable relation to the economic value of the product supplied."[39] The result is that all excessive pricing cases in Europe have involved some discussion of what the "economic value" of the product is.

The difficulty for an economist is that "economic value" has no meaning in economics. When economists are pushed on this, we end up saying that the economic value of a product to a user is what that user is willing to pay for the product. This is the same as saying that the demand curve for the product maps out the economic value of the product to different consumers. This implies that no product would ever be sold for more than the economic value of the product to the buyers, which means that under this test there could never be excessive pricing.

The only observation that we will make on the economic value discussion in these cases is that it highlighted the different attitudes of the Parties and the CMA to the high prices. The Parties argued that the willingness of the health service to pay those high prices indicated how valuable the product was to patients and consequently indicated very high economic value. The CMA's view (and ours) is that the willingness to pay high prices was indicative of the market power by the Parties when selling drugs that were essential to their users. This is the exercise of hold-up market power; it is not, in our view, indicative of why firms should be allowed to charge prices that are vastly above costs for long off-patent drugs.

---

37 *See* Figure 1.5 of the CMA decision.
38 *United Brands v. Commission* C-27/76.
39 Para. 250, *Op. Cit.*

## D. Arguments about Costs

Since the starting point for a concern about excessive prices is the relationship between costs and prices, it is not surprising that in all of these cases there was much discussion about the correct measurement of costs. Most of these were the standard fare of any regulatory discussion about price controls: the correct measurement of direct costs; how to measure indirect costs; how to allocate common costs; what is a reasonable cost of capital; are there any intangibles that need to be included; and so on. None of these raised novel issues in our cases, so we will not discuss them in this chapter.

However, there was one cost-related issue that the Parties raised in *Liothyronine* that is novel and hence worth mentioning. This relates to the fact that the market for liothyronine was small, with significant fixed costs of entry. The Parties argued that in a competitive market there would be multiple suppliers of liothyronine. Each of these suppliers would have higher unit costs than a monopolist because of the need to cover their fixed costs over a smaller volume of sales. The implication is that any benchmark for an excessive price should be based on the unit costs of each firm in a multi-firm market.[40]

This argument suffers from similar flaws to the one discussed above about the entry-incentivizing price. First, it implies that the higher are the fixed costs of entry, the more an incumbent monopolist should be allowed to charge. That seems contrary to the purpose of competition law, which is to stop firms from being able to exercise market power. Second, it means that the benchmark would differ depending on how many firms the competition authority thinks ought to be in the market. The more firms that one thinks ought to be in the market, the higher would be the benchmark for an excessive price. That seems counter-intuitive.

In *Liothyronine*, Advanz's actual prices were substantially above costs even if a multi-firm adjustment were made. The CMA calculated that a three-firm adjustment would raise unit costs to £12.64 per pack in 2009, rising to £17.89 per pack in 2017. These figures are still substantially below the prices that Advanz actually charged over that period: Rising to nearly £250 per pack by the end of the period.

## VI. CONCLUSIONS

This chapter has presented three UK cases that involved excessive pricing in generic pharmaceuticals. The economics of these cases are simple and in many ways are textbook illustrations of the exploitation of market power. All of the cases involved monopoly suppliers of a drug that were protected by very high barriers to entry and

---

40 A separate but related point was that Advanz benefitted from low manufacturing costs through the historical advantage of having acquired the rights to manufacture liothyronine for a very low price. However, the costs of replicating these manufacturing costs were significantly in excess of Advanz's actual costs – partly because regulatory requirements with respect to the manufacturing of liothyronine have tightened, which have made it more costly for new entrants to acquire the relevant authorization. The CMA calculated per unit costs on the basis of the costs of a new entrant. This showed that even if Advanz had priced at that level, it would still have earned windfall profits.

that increased prices by thousands of percent in a context of highly inelastic demand. Consumer detriment – in the form of higher prices to the NHS – was very high as a result. While entry did eventually occur in all three cases, this was only because prices had increased to such an extent that entry became profitable despite the very high barriers to entry.

In all three cases, the monopoly supplier exploited a gap in the regulation of drug prices. Unbranded generic drug prices are unregulated because the expectation is that rapid entry by generic suppliers will drive prices down to costs, which is what happens for the large majority of generics. However, where, as is the case here, the barriers to entry are very high or insurmountable, the opposite happened: De-branding the drug allowed the suppliers to increase prices substantially.

While there are good reasons for competition authorities to be cautious with respect to excessive pricing cases, we have argued in this chapter that the benefits of intervention can far outweigh any costs of intervention in these three cases. The drugs in question were long off-patent and the firms that did the de-branding had done nothing to earn the monopoly position of the drugs beyond acquiring the rights to sell the drug, so the high prices were not a reward for innovation by the owners. There were high benefits from intervention, through lower prices, whereas the potential costs of intervention – from a reduction in innovation incentives and dynamic competition – were absent.

Motta & de Streel's 2007 paper is entitled "Excessive pricing in competition law: never say never?." They have a question mark at the end of this title. The cases discussed in this chapter explain why that question mark should be removed. Excessive pricing cases should be rare in competition law; but we should never rule them out completely.

## REFERENCES

Evans, D. & Padilla, J. (2004). "Excessive prices: using economics to define administrable legal rules" *Journal of Competition Law and Economics.*

Fletcher, Amelia & Alina Jardine (2008). "Towards an appropriate policy for excessive pricing" in *European Competition Law Annual 2007: A reformed approach to Article 82 EC*, edited by Claus-Dieter Ehlermann and Mel Marquis.

Jenny, F. (2018). "Abuse of dominance by firms charging excessive or unfair prices: an assessment" in Excessive pricing and competition law enforcement, Katsoulacos and Jenny.

Motta, Massimo & Alexandre De Streel (2007). "Excessive pricing in competition law: never say never?" in *The pros and cons of high prices*, Swedish Competition Authority.

Oxera (2019). "The supply of generic medicines in the UK." Report prepared for The British Generics Manufacturers Association.

Röller, L. (2008). "Exploitative abuses" in A reformed approach to Article 82 EC, Ehlemann and Marquis.

# CHAPTER 12
# Extension of Its Search Monopoly: The EC Case against Google Android

*By Cristina Caffarra & Federico Etro*[1]

## I. BACKGROUND AND INTRODUCTION TO "THE ANDROID CASE"

In July 2018 the European Commission ("EC") issued a "cease and desist" order – together with a €4.34bn fine – to Google for imposing anti-competitive restrictions on Original Equipment Manufacturers ("OEMs") that supply devices with an Android operating system ("OS"). The restrictions had the purpose of cementing Google's dominant position in general internet search – extending in particular its quasi-monopoly in the desktop environment to mobile devices (Case AT.4099 – *Google Android*).[2]

The "*Android* case" generated wide debate with respect to the anti-competitive mechanisms that were at play, and prompted formal economic work that extended traditional theories of harm that were based on tying, network effects, and naked exclusion so as to incorporate multi-sidedness markets with monetization on one side. This in turn established the foundations for ongoing work on the economics of platforms that do not charge users for services but instead monetize through advertising: the "zero-price constraint," which is typical ad-funded business models; see in particular Etro & Caffarra (2017); Choi & Jeon (2021); De Cornière & Taylor (2021); and Bisceglia & Tirole (2022).

Monetization through online advertising – including search and display – has traditionally driven much of Google's business strategy. Google provides multiple products and services to users free of charge: the Chrome Brower, Google Maps, YouTube, Gmail, and many more. Google then leverages users' data from its apps and services to improve and strengthen its search and display products.

While Google's early business was in a PC/web browser environment, by the mid-2000s it recognized the opportunities and risks of a rapidly developing mobile smartphone market. Google risked losing millions of mobile searches to competing search

---

[1] We advised Yandex, a complainant, throughout the EC investigation and prior to that in the investigation by the Russian Federal Antimonopoly Service ("FAS"). We are not aware of economic analyses submitted by Google in the proceedings to counter the theory of harm. None is in the public domain in any event. Caffarra also advised a group of U.S. state attorneys general in the early stages of preparation of their *Google Search* complaint.

[2] Case AT 40099, *Google Android, see* https://ec.europa.eu/competition/antitrust/cases/dec_docs/40099/40099_9993_3.pdf.

browsers or applications if it did not have products and technologies for the mobile search market. To capture mobile search users, Google acquired the Android mobile operating system in 2005, and entered into various agreements with OEMs – as well as with Apple – to become the default search engine on smart mobile devices and iOS.

The EC formally opened proceedings in 2015, although the informal investigation had started a year or so earlier. The focus of the case was a suite of contractual agreements that Google had entered into with OEMs that produced mobile devices with an Android OS: "anti-fragmentation agreements" ("AFAs"), "mobile application distribution agreements" ("MADAs"), and "revenue sharing agreements" ("RSAs"). In practice, the agreements allowed OEMs to pre-install Google's app store (Google Play) – a must-have for a consumer that bought an Android device – on condition that Google Search ("GS") was pre-installed as the default search engine on the device.

The concern was that together these agreements *de facto* involved a tie of Google's app store with its search engine, which induced OEMs to pre-install GS on their devices and foreclosed all alternatives. This tie thus protected Google's dominance in search advertising and extended its power into the emerging market for mobile search. In particular, the concern was that Google used these agreements and associated financial incentives as a means to ensure exclusive pre-installation of its search engine as the default on Android devices, thereby foreclosing the installation of rival search engines, as well as hindering the growth of OEMs that produced so-called "forked" Android devices – devices that used the Android OS without Google Play and other key apps by Google – in a way that reduced both consumer surplus and social welfare to Google's own advantage.

The EC concluded in 2018 that Google was dominant in the markets for: (i) general internet search services; (ii) licensable smart mobile OS; and (iii) app stores for the Android mobile OS. Google was deemed to have engaged in three illegal practices, all of which denied rival search engines the possibility to compete on the merits and therefore constituted an abuse of its dominant position: (i) tying of Google's search and browser apps to its popular app store; (ii) revenue-share payments that were conditional on exclusive pre-installation of Google Search; and (iii) obstruction of development and distribution of competing Android operating systems ("Android forks") through anti-fragmentation agreements that were signed between Google and the OEMs and also between Google and mobile network operators ("MNOs").

While the EC case was (in our view) strong, the lengthy process of negotiating remedies with Google post-decision has not led to any change on the ground since the decision was reached in 2018: Google has succeeded in preserving and defending its mobile search monopoly without material progress by rivals. Google had also appealed the EC decision, and in September 2022 the European General Court issued a judgment that largely confirmed the original decision. This judgment has been also appealed by Google to the higher court – the European Court of Justice ("ECJ") – in December 2022. Hence a further round of hearings and a final judgment are still pending.

This chapter first discusses the evidence that was relied upon by the EC to support the threshold claim that Google was dominant in various markets: a dominance that could be leveraged into mobile search so as to protect Google's newly acquired position there. It then discusses the theory of harm and expands on the economic substance of the case: in particular the leveraging mechanism that was at play. We then describe the failures of the remedy process, and conclude with a brief discussion of the General Court's judgment in September 2022 that upheld the EC's decision. As a postscript, we briefly refer to the Search complaint that is being pursued by the U.S. Department of Justice and a number of U.S. state attorneys general, which covers *inter alia* the *Android* case.

## II. GOOGLE LEVERAGED "DOMINANCE" FROM MULTIPLE RELEVANT MARKETS

The EC concluded that Google was dominant in the markets for: (i) general internet search services; (ii) licensable smart mobile OS; and (iii) app stores for the Android mobile OS; as well as (iv) the market for non-OS-specific mobile web browsers. We briefly describe below the analyses and evidence that were relied upon for the first three.

### A. Google's Dominant Position in the Market for the Licensing of Smart Mobile OSs[3]

The EC investigation concluded that the licensing of smart mobile OSs constituted a separate relevant product market, in which Google had held a dominant position globally since 2011. The EC excluded from the relevant market PC OSs, basic and feature phone OSs, and non-licensable OSs (such as Apple's iOS or BlackBerry OS). The worldwide share of Google Android OS (excluding forks and excluding China) for "licensable smart mobile OSs" was 72 percent in 2011 and over 90 percent in 2013-16. Android also enjoyed the largest installed base of smart mobile OSs: 2,156m Google Android smartphones, compared to 518m iOS and 24m Windows Mobile in July 2016.

Google challenged the EC's position and claimed that iOS and Android were part of a single market for mobile devices. The EC argued instead that: (i) iOS and Android did not compete to attract users and app developers; and (ii) the respondents to the investigation and Google's internal documents did not indicate that iOS and Android OS were substitutes from an OEM perspective.

The EC calculated the shares of Google and competing developers of licensable smart mobile OSs from the evidence that included internal Google documents as well as OEMs' and MNOs' responses to the EC's "requests for information" ("RFIs") on high barriers to entry and lack of countervailing buyer power). Although the EC was not required to carry out a SSNIP test, nonetheless it assessed the extent of user and developer switching in response to a "small but significant, non-transitory quality degradation" of the licensable smart mobile OS and found that this quality degrada-

---

[3] See Section 9.3 of the EC *Google Android* decision. Smart mobile OSs include both smartphones and tablets.

tion would not induce enough switching. The EC had not previously defined a single market for smart mobile OSs, in particular in the *Google/Motorola Mobility* merger decision.

## B. Google's Dominant Position in the Market for the Licensing of Android App Stores

The EC concluded that Android app stores constituted a separate relevant product market, in which Google had held a dominant position globally since 2011. The market included different app stores for Google Android,[4] since from a demand-side perspective, an OEM could choose from a number of different Android app stores. The EC however excluded from the market app stores for non-Android licensable smart mobile OSs, and app stores for other non-licensable smart mobile OSs (*e.g.*, Apple's AppStore). Volume shares of pre-installed app stores were calculated based on total sales of smartphones and tablets that use Android OS: Google's Play Store was found to have been pre-installed on over 90 percent of Android OS smart mobile devices and accounted for over 90 percent of all downloaded apps since 2011 (global excl. China).

Google challenged the EC's conclusion by claiming that users and developers would switch away – to Apple devices in particular – in response to a decline in the quality of the app store. In response, the EC noted that switching costs and OS loyalty were high and that there was in any event only a limited number of alternative licensable OSs to switch to. Apple's and BlackBerry's app stores had been specifically developed for iOS and BlackBerry OS and could not run on Android; and from a supply-side perspective, developers of app stores for non-licensable smart mobile OSs were unlikely to start developing app stores for Android due to their vertically integrated business model. For example, neither Apple nor BlackBerry had developed or announced any plan to develop and license an app store for Android.

## C. Google's Dominant Position in the Market for the Provision of General Search[5]

The EC further concluded that the provision of general search services constituted a separate relevant product market, in which Google held a dominant position in each national EEA market since 2011. The EC noted that general search services belonged to a different product market relative to other online services (*e.g.*, content sites, specialized search services, and social networks). At the same time, the product market included: (i) PC and smart mobile devices; (ii) all different smart mobile OSs; and (iii) all "entry points."

The EC argued that from a demand-side perspective, users expected to receive the same general search services regardless of device (PC versus smart mobile). From

---

4 Including Google's Play Store, the Amazon AppStore, Samsung's Galaxy App store, Opera, Yandex store, and Aptoid.

5 *See* Section 9.5 of the EC *Google Android* decision. Other evidence includes network effects and the high investments and queries volume that were needed to build a viable general search engine.

a supply-side perspective, the same undertakings offered search services on both PCs and smart mobile devices: Google, Bing, Yandex, Yahoo, and DuckDuckGo. The EC found that Google's general search share had been above 80-90 percent across all EEA countries since 2011. It also noted there were high barriers to entry, with several companies abandoning their own search technology (*e.g.*, Ask.com and Yahoo!), while Microsoft (Bing) had been the only significant EEA entrant since 2007 (with less than 6 percent share in any EEA country). Further, the EC found it unlikely that a substantial proportion of Google users would switch search service in the event a small but significant non-transitory deterioration of the Google's search quality.[6]

Google argued that specialized search services should be included in the market as they exercised a constraint on general search services for the categories of queries for which their search functionalities overlap. The EC rejected this claim since general and specialized search services did not offer the same functionalities even with respect to the overlapping queries: For instance, for services that specialize in travel, users may look for hotels within a certain number of stars or certain part of the city, and these functionalities are not available to the same extent on a general search service.

Further, while the EC did examine iOS in the context of the market for mobile licensing, this case was not one of "Android versus iOS operating system." There was no indication that iOS would be a channel for a competing search engine to enter; and in any event Google was announced as the default Search and Maps provider at the 2007 launch of the iPhone.[7]

## III. THE ABUSIVE CONDUCT AND ITS IMPACT

The EC concluded that Google's requirement that OEMs pre-install the Google Search app and Chrome as a condition for licensing the Play Store[8] amounted to tying Google Search app with the Play Store, which had exclusionary effects and thus constituted an abuse of Google's dominant position in the market for Android app stores. Similarly, the tying of Google Chrome with the Play Store and the Google Search app was deemed an abuse of Google's dominant position in the global market for Android app stores and in national EU markets for general search services.

Google argued in response that the tying of the Google Search app and Chrome were required to allow Google to monetize its investment in a freely distributed open

---

6 For this the EC relied on a Microsoft survey that indicated that only 20 percent of consumers multi-homed (defined as conducting more than 5 percent of queries on at least two search engines) between multiple search engines in France, Germany, Italy, Spain, and the UK. Google primary search users multi-homed approximately seven times less than did the primary users of Bing/Yahoo. This suggested that there was little scope to believe that users would switch their search away from Google to any additional search services that they might be using.

7 "Apple Reinvents the Phone with iPhone," Apple Press Release. January 9, 2007.

8 European Commission, "Antitrust: Commission fines Google €4.34 billion for illegal practices regarding Android mobile devices to strengthen dominance of Google's search engine," July 18, 2018 press release.

source OS such as Android, as well as in a freely distributed app store such as Google Play. Further, Google argued that its development and stewardship of the Android ecosystem was pro-competitive: Google's model gave OEMs all the software that they needed to develop a smart mobile device for free – the Android Open Source Project ("AOSP") – as well as wide latitude to customize Android devices. The model offered an open platform with a minimum compatibility baseline that allowed app developers to write a single app that could run on all Android devices that met this baseline. As a result, OEMs could modify Android to produce their own variants of the platform, and could in fact produce differentiated Android devices.

Making Android open source gave OEMs and MNOs important assurances that induced them to embrace and invest in Android, as it meant that Google could not, at some later stage, degrade the platform. Google further argued that the pre-installation requirements with OEMs were what enabled Google to continue to offer the Android platform for free; OEMs received the OS for free in exchange for the promotion of Google services.

Critical to the EC's analysis was the effect of pre-installation for Google's usage and revenues. The EC argued that pre-installation was critical because it increased significantly and on a lasting basis the usage of the service that was provided by the app and by the web browser. This was the reason why Google remunerated OEMs and MNOs for pre-installing the search app, setting its service as the default ("default setting"), and placing it in a premium position on smart mobile devices ("premium placement"). Especially when consumer inertia is important and placement on a main screen can be considered a scarce resource, an incumbent monopolist can outbid potential rivals for access to the scarce resource and preserve its lead.

On the premium placement point, app placement is a scare resource, as only a few apps can occupy the first screen and only one search engine can be a default search engine. Google did allow its default search engine to be changed; but this was a case of user "inertia," where users are more likely to stick with a pre-installed search engine – as was seen by Bing and Yahoo in markets where their engines were preinstalled. Google could exclude entrants by offering RSAs to major OEMs in exchange for exclusive pre-installation of its search engine.

Premium placement, default search, and dominance taken together were an unbeatable combination for Google to outbid potential rivals in agreements with OEMs. The result was a classic pre-emption mechanism: The incumbent has more to lose than entrants have to gain when there is free entry in a bidding competition, and therefore the incumbent outbids its rivals; see Gilbert & Newbery (1982).

### A. Pre-installation and Default Setting were Important for the Distribution of General Search Apps (e.g., Google Search) and Significantly Increased their Usage[9]

The EC used multiple examples of how pre-installation of the search apps affected search engines' popularity in various countries in different periods. Analysis from

---

9 *See* Section 11.3 of EC *Google Android* decision.

complainant Yandex indicated that Yandex's general search share in Russia in May 2015 was two-to-five times higher on Android devices on which its search widget was pre-installed on the home screen, and set as default in the pre-installed mobile web browser. Figure 1 illustrates Yandex's share of general search queries' depending on installation status.

**Figure 1: Yandex's Share of General Search Queries on Smart Mobile Devices as a Function of Various Scenarios for Pre-installation and Default Setting**

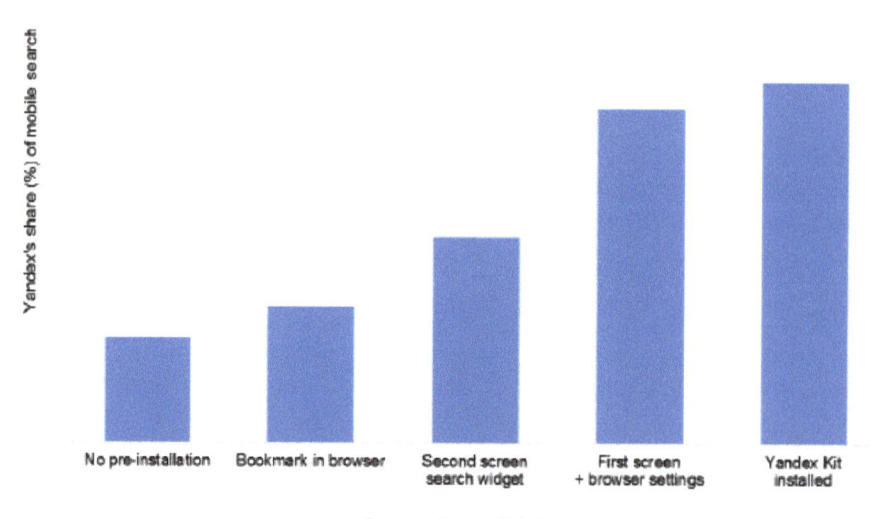

**Relation between Yandex's share of search and degree of pre-installation, May 2015**

**Source:** Figure 18 of the EC Google Android decision

The EC concluded that Google enjoyed higher usage and revenues from mobile devices that pre-installed Google apps. For instance, the Google Search app was used by 76 percent users of Google Android (pre-installed) versus 17 percent iOS (not pre-installed, must download).

The EC also calculated that competing general search apps – such as Naver, Natc, Daum, Yandex, Bing, DuckDuckGo, Yahoo, Seznam were downloaded on Google's Play Store on only 0-10 percent of new devices sold where the Google Search app was pre-installed. This held true on a worldwide basis and across the EEA. *See* Figure 2.

## Figure 2: Number of Competing General Search Apps' Downloads from the Play Store

**Number of downloads of competing general search apps worldwide from the Play Store in 2011-2016 (in thousands)**

| General search apps | 2011 | 2012 | 2013 | 2014 | 2015 | 2016 |
|---|---|---|---|---|---|---|
| Total number of Google Search pre-installations | 215,092 | 379,425 | 594,272 | 808,200 | 916,293 | 917,909 |
| Total as % of Google Search pre-installations | [0-5]% | [5-10]% | [0-5]% | [0-5]% | [0-5]% | [0-5]% |

**Source:** Tables 14 of the EC *Google Android* Decision.

## B. Pre-installation was also an Important Channel for Distribution of General Web Browsers (e.g., Google Chrome)[10]

The EC also concluded that pre-installation and default settings for web browsers significantly boosted the usage of these services. For instance, the EC relied on Opera's 2013 survey that indicated that 72 percent of the 1,500 respondents in Germany, Poland, and the UK regularly used the pre-installed mobile web browser. Further, both Bing and Yahoo experienced increases in their search queries after preinstallation in specific markets and browsers.[11] The EC also estimated that pre-installation increased Google's revenues from its Chrome browser, similar to the effects of pre-installation of search apps.[12]

Downloads could not be compared in reach and effectiveness to pre-installation of Google Chrome. The EC calculated that in 2013-16 competing non-Google web browsers were downloaded only on a portion of mobile devices that had the Google Chrome browser pre-installed: less than 40-50 percent worldwide and less than 10-20 percent in the EEA. The results are shown in Figure 3.

---

10 *See* Section 11.4 of EC *Google Android* decision.

11 Second, there were multiple examples of pre-installation's driving up usage shares and being key to web-browsers' success in different countries across different time periods: (i) Six months after Bing was preinstalled in Mexico (July 2013) Bing's query share increased from 0-10 percent to 50-60 percent; (ii) Mozilla changed its U.S. default from Google in Firefox 33 to Yahoo in Firefox 34. As a result, Yahoo's (Google's) query shares were 29 percent (63 percent) on Firefox 34 versus 10 percent (82 percent) on Firefox 33; (iii) Shares of Yandex in Russia were 5-10 percent versus 20-30 percent on the devices where the Yandex browser was not pre-installed versus when it was pre-installed; (iv) Bing's pre-installation on Nokia in India and Brazil drove its query shares to 20-40 percent compared to 0-10 percent in any EEA country.

12 Worldwide revenues from general search queries on Google Android devices in 2014-16 via Google Chrome (pre-installed) were higher than those obtained via other mobile web browsers (nor pre-installed); worldwide revenues from general search queries on iOS devices in 2014-16 via Safari (pre-installed) were higher than those obtained via Google Chrome (not pre-installed).

### Figure 3: Number of Competing Web Browsers' Downloads from the Play Store

Number of downloads on GMS devices of competing non OS-specific mobile web browsers worldwide from the Play Store in 2013-2016 (in thousands)

| Mobile browsers | 2013 | 2014 | 2015 | 2016 |
|---|---|---|---|---|
| Total number of Google Chrome pre-installations | 594,272 | 808,200 | 916,293 | 917,909 |
| Total as % of Google Chrome pre-installations | [10-20]% | [20-30]% | [30-40]% | [40-50]% |

Number of downloads on GMS devices of competing non OS-specific mobile web browsers in the EEA from the Play Store in 2013-2016 (in thousands)

| Mobile browsers | 2013 | 2014 | 2015 | 2016 |
|---|---|---|---|---|
| Total number of Google Chrome pre-installations | 174,217 | 196,349 | 203,740 | 197,375 |
| Total as % of Google Chrome pre-installations | [5-10]% | [5-10]% | [10-20]% | [10-20]% |

**Source:** Tables 17 and 18 of the EC *Google Android* decision.

## C. The Conduct: Google Licensed the Play Store and Google Search Apps Conditionally on Contractual and Anti-fragmentation Obligations[13]

The EC argued that since at least January 1, 2011 (but in fact earlier), Google had made the licensing of the Play Store and the Google Search app conditional on OEMs' agreeing to multiple agreements and that this constituted an abuse of its dominant positions in the global market for Android app stores and the national markets for general search services. It was a common view among observers at the time that as a result of the anti-fragmentation and other contractual agreements, "Android is open – except for all the good parts."[14]

### 1. Anti-Fragmentation Agreements ("AFAs")

Anti-Fragmentation Agreements were agreements between Google and OEMs that prevented OEMs from selling "forked" Android devices, in exchange for which OEMs had access to the Android OS system and brand. Because AFAs were applied at the company level, OEMs could not diversify production with normal and forked Android devices for different markets or in different periods. As a result, few OEMs attempted to distribute forked devices.

---

13 *See* Section 12 of the EC *Google Android* decision.

14 Amadeo, Ron, "Google's iron grip on Android: Controlling open source by any means necessary," *ARS Technica*, July 21, 2018.

The EC calculated that anti-fragmentation agreements between Google and OEMs covered 90-100 percent of worldwide (excl. China) smart mobile devices in 2013-2016 (excl. non-licensable OSs such as Apple),[15] and that this prevented the entry entrance of multiple differentiated Android OSs – "forks" – of which Amazon's Fire OS was the most prominent example. Despite the fact that, as of 2013, 75 percent of apps in Google Play were compatible with Fire OS and 700,000 – 900,000 apps were developed for Fire OS, Amazon was unable to secure production from any OEM.

Google argued that these AFAs were necessary to ensure that apps worked across different Android devices, and preserved a minimum quality standard and a common user experience for customers of those devices. Other open source systems such as Symbian and Unix had failed – Google argued – due to fragmentation, and AFAs were intended to ensure compatibility for the Android ecosystem as a whole. Allowing a fragmentation risk with Android would have damaged the platform, both functionally and reputationally.

## 2. *Mobile Application Distribution Agreements ("MADAs")*

By signing a Mobile Application Distribution Agreements ("MADA") to produce a normal Android device, an OEM accepted a number of restrictions on the applications that could be pre-installed on its mobile devices. The role of pre-installed applications is crucial in mobile devices because most online traffic originates from access through these dedicated applications – due to both an easier user experience and a technological advantage as compared with traditional access through internet navigation.

The first main requirement of a MADA was that the OEM must pre-install certain applications – that were specified by Google – on the device and display them in a prominent position (such as on the default home screen or in the next panel). While the list of specified Google applications could change over time, the main ones included YouTube, Google Maps, Chrome, Google Search, and Google Play.

The second key requirement of a MADA was that Google Search must be set as the default search provider, and it must also be the default search engine for the voice search function, the hardware-button-activated search function, and other advanced options in recent smartphones. The same occurred for the Chrome browser, which in turn incorporated Google Search as default search engine and was a main access point to search for most users. These requirements contributed to providing a common user experience that was based on Google products on all normal Android devices; but they also limited OEMs from mixing and matching applications according to market demand, and reduced opportunities for product differentiation. By signing a MADA, OEMs gained access to Google Mobile Services ("GMS"), Google apps, and

---

15 *See* Table 1 of the EC *Google Android* decision. Smart mobile OSs are developed by vertically integrated OEMs such as Apple or BlackBerry for use on their own smart mobile devices ("non-licensable smart mobile OSs"), or by providers such as Google or Microsoft which then license their smart mobile OSs to OEMs ("licensable smart mobile OSs").

associated applications programming interfaces ("APIs") and software development kits ("SDKs").

Google stated that by pre-installing apps consumers would have a suite of useful apps "out of the box." Furthermore, Google argued that pre-installation better positioned manufacturers of Android devices to compete with Apple, Microsoft, and other mobile ecosystems that came preloaded with similar baseline apps. Finally, Google argued that the preinstalls did not prevent OEMS or consumers from installing other apps.[16]

3. *Revenue Share Agreements ("RSAs")*

Google further offered Revenue Sharing Agreements ("RSAs") to a selected group of major OEMs of Android-based devices and to MNOs – in exchange for exclusivity. RSAs prevented these parties from pre-installing competing search engines anywhere on their devices. These agreements could be based on exclusive pre-installation on a portfolio of products or on precise devices; but, in either case, the purpose was to make it convenient for OEMs to pre-install Google Search as the only search engine at any entry point on all of their devices. The EC estimated that competing general search could not have offered OEMs and MNOs enough revenues to compensate for the loss of Google's portfolio-based revenue share payments across the entire portfolio of Google Android devices.[17]

## D. Impact of the Conduct: Google's Conduct Harmed Consumers as it Increased Barriers to Entry and Expansion and Reduced Innovation and Consumer Choice in General Search Apps, Web Browsers, and Alternative Android OSs[18]

1. *Google's Tying Practices had Exclusionary Effects*

The EC concluded that the tying of the Play Store and the Google Search app as well as the tying of Chrome with the Play Store and the Google Search app erected a major barrier to rivals' entry and expansion, and reduced competitors' incentives to innovate and invest in improvements such as algorithms and user experience design for both their search apps and web browsers. This is because Google's pre-installation significantly boosted its usage, which made it harder for competing general search services and web browsers to gain search queries and the respective revenues and data that they needed to improve their services. The conduct further increased barriers to entry by making it harder for competitors to challenge Google's dominant position in general search services as competitors would need to spend substantial resources to overcome the status quo advantage of pre-installation. The

---

16 Google, "Android has helped create more choice and innovation on mobile than ever before," April 15, 2015.
17 Section 13.4.1.2 of the EC *Google Android* decision.
18 *See* Sections 11.3.4.2, 11.4.4.2, 12.6.6 and 13.4.2 of the EC *Google Android* decision.

conduct therefore harmed consumers, who would see less choice of general search services and web browsers.

### 2. *The Anti-fragmentation Obligations Prevented the Development of New Variants*

The EC further concluded that Google's anti-fragmentation obligations reduced the incentives of market participants to develop Android OS variations ("Android forks") and provide distinctive features and additional functionalities to smart mobile devices. It therefore tended to harm – directly or indirectly – consumers, who as a result of Google's interference with the normal competitive process would see less choice of smart mobile OSs that would be suitable for their needs.

In particular, the EC pointed to consumers' being unable to purchase devices based on Fire OS: A forked version of Android that was developed by Amazon that was generally considered at the time to be a high-quality Android fork and that was prevented from finding even a single distribution channel: OEMs were hesitant to manufacture Fire OS devices as this would have breached Google's anti-fragmentation obligations. Amazon's plans to license its Fire OS were eventually withdrawn and the EC found that Amazon's internal documents as well as its correspondence with OEMs demonstrated that the anti-fragmentation obligations were an important cause of the failure of Amazon's efforts to license Fire OS.

### 3. *The Incentive Payments ("RSAs") Were a Further Barrier to Entry for Rival Search Providers*

The EC concluded overall that Google's exclusivity portfolio-based revenue share payments deterred innovation to the detriment of consumers: Other general search services with more focused offerings would not have been able to achieve the scale and access to users that would allow them to invest in R&D. Google prevented competing search services from gaining incremental search queries and the respective revenues and valuable user data that they needed to improve and develop innovative features such as innovation in algorithms and in user-experience designs. The portfolio-based revenue share payments also reduced Google's incentives to improve the quality of its general search service as it did not compete on the merits with other search services. Competitors could not match Google's revenue share payments due to both Google's strong position in search services and competitors' low pre-installation levels.

## IV. THE ECONOMIC THEORY OF HARM[19]

This section reviews the economic theory of harm that underpinned the *Android* case. A wide debate developed at the time as to the anti-competitive mechanism that was at play. This promoted academic work that extended traditional theories of harm

---

19 The analysis in this section is based on Etro & Caffarra (2017).

based on tying and naked exclusion to incorporate multiple important features of the case. Critically, this was the first time that economic theories of exclusion that were based on a tying mechanism were adapted to a multisided environment, in which the service that was supplied was free to end users and monetization occurred on the advertising side; see in particular the discussions in Choi & Jeon (2021); De Cornière & Taylor (2021); and Iacobucci & Ducci (2019).

Multiple papers are now developing models that incorporate "zero-price constraints" on one group of users when analyzing the potential for exclusion and foreclosure, as well as potential implications for regulatory approaches; see in particular the recent work of Bisceglia & Tirole (2022). The *Android* case was the first time that these features were incorporated in the analysis combined with more standard mechanisms.

## A. Traditional Anti-competitive Mechanisms

Multiple insights of the traditional antitrust literature on tying apply directly to the *Android* case. The classic analysis is that of Whinston (1990), which tells us that tying a primary product that is supplied by a monopolist (here Google, as a dominant provider of the Google Play suite) with a secondary product (here its search engine) can be an aggressive strategy that can foreclose entry in the secondary market. Given the high fixed costs that are involved in developing a search engine and reaching a viable scale in search, a bundling strategy that reduces the profits of an entrant can deter entry and allow Google to extend its market power to mobile search.

Dynamic theories by Carlton & Waldman (2002), as well as Choi & Stefanadis (2001) also analyzed how tying can be used against the threat of entry in both the primary and secondary market and can provide the foundations for a theory of harm in the *Android* case: As long as Google's rivals could compete against its bundle only by providing both an app store and a search engine pre-installed as default, it was harder for third-party suppliers to offer such an alternative package on Android based devices. At the very least, the bundling strategy increased their costs and degraded the quality of their potential offers.

The mechanism of Choi & Stefanadis, in particular, holds when primary and secondary products are complements and is particularly relevant to the *Android* case. In their approach, bundling reduces the incentives to invest in the development of a better application store and a better search engine because each innovation will be profitable (against the bundle) only if the other will also be successful (otherwise buyers would use the bundle). By developing a high-quality app store and committing to distribute it for free to OEMs if it is bundled with Google Search, Google attracted more apps than any other app store, and increased the investment that any potential entrant had to face to build a competitive package that included an alternative app store and a search engine. Accordingly, the bundling strategy could be sufficient to deter entry.

While useful, these "work horse" theories did not incorporate the specificities of search engines and application stores as *two-sided markets* – where providers are potentially able to monetize their services by charging either advertisers and app developers, or consumers and OEMs.

## B. Extending the Analysis to Fit the Case

### 1. The Choi & Jeon Mechanism

An important contribution by Choi & Jeon (2021) filled the gap, by showing that a dominant firm in a two-sided primary market can tie its primary good with a secondary good that is produced in a competitive two-sided market, and deter entry in the latter in a profitable way – as long as there are some constraints on the prices that can be charged for the service.

Choi & Jeon used the *Android* case as an illustration of their framework. They showed that if a new superior search engine could subsidize consumers to use its product and finance this through the rents that are obtained on the advertising side, entry could be successful and challenge Google's dominance. However, when subsidies to consumers are not feasible – for instance because consumers cannot be directly paid for installing applications (the zero-price constraint), otherwise they would install applications that they do not use – Google had an easy mechanism with which to tie Google Search with the Google Play suite and attract consumers with a low enough price for the bundle. The intuition is that, without tying, the zero-price constraint softens competition and increases the rents that the rival search incumbent can extract; but with tying the price constraint makes it harder for the rival search engine to compete against Google.

However, the original Choi & Jeon model has two main limitations when applied to the *Android* case: The first is its main assumption that firms cannot pay buyers to adopt their secondary product: While this is realistic when perhaps considering consumers (as it is unusual for search engines to pay consumers to use or install them), it is less realistic when the "customers" are OEMs. The model assumes implicitly that search engines cannot pay OEMs to have the search engine pre-installed on their mobile devices. But payments for pre-installation and for default position do actually take place in the market, and certainly Google makes such payments to OEMs.

Another limitation when applying Choi & Jeon to the *Android* case is that while the analysis finds that foreclosure is profitable and reduces total welfare, it also finds that consumer surplus is actually increased by tying. This happens because without tying competition is reduced, as search engines cannot subsidize adoption, while under tying competition is increased, and both the price of mobile devices and their price-quality ratio decrease, which makes consumers better off.

### 2. The Etro & Caffarra Mechanism

We have provided an alternative but related foreclosure mechanism that more closely fits the facts of the *Android* case; *see* Etro & Caffarra (2017).[20] The key ques-

---

20 *See also* the discussion by Choi & Jeon (2021, pp. 323-325) and related work by De Cornière & Taylor (2021).

tion in the case was whether an efficient rival search engine that offered equivalent (or better) quality relative to Google Search could outbid Google, be pre-installed on Android devices, and challenge dominance in search. We argued that when Google ties the Google Play ("GP") suite to Google Search it can outbid a more efficient search engine, and therefore deter entry, as long as it has committed to distributing Android with the GP suite without charging the OEMs.

This commitment generates a "quality gap" compared to "bare" Android devices that do not include the GP suite. This fits what is observed in the market, where Google committed to providing to OEMs both Android and its GP suite for free. As noted by Choi & Jeon (2021, p. 324) this implies that "Google has a "surplus slack" in the tying good market (due to its free availability), which can be leveraged to the tied good market via bundling."

Our mechanism emerges in a situation where OEMs produce hardware devices (as they do), and Google provides Android to OEMs for free (as it does). In addition, let us assume that search engines can be provided by two firms: Google provides Google Search, and an entrant provides a search engine of superior quality. Search advertising gains can be collected by each search engine that is used by a consumer, and we assume that both search engines can extract the same revenues from online advertising.

We compared two scenarios: In the first scenario there is no tying, so Google provides the GP suite as a standalone product and competitive bidding for exclusive pre-installation of search engines takes place. As long as a rival search engine provides a superior offer, it can outbid Google Search for pre-installation. Then, the outcome is that OEMs "mix and match" products (Google suite with the rival search engine).

The second scenario involves Google's tying its suite with Google Search. This mirrors what happened in practice. While an entrant can still bid for exclusive pre-installation on forked Android devices without GP, the difference in quality makes it possible for Google to pay OEMs enough to use its bundle. In practice this happens through the RSAs. Under some additional conditions, the analysis shows that this strategy can deter entry, be profitable for Google, and worsen the price-quality ratio of mobiles compared to the previous situation without tying. Accordingly, consumer surplus decreases because of tying.

The key condition for the breakdown of the One Monopoly Profit theorem here is that in the absence of tying, Google forgoes collecting some surplus from OEMs through its commitment to a zero price for the GP suite. This "uncollected surplus" is then used to capture the tied good market. In practice, the difference in quality between "normal" Android devices with the GP suite, and "bare" Android devices without it is so large that through small financial incentives Google can convince OEMs to adopt the GP suite, and rival search engines cannot outbid Google. Notice that if Google had set a monopolistic price for the standalone GP suite, assuming homogeneous consumers in their valuations, the price would equal the incremental value of the GP suite relative to an alternative suite, and exclusive tying would no longer be profitable. However, when there is a constraint on pricing the product in the primary market, the One Monopoly Profit Theorem breaks down.

An additional finding of our model is that tying deters entry of a rival search engine when the extra gains for consumers from the GP suite are greater than the difference in quality between search engines. Moreover, foreclosure requires financial incentives for OEMs to adopt the bundle if the total surplus that is generated by the rival search engine (for both consumers and firms) is greater than the consumer surplus that is generated by the tying product.

Finally, we have shown that anti-competitive tying can also emerge after relaxing the zero-price constraint and allowing some form of monetization of the tying product. In particular, when consumers are heterogeneous in their valuations of the suites, tying remains anti-competitive also when Google sets an optimal linear price for the GP suite as a standalone product. The intuition is that a linear price for the GP suite without tying does not allow Google to extract all of the surplus of heterogeneous consumers. Then tying allows some forked devices to be supplied with the rival search engine pre-installed, but Google can still profit from this strategy if the revenues from app developers and in-app advertising are low enough (since these are lost on the forked devices) and the quality gap between search engines is low enough (since this limits the payments to OEMs to accept the bundle). When profitable, tying can still reduce consumer surplus when the revenues from app developers and in-app advertising are low enough and the quality gap between search engines is low enough. Therefore, the anti-competitive essence of Google's tying strategy holds under rather general conditions.

## C. Network Effects and Naked Exclusion Mechanisms

Exclusionary effects could be further reinforced by an additional mechanism that is well known in the antitrust literature. It has to do with what is usually referred to as the 'naked exclusion' of rivals through exclusive dealing contracts. Google signed RSAs with a group of selected large OEMs. These RSAs can be decisive to foreclose entry, yet Google can also exploit its dominance by bargaining with OEMs in a way that minimizes its payments.

Essentially, this is a "divide and conquer" strategy: Google had technological leadership in search, and dominance of online advertising that could be threatened only if a competing search engine manages to develop a sufficient scale to endogenously improve its search algorithms (known as "scale in search"), and to attract enough search queries to expand revenues in online ads and further invest in innovation ("network effects"). Both these elements explain why a rival search engine could compete with Google Search only if the rival achieved a large enough scale: reached a large enough number of users.

A dominant firm can adopt a network of exclusive dealing arrangements to deter entry of existing or potential rivals and harm consumers: This is usually defined as "naked exclusion." The mechanism behind this form of vertical foreclosure is due to Rasmusen, Ramseyer & Wiley (1991) and applies in the present context when appropriately modified. The additional aspects that must be introduced are "scale economies" in search, and network effects. Competing search engines can enter the market or expand their market share by building "scale in search" only if they reach a high enough share of users. Contracts for pre-installation of their search engine on some OEMs' devices are a viable opportunity (in practice the only one) for this. However, dominance in search puts Google in an asymmetric position compared to rival search engines.

Overall, a variety of traditional and new economic mechanisms have been deployed and developed to underpin formally the concern that Google was profitably foreclosing the entry and expansion of rival search engines through its tying strategy, and that consumers were deprived of the benefits that would have arisen from the provision of better or differentiated search engines.

Interestingly Google did not seek to counter this body of economic work with economic analyses of its own, to the best of our knowledge. It argued qualitatively that there was undoubtedly significant innovation and new entry in search, or rather "in how people access information today." Google argued that consumers "look for news on Twitter, flights on Kayak and Expedia, restaurants on OpenTable, recommendations on Instagram and Pinterest" – all of which were outside the Google search engine.[21]

The EC wrapped up the case in 2018 with a finding of infringement, and a large fine at the time: €4.34 bn. The decision also contained a "cease and desist" order whereby Google was to desist from adopting the contractual restrictions – MADA, AFA, RSA – that were the focus of the investigation and not adopt alternative conduct that could have the same effects. The case was a straightforward leveraging/tying case along the lines of the original 2001 *Microsoft Media Player* case (a favorite of the EC), which was updated to the age of multisidedness and zero-price constraints.

How have things fared since?

## V. WHY HAS EUROPEAN ENFORCEMENT FAILED TO BRING ABOUT CHANGE?

Notwithstanding strong theories of harm and good evidence, European infringement decisions against Google have generally struggled to achieve any real change. This is the unfortunate reality also for *Android*.

Just as was true for the earlier decisions in the *Search (Shopping)* case,[22] the *Android* decision contained a "cease and desist" order: to stop the conduct at issue, and not do anything that would lead to equivalent outcomes.[23] There were very limited indications in the decision as to what an appropriate remedy could look like: The decision mandated Google not to tie the Play Store with Search, or engage in equivalent

---

21 Google, "A deeply flawed lawsuit that would do nothing to help consumers," October 20, 2020.
22 Case T-612/17 *Google and Alphabet v. Commission* (*Google Shopping*). See also the chapter in this volume by Andrea Amelio.
23 *Google Android,* para. 1393: "Google and Alphabet should be required to bring (…) the "Infringement" effectively to an end (…), and to refrain from adopting any practice or measure having an equivalent object or effect," see https://ec.europa.eu/competition/antitrust/cases/dec_docs/40099/40099_9993_3.pdf.

conduct.[24] This means the onus is then on the infringer to put forward a proposal for an alternative approach. And with huge information asymmetries between the company and the agency, and incentives to perpetuate the conduct remaining exceptionally strong given that it is so lucrative, the process tends to lead to a protracted game of "cat and mouse": A proposed solution; a market test that draws negative comments from complainants; another solution being proposed; and so on.

In practice in this case, Google responded by first engaging in a *"de facto"* tie: no longer formally tying the Play Store with Search and Chrome, but offering the former to OEMs at a positive price and the latter at an *equivalent* discount, so that OEMs continued to be able to pre-install Google Play effectively at zero cost – on condition that they also pre-installed the Search app or Chrome.

Following negative reactions by complainants and observers, the "proposed solution" then veered towards an auction in which alternative search engines could bid to get a place in the range of choices that the owner of a new phone in Europe would face on the homepage when getting the device out of the box. In practice, however, Google is always in the list while others (Bing, DuckDuckGo) have to pay for inclusion. And though a few names made it to the list, not much is (inevitably) happening in terms of consumers' actually choosing to pre-install alternatives to Google Search.

This was predictable: While relying on auction-type logic for "inclusion" in a set of choices – and on margin squeeze tests for policing anticompetitive behavior – sounds fine in principle, it could not "move the dial." Where strong economies of scale/network effects are *reinforced* by vertical links to other products in which the incumbent is dominant, the ability and incentive to game and circumvent a margin squeeze test are too strong. And to reward through auctions the company that achieved dominance by illegal means is problematic *per se*: Good policy should not allow a company to price its market power and extract the associated rents from others.[25]

But critically, firms that are nascent or that have been weakened and marginalized as a result of years of the conduct will simply not gain visibility in this way. Relying on *consumers* then spontaneously to select weak alternatives to the super dominant choice is not going to achieve pro-competitive outcomes – given all that we know about behavioral factors. Lack of familiarity with alternatives will continue to drive consumers towards the dominant firm – especially if the alternative is still in some measure disadvantaged by less attractive placement and other constraints.

---

24 *"Google and Alphabet should refrain from licensing the Play Store to hardware manufacturers only on condition that they pre-install the Google Search app [and Google Chrome]* (paras. 1394-5), and *"(1) (...) cannot make the obtaining by hardware manufacturers and users of the Google Search app [or Google Chrome] with the Play Store conditional on any payment or discount that would remove or restrict the freedom of hardware manufacturers and users to pre-install the Play Store without the Google Search app [or Google Chrome]; (2) (...) cannot punish or threaten hardware manufacturers and users that pre-install the Play Store without the Google Search app [or Google Chrome]"* (para. 1396)). There is similar language prohibiting the conditioning of a Play Store license on the OEM entering into Anti-Fragmentation obligations, and language prohibiting exclusive pre-installation payments *("(must) refrain from granting payments to OEMs and MNOs on condition that they pre-install no competing general search service on any device"* (para. 1401).

25 *See also* Ostrovsky (2020) for a discussion of the potential problems with such auctions.

With a "cease and desist" order that has only very mild principles of non-discrimination, the latitude has been enormous for Google to propose changes that appeared to create the semblance of competition, but that are inherently incapable of having any effect. If companies that depend on traffic or rely on the platform of the dominant company to provide an alternative to its service are suppressed for a protracted period, "solutions" that could send some traffic their way but in practice to do not increase their visibility after years of degradation are not going to achieve success – even more so if there is "grit" in the system such that the traffic is minimal, and visibility remains low.

It does not need to be thus. The EC has occasionally adopted remedies that require positive obligations that go beyond a cease and desist order. For instance, in the *Microsoft Media Player* case, Microsoft was ordered to offer a full-functioning version of its Windows client PC operating system that did not incorporate Windows Media Player. What appears to be standing in the way is a mixture of uncertainty over what could be an effective remedy, and a sense that to mandate a big and disruptive solution to a giant non-European firm would be politically difficult.[26]

The inevitable outcome of the frustration in Europe with the duration and lack of effects of antitrust enforcement cases against Google ultimately accelerated political momentum towards regulation. The Digital Markets Act ("DMA") – which was adopted by the European Parliament in record time and is in the process of being implemented – is a direct consequence of this sentiment.

## VI. THE EC DECISION HAS BEEN UPHELD BY THE GENERAL COURT

Google appealed the EC decision immediately in 2018: Google claimed that Android "created more choice for everyone, not less."[27] The first round of appeals of the EC decision by Google ended with a judgment by the General Court of the EU in September 2022,[28] which upheld the decision and confirmed the 2018 findings. This was a critical victory for the EC – at a time when the Court had been patchy in its support. The Court (mostly) endorsed the Commission's analysis and use of evidence; the Court rejected Google's efficiency justifications.

A few general reflections arise from the Court's endorsement:[29] First, the Court generally embraced the EC's analysis but rejected one of the grounds of infringement: the claim that Google's RSAs with OEMs gave rise to exclusionary effects. The Court struck down the notion that the RSAs had exclusionary effects by running its own version of an "as efficient competitor" test. The significance of this is that it would

---

26 As expressed by Commissioner Vestager, "with hindsight" she would have taken a different view: "If I knew what I know now about Google, I would be bolder" (Politico conference December 8, 2020). She has since referred repeatedly to the need to contemplate more "restorative" remedies.

27 Google, "Android has created more choice, not less," blog, July 18, 2018.

28 Judgment of the General Court, September 14, 2022, *see* https://ec.europa.eu/competition/antitrust/cases/dec_docs/40099/40099_9993_3.pdf.

29 *See also* Caffarra (2022).

appear that the Courts have developed an appetite for engaging with price-cost tests, and that these will be taken seriously if they are relied upon at all. This will be a deterrent to agencies' bringing cases with a price-cost aspect; and at the margin it will weaken the appetite for enforcement in cases that involve exclusivity.

Second, and more generally, while the judgment has been a much-needed boost to the EC's posture and appetite for risk, the case is also most emblematic of the inherent challenges and failures of *ex post* enforcement. Google's practices had succeeded in moving the Search monopoly from the desktop to the mobile environment long before the case was formally opened. The major "pivot" into mobile technology could have provided in principle a major opportunity for challenging the incumbent in the previous technology (desktop search). Yet monopolization of mobile search was long accomplished by the time the investigation even began. Nearly 10 years after concerns were first expressed, there is yet another round of appeal – to the ECJ.

Third, the case is also emblematic because – notwithstanding a straightforward theory of harm, fines, and a "remedy" – there has been absolutely no change on the ground. In practice the "remedy" could not realistically undo the harm in a digital market that has tipped. And the Court judgment cannot change that. The Court does not engage (of course) with the failure of the EC remedies. But this is an endemic failure, because when markets have tipped, they cannot be "untipped" through these remedies.

The pivot to digital regulation in the past two years – with the adoption in record time of the DMA – has reflected deep frustration at the political level with all the above. The Court judgment on Android confirms that the case was good law, and that the Court believed that it was also good economics – and yet we are no closer to creating competition in mobile search.

## VII. CONCLUSION

In the *Android* case, the EC concluded that Google's contractual practices with OEMs – which made the supply of Google's Play Store contingent on the pre-installation of Google Search as the default at every entry point to the device – were anticompetitive and an abuse of Google's dominant positions in smart mobile OS, Android app stores, and general search. The case attracted significant interest from economists as to the anticompetitive mechanism that was at play and prompted work that extended traditional theories of harm that were based on tying, network effects, and naked exclusion to incorporate multisidedness and zero-price constraints in ad-funded business models. This initial work is now being expanded to underpin the assessment of further practices by digital platforms that operate under a zero-price constraint (*e.g.*, app store terms and commissions), as in recent work by Bisceglia & Tirole (2022).

The courts have so far upheld the decision, and while it is subject to a further round of appeals at the ECJ, we believe that it will be upheld again. Yet the case is a poster child for how ex post enforcement was inadequate to prevent the extension of monopoly – an especially grave loss at times of pivotal technological change. It is also a poster child for how markets that have "tipped" cannot be "untipped" with remedies. Overall, the legacy of the *Android* case is that enforcement against the conduct of digital giants continues to achieve very little because it has not been timely, and remedies have been inadequate to overcome a loss of competition that was pretty much complete.

The slow grinding of the antitrust wheels in this (and other) cases has solidified the view in Europe that *ex ante* regulation – the DMA – was an urgent and necessary complement to *ex post* enforcement. Digital enforcement has thus strongly shifted to a huge experiment in digital regulation. Is this more likely to succeed? DMA regulation requires "gatekeepers" themselves to come forward with proposed "solutions" to the "obligations" that are identified in the new law. Is this going to be more effective? Can competition be preserved? Can it be restored in a more timely fashion? Are any of these interventions going to do more than enforce some fairness?

The experiment is underway.

## VIII. POSTSCRIPT: THE ONGOING GOOGLE "SEARCH" CASE IN THE U.S.

In October 2020, the United States Department of Justice ("DOJ") and several state attorneys general brought legal action against Google under Section 2 of the Sherman Act.[30]

The case as outlined in the DOJ's and states' complaints is broader than Android. The precedent of the EC *Android* case clearly provided a blueprint for the Android part of the U.S. case. The complaints identify Google's implementation and enforcement of a series of exclusionary agreements with distributors as the key mechanisms for the anti-competitive conduct. The complaints allege that these agreements locked up search distribution both in mobile and in browsers: Google captured essentially all of the mobile search market – enabled by agreements with Apple for iOS distribution, as well as its own Android licensing terms.

As in the EC case, the DOJ points to Google's control of the Android mobile distribution channel with its distributor agreements and owned-and-operated distribution properties. The AFAs, MADAs, and RSAs are identified as the mechanisms for Google to control distribution on Android.

A major difference with the European case is that the EC did not cover Google's agreements with Apple in its case. Google has had a series of search distribution agreements with Apple, which involved setting Google as the pre-set default general search engine for Apple's Safari browser (Mac and iOS) in exchange for a $8–12bn slice of its advertising revenues a year. Google also has a separate RSA with Mozilla's Firefox to make Google the default search option on the browser. Over 85 percent of all browser usage in the U.S. occurs on Google's own Chrome browser or on one of the browsers that are covered by these RSAs.

---

30 "…bring this action under Section 2 of the Sherman Act, 15 U.S.C. § 2, to restrain Google LLC (Google) from unlawfully maintaining monopolies in the markets for general search services, search advertising, and general search text advertising in the United States through anticompetitive and exclusionary practices, and to remedy the effects of this conduct." *United States v. Google LLC*, October 2020.

The DOJ's complaint also tries to capture the perennial problem that once enforcers pursue Google for a specific conduct, it is too late. The complaint alleges that Google positioned itself as a search distributor beyond mobile and browser and points to agreements with car manufacturers, smart watch manufacturers, and "internet-of-things ("IoT") device manufacturers. The complaint argues that through agreements with "next-gen" manufacturers, Google is well positioned to continue to extend its search monopoly in the future.

Google replied that consumer use Search "because they choose to, not because they're forced to, or because they can't find alternatives."[31] It argued that the complaints are against consumers' interests, and serve only to prop up lower-quality search alternatives artificially, raise device prices, and make it harder for consumers to get the search services that they want to use. Its agreements were free negotiations with other companies, and pre-installation did not preclude consumers from accessing competitor products. Indeed, changing a default search engine was easy on a browser, and Android often came pre-loaded with OEMs' app stores (*e,g,*, the Samsung Galaxy Store) in addition to the Google Play Store. Google also pointed to evidence that 204 billion apps were downloaded in 2019 – hence consumers are savvy enough to download the apps that they actually want.[32]

The trial is tentatively set to start in September 2023.

# REFERENCES

Bisceglia, Michele & Jean Tirole (2022). "Fair Gatekeeping in Digital Ecosystems," mimeo, Toulouse School of Economics.

Caffarra, Cristina (2022). "The EU General Court Confirms Android Abuse of Dominance through Tying, with the Real Legacy of the Case Extending Far Beyond (Google Android)." Concurrences, September 14.

Carlton, Dennis W. & Michael Waldman (2002). "The Strategic Use of Tying to Preserve and Create Market Power in Evolving Industries." *RAND Journal of Economics*, 33.2: 194-220.

Choi, Jay Pil, & Doh-Shin Jeon (2021). "A Leverage Theory of Tying in Two-sided Markets with Nonnegative Price Constraints." *American Economic Journal: Microeconomics* 13.1: 283-337.

Choi, Jay Pil & Christodoulos Stefanadis (2001). "Tying, Investment, and the Dynamic Leverage Theory." *RAND Journal of Economics*, 32.1: 52-71.

De Cornière, Alexandre & Greg Taylor (2021). "Upstream Bundling and Leverage of Market Power." *The Economic Journal* 131.640: 3122-3144.

Etro, Federico & Cristina Caffarra (2017). "On the Economics of the Android Case." *European Competition Journal*, 13.2-3: 282-313.

---

31 https://blog.google/outreach-initiatives/public-policy/response-doj/.

32 Google, "A deeply flawed lawsuit that would do nothing to help consumers," October 20, 2020.

Gilbert, Richard J. & David M.G. Newbery (1982). "Pre-emptive Patenting and the Persistence of Monopoly." *The American Economic Review*, 72.3 514-526.

Iacobucci, Edward & Francesco Ducci (2019). "The Google Search Case in Europe: Tying and the Single Monopoly Profit Theorem in Two-sided Markets." *European Journal of Law and Economics*, 47.1: 15-42.

Ostrovsky, Michael (2020). "Choice Screen Auctions," NBER Working Paper No. w28091.

Rasmusen, Eric B., J. Mark Ramseyer & John S. Wiley Jr. (1991). "Naked Exclusion," *American Economic Review*, 81.5: 1137-45.

Whinston, Michael D. (1990). "Tying, Foreclosure, and Exclusion," *American Economic Review*, 80.4: 837-59.

## CHAPTER 13
# Targeted Below-Cost Pricing in the Semiconductor Industry: The *Qualcomm Predation* Case

*By Liliane Giardino-Karlinger*[1]

## I. INTRODUCTION

In the late 2000s, Qualcomm – the leading developer of wireless technology products and services – was selling certain chipsets to two Chinese manufacturers of mobile devices, Huawei and ZTE, who were of particular importance in the segment for chipsets offering advanced data rates.

The European Commission argued that some of these sales were at prices that were below cost – with the intention of eliminating Icera, which was a small and financially constrained start-up that was competing with Qualcomm in the leading-edge segment at the time. By containing Icera's growth with respect to the two key customers in this segment, Qualcomm intended to prevent Icera from gaining the reputation and scale necessary to challenge Qualcomm's dominance in the "universal mobile telecommunications system" ("UMTS") chipset market. This targeted predatory attack took place between 2009 and 2011, at a time when the global take-up of smart mobile devices created expectations of large growth for chipsets with advanced data rate performance.

To substantiate this theory of harm, the European Commission conducted an in-depth analysis of Qualcomm's pricing decisions at the time as reflected in its internal documents, and carried out a price-cost test comparing Qualcomm's prices to Huawei and ZTE for certain leading-edge chipsets with the relevant long-run average incremental costs of these products.

In July 2019, the European Commission imposed a fine of EUR 242 million on Qualcomm (the "Decision"). Qualcomm lodged an application for annulment of the Decision in November 2019, which is currently (as of August 2022) pending before the General Court.

The remainder of this chapter describes the companies and the industry concerned by this case; Qualcomm's strategy and practices; the law and economics of pre-

---

[1] The author of this chapter was involved in the investigation in this case while at the European Commission's Chief Economist Team at DG COMP. The views that are expressed in this chapter are those of its author and may not in any circumstances be regarded as stating an official position of the European Commission.

dation; the European Commission's case against Qualcomm; Qualcomm's arguments in its defense; and the outcome of the case.

## II. THE SMART MOBILE REVOLUTION

The term "mobile" refers to all technologies that enable voice and data services via cellular connectivity. The different "eras" of mobile technology are typically identified by the prevailing telecommunications standard; these eras are divided into the analog standard (1G), second generation (2G), third generation (3G), fourth generation (4G), and now fifth generation (5G) networks. The relevant standard in the Qualcomm (predation) case is the UMTS standard, which is a 3G communications standard. To connect a mobile device (*e.g.*, a smartphone or tablet) to the cellular network, the device must contain a "baseband chipset" that supports the same standard as the cellular network to which the device is to be connected. The relevant market in this case is the merchant market for baseband chipsets compliant with different iterations of the UMTS standard.

Figure 1 below provides an overview of the various technology developments over time that merged into the modern smartphone as we know it.

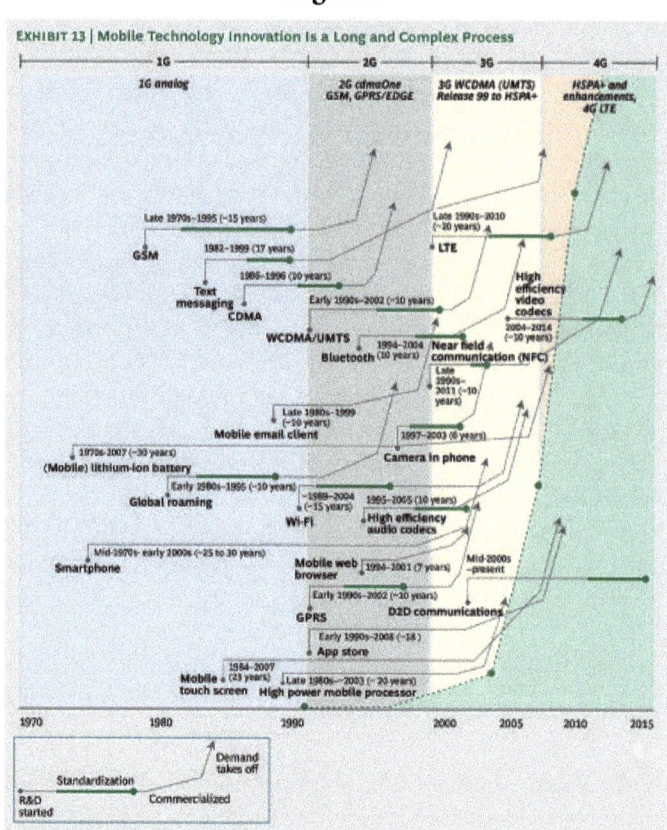

**Figure 1**

**Source:** Bock et al. (2015)

The leading communications technology developer – Qualcomm – is headquartered in San Diego, California, and had 45,000 employees in 2021 generating about 33.57 billion U.S. dollars in revenue. Qualcomm develops semiconductors, software, and services that are related to wireless technology, and sells its semiconductor products in a fabless manufacturing model, meaning that the physical manufacturing of the chipsets designed by Qualcomm is not carried out by Qualcomm itself, but is outsourced to independent chipset manufacturers called foundries. Qualcomm owns patents that are critical to the 5G, 4G, CDMA2000, TD-SCDMA, and WCDMA mobile communications standards, the latter including the UMTS standard that is relevant for this case.

The main customers for the chipsets of interest for the case were China-based device makers Huawei and ZTE. The complainant in the case was the UK-based company Icera, which was founded in 2002 by four European semiconductor executives, with its headquarters in Bristol, UK. Icera developed chipsets for devices that provided mobile communications that are based on the UMTS standard, including: datacards (for example USB sticks); laptops; netbooks; tablets; and e-book readers.

Although a number of technologies that were necessary for the creation of the smartphone had already been developed in the 1990s, the 2G networks that were deployed at the time (and even the 3G networks that dominated the early 2000s) had not been optimized for data transmission, but for voice transmission. The great leap forward in data rates came with the HSPA+ and LTE networks, which represented a 12,000-times improvement in capacity relative to 2G, with maximum download speeds of 250 megabits per second ("Mbps"), as opposed to 20 kilobits per second ("Kbps") for 2G. As data rates improved dramatically, retail prices for data usage fell exponentially (*see* Figure 2), which made mobile internet access affordable for ever broader segments of the population.

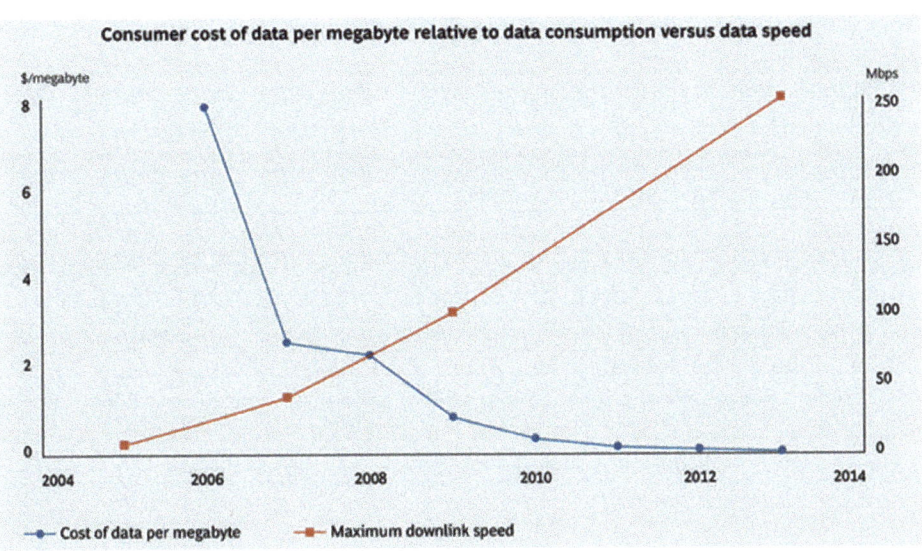

**Figure 2**

Consumer cost of data per megabyte relative to data consumption versus data speed

**Source:** Bock et al. (2015)

The smartphone revolution really started in 2007 with the launch of the iPhone, the first handset to fully integrate the phone with an internet communications device. Since then, consumer adoption of the smartphone has seen a dramatic evolution, with an estimated 3.5 billion people using smartphones worldwide in 2021. By the end of 2016, mobile and tablet had surpassed desktop computers as the primary access point for the internet.[2]

## III. QUALCOMM'S STRATEGY AND PRACTICES

The Commission found Qualcomm's pricing policy for certain chipsets between July 2009 and June 2011 to have violated EU antitrust laws because it constituted predatory pricing. As a predation case this decision is something of a rarity: It is the first one since 2003, when the Commission found that French broadband provider Wanadoo Interactive had charged predatory prices for its eXtense and Wanadoo ADSL services as part of a plan to preempt the market in high-speed Internet access during a key phase in that market's development.[3]

Similar to the *Wanadoo* case, the infringement in the *Qualcomm Predation* case occurred at a key juncture in the development of the market: The early 2000s were the period of the introduction of "slim" modems: stand-alone UMTS-compliant chipsets that provide only connectivity, but that do not have any application processing functionality. Slim modems use less silicon and are therefore less expensive than integrated chipsets with equivalent baseband characteristics. They are also smaller than integrated chipsets and are less power hungry, which makes them commercially interesting for use cases that require only connectivity. One such category of products are Mobile Broadband ("MBB") devices: in particular "data cards" with cellular access, typically in the form of USB sticks ("dongles"), which allow a PC or a router to receive wireless internet access via a mobile broadband connection instead of using telephone or cable television lines.

Slim modems have eventually prevailed in MBB devices, but they are also widely used in smartphones and tablets, when a device maker prefers to have the baseband processor and the application processor residing in different chips; this is a concept that is known as "two-chip" architecture.

Icera entered the UMTS chipset market with sales of the first slim modem in 2006; Icera targeted the MBB segment. Shortly thereafter, Qualcomm followed Icera in the development and launch of slim modems. Other companies – such as Intel/Infineon, Mediatek, and HiSilicon – later also developed slim modems, in parallel with their integrated chipsets.

The key parameter for such data-centric baseband chipsets – whether they are slim or integrated – is their data rate performance. In the "leading-edge segment" – the segment of chipsets that offered advanced data rate performance – Icera had

---

[2] StatCounter, *available at* https://gs.statcounter.com/press/mobile-and-tablet-internet-usage-exceeds-desktop-for-first-time-worldwide (accessed July 12, 2022).

[3] *See* Case COMP/38.233 - *Wanadoo Interactive* (Commission Decision of July 16, 2003).

started to gain traction in 2008/2009 due to the software upgradability of its chipsets to leading edge data rates (meaning that these chipsets could be adapted to higher download speeds by means of software updates at a later stage, even after the chip had been incorporated into an end device and sold on, without the need to change the silicon itself) and its competitive pricing.

Qualcomm's pricing strategy focused selectively on UMTS chipsets in the leading-edge segment, while the objective of its conduct was to protect Qualcomm's dominance in the entire UMTS chipset market – and in particular its strong position in the high-volume segment of baseband chipsets for use in mobile phones. While the sales of MBB devices were relatively small compared to the overall sales of mobile phones, the MBB segment was particularly important for the leading-edge chipsets that were supplied by Icera and Qualcomm.

The two strategically most important customers for leading-edge UMTS chipsets during the Relevant Period were Huawei and ZTE: They were the main manufacturers of MBB devices at the time, into which almost all leading-edge chipsets were incorporated in this period. By containing Icera's growth in sales to these two key customers in this segment, Qualcomm intended to prevent Icera – a small and financially constrained start-up – from gaining the reputation and scale that were necessary to challenge Qualcomm's dominance in the wider UMTS chipset market. Qualcomm was particularly concerned by Icera's threat because of the expected growth potential of the leading-edge segment due to the global take-up of smart mobile devices.

The theory of harm in the Qualcomm predation case was thus essentially one of "selective" targeting: Qualcomm's below-cost pricing applied to only a small part of the UMTS chipset market; but this pricing had an (intentionally) adverse impact on the entirety of the market that the strategy intended to foreclose.

This selective element is not typically captured by standard economic models of predatory pricing, which generally assume that the predatory prices are applied to all of the units that are sold in the market that the predator wishes to defend.[4] As such, this broad pricing strategy is very costly, and much more difficult to rationalize, as it fully depends on the possibility of "recoupment" in the same product market in a possibly distant and uncertain future. It is therefore not surprising that enforcers have rarely found instances where a predatory strategy was implemented in this extreme form. Predation cases are often considered as *"something between a white tiger and a unicorn."*[5]

But predation may also involve a dynamic strategy where market entrants can at first compete only in a segment of the market, which may become the theatre of a predatory attack to protect future markets or contemporaneous neighboring markets or segments. This mechanism is reminiscent of the "divide and conquer" strategies that have been studied in the literature on exclusive dealing.[6] In the context of preda-

---

[4] *See* section below on the economics of predation.
[5] Baker (1994).
[6] Rasmusen et al. (1991), Segal & Whinston (2000), Fumagalli & Motta (2006).

tion, this notion has been explored only sparsely in the economic literature,[7] and has yet to affirm itself in enforcement practice.[8]

In the *Qualcomm Predation* case, the future market that was likely affected by Qualcomm's conduct was the fledgling LTE (or 4G) chipset market. With revenues from MBB sales in the UMTS chipset market falling below its targets, Icera was forced to scale back its R&D in voice functionality/LTE, which was crucial for Icera to be able to enter the LTE smartphone segment as scheduled by the end of 2011. Instead, Icera's entry into the LTE smartphone segment was delayed to February 2013, by which time Icera had already lost the commercial opportunity of early entrance in this segment; and its acquirer, Nvidia, eventually wound down Icera's modem operations in May 2015.

## IV. THE LAW AND ECONOMICS OF PREDATION

### A. The Economics of Predation

Predation is typically defined as a strategy where, in the short run, a dominant firm sacrifices part of the profit that could be earned under competitive circumstances in order to induce the exit of a rival (or prevent entry) and subsequently gain (or maintain) additional monopoly profits in the long run (Ordover & Willig, 1981). The interest of economists in predation as an exclusionary strategy dates back at least to McGee's seminal contribution of 1958, discussing the *Standard Oil* case of 1910.[9] The often-critical position of economists towards the legal practice in predation cases culminated in the Chicago School criticism (McGee, 1958; Easterbrook, 1981), which essentially claimed that predation could not be a rational strategy. Subsequent research showed that this claim builds on a number of strong assumptions, the most fundamental being that of perfect information. When this assumption is violated, there is room for predatory pricing as a way of making a rival believe that the market is less profitable than it initially believed, thus prompting the rival's exit.

The modern economic models of predation can be grouped into three categories: First the predator may want to build a reputation for being tough, which can then be used to extend the reputational effects of predation to other markets (Yamey, 1972; Posner, 1976; Scherer, 1980; Bolton et al., 2000). Second, the predator can charge predatory prices to signal that it has very low costs or that demand is too low to sustain an entrant, even if this is not the case (Milgrom & Roberts, 1982). Third, the predator can exploit imperfect information in capital markets by inflicting losses on the prey which will then induce its investors to withdraw their support, because they cannot distinguish losses due to predatory attacks from losses due to inefficiency or underperformance (Telser, 1966; Bolton & Scharfstein, 1990).

This latter model is directly relevant for the theory of harm in the *Qualcomm Predation* case. Another directly relevant model is that of Fumagalli & Motta (2013),

---

[7] *See* Bolton et al. (2000); *see also* Bolton & Scharfstein (1990), Fumagalli & Motta (2013).
[8] *See* Crocioni & Giardino-Karlinger (2022).
[9] *See* McGee (1958).

who showed that a dominant firm that has already sunk some costs, can predate a more efficient entrant on early buyers in order to deprive the latter from the required economies of scale, recouping its losses on monopoly sales to later buyers.

## B. The Legal Standard for Predation Cases

In the U.S., the legal standard for finding predatory pricing is based on the "Areeda-Turner" test, which requires that prices be below short-run average variable costs ("AVC"), and that recoupment is at least possible.[10] This is a stringent standard – in particular in industries where the variable costs tend to be low, and the fixed costs are high. This is particularly true of innovative and high-tech industries, where a large part of operating costs is incurred for R&D and other non-variable cost components. Under the U.S. legal standard, there is a risk of underenforcement, in the sense that predatory attacks at prices above AVC, or with doubtful recoupment, will go unpunished and are hence not deterred.

On the other hand, the Areeda-Turner test minimizes the risk of overenforcement: of conflating a "healthy" pro-competitive price cut by an incumbent that follows entry by new rivals with a predatory attack. Such overenforcement can have a chilling effect on competition, as incumbents may hesitate to react pro-competitively to entry for fear of triggering an antitrust investigation. It is therefore vital to strike the right balance between rigorous antitrust enforcement and encouraging pro-competitive behavior where adequate.

The legal framework for predation cases under EU law builds on two different tests: the AKZO I and AKZO II tests. With respect to the relevant cost benchmark, the case law states that "*first, […] prices below average variable costs must be considered prima facie abusive inasmuch as, in applying such prices, an undertaking in a dominant position is presumed to pursue no other economic objective save that of eliminating its competitors.* [AKZO I] *Secondly, prices below average total costs but above average variable costs are to be considered abusive only where they are fixed in the context of a plan having the purpose of eliminating a competitor.*" [AKZO II][11]

The AKZO I test is reminiscent of the Areeda-Turner test in the U.S., insofar as the relevant cost standard is AVC under these two tests. However, in the European variant, prices below AVC give rise to a presumption of illegality: No further evidence is needed to find an infringement.

The main departure from U.S. practice is that in Europe, even prices above AVC (but below average total costs, or "ATC") may be found abusive – provided that there was exclusionary intent (AKZO II). While prices above AVC do not generally give rise to antitrust concerns (as they are compatible with many forms of pro-competitive behavior), they are not a safe haven in the EEA, as the existence of evidence on intent may give rise to a finding of abusive pricing nonetheless. Another important differ-

---

10 *See* Areeda & Turner (1975), Hovenkamp (2015).

11 Case C-62/86, *AKZO v. Commission* (Court of Justice judgment of July 3, 1991), para. 72; Case C-333/94, *Tetra Pak v. Commission* (Court of Justice judgment of November 14, 1996), para. 41; Case C-202/07 P, *France Télécom v. Commission* (Court of Justice judgment of April 2, 2009), para. 109.

ence between the U.S. and Europe is that it is not necessary to show recoupment (or the possibility thereof) under either the AKZO I or AKZO II test to sustain a finding of predation.

While the AKZO II test has been part of the case law since the early 1990s, most predation cases in the EU relied mainly or exclusively on the AKZO I standard. The 2003 *Wanadoo* case that was mentioned above is no exception, as the majority of the predatory prices were found to be below AVC, and only a small part above AVC (but below average total costs [ATC]).

The Qualcomm predation case instead is the first case where (almost) all predatory prices were found to be between AVC and ATC:[12] This case is the first to rely fully on the AKZO II test. In this context, the documentary evidence that substantiated the existence of a "*plan having the purpose of eliminating a competitor*" was therefore a key component of the Decision's findings.

## V. THE COMMISSION'S CASE AGAINST QUALCOMM

When Icera entered the market with its first chipset in 2006, it was initially faced with the challenge of having to earn the trust of device manufacturers, who attach great importance to the reliability of their chipset suppliers and those suppliers' products. After initial teething problems, however, Icera's chipsets quickly gained traction in the market – especially among manufacturers of MBB devices. Icera's strength was in its focus on chipsets without a built-in application processor (slim chipsets), which enabled Icera to offer attractive prices and the promise of software upgradability of its chipsets. The latter in particular was perceived by the market as an innovative and attractive feature that set Icera's chipsets apart from Qualcomm's products.

In order to contain Icera's growth, Qualcomm decided to take "*preventive measures*" in the form of targeted price reductions. These were needed because – in contrast to Icera's market acceptance and a growing number of orders for its chipsets from key customers – Qualcomm's product offering in the leading-edge segment was only marginally competitive at the time. It essentially consisted of a chipset model called MDM8200, which enabled particularly high download speeds of up to 28 Mbps, but otherwise suffered from technical defects that Qualcomm attributed to a rushed market launch. The MDM8200 chipset was the first chipset that was compatible with HSPA+ on the market, but it was not an attractive product due to increased power consumption, overheating issues that delayed the market launch, and the lack of widespread support for such high download speeds by mobile phone networks.

In this context, Qualcomm identified a "*competitive gap*" vis-à-vis Icera in the leading-edge segment. To fill this gap until more competitive chipset models were launched, Qualcomm was willing to "*make price a non-issue to let MDM8200 fill the void*" in its sales negotiations for the MDM8200 chipsets. In the first half of 2010, Qualcomm released its highly anticipated new chipset models in the leading-edge

---

12 *See* Appendix for tables showing prices, AVC, gross margins, and the Commission's cost benchmark and calculated price shortfall.

segment – the MDM6200 and the MDM8200A – with some delay. However, it soon became apparent that Qualcomm's new chipset offering was not attractive enough to catch up with Icera. This was also due to the fact that Icera was now offering an enhanced variant of its top chipset (ICE8042 chipset) at an aggressive unit price for all download speeds up to 21 Mbps.

According to Qualcomm's assessment, Icera's ability to survive depended crucially on whether Icera would succeed in establishing itself as a chipset supplier for at least one of these companies ("*Icera has to win either of the two or it cannot survive*"). Accordingly, Qualcomm's goal was to prevent Icera from establishing a business relationship with either Huawei or ZTE and thus generating stable and sustainable sales ("*Penetration in Huawei and ZTE would bring Icera stable and sustainable business*").

Qualcomm's strategy initially focused on Huawei ("*the undisputed king of data card with >50% market share worldwide*"). Not only should any overtures by Icera towards Huawei be nipped in the bud ("*not give Icera any opportunity in Huawei strategically*"), but Qualcomm's low prices for Huawei should also ensure that if Icera were to push ahead with ZTE, then Huawei's devices would outperform ZTE's in terms of price; this would divert downstream demand away from end devices that contained Icera chipsets and towards Qualcomm-based devices ("*push ZTE back by working with Huawei in the market place*").

Despite Icera's already precarious financial situation, Qualcomm continued to pursue its predatory pricing strategy throughout 2010 and well into the first half of 2011. After Nvidia acquired Icera in May 2011, Qualcomm was uncertain about Icera's future direction, and so decided to reduce prices further in order to exclude Icera from doing business with Huawei and ZTE even after Icera's acquisition by Nvidia. Qualcomm's internal documents at the time indicate that as of the second half of 2011, competition from Icera as a driver of Qualcomm's pricing became less important as other considerations in this regard gained prominence. Based on Qualcomm's internal documents, the Commission used the last day of the quarter in which the price-cost test (see below) indicated the presence of below-cost pricing as the end date of the infringement.

In June 2009, Icera lodged a first formal complaint with the European Commission regarding Qualcomm. However, it was only in 2012 that allegations of predatory pricing began to feature prominently in these submissions. As is often the case in B2B markets, where bilateral contracts tend to be unobservable for any third party, Icera did not have full visibility of Qualcomm's conduct *vis-à-vis* its customers. Icera therefore had to rely on indirect evidence to identify the conduct that triggered the complaint. What followed was an in-depth investigation of Qualcomm's conduct, notably its pricing decisions, during the period of interest. The resulting infringement decision builds on the evidence on intent contained in Qualcomm's internal documents as well as on a price-cost test for the three products concerned by the predatory strategy, namely the MDM8200, the MDM6200 and the MDM8200A, which were launched at different points in time during the relevant time frame encompassing the years 2009 to 2011.

A price-cost test is an indispensable element to build a predation case under EU law. While this may seem to be a straightforward exercise, it often involves a fair amount of data processing before the actual test can be conducted. This applies both to the price and the cost side of the test, although the cost side usually requires more attention.

## VI. THE COMMISSION'S PRICE RECONSTRUCTION

As far as prices are concerned, the commonly used concept of "unit price" in economic models is drawn from the world of spot markets, where prices are effectively quoted on a unit basis, and the total transaction value is given by the product of price and quantity. However, in long-run B2B relationships, such flat unit pricing is rare. Instead, the trading partners typically agree on a list price that is in place for a certain time period, and later negotiate a number of discounts that apply to some or all of the units that have been traded within this period. Some of these discounts may be conditional on future events, such as the price at which a customer will resell the product or the end product into which a certain input is incorporated.

Such discounts drive a wedge between the revenue that is recorded in a given period, and the revenue that is effectively generated by the units that are shipped in this same period: The discounts may trigger adjustments to the effective revenue that will be recorded long after the sales to which these discounts apply have been carried out. In each period, the accounting revenue is therefore composed of the (yet to be adjusted) revenue of the units that were sold in that period, and also the adjustments that refer to certain units that were sold in previous periods. In order to identify the correct unit price that applies to the units that are sold in a given reference period (quarters in the *Qualcomm* case), these adjustments have to be matched with the quarter in which the sales occurred that triggered the adjustment, rather than the quarter in which the adjustment was recorded.

In other words, the Commission based its price-cost test on *ex post* realized prices rather than any *ex ante* expected prices, taking into account all information on entitlement for discounts that became available after the relevant units were sold. This approach was in Qualcomm's favor, because the *ex ante* prices as recorded in Qualcomm's accountings always assumed full entitlement for all discounts. Thus, the *ex post* realized prices were, if anything, higher than the *ex ante* prices, namely in those cases where the customer eventually did not qualify for a certain rebate, so that the non-disbursed rebate was recorded later on as additional revenue. Where this was the case, the Commission took this additional revenue fully into account in its price reconstruction.

It turns out that these reconstructed prices often closely match the price points that are discussed in contemporaneous internal documents from managers with price-setting authority. This matching demonstrates that the "*preventive measures*" in the form of below-cost prices envisaged in Qualcomm's internal documents had actually been implemented.

Furthermore, during its investigations, the Commission discovered two one-off payments that Qualcomm had made to Huawei and ZTE, respectively. In Qualcomm's accounting, these one-off payments were allocated to a specific chipset model. However, internal documents from Qualcomm – which were supported in part by third-party documents – revealed that these one-off payments were intended as a discount for certain quantities of other chipsets for which Qualcomm did not want directly to reduce the price further at the time. The Commission therefore allocated the relevant one-off payments to the transactions based on the documents in question, which in some cases significantly reduced the unit price that was actually paid for the relevant sales.

## A. The Commission's Cost Benchmark

On the cost side of the test, the first cost benchmark that had to be identified was AVC, as this cost metric represents the dividing line between the AKZO I and AKZO II tests. Since Qualcomm did not manufacture its chipsets itself, but outsourced manufacturing to foundries, the AVC was calculated on the basis of the purchase price that Qualcomm paid to the foundries for the deliveries of the respective chipset volumes. In order to take into account the fact that not all of the chipsets were resold immediately, but were sometimes kept in stock for some time, the Commission calculated the respective stock levels in order to allocate the correct purchase price to the corresponding chipset sales on Qualcomm's side, applying the first-in-first-out ("FIFO") principle.

As was already mentioned, the unit prices that were effectively paid by Huawei and ZTE were always above the AVC that was calculated by the Commission, with very few exceptions. The applicable legal standard is therefore the AKZO II standard: Prices between AVC and ATC can also be abusive if these prices were intended to drive a competitor out of the market.

This begs the question of which cost benchmark to apply in such an AKZO II scenario. None of the modern economic models of predation discussed above suggests any specific cost benchmark, such as short-run marginal cost, for a predator to successfully deter entry or induce exit. The appropriate cost benchmark does depend on the applicable legal test, where the AKZO II test is less prescriptive than the AKZO I test regarding the appropriate cost benchmark. In the *Qualcomm Predation* case, the Commission considered long-run average incremental costs ("LRAIC") – the average of all (variable and fixed) costs that Qualcomm incurred in the production of the products under investigation – as the most appropriate cost measure for the purposes of this case.

This approach is in line with Baumol (1996), who called for an avoidable cost standard in predation cases, taking into account both the short- and longer-run time frame. To assess the short run costs, Baumol suggested to replace AVC by Average Avoidable Costs (or "AAC"), while using LRAIC to assess those cost components that are variable in the long-run.

LRAIC is below ATC because Qualcomm is a company that supplies a range of different products, of which only three specific chipset models were relevant to the implementation of its predatory strategy against Icera. In a multi-product company, in addition to the costs that can be attributed to the production of certain products, there are also so-called real common costs (such as selling and advertisement costs) that would not have been avoidable if a single product had not been produced. Such common costs are therefore not included in the calculation of LRAIC, but would be fully included in the calculation of ATC. LRAIC therefore represents a conservative cost benchmark compared to ATC in the context of a predatory pricing case.[13]

To calculate the LRAIC for the chipsets under consideration, the Commission relied (in addition to the AVC) on product-specific development costs, which resulted from internal Qualcomm documents. The latter costs do not vary with the short-term sales volume (and are therefore not part of the variable costs), but are unavoidable in the long term in order to achieve the relevant chipset sales in their entirety. Since the majority of these development costs precede the sale of the chipsets, the Commission needed a methodology for allocating these development costs to the relevant chipset sales.

The Commission used a revenue-based allocation method. This approach recognizes that leading-edge chipsets generally generate the highest margins early in their life cycle, as the innovative value of these products is greatest at launch. Thus, these products tend to generate the highest revenues in the first half of the product life cycle, when volumes are still relatively low, while they generate the highest volumes towards the end of their life cycle, when they are already "commoditized" and therefore sell at very low margins.

In such a context, using a quantity-based allocation – as is often found in corporate cost accounting – instead of a revenue-based allocation would greatly increase the LRAIC for such products towards the end of their life cycle, and may thus lead to a spurious finding of below-cost prices in later periods, even if there was in fact no intention to charge predatory prices. For products whose margins are subject to such innovation-related fluctuations over the course of their life cycle, a revenue-based allocation allows the calculated minimum margin to reflect the influence of these life-cycle dynamics in a realistic way. This approach also allowed the Commission to take into account so-called spillovers between two of the three products that were examined.

It should be noted that the conduct that is being examined – in this case predatory pricing – has an impact on the revenue that is generated in any given period, and hence on the way that the non-variable components of LRAIC are allocated to these periods. Arguably, the revenue that is generated by a company during those periods where it engages in predatory pricing is *lower* than it would have been absent the anticompetitive conduct. As a result, the costs that are allocated to the relevant quarters under a revenue-based allocation will be lower than in the counterfactual, which makes it thus *more* likely that the price-cost test is passed in a period where prices were in fact predatory.

## B. Results of the Commission's Price-cost Test

As a final step in the test, the Commission compared the effectively paid prices with the reconstructed LRAIC. This comparison was performed on a quarterly basis for each of the three chipset models that were examined and for each of the two key customers. The test showed that almost all sales to Huawei and the majority of sales to ZTE were made at prices that were below the respective LRAIC (see Table 59 extracted from the Commission's decision below, and the full results tables in the Appendix).

---

13 For such multi-product firms, Baumol (1996) proposed the so-called "combinatorial tests" whereby any combination of products must also be collectively priced to yield revenues that cover the combined incremental costs.

Table 59: Percentage of predatory sales to Huawei and ZTE in the leading edge segment (1 July 2009 to 30 June 2011)

|  | MDM8200 | MDM6200 | MDM8200A | Total |
|---|---|---|---|---|
| Sales to Huawei | 100% | 0% | 100% | 99% |
| Sales to ZTE | 43% | 91% | 100% | 68% |
| Sales to Huawei and ZTE | 85% | 64% | 100% | 92% |

**Source:** Case COMP/39.711 *Qualcomm (predation)* (Commission Decision of July 18. 2019)

The total revenue that was generated by Qualcomm from these predatory sales was significantly higher than Icera's *total* revenue in 2011 (the last year of the investigated period), further illustrating the potential impact that Qualcomm's predatory pricing had on Icera.

Figure 33 (extracted from the Commission's decision) illustrates the evolution of predatory sales (in volumes) over time, with bars above the horizontal axis (bold) represent above-LRAIC sales, and bars below the axis represent below-LRAIC sales.[14] The small quantities of chipsets that were sold to ZTE at prices that were above LRAIC all occurred at the beginning of the Relevant Period, when Icera had already established a sales relationship with ZTE. At this point Qualcomm's strategy was to sell its chipsets primarily to Huawei to enable the latter to crowd out ZTE's Icera-based end products in the downstream market: to the main buyers of MBB devices, in particular telecom operators.

Figure 33: Evolution of Qualcomm's sales to Huawei and ZTE made below and above cost during the infringement period

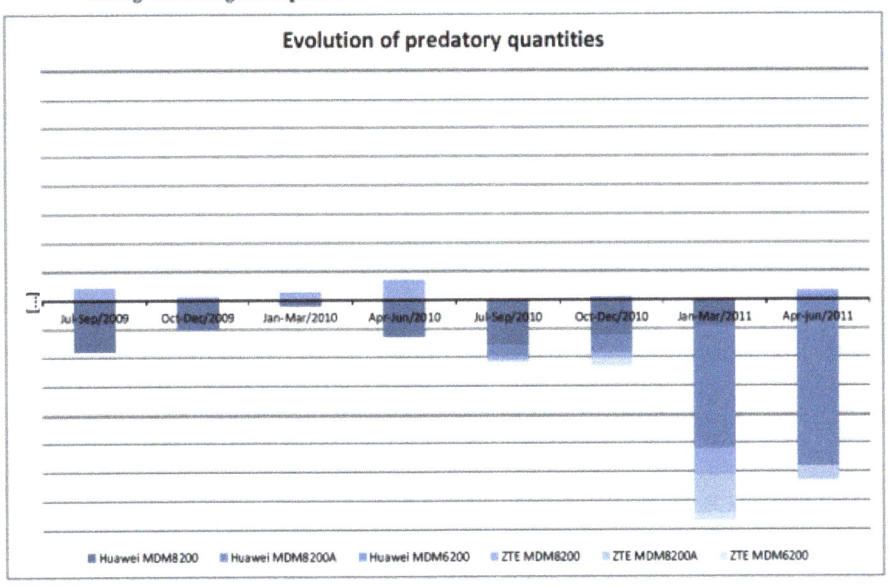

**Source:** Case COMP/39.711 *Qualcomm (predation)* (Commission Decision of July 18, 2019)

---

14 For confidentiality reasons, this figure is shown without a scale on the vertical axis.

Nevertheless, in addition to the price-cost test that was explained above, the Commission also examined the question of whether the analyzed chipsets had fully recovered their respective aggregated LRAIC when the total life cycle revenues are considered. The main differences between the lifetime profitability analysis and the price-cost test above were as follows: (1) The Commission took into account the entire life cycle of the products, including the period that was already outside the investigated period, in which two of the three chipsets examined were still available on the market; (2) the Commission also took into account all of the revenues that were generated from all of the other customers of these three products (not just Huawei and ZTE); and (3) the Commission carried out the test not only for each individual chipset, but also at the chipset family level, for which both the revenues and the development costs of the MDM8200 and the MDM8200A were aggregated into a single metric.[15]

Although this life-cycle analysis considered far higher revenues than the price-cost test above, the investigation revealed that only the MDM8200A as a stand-alone product – but not the MDM8200 individually and especially not the product family as such – had fully recovered their respective product-specific life-time costs (including the development costs), and even for the MDM8200A, the life-time revenues are probably overstated, and its lifetime costs understated, in this exercise. This result does not depend on the specific assumptions that were made in allocating the development costs to particular quarters or products and thus reinforces the result of the price-cost test in this case.

## VII. QUALCOMM'S VIEW OF THE CASE

EU case law has established that a dominant company that is investigated for abuse of dominance can invoke objective justifications to escape the application of Art. 102. In the *Qualcomm (predation)* case, Qualcomm presented the following objective justifications:

- *Qualcomm's pricing practices were both rational and profit maximizing, as every unit was sold at a price that was above AVC and thus was sold at a profit that contributed towards the recovery of Qualcomm's fixed costs.*

While it is true that pricing *below* AVC represents a deviation from short-run profit maximization, and therefore triggers a presumption of illegality in the EU legal order, the presence of *above*-AVC prices does not automatically show proof of profit-maximizing conduct. While non-dominant firms that charge prices that are above AVC will not attract any further scrutiny, a dominant firm that charges prices that are above AVC but that are part of a plan to eliminate a competitor still infringes Art. 102. Therefore, Qualcomm cannot escape the application of Art. 102 even if its pricing strategy was at least *prima facie* compatible with short-run profit maximization.

---

15 The MDM8200A was based on the MDM8200 architecture, and therefore belonged to the same chipset family, along with several other models that shared similar features. This exercise is somewhat reminiscent of Baumol's (1996) "combinatorial tests." The MDM6200 belonged to a different chipset family and was thus not included in this exercise.

- *Regarding the sales of the MDM8200 to Huawei, Qualcomm's pricing strategy was meant to help Huawei reduce the inventory and backlog of orders of this chipset that it had accumulated as a result of a number of factors, including lower than expected sales of end devices that were due to: (i) technical difficulties and delivery delays that were experienced with the MDM8200 based chipset; (ii) the slower than anticipated roll-out of HSPA+ networks; and (iii) the expected imminent availability of the MDM6200 and the MDM8200A based chipsets. The "firesale" that was offered by Qualcomm was thus a rational commercial response to the difficulties that were encountered by this specific chipset model in the market and had nothing to do with the emergence of Icera in that same market.*

There are several factual problems with this "firesale" defense: To begin with, it appears that there was continued demand for the MDM8200 throughout the Relevant Period which contradicts Qualcomm's portrayal of the MDM8200 as a complete commercial failure. Moreover, the internal documents that discuss the pricing strategy for the MDM8200 clearly point towards the "*Icera threat*" and the desire to contain it as being the main drivers behind the various price moves.

Qualcomm's critique of the Commission's economic analysis in the case centers on the following points:

- *The Commission's market definition[16] is too narrow as it excludes different standards (or certain iterations of a given non-UMTS standard) with similar performance characteristics as UMTS chipsets, as well as captive sales of UMTS chipsets by vertically integrated device manufacturers who have in-house capabilities for baseband chipset production. A wider market definition would have called into question the Commission's dominance finding.*

Neither the chipsets supporting different standards nor the captive sales of UMTS chipsets were found to exert an effective competitive constraint on the merchant market for UMTS baseband chipsets, so that they were correctly excluded from this market.

- *The chipset sales relevant for this case only account for a small share of the overall sales in the UMTS chipset market as defined by the Commission. An equally efficient competitor should be able to replicate the dominant firm's entire product offering, and not just a small subset of the latter.*

As explained above, the Commission's theory of harm is based on the notion that entrants typically do not enter all segments of a large market simultaneously. Instead, entrants make a name for themselves in a small niche of the market – such as the leading-edge segment in Icera's case – where they have a competitive advantage *vis-à-vis* the incumbent, before expanding into other segments. The Commission's price-cost test was designed to verify if Qualcomm's pricing would have allowed an equally efficient competitor to recover its long-run production costs for those sales

---

16 Recall that the relevant market in this case was defined as the merchant market for slim and integrated chipsets that comply with different iterations of the UMTS standard.

that were contestable to such competitor at the time when the targeted predatory attack occurred, *i.e.*, before Icera had a chance to broaden its product portfolio and challenge Qualcomm also on other segments in the UMTS baseband chipset market.

- Qualcomm argued that *"Icera's technology and knowhow were transferable, as proved by NVidia's acquisition of Icera"* so that the alleged predation *"could not have removed, and, in fact, did not remove the alleged competitive pressure exerted by Icera's technology."*

Internal documents show that Qualcomm was uncertain about the extent of the competitive threat that Icera would still represent for Qualcomm's chipset business in the period that followed Nvidia's acquisition of Icera. Qualcomm considered it necessary to continue granting further price reductions to address competition from Icera beyond that date and after the public announcement of the acquisition of Icera by Nvidia on May 9, 2011. It was only after June 2011 that other considerations came to the fore in Qualcomm's pricing decisions for the investigated chipsets.

- *Qualcomm does not consider LRAIC to be the appropriate cost measure to assess alleged predation in R&D-intensive industries such as the semiconductor industry, and instead advocates the use of the equivalent of AVC as the relevant cost measure. Qualcomm emphasized the significant intertemporal and contemporaneous cross-product R&D spillovers that are typical in R&D-intensive industries, and that make it difficult to identify and measure product-specific incremental costs in such industries. Qualcomm also pointed to the presence of sunk costs in the LRAIC measure that are irrelevant for price-setting and hence should not be present in a price-cost test.*

However, EU case law, and more specifically the AKZO II test, explicitly allows for a cost benchmark above AVC (and below ATC) in a price-cost test, provided that certain conditions are met. LRAIC encompasses product-specific costs that are incurred both before and during the period in which the abusive conduct took place, and a failure to cover LRAIC indicates that the dominant undertaking is not recovering all of the (attributable) variable and fixed costs of producing the good or service in question. An equally efficient competitor (sustaining the same costs as the incumbent by definition) would therefore not be able to cover its product-specific costs either and could be foreclosed from the market.

In an industry such as the semiconductor industry – which is characterized by low variable costs and high fixed costs that are mostly sunk by the time the products are commercialized – a failure to include the product-specific sunk costs in the LRAIC measure would make it very difficult, if not impossible, to detect any such foreclosure of an equally efficient competitor in a price-cost test.

- *The alleged predation would not have been rational for Qualcomm, as there was no scope for recoupment, given that at the end of the investigated period, the products under investigation where either no longer on the market, or sold at very low margins since they were no longer at the technological frontier at that point in time.*

According to established case law in the EU, evidence of recoupment following a predatory episode is not necessary. In the *Qualcomm* case, however, the internal documents of the dominant company showed that such recoupment over the remaining life cycle of the products would not have been possible and was not planned, since (as was already described above) the margins of leading-edge chipsets fall rapidly after a short time even absent any predatory pricing.

The objective of Qualcomm's strategy was to prevent Icera's imminent entry into the far larger and more lucrative smartphone chipset segment, which would have meant a far more serious profit loss for Qualcomm than that caused by the predatory pricing episode in the much smaller MBB device segment. This was the recoupment that Qualcomm intended – and achieved.[17]

## VIII. THE OUTCOME OF THE CASE

On the day of the adoption of the *Qualcomm Predation* decision by the EC, Qualcomm lodged an application for annulment of the decision.[18] Qualcomm's appeal is mainly based on the following claims:

(i) a lack of perceived competitive threat from Icera, since customers turned to Qualcomm's products not because of their price but because rival chipsets were (according to Qualcomm) technologically inferior;

(ii) a lack of precedent and economic rationale for the Decision's theory of harm, which is based on alleged below-cost pricing over a very short time period and for a very small volume of chips; and

(iii) a lack of anticompetitive harm to Icera from Qualcomm's conduct, given that Icera was later acquired by Nvidia and continued to compete in the relevant market for several years after the end of the alleged conduct.

The appeal is currently (as of August 2022) awaiting the hearing and the judgment by the General Court.

In the meantime, several significant events have occurred, which fundamentally transformed the chipset industry and the competitive equilibria in the market: In May 2011, U.S.-based Nvidia – the leading developer of graphics processors – acquired Icera: Nvidia hoped to position itself in the baseband chipset market by combining Icera's chipset technology with Nvidia's Tegra processor; this would have allowed Nvidia to provide "integrated baseband chipsets."[19] Such an architecture is particularly interesting for smartphones and tablets, which – unlike laptops – often do not have any built-in application processors that allow applications such as browsers or email clients to run on a device. Four years after the acquisition, however, in May 2015 Nvidia announced that it would wind down its Icera modem operations; Nvidia

---

17 *See also* the discussion of the economics of predation above.

18 *See* Case T-671/19, first application lodged on October 1, 2019, final version on November 22, 2019.

19 *See* Nvidia's press release "NVIDIA to Acquire Baseband and RF Technology Leader Icera," *available at* https://nvidianews.nvidia.com/news/nvidia-to-acquire-baseband-and-rf-technology-leader-icera-6622925 (accessed July 12, 2022).

thus effectively exited the baseband chipset market before the Commission could conclude its investigation.

Nvidia was not the only competitor to "throw in the towel" in this period: Another historic baseband chipset provider that had tried a comeback in the LTE (4G) chipset market was Intel. In April 2019, on the same day that the settlement in a major patent dispute between Qualcomm and Apple was announced, Intel exited the 5G modem market for phones; Intel's chipset business was subsequently acquired by Apple. This created in-house capabilities for the device maker, which had until then fully relied on third-party supplies – notably from Qualcomm and Intel. This trend away from the merchant market and towards in-house development of chipsets is also observable for other major device makers, for instance Samsung and Huawei, who both operate their own chipset subsidiaries. The contracts between Qualcomm and Apple that had governed their supply relationship between 2011 and 2016 were under antitrust scrutiny both in the U.S. (*see* Chapter 15. Using and Misusing Microeconomics: *Federal Trade Commission v. Qualcomm* (Carl Shapiro & Keith Waehrer)) and in Europe; the latter led to an infringement decision that was issued in January 2018,[20] which was annulled by the General Court in June 2022.

## IX. CONCLUSION

With the *Qualcomm Predation* decision, the European Commission broke new ground on a number of issues: For one, it is the first predation decision in Commission practice to rely fully on the AKZO II test in its findings: on prices above AVC (yet below LRAIC). Second, its theory of harm broadens the existing understanding of predation to accommodate strategies where the predatory conduct is selective – both with regard to the products and to the customers that are affected by it – while unfolding its anticompetitive effects on a much wider market. Such selective and targeted conduct is possible where an imbalance in size and footprint between the predator and the prey do not allow the latter to challenge the incumbent in other segments until it first succeeds in the segment(s) where the predatory attack (naturally) occurs.

Third, the Qualcomm (predation) decision illustrates how, in addition to "direct" predation at the device-maker level, there can also be instances of "indirect" predation where the predatory prices that are offered to one customer allow the latter to beat other downstream rivals at the next level in the supply chain, which thus undermines the demand for the upstream rival's products. Fourth, the analysis of predation in a B2B context and the reallocation of discounts to different revenue streams is also an element of novelty of the case.

Finally, the *Qualcomm Predation* decision is testament to the importance of internal documents to gain an in-depth understanding of how pricing and R&D decisions are made, and what motivates these different business decisions, which is crucial to be able to analyze such conduct from an antitrust enforcement perspective.

---

[20] This case is commonly referred to as the *Qualcomm (exclusivity)* case, to distinguish it from the *Qualcomm (predation)* case that is the subject of this chapter.

# APPENDIX

The tables below show the results of the European Commission's price-cost test for each of the three products[21] and two customers subject of the investigation. The respective sales volumes in each quarter are confidential and therefore redacted. Column "Price" shows the average sales prices resulting from the Commission's reconstruction. Column "AVC" shows the reconstructed average variable costs, column "R&D" indicates the non-variable costs attributable to each product, resulting from a revenue-based allocation. Next, columns "LRAIC" represents the sum of AVC and R&D, *i.e.*, the total long-run incremental costs. Column "TEST" shows the difference between price and LRAIC, with a negative result indicating an incidence of predatory pricing. Finally, column "GROSS MARGIN" shows the difference between price and AVC, expressed as a percentage of price.

Table 55: MDM8200 - Results of the revised price-cost test

1) Huawei – MDM8200

| Calendar Quarter | Volume | Price | AVC | R&D | LRAIC = AVC + R&D | TEST = Price - LRAIC | GROSS MARGIN = 1 - AVC/Price |
|---|---|---|---|---|---|---|---|
| Jul-Sep/2009 | [...] | $33.55 | $20.74 | $14.53 | $35.27 | -$1.72 | 38.19% |
| Oct-Dec/2009 | [...] | $22.61 | $18.31 | $15.26 | $33.57 | -$10.97 | 19.01% |
| Jan-Mar/2010 | [...] | $23.16 | $16.57 | $18.26 | $34.83 | -$11.67 | 28.47% |
| Apr-Jun/2010 | [...] | $15.67 | $14.64 | $9.28 | $23.92 | -$8.25 | 6.60% |
| Jul-Sep/2010 | [...] | $16.72 | $13.93 | $16.54 | $30.48 | -$13.76 | 16.68% |
| Oct-Dec/2010 | [...] | $16.56 | $12.92 | $7.34 | $20.26 | -$3.70 | 21.99% |
| Jan-Mar/2011 | [...] | $17.33 | $12.28 | $7.91 | $20.19 | -$2.86 | 29.13% |
| Apr-Jun/2011 | [...] | $17.25 | $12.11 | $6.06 | $18.17 | -$0.92 | 29.83% |

2) ZTE – MDM8200

| Calendar Quarter | Volume | Price | AVC | R&D | LRAIC = AVC + R&D | TEST = Price - LRAIC | GROSS MARGIN = 1 - AVC/Price |
|---|---|---|---|---|---|---|---|
| Jul-Sep/2009 | [...] | $40.21 | $20.74 | $14.53 | $35.27 | $4.94 | 48.43% |
| Oct-Dec/2009 | [...] | $39.75 | $18.31 | $15.26 | $33.57 | $6.18 | 53.95% |
| Jan-Mar/2010 | [...] | $39.42 | $16.57 | $18.26 | $34.83 | $4.60 | 57.98% |
| Apr-Jun/2010 | [...] | $25.57 | $14.64 | $9.28 | $23.92 | $1.65 | 42.75% |
| Jul-Sep/2010 | [...] | $17.25 | $13.93 | $16.54 | $30.48 | -$13.22 | 19.26% |
| Oct-Dec/2010 | [...] | $18.63 | $12.92 | $7.34 | $20.26 | -$1.63 | 30.67% |
| Jan-Mar/2011 | [...] | $18.65 | $12.28 | $7.91 | $20.19 | -$1.54 | 34.13% |
| Apr-Jun/2011 | [...] | $18.53 | $12.11 | $6.06 | $18.17 | $0.36 | 34.66% |

---

21 MDM8200, MDM6200, and MDM8200A.

Table 56: MDM6200 - Results of the revised price-cost test

1) Huawei – MDM6200 – Configuration 1

| Calendar Quarter | Volume (aggregate over both configs.) | Configuration 1 ||||||
|---|---|---|---|---|---|---|---|
| | | Price | AVC | R&D | LRAIC = AVC + R&D | TEST = Price - LRAIC | GROSS MARGIN = 1 - AVC/Price |
| Jul-Sep/2010 | [...] | $16.62 | $12.50 | $0.96 | $13.46 | $3.16 | 24.77% |
| Oct-Dec/2010 | [...] | $16.62 | $10.79 | $0.85 | $11.64 | $4.98 | 35.06% |
| Jan-Mar/2011 | [...] | $13.23 | $6.65 | $0.95 | $7.60 | $5.63 | 49.74% |
| Apr-Jun/2011 | [...] | $13.18 | $6.26 | $0.90 | $7.16 | $6.02 | 52.49% |

2) Huawei – MDM6200 – Configuration 2[1348]

| Calendar Quarter | Volume (aggregate over both configs.) | Configuration 2 ||||||
|---|---|---|---|---|---|---|---|
| | | Price | AVC | R&D | LRAIC = AVC + R&D | TEST = Price - LRAIC | GROSS MARGIN = 1 - AVC/Price |
| Jul-Sep/2010 | [...] | | | $0.96 | | | |
| Oct-Dec/2010 | [...] | | | $0.85 | | | |
| Jan-Mar/2011 | [...] | $11.88 | $6.47 | $0.95 | $7.42 | $4.46 | 45.51% |
| Apr-Jun/2011 | [...] | $11.82 | $6.10 | $0.90 | $7.00 | $4.82 | 48.37% |

3) ZTE – MDM6200 – Configuration 1

| Calendar Quarter | Volume (aggregate over both configs.) | Configuration 1 ||||||
|---|---|---|---|---|---|---|---|
| | | Price | AVC | R&D | LRAIC = AVC + R&D | TEST = Price - LRAIC | GROSS MARGIN = 1 - AVC/Price |
| Jul-Sep/2010 | [...] | $10.89 | $12.50 | $0.96 | $13.46 | -$2.57 | -14.81% |
| Oct-Dec/2010 | [...] | $7.21 | $10.79 | $0.85 | $11.64 | -$4.43 | -49.71% |
| Jan-Mar/2011 | [...] | $6.33 | $6.65 | $0.95 | $7.60 | -$1.27 | -5.05% |
| Apr-Jun/2011 | [...] | $13.08 | $6.26 | $0.90 | $7.16 | $5.92 | 52.13% |

4) ZTE – MDM6200 – Configuration 2[1349]

| Calendar Quarter | Volume (aggregate over both configs.) | Configuration 2 ||||||
|---|---|---|---|---|---|---|---|
| | | Price | AVC | R&D | LRAIC = AVC + R&D | TEST = Price - LRAIC | GROSS MARGIN = 1 - AVC/Price |
| Jul-Sep/2010 | [...] | | | $0.96 | | | |
| Oct-Dec/2010 | [...] | | | $0.85 | | | |
| Jan-Mar/2011 | [...] | $4.97 | $6.47 | $0.95 | $7.42 | -$2.45 | -30.24% |
| Apr-Jun/2011 | [...] | $11.81 | $6.10 | $0.90 | $7.00 | $4.81 | 48.33% |

### Table 57: MDM8200A - Results of the revised price-cost test

#### 1) Huawei – MDM8200A – Configuration 1

| Calendar Quarter | Volume (aggregate over both configs.) | Configuration 1 | | | | | |
|---|---|---|---|---|---|---|---|
| | | Price | AVC | R&D | LRAIC = AVC + R&D | TEST = Price - LRAIC | GROSS MARGIN = 1 - AVC/Price |
| Jul-Sep/2010 | [...] | $24.93 | $10.58 | $21.03 | $31.61 | -$6.68 | 57.56% |
| Oct-Dec/2010 | [...] | $14.37 | $9.19 | $11.05 | $20.25 | -$5.88 | 36.01% |
| Jan-Mar/2011 | [...] | $13.57 | $7.80 | $7.91 | $15.71 | -$2.14 | 42.52% |
| Apr-Jun/2011 | [...] | $13.56 | $7.36 | $7.16 | $14.51 | -$0.95 | 45.74% |

#### 2) Huawei – MDM8200A – Configuration 2[1354]

| Calendar Quarter | Volume (aggregate over both configs.) | Configuration 2 | | | | | |
|---|---|---|---|---|---|---|---|
| | | Price | AVC | R&D | LRAIC = AVC + R&D | TEST = Price - LRAIC | GROSS MARGIN = 1 - AVC/Price |
| Jul-Sep/2010 | [...] | | | $21.03 | | | |
| Oct-Dec/2010 | [...] | | | $11.05 | | | |
| Jan-Mar/2011 | [...] | $12.22 | $7.84 | $7.91 | $15.75 | -$3.53 | 35.84% |
| Apr-Jun/2011 | [...] | $12.20 | $6.98 | $7.16 | $14.14 | -$1.94 | 42.80% |

#### 3) ZTE – MDM8200A – Configuration 1

| Calendar Quarter | Volume (aggregate over both configs.) | Configuration 1 | | | | | |
|---|---|---|---|---|---|---|---|
| | | Price | AVC | R&D | LRAIC = AVC + R&D | TEST = Price - LRAIC | GROSS MARGIN = 1 - AVC/Price |
| Jul-Sep/2010 | [...] | $25.63 | $10.58 | $21.03 | $31.61 | -$5.98 | 58.72% |
| Oct-Dec/2010 | [...] | $14.95 | $9.19 | $11.05 | $20.25 | -$5.30 | 38.50% |
| Jan-Mar/2011 | [...] | $14.49 | $7.80 | $7.91 | $15.71 | -$1.22 | 46.17% |
| Apr-Jun/2011 | [...] | $14.26 | $7.36 | $7.16 | $14.51 | -$0.25 | 48.40% |

4) ZTE – MDM8200A – Configuration 2[1355]

| Calendar Quarter | Volume (aggregate over both configs.) | Configuration 2 ||||||
|---|---|---|---|---|---|---|---|
| | | Price | AVC | R&D | LRAIC = AVC + R&D | TEST = Price - LRAIC | GROSS MARGIN = 1 - AVC/Price |
| Jul-Sep/2010 | [...] | | | $21.03 | | | |
| Oct-Dec/2010 | [...] | | | $11.05 | | | |
| Jan-Mar/2011 | [...] | $13.13 | $7.84 | $7.91 | $15.75 | -$2.62 | 40.28% |
| Apr-Jun/2011 | [...] | $12.99 | $6.98 | $7.16 | $14.14 | -$1.15 | 46.27% |

# REFERENCES

Areeda, Phillip E. & Donald F. Turner (1975). "Predatory pricing and related practices under Section 2 of the Sherman Act." *Harvard Law Review* 88(4): 697–733.

Baker, Jonathan B. (1994). "Predatory Pricing After Brooke Group: An Economic Perspective." *Antitrust Law Journal* 62 (3): 585–603.

Baumol, William J. (1996). "Predation and the Logic of the Average Variable Cost Test." *Journal of Law and Economics* 39(1): 49–72.

Bock, Wolfgang, François Candelon, Steve Chai, Ethan Choi, John Corwin, Sebastian DiGrande, Rishab Gulshan, David Michael & Antonio Varas (2015). "The Mobile Revolution." BCG Report commissioned by Qualcomm, *available at*: https://www.bcg.com/publications/2015/telecommunications-technology-industries-the-mobile-revolution, accessed July 12, 2022.

Bolton, Patrick, Joseph F. Brodley & Michael H. Riordan (2000). "Predatory Pricing: Strategic Theory and Legal Policy," *Georgetown Law Journal* 88(8): 2239-2330.

Bolton, Patrick & David S. Scharfstein (1990). "A Theory of Predation Based on Agency Problems in Financial Contracting." *American Economic Review* 80(1): 93-106.

Crocioni, Pietro (2018). "On the Relevant Cost Standard for Price-Cost Test in Abuses of Dominance." *Journal of Competition Law & Economics* 14 (2): 262–291.

Crocioni, Pietro & Liliane Giardino-Karlinger (2022). "Predation as a leveraging abuse – filling the gap between economic theory and antitrust enforcement?" *CPI Antitrust Chronicle – Predatory Pricing* Winter 2022 1 (1).

Easterbrook, Frank H. (1981). "Predatory Strategies and Counterstrategies." *University of Chicago Law Review* 48(2): 263–337.

Fumagalli, Chiara & Massimo Motta (2006). "Exclusive Dealing and Entry, when Buyers Compete." *American Economic Review*, 96 (3): 785-795.

Fumagalli, Chiara & Massimo Motta (2013). "A Simple Theory of Predation." *Journal of Law and Economics* 56 (3): 595–631.

Hovenkamp, Herbert (2015). "The Areeda-Turner Test for Exclusionary Pricing: A Critical Journal." *Review of Industrial Organization* 46 (3): 209–228.

Karlinger, Liliane, Dimitrios Magos, Pierre Régibeau & Hans Zenger (2020). "Recent Developments at DG Competition: 2019/2020." *Review of Industrial Organization* 57: 783–814.

McGee, John S. (1958). "Predatory Price Cutting: The Standard Oil (N.J.) Case." *Journal of Law and Economics* 1: 137–169.

Milgrom, Paul & John Roberts (1982). "Predation, Reputation, and Entry Deterrence." *Journal of Economic Theory* 27(2): 280–312.

Motta, Massimo (2004). "Competition Policy – Theory and Practice." Cambridge: Cambridge University Press.

Nvidia Press Release (2011). "NVIDIA to Acquire Baseband and RF Technology Leader Icera," *available at* https://nvidianews.nvidia.com/news/nvidia-to-acquire-baseband-and-rf-technology-leader-icera-6622925 (accessed July 12, 2022).

Ordover, Janusz A. & Robert D. Willig (1981). "An Economic Definition of Predation: Pricing and Product Innovation." *The Yale Law Journal* 91(1): 8-53.

Posner, Richard A. (1976). *Antitrust Law: An Economic Perspective*. Chicago: Chicago University Press.

Rasmusen, Eric B., J. Mark Ramseyer & John S. Wiley, Jr. (1991). "Naked Exclusion." *American Economic Review* 81(5): 1137-1145.

Scherer, Frederic M. (1980). *Industrial Market Structure and Economic Performance*. Rand McNally & Co, U.S., Chicago.

Scholz, Marieke, Peter Schedereit & Liliane Giardino-Karlinger (2020). "Wenn der Zweck den Mitteln im Wege steht. Der Kommissionsbeschluss zu Qualcomms Kampfpreisstrategie gegen Icera." *Europäisches Wirtschafts- und Steuerrecht* 31 (5): 241–247.

Segal, Ilya R. & Michael D. Whinston (2000). "Naked Exclusion: Comment." *American Economic Review* 90 (1): 296-309.

Telser, Lester G. (1966). "Cutthroat Competition and the Long-Purse." *Journal of Law and Economics* 9: 259–277.

Yamey, B.S. (1972). "Predatory price cutting: Notes and Comments." *Journal of Law and Economics* 15: 129–142.

# CHAPTER 14
# Advertising, Customer Data, and Competition: The German *Facebook* Case

By Rupprecht Podszun

## I. INTRODUCTION

The German *Facebook* case deals with the combination of user data from different sources. Facebook (now Meta) is accused of building "super profiles" of users, thereby violating data protection rules *and* competition rules. The national competition agency in Germany – the Federal Cartel Office ("FCO," "*Bundeskartellamt*") – held that this amounts to an exploitative abuse of a dominant position, which is prohibited under German law according to section 19 (1) of the German competition act.[1]

The case is seen as one of the most important European competition law cases in recent times. At the time of writing (August 2022), it is still pending with the courts so the final outcome has yet to be determined.

For three reasons, this case proves significant far beyond German borders: First, it is one of the few Big Tech cases that really seem to hit a point: For a while, the *Facebook* case was the focal point of antitrust enforcement against Big Tech in Europe. It aims at the heart of Facebook's business model of selling targeted advertising, based on user data. The case also triggered legislation at the German and the European level – making competition law fit for the digital age.

Second, it is a prime example of a case that ventures into fields beyond the mere protection of competition or consumer welfare. What are the boundaries of antitrust law? Where does competition law end, and what do its proponents have to contribute to the issues of our time? This case explores the intersection of competition law with privacy. It illustrates the (controversial) agenda of a more progressive antitrust movement that speaks out in favor of integrating issues such as sustainability, inequality, privacy, or fairness into antitrust (Khan (2018); Hovenkamp (2018)).

Third, the limited economics of the case are noteworthy: The agency that led the case in public enforcement and all of the courts that have looked into it so far have largely refrained from applying standard competition economics. The case has (thus far) been resolved without recourse to modelling efficiency effects. Consumer welfare – which is often defined as the ultimate goal of antitrust – will hardly be recognizable

---

[1] The provision in the *Gesetz gegen Wettbewerbsbeschränkungen* ("GWB") reads: "Any abuse of a dominant position by one or several undertakings is prohibited." This is equivalent to the European provision in Art. 102 of the Treaty on the Functioning of the European Union ("TFEU").

to U.S. scholars who examine this case. Thus, the *Facebook* case offers an opportunity to dive into European concepts of competition.

While the lack of post-Chicago analysis is not necessarily representative of all German or EU cases, it points to an important transatlantic divide in the approach to competition law: The U.S. has established antitrust as a field where consumer welfare is the yardstick and where economists have an important role to play. In Europe, applying competition law is first and foremost the realm of lawyers who try to determine, with their legal expertise and doctrinal concepts, whether a statute covers the case under investigation. The European economic tradition is different, and this is particularly true for Germany.

The Facebook saga is a telling example of a distinct European and specifically German way of applying antitrust law, even though the connections with the FTC antitrust case against into Facebook are obvious.[2] Whether *Facebook* is seen as a backslide that is out of touch with (post)modern economics or as a future-proof progressive approach, lies in the eye of the beholder.

## II. FACTS OF THE CASE

The German Federal Cartel Office (*Bundeskartellamt*) formally launched proceedings against Facebook in March 2016. At the time, skepticism in Germany against Big Tech-companies had grown considerably. The FCO had early on looked into data issues and the nature of multi-sided platforms (Bundeskartellamt (2016); Autorité de la Concurrence/Bundeskartellamt (2016)) and had a track record in the digital field that was balanced: It sided with and also against platforms from time to time.

The move to challenge Facebook over data abuses still seemed somewhat strange. First, the *Facebook* case could have been dealt with by the European Commission, the sister authority that usually covers the cases that concern all of Europe. Second, the case surprised many since the FCO decided to take on Facebook for its practices in the field of data. At first sight, this looked like a privacy case – which would fall into the jurisdiction of privacy regulators – and not a competition case. However, the competent Irish data protection authority displayed a certain reluctance to investigate Facebook (which has its European headquarters in Ireland).

Facebook (now Meta) is one of the world's leading digital companies; it runs applications such as Facebook, Instagram, and WhatsApp. Its business model essentially relies on advertising – the value of which is increased through the use of personal data. The use of personal data is regulated in the European Union according to the General Data Protection Regulation ("GDPR").[3] Under this statute, the processing of personal data is subject to conditions and usually requires the consent of the data subjects (Art. 6 GDPR). This consent must be "a freely given, specific, informed and unambiguous indication of the data subject's wishes" (Art. 4 (11) GDPR). Without proper consent, the exploitation of user data is illegal and can be penalized.

---

2   For the state of play *see* https://www.ftc.gov/legal-library/browse/cases-proceedings/191-0134-facebook-inc-ftc-v.

3   Regulation (EU) 2016/679.

The key issue of this case, as presented by the FCO, was the question of whether Facebook violated competition rules by combining the personal data of users in a way that was incompatible with the GDPR.[4] Facebook compiles personal data of users into "super-profiles," which combine data from different sources: data from the use of the social network Facebook; data from other Facebook-owned services such as Instagram or WhatsApp; and "off-Facebook-data": data from third-party websites. Off-Facebook data are collected via Facebook Business Tools. These interfaces allow the company to collect user or device-related data from users once these tools are integrated into other websites: for example, as a social plugin or as measurement and analysis services (based on Facebook Pixel, for example).

With its decision, the FCO claims that this combination of user data – without user consent – constitutes an abuse of dominance for which Facebook is liable under competition law. The case links data protection and competition.

The data combination issue had already surfaced in the 2014 decision of the European Commission on the *Facebook/WhatsApp* merger. When Facebook acquired WhatsApp, the Commission investigated a "possible theory of harm" that:

> "post-Transaction, the merged entity could start collecting data from WhatsApp users with a view to improving the accuracy of the targeted ads."[5]

The Commission dismissed this concern, partly based on Facebook's statement that it would be technically difficult to integrate WhatsApp data with Facebook data (at 139). This proved to be misleading. The Commission later fined Facebook for wrongful statements in the proceedings.[6] The merger itself was left untouched, and the integration of the data was not re-considered.

## III. PROCEDURAL TWISTS AND TURNS

As was stated above, the FCO made the investigation public in March 2016. The procedural twists and turns that the case took are a gripping story of litigation in itself. On February 6, 2019, the FCO issued a decision against Facebook prohibiting said behavior and obliging Facebook to terminate the behavior within 12 months and to present an implementation plan after four months. The decision was immediately enforceable under German law.

Facebook successfully appealed to the Düsseldorf Court of Appeal (*Oberlandesgericht* Düsseldorf) that halted the immediate effect of the decision with an order on August 26, 2019 against the FCO.[7] This injunction decision is unsparing in its wording: The decision shredded the reasoning of the FCO. The Düsseldorf decision was an enormous setback for the FCO in this high-profile case.

---

4  On the competitive effects of the GDPR itself *see* Gal & Aviv (2020).

5  European Commission, 3.10.2014, decision M.7217 – *Facebook/WhatsApp* at para. 180.

6  European Commission, 17.5.2017, decision M.8228 – *Facebook/WhatsApp*.

7  Düsseldorf Court of Appeal, Decision VI-Kart 1/19 (V) of Aug. 26, 2019.

The FCO took the case to the German Federal Court of Justice (*Bundesgerichtshof*), seeking to overturn the Düsseldorf ruling. It succeeded in this endeavor. On June 23, 2020, the Cartel Senate of the Federal Court of Justice declared the decision enforceable again.[8] However, it slightly changed the reasoning of the FCO's case. All this took place in interim proceedings. There were further procedural surprises.[9] In main proceedings, the Court of Appeal sent the case to the European Court of Justice for a preliminary ruling on details of European law. When this Court issues its opinion, the Düsseldorf Court of Appeal will give another ruling that may be appealed to the Federal Court of Justice again.

## IV. THE CASE AGAINST FACEBOOK

To establish an abuse of dominance by exploitative conditions towards users (as an equivalent to excessive pricing), the FCO had to prove that Facebook holds a dominant position in a market and abuses this dominant position by imposing abusive business terms with no justification. Also, there must be some form of causal link between the dominant position and the abuse. Finally, a remedy had to be found.

### A. *Market Definition and Dominance*

Facebook was seen as dominant by the FCO on the market for social networks. The service in question was defined as enabling users to find and network with other people on a daily basis, exchanging experiences, opinions, and content. Providers meet the demand by granting users a "rich social experience."[10] Services like YouTube, Twitter or LinkedIn were not seen as part of the market since they do not provide a similar user experience.[11] The same applied to Snapchat, as a potential competitor, where the FCO did not find sufficient supply-side substitutability with Snapchat, based on its limited flexibility to adapt its services at short notice and at reasonable economic cost.[12] Facebook's submission that the relevant market is an attention market where companies compete for user attention, a concept put forward by Facebook with an opinion by David S. Evans (cf. Evans (2020)), was dismissed. Assuming an attention market would turn the user into the product, the FCO argued.[13] Defining the market from the demand side perspective of the user means that the core functionalities of the product (*i.e.*, the social network) are the characteristic feature. Otherwise, so the FCO argued, in non-zero-price-markets all companies would compete in one market for income.[14]

---

8  Federal Court of Justice, Decision KVR 69/19 of June 23, 2020.

9  For a complete list of documents and reports from the different court proceedings, *see* https://www.d-kart.de/en/der-fall-facebook/.

10  Federal Cartel Office, Decision B6-22/16 of Feb. 6, 2019, para. 249.

11  Federal Cartel Office, Decision B6-22/16 of Feb. 6, 2019, para. 264.

12  Federal Cartel Office, Decision B6-22/16 of Feb. 6, 2019, para. 300 – *Facebook*.

13  Federal Cartel Office, Decision B6-22/16 of Feb. 6, 2019, para. 246; confirmed by Federal Court of Justice, Decision KVR 69/19 of June 23, 2020, para. 22.

14  Federal Cartel Office, Decision B6-22/16 of Feb. 6, 2019, para. 246.

The FCO placed major emphasis on network effects and relied on the economic literature on this: *e.g.*, by Rochet & Tirole (2006) and Katz & Shapiro (1985).[15] The network effects lead to lock-in effects and therefore hinder the substitutability of Facebook with Google+ (the – at the time – still existing Google alternative to Facebook).[16]

Where the U.S. Supreme Court in *Amex* had held with a majority that transaction platforms constitute a single market with two relevant market sides,[17] the Federal Court of Justice stated that one single uniform market definition is justified only if both market sides have the same demand.[18] Otherwise, as in the case of Facebook, competitive effects differ, and thus, markets need to be defined separately.

Regarding dominance, the FCO had to overcome the problem of how to measure dominance in a zero-price market. The FCO identified the share of daily active and monthly active users of social networks and the number of registered users of the services. The figure of daily active users was seen as "the most significant metric in the assessment of the market position."[19] Since the market that was defined by the FCO comprises only real social networks that offer all of the features that Facebook offers, there is little competition left: The remaining social networks – such as Google+ – had only negligible success in the German market.

Other indicators of dominance that were considered by the FCO included the installed base (a concept put forward by Farrell & Saloner (1986) and Malueg & Schwartz (2011)).[20] The installed base of a network consists of the number of users and their opportunities to switch.

Facebook would have preferred to consider monthly active users as the "industry standard"; but according to the FCO this metric does not reflect typical user behavior and is not even used in Facebook's own reporting.[21]

Facebook did not succeed in challenging the assumption of dominance – not least since there had not been any significant developments over the past seven years that endangered its entrenched market position.[22]

## B. Abuse

With dominance comes a "special responsibility" for competition in markets. The European courts continuously say that a dominant company must not allow

---

15 Federal Cartel Office, Decision B6-22/16 of Feb. 6, 2019, para. 215 – *Facebook*.
16 Federal Cartel Office, Decision B6-22/16 of Feb. 6, 2019, para. 276 – *Facebook*.
17 *Ohio et al v. American Express Co.*, 138 S.Ct. 2274, 2278 (2018).
18 Federal Court, Decision KVR 69/19 of June 23, 2020, para. 31. Cf. *Ohio v. Am. Express Co.* 138 S. Ct. 2274, at 2286.
19 Federal Cartel Office, Decision B6-22/16 of Feb. 6, 2019, para. 389 – *Facebook*.
20 Federal Cartel Office, Decision B6-22/16 of Feb. 6, 2019, paras. 405, 428 – *Facebook*.
21 Federal Cartel Office, Decision B6-22/16 of Feb. 6, 2019, para. 409 – *Facebook*. Confirmed by Federal Court, Decision KVR 69/19 of June 23, 2020, para. 38.
22 Federal Court, Decision KVR 69/19 of June 23, 2020, para. 52.

its conduct to impair genuine undistorted competition.[23] On the question of how Facebook's data practices distort competition, the FCO and the Federal Court offered different theories of harm.

### 1. *Abusive Conditions*

The FCO held that the use of data by Facebook constituted an abusive exploitation of customers through business conditions.

German and European competition law has acknowledged the concept of exploitative business terms as part of competition law ever since the provisions of European competition law entered into force in the 1950s. Art. 102 TFEU – a central provision of European antitrust law – expressly states that an abuse of dominance may consist of:

> "directly or indirectly imposing unfair purchase or selling prices or other unfair trading conditions."

The two limbs of this rule relate to prices on the one hand and conditions on the other. The rule is not primarily driven by welfare economics (even though there is a case for a loss of consumer welfare), but it is rooted in the principle of equal chances in the competitive process for all market participants. Where competition does not occur in markets, dominant actors should behave *as if* they were under competitive pressure. "As if-competition" is the yardstick for excessive pricing cases. In practice, excessive pricing cases are rare, and agencies usually rely on market solutions instead of stepping in to regulate prices.

Transferring the idea of exploitation to conditions (instead of prices) means that an "as if competition" standard has to be found as well. The FCO's reasoning is that Facebook engages in supra-competitive data collection and usage – which can be seen as equivalent to excessive pricing and can be enforced only because of its dominant position (Budzinski et al., 2021, p. 59). This is all the more convincing if data provided by users is seen as consideration for the social networking service. The "excess" is not measured with an economic monetary standard but with a view to the normative role of competition as the force in markets to discipline dominant actors.

### 2. *The Benchmark for Excess*

Once it is accepted that exploitative business terms may amount to an abuse of dominance, the key question is where to set the point at which terms become exploitative.

For excessive pricing, competition agencies usually consider roughly comparable – but competitive – markets, and try to take commonalities and differences into account. When they find a significant difference of pricing in competitive and non-competitive markets, they may identify the latter as an abusive practice (Botta, 2021).

---

23 European Court of Justice, Decision 322/81 of Nov. 9, 1983, para. 57 – *Michelin*.

A second concept for finding excesses, at least in theory, is the concept of limiting profit margins: Agencies could compare costs and prices to find the profit margin and declare this as inappropriate and excessive. The European Court of Justice in 1978 alluded to this concept in *United Brands*.[24] This concept has not been taken up.

In the *Facebook* case, the FCO takes a legal standard as the benchmark for the conditions that become excessive. Its argument is based on precedent set by the Federal Court of Justice that dominant actors act abusively if they do not respect the provisions in the legal system governing situations of imbalanced bargaining power.[25]

In the view of the FCO, a violation of the GDPR by Facebook therefore amounts to an abuse of dominance in that the company does not respect rules protecting consumers in an unbalanced bargaining position. Large parts of the decision (paras. 166-244) deal with the violation of GDPR rules. Facebook disputes these findings, and also raises doubts as to the authority of the FCO even to consider data protection issues. These are, so the company states, different fields of law with different institutions in charge. This latter argument is currently (as of September 2022) under consideration by the European Court of Justice. Srinivasan (2019) argues that the history of Facebook may be read as a move from privacy protection to wide-scale commercial surveillance.

On the question whether all violations of laws by a dominant company trigger the application of competition law the FCO confines the authority of competition law to such rules that govern unbalanced negotiating situations.

### 3. *Competitive Harm?*

The FCO's decision was heavily criticized by the Düsseldorf Court of Appeal in the interim proceedings for an absence of showing competitive harm. The Düsseldorf Court does not question that inappropriate conditions could possibly be a case for a competition law assessment, but only if those conditions would not have appeared in a hypothetical scenario of competition. The Court does not see any indication that Facebook, in a competitive situation, would have adopted different terms for users. The FCO had failed to provide scenarios of as-if-competition (cf. Budzinski et al., 2021, p. 63), and it had not provided evidence for competitive harm.

The discussion by the Düsseldorf Court reveals a fundamental disagreement on the notion of competition: For the Düsseldorf Court, a violation of competition requires either quantitative effects (for which there was no evidence) or a comparison of the actual scenario with a scenario in a comparable situation of as if-competition. One may take the view that the building of super profiles in this case is a deterioration of quality equivalent to a price increase in a zero-price market.

For the FCO, the harm to competition starts at the point when one market side imposes its rules on the other market side, which then finds itself in a "take-it-or-leave-it" scenario (Budzinski et al., 2021, p. 63). This is based on the archaic idea

---

24 European Court of Justice, Decision 27/76 of Feb. 14, 1978 – *United Brands*.
25 Federal Cartel Office, Decision B6-22/16 of Feb. 6, 2019, para. 526 – *Facebook*.

of a market economy where different actors meet on a level playing field and start to negotiate in the marketplace. Essentially, the FCO stipulates that consumers are empowered *vis-à-vis* dominant companies as a prerequisite for a working competitive process. If the terms and conditions that are enforced by a company upon which the user is dependent corrupt this model, the market economy is at risk – and the competition agency has to restore the starting conditions for all actors that are involved. That is the core idea of this line of reasoning.

The reading of preceding court cases proposed by the FCO may be considered as innovative or far-reaching. The case that the FCO primarily relied upon addressed very specific and complex circumstances in cases where a professional association of medical doctors sued the governmental pension institution.[26]

It is only in a short paragraph that the FCO deals with competitive harm. It states that the combination of data leads to more tailor-made advertising. This makes it hard for new entrants to enter: whether as a social network or in the advertising market. Again, the normative argument of a level playing field for all actors comes up. Competitors are at a competitive disadvantage if they respected the GDPR.[27]

### 4. *Compulsory Tying*

The decision of the Federal Court of Justice, intervening after the damaging setback for the FCO by the Düsseldorf Court of Appeal irons out some of the flaws of the FCO decision. This 55-page-long decision is seen as a landmark opinion that shapes the approach towards Big Tech. The Court slightly reframed the abuse. It moved away from the violation of privacy standards and instead focused on an abuse that may be summarized as "compulsory tying": Facebook imposed a service on the user that she does not necessarily wish to have – but that she has to pay for with extensive data revelation and combination. While users seek a social network service, what they get is a highly personalized experience that includes extensive data revelation. They are not given the choice as to what to consume and what to give for it. They are pushed into a data-intense network which is quasi-monopolistic.

On the matter of anti-competitive effects, the Court states:

> "(…) as in the case of a compulsory tying of products or services, anti-competitive effects may arise both in the vertical relationship and in the horizontal relationship if the imposed extension of the scope of services proves to be an exploitation of customers or an obstacle to competition (…). The anti-competitive nature of the imposed extension of services results here both from the exploitation of customers and from its anti-competitive effect."[28]

---

26 In particular Federal Court of Justice, Decision KZR 47/14 of Jan. 24, 2017 – *VBL Gegenwert II*.
27 Federal Cartel Office, Decision B6-22/16 of Feb. 6, 2019, para. 888 – *Facebook*.
28 Federal Court of Justice, Decision KVR 69/19 of June 23, 2020, para. 64.

The Court thereby bases the case on exploitation of users, but also on the anti-competitive effects for other social networks and advertising clients.

This is close to the established European case law on tying, as in the *Microsoft* case, where the European General Court accepted four requirements for finding an anti-competitive tying: (1) the tying and tied products are two separate products; (2) the undertaking concerned is dominant in the market for the tying product; (3) the undertaking concerned does not give customers a choice to obtain the tying product without the tied product; and (4) the practice in question forecloses competition.[29]

The tying and tied product could be identified as the social network experience in its raw form, and the rich personalized data revelation form. Obviously, even a dominant company does not need to cater to all possible user preferences. Yet, if there is a considerable user demand for a less data-intense social network (a fact that the FCO had uncovered in a survey), it could be expected that – under competitive parameters – an offer for the separate product would be created in the market.

### 5. *Consumer Choice*

With regard to the vertical anticompetitive effect, the Court argues that competition is weakened when the opposite market side loses choice. This relates to the consumer choice approach as advanced by authors before (Nihoul, 2016; Averitt & Lande, 2007). Consumer choice implies that market actors can interact on a decentralized level, taking into account their individual preferences and decisions (Budzinski et al., 2021, p. 63).

This is close to a Hayekian understanding of markets as the spontaneous order and mirrors the approach of the FCO: Protecting the opposite market side becomes a key component of competition law (Zimmer, 2012). The customer as the "referee in markets" makes the decisions as to who wins the competition. These decisions remain subjective and are in the hands of consumers who have choice. This understanding of competition emphasizes the consumer as a sovereign. In post-Chicago economics, the consumer is introduced as the beneficiary of welfare effects. The latter view of the role of consumers in the market economy seems less holistic and reduces consumers from active market players to passive beneficiaries of welfare effects.

### 6. *Foreclosure*

With regard to the horizontal dimension of the data combination, the Court elegantly connects the two market sides of the platform; this is an aspect that had not been fully developed in the FCO decision. With data collected and combined unlawfully, the chances for actual or potential competitors are reduced and market entry barriers are raised. With more data at its disposal, Facebook can offer more targeted advertising and raises data-based market entry barriers next to the network effects that make it hard to contest the market anyway.[30]

---

29 European General Court, Decision T-612/04 of Sept. 17, 2007, paras. 850 et seqq. – *Microsoft*.
30 Federal Court, Decision KVR 69/19 of June 23, 2020, para. 94.

Accordingly, the Court sees the exclusionary effects – which are produced by data access and network effects – as equally important for the assessment of the behavior. With the Court addressing this aspect in greater detail, one of the weaknesses of the FCO decision is cured. The relationship of Facebook with third-party websites that make use of Facebook Business Tools remains completely underexplored (Budzinski et al., 2021, p. 66).

## C. Causal Link

A major legal debate ensued regarding the question of causality. Facebook had argued that the practices were independent from any dominant position. Some scholars and the Court of Appeal advanced the argument that a strict causal link between dominance and behavior is necessary, so that only dominant companies can execute these practices. With other companies in the digital sphere using similar terms and conditions as Facebook it seems that the causality requirement was not met. Facebook called its practices an "established industry standard."

This argument was rejected on the basis that it was Facebook that was a frontrunner in establishing these "industry standards" in the first place. If the leading companies ignore the right of users to have a "substantial say in deciding how personal data are used," such behavior is easily imitated by other, smaller companies, while consumers lack the imagination that this is not a necessity in such markets. Facebook and the other digital giants set the standard – that is why the (allegedly unlawful) data practices appear to be an industry standard.[31] The FCO and the Federal Court of Justice let it suffice that there is some causal link between the dominance and the anti-competitive results in the market. With the Federal Court's decision and a later amendment of the German abuse law provisions, it is now clear that such a causal link suffices for finding an abuse in such a case.

## D. Balancing of Interests

At the stage of justification, the court took a balancing of interests for finding out whether Facebook's practices could be justified.

### 1. *Efficiencies*

Facebook submitted that users profit from "super profiles." The undertaking tried to quantify efficiencies for users with an expert opinion by Professor Evans.

The FCO replied – in a surprisingly old-fashioned way of treating competition economics – that "an economic quantification of abusive behavior hardly seems possible."[32] In any case, the efficiencies from personal advertising, based on data collection,

> "do not outweigh the interests of the users when it comes to processing data from sources outside of the social network. This applies in particular

---

31 Federal Court, Decision KVR 69/19 of June 23, 2020, para. 90.
32 Federal Cartel Office, Decision B6-22/16 of Feb. 6, 2019, para. 908.

where users have insufficient control over the processing of their data and the assignment of this data to their Facebook user accounts."[33]

Data collection could lead to economic harm by making users change their behavior in order to please other users or public bodies. Also, the Cambridge Analytica scandal where Facebook user data were leaked to a consulting firm that used it for political advertising (Confessore (2018)) and other unwanted data flows were referenced to show that users are exposed to risks, including financial harm, from extensive data exploitation.[34] These risks are negative external effects that Facebook does not need to bear. The FCO saw a gross imbalance of profits and risks from data harvesting, with increased monetization potential on the side of Facebook and no responsibility of Facebook for financial and intangible costs for users.[35] Such externalities weigh against Facebook.

## 2. *The Turn to the Constitution*

The Federal Court of Justice added another aspect to the balancing test: The Court weighed the pros and cons of the case from a constitutional law perspective. This had never been done expressly in a competition case, and it is a ground-breaking step in addressing Big Tech.

Facebook's social network has become an important forum for exchange and communication in society. Starting from this observation, the court argues that fundamental rights need to be respected, in particular, the right to privacy or to self-determination in a digital society. The GDPR is one consequence of this constitutional right. If not respected, this heavily weighs against the company.

The Court goes very far in binding Facebook to respect the fundamental rights. Doctrinally, fundamental rights primarily bind public actors – the state – and not directly private companies. But in the words of the Court:

> "Depending on the circumstances, especially when private companies - as in this case - move into a dominant position and take over the provision of the framework conditions for communication themselves, the binding of private companies by fundamental rights may in fact be more similar or even equivalent to the binding of the state."[36]

Facebook is thus seen as a company that provides an infrastructure for communication in society, and it is therefore held liable for guaranteeing fundamental rights as if it were a state actor. Similarly, on the European level, the European General Court had called Google "ultra-dominant" and "superdominant" with its search-engine.[37] This goes beyond the traditional "special responsibility" of dominant companies, and

---

[33] Federal Cartel Office, Decision B6-22/16 of Feb. 6, 2019, para. 965.
[34] Federal Cartel Office, Decision B6-22/16 of Feb. 6, 2019, paras. 906 et seqq. – *Facebook*.
[35] Federal Cartel Office, Decision B6-22/16 of Feb. 6, 2019, para. 911 – *Facebook*.
[36] Federal Court, Decision KVR 69/19 of June 23, 2020, para. 105.
[37] European General Court, Decision T-612/17 of Nov. 10, 2021, paras. 180, 182 – *Google Shopping*.

limits the possibility to advance economic arguments of efficiency. These companies and their "core platform services" (to use the terminology of the EU Digital Markets Act) are not just your everyday dominant actor.

With its statement, the Federal Court of Justice acknowledges the role of services such as Facebook for society as a whole – and it opens the door for connecting the dots of economic power, as tackled by antitrust, and social values as protected by the constitution as the ultimate legal authority in every case. This view of antitrust opens up the door for privacy arguments, and it also acknowledges that competition cannot be isolated from other aspects of the economy.

## V. THE OUTCOME, AND SUBSEQUENT DEVELOPMENTS

In mid-2022, six years after the case had started, there is neither a final decision in courts, nor any palpable outcome in the markets. The FCO had obliged Facebook to present an implementation plan within four months and material changes within 12 months; but nothing has happened so far (as of September 2022). This is all the more stunning since the decision is immediately enforceable and has been approved by the highest German competition law court. Yet, as stated before, main proceedings are still pending in courts which may make the FCO hesitant to enforce.

Developments based on the case have happened in the legislative arena.

Germany amended its competition act and introduced Section 19a as a specific provision for undertakings with paramount significance for competition across markets. These are the digital infrastructure providers or gatekeepers. According to Section 19a (1), the FCO can designate a company to be such an undertaking; and, in a second step, the FCO can activate specific prohibitions and requirements – which are specified in 19a (2) – that these companies have to respect. No. 4a of Section 19a (2) prohibits:

> "creating or appreciably raising barriers to market entry or otherwise impeding other undertakings by processing data relevant for competition that have been collected by the undertaking, or demanding terms and conditions that permit such processing, in particular (a) making the use of services conditional on the user agreeing to the processing of data from other services of the undertaking or a third-party provider without giving the user sufficient choice as to whether, how and for what purpose such data are processed."

This is the lawmakers' direct answer to the *Facebook* case: With the new Section 19a, super-profiling without meaningful consent becomes a distinct violation of competition law. Obviously, such specific obligations are close to regulation; but the undertakings still have an efficiency defense. The FCO has already declared Meta to be an undertaking in the sense of Section 19a (1).[38]

The European Parliament reacted to the *Facebook* case and the new German legislation in the Digital Markets Act ("DMA"), a new regulatory framework for digital gatekeepers. According to Art. 5 (2) (b) of the DMA, the gatekeeper shall not:

---

38 Federal Cartel Office, Decision B6-27/21 of May 2, 2022 – *Meta*.

"combine personal data from the relevant core platform service with personal data from any further core platform services or from any other services provided by the gatekeeper or with personal data from third-party services (...) unless the end user has been presented with the specific choice and has given consent within the meaning of [the GDPR]."

This is a direct reference to the *Facebook* case on the European level. As stated earlier, the German Parliament (*Bundestag*) also clarified the causality issue.

Finally, the German Parliament decided that appeals of FCO decisions under Section 19a should go directly to the Federal Court of Justice. The Düsseldorf Court of Appeal that had been so critical of the FCO's initial Facebook decision is cut out of the appeals process for this category of cases. Whether such a short-cut in the legal system is the right answer to the long duration of cases (and to courts that some perceive as stubborn) is a matter of taste.

## VI. CONCLUSION

The *Facebook* case is exemplary for answering three questions: Does competition law cope with the phenomena of the digital economy? What is the German or European approach to antitrust? Does competition law have anything to say for solving problems of privacy – and potentially other fields?

### A. Antitrust and Big Tech

The *Facebook* case stands for tackling the competitive issues posed by platforms. It is seen as a landmark case in the digital arena – but also beyond. The presiding judge in the case called it the most important one of his 20-year tenure.

With respect to the outcome, the case shows a mixed picture in many regards: While it holds an innovative and, in some respects, fascinating development on substance, it has not yet managed to open the market or to place users of Facebook in a better bargaining position. Finding suitable remedies remains a key problem for antitrust enforcement (Botta & Wiedemann, 2019). It seems that the procedures of antitrust are too slow and too susceptible to litigious imbroglio – at least if one is launching a monopolization case *ex post* against one of the most powerful firms on earth.

However, it would be one-sided to roll one's eyes with a view to agencies and courts that take their time. The law needs time to unfold. Quick decisions based on superficial investigations and reduced rights of defense are not a choice to go for. The case also shows that with every step in the proceedings, the discourse can become more nuanced. The Court of Justice's decision would never have been as impressive as it is if the Court of Appeal had not pointed out the shortcomings of the agency's decision.

Perhaps the case served its aims perfectly. Abuse cases often offer a possibility to analyze a specific behavior in detail. It has never been the strength of abuse cases to remedy complicated problems; but the cases have often been an opportunity to highlight weaknesses in the current legal framework. In this regard, the case was seminal:

It triggered legislation that moved the agenda forward. Section 19a and the DMA would not have come into existence without the FCO's *Facebook* case.

The case also shed light on the power of merger control. If the European Commission had prohibited the *Facebook/WhatsApp* merger in 2014, the whole issue of super profiles may not have happened (cf. Deutscher, 2018). Merger cases are often more effective than abuse cases. Ever since the experiences with Facebook, the European Commission and the national regulators have been working on better enforcement of merger control.

In summary, the case may look like a failure regarding the outcome in markets – but it is a healthy one that made politicians and enforcers rethink the institutional design of economic law.

## *B. Antitrust with Different Economics*

In 2016, when Germany's confident and powerful competition agency started the case, many observers asked for a theory of harm in traditional competition economics that they were not able to identify. The case seemed to confirm the prejudice against German competition law application as being out of tune with economics.

This is a misrepresentation. German competition law has always followed an economic approach, but one that slightly differs from the economic approach in the United States. Germany never had a Robert Bork, and never was heavily influenced by the Chicago School. The *Facebook* case points to the very roots of continental antitrust law: The German competition act was introduced in 1958. Germany had been pushed by the U.S. to have a proper competition law regime. This was not only or even primarily based on the belief that competition law brings about efficiencies, but also by the aim to break up German cartels and conglomerates that had played a role in the horror of Nazi times. Antitrust was a piece of liberation. Introducing it was about freedom. This political motive resonated with the ordoliberal (or neo-liberal) economists such as Walter Eucken (Behrens, 2015; Gerber 1998).

The individual's freedom and her choice as to how to engage in the economy were fundamental, a thought that can be traced back to the idealistic tradition of Immanuel Kant's philosophy. Friedrich von Hayek – who later championed the free spirit of competition ("competition as a discovery procedure") – came from this tradition. There are also links to the Harvard School ideas with its structural approach. There are few links to a laisser-faire approach that is sometimes camouflaged by indefinite calculations.

Therefore, the economics of the *Facebook* case may not be in tune with mainstream Anglo-Saxon IO, but are firmly grounded in an economic understanding of individual decisions on a level playing field that shape market outcomes. The very principled economic approach at play requires that all market actors stand a fair chance in this process. Also, the application of economics in the realm of the law is not detached from the constitution.

At the beginning of the 2000s, there was a movement in Europe to integrate more findings of consumer welfare economics into antitrust. This has often been labelled as a "more economic approach." For abuse cases it culminated in a 2009 Guidance Paper by the European Commission.[39] The key aspects of this movement were the focus on efficiencies and on proving effects.

While it is widely accepted nowadays that economic theory needs to inform law-making, there are still disputes as to whether concrete economic models and theories should play a defining role in specific cases.[40] Increasing numbers of European scholars and practitioners nowadays believe that some of the excrescences of the "more economic approach" in case application lead to an under-enforcement of antitrust rules – particularly in digital markets (cf. Valletti, 2021).

Whether the leading European institutions subscribe to the "more economic approach" is hard to tell (Witt, 2019). For a long time, the European Court of Justice had stayed with the concept that EU competition law protects competition, and that it is not necessary to show negative effects for consumer welfare. In 2022, however, the lower European court (the General Court) in some rulings relied heavily on a model-based economic approach to cases of abuse of dominance.[41] Yet, in *Google Shopping* a belief in this specific type of economics was not on display.[42]

## C. The Boundaries of Antitrust Law

For the current debate on competition policy, the question is paramount as to what antitrust can do to solve problems in society – be it privacy, sustainability, inflation, or inequality. The Facebook case stands for the intersection of privacy and competition. Expectations, however, should not grow too high that the tools of competition law can ultimately remedy the problems of society.

It seems trivial to state that competition law always needs to address competition issues; indeed, that is its essential task. In *Facebook*, the Court of Appeal doubted that the connection with competition was sufficiently strong. Some critics think that the FCO overstepped its boundaries and intruded into the competencies of data protection agencies.

Three aspects need to be taken into account. First, data has become an important parameter of competition. Access to data is a resource that defines competitive positions. Use of essential resources has to be a topic of competition law – and it always has been. Separating data issues from competition issues would miss the point of the data economy (Kerber & Zolna (2022)).

In the *Facebook* case, the connection was established when the exploitation of one side of the market (users) was considered to provide a competitive edge with respect to the other market side of the platform (advertising). Privacy rules – while aiming at indi-

---

[39] European Commission, Guidance on the Commission's enforcement priorities in applying Article 82 of the EC Treaty to abusive exclusionary conduct by dominant undertakings, 2009 O.J. (C 45/7).

[40] It needs to be pointed out that continental Europe has a strong tradition of working with statute. It is less case-based than Anglo-American legal traditions.

[41] European General Court, Decision T-286/09 RENV of Jan. 26, 2022 – *Intel;* European General Court, Decision T-235/18 of June 15, 2022 – *Qualcomm.*

[42] European General Court, Decision T-612/17 of Nov. 10, 2021– *Google Shopping.*

vidual liberties in the first place – define the boundaries of the use of personal data as a resource in competition. The complex relationship between both fields remains a difficult issue – but the two cannot be separated (Kerber, 2022; Robertson, 2020; OECD, 2020; Podszun, 2019; Graef et al., 2018; O'Callaghan, 2018; Costa-Cabral & Lynskey, 2017).

Second, it could be argued that without competition the problems that are associated with data – surveillance, exploitation, depriving individuals of their right to self-determination – are aggravated. In the *Facebook* case, the FCO and the Court of Justice assume (on the basis of surveys) that users are interested in less data-intense social networks. If competition was working well, this demand would be catered to.

This is an idea that applies to many of the fields that nowadays attract the interest of progressive antitrust advocates: Competition rules are not the prime tool to tackle climate change or inflation or inequality – but without competition these problems would even be more severe. Kerber & Zolna (2022) argue that these are cases where two market failures (typically competition problems and behavioral biases or information asymmetries) are combined. Enhancing competition can have positive effects for solving one of the market failures, yet the interdependencies with the other issues need to be taken into account.

For the *Facebook* case, Kerber & Zolna (2022) argue that the objective privacy risks and a lower fulfilment of heterogeneous privacy preferences lead to negative effects on consumer welfare. Consumer choice could help – they thereby approve of the approach that has been taken by the Federal Court of Justice. This is not true for all instances, however, but *Facebook* shows that antitrust enforcement can support the progressive agenda.

Third, the case is a perfect example of the diverse paths that competition law may take. The goals, tools, considerations, procedures, and mechanisms of antitrust enforcement are on full display in this hard case. Stylianou & Iacovides (2022) identified seven broad goals that are simultaneously pursued by European competition law – including efficiency and welfare – but also freedom to compete, protecting the competitive process, market structure, fairness, and European integration.

This is a "multitude of goals and values that European competition law aims to advance" (Ezrachi, 2018). For some, competition is a mere tool to ensure consumer welfare; for others, it is a defining feature of freedom in society. Some understand competition law as applied economics; others adhere to the supremacy of law. Some look at short-term effects; others at long-term effects; and yet others at principles, not effects. Even the German institutions varied in their approach. What better could happen to a field of law than to have *competing* ideas in changing times?

# REFERENCES

Autorité de la Concurrence/Bundeskartellamt (2016). "Competition Law and Data."

Behrens, Peter (2015). "The ordoliberal concept of "abuse" of a dominant position and its impact on Article 102 TFEU." Discussion Paper No. 7/15, Europa-Kolleg Hamburg, Institute for European Integration, Hamburg.

Botta, Marco & Klaus Wiedemann (2019). "Exploitative Conducts in Digital Markets: Time for a Discussion after the Facebook Decision." *Journal of European Competition Law & Practice*: 2019–465.

Botta, Marco (2021). "Sanctioning unfair pricing under Art. 102(a) TFEU: yes, we can!." *European Competition Journal*, 17:1, 156.

Budzinski, Oliver, Marina Grusevaja & Victoriia Noskova (2021). "The Economics of the German Investigation of Facebook's Data Collection." *Market and Competition Law Review* V(3), 43.

Bundeskartellamt (2016). "Working Paper: Market Power of Platforms and Networks."

Confessore, Nicholas (2018). "Cambridge Analytica and Facebook: The Scandal and the Fallout So Far," New York Times, 4 April 2018. https://www.nytimes.com/2018/04/04/us/politics/cambridge-analytica-scandal-fallout.html

Costa-Cabral, Francisco, & Orla Lynskey (2017). "Family Ties: The Intersection between Data Protection and Competition in EU Law." 54 *Common Market Law Review* 11.

Deutscher, Elias (2018). "How to measure privacy-related consumer harm in merger analysis?." EUI Working Paper LAW 2018/13.

Evans, David S. (2020). "The Economics of Attention Markets." https://ssrn.com/abstract=3044858.

Ezrachi, Ariel (2018). "EU Competition Law Goals and the Digital Economy." BEUC Discussion Paper.

Farrell, Joseph & Garth Saloner (1986). "Installed Base and Compatibility: Innovation, Product Preannouncements, and Predation." *The American Economic Review*, 76(5), 940.

Gal, Michal & Oshrit Aviv (2020). "The Competitive Effects of the GDPR." *Journal of Competition Law and Economics*, 16(3), 349.

Gerber, David J. (1998). Law and Competition in Twentieth Century Europe: Protecting Prometheus. Oxford: Clarendon.

Graef, Inge, Damian Clifford & Peggy Valcke (2018). "Fairness and enforcement: bridging competition, data protection, and consumer law." *International Data Privacy Law*, 8(3), 200.

Hovenkamp, Herbert (2018). "Progressive Antitrust." 1 *University of Illinois Law Review* 72.

Katz, Michael & Carl Shapiro (1985). "Network Externalities, Competition, and Compatibility." *The American Economic Review*, 75(3), 424.

Kerber, Wolfgang (2022). "Taming Tech Giants: The Neglected Interplay between Competition Law and Data Protection (Privacy) Law." 67 *Antitrust Bulletin* 280.

Kerber, Wolfgang & Karsten K. Zolna (2022). "The German Facebook Case: The Law and Economics of the Relationship between Competition and Data Protection Law." *European Journal of Law and Economics* 2022. https://papers.ssrn.com/sol3/papers.cfm?abstract_id=3719098.

Khan, Lina M. (2018). "The New Brandeis Movement: America's Antimonopoly Debate." 9 *Journal of European Competition Law and Practice* 131.

Lande, Robert H. & Neil W. Averitt (2007). "Using the 'Consumer Choice' Approach to Antitrust." *Antitrust Law Journal*, Vol. 74, 175.

Malueg, David & Marius Schwartz (2006). "Compatibility Incentives of a Large Network Facing Multiple Rivals." *Journal of Industrial Economics*, 54(4), 527.

Newman, John M. (2020). "Antitrust in Attention Markets: Objections and Responses." 59 *Santa Clara Law Review* 743 (2020). https://digitalcommons.law.scu.edu/lawreview/vol59/iss3/9/.

Nihoul, Paul (2016). "'Freedom of choice': the emergence of a powerful concept in European competition law, in: Paul Nihoul, Nicholas Charbit, Elisa Ramundo (eds), Choice: A New Standard for Competition Law Analysis?, 9.

O'Callaghan, Louise (2018). "The Intersection between Data Protection and Competition Law: How to Incorporate Data Protection, as a Non-Economic Objective, into EU Competition Analysis." 21 *Trinity College Law Review* 109.

OECD – Organisation for Economic Co-operation and Development (2020). "Consumer Data Rights and Competition – Background note." DAF/COMP(2020)1. https://one.oecd.org/document/DAF/COMP(2020)1/en/pdf.

Podszun, Rupprecht (2019). "Regulatory Mishmash? Competition Law, Facebook and Consumer Protection." *Journal of European Consumer and Market Law*: 2019–49.

Robertson, Viktoria H.S.E. (2020). "Excessive data collection: Privacy considerations and abuse of dominance in the era of big data." 57(1) *Common Market Law Review*, 161-190.

Rochet, Jean-Charles & Jean Tirole (2006). "Two-sided markets: a progress report." *RAND Journal of Economics*, 37(3), 645.

Srinivasan, Dina (2019). "The Antitrust Case Against Facebook," 16 *Berkeley Business Law Journal* 39.

Stylianou, Konstantinos & Marios Iacovides (2022). "The goals of EU competition law: A comprehensive empirical investigation." *Legal Studies*, 1-29.

Valletti, Tomasso (2021). Interview: "The European System of Monopoly." *The Counterbalance*, Apr 20, 2021, *available at* https://thecounterbalance.substack.com/p/the-european-system-of-monopoly.

Witt, Anne C. (2019). "The European Court of Justice and the More Economic Approach to EU Competition Law – Is the Tide Turning?." 64(2) *Antitrust Bulletin* 172.

Zimmer, Daniel (2012). "The Basic Goal of Competition Law: To Protect the Opposite Side of the Market," in: Daniel Zimmer, The Goals of Competition Law, Cheltenham: Edward Elgar.

# CHAPTER 15
# USING AND MISUSING MICROECONOMICS: *FEDERAL TRADE COMMISSION v. QUALCOMM*

*By Carl Shapiro & Keith Waehrer*[1]

## I. INTRODUCTION

In January 2017, the Federal Trade Commission ("FTC") voted 2-1 to challenge a number of Qualcomm's business practices. Qualcomm had long been the leading supplier of modem chips, the components of cell phones that allow them to communicate over cellular networks. Qualcomm also was a major innovator in developing cellular technologies and the owner of many patents that were essential to complying with 3G and 4G telecommunications standards.

At the heart of the FTC's case was Qualcomm's "no-license/no-chips" policy. Under this policy, Qualcomm refused to sell its modem chips to cell-phone manufacturers such as Apple, Samsung, and Motorola unless they had agreed to pay Qualcomm's preferred royalty for its standard-essential patents on devices containing the modem chips sold by Qualcomm's competitors. While the same royalty applied to devices containing Qualcomm modem chips, as we explain below, given Qualcomm's ability to adjust to the price of its own modem chips, the royalty applied to devices containing those modem chips is irrelevant to the analysis.

The FTC alleged that Qualcomm's no-license/no-chips policy enabled Qualcomm to use its monopoly power over modem chips to get cell-phone manufacturers to pay unreasonably high royalties for its standard-essential patents for devices containing modem chips of its competitors. Critically, Qualcomm had previously committed to license those patents on reasonable terms. The FTC alleged that Qualcomm's elevated royalties acted like a tax on modem chips sold by Qualcomm's *rivals*, raising their costs. The alleged effect of those higher costs was a weakening of Qualcomm's modem-chip rivals, higher costs for cell-phone makers, and ultimately higher cell-phone prices for consumers. Qualcomm, in its defense, claimed that its royalties were a legitimate effort to charge appropriate fees for its superior technology and in any event were not assessed against Qualcomm's rivals.

---

[1] Shapiro testified as an economic expert witness on behalf of the FTC; Waehrer led the team of economists supporting that testimony.

The FTC's case against Qualcomm was one of the most important enforcement actions in recent years at the intersection of antitrust law and intellectual property law. The case was controversial from the outset, as reflected in the sharp, public dissent by one of the three FTC commissioners. In an extraordinary rupture between the FTC and the U.S. Department of Justice ("DOJ"), the Antitrust Division of the DOJ later intervened vigorously in the case on behalf of Qualcomm.

The case went to trial in January 2019. In May 2019, the District Court gave the FTC a complete victory. However, the Appeals Court reversed the District Court's judgment, leaving Qualcomm as the ultimate victor.

The case provides an exceptional opportunity to see how basic microeconomics can be used – and misused – in antitrust litigation. In this paper, we identify the microeconomic issues underlying the FTC's case against Qualcomm. We then explain how the Appeals Court, with assistance from the Antitrust Division of the Department of Justice, essentially ignored the relevant microeconomics. Section II provides brief background information about Qualcomm. Section III describes the relevant aspects of the FTC Complaint. Section IV explains the economic effects of Qualcomm's no-license/no-chips policy, as argued by both the FTC and Qualcomm experts. Section V reports the pertinent parts of District Court's decision, which closely tracks our analysis. Section VI explains the errors made by the Appeals Court, and Section VII offers concluding remarks.

## II. QUALCOMM'S STANDARD-ESSENTIAL PATENTS AND MODEM CHIPS

The FTC's case against Qualcomm related to the cellular devices that have become ubiquitous over the past two decades. The case involved two critical components of cellular devices:

**Qualcomm's Portfolio of Standard-Essential Patents**: Standard-essential patents ("SEPs") are patents that must be practiced to produce cellular devices compatible with modern cellular networks.

**Qualcomm's Modem Chips**: Modem chips are the components of cellular devices that enable them to communicate with each other across cellular networks.

Cellular networks rely on compatibility standards. A mobile device must comply with the compatibility standard used by a given carrier to operate on that carrier's network. The relevant standards in this case are those governing 3G and 4G cellular networks.

Qualcomm owned a large number of SEPs for 3G and 4G cellular standards. Like other SEP owners, Qualcomm made a "FRAND commitment," when those standards were being developed, to license its SEPs on "fair, reasonable and non-discriminatory" ("FRAND") terms.

Qualcomm licensed its SEPs to original equipment manufacturers ("OEMs") of mobile devices, such Apple and Samsung. Qualcomm did *not* offer licenses to its SEPs to rival suppliers of modem chips, such as Intel, Broadcom, and MediaTek. Nor did Qualcomm enforce its patents against these rivals, even though their products infringed Qualcomm's SEPs. Instead, Qualcomm chose to collect its SEP royalties further downstream, from OEMs.[2]

Qualcomm also was a major supplier of modem chips. The FTC's case against Qualcomm involved two types of modem chips: those compatible with CDMA standards ("CDMA modem chips"), and those used in premium "long-term evolution" (LTE) 4G devices ("premium LTE modem chips").

While it faced some competition from other chip manufacturers such as Intel, the FTC alleged that Qualcomm had monopoly power over these two types of modem chips. Qualcomm disputed that allegation, but the District Court agreed with the FTC, and the Appeals Court accepted these factual findings by the District Court. "From 2006 to 2016, Qualcomm possessed monopoly power in the CDMA modem chip market, including over 90 percent of market share. From 2011 to 2016, Qualcomm possessed monopoly power in the premium LTE modem chip market, including at least 70 percent of market share."[3] In this paper, we take as given these factual findings relating to monopoly power; we do not discuss the related evidence or arguments.

## III. THE FTC'S COMPLAINT

The centerpiece of the FTC's case against Qualcomm involved Qualcomm's no-license/no-chips policy. Under that policy, Qualcomm refused to sell modem chips to an OEM unless and until the OEM signed a patent license agreement covering Qualcomm's SEPs. To enforce this policy, Qualcomm threatened to withhold an OEM's chip supply until that OEM signed a patent license on Qualcomm's preferred terms.[4] Critically, these patent licenses set not only the royalty paid on devices that contained Qualcomm modem chips, but also the royalty paid on devices that contained the modem chips of rival manufacturers such as Intel and MediaTek.

The FTC alleged that Qualcomm's no-license/no-chips policy had enabled Qualcomm to illegally maintain its monopolies over CDMA modem chips and premium LTE modem chips.[5]

The FTC alleged that Qualcomm's no-license/no-chips policy enabled Qualcomm to charge unreasonably high royalties for its SEPs. In particular, the FTC Complaint (p. 3) alleged that the result of Qualcomm's no-license/no-chips policy was that "Qualcomm's customers have accepted elevated royalties and other license

---

2 Under the legal doctrine of patent exhaustion (also described in Section 4.E) if Qualcomm had licensed its SEPs to rival modem chip suppliers, OEMs would not have needed a license from or to pay royalties to Qualcomm for those SEPs for phones containing the modem chips of rivals.

3 Appeals Court at 983.

4 District Court at 698.

5 The FTC also challenged Qualcomm's refusal to license its SEPs to its competitors, which the FTC viewed as a violation of Qualcomm's FRAND commitments, and Qualcomm's arrangements with Apple, which the FTC considered to be a form of exclusive dealing. We do not address those allegations here.

terms that do not reflect an assessment of terms that a court or other neutral arbiter would determine to be fair and reasonable."

The FTC alleged that by charging unreasonably high royalties for its SEPs Qualcomm excluded its modem-chip rivals and thus maintained its modem-chip monopolies.

> "By using its monopoly power to obtain elevated royalties that apply to baseband processors supplied by its competitors, Qualcomm in effect collects a "tax" on cell phone manufacturers when they use non-Qualcomm processors. This tax weakens Qualcomm's competitors, including by reducing demand for their processors, and serves to maintain Qualcomm's monopoly in baseband processor markets." (FTC Complaint, p. 3)

Our analysis focuses on this allegation about the economic effects of Qualcomm's no-license/no-chips policy, which was hotly disputed by Qualcomm and its experts.

The FTC's case relied on two undisputed facts relating to Qualcomm's SEPs: (1) Qualcomm had made a commitment to charge "reasonable royalties" for its SEPs; and (2) if Qualcomm and an OEM could not agree on the "reasonable royalties," either party could go to court to get a "FRAND determination" setting the royalty rate, which would then be binding on both parties. As a factual matter, no OEM obtained such a FRAND determination. All of the SEP royalties that OEMs paid to Qualcomm resulted from agreements Qualcomm negotiated with OEMs.

The economics of FTC's case against Qualcomm does not rely on (a) any conclusion regarding the specific level of royalties that would have been reasonable for Qualcomm's SEPs; or (b) whether Qualcomm had breached its FRAND commitment by refusing to license its SEPs to rival suppliers of modem chips (as alleged by the FTC).

## IV. ECONOMIC ANALYSIS OF QUALCOMM'S NO-LICENSE/NO-CHIP POLICY

This section focuses on two economic issues that were critical at trial and upon appeal. First, did Qualcomm's no-license/no-chip policy result in higher royalties? Second, if so, did those higher royalties have anticompetitive effects? We also briefly discuss an issue that is of interest to many economists but was not a prominent issue in the litigation: why would OEMs agree to elevated royalties that fortified Qualcomm's monopoly? As part of this description, we include the relevant arguments put forward by Qualcomm and its economic experts on these issues.

### A. Qualcomm Charged OEMs a Royalty Surcharge

There was abundant evidence that Qualcomm had used the threat to withhold modem chips in its negotiations with OEMs over royalties. The evidence presented at trial by the FTC and accepted by the Court showed that this threat enabled Qualcomm to extract a far higher royalty from OEMs than it could have obtained without that threat. That conclusion fits well with basic bargaining theory, under which Qualcomm and an OEM share the gains from trade from reaching an agreement.

Qualcomm's no-license/no-chips policy made it far more costly for an OEM to disagree with Qualcomm and seek a judicial determination of the FRAND royalty rate, because this OEM's business would be crippled for an extended period. Qualcomm's no-license/no-chips policy also increased the cost of disagreement for Qualcomm, but not by nearly as much, because a significant portion of Qualcomm's lost chip sales to any one OEM, if Qualcomm stopped selling chips to that OEM, would likely divert to other OEMs, due in part to Qualcomm's monopoly power, leaving Qualcomm's total chip sales largely unchanged. Assuming that the interruption in chip supply would be quite costly to the OEM given Qualcomm's market power and not very costly to Qualcomm, bargaining theory predicts that Qualcomm's no-license/no-chips policy increases the royalty the OEM and Qualcomm would negotiate.

A large portion of testimony of one of Qualcomm's economic experts argued that the no-license/no-chips policy had no apparent impact on the royalty rate. That expert looked at the contract royalty rates negotiated over time and across different OEMs. He attempted to exploit two types of variation in the effectiveness of the no-license/no-chips policy: variation in Qualcomm's alleged market power in modem chips over time, and variation in different OEM's vulnerability to the threat of Qualcomm withhold modem chips.

The FTC alleged that Qualcomm had market power in CDMA chips from 2006 to 2016 and WCDMA chips from 2011 to 2016. Qualcomm's expert therefore argued that royalty rates should have been lower when Qualcomm was not alleged to have market power than during the period where it could use its market power in CDMA chips to extract higher royalties. Finding that negotiated royalties as a percentage of the handset price remained mostly the same in the period with and without market power, he concluded that the "data do not support" the predictions that the no-license/no-chips policy led to higher royalty rates.[6]

As a proxy for an OEM's vulnerability to the no-license/no-chips threat, Qualcomm's expert used that OEM's purchases of Qualcomm chips in the two years following the signing of a licensing agreement as a share of its total chip purchases. According to the expert, if the no-license/no-chips policy allowed Qualcomm to charge higher royalties, one would expect OEMs that relied more heavily on Qualcomm chips to have paid higher royalties than other OEMs. However, he found no correlation between his reliance measure and the negotiated royalty.

This empirical work was disputed by the FTC and found not "reliable" by the court.[7] The vast majority of negotiations resulted in the same royalty rate as a percentage of net handset revenue. Despite varying conditions over time and across OEMs, the lack of variation in Qualcomm's royalty rate was not seen by the court as an argument for its reasonableness. Looking over time, evidence was presented that one could reasonably have expected the royalty rate to fall over time rather than remaining constant.[8] Critically, many of the OEMs classified as not reliant on Qualcomm modem chips were in fact purchasing CDMA chips from a rival chip supplier that had agreed

---

6  Trial Transcript, page 1866, lines 3–5.

7  District Court at 786.

8  District Court at 783-786.

not to sell chips to unlicensed OEMs, so those OEMs would have suffered a similar interruption in supply without a license.[9] In addition, Qualcomm's agreements with OEMs also included marketing funds, cross-licenses, and the exchange of other valuable consideration that one would need to control for to make proper comparisons across OEMs. Given the uniqueness of each negotiation and difficulty accounting for these other exchanges of value, and Qualcomm's incentive to maintain a uniform headline royalty rate, it was therefore not possible to reliably measure the effect on the policy along the lines pursued by Qualcomm's expert.

However, other evidence supported the intuitive idea that Qualcomm's no-license/no-chips policy enabled Qualcomm to negotiate higher royalties. Numerous OEM witnesses testified that Qualcomm's threat to withhold its modem chips forced them to agree to higher royalties than they would otherwise have accepted. The District Court describes this evidence in great detail.[10]

Qualcomm's own documents strongly supported this same conclusion. The District Court cited two high-level Qualcomm analyses of whether to divest Qualcomm's licensing business unit, Qualcomm Technology Licensing ("QTL"), from its chip and software business unit, Qualcomm CDMA Technologies ("QCT"). These were "Project Berlin" in 2007 and "Project Phoenix" in 2015. Both times, Qualcomm decided *not* to split QTL from QCT. Both times, top Qualcomm executives recognized that Qualcomm's no-license/no-chips policy gave Qualcomm powerful bargaining leverage in licensing negotiations, so splitting QCT from QTL would undermine QTL's ability to maintain the royalty rates it had been getting from OEMs.[11]

We define Qualcomm's *royalty surcharge* as the per-device difference between the royalty that Qualcomm was able to achieve under its no-license/no-chips policy and the per-device FRAND royalty for Qualcomm's SEP portfolio. The FRAND royalty for Qualcomm's SEP portfolio is the royalty that Qualcomm would have been able to achieve in negotiations with OEMs where disagreements lead to a court-determined FRAND rate *without* any withholding of Qualcomm's modem-chip supply during the pendency of the FRAND dispute.

Therefore: **Qualcomm Actual Royalty = Reasonable Royalty + Royalty Surcharge**

## B. The Royalty Surcharge Acts Like a Tax on OEM Purchases of Modem Chips from Qualcomm's Rivals

We now discuss the economic effects of Qualcomm's royalty surcharge. This analysis builds on the Court's finding that Qualcomm was in fact able to charge OEMs a substantial royalty surcharge (see below).

One important economic question in the litigation related to the apparent disconnect between (a) the FTC's allegation that the royalty surcharge harmed Qual-

---

9  Transcript at 1884-1885 and District Court at 743-744.

10 District Court at 697-744.

11 District Court at 773-775.

comm's modem-chip rivals and diminished their ability to compete by imposing an extra "tax" on them, and (b) the fact that Qualcomm actually collected the royalty surcharge from OEMs, not from Qualcomm's modem-chip rivals.

The FTC's expert explained that Qualcomm's royalty surcharge acts like a tax on transactions between OEMs and rival chip manufacturers.[12] The only economic difference is that the tax is collected by Qualcomm rather than by a conventional taxation authority.[13]

Figure 1 below is drawn from the trial demonstratives used by the FTC to explain the effects of a royalty surcharge. In Figure 1, the value of the rival's modem chip to the OEM is $40, and the rival chip maker's cost of supplying that chip is $5. The SEP royalties charged by Qualcomm for the use of its technologies represent an additional cost of using these chips. In the left-hand panel, Qualcomm is assumed to charge the FRAND royalty of $10. In that case, the gains from trade for the OEM and the rival are $25. If these gains from trade are split equally, the rival's variable profit is $12.50 and the all-in price of the chip (the price of chip plus the royalty paid to Qualcomm) is $27.50. One can think of this in two ways that are economically identical: (1) the OEM pays the rival $17.50 for the chip and $10 to Qualcomm, or (2) the OEM pays the rival $27.50 and the rival pays $10 to Qualcomm. Under (1), Qualcomm collects its FRAND royalty from the OEM. Under (2), Qualcomm collects its FRAND royalty from the rival.

**Figure 1: Effect of a Royalty Surcharge on the Gains from Trade Between an OEM and a Rival Chip Maker**

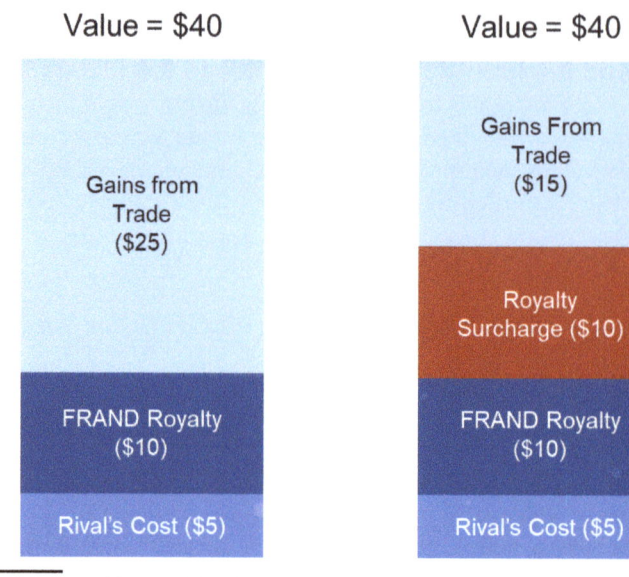

---

[12] Qualcomm's reasonable royalties for the use of its technologies also impose a "tax" on Qualcomm's modem-chip rivals, but the FTC was not disputing a tax of that magnitude. The reasonable royalties by definition reflect the reasonable value of Qualcomm's SEP portfolio, which itself reflects Qualcomm's R&D investments that led to those patents.

[13] Trial Transcript at 1124 and following.

Now consider the effects of adding a royalty surcharge of $10, as depicted on the right-hand side of Figure 1. Assuming the same chip value of $40, this royalty surcharge reduces the gains from trade to $15. If these reduced gains are again split equally, the rival's variable profit falls to $7.50 and the all-in price of the modem chip to the OEM increases to $32.50. In this example, the incidence of the $10 royalty surcharge is borne equally by the OEM and the rival chip supplier; each is harmed by $5. Note that the effect of the $10 royalty surcharge is exactly the same as the effect of a $10 tax.

The FTC argued that this pricing practice had the same effects as a government tax. Basic microeconomics teaches that the economic effects of a tax on a transaction are independent of whether the tax is collected from buyers or sellers.[14]

Applied here, this basic principle teaches us that the economic effects of Qualcomm's royalty surcharge are exactly the same, regardless of whether the OEM or the rival chip supplier pays that surcharge to Qualcomm. *The economic effect of the royalty surcharge is therefore to raise the marginal costs of Qualcomm's modem-chip rivals by the amount of the surcharge.*

Formally, suppose that the modem-chip supplier has marginal cost $c$ and faces demand $D(\bullet)$, which is a function of the per-unit cost of its modem chips to OEMs. If OEMs pay a royalty $r$ per modem chip and a price of $p$ to the modem-chip supplier, the quantity demanded given the price and royalty would be $D(p + r)$ and the modem-chip supplier's profits are $[p - c] \, D(p + r)$.

Now suppose instead that the royalty is collected directly from the modem-chip supplier. Let $x$ denote the price charged by the modem-chip supplier. We call $x$ the "all-in" price of modem-chips because it also covers any royalties associated with Qualcomm's SEPs. Thus, quantity demanded would be $D(x)$ and the modem-chip supplier's profit would be $[x - r - c] \, D(x)$.

Notice that the economic outcome in terms of the modem-chip supplier's profit and output are the same in the two cases if $x = p + r$. This application of the textbook result shows that the economic impact of the royalty on the modem-chip supplier does not depend on whether Qualcomm collects that royalty from OEMs or from rival modem-chip suppliers.[15] Therefore, the effect of any royalty surcharge is the same as an increase in the margin costs of rival modem-chip suppliers. The surcharge will tend to increase $p + r$, the all-in price OEMs pay for rival modem-chips, while weakening them as competitors to Qualcomm.

## C. Decomposing Qualcomm's Prices

Qualcomm charged OEMs two prices: a price $p_Q$ for its modem chips, and a per-device royalty rate $r$ for its SEPs. Let $\bar{r}$ denote the FRAND royalty for Qualcomm's

---

[14] *See, for example,* Lipsey, Courant & Ragan (1999, p. 102) "A straightforward application of demand-and-supply analysis will show that tax incidence has nothing to do with whether the government collects the tax directly from consumers or from firms."

[15] Likewise, it is not hard to show that for a given $r$, the profit-maximizing all-in price $x^*$ is equal to $p^* + r$ where $p^*$ is the profit-maximizing price in the case where the royalty is collected from OEMs. In addition, a higher royalty increases the rival manufacturer's profit maximizing all-in price and lowers its profit margin.

SEPs. By definition, Qualcomm's royalty surcharge is $s = r - \bar{r}$. We assume that $s > 0$ and examine the case where $s$ is substantial in size.

Rather than focus on $p_Q$ and $r$, it is illuminating to consider a different pricing pair: how much an OEM pays Qualcomm when the OEM makes and sells a device containing a Qualcomm chip, and how much an OEM pays Qualcomm when the OEM makes and sells a device containing a non-Qualcomm chip.

When an OEM sells a device containing a Qualcomm chip, the OEM pays Qualcomm $p_Q + r$. We call this the "all-in price" of Qualcomm's modem chips, which we denote by $x_Q$. When an OEM sells a device containing a non-Qualcomm chip, the OEM pays Qualcomm $r$. We describe Qualcomm's prices with the pair $[x_Q, r]$.

Normally, we do not think that a supplier can charge its customers when they purchase from that supplier's *rivals*. For example, when an airline passenger purchases a ticket from United Airlines, Delta Airlines does not also charge that passenger (or United). Indeed, if Delta had a dominant position on a given route where United was trying to compete, it would be highly suspicious for Delta to charge a fee to customers who are flying United on that route.

In fact, this very issue arose in the 1990s when Microsoft entered into "per processor" licenses with computer OEMs. The DOJ explained how those licenses operated: "'Per processor' licenses require OEMs to pay a royalty for each computer the OEM sells containing a particular processor (*e.g.*, an Intel 386 microprocessor) whether or not the OEM has included a Microsoft operating system with that computer."[16] The DOJ told the court that "Microsoft's licenses impose a penalty or 'tax' paid to Microsoft upon OEMs' use of competing PC operating systems."[17]

One can think of Microsoft charging computer OEMs a price $p_M$ for computers including Microsoft's operating system and a price $z$ for computers not including Microsoft's operating system. In terms of the price pair $[p_M, z]$, the DOJ did not object to Microsoft setting $p_M$, but the DOJ argued that Microsoft should not be allowed to charge OEMs anything for computers not containing Microsoft's operating system, *i.e.*, that $z$ should be zero.

In Qualcomm's case, the FTC was not arguing that $r$ should be zero, but rather that $r$ should be no larger than $\bar{r}$, so the *royalty surcharge* $s = r - \bar{r}$ should be zero. As a matter of economics any *royalty surcharge* $s = r - \bar{r}$ operates just like the licensing fee $z$ that Microsoft charged OEMs for computers not containing its operating system.[18] Both are examples of a supplier with monopoly power imposing a fee on its customers when they purchase products from *rival* suppliers. We next explain why such fees raise rivals' costs and harm competition.

---

16 *United States of America v. Microsoft*, Complaint, July 15, 1994. For further elaboration, *see* the DOJ's Competitive Impact Statement.

17 Microsoft's per processor licenses were also challenged in a private antitrust case against Microsoft. *Caldera v. Microsoft*, 87 F. Supp. 2d 1244 (District Court of Utah, 1999). The District Court in that case recognized the potential for Microsoft's per processor licenses to harm competition by excluding its operating-system rivals.

18 The FTC's expert explained this to the Court. Trial Transcript, at 1124-1125.

## D. How a Seemingly Neutral Royalty Surcharge Weakens Chip Competitors and Raises Prices to Consumers

Based on this analysis, the FTC concluded that Qualcomm's royalty surcharged effectively raised the costs of its modem-chip rivals, putting them at a competitive disadvantage, while also harming Qualcomm's customers, OEMs. However, Qualcomm denied that such a royalty surcharge would weaken its modem-chip rivals. Qualcomm persistently claimed that its SEP royalties were "chip agnostic" because they applied equally to handsets that used Qualcomm and non-Qualcomm chips. Therefore, according to Qualcomm, any royalty surcharge would not disadvantage Qualcomm's rival modem-chip suppliers, and not harm competition in the markets for modem chips.

As discussed below, the Appeals Court was convinced by this argument. We believe that confusion on this issue derived from a failure to recognize that when a tax is imposed on a transaction, its economic effects do not depend on whether that tax is collected from the buyer or from the seller.

Once one recognizes that one can treat any royalty surcharge as if it were paid by Qualcomm's modem-chip rivals, the seeming neutrality of Qualcomm's royalty surcharge completely evaporates. Furthermore, the equality of the royalty is irrelevant to the analysis. Qualcomm's royalty surcharge raises its rivals' costs, but not its own. In terms of the price pair $[x_Q, r]$, the FTC agreed that Qualcomm could freely set the all-in prices for its chips, $x_Q$, but objected to Qualcomm using its power over modem-chips to set $r > \bar{r}$.

The situation here is similar in effect to a vertically integrated supplier facing competition downstream. The economic effects of an increase in the input price charged by a vertically integrated supplier are not neutral, even if the integrated supplier's upstream division facially charges that same input price to its own downstream division. It would be nonsensical to claim that increasing the price charged to a downstream rival for an input would not have a foreclosure effect as long as the integrated firm charges the same amount to its downstream division.

The royalty surcharge on rival chips allows Qualcomm to profitably raise the all-in price for its own modem chips. Contrary to Qualcomm's arguments, this effect holds whether the royalty applied to its own chips is equal, above, or below the royalty applied to rival chips. To see why, define Qualcomm's chip price and all-in price as $p_Q$ and $x_Q$ where $x_Q = p_Q + r_Q$ and let $p_R$ and $x_R$ denote the chip and all-in prices for the rival chip maker. Here we have introduced notation allowing for different SEP royalties for devices containing Qualcomm chips ($r_Q$) and rival chips ($r_R$) to demonstrate that the equality of these rates is economically irrelevant.

First consider the case in which Qualcomm does not face any chip rivals and thus has a secure monopoly. Under this assumption Qualcomm's profit can be written as:

$$\left[p_Q + r_Q - c_Q\right] D_Q\left(p_Q + r_Q\right) = \left[x_Q - c_Q\right] D(x_Q).$$

Here, for any given all-in price $x_Q$, Qualcomm's profit does not depend on how the all-in price is split between the chip price and the royalty. In the absence of any actual or potential rivals, a royalty surcharge has no effect, as Qualcomm would simply lower its chip price by an amount equal to the surcharge to maintain the same profit-maximizing all-in price.

Now suppose that Qualcomm faces some competition in the modem-chip market. The demand for Qualcomm chips and rival chip maker chips will be functions of both all-in prices. Qualcomm's profit in the presence of a chip rival is equal to:

$$\left[x_Q - c_Q\right] D_Q\left(x_Q, x_R\right) + r_R D_R\left(x_Q, x_R\right).$$

Because Qualcomm can freely adjust its chip price $p_Q$ to set its all-in price $x_Q$ at its profit-maximizing level in response to changes in $r_Q$, the level of $r_Q$ has no effect on Qualcomm's profits or its profit maximizing all-in price, $x_Q$. However, the level of the royalty charged the rival does impact Qualcomm profits. The anticompetitive effect of the surcharge derives entirely from the impact on the royalty applied to devices containing rival modem chips and not on a comparison with the royalty applied to devices containing Qualcomm chips.

This analysis shows that Qualcomm's argument that their royalties are benign because they are "chip agnostic," which was picked up by the DOJ and accepted by the Appeals Court, is incorrect as a matter of basic microeconomics.

### E. Patent Exhaustion

Under the legal doctrine of patent exhaustion, if a component part is licensed to use a certain patent, then the owner of that patent cannot collect damages for infringement from a downstream firm selling products that practice that patent by virtue of containing that licensed component.

Qualcomm argued that its no-license/no-chips policy was justified because without that policy it would have been required to sell chips to an OEM that was infringing its patents. Qualcomm correctly pointed out that it would then not be able to sue that OEM for infringing Qualcomm's SEPs by selling devices containing Qualcomm chips, due to the doctrine of patent exhaustion. Qualcomm argued that its no-license/no-chips policy was thus necessary for it to earn reasonable royalties on its SEPs.

However, Qualcomm's argument fails logically because Qualcomm could and would simply include the reasonable royalties for its SEPs in the (all-in) price its charges the OEM for its modem chip. Qualcomm would therefore not be prevented from earning reasonable royalties for its SEPs on devices containing Qualcomm chips.

### F. Why did OEMs Agree to Pay a Royalty Surcharge?

We now address the question of how Qualcomm was able to induce OEMs to pay a royalty surcharge that weakened Qualcomm's modem-chip rivals. After all, OEMs are seemingly harmed in the near term by a royalty surcharge, plus they become more vulnerable to Qualcomm's monopoly power over time if Qualcomm's modem-chip rivals reduce or cease their investments in developing modem chips.

This analysis can usefully be separated into two parts. First, is agreement between Qualcomm and OEMs regarding a royalty surcharge impossible or unlikely because Qualcomm's gain from the royalty surcharge is less than the loss suffered by the OEMs? Second, if Qualcomm and OEMs collectively benefit from a royalty surcharge, are there available mechanisms by which Qualcomm can induce OEMs to agree to pay that surcharge?

### 1. *Qualcomm's Royalty Surcharge Raises Joint Profits*

Qualcomm's increase in profit from a royalty surcharge very likely exceeds the loss to OEMs. To see why, note that if handset prices are below the fully integrated or cartelized monopoly price, the joint industry profit – the sum of the profits of Qualcomm, its modem-chip rivals, and OEMs – would increase if handset prices were to increase. (Qualcomm was certainly not arguing that handset prices were at fully cartelized levels.) As described above, an increase in Qualcomm's royalty has the effect of raising all-in chip prices, increasing the costs of handset OEMs. This leads to higher handset prices for consumers. Thus, an increase in Qualcomm's royalty increases Qualcomm's profit by more than the joint losses to the OEMs. The reason is that the royalty surcharge will be passed through to consumers, raising industrywide profits.

The FTC contended that this situation is very different from the canonical setting in which a monopolist cannot profitably induce its customers to enter into exclusionary contracts. Economists use the following example to illustrate the argument put forward by Bork (1978, pp. 306-307), where an incumbent monopolist is not able to exclude entrants.[19] The example involves three players: an incumbent, an entrant, and a consumer. In that simple example, the loss to the consumer from agreeing to purchase exclusively from the incumbent exceeds the increase in the profit to the incumbent from excluding the entrant. As a result, in that example it is not possible for the incumbent to "buy" the consumer's agreement to exclude the entrant.

The Qualcomm situation is fundamentally different because Qualcomm and OEMs collectively *benefit* from the imposition of a royalty surcharge. As pointed out by many economists, when the victims are not at the bargaining table, the so-called Chicago critique need not hold. As a result, thus there is a large collection of models or mechanisms in which customers accept anticompetitive agreements that harm them or others (including downstream consumers) relative to a world in which such agreements are prohibited.[20]

### 2. *A Mechanism to Induce OEMs to Pay a Royalty Surcharge*

One such mechanism was presented at trial. There was abundant evidence that OEMs were sufficiently afraid of being cut off from their supply of modem chips from Qualcomm that they agreed to substantially higher royalties than they otherwise would have accepted.

---

19 *For example, see* Whinston (2008, pp. 136-139).

20 Whinston (2008, pp. 140-178) discusses a whole collection of models where exclusionary contacts are profitable.

What does that imply about the counterfactual world in which Qualcomm was prohibited from bringing its modem-chip monopoly power to bear in its royalty negotiations with OEMs?

One possibility is that Qualcomm would instead have used it modem-chip power to extract a large fixed fee from OEMs. Compared with that but-for world, Qualcomm waived its fixed fees in exchange for OEMs agreeing to pay the royalty surcharge. Viewed this way, Qualcomm paid OEMs a large fixed fee (waiving the fee it otherwise would have charged) in exchange for their agreement to pay Qualcomm an additional amount (the royalty surcharge) every time they purchase a modem chip from another manufacturer. Such contracts clearly harm competition in the supply of modem chips. However, extracting large fixed fees from OEMs might not be a practical, for a number of reasons.[21] Therefore, in that counterfactual world Qualcomm might not have been able to extract as much from OEMs as it was able to obtain using a royalty surcharge.

## G. Summary of the Effects of Qualcomm's Royalty Surcharge

We are now able to summarize the economic effects of Qualcomm's royalty surcharge:

- Qualcomm's rivals are harmed by the royalty surcharge, which raises their costs, reduces their unit sales, and reduces their profit margins on their remaining sales. This in turn reduces their incentives to invest in R&D to develop next-generation modem chips.
- The all-in price of rival modem chips rises, harming OEMs making devices containing those chips and and/or consumers purchasing them.
- Qualcomm benefits directly from the royalty surcharge because it collects a higher royalty on devices containing non-Qualcomm modem chips.
- Qualcomm benefits indirectly from the royalty surcharge due to the increased demand for Qualcomm's chips resulting from the higher all-in price of rival chips. In response, Qualcomm will raise the all-in price of its own chips, but likely by less than the price increases of its rivals. This allows Qualcomm to sell more modem chips and to earn more on each chip it sells.
- The royalty surcharge additionally decreases Qualcomm's incentive to compete, similar to if Qualcomm held a minority ownership share in its rivals. Qualcomm effectively bears an opportunity cost in the form of forgone royalty income when Qualcomm wins modem-chips sales from its rivals.[22]

---

21 Determining the size of the fixed fee for each OEM might be difficult. Costly bargaining impasses could result. Charging a sizeable fixed fee also shifts significant risk to OEMs. An OEM would have to commit to a large fixed payment to Qualcomm before it likely knows what its sales will be. These problems do not arise under Qualcomm's no-license/no-chips policy.

22 Qualcomm's per-unit opportunity cost is less than the royalty surcharge, because some sales that Qualcomm gains by lowering its all-in price do not come at the expense of sales by rivals. Instead, they result from end users deciding to purchase more mobile devices, *e.g.*, by increasing the frequency with which they replace their cell phones.

- The all-in price of Qualcomm's chips rises, harming OEMs making devices containing those chips and/or consumers purchasing them.

The FTC's expert explained that all of these effects were present, including the two key elements that establish harm to competition from exclusionary conduct: A weakening of competitors and harm to customers.

## V. THE DISTRICT COURT'S DECISION

The District Court ruled in favor of the FTC on virtually every disputed issue, closely tracking the economic analysis presented to the court by the FTC expert. The District Court rejected the arguments put forward by Qualcomm, finding the testimony of many Qualcomm executives to be lacking credibility.[23]

A critical point of dispute was whether as a result of its conduct Qualcomm's SEP royalties were unreasonably high. The District Court answered this factual question with a clear "yes."

The District Court provided extensive detail about how Qualcomm used its threat to stop supplying modem chips to OEMs to obtain higher royalty rates than Qualcomm would otherwise have been able to negotiate. Based on a substantial body of evidence, from OEM and Qualcomm documents and OEM testimony, the District Court described how this dynamic played out over more than twenty years for each of many OEMs, including LG Electronics, Sony, Samsung, Huawei, Motorola, Lenovo, Blackberry, Apple, ZTE, and Nokia.[24] The District Court also cited numerous other categories of evidence in support of its conclusion that Qualcomm's royalty rates were elevated by Qualcomm's threat to withhold its modem chips from OEMs.

Importantly, Qualcomm's own internal analysis strongly supported this conclusion. The District Court's description of this evidence is described above in Section IV.A.

The District Court also concluded that Qualcomm's royalty surcharge raised rivals' costs and fortified Qualcomm's monopoly power, for the reasons given in Section IV above.[25]

The District Court further explained how Qualcomm's royalty surcharge harmed competition.[26]

---

23 *See* Section II.E, "Credibility Determinations." "The Court finds Qualcomm's internal, contemporaneous documents more persuasive than Qualcomm's trial testimony prepared specifically for this litigation. ... Specifically, many Qualcomm executives' trial testimony was contradicted by these witnesses' own contemporaneous emails, handwritten notes, and recorded statements to the Internal Revenue Service ('IRS')." District Court at 676.

24 District Court at 698-742.

25 District Court at 790. When the District Court states that the royalty surcharge "results in exclusivity," we interpret this to mean that the royalty surcharge excludes Qualcomm's modem-chip rivals from the relevant modem-chip markets by lowering their margins, reducing their unit sales, and reducing their profits, thus making it more difficult for them to sustain the investments necessary to offer modem chips that can match Qualcomm's in terms of quality and performance. During the relevant period of time, a number of Qualcomm's modem-chip rivals ceased selling modem chips.

26 District Court at 792.

> "Because the surcharge also raises the market price of rivals' chips, Qualcomm prevents rivals from underbidding Qualcomm, so that Qualcomm can maintain its modem chip market power. The surcharge affects demand for rivals' chips because as a matter of basic economics, regardless of whether a surcharge is imposed on OEMs or directly on Qualcomm's rivals, 'the price paid by buyers rises, and the price received by sellers falls.' N. Gregory Mankiw, Principles of Microeconomics, Vol. 1 156 (7th ed. 2014). Thus, the surcharge 'places a wedge between the price that buyers pay and the price that sellers receive,' and demand for such transactions decreases. Id. Rivals see lower sales volumes and lower margins, and consumers see less advanced features as competition decreases."

As noted above in Section IV, Qualcomm had denied that Qualcomm's royalty surcharge acted like a tax on rival modem chips purchased by OEMs, because the surcharge was paid by OEMs and because the surcharge also applied to devices containing Qualcomm modem chips. The District Court recognized that this was a specious economic argument. The District Court also recognized that Qualcomm's royalty surcharge operates very much like Microsoft's per-processor license to raise rivals' costs.[27]

In summary, the District Court found that Qualcomm's no-license/no-chips policy allowed Qualcomm to impose a royalty surcharge for its SEPs on OEMs, and that "Qualcomm's surcharge increased the effective price of rivals' modem chips." By imposing a tax on OEMs when they purchased rival modem chips, Qualcomm raised rivals' costs, reduced the effective price that Qualcomm's rivals could obtain for their modem chips (for any given all-in price and quality of Qualcomm own modem chips), and increased the all-in price of modem chips to OEMs. The FTC had thus proven the central elements of a violation of Section 2 of the Sherman Act: monopoly power and the use of that power to exclude rivals and harm customers.

The District Court ordered Qualcomm to modify its business practices to comply with antitrust law. Here is the key provision of the District Court's injunction relating to Qualcomm's no-license/no-chips policy:

> "(1) Qualcomm must not condition the supply of modem chips on a customer's patent license status and Qualcomm must negotiate or renegotiate license terms with customers in good faith under conditions free from the threat of lack of access to or discriminatory provision of modem chip supply or associated technical support or access to software."[28]

This injunction was well designed to end Qualcomm's no-license/no-chips policy. Note that this requirement does not prevent Qualcomm from obtaining reasonable royalties for its SEPs. Nor does it impose any limit on what Qualcomm can charge for its modem chips, so long as those charges do not depend on whether the OEM has signed a license to Qualcomm's SEPs.

---

27 District Court at 792.

28 District Court at 820.

# VI. THE APPEALS COURT'S DECISION

The Appeals Court took a very different view of Qualcomm's no-license/no-chips policy:

> "Qualcomm's patent-licensing royalties and 'no license, no chips' policy do not impose an anticompetitive surcharge on rivals' modem chip sales. Instead, these aspects of Qualcomm's business model are 'chip-supplier neutral' and do not undermine competition in the relevant antitrust markets."[29]

In this section, we explain how the Appeals Court reached the erroneous conclusion that a royalty surcharge would be "chip-supplier neutral."

## A. Qualcomm's Appeal Briefs

Qualcomm's briefs to the Appeals Court repeated a number of arguments relating to its no-license/no-chips policy that the District Court had rejected after hearing the economic expert testimony presented in court on behalf of the FTC and Qualcomm. Notably, Qualcomm's brief made the following argument:

> "The District Court next held that Qualcomm's royalties, paid by OEMs, are 'unreasonable' and act as a 'surcharge' on the chip sales of its rivals, reducing the money they have available to innovate and thus compete. As a threshold matter, that defies common sense because Qualcomm imposes no 'surcharge' on its competitors; it is undisputed that competing chipmakers do not pay any royalties to Qualcomm."[30]

> "Put simply, Qualcomm's license fees imposed no obstacle to its rivals' ability to compete on the merits—by offering better chips at lower prices."[31]

These arguments failed to recognize the basic economics of tax incidence: the economic effects of the higher royalties do not depend on which party actually remits those royalties to Qualcomm.

## B. Intervention by the U.S. Department of Justice

The DOJ intervened three times in the case in favor of Qualcomm.[32] The DOJ's challenging its sister antitrust enforcement agency in a major enforcement action was truly extraordinary.[33]

---

[29] Appeals Court at 1005.

[30] Qualcomm Opening Brief, p. 26.

[31] Qualcomm Opening Brief, p. 29.

[32] In addition, a sitting FTC Commissioner, Christine Wilson, publicly attacked the District Court's decision in favor of her own agency while it was on appeal. *See* Wilson (2019a) and (2019b).

[33] Qualcomm had been a major client of the leader of the Antitrust Division before he joined the DOJ: "Makan Delrahim, a tech lobbyist turned enforcer," *Financial Times*, July 26, 2019.

First, the DOJ intervened at the District Court level, urging the District Court to hold an evidentiary hearing before imposing any remedy. The DOJ expressed concern that "an overly broad remedy in this case could reduce competition and innovation in markets for 5G technology and downstream applications that rely on that technology."[34]

Next, the DOJ filed a brief urging the Appeals Court to order a stay to prevent the District Court's injunction from going into effect.[35] The opening passage from that brief states:

> "The district court's ruling threatens competition, innovation, and national security. Its liability determination misapplied Supreme Court precedent, and its remedy is unprecedented. Immediate implementation of the remedy could put our nation's security at risk, potentially undermining U.S. leadership in 5G technology and standard-setting, which is vital to military readiness and other critical national interests."

Despite these dire warnings, the DOJ did not explain why requiring Qualcomm to negotiate its SEP licenses without the threat of cutting OEMs off from their supply of Qualcomm's modem chips would have any of these feared effects.

Third, and most dramatically, the DOJ strongly supported Qualcomm's appeal, urging the Ninth Circuit to reverse the District Court.[36] The heart of the DOJ's argument was that Qualcomm was simply charging high royalties, which is not an antitrust violation.

> "The court erroneously reasoned that Qualcomm's practice was anticompetitive because it allowed Qualcomm to charge OEMs purportedly high prices. ... Premising liability on 'unreasonably high' prices, as the court did here—instead of harm to competition—can radically undermine important incentives to innovate. 'The opportunity to charge monopoly prices—at least for a short period—is what attracts 'business acumen' in the first place; it induces risk taking that produces innovation and economic growth.' *Trinko*, 540 U.S. at 407."[37]

As explained above, this argument overlooks Qualcomm's practice of charging unreasonably high royalties for its SEPs on devices containing *rival* modem chips. This case is thus distinguished from situations in which a dominant firm merely charges a high price. Furthermore, the case relies on Qualcomm's promise to license its SEPs on FRAND terms, which is a fundamental distinction from situations in which a dominant firm merely charges a high price.

---

34 Statement of Interest of the United States of America, May 2, 2019.

35 Statement of Interest Concerning Qualcomm's Motion for Partial Stay of Injunction Pending Appeal, July 16, 2019.

36 Brief of the United States of America as Amicus Curiae in Support of Appellant and Vacatur, August 30, 2019.

37 *Ibid.* at 8.

The DOJ also argued that Qualcomm's no-license/no-chips policy could not harm competition because it was directed at Qualcomm's customers, OEMs, not Qualcomm's modem-chip rivals.

Lastly, the DOJ attempted to distinguish Qualcomm's royalty surcharge from Microsoft's per-processor licenses:

> "In *Caldera*, however, '[t]he effect of [a per-processor licensing] arrangement was that an OEM who chose to install [a competing system] would pay two royalties on the same machine.' 87 F. Supp. 2d at 1250. Thus, the per-processor arrangement could serve as a disincentive for OEMs to purchase or invest in competing systems. Here, by contrast, OEMs pay for use of Qualcomm's SEPs that are essential to every cellular device produced, regardless of which supplier's chip is used." [38]

This argument makes sense for the reasonable royalties that Qualcomm charges OEMs but not when applied to the royalty surcharge. The DOJ seems to be assuming away the issue by simply assuming there was no royalty surcharge. As explained above, Qualcomm's surcharge acted to raise rivals' costs, just like Microsoft's per-processor licenses.

## C. Pinpointing the Errors

The Appeals Court was convinced by the arguments put forward by Qualcomm and endorsed by the DOJ. Critically, the Appeals Court argued that a royalty surcharge by Qualcomm would not cause harm to competition because it was paid by Qualcomm's customers, the OEMs.

> "Finally, even assuming that a deviation between licensing royalty rates and a patent portfolio's 'fair value' could amount to 'anticompetitive harm' in the antitrust sense, the primary harms the district court identified here were to the OEMs who agreed to pay Qualcomm's royalty rates—that is, Qualcomm's *customers*, not its *competitors*. These harms were thus located outside the 'areas of effective competition'—the markets for CDMA and premium LTE modem chips—and had no direct impact on competition in those markets."[39]

Here, the Appeals Court failed to understand that the textbook proposition that the economic effects of a tax do not depend upon whether the tax is collected from the buyer or the seller. The Appeals Court also failed to appreciate that a tax on a transaction typically harms both parties to that transaction. The District Court had heard expert testimony on precisely that point.

The Appeals Court also attempted to distinguish Qualcomm's royalty surcharge from Microsoft's per processor licenses.

---

38 *Ibid.* at 18, footnote omitted, emphasis supplied.
39 Appeals Court at 999 (citations omitted).

"Qualcomm's licensing royalties are qualitatively different from the per-unit operating-system royalties at issue in *Caldera*. When Qualcomm licenses its SEPs to an OEM, those patent licenses have value—indeed, they are necessary to the OEM's ability to market and sell its cellular products to consumers—regardless of whether the OEM uses Qualcomm's modem chips or chips manufactured and sold by one of Qualcomm's rivals." [40]

At this critical point, the Appeal Court again overlooked the distinction between Qualcomm's FRAND royalty and an additional royalty surcharge.

To illustrate the arithmetic, suppose that Microsoft charged OEMs $50 per device for Windows, but also $50 for each device they ship without Windows. In our notation, $[p_M, z] = [50, 50]$. Microsoft has the right to set the price for Windows at $p_M = 50$, but Microsoft does not have the right to charge OEMs for computers that do not run Windows, so $z$ should equal zero. Put differently, Microsoft's "reasonable royalty" for Windows for a non-Windows machine is zero, as recognized by the Appeals Court. So, Microsoft's $50 charge for non-Windows machines is a royalty surcharge. The Appeals Court accepts that such a charge excludes rivals.

What about Qualcomm? Suppose that the reasonable royalty rate for Qualcomm's SEP portfolio is $\bar{r} = 1\%$ of the device price but Qualcomm is charging $r = 5\%$ of the device price. The royalty surcharge is $s = 4\%$ of the device price. The Appeals Court correctly observed that Qualcomm's SEPs "have value in such devices," but then incorrectly asserts based on this observation that the full 5 percent royalty rate cannot be exclusionary. Remember, at this point in its opinion, the Appeals Court is assuming that Qualcomm *did* obtain unreasonably high royalty rates and is arguing that such rates would not harm competition.

The Appeals Court also accepted Qualcomm's justification for its no-license/no-chips policy based on patent exhaustion.

"Otherwise, because of patent exhaustion, OEMs could decline to take licenses, arguing instead that their purchase of chips from Qualcomm extinguished Qualcomm's patent rights with respect to any CDMA or premium LTE technologies embodied in the chips. This would not only prevent Qualcomm from obtaining the maximum value for its patents, it would result in OEMs having to pay more money (in licensing royalties) to purchase and use a competitor's chips, which are unlicensed. Instead, Qualcomm's practices, taken together, are 'chip supplier neutral'—that is, OEMs are required to pay a per-unit licensing royalty to Qualcomm for its patent portfolios regardless of which company they choose to source their chips from."[41]

In this passage, the Appeals Court overlooks the fact that even without its no-license/no-chips policy, Qualcomm could still freely set the all-in price for its modem chips, so that policy is not needed to allow Qualcomm to benefit from the technolo-

---

[40] Appeals Court at 1000.
[41] Appeals Court at 985.

gies embodied in those chips. Note that the Appeals Court embraces the idea that Qualcomm should not be prevented "from obtaining the maximum value for its patents," but that perspective is directly contrary to Qualcomm's FRAND commitment. Lastly, the Appeals court repeats the erroneous proposition that Qualcomm's royalties are "chip supplier neutral."

## VII. CONCLUSION

Several factors contributed to Qualcomm's victory on appeal.

First, the DOJ intervened strongly in favor of Qualcomm. They expressed a fear that requiring Qualcomm to drop its no-license/no-chips policy would pose a threat to national security. The DOJ emphasized that Qualcomm was a national champion and raised the specter that imposing restraints on Qualcomm would be a gift to China in its economic rivalry with the United States. Surely these warnings from the DOJ and the Department of Defense gave the three appellate judges pause about affirming the District Court's decision and ordering Qualcomm to drop its no-license/no-chips policy.

Second, even the FTC had to concede that the District Court had made a legal error in its finding that Qualcomm's refusal to license its SEPs to Qualcomm's modem-chip rivals was a stand-alone violation of the Sherman Act.[42] That error may well have undermined the Appeals Court's confidence in the District Court's legal analysis.

Third, the Appeals Court was convinced by specious economic arguments put forward by Qualcomm, as we have explained in some detail. Additional economics training for appellate judges would help reduce the incidence of such errors.

Fourth, the three appellate judges, facing a novel business practice that they found difficult to understand, defaulted in favor of the defendant. Here is a telling passage from their decision:

> "Furthermore, novel business practices—especially in technology markets—should not be 'conclusively presumed to be unreasonable and therefore illegal without elaborate inquiry as to the precise harm they have caused or the business excuse for their use.' *Microsoft*, 253 F.3d at 91 (citing N. Pac. Ry. Co., 356 U.S. at 5)."[43]

In reality, however, Qualcomm's no-license/no-chips policy *had* been subject to an "elaborate inquiry" in the form of a detailed investigation by the FTC, a full trial on the merits, and extensive factual findings by the District Court after hearing economic expert testimony from both sides. The Appeals Court's reversal of the District Court was an unfortunate outcome in terms of the use of microeconomics in antitrust cases.

---

42 The key Supreme Court precedents regarding a monopolist's duty to deal with a rival are *Aspen Skiing v. Aspen Highlands*, 472 U.S. 585 (1985) and *Verizon v. Trinko*, 540 U.S. 398 (2004).

43 Appeals Court, 990-991.

# REFERENCES

Bork, Robert (1978). *The Antitrust Paradox*, New York, Free Press.

Contreras, Jorge & Richard J. Gilbert (2015). "A Unified Framework for RAND and Other Reasonable Royalties," *Berkeley Technology Law Journal*, 30(2), 1447-1499.

Easterbrook, Frank (1984). "The Limits of Antitrust," *Texas Law Review*, 63, 1.

*Federal Trade Commission v. Qualcomm* (2017), Complaint.

*Federal Trade Commission v. Qualcomm* (2017), Dissenting Statement by Commissioner Ohlhausen.

*Federal Trade Commission v. Qualcomm* (2019), 411 F. Supp. 3d 658, ("District Court").

*Federal Trade Commission v. Qualcomm* (2020), 969 F. 3d. 974, ("Appeals Court").

Lemley, Mark & Carl Shapiro (2007). "Patent Holdup and Royalty Stacking," *Texas Law Review*, 85, 1991-2049

Lemley, Mark & Carl Shapiro (2013). "A Simple Approach to Setting Reasonable Royalties for Standard-Essential Patents," Berkeley Technology Law Review," 28, 1135-1166.

Lipsey, Richard, Paul Courant & Christopher Ragan (1999). *Economics*, 12th ed., New York, Addison-Wesley.

Manne, Geoffrey & Joshua Wright (2010). "Innovation and the Limits of Antitrust," *Journal of Competition Law & Economics*, 6, 153.

National Research Council (2013). *Patent Challenges for Standard Setting*, National Academies Press.

Shapiro, Carl (2010). "Injunctions, Hold-Up, and Patent Remedies," *American Law and Economics Review*, 12, 280-318.

Shapiro, Carl (2021). "Antitrust: What Went Wrong and How to Fix It," *Antitrust Magazine*.

Shapiro, Carl & Mark Lemley (2020). "The Role of Antitrust in Preventing Patent Holdup," University of Pennsylvania Law Review," 168, 2019-2063.

Wilson, Christine (2019a). "A Court's Dangerous Overreach," *Wall Street Journal*, May 28.

Wilson, Christine (2019b). "Antitrust and Innovation: Still Not a Dynamic Duo," Remarks at the Stanford Essential Patents Symposium, September 10.

Whinston, Michael D. (2008). *Lectures on Antitrust Economics, Cambridge*, The MIT Press.

# CHAPTER 16
# Platform Price Parity Clauses: The Hotel Booking Industry

## By Thibaud Vergé[1]

The massive development of the internet and of online commerce from the 1990s onwards has profoundly transformed the marketing of hotel nights. In parallel with this development, the first online travel agencies ("OTAs") appeared. They act as on-line intermediaries that offer rooms to final consumers on behalf of partner hotels.

This development has resulted in some new pricing practices, notably the switch from the merchant model (where the intermediary – *e.g.*, a travel agent – acquires rooms that it then resells directly to final consumers at a price it controls) to the agent model (where the intermediary does not acquire rooms and the hotel keeps control over the prices it charges) and the introduction of price parity clauses linking the prices set by a hotel for sales through different intermediaries.

These practices have been scrutinized by competition agencies worldwide. This chapter will discuss the economics and the (not always consistent) policies or antitrust decisions toward these practices.

## I. INTRODUCTION

The two largest OTAs entered the market at the same time: *Booking* – currently the largest OTA worldwide – was created in 1996 in the Netherlands. It was acquired in 2005 by *Priceline Group* and now offers rooms in 1.7 million hotels worldwide. *Expedia* – which is strongest in the U.S. market, and a close second on the Asia-Pacific market, but now a distant second in Europe – was launched in 1996 as a division of *Microsoft* before being spun off in 1999. It later acquired Travelocity and now operates many well-known platforms: *Expedia.com* but also *Hotel.com*, *eBookers*, *Travelocity*, and *Orbitz*. HRS (Hotel Reservation Services) – which now lags behind the two largest OTAs – had initially been the market leader in German-speaking countries (Germany and Austria, and to a smaller extent in Switzerland).

The development of OTAs has profoundly modified the way that hotels sell their rooms. In 2001, 5 percent of all travel bookings (including hotel rooms) took place online in the U.S. In 2009, more than half of all travel bookings were made through these channels, including about 45 percent of hotel bookings. In 2009, OTAs ac-

---

[1] I was, for a brief period, part of CRA's team that advised *Expedia* in France. My research work on the topic (with Bjørn Olav Johansen) received financial support from the Norwegian Competition Authority and from the ANR Investissements d'Avenir program under the ANR-11-LABEX-0047 grant. The views expressed in this paper of solely mine.

counted for just 13 percent of online bookings of hotel rooms, but this share increased to more than 66 percent by 2017. For European hotels (according to D-Edge), revenue that is generated through OTAs increased by more than 50 percent between 2014 and 2018, while revenue that is generated directly through the hotel (or chain) website increased by only 12 percent.

Selling through OTAs is a great opportunity for hotels – especially for small independent hotels that can more easily market their room (and especially to new categories of consumers); but this opportunity also comes at a cost: Hotels pay a commission on each booking that is done through an OTA, which is a cost that is often higher than the cost of selling directly; and the hotels face higher cancellation rates on these platforms. According to D-Edge, one of two bookings made through *Booking* in European hotels was cancelled before arrival in 2018. The figure is lower for Expedia with only one cancellation out of four bookings; but this is still above the rate that is observed for direct online sales through the hotel website (about 18 percent).

OTAs – notably *Expedia* – initially operated under the merchant's (or wholesale) model: The OTA agrees with the hotel on a wholesale price for each room sold – the net revenue for the hotel – and the OTA is then free to set the price at which the room is offered on its platforms. OTAs have abandoned this model (about 10 years ago in the case of *Expedia*) or never adopted it when they entered on the market.

OTAs now work almost exclusively under the so-called agency model: OTAs never acquire hotel rooms but act as an online intermediation service that helps connect hotels and consumers. They offer an online environment where hotels can offer their rooms, and where consumers can search and compare hotels before booking a room. Though the room can be booked on the OTA's platform, the transaction may take place directly between the hotel and the final consumer who may even pay the room directly to the hotel.

In this intermediated model, the hotel keeps control of room prices: It sets the prices at which it sells rooms in all online distribution channels, and the OTA simply charges a commission – usually expressed as a share of the room price – to the hotel whenever a room is booked through its platform.

Because hotels pay a commission only if the sale is effectively done through the OTA, the intermediary may fear that hotels will use the OTA as a (cheap) marketing tool and eventually try to "convince" consumers to book directly on the hotel website rather than through the OTA, so as to avoid paying commissions.[2] It could also try to steer consumers to cheaper OTAs – by setting lower room prices – so as to pay lower commissions than on some more expensive OTAs.

Feeling that they needed to prevent such opportunistic behavior by hotels, OTAs have introduced additional clauses in their contracts with hotels to guarantee themselves the "best available conditions." The conditions are often referred to as platform parity clauses or "most-favored nation" ("MFN") clauses.[3] These clauses most often reference the prices that are set by hotels, but the clauses may also be related to availability or booking conditions (such as cancellation policy). The goal is to ensure that

---

[2] This is sometimes described as "showrooming."

[3] The MFN terminology comes from international trade agreements.

the rooms that are available on the OTA have similar conditions as those that are on other OTAs or on the hotel's direct sales channel.

Two types of price parity clauses have been distinguished depending on the constraints that they force on hotels:

A "wide price parity" clause that is imposed by an OTA prevents the hotel from setting a lower price for sales through any other distribution channel than the price that it sets for sales through that OTA. Such a clause thus links the price that is charged on the OTA that imposes it to the prices that are set on rival OTAs but also to the price that is charged by the hotel on its own direct distribution channel. This type of parity requirement has been common in contracts between hotels and major OTAs until 2015.

Following the antitrust investigations that will be discussed in this chapter, OTAs switched to a less restrictive type of clause: OTAs no longer prevent hotels from setting better prices on rival OTAs; but the clauses continue to prevent the hotel from offering better terms on its own direct distribution channel. This type of contractual restriction is often referred to as a "narrow price parity" clause.

In this chapter, I will discuss the competitive effects of wide and narrow price parity requirements imposed by platforms and describe how competition agencies (with a special focus on the different European cases) have treated such clauses in the context of OTAs/hotels relationships. To keep the presentation simple, I will most often focus on price parity requirements; but the analysis easily extends to availability or condition parity requirements.

## II. ECONOMICS OF PRICE PARITY CLAUSES

### A. Standard MFN clauses

MFN clauses have been widely used by firms way before intermediary platforms became widespread. They have for instance taken the form of price-matching guarantees offered to final consumers by retailers (in this context, a retailer commits to match – or even to beat – the price offered for the same product by competing retailers in the local area) but have also been used in vertical agreements between suppliers and wholesalers/retailers (in which case, the supplier promises to one buyer not to sell to any other customer at a lower price).

These clauses seem at first glance to obviously benefit consumers as they promise low prices. However, economists have extensively discussed the potential anti-competitive effects of such clauses and antitrust authorities have investigated these clauses that have in some instances been prohibited.[4]

---

[4] For instance, the U.S. Department of Justice successfully managed to prohibit the "coordinated" use of MFNs by *General Electric* and *Westinghouse* (*United States v. Gen. Elec. Co.*, No 28228, 1977 WL 1474 (E.D. Pa. 1977), September 16, 1977). More recently, the Department of Justice's cases against *Delta Dental* (*United States v. Delta Dental of Rhode Island.*, 943 F. Supp. 172 (D.R.I. 1996), October 2, 1996) and *Blue Cross Blue Shield of Michigan* (*United States v. Blue Cross Blue Shield of Michigan*, 809 F. Supp, 2nd 665 (E.D.Mich.2011), August 12, 2011) focused on exclusionary effects of MFNs.

Though MFN clauses include a promise to offer the lowest possible price to some consumers, they may harm consumers as they reduce the seller's incentives to offer a discounter price to one (or more) buyers. If the seller offers a discounted price to some buyers, it indeed will be constrained to offer that same discount to all buyers covered by the MFN provision. This substantially increases the cost of offering discounts and may ultimately soften price competition between sellers leading to higher prices. In a dynamic price stetting context, MFN clauses may also facilitate tacit collusion (again leading to higher prices), discouraging discounting and leading to stable high prices.

MFN clauses may also have exclusionary effects when they are required by dominant firms. Suppose for instance a dominant downstream firm (or a group of collectively dominant firms) require sellers to guarantee the lowest price. If an entrant on that downstream market were to try to obtain a discount from the suppliers, the suppliers would have to also offer that low price to dominant incumbent making it too costly. Entry could thus be prevented by the price-matching guarantee imposed by the dominant buyer.

Though MFN clauses can have competitive effects, economists have also exhibited situations in which these clauses could instead be pro-competitive, for instance by mitigating hold-up problems or reducing transactions costs. [5]

## B. *Platforms and Parity Clauses*

Price parity requirements imposed by platforms are different from standard MFN clauses in that they are related to price paid by final consumers and not to intermediate prices. For these reasons, they have also sometimes been called "retail MFNs." However, they may raise similar anticompetitive concerns.

### *1. Intra-brand Competition Dampening*

A first possible concern is that price parity clause may reduce competition between platforms over commissions charged to sellers using their services. Such theories of harm have been developed by Boik & Corts (2016) and Johnson (2017): Consider a simple setting with one hotel (but the model easily extends to multiple hotels) and two OTAs. The OTAs first simultaneously set commission levels.[6] Having observed the level of the commissions, the hotel sets its prices on the two platforms.

In a world without price parity requirements, the hotel freely sets its prices in the two distribution channels as functions of the commissions that it faces. Therefore, when an OTA decreases its commission, the hotel reacts by decreasing the price that it charges through that channel; and possibly – but to a smaller extent – it decreases its

---

5 See for instance Baker & Chevalier (2013) and Hviid (2015) for more detailed reviews of the economic literature on the competitive effects of MFN clauses.

6 In the Boik & Corts (2016) model, commissions level are per-unit fees that do not depend on the room price; whereas Johnson (2017) looks at both per-unit fees and revenue sharing (the commission is then proportional to the room price). But the main mechanism does not depend on whether fees are per-unit or revenue sharing.

price also on the second channel. Therefore, sales increase through the OTA that has become relatively cheaper to the detriment of the rival OTA. OTAs thus compete on commission level so as to maximize their own profits; and, in this unrestricted pricing equilibrium, commissions depend on the degree of substitution between OTAs.

In equilibrium, the level of commission is such that, if an OTA were to increase its commission marginally, the gains from the increased margin (earned on all units) would just be compensated by the marginal loss due to the decrease in quantities sold. To simplify, the discussion, I assume in what follows that the market is originally symmetric, so that equilibrium commissions and equilibrium prices are also symmetric.[7]

If we start from this competitive equilibrium, suppose now that one of the two OTAs ("$A$") decides to impose a parity requirement. If that OTA increases its commission above the "competitive" level, the hotel can no longer freely adjust its prices by penalizing platform $A$. Because of the price parity requirement, if the hotel decides to increase the price that it charges for sales through platform $A$, it must similarly increase the price that it charges for sales through the rival platform ("$B$"). The price thus increases to remain symmetric; this implies that, though total sales may decrease, the platforms' market shares remain unaffected. Therefore, the negative impact on platform $A$'s sales is now smaller than in the unrestricted pricing regime; thus platform $A$ has an incentive to increase its commission when it introduces a price parity requirement.

In equilibrium, commissions increase when at least one price parity requirement is introduced; commissions increase even more if both platforms impose price parity requirements. Commissions affect the hotel's distribution cost: Accordingly, any increase in the commission rates is likely to be passed-on (at least partially) to final consumers who consequently will face higher room prices.

The same argument applies also if the hotel is allowed to sell directly to final consumers: In essence, the direct distribution channel of hotels is a non-strategic platform where the commission remains fixed. But because, in this simple setting, when an OTA introduces a price parity clause, it has a unilateral incentive to increase its commission above the "competitive" level, the theory of harm applies whether the hotels can sell directly or not.[8]

## 2. *Exclusionary Effects*

Boik & Corts (2016) also developed a related concern of exclusionary effects of price parity requirements. This argument relies on the idea that a platform does not benefit from offering low commissions because sellers are not able to set lower

---

[7] If equilibrium room prices are not symmetric in the unconstrained pricing regime, introducing a price parity requirement (which is imposed by the platform on which the hotel sets higher prices – otherwise the requirement is not binding) necessarily has an impact on room prices (most likely the price on the expensive platform decreases whereas the price on the cheap platform increases to reach a common level on both platforms) even if commissions are left unchanged. The effects on final consumers are then like the effects of bans on price discrimination.

[8] *See* for instance Carlton & Winter (2018), who develop a similar argument in the context of no-surcharge rules for the credit card market.

prices on that platform (due to the price parity requirements that are imposed by the more expensive OTAs). Therefore, if there exists an incumbency advantage for early entrants – because consumers are aware of these platforms and because a newcomer needs to convince enough sellers to join to be able to propose an attractive package (in terms of choice but also prices) to consumers – price parity requirements make it difficult if not impossible for a new entrant to develop with a low commission/low prices strategy. Any entrant would thus have to impose equally high commissions and face equally high final prices as is true for existing platforms. This may a priori seem attractive as platforms' margins are then relatively high; but it also means that an entrant cannot differentiate itself from the incumbents and may thus find it difficult to convince suppliers and consumers to switch to their new (and untested) offer.

### 3. *The Role of Inter-brand Competition*

The anticompetitive theory developed by Boik & Corts (2016) and Johnson (2017) relies on the important assumption that a supplier is always active on all OTAs: more specifically, their model imposes that the supplier is either active on both platforms, or is simply out of the market altogether.

This is a strong assumption that has potentially important consequences; Johansen & Vergé (2017) relax that assumption: They allow a supplier to drop out of a platform if that platform's commission becomes "excessive"; and they show that it may no longer be the case that price parity clauses lead to higher commissions. Important factors that influence how price parity requirements affect equilibrium commissions, prices, and profits are the direct channel's market share and the degree of substitutability – from the viewpoint of consumers – of suppliers: the degree of inter-brand competition (*e.g.*, between hotels).[9] The basis for this alternative outcome is as follows:

When inter-brand competition is weak or when the supplier's direct distribution channel – *e.g.*, its own website – accounts for a small share of the sales, then price parity requirements harm consumers: Equilibrium commissions increase due to the lack of intra-brand competition, and this leads to higher prices. However, when inter-brand competition and suppliers' direct sales are more significant, price parity may yield lower commissions and benefit consumers. If inter-brand competition is fierce, suppliers set prices – in the absence of price parity requirements – that include distribution margins that are close to the commissions that they face on the platforms and close to their marginal distribution cost for direct sales (it is assumed that this cost is smaller, which thus provides incentives to reduce the price for direct sales).

Suppose now that platforms introduce price parity requirements. If all suppliers remain active in all channels, each supplier sets a price – the same in all channels – that is inclusive of its approximate average distribution cost. If commissions are relatively high, an individual supplier has a strong unilateral incentive to drop out of expensive platforms: It thereby drastically reduces its average distribution cost

---

9 *See also* Vergé (2018) for a summary of the theoretical and empirical literature on platform price parity clauses.

and can undercut the other suppliers through its direct distribution channel. It loses the sales that it used to make through platforms (but its margin was smaller on those sales); but it substantially increases its margin as well as its sales on the direct distribution channel. If inter-brand competition is fierce enough, the second effect dominates, and the supplier stops selling through platforms unless they substantially lower their commissions.

Thus, in the presence of strong inter-brand competition and credible direct distribution channels, the suppliers' participation constraints become crucial and serve as a disciplining device for platforms' commissions. If inter-brand competition is sufficiently fierce, platforms do not find it profitable to introduce price parity requirements: If this decision is endogenized, price parity clauses would not be observed in equilibrium. But Johansen & Vergé (2017) show that there exist situations – with strong but not extreme inter-brand competition – where platforms want to impose price parity requirement, even though it leads to lower equilibrium commissions (they benefit through higher market shares), and consumers also benefit.

Market structure thus seems to matter when determining whether price parity clauses are anticompetitive or not. In markets, where suppliers have no choice but to rely on platforms to market their products or suppliers are sufficiently differentiated, price parity clauses are likely to lead to higher commissions and to increase prices.

## 4. *Narrow vs. Wide-price Parity Clauses*

A few models consider direct sales by suppliers and thus allow to look separately at the effects of wide and narrow price parity clauses. Johansen & Vergé (2017) argue that narrow price parity clauses have the same effects as wide price parity clauses, at least when they are used by all platforms in one market. When wide price parity clauses are used by all platforms in the industry, they force suppliers to set the same price in all distribution channels. When wide clauses are replaced by narrow, suppliers will only be constrained to set a price on their direct channel that is equal to the highest price they set on other platforms. Suppose for simplicity that they are only two platforms, and that when wide price parity is used, the equilibrium commission is $ 15 per unit (and for simplicity, there are no direct distribution costs). In this case, each supplier sets a price based on an average distribution cost of $ 10.

Suppose now that wide clauses are replaced by narrow clauses and look at the incentives for one platform, say platform $A$, to lower its commission level (assuming that platform $B$ continues to set a commission of $ 15). The supplier will then set two prices: one for sales through platform $A$ and one common price for sales through the direct channel and platform $B$, where assuming that symmetry still holds, the average distribution cost is $ 7.50. For the supplier to lower the price below the price its charges on platform $A$, platform $A$ would have to lower its commission below $ 7.5. At this level, sales would not yet increase. It is therefore unlikely that a platform would unilaterally decrease its commission as it has to decrease too much before sales made through the platform would substantially increase.

Wang & Wright (2020a) obtain different results in a search model with showrooming: consumers search on one platform to identify the product that they willing to buy and then observe prices for that product on all distribution channels (competing platforms as well at the direct channel) at no cost. This generates incentives for showrooming, *i.e.*, a situation where the suppliers use the platform as an advertising channel to help consumers evaluating the quality of its offer, and to propose a lower on their direct sales channels so as to induce consumers to buy directly rather than through the platforms. Showrooming thus creates the risk that platform may not be viable as it faces the cost of providing the search services to consumers but does not generate any sale (and thus any revenue). Price parity clauses are thus used by platforms to prevent the suppliers' free-riding and maintain the platform's viability. Even when consumers have a preference for buying through the platforms, wide price parity clauses always harm consumers as platforms will anyway extract the buyers' additional benefit through higher commissions. However, they also show that narrow price parity clauses may sometimes benefit consumers because the collusive effect of wide price parity clauses is now avoided (platforms compete against each other) while the narrow clauses preserve the platforms' viability.[10]

## III. ANTITRUST CASES AND SPECIFIC LEGISLATIVE AND REGULATORY ACTIONS

Over the last decade, many competition authorities have investigated the competitive effects of the parity requirements imposed by platforms.[11] One specific sector that has drawn the attention of competition agencies, regulators and legislators worldwide is the hotel booking sector and in particular the largest OTAs active on that market. Even within the European Union, where national agencies have all looked into the application of the Article 101 (regarding anticompetitive effects of agreements between firms) of the Treaty on the Functioning of the European Union ("TFEU"), the outcome has not always been identical. In this section, we briefly discuss the different cases and present the various outcomes.

---

10 *See also* Wals & Schinkel (2018) who show that the combination of narrow price parity clauses and best price guarantees have the same anticompetitive effects as wide clauses. Edelman & Wright (2015) and Wang & Wright (2020b) extend the model by allowing platforms to invest in the quality of services they provide. They show that price parity requirement still tends to be anticompetitive and may lead to excessive investment. *See also* Maruyama & Zennyo (2020) who focus on demand-increasing investment and find more nuanced results.

11 *See* for instance the multiple investigations related to insurance markets (*see* the UK's CMA *Digital Comparison Tools Market Study* of 2017), interchange fees set by debit/credit cards networks (*United States* v. *Am. Express Co.*, 88 F. Supp. 3d 143, 165 (E.D.N.Y. 2015) or *Ohio* v. *Am. Express Co.*, 138 S. Ct. 355 (2017); MasterCard, COMP/34.579, Commission Decision of 19 December 2007 or the *2013 Payment Services Directive and Interchange Fees Regulation* from the European Commission) or cases opened against Amazon (Germany, UK) or Apple in relations with provision of e-Books (for instance, *United States* v. *Apple Inc.*, 952 F. Supp. 2d 638 (S.D.N.Y. 2013). Baker & Scott-Morton (2018) discuss antitrust enforcement of platform MFNs in these cases.

## A. United Kingdom

In September 2010, the Office of Fair Trading ("OFT") opened an investigation into the specific arrangements that were included in contracts that had been negotiated between hotels and OTAs. In January 2014, the OFT accepted commitments that were offered by *Booking*, *Expedia*, and the *Intercontinental Hotels Group* to remove restrictions on discounts that OTAs were allowed to offer to final consumers.[12]

The OFT's investigation did not directly focus on the parity clauses but instead on the OTAs' ability to pass-on to final consumers part of the commission that they received from the hotels through discounts. In September 2014, following an appeal by *Skyscanner Limited*, the Competition Appeals Tribunal quashed the OFT's decision and remitted the case back to the Competition and Markets Authority ("CMA").[13] Following changes that were introduced by *Booking* and *Expedia*, the CMA closed the case in September 2015.

## B. Germany

In January 2010, following a complaint from a hotel against *HRS* (then the leading OTA on the German market), the *Bundeskartellamt* ("BKartA") opened an investigation of *HRS*'s vertical agreements with hotels. On December 19, 2013, the BKartA informed *Expedia* and *Booking* that it was also investigating their contractual arrangements with hotels in Germany.

On December 20, 2013, the BKartA concluded that all parity clauses – price parity but also availability parity – that were imposed by *HRS vis-a-vis* German hotels (at least as stated in the 2010 and 2012 contractual terms) were infringing competition law. They were then ordered to remove the clauses from their general terms and conditions by March 1, 2014. This decision was later confirmed by the Düsseldorf Higher Regional Court (OLG Düsseldorf).[14]

In December 2015, the BKartA also concluded that all price parity clauses – including narrow parity clauses – that were imposed by *Booking* were infringing competition law and ordered *Booking* to remove these clauses from its contracts with German hotels. Though it had initially broadly approved the BKartA's analysis, the OLG Düsseldorf partially overturned the infringement decision in June 2019. The court then decided that while wide parity clauses were indeed anticompetitive, this was not the case with respect to narrow price parity clauses. However, in May 2021 the German Federal Court of Justice overruled the OLG Düsseldorf and sided with the BKartA; this decision thus confirmed the illegality of *Booking*'s narrow price parity clauses.[15]

---

12 Office of Fair Trading, Decision 1514, *Hotel online booking: Decision to accept commitments to remove certain discounting restrictions for Online Travel Agents*, January 31, 2014.

13 Competition Appeals Tribunal, CAT 16, *Skyscanner Ltd. v. CMA*, September 26, 2014.

14 Bundeskartellamt, B9-66/10, December 20, 2013 and OLG Düsseldorf, VI-Kart 1/14 (V), January 9, 2015.

15 OLG Düsseldorf, VI-Kart 1/16(V), May 4, 2016 and VI-Kart 2/16(V), June 4, 2019; Bundesgerichtshof, KVR 54/20, May 18, 2021.

In a private enforcement case, the Cologne District Court decided in February 2017 that *Expedia*'s wide price parity clauses were covered by the 2010 Vertical Block Exemption Regulations ("VBER")[16] under European Competition Law as *Expedia*'s market share was below 30 percent. This judgment was upheld by the OLG Düsseldorf later that year.[17]

## C. Other European Countries

In 2013 and 2014, other national competition agencies within the EU – notably in France, Italy, and Sweden – launched their own investigations of OTAs' parity clauses. In April 2015 the three national agencies simultaneously accepted commitments that were offered by *Booking*.[18] In Sweden, the commitment decision also included a fine of about 3.3 million euros (35 million SEK). Three types of commitments were offered:

1. *No availability parity requirement.* *Booking* would stop requiring hotels to guarantee on its platforms the same availability as on any other platform including the hotel's own booking system.
2. *Switching from wide to narrow price parity (online sales only).* *Booking* would stop requiring the hotels to offer better prices on its platforms than on any other OTA. However, it would continue to prevent hotels from offering better deals on their direct sales channels.
3. *No parity requirement regarding offline sales.* Hotels would now be free to offer better deals (than on *Booking*) for offline sales: sales that were made by phone or directly at the hotel.

When negotiating with the French, Italian, and Swedish agencies, *Booking* announced that the changes with regard to contractual obligations that were offered as binding commitments would apply widely across Europe as of July 1, 2015. On July 1, 2015, *Expedia* unilaterally announced that it would also abandon availability parity requirements and switch from wide to narrow price parity clauses in their negotiations with European hotels. As a result, most national competition authorities decided to close their investigations or – like the Irish Competition and Consumer Protection Commission – accepted similar commitments.

Some agencies continued to investigate; in December 2018, the Czech Office for the Protection of Competition found that *Booking* had entered into unlawful vertical agreements with hotels in Czech Republic between May 2009 and June 2015. *Booking* was fined about 0.32 million euros for the infringement (8.3 million CZK).[19]

---

16 The VBER exempts vertical agreements from the application of Article 101(1) of the Treaty [prohibiting anticompetitive agreements] as long as the agreements do not contain certain severe restrictions of competition (*e.g.*, resale price maintenance or restriction of online sales) and each party to the agreement has a market share that does not exceed 30 percent.

17 LG Köln, 88 (O) Kart 17/16, February 16, 2017 and OLG Düsseldorf, VI-U (Kart) 5/17, December 4, 2017.

18 Autorité de la concurrence, Decision n° 15-D-06, April 21, 2015; Autorità Garante della Concorrenza e del Mercato, I-774, April 21, 2015; Konkurrensverket, n° 596/2013, April 15, 2015.

19 UOHS (Czech Office for the Protection of Competition), S0664/2015, December 18, 2018.

In Sweden, the case against (narrow) parity clauses continued after the 2015 commitment decision. In July 2018, following a complaint by *Visita* (representing the Swedish tourism industry), the Swedish Patent and Market Court held that narrow price parity clauses were anticompetitive. However, this judgment was later overturned by the Swedish court of appeals.[20]

In some European countries, governments – often after intense lobbying by hotels that were unhappy with the outcome of the antitrust investigations – passed more restrictive laws. This started in France in August 2015, when under the so-called "Macron law" (law n°2015-990, August 6, 2015), any kind of parity obligation imposed by hotel booking platforms became illegal. Italy, Austria, Belgium, and more recently Portugal later adopted similar legislation.

It is also worth mentioning that prior the April 2015 commitment decision, the French Ministry of the Economy had launched legal actions against *Booking* and *Expedia* in order to put an end to the platforms' parity requirements under the unfair practices legislation. In May 2015, the Paris Commercial Court found that the availability parity and wide price parity clauses that were required by *Expedia* were abusive.[21] In June 2017, the Paris Court of Appeals confirmed this decision and fined *Expedia* 1 million euros; but this judgment was later quashed by the Cour de Cassation, and the case is still pending (as of August 2022).[22] In November 2016, the Paris Commercial Court found that the parity requirements that were imposed by *Booking* were also abusive. However, as *Booking* had already removed the clauses (commitments accepted by the Autorité de la concurrence), it avoided any fine.[23]

## D. Other Jurisdictions

Outside the European Union, multiple jurisdictions also investigated the competition effects of the parity clauses that have been imposed by the largest OTAs. In October 2015, the Swiss Competition Commission ruled that wide parity clauses were violating the Swiss Cartel act and prohibited them. In June 2022, the Swiss parliament approved new legislation that bans all kinds of parity requirements. Narrow price parity clauses are now deemed illegal too, as are availability and condition parity requirements.

In September 2016, the Australian Competition and Consumer Commission approved commitments that were offered by *Booking* and *Expedia* to abandon wide price parity and availability parity requirements. It also considered that narrow price parity clauses were not anticompetitive. Similar decisions have since been taken in Brazil, Hong-Kong, New-Zealand, and South Korea.

In the U.S., though the antitrust agencies have investigated cases that have involved price parity or similar clauses that have been set by platforms, they have not investigated parity requirements that have been imposed by OTAs.

---

20 Stockholms Tingsrätt, PMT 13013-16, July 20, 2018 and Svea Hovrätt, PMT 7779-18, May 9, 2019.
21 Tribunal de Commerce de Paris, n° 2015000040, May 7, 2015.
22 Cour d'appel de Paris, n° 15/18784, June 21, 2017; Cour de Cassation, 17-31.536, July 8, 2020.
23 Tribunal de Commerce de Paris, n° 2014027403, November 29, 2016.

Private plaintiffs first filed complaints against OTAs and major hotel chains in August 2012, and these complaints were consolidated in March 2013. The plaintiffs claimed that large chains and OTAs had been *"engaging in an industry-wide conspiracy to uniformly adopt resale price maintenance agreements, containing most favored nation clauses, in an effort to eliminate price competition among hotel room booking websites."* In February 2014, the Northern District of Texas District Court dismissed the case on the basis that the plaintiffs failed to allege sufficient facts that would plausibly demonstrate the existence of a price-fixing conspiracy.[24] Having rejected the claim on this basis, the court did not need to discuss whether price parity clauses were anti-competitive or not.

## IV. LEGAL ASSESSMENT IN EUROPEAN CASES

There have been two distinct ways to assess the legal status of the vertical contractual terms between OTAs and hotels: The UK's OFT decided to treat these agreements as akin to resale price maintenance: Though the consumers book their hotel rooms through OTAs, the room prices were set by the hotels and prevented OTAs from offering rebates (using their commissions) to consumers. This allowed the OFT to treat these agreements as hardcore restrictions under European competition law: Hardcore restrictions (or "black clauses") are serious restrictions of competition that are very likely to harm consumers, and thus violate Article 101(1) TFEU and are very unlikely to fulfill the requirements for an individual exemption under Article 101(3) TFEU.

The other national competition authorities in the EU did not treat parity requirements as hardcore restrictions (though the BKartA indicated in the HRS case that *"it can thus be left open whether the MFN clauses are hardcore restrictions,"* BKartA, B9-66/10, para. 187). A first important step of the analysis was thus to define relevant markets and compute market shares to check whether the 2010 Vertical Block Exemption Regulation ("VBER") applied to agreements between hotels and the largest OTAs, or not.

Indeed, under EU law in force at the time of the investigations, vertical agreements that did not include restrictions seen as *per se* anticompetitive (such as RPM or restrictions on online sales) were exempted from the application of Article 101(1) TFEU (prohibiting agreements that restrict competition) according to the 2010 VBER as long as the participants' market shares remained below 30 percent.[25]

### A. Market Definition

In most cases, market definition has thus been a central issue. However, except in the German cases, the discussion has eventually remained limited given that cases

---

24 *In re Online Travel Co. (OTC) Hotel Booking Antitrust Litig.*, 997 F. Supp. 2d 526 (N.D. Tex., 2014).

25 Commission Regulation (EU) n° 330/2010 of 20 April 2010 on the application of Article 101(3) of the Treaty on the Functioning of the European Union to categories of vertical agreements and concerted practices.

were most often closed with a commitment decision, in which event the competition authority only needs to raise its concerns but does not need to prove an infringement. I will thus now focus on the discussion that occurred in the first German case: BKartA's investigation of *HRS* in 2010-2013.

## 1. **Product Market**

*HRS* and the BKartA disagreed on the relevant market definitions, for both product and geographic markets. According to *HRS*, hotel booking platforms "*belong to a broad* [product] *market which, in addition to the providers of typical bundle of services of a hotel portal ("search, comparison and booking"), also includes all providers of services possibly leading to a booking*" (BKartA, B9-66/10, para. 70). *HRS* thus wanted to include a wide range of actors: offline sellers (*i.e.*, travel agents but also sales of rooms by telephone or e-mail); hotels' own websites; tour operators and other specialized portals; meta-search engines that specialize on travel or hotel services (*e.g.*, *Tripadvisor*, *Kayak*, *Trivago*); and also, general information engines such as *Google* (including *Google*'s hotel finder). In such a very widely defined market, *HRS* was a relatively limited actor and most likely did not to reach the 30 percent market share threshold.

The BKartA disagreed with this wide market definition and argued instead (as did all other national competition agencies) for a much narrower definition: It decided to restrict the market to "*the market for the sale of hotel rooms via hotel portals*" (BKartA, B9-66/10, para. 69), which excluded not only specialized meta-search engines but also sales via the hotels' own websites. The reasoning that underlay BKartA's decision is worth noting.

Specialized meta-search engines allow consumers to compare prices for a given room on different portals and possibly on the hotel's own real-time booking website. However, consumers cannot directly book a room and will be redirected to either a hotel booking platform or to the hotel's own website to complete the booking. In many cases, meta-search engines do not have contractual ties with individual hotels and never deal directly with the final consumers. The BKartA concluded that "*from the viewpoint of hotels, meta search engines are not a substitute for hotel portal because they do not provide the comprehensive service expected of a hotel portal by hotels (search, comparison and booking).*" (BKartA, B9-66/10, para. 99).

This notion of a comprehensive service that allows consumers to search, compare, and book has proved central in the market definition exercise. It was also used to exclude hotels' own websites from the relevant product market. The key element here was that a hotel's own website allows a consumer to book a room only in that specific hotel (sometimes possibly within a few hotels when the hotel belongs to a chain) – but does not allow the consumer to search and compare hotels more widely. Thus, hotels' own websites "*are not substitutes for hotel portals because they do not offer the same bundle of services for hotel consumers that hotel portals do.*" (BKartA, B9-66/10, para. 88).

The relevant product market has thus always been limited to include only hotel room bookings made through hotel booking platforms – specialized OTAs (*e.g.*, *HRS*,

*Hotels.com* and *Booking*) or more generalist OTAs (*e.g.*, *Expedia*) – that may sell other products in addition to hotel rooms.[26]

## 2. Geographic Market

*HRS* and the *BKartA* also disagreed on the delineation of the relevant geographic market. *HRS* claimed that the market should be defined as Europe-wide since providers (especially hotel booking platforms) operate Europe-wide; products are standardized at the European level; and the terms and the conditions that are applicable between hotels and hotel booking platforms tend to be uniform across Europe. The BKartA disagreed considering that "*within Europe, the economic focus of hotel portals which are major market players in Germany varies*" and thus arguing that the "*market developments also show that one should presume a separate German hotel portal market in the present case.*" (BKarta, B9-66/10, para. 111).

The BKartA argued for instance that hotel portals have a strong local presence in Germany with a registered office that employs several hundred staff whose objective is to recruit hotels and maintain business relationships with hotels. Advertising by the platforms is also done at the national rather than European level. On the consumer side, portals adapt to the local market by offering local language versions of their websites and target customers through specific country-specific domain names: For instance, *Expedia.de* and *Expedia.co.uk* advertise different "domestic hotels."

The BKartA thus decided that, at the geographic level, the market was national. The other national authorities reached similar conclusions: The Swedish Konkurrensverket defined a "*market for the provision of online travel agency services with respect to hotels located in Sweden*" (that covers only such OTAs that enable booking directly on the platforms) [Decision 596/2013, para. 15]; the French Autorité de la Concurrence also defined a market for hotel room booking services through OTAs (excluding direct sales by the hotels) of national dimension: services that are offered to hotels located in France whether bookings are made by French or international clients.

## 3. Market Shares

Having defined the relevant product and geographic markets, each national competition authority was then able to compute market shares and thus to check whether the agreements between an OTA and hotels was or not exempted under the 2010 VBER.

---

26 BKartA distinguished online travel agencies from hotel portals. From the viewpoint of BKartA, online travel agents (*e.g.*, *Opodo*) offer a comprehensive range of products that include last-minute offers, packages, car rentals, etc., and primarily address demand from holiday travelers. They are thus different from hotel portals that sell hotel rooms to individual travelers. Other agencies have defined a market for "hotel room bookings through OTAs"; but ultimately all enforcement agencies include the same actors within the relevant markets – *HRS*, *Booking*, and *Expedia* – that account for the largest share of that product market. In the rest of the text, I often use the two terminologies (OTAs and hotel portals) for platforms that allow individual customers to search, compare, and book hotel rooms.

The BKartA evaluated market shares based on revenues (*i.e.*, commissions for most OTAs, margin income as some still operated – at least partly – on the merchant's model) but also based on number of booked bed-nights.[27] *HRS* – including the portal *Hotel.de*, since *HRS* took control of that portal in October 2011 – had a market share that exceeded 40 percent in 2009 and 2010, and exceeded 30 percent in 2011 and 2012. Its market share was even higher for bed-nights rather than commissions: over 50 percent in 2009 and 2010, over 40 percent in 2011 and 2012. On this basis, the BKartA considered that the vertical agreements between *HRS* and German hotels did not benefit from the 2010 VBER.

It is nevertheless interesting to examine the evolution of the three main portals' markets shares in the German market. These market shares (or at least intervals) were published by the BKartA in the *HRS* decision in 2013 but also in a later study that evaluated the effects of the different decisions on the hotel portals market. The evolution of these market shares based on commission revenue are presented in Figure 1.

**Figure 1: Evolution of OTAs (revenue-based) market shares on the German hotel portal market**

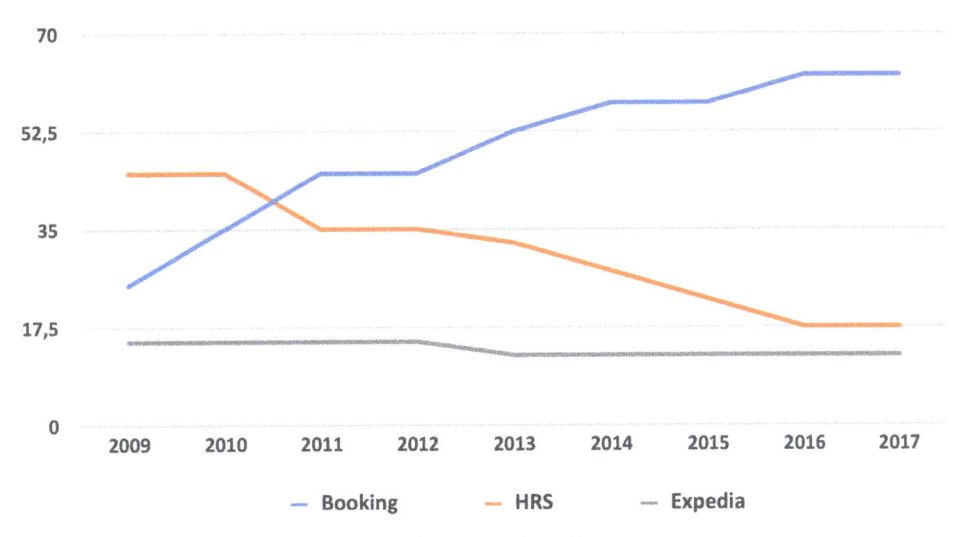

**Source:** BKartA, decision B9-66/10 and BKartA (2020).

*Note:* The BKartA document only present intervals for the market shares, the Figure has been drawn used the mid-point of each interval. Market shares from the decision B9-66/10 and the 2020 study have been used for the periods 2009-2012 and 2013-2017 respectively.

It is interesting to note that *Expedia*'s market share has never exceeded 15 to 20 percent in the German market. This explains why *Expedia*'s parity requirements have never

---

[27] Though market definition may appear simple in theory, in practice it remains an often controversial exercise. Moreover, even when parties agree on the delineation of product or geographic markets, computing market shares may also be questionable (for instance it is not always obvious whether market shares should be computed based on revenues or volumes).

been treated as infringing competition rules in Germany. The courts that examined them considered that *Expedia*'s agreements benefitted from the 2010 VBER given that *Expedia*'s market share did not exceed 30 percent, even in that narrowly defined market.

The BKartA initially investigated the market leader's (*HRS*) contracts before examining *Booking*'s contractual terms. *Booking*'s market share had been steadily increasing over time as it gained leadership in many European markets – in Germany primarily to the detriment of *HRS*, which had initially benefitted from its well-known brand in the offline travel agency market.

If *HRS* could not benefit from the 2010 VBER when the BKartA started to investigate the effects of parity clauses, one may wonder what would have happened if it had decided to reintroduce such clauses after its market share had dropped below 30 percent. Would the BKartA have attempted to remove the benefit from the exemption that was granted by the 2010 VBER?

If *HRS* had initially been the market leader in German-speaking countries (Germany and Austria), *Booking* and *Expedia* were larger than *HRS* in many other European markets. According to the figures that were published by D-Edge (based on a sample of D-Edge hotel clients in Europe), *Booking* has been a dominant player in the OTA market in Europe with a market share that was consistently in excess of 60 percent between 2014 and 2018 – far ahead of *Expedia*, which was a distant second with a market share that varied between 20 and 27 percent.[28] Though it is likely that market shares differ across Europe, this strong leadership for *Booking* most likely explains why the national competition agencies focused on *Booking* and rapidly closed cases against *Expedia* after it unilaterally announced that it would also abandon wide price parity and availability parity requirements.

## B. Theory of Harm

The national competition authorities have been concerned that parity obligations between OTAs and hotels are likely to have anticompetitive effects by reducing the OTAs' incentives to compete on commissions that are charged to hotels, which would ultimately lead to higher room prices for consumers.

The mechanism through which the anticompetitive effects materialize is similar to that developed in Boik & Corts (2016) or Johnson (2017):

> "The provision that hotels may not offer better prices via Booking.com's competitors than they do via Booking.com, the horizontal price parity, does, however, have an impact on the competition between Booking.com and other online travel agencies, in other words the competition between companies in the same relevant market. (…) Booking.com's price parity clause implies that increases in Booking.com's commission rate cannot lead to a higher room rate on Booking.com than that available through its competitors, which means that Booking.com can raise its commission rate without losing customers to its competitors. The price parity clause, combined with the fact that hotels generally want to enlist on several com-

---

28 Statista figures are even more extreme: *Booking*'s and *Expedia*'s shares were estimated in 2019 at 68 percent and 16 percent respectively, and *HRS* was a distant third at 6 percent.

*peting platforms, thus implies that Booking.com has less inventive, than would otherwise be the case, to compete by offering low commission rates. This risks leading to higher commission rates, which in turn risks leading to higher room prices."* (Konkurrensverket, decision 596/2013, paras. 20 and 21).

Competition agencies also developed a related theory of exclusionary effects of price parity requirements on the OTA market. For instance, the Swedish competition authority considered that:

*"Booking.com's price parity clause may also constitute a barrier to entry into the market as on online travel agency cannot enter or expand on the market by competing on low commission rates in exchange for hotels setting lower prices on that operator's channel."* (Konkurrensverket, decision 596/2013, para. 23).

The theory of harm that was developed by the competition agencies in the cases against *Booking* (and against *HRS* in Germany) relies on sound economic arguments though we may wonder whether the role of market structure, and more specifically of inter-brand competition as well as the importance of direct sales by hotels, should have been given more consideration.

For instance, the theory developed in Johansen & Vergé (2017) suggests that price parity clauses that are imposed on small independent hotels may well be anticompetitive but that we could expect a different outcome when a small number of large chains of hotels compete for consumers. Consumers tend to be more aware of the existence of the large chains and can thus start searching directly on a chain's website. In this case, a large chain can more easily withdraw from any OTA that would charge a commission that the chain considers to be excessively high. Dropping out of a large platform to rely instead on direct sales may however be more difficult for a small independent hotel.

Cazaubiel et al. (2020) discuss an interesting case in the Scandinavian market: In 2012, several large hotels chains decided to stop offering rooms on *Expedia*, which forced the platform to renegotiate its commission rates and (at least partially) to abandon price parity requirements.

## C. Efficiency Defense

Although all of the competition authorities that investigated the price parity clauses considered wide price parity as being anticompetitive, they partially disagreed on the overall effects of the narrow price parity clauses. This was due to differences in approaches with regard to efficiency considerations and the free-rider argument that was put forward by the OTAs. Most competition agencies considered that – although narrow price parity clauses had the potential to soften competition on commissions to the detriment of consumers – it also prevented hotels from free-riding on OTAs' investments through "showrooming." The Swedish competition authority – in line with its French and Italian counterparts – argued that free-riding was an issue and that solving it was to the benefit of consumers:

*"If the hotel was completely free to control the relationship between prices on the hotel's own channels and prices on Booking.com, the hotel would have the possibility to free-ride on Booking.com's investments. Booking.com would therefore face significant risk of not being compensated for the services it provides to the hotels. (…) The Competition Authority's assessment, which is supported by analyses and the above-mentioned surveys supplied by Booking.com, is in view of the above that the vertical price parity substantially reduces the risk that hotels free-ride on investments made by Booking.com. This in turn allows Booking.com to receive remuneration for its search and compare services so that the services can continue to be offered on the market to the benefit of consumers."* (Konkurrensverket, decision 596/2013, paras. 28 and 30)

The three authorities thus approved *Booking*'s proposed switch from wide to narrow price parity clauses in their decisions.

BKartA did not follow suit and decided that the efficiency argument was not sufficiently convincing and that the narrow price parity clauses that were imposed by *Booking* thus had anticompetitive effects and could not be exempted under Article 101(3) TFEU. It considered in particular that:

*"Booking is also unable to provide sufficient proof that deleting the narrow best price clauses would result in such a relevant decline in sales that as a result, by reverse logic, there would be an advantage of the narrow best price clauses in terms of an efficiency gain. (…) [I]t is also not further demonstrated the extent to which the current business model might have to be modified in the medium term"* (BKartA, Decision B9-121/13, para. 266)

Ultimately, BKartA judged that there was no sufficient proof that free-riding was really a key issue, and – more important – that there was no evidence that this free-riding would lead to reduced incentives to invest in the platform's quality or would limit advertising investment by the platform to the detriment of the listed hotels. In addition, BKartA argued that the narrow price parity clause was not indispensable to solve the alleged free-riding issue. It noted that *Booking* not only failed to prove that the price parity clause was indispensable under the commission-based business model but also that it did not show that other business models (where *Booking* could be remunerated by hotels through other means than the existing revenue sharing mechanism) would be less efficient.

The differences in outcome in different European countries thus comes primarily from different stances with regard to efficiency claims and the need to solve the free-riding (or showrooming) issue.

## V. THE 2022 VERTICAL BLOCK EXEMPTION REGULATION

The 2010 Vertical Block Exemption Regulation ("VBER") expired in May 2022. In October 2018, the European Commission launched a review of the existing Regulation to decide whether to let it lapse, extend its duration, or revise it. After a lengthy process (evaluation, impact assessment phase, public consultation), the Commission adopted on May 10, 2022, the 2022 Vertical Block Exemption Regulation and the 2022 Vertical Restraints Guidelines.[29]

The new regulation and guidelines clarify the Commission's assessment of vertical arrangements between online intermediaries (such as OTAs) and suppliers that sell through these intermediaries. In the context of online intermediaries, the Commission considers that the seller (*e.g.*, a hotel) is the buyer of online intermediation services sold by the online intermediary (*e.g.*, an OTA). Therefore, even though the Commission considers that an agreement between a seller and an online platform cannot be categorized as a genuine agency agreement (which fall outside the scope of Article 101(1) TFEU), such an agreement cannot be treated as RPM when the supplier keeps control of prices at which its products are sold through the online intermediaries. This thus allows hotels freely to set the prices at which its rooms are sold through different OTAs without infringing competition rules.

More important, the Commission decided to include wide price parity agreements in the list of excluded restrictions. This means that wide price parity clauses can no longer be exempted under the new VBER even if imposed by OTAs with limited market shares. However, there is no presumption of illegality: Instead, it is up to the competition authorities to prove the existence of (at least potential) anticompetitive effects of the clauses. Narrow price parity clauses continue however to benefit from the VBER and can thus be used by OTAs with a market share below 30 percent.

Some countries had pushed to include price parity clauses in the list of hardcore restrictions, while others favored a softer approach. Ultimately, the European Commission adopted a balanced approach when revising the VBER: This approach is broadly consistent with the conclusions that can be drawn from the existing academic literature.[30]

## VI. CONCLUDING REMARKS

Though most competition authorities agreed on the competitive effects of wide price parity clauses in the hotel booking industry, disagreements still exist on the effects of narrow parity clauses. Trying to harmonize decisions across the European Union, the European Commission – through the European Competition Network (which is composed of all of the EU national competition agencies) – carried out a monitoring exercise trying the evaluate the effects of the recent decisions. Unfortu-

---

29  Commission Regulation (EU) 2022/720 of 10 May 2022 on the application of Article 101(3) of the Treaty on the Functioning of the European Union to categories of vertical agreements and concerted practices (VBER) and Guidelines on Vertical Restraints (2022/C 248/01) setting out the principles for the assessment of vertical agreements under Article 101 of the Treaty on the Functioning of the European Union.

30  In its response to the public consultation, a subgroup of the Economic Advisory Group for Competition Policy ("EAGCP") reviewed the existing literature and initially suggested to include all types of parity clauses in the list of excluded restrictions (including narrow parity clauses).

nately, because it is extremely complex to estimate the direct effects of the changes on prices, most empirical evaluations that were published after these decisions, including the Commission's monitoring exercise, essentially focus on the impact on price dispersion. But this does not tell much, since removing constraints on price differentiation is likely to lead to more price dispersion whether it is to the benefit of final consumers or not.

But a few notable exceptions should be mentioned. Mantovani et al. (2021) compared the evolution of hotel room prices posted on Booking.com by hotels in the islands of Corsica (France) and Sardinia (Italy) before and after France banned narrow price parity clauses in 2015. Their results show a short-run price reduction of 2.6 percent for hotels in Corsica (relative to hotels in Sardinia). The impact is slightly smaller in the medium run but still confirms a price reduction (of 1.6 percent). Ennis et al. (2020) also provide some evidence that the switch from wide to narrow led to a price decrease on direct channels, notably for more expensive hotels. Hunold et al. (2018) do not look directly at price levels but find that the prohibition of price party clauses by the BKartA incentivized German hotels to increase room availability on OTAs (or even to participate to new platforms).

Because of lack of data availability (accessible to academic researchers), the empirical academic papers have not been able to discuss the validity of the theory of harm applied in the OTA cases, *i.e.*, not been able to analyze the evolution of commissions charged by OTAs. A recent market study realized for the European Commission looked – among other points – at this evolution and concluded that:[31]

> *"[a]ll in all, the six study countries experienced a slight decreasing trend in OTA basic and effective commission rates over the period 2017-2021, but the levels and patterns observed for Austria and Belgium do not appear to differ significantly from those observed across the other study countries."* (European Commission (2022), page 74)

More recently, empirical studies have demonstrated the importance of algorithms and rankings in this industry. Hunold et al. (2020) show (for instance) that setting higher prices on *Booking* (or *Expedia*) than on the hotel's own website has a significant negative effect on the hotel's ranking on that platform, which in turn is likely to lead to lower sales through the platform. Because the largest platforms are vertically integrated with the most important specialized meta-search engines,[32] this negative effect is made even worse as meta-search engines tend to favor hotels that offer better prices on their "in-house" platforms (Cure et al., 2022). One may then wonder whether OTAs have replaced price parity requirements with rankings and whether the recent changes brought by the VBER are likely to matter that much. As is often the case, it seems that he affected enterprises are one step ahead of the law.

---

31 Unfortunately, the report does not provide detailed information on the evolution of these commissions, other than mentioning that the average commission paid by hotels in any of the six study countries in any of the years 2017 to 2021 is between 10 percent and 20 percent.

32 In 2013, two of the largest meta-search engines in that industry, *Kayak* and *Trivago*, have respectively been acquired by the *Priceline Group* (owner of *Booking*) and by *Expedia*.

# REFERENCES

Baker, Jonathan & Judith Chevalier (2013). "The Competitive Consequences of Most-Favored-Nation Provisions." *Antitrust* 27(2): 20-26.

Baker, Jonathan & Fiona Scott Morton (2018). "Antitrust Enforcement Against Platform MFN." *Yale Law Journal* 127(7): 2176-2202.

Boik, Andre & Kenneth Corts (2016). "The Effects of Platform Most-Favored-Nation Clauses on Competition and Entry." *Journal of Law and Economics* 59(1): 105-134.

Bundeskartellamt (2020). "The effects of narrow price parity clauses on online sales – Investigation results from the Bundeskartellamt's Booking proceeding." *Series of papers on Competition and Consumer Protection in the Digital Economy* 7.

Carlton, Dennis & Ralph Winter (2018). "Vertical Most-Favored-Nation Restraints and Credit Card No-Surcharge Rules." *Journal of Law and Economics* 61(2): 215-251.

Cazaubiel, Arthur, Morgane Cure, Bjørn Olav Johansen & Thibaud Vergé (2020). "Substitution between online distribution channels: Evidence from the Oslo hotel market." *International Journal of Industrial Organization* 69: 102577.

Cure Morgane, Matthias Hunold, Reinhold Kesler, Ulrich Laitenberger & Thomas Larrieu (2022). "Vertical integration of platforms and product prominence." *Quantitative Marketing and Economics* forthcoming.

Edelman, Benjamin & Julian Wright (2015). "Price Coherence and Excessive Intermediation." *Quarterly Journal of Economics* 130(3): 1283-1328.

Ennis, Sean, Marc Ivaldi & Vicente Lagos (2020). "Price Parity Clauses for Hotel Room Booking: Empirical Evidence from Regulatory Change." TSE Working Paper n° 20-1106.

European Commission (2016). *Report on the monitoring exercise carried out in the online hotel booking sector by the EU Competition Authorities in 2016.*

European Commission (2022). *Market study on the distribution of hotel accommodation in the EU – Final Report.* COMP/2020/OP/002.

Hunold, Matthias, Reinhold Kessler & Ulrich Laitenberger (2020). "Rankings of Online Travel Agents, Channel Pricing, and Consumer Protection." *Marketing Science* 39(1): 92-116.

Hunold, Matthias, Reinhold Kesler & Frank Schlütter (2018). "Evaluation of Best Price Clauses in Hotel Booking." *International Journal of Industrial Organization* 61: 542-571.

Hviid, Morten (2015). "Vertical agreements between suppliers and retailers that specify a relative price relationship between competing products or competing retailers." OECD Competition Committee Paper DAF/COMP(2015)6.

Johansen, Bjørn Olav & Thibaud Vergé (2017). "Platform price parity clauses with direct sales." *Working Papers in Economics 01/17, University of Bergen.*

Johnson, Justin (2017). "The agency model and MFN clauses." *The Review of Economic Studies* 84(3): 1151-1185.

Mantovani, Andrea, Claudio Piga & Carlo Reggiani (2021). "Online platform price parity clauses: Evidence from the EU Booking.com case." *European Economic Review* 131: 103625.

Maruyama, Masayoshi & Yusuke Zennyo (2020). "Platform Most-Favored-Customer Clauses and Investment Incentives." *International Journal of Industrial Organization* 70: 102617.

Vergé, Thibaud (2018). "Are Price Parity Clauses Necessarily Anticompetitive?" *CPI Antitrust Chronicle* January 2018.

Wals, Francisca & Maarten Pieter Schinkel (2018). "Platform monopolization by narrow-PPC-BPG combination: Booking et al." *International Journal of Industrial Organization* 61: 572-589.

Wang, Chengsi & Julian Wright (2020a). "Search platforms: showrooming and price parity clauses." *Rand Journal of Economics* 51(1): 32-58.

Wang, Chengsi & Julian Wright (2020b). "Platform investment and price parity clauses." *Journal of Industrial Economics,* forthcoming.

# III. ANTICOMPETITIVE AGREEMENTS

# CHAPTER 17
# No-Poaching Agreements as Antitrust Violations: Animation Workers Antitrust Litigation

By Orley Ashenfelter & Ruth Gilgenbach[1]

## I. INTRODUCTION

The last decade has witnessed a number of remarkable developments in public policy, laws, and law enforcement that are associated with failures of competition in U.S. labor markets. These include: (1) enforcement actions and antitrust lawsuits with regard to explicit conspiracies to suppress competition in labor markets; (2) the documentation and forced abolition of franchise contracts that include worker "no-poaching" clauses; (3) explicit discussion of the regulation of mergers that affect labor market competition; and (4) legislation and regulation that affect "non-compete" and "non-solicit" clauses in employment contracts.

It is difficult to pinpoint the reasons for this rebirth of interest in competition in labor markets. It is likely that one factor at work is the stagnation of real wage rates. Wage rate growth has a natural benchmark: productivity growth. In the three decades that followed World War II, productivity growth and real wage growth were similar. But in the four decades since that time, productivity growth has been four to five times as high as wage growth. The gap between wage growth and productivity growth implies that the share of aggregate real income paid to workers has declined. Despite elaborate explanations for this gap that rely on assumptions about technology, a decline in labor market competition is one obvious explanation for this development.

In addition, there have been some highly visible examples of explicit collusion in labor markets, and these have raised questions about the extent to which competition has been damaged. This chapter covers one such alleged conspiracy to reduce labor market competition among workers in the studio animation industry.[2]

---

[1] Orley Ashenfelter served as the Plaintiffs' testifying economic expert in the *Animation Worker's* antitrust case; Ruth Gilgenbach worked as a non-testifying expert in the case. The authors would like to thank Maria Kozhevnikova, Michael LeFors, Kelly Eakin, Tim Huegerich, and Michael Naaman.

[2] As will be discussed below, the Defendants in this case eventually settled with the Plaintiffs. Although the parties agreed to a cash settlement, the Defendants did not acknowledge any wrongdoing. Consequently, in the discussion of the actions that the Plaintiffs considered to be at the heart of their case, we will use the word "alleged" extensively.

## II. BACKGROUND AND PARTIES

This case was initiated in 2014 by Plaintiffs who represented a group of animation workers at several major animation studios in the United States.[3] The Plaintiffs claimed that these studios conspired to suppress workers' compensation during the specific period 2001-2010 (although the conspiracy likely began in the 1980s).

The details of the alleged conspiracy will be discussed at greater length below, but there were two main prongs to the alleged conspiracy: that the studios had agreements not to solicit each other's employees; and that the studios had agreements to exchange detailed compensation information with each other. The Plaintiffs argued that these agreements were *per se* violations of the antitrust law, putting this behavior in the same category as naked price- or wage-fixing agreements between competitors.[4] However, because each Defendant settled with the Plaintiffs prior to or shortly after the Court granted class certification (and in all cases before the liability phase of expert reports), this chapter will focus on issues of class certification in addition to issues of Defendants' antitrust liability and damages.

The Defendants in this case were the following animation studios:

- *Blue Sky Studios, Inc.* At the time of the case, Blue Sky was a subsidiary of Twentieth Century Fox. It is best known for the *Ice Age* movies. It has since been purchased by Disney and was closed in 2021.
- *DreamWorks Animation.* DreamWorks Animation was founded as a division of DreamWorks, LLC, which was founded in 1994 by Steven Spielberg, Jeffrey Katzenberg, and David Geffen. It is best known for the *Shrek* movies. It was purchased by NBC Universal in 2016.
- *ImageMovers Digital* was a joint venture of ImageMovers and Disney, and sometimes operated under the name Two Pic MC LLC. IMD produced two films (an animated version of *A Christmas Carol* and *Mars Needs Moms*). Disney closed IMD in 2010.
- *Lucasfilm* was founded by George Lucas in 1971. Industrial Lights and Magic ("ILM") is their motion picture visual effects company. ILM did the visual effects work for the *Star Wars* series, the *Iron Man* series, the *Pirates of the Caribbean* series, *Avatar*, and more. Disney purchased Lucasfilm and ILM in 2012.
- *Pixar* was founded by Steve Jobs in 1986 and was formed when Jobs purchased the Computer Graphics Division of Lucasfilm from George Lucas. Pixar films include the *Toy Story* series, *Monsters, Inc., Cars, Finding Nemo, Up, Inside Out, Wall-E* and others. Disney purchased Pixar in 2006.
- *Sony Picture Animation* and *Sony Pictures Imageworks* are owned by Sony Pictures Entertainment. Films produced by Sony include *Open Season, Cloudy with a Chance of Meatballs,* and *Smurfs.*

---

3 *In Re: Animation Workers Antitrust Litigation.* Second Consolidated Amended Class Action Complaint. Case No. 5:14-cv-04062-LHK. ("Complaint"). Most of the details in this chapter are based on Judge Lucy Koh's Order Granting-in-Part and Denying-in-Part Plaintiffs' Motion for Class Certification ("Class Certification Order"), dated May 25, 2016.

4 *See* Complaint at ¶¶ 1, 205-213.

- *Walt Disney Studios* is a division of the Walt Disney Company, and produces, markets, and distributes films and other products. Disney purchased Pixar in 2006, Lucasfilm in 2012, and Blue Sky in 2019. At the time of the *Animation Workers* case, recent Disney films included *Tangled* and *Big Hero 6*.

The *Animation Workers* case was related to the High-Tech Employee Antitrust Litigation ("*High-Tech*"). That case was initiated by the U.S. Department of Justice ("DOJ") in 2010 against Adobe, Apple, Google, Intel, Intuit, and Pixar (and subsequently, Lucasfilm).[5] The DOJ complaints alleged violations of Section 1 of the Sherman Act in establishing a series of bilateral "no cold call" (*i.e.*, no solicitation) agreements. The parties agreed to settlements with the DOJ that ended these practices. In 2011, private plaintiffs brought a related class action lawsuit that involved the same parties and the same allegations, which was eventually settled for $415 million in 2015.[6] Judge Lucy Koh of the Northern District of California presided over both the *High-Tech* and the *Animation Workers* cases.

Successful certification of a class is critical for most antitrust actions that are not pursued by government enforcement agencies (*e.g.*, DOJ, FTC, or state antitrust agencies). Class action lawsuits, where one or several Plaintiffs represents the interests of all similarly-situated individuals, are typically pursued when there are relatively small damages incurred by any individual plaintiff, but these damages are large in aggregate. In this case, total damages paid by all Defendants per class member averaged approximately $17,000 per person, far below the cost for an individual employee to litigate.[7] If the Plaintiffs fail to certify a class, claimants may proceed on an individual basis, but it is rarely feasible to do so.

Class actions in Federal courts in the United States are governed by Rule 23 of the Federal Rules of Civil Procedure. Under Rule 23, for a class to be certified, all four of the following conditions from Rule 23(a) must be met:

- *Numerosity:* The class is so numerous that joinder of all members is impracticable;
- *Commonality:* There are questions of law or fact common to the class;
- *Typicality:* The claims or defenses of the representative parties are typical of the claims or defenses of the class; and
- *Adequacy of representation:* The representative parties will fairly and adequately protect the interests of the class.

---

5 *United States v. Adobe Systems, Inc., Apple, Inc., Google Inc., Intel Corporation, Intuit, Inc., and Pixar,* Case 1:10-cv-01629; *United States v. Lucasfilm LTD.*, Case 1:10-cv-02220.

6 *In Re: High Tech Employee Antitrust Litigation*, Case No.: 11-cv-02509-LHK. Order Granting Plaintiffs' Motion for Preliminary Approval of Class Action Settlement with Defendants Adobe Systems Incorporated, Apple Inc., Google Inc., and Intel Corporation, Approving Form and Manner of Notice and Scheduling Final Approval Hearing ("*High-Tech* Settlement Order") at ¶ 7. The parties had originally negotiated a $324.5 million settlement, which was rejected by the Court. *High-Tech* Settlement Order at ¶ 4.

7 Total damages collected from the Defendants totaled $169.5 million. *See* Outcome section of this chapter. There were approximately 10,000 class members. *See* Class Certification Order at 18:5.

If all of the conditions of Rule 23(a) are satisfied, in order to certify a class, the Court must also find that the plaintiffs satisfy at least one of the three subsections of Rule 23(b).[8]

The Plaintiffs in this case sought class certification under Rule 23(b)(3), which requires that "the Court finds that questions of law or facts common to the class predominate over any questions affecting only individual members, and that a class action is superior to other methods for fairly and efficiently adjudicating the controversy."[9] These requirements are respectively called "predominance" and "superiority."

Because each Defendant settled during or shortly after the class certification phase, the arguments presented by the Plaintiffs' and Defendants' experts and described in the remaining sections of this chapter are focused largely on issues critical to class certification, mostly issues of predominance.[10] The Defendants argued that Plaintiffs' proposed class did not satisfy the predominance requirement because antitrust impact and antitrust damages cannot be proven on a classwide basis.[11] The Plaintiffs' economic arguments at the class certification phase, therefore, focused largely on whether or not the Defendants' alleged anti-solicitation agreements and collusion over compensation policies would have the effect of suppressing compensation for all or nearly all members of the class. The Court agreed with the Plaintiffs and certified a class of animation workers in May 2016.

## A. "No-Poach" Agreement

The roots of the alleged conspiracy to reduce labor market competition for animation workers – the central case for this chapter – dates to the 1980s.[12] In 1986, George Lucas (then-CEO and Chairman of the Board of Lucasfilm) sold Lucasfilm's Computer Graphics Division to then-recently departed Apple CEO Steve Jobs, who turned this division into a new company: Pixar. Pixar and Lucasfilm quickly entered

---

[8] In addition to the four rules explicitly outlined in Rule 23(a), courts have also held that Rule 23(a) implicitly requires that the class be *ascertainable*, or that the description of the class is "definite enough so that it is administratively feasible for the court to ascertain whether an individual is a member." See Class Certification Order at pp. 22:24-23:3. In this case, the class definition explicitly incorporated a list of job titles of class members, which satisfied the Court's ascertainably requirement. See Class Certification Order at pp 22-26.

[9] Federal Rules of Civil Procedure at Rule 23.

[10] The Defendants did not contest that the requirements for numerosity were satisfied, nor that the allegations of antitrust conspiracy present common legal and factual issues. See Class Certification Order at 18:4 and 19:4-5. The Defendants claimed that because some class members had arbitration or release agreements with some Defendants, and the named Plaintiffs were not party to these agreements, that the named Plaintiffs' claims were not typical of the class. The Court found that because all class members were injured by the same alleged antitrust conspiracy and incurred the same alleged injury, the typicality requirement was satisfied. See Class Certification Order at pp 19-21.

[11] See Class Certification Order at 26:15-20. The Defendants also argued that fraudulent concealment and issues regarding arbitration or release of claims agreements could not be proven on a classwide basis. However, these arguments are primarily legal in nature and are of little economic interest so they will not be discussed in this chapter.

[12] Complaint at ¶ 47.

into a "gentleman's agreement" to restrain competition for each other's employees.[13] George Lucas testified that Lucasfilm had a policy that "we would not actively go out and recruit from other companies."[14] According to Lucas, Lucasfilm "had a general policy, because we were out to promote other digital companies and help them, that the — we weren't going to try to recruit people from them....It's not a normal industrial competitive situation."[15]

Pixar and Lucasfilm allegedly reached an agreement to: (1) not cold call each other's employees; (2) notify each other when making an offer to an employee of the other company, and (3) treat any offer by the potential new employer as "final" and not capable of being improved in response to a counteroffer from the employee's current employer.[16] These policies appear to have been operative: A Pixar document stated that Pixar would "never counter if the candidate comes back to us with a better offer from Lucasfilm;" similarly emails from within Lucasfilm's HR department confirmed that Lucasfilm followed these procedures and had "actually cancelled offers to people that Pixar said were 'essential.'"[17]

Evidence indicates that DreamWorks joined Pixar and Lucasfilm's conspiracy by 2003: A 2003 email from a Pixar employee to Steve Jobs confirmed that Pixar had an "agreement with DreamWork[s] to not poach their people."[18] In 2004, Pixar President Ed Catmull reported to Steve Jobs that Pixar's "no-raid agreement" with DreamWorks had "worked quite well."[19]

In 2004, Disney joined the alleged conspiracy. A 2004 email among Pixar's HR department identified Pixar as having anti-solicitation agreements with DreamWorks, Disney, and ILM (Industrial Light and Magic, a division of Lucasfilm).[20] Another 2004 Pixar email identified "gentleman's agreements" with Disney and ILM with regard to recruiting.[21] In 2007 (after Disney's 2006 purchase of Pixar), Pixar President Ed Catmull wrote an email to Disney's Chairman describing that Northern California animation studios "have conscientiously avoided raiding each other" because recruiting from other studios "seriously messes up the pay structure."[22]

The Plaintiffs alleged that Sony also joined the conspiracy in 2004. A 2004 email from Pixar's President Ed Catmull to Steve Jobs noted that "We don't have a no raid agreement with Sony.... I probably should go down and meet with...Sony to reach some agreement. Our people are become [sic] really desirable and we need to nip

---

13 Class Certification Order at 29:16-17.
14 *Ibid.* at 29:19-20.
15 *Ibid.* at 29:21-23.
16 *Ibid.* at 6:6-10.
17 *Ibid.* at 29:24-30:3.
18 *Ibid.* at 30:8-9.
19 *Ibid.* at 30:10-11.
20 *Ibid.* at 30:19-21.
21 *Ibid.* at 30:21-23.
22 *Ibid.* at 30:23-26.

this in the bud."[23] A 2005 email indicated that Catmull did meet with Sony in 2004 and "asked Sony to quit calling all [Pixar's] employees."[24] Later, a Pixar HR executive stated that she would contact Sony about their anti-solicitation agreement with Pixar to "make sure they're still honoring it as they may have had some turnover in their Recruiting team."[25]

By 2005, evidence indicated that Blue Sky joined the conspiracy. In 2005, a Pixar email described Pixar's "gentleman's agreements not to directly solicit/poach" from Lucasfilm, Sony, or Blue Sky, and that these agreements were mutual.[26] In 2007, Pixar's Ed Catmull approached IMD's founder to discuss "how important it is that we not have a hiring war."[27] In that conversation, the IMD founder said that he had agreed with George Lucas that IMD would not recruit from Lucasfilm.[28]

Additionally, there is evidence that the Defendants took steps to police their no-poach agreements. In 2006, a DreamWorks executive emailed a Pixar executive asking her to ensure that Pixar recruiters would not solicit DreamWorks' employees. In response, the Pixar executive said she'd "put a stop to it!"[29] Similarly, Disney's Director of Animation Resources emailed an ILM recruiter to ask ILM to abide by the "Gentle*women's* agreement" between Disney and ILM.[30] Blue Sky emails indicate that Blue Sky stopped Disney from holding a recruiting event in New York, near Blue Sky's headquarters.[31] The President of Pixar personally emailed a DreamWorks recruiter who had contacted a Pixar employee to chastise the recruiter for violating Pixar's "agreement with DreamWorks not to actively pursue each other's employees."[32]

## B. *Discussion of, and Agreement on, Compensation Ranges*

In addition to the alleged no-poach conspiracy, the Plaintiffs additionally alleged that the Defendants exchanged sensitive compensation information (both contemporaneous and forward-looking) and engaged in fixing the compensation ranges of class members. A large portion of the allegedly improper information exchange occurred in and around meetings of a compensation consultancy, the Croner Company. Croner is a third-party compensation consulting company that collects industry-specific compensation data and provides annual and customized compensation surveys to clients.[33]

---

23 *Ibid.* 31:1-4.
24 *Ibid.* at 31:4-6.
25 *Ibid.* at 31:6-8.
26 *Ibid.* at 31:9-13.
27 *Ibid.* at 31:19-20.
28 *Ibid.* at 31:21-22.
29 *Ibid.* at 38:16-19.
30 *Ibid.* at 38:20-22.
31 *Ibid.* at 38:22-24.
32 *Ibid.* at 38:25 -39:1.
33 https://www.croner.com/about-us.

In addition to participating in salary surveys, the Defendants also attended annual meetings that were hosted by Croner. The Plaintiffs alleged that during meals, over drinks, and at other social gatherings connected to these meetings, recruiting personnel from the Defendants would discuss, agree upon, and set wage and salary ranges.[34] For example, notes from a 2006 dinner that included participants from DreamWorks, Disney, Pixar, and Blue Sky, Sony, and Lucasfilm indicated that compensation had been discussed in detail, with "Salary Increases" as a topic of conversation, noting that "[a]ll of the companies give out 4% increases on average."[35] A 2007 email between Pixar (which at by this time had been purchased by Disney) and Disney executives explaining the schedule for the upcoming Croner meeting, "Friday is HR Directors networking day (we get the group together twice a year to talk/visit/compare/benchmark stuff."[36]

In addition to meeting in-person to discuss compensation plans, the Plaintiffs alleged that the Defendants also exchanged information outside of these meetings: In 2006, a Pixar HR executive wrote to her counterparts at DreamWorks, Sony, Lucasfilm, Disney, and Blue Sky and asked for their companies' budgets for salary raises for 2007. She informed them that Pixar's budget was "4% but we may manage it closer to 3% on average."[37] A Sony executive responded that Sony was "doing the same, 4% but trying to manage to 3% when we can."[38] Another email sent by the same Pixar executive explained that Pixar would "share salary ranges with other employers/HR folks who write or call and ask us about how we compensate positions that are the same as theirs," particularly for other animation studios.[39] An "Executive Review" document from Lucasfilm in 2006 included budgets for merit raises for Disney, Pixar, Sony, and DreamWorks for 2005 and 2006.[40]

Once the DOJ began its investigation into the *High-Tech* conspiracy (which included Pixar and Lucasfilm), the Defendants began changing their behavior: They limited or ended many of their in-person meetings and email exchanges. In November 2009, a Pixar HR executive emailed her counterparts at Sony and Disney and stated that she was "not planning to attend the Croner meeting," and that it was "time for me to let go and bring a close to that era. I have a capable team who can/should represent us and without some of the other cronies it doesn't make sense."[41] Then, in 2010 the same Pixar executive wrote to a former DreamWorks employee that "[s]ince the DOJ rained on our parade of getting together with other companies, there's not really a good reason for me to go" to the Siggraph conference, a major visual effects industry conference.[42]

---

34 Complaint at ¶ 89.
35 Class Certification Order at 32:22-26.
36 *Ibid.* at 33:4-7.
37 *Ibid.* at 33:9:12.
38 *Ibid.* at 33:12-13.
39 *Ibid.* at 33:13-16.
40 *Ibid.* at 33:17-20.
41 *Ibid.* at 33:23-34:2.
42 *Ibid.* at 34:2-4.

Evidence also suggests that the Defendants ceased discussion of compensation. For instance, in 2011 a Senior Recruiter at Pixar wrote to Sony's Director of Recruiting and explained that Pixar could no longer respond to requests for information about salary ranges. This was because of the Consent Decree that Pixar had signed with the DOJ, wherein Pixar had agreed not to engage in no-poach agreements or other anticompetitive behavior; Pixar's Senior Recruiter wrote that "the prospect of any direct communication with another company about salary ranges makes our lawyers nervous."[43]

## III. THE PLAINTIFFS' ECONOMIC ARGUMENTS

In order to demonstrate that the Defendants' alleged anti-solicitation agreements and collusion overcompensation policies would have had the effect of suppressing workers' compensation class-wide, the Plaintiffs made an argument in two stages: First, the Plaintiffs provided evidence that the alleged conspiracy would have suppressed compensation for *some* class members. Second, the Plaintiffs argued that through the Defendants' general compensation policies and use of semi-rigid compensation structures, this compensation suppression would have spread classwide and affected all or nearly all members of the class.

The goal of monopsonistic collusion between rivals in a labor market is the same as the goal of monopolistic competition between rivals in a product market: to maximize profits. If the goal of a conspiracy among product market competitors is to behave like a monopolist, the goal of a conspiracy among labor market competitors is to behave like a monopsonist.

A monopsonist employer will hire workers as long as the marginal value of labor exceeds the marginal cost of hiring another unit of labor.[44] In order to hire an additional worker, the monopsonist must not only increase its wage rate paid to that worker, but must also increase the wage paid to all other workers, because only by increasing the wage it pays can the monopsonist induce additional labor supply to enter the market.

This situation is illustrated in Figure 1. The firm's demand curve for labor is downward sloping. The labor supply curve is upward sloping, indicating that in order to hire an additional unit of labor, the monopsonist must increase wages. The marginal cost curve for labor lies above the supply curve, because the monopsonist must increase wages to all workers in order to hire an additional worker. A profit maximizing monopsonist will hire $L_M$ workers, where the marginal benefit (described by the demand curve) is equal to the marginal cost of hiring an additional worker, and will pay $w_M$, the wage necessary to hire $L_M$ workers. Both the prevailing wage and number

---

43 *Ibid.* at 34:5-9. Pixar's agreement with the DOJ prohibited "attempting to enter into, entering into, maintaining or enforcing any agreement with any other person to in any way refrain from, requesting that any person in any way refrain from, or pressuring any person in any way to refrain from soliciting, cold calling, recruiting, or otherwise competing for employees of the other person." Final Judgement. *U.S. v. Adobe Systems, Inc., Apple, Inc., Google, Inc., Intel Corporation, Intuit, Inc., and Pixar.* Case 1:10-cv-01629 at Section IV.

44 This discussion is adapted from Carlton & Perloff (2005) at pp. 107-108.

of workers hired is lower under monopsony than under a competitive market ($w_M <  w_C$ and $L_M < L_C$, respectively).

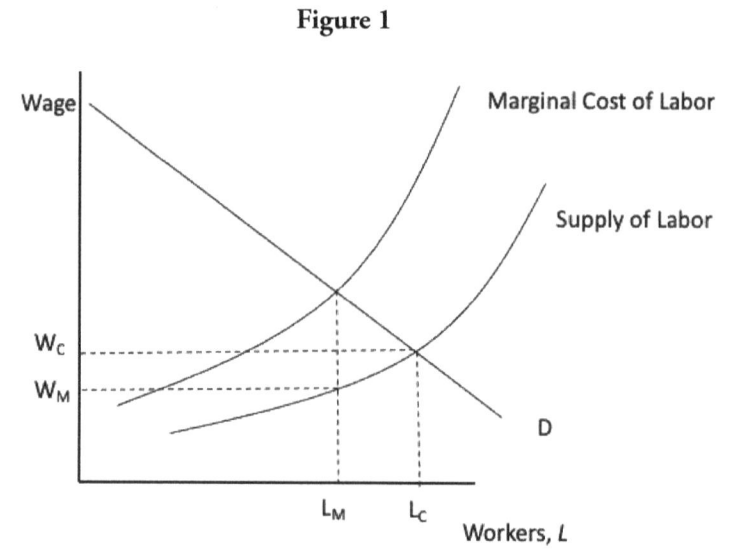

**Figure 1**

## A. The Conspiracy Suppressed Compensation for Some Class Members

The first step in the Plaintiffs' economic argument was that the alleged conspiracy suppressed compensation for some members. The Plaintiffs' expert presented three categories of evidence that can be used to show that the alleged conspiracy suppressed class compensation generally. These three categories are (1) the economic theory of negotiations under asymmetric information; (2) evidence from Defendants' documents showing that the purpose and effect of the alleged conspiracy was to suppress compensation across the class; and (2) a regression analysis that estimates the level of undercompensation caused by the alleged conspiracy.

## B. The Defendants' Conspiracy Increased Information Asymmetry between Employers and Class Members

The Defendants' alleged conspiracy was twofold: first, a series of agreements to restrict recruitment and hiring of other conspiracy members' employees; and second, the exchange of detailed compensation information. The former had the effect of decreasing the amount of information that was available to class members, while the latter had the effect of increasing the amount of information that was available to employers. One effect of this conspiracy was to increase the degree of information asymmetry in favor of the Defendants, which allowed the Defendants to pay lower compensation than they would have in the absence of the conspiracy.

Employers are likely to have better information about the prevailing wage rates for a job or industry than do workers. Employers – especially large employers – have information about the wages and salaries that are paid to their own employees (across a variety of job titles and for hundreds or thousands of employees); and employers engage with consultants to determine the compensation that is paid by competitors. Additionally, here the Defendants are alleged to have communicated with each other directly to determine the compensation that was being paid by their competitors – including current and future compensation. Workers, by contrast: know their own compensation history; may consult salary-tracking websites such as Glassdoor.com or Payscale.com; may rely on informal conversations with friends and colleagues (who may work for their employer or for other employers) to discover pay information for specific or related jobs; and, if they are members of a union, may receive information from union salary surveys – though these will tend to cover only other unionized workers, not all workers in all positions.

Because workers do not have access to the same information as do employers, receiving cold calls is a key avenue by which workers can obtain accurate and timely information about the value of their services. An employee who receives a cold call knows that the firm that is cold-calling him is interested in hiring workers with his skill set and is provided information about the level of compensation that the cold-calling firm is willing to offer. Thus, an agreement among the Defendants to refrain from cold calling each other's employees would work to limit the information that is available to workers about potential outside opportunities.

Furthermore, the information that is provided by the cold call is not limited to the individual who receives the call. Rather, when employees receive such information, they tend to discuss it with their friends and colleagues, which thus provides a mechanism by which information can spread beyond the original cold-call recipient. By agreeing not to solicit each other's employees, as the Defendants were alleged to have done, the Defendants were able to stop the spread of information about compensation to the workforce before it could start.

In addition to decreasing the amount of information that was available to class members, the Defendants' alleged collusion on compensation also increased the amount of information that was available to the Defendants. The Plaintiffs alleged that, in addition to an agreement not to solicit each other's employees, the conspiracy among the Defendants to suppress their employees' compensation included coordination on compensation, including: current salaries; future salaries; annual budgets for salary increases; and benefits. This increased flow of information allowed the Defendants to coordinate on compensation, and to target compensation offers so as to avoid paying more than was needed to attract workers.

While the anti-solicitation agreement reduced the information that was available to employees, the alleged conspiracy – through the direct and indirect communications among Defendants on compensation – had the effect of increasing the amount of information that was available to the Defendants. By systematically and frequently sharing information about their employees' compensation, the Defendants were increasing their own information about "market" compensation for class members. This increased information would have augmented the Defendants' bargaining power when negotiating salary with their employees and candidates.

The Defendants' documents acknowledge that the purpose of colluding on compensation was to enable them to negotiate lower wages and benefits. For example,

Lucasfilm's President explained in an email that the purpose of the industry surveys was to "keep[] a lid on rising labor costs."[45] Similarly, Pixar's Lori McAdams explained to an HR executive at Lucasfilm that "[s]ince money can always be a factor, that's the other thing we should consider (*e.g.*, we wouldn't want to offer a lateral move more than you, and vice versa)."[46]

In line with the concerns that are raised by asymmetrical information between employers and employees, the DOJ, and the U.S. Federal Trade Commission ("FTC") discussed the potential for anti-competitive collusion in this area in their 1996 Statements of Antitrust Enforcement Policy in Healthcare. Though these guidelines were developed for the healthcare industry, the FTC notes that "the principles in these guidelines are broadly applicable to other industries as well."[47] These guidelines are clear that "[e]xchanges of…future compensation of employees are very likely to be considered anticompetitive. If an exchange among competing providers of price or cost information results in an agreement among competitors as to the…wages to be paid to…employees, that agreement will be considered unlawful per se."[48] The Defendants' alleged collusive coordination on future compensation, such as salary ranges or merit increase budgets, is the sort of conduct that the DOJ and FTC recognize as "very likely" to have anticompetitive effects.

## C. Cold Calling

The Plaintiffs produced documentary evidence that the Defendants valued cold calling as a way of recruiting "passive" candidates: those individuals who are currently employed and are not actively seeking new employment, but who might be interested in an offer if contacted by a recruiter. An internal Disney recruiting guide stated that "[g]enerating interests from passive candidates" was one of Disney's challenges.[49] A Disney summary of the "Future of Recruiting" noted that passive candidates represented 70 percent of the population.[50] Likewise, an internal Sony email noted that they viewed workers who are currently employed by another firm as more valuable than unemployed workers because "if we limit our offers only to people who are unemployed then we're basically limiting our talent pool to artists who are not in demand."[51] A 2007 Lucasfilm presentation described "Passive Talent" as "difficult to find" and said that Lucasfilm should "[c]hange recruiting strategy from gatherer to hunter" to "get the best and brightest."[52]

---

45 Class Certification Order at 42:14-15.

46 *Ibid.* at 42:15-18.

47 https://www.ftc.gov/advice-guidance/competition-guidance/guide-antitrust-laws/dealings-competitors/spotlight-trade-associations.

48 Department of Justice and Federal Trade Commission. Statements of Antitrust Enforcement Policy in Healthcare (1996, p. 51).

49 Class Certification Opinion and Order at 37:24.

50 *Ibid.* at 37:25-26

51 *Ibid.* at 37:26-38:2.

52 *Ibid.* at 38:3-5.

Even though the Defendants considered passive candidates to be "the best and brightest," most desirable recruiting targets, Plaintiffs allege that they nevertheless entered into anti-solicitation agreements not to cold call each other's employees. Recruiters that were subject to these anti-solicitation agreements complained that it was difficult to recruit talent with these restrictions in place, and that these agreements did in fact stifle recruitment of passive candidates by the Defendants. For instance, a 2008 recruiting summary prepared for IMD states that IMD recruiters are unable "to go into about 90% of the companies that we would want as there are 'no recruit' agreements in place with our studio and the top studios in Southern and Northern California."[53]

Given that the Defendants highly valued passive candidates, it would have been irrational for the Defendants to forgo this recruitment unless they received something of equal or greater value in return. What the Defendants obtained from the alleged conspiracy was not having their own employees poached by rival firms and preventing the spread of information from employer to employee – each of which had the effect of suppressing their workers' salaries.

It would also be irrational for any Defendant unilaterally to provide compensation information to the other Defendants if it did not expect that the other Defendants would provide the same information in return and coordinate their compensation accordingly. If an employer were unilaterally to provide its competitors with information on its planned offers to candidates, that information would allow its rival to tailor its offers so as to just outbid the first firm. Meanwhile, the firm that provided its compensation information unilaterally to its rivals would face either losing out on key talent or making higher-than-anticipated compensation offers. This is a variation on the classic prisoner's dilemma, where absent coordination between parties (here, rival animation studios), each studio's profits are maximized in a non-cooperative Nash equilibrium where they do not share information with the other party. However, if they are able to coordinate (collude) successfully and exchange this information, this cooperative outcome increases profits over the non-cooperative Nash equilibrium.

Similarly, if a firm were unilaterally to provide wage information for their current employees to a rival firm, that firm would be providing their rival with critical information on the lowest compensation at which their employees or other prospective employees could reasonably be hired. In neither case is this rational behavior from a firm that is behaving unilaterally. These types of discussions benefit a firm that is providing information to its rivals only if this information is used to facilitate effective collusion on compensation.

Indeed, the Defendants' documents indicate that the purpose of the anti-solicitation and information exchange agreements was to suppress compensation. Emails between the Defendants indicated that the Defendants participated in a salary survey for the purpose of "keeping a lid on rising labor costs"[54] and that competition for employees "messes up the pay structure" by making pay "very high."[55]

---

53 *Ibid.* at 38:11-14.
54 *Ibid.* at 45:13-15.
55 *Ibid.* at 45:15-16.

That the Defendants would have engaged in increased solicitation in the absence of ("but for") the alleged conspiracy is demonstrated by the fact that after the DOJ began its investigation into the *High-Tech* conspiracy (which had Pixar and Lucasfilm in common as alleged participants), the Defendants began to solicit and hire each other's employees once more. In late 2009, a Blue Sky employee was "poached by Sony," prompting an internal email at Blue Sky "and so it begins... ..."[56] In 2010, DreamWorks prepared a list of Disney employees to "proactively call."[57] In late 2010, a Disney recruiter noted "I guess the theme of this year's expo is 'Poach What You Want.'"[58] By resuming solicitation of each other's employees after the end of the alleged conspiracy, the Defendants demonstrated that such solicitation was a valuable recruiting tool that they would have used but for their anti-solicitation agreements.

## D. The Compensation Suppression Spread to All or Most Class Members

To demonstrate that compensation suppression was likely to spread beyond just individual employees who – but for the alleged conspiracy – would have been contacted by a recruiter from a rival firm, Plaintiffs presented evidence that the Defendants had compensation structures that prioritized both "internal" (intrafirm) and "external" (interfirm) equity.

The Plaintiffs argued that the Defendants maintained formal compensation structures and prioritized maintaining internal equity within these compensation structures. The Plaintiffs provided documentary and testimony from members of the Defendants' human resources ("HR") departments that indicated that the Defendants assigned employees to specific pay bands and ranges based on their job titles. For instance, the Director of Human Resources at Lucasfilm explained that "we had identified levels of positions within our salary structure all the way through nonexempt up to executive level." Lucasfilm would then consult the pay ranges for each position within the salary structure to ensure that compensation remained equitable across positions.

The Defendants took "internal equity" – workers' receiving similar pay for similar work – into account when considering salaries. For instance, an email from Lucasfilm discussed whether or not they should increase the compensation for one job title in response to increasing the pay for another job title, noting that the second "should be valued more highly" than the first.[59] Internal equity is critical for morale, with one Defendant (Blue Sky) noting that they needed to make salary adjustments for their current workforce to adjust for a class of new employees with higher salaries being described as necessary because "salary inequality breeds huge morale problems with

---

56 *Ibid.* at 39:2-5. Ellipsis in original.

57 *Ibid.* at 39:6.

58 *Ibid.* at 39:7-9.

59 *Ibid.* at 40:5-6.

the floor."[60] DreamWorks described "closely monitor[ing] salaries to ensure internal equity and fairness among our employees."[61]

Because of the Defendants' formal compensation structures and desire for internal equity, compensation increases that were caused by a worker's receiving a cold call – whether he took a job at the cold-calling firm, or he negotiated a pay increase at his current employer – would spread beyond the employee who received a cold call: the information that was conveyed through cold calls would percolate throughout the salary structure. Thus, the Plaintiffs argued, the suppression of individual employee's salaries – who, absent the no-poach conspiracy, would have received cold calls that would have solicited them to work for rival firms – would also affect other employees who were paid similar compensation and in similar job titles at each Defendant.

The Plaintiffs' expert confirmed the presence of the Defendants' formal compensation structure by estimating earning models for all Defendants taken as a group (industry wide). These analyses regressed each member's log total annual compensation on: his or her age and age squared; experience with the defendant (tenure) and tenure squared; gender; an indicator for job title; and an indicator for each Defendant in the industry-wide model. This analysis produced $R^2$ statistics that ranged from 0.63 to 0.78, which indicated that the Defendants' formal job compensation structures along with standard human capital controls were able to explain between 63 and 78 percent of the variation in class members' compensation across all of the Defendants for the years that were encompassed by the alleged conspiracy.[62] This, according to Plaintiffs, was evidence that the Defendants had systematic pay structures that persisted over time (and thus that cold calling would have had effects that would have spread beyond that the target of a cold call).

The Defendants were also concerned about *external* equity, which seeks to ensure that individuals who perform similar work across the Defendants receive similar compensation. For instance, an internal DreamWorks email from 2006 explained that employees' total pay packaged would be driven in part by "The Market—Comparing our Total Pay package to other companies where we compete for talent."

The Plaintiffs argued that the Defendants entered into anti-solicitation agreements and colluded on compensation policies in order to reduce competition for labor and combat increasing wages. If the Defendants were successful in this collusion, they were able to pay lower compensation than they would have had to in the absence of their alleged conspiracy.

In short, the Plaintiffs argued that the Defendants' no-poach conspiracy had the following impact:

1. There was the direct effect of suppressing the compensation of some workers: those who, but for the alleged conspiracy, would have been recruited by a rival firm, which would have led to the worker's either accepting a higher-paid or

---

60 *Ibid.* at 41:8-9.
61 *Ibid.* at 40:17-18.
62 *Ibid.* at 47:3-22.

otherwise more preferable job at the rival firm, or using that offer to negotiate higher pay or other benefits at his current employer.
2. Because the compensation of these directly affected workers was lower than it would have been but for the alleged conspiracy, the forces of internal equity caused this compensation suppression to spread beyond the directly affected workers inside each firm.
3. Additionally, the defendants' goal of maintaining external (interfirm) pay equity would allow pay suppression to propagate across defendants.

Together, the effects of internal and external equity worked to spread the effects of the conspiracy to all or nearly all members of the class.

### E. Econometric Analysis Shows That Compensation Was Generally Reduced

The Plaintiffs' economics expert performed a regression analysis, described in greater detail in the appendix to this chapter. Because the conspiracy was alleged to have begun – at least as to between Pixar and Lucasfilm – in the 1980s, benchmark data from a true "pre-conspiracy" period did not exist. Therefore, in order to determine the amount by which compensation was reduced, the Plaintiff's expert performed a "during-after" regression analysis.

This regression used data from 2001-2013, with the post-conspiracy benchmark period beginning in 2011. The Plaintiffs' expert found that, in all periods, compensation was suppressed relative to the post-conspiracy benchmark, and this suppression was statistically significant in each period. The magnitude of this estimated compensation suppression varied over time (with the number of Defendants that participated in the alleged conspiracy) and ranged from 5 percent to 31 percent.[63]

These regression results translated to an estimated classwide loss of earnings of approximately $646 million.[64]

## IV. THE DEFENDANTS' ARGUMENTS

The bulk of the Defendants' economic and econometric analyses attempted to rebut the Plaintiffs' predominance arguments regarding class certification: The Defendants argued that individual inquiries with regard to the antitrust impact would dominate at trial – rather than the antitrust impact's being felt classwide. The Defendants also argued (in the event that the class was allowed to be certified) that the Defendants' actions were unlikely to have substantial effects in suppressing the animation workers' compensation.

### A. The Defendants' Criticisms of the Plaintiffs' Arguments

The Defendants' economics expert focused on issues of class certification, particularly arguing that issues of individual inquiry with regard to antitrust impact would

---

63 *Ibid.* at 56:12-21.
64 *Ibid.* at 56:25.

predominate – and so the class should not be certified). The Defendants' expert concluded that documentary evidence, economic theory, and the nature of the labor market for animation workers all undermined the Plaintiffs' theories with regard to class-wide impact. The Defendants' expert also critiqued the Plaintiffs' expert's methodology for conducting analyses of classwide impact.

The Defendants argued that the Plaintiffs' documentary evidence did not show that compensation changes for one job title at a given Defendant necessarily require compensation changes for other job titles within that Defendant. The Defendants' expert cited the Defendants' documents that showed that some employees received raises while others did not, and that the decision of whether or not to increase an employee's compensation was based on factors beyond solely internal equity concerns. Additionally, Defendants pointed to the 2010 Croner Survey, which found that compensation for some job titles increased while compensation for other titles decreased.[65]

As further support for the claim that there was substantial variation in compensation – which would undermine Plaintiffs' theory of internal equity and thus weaken the Plaintiffs' argument for class certification – the Defendants' expert performed an exercise where he identified five job titles at each company where he argued that there was substantial variation in pay between the highest- and lowest-paid workers within each title.[66] Similarly, he identified a single job title at Sony for which some employees appeared to receive raises while other employees saw their compensation fall sharply.[67] He also examined compensation changes over time for three job titles at DreamWorks and found that these three job titles did not experience simultaneous compensation changes.[68]

The Defendants' expert also argued that because of the structure of the labor market for animation workers, class members did not require cold calls to obtain information about market wages. In particular, he asserted that because many class members were members of unions, the result of union compensation surveys were available to all class members. Additionally, he argued, that because the union engaged in collective bargaining, union executives were well-informed about compensation in the animation and related industries and took steps to disseminate this information to union members. The function of unions as an alternative source of compensation information, the Defendants' expert argued, meant that cold calls were not necessary to spread compensation information to class members.[69]

Additionally, the Defendants' expert argued that many animation workers were employed on a short-term project basis. Because of this, many class members looked

---

65 *Ibid.* at 49:1-5.

66 *Ibid.* at 49:27-50:3.

67 *Ibid.* at 50:3-5. The Plaintiffs' expert examined these claims and found that the Defendants' expert failed to account for overtime hours worked, so that the Defendants' expert identified changes in compensation that were unrelated to changes in employees' pay.

68 *Ibid.* at 50:6-9. The Plaintiffs' expert examined this analysis and found that it did not account for employee turnover, nor did it account for human capital factors such as age and experience. He examined the compensation trends for these job titles after controlling for employee turnover and found that they followed similar trends over time.

69 *Ibid.* at 51:2-4.

for work frequently during the class period, and there was a high degree of "cross-hiring" where a worker was employed by multiple Defendants during the course of the class period.[70] Indeed, two of the three named Plaintiffs worked for multiple Defendants during the class period.[71]

In addition to the criticisms above, the Defendants' expert criticized the Plaintiffs' expert's statistical and econometric analyses in several ways. What follows is a condensation of the Defendants' primary criticisms of the Plaintiffs' expert's report. This discussion elides many of the technical details for the sake of brevity.

The Defendants' expert criticized the Plaintiff's human capital regressions (which explained a large proportion of the variation in compensation stemming from standard controls, including job titles) as being driven by differences across job titles, inclusion of which he argued was improper, and which served to improperly inflate the measured effect. He also argued that the variables used by Ashenfelter in his human capital model would show that all industries, and the economy as a whole, exhibit a semi-rigid compensation structure.[72]

Additionally, the Defendants' expert claimed that because the average compensation at each Defendant did not increase after the end of the alleged conspiracy, this is evidence that the Plaintiff's regression analysis cannot show that compensation was suppressed during the alleged conspiracy. However, this claim was based on taking the sum of total compensation for all class members at each Defendant in each year divided by the number of class members at that Defendant, and did reflect widespread compensation decreases for individual employees.[73]

The Defendants' expert criticized the Plaintiffs' damages analysis in several ways. In particular, the Defendants' expert argued that the Plaintiffs' use of post-conspiracy benchmark period was inappropriate; that the way that the Plaintiffs' analysis accounted for Defendants to enter the alleged conspiracy over time was inappropriate, that the post-conspiracy period should have begun a year earlier than the Plaintiffs' expert's analysis allowed, and that the Plaintiff's expert's model did not properly account for increased market concentration due to mergers of Disney and Pixar in 2006, and between Disney and Lucasfilm in 2012.

The Defendants' expert criticized the Plaintiffs' expert for not controlling for the effects of the *High-Tech* conspiracy, which shared two members (Pixar and Lucasfilm)

---

70 *Ibid.* at 51:5-11.

71 Robert Nitsch worked for Sony Pictures Imageworks in 2004 and DreamWorks from 2007-2011. Georgia Cano worked for Walt Disney Feature Animation from 2004 to 2005, and IMD in 2010. *Ibid.* at 3:8-11.

72 *Ibid.* at 52:16-22. In reply, the Plaintiff's expert argued, and the court agreed, that the fact that job titles explain a large portion of variation in compensation supports rather than undermines the Plaintiffs' conclusions, because it shows that the Defendants had compensation structures that enforced internal equity. He also asserted that it was unremarkable that most companies would exhibit rigid pay structures because "most companies in most industries pay their employees based on a formal salary structure" and his analyses merely confirmed that the Defendants participated in such an industry. *Ibid.* at 52:23-53:6.

73 *Ibid.* at 57:24-58:4.

in common with the animation workers' conspiracy, and which covered an overlapping time period. He also argued that under the Plaintiffs' theory, even before Defendants joined the alleged conspiracy, they were part of the competitive fringe and were paying lower compensation than they would have absent a conspiracy. Undercompensation at Pixar and Lucasfilm that resulted from the *High-Tech* conspiracy would have led to under-compensation at the animation studios, even in the absence of a separate conspiracy among the animation studios.

The Court disagreed with this argument, finding that "there are significant differences between the proposed class in the [animation workers] case and the *High-Tech* class members."[74] Furthermore, the Court found that the Defendants' argument that any undercompensation to class members in the animation workers case was caused by the *High-Tech* conspiracy and not by any wrongdoing from Defendants was undermined by substantial evidence from the Plaintiffs that the animation studio Defendants colluded to suppress class members' compensation and that this collusion had a classwide impact.[75]

## V. OUTCOME

The Court ruled in favor of certifying the Plaintiffs' class on May 25, 2016. Between March 2016 and January 2017, each of the Defendants reached settlements with the Plaintiffs; collectively the Defendants paid a total of $168.95 million.[76] The last of these settlements was approved on June 5, 2017.

No Defendants ever acknowledged wrongdoing.

## VI. CONCLUSIONS

The antitrust agencies have indicated that they are taking seriously the threat of collusion in labor markets. In October 2016, the DOJ and FTC published "Antitrust Guidance for Human Resources Professionals."[77] This document includes guidance that "An individual is likely breaking the antitrust laws if he or she:

- agrees with individual(s) at another company about employee salary or other terms of compensation, either at a specific level or within a range (so-called wage-fixing agreements), or
- agrees with individual(s) at another company to refuse to solicit or hire that other company's employees (so-called "no-poaching agreements").

In this guidance, the DOJ stated its intention to "proceed criminally against naked wage fixing or no-poaching agreements"; it noted that "[t]hese types of agreements

---

74 *Ibid.* 61:15-17.

75 *Ibid.* 62:1-5.

76 Blue Sky settled for $5.95 million; Sony settled for $13 million; DreamWorks settled for $50 million; and Disney settled for $100 million (which covered claims against Disney, Pixar, Lucasfilm, and IMD).

77 https://www.justice.gov/atr/file/903511/download.

eliminate competition in the same irredeemable way as agreements to fix product prices or allocate customers, which have traditionally been criminally investigated as hardcore cartel conduct."[78]

Indeed, recently the DOJ has brought several criminal cases based on alleged no-poach conspiracies, including in the healthcare[79] and aerospace industries.[80] However, as of September 2022, the DOJ had yet to secure a criminal conviction for violations of the antitrust laws in any of these cases.[81]

There is an irony to the animation workers' case: During and after the period of the alleged conspiracy, Disney purchased many of its labor market competitors – including several co-Defendants. Disney acquired Pixar in 2006, Lucasfilm in 2012, and Blue Sky in 2019 (as part of Disney's acquisition of 21st Century Fox). Of course, once these studios are owned in common, then the practices that were the basis for this litigation would no longer be illegal, as they would take place within the single, larger entity.

There are several recent papers that have considered the effect of the role of concentration in labor markets on wages. Azar, Marinescu & Steinbaum (2022) examine 8,000 geographic-occupational labor markets in the U.S., and find that moving from the 25th percentile to 75th percentile of market concentration is associated with a five to 17 percent decline in posted wages; Benmelech, Bergman & Kim (2022) analyze how monopsony power affects wage behavior in the U.S. manufacturing sector, and finds that the elasticity of wages with respect to productivity growth is smaller in more concentrated markets. Rinz (2022) develops measures of market concentration and uses individual earnings data from income tax records to study the effect of market concentration on wages. Rinz finds that, on average, measures of local concentration of the stock of employment by industry and commuting zone have declined in the United States.[82] Yeh et al. (2022) uses administrative data to estimate plant-level wage markdowns, and find that most manufacturing plants operate in a monopsonistic environment, and that the aggregate markdown decreased between the 1970s and the early 2000s but has been increasing over the last two decades. Arnold (2020) used matched employer-employee data to estimate the direct and indirect effects of mergers and acquisitions on worker outcomes. Arnold finds that the implied elasticity of earnings with respect to local concentration is 0.22; this implies that relative to

---

78 Antitrust Guidance at p. 4.

79 *U.S. v. DaVita Inc, and Kent Thiry*, 1:21-cr-00229RBJ; *U.S. v. Surgical Care Affiliates, LLC and SCAI Holdings, LLC*, 3:21-cr-00011-L; *U.S. v. Neeraj Jindal*, 4:20-cr-00358-ALM-KPJ.

80 *U.S. v. Mahesh Patel et al.*, 3:21-cr-00220-VAB.

81 In *Jindal*, the jury found the Defendants not guilty of the alleged conspiracy, but they were found guilty of obstruction of justice after lying to FTC officials. In *DaVita*, both DaVita and its CEO were acquitted on all counts. https://www.natlawreview.com/article/doj-faces-two-strikeouts-first-healthcare-wage-fixing-and-no-poach-prosecutions.

82 The aforementioned three papers, along with eight others, were originally presented at the Sundance Conference on Monopsony in Labor Markets and were compiled into a special issue of the Journal of Human Resources: "Monopsony in the Labor Market: New Empirical Results and New Public Policies."

a competitive benchmark, local concentration reduces wages by approximately four to five percent. Prager & Schmitt (2021) examine wage growth following employer consolidation following hospital mergers. They find evidence of reduced wage growth in cases where the increase in market concentration resulting from the merger is large, and when workers' skills are industry-specific. They also find that wage growth slowdowns are attenuated in labor markets with strong labor unions.

This growing literature suggests the possible importance of merger policy for labor market competition. The DOJ and the FTC have begun investigating these issues. A Public Workshop on Competition in Labor Markets summarized many of the key issues.[83] Whether public policy toward mergers and their effect on labor market competition, which is governed by the regulatory authority enabled by the Clayton Act, will change is unclear.

## APPENDIX: EMPIRICAL ANALYSIS OF COMPENSATION

The economics experts who examined the effect of the alleged conspiracy on compensation reviewed payroll data from 2001-2013 from each of the Defendants. As Pixar and Lucasfilm were alleged to have been engaged in a non-solicitation conspiracy since the 1980's, benchmark data from a true "pre-conspiracy" period did not exist. Therefore, in order to determine the amount by which compensation was reduced, the Plaintiffs' expert performed a "during-after" regression analysis, using data from after the conspiracy is believed to have ended as a benchmark. The DOJ began its investigation into the *High-Tech* conspiracy (which included Pixar and Lucasfilm) and filed its complaint in 2010. The Plaintiffs chose the period 2011-2013 as the post-conspiracy benchmark because by 2011 any wage suppressing effects of the alleged conspiracy were likely to have dissipated.[84]

This regression used individual-level compensation data from 2001 through 2013. The regression explains class members' total (log) compensation using a variety of individual, firm, and economy-wide effects:

- Conspiracy Effect: How the Defendants' challenged conduct impacted annual compensation over time, allowing for this effect to vary as additional Defendants entered the alleged conspiracy.[85]
- Employee Effects: How compensation varies across workers based on their individual characteristics. These variables include each employee in each

---

[83] www.justice.gov/atr/events/public.

[84] Finkelstein et al. (1983) write that a post-conspiracy period is commonly used, "since the ending of the conspiracy is usually a fairly dramatic event."

[85] The conspiracy periods were as follows: Conspiracy 2001-2002 (measures the conspiracy effect limited to Pixar and Lucasfilm, participants in the alleged conspiracy in 2001 and 2002 ); Conspiracy 2003 (Adds DreamWorks); Conspiracy 2004 (Adds Disney and Sony); Conspiracy 2005-2006 (Adds Blue Sky. Because no additional Defendants were alleged to have joined in 2006, the effect is assumed to be the same in 2005 and 2006); Conspiracy 2007-2008 (Adds IMD). Because no additional Defendants were alleged to have joined in 2008, the effect is assumed to be the same in 2007 and 2008); Conspiracy 2009 (The final year of the alleged conspiracy, when DOJ began its investigation into High Tech); Wind Down 2010.

year; age squared; tenure with current employer squared; share of year worked; previous year's total compensation; and an employer-employee fixed effect.
- Employer Effects: How compensation varies across firms. These variables include for each Defendant in each year: total number of employees; annual worldwide box office revenue; and the ratio of the number of new in-class hires to the previous year's total in-class employment.
- Macroeconomic Effects: How compensation varies according to changes in the broader economy. These variables include: growth in U.S. GDP; the consumer price index; and a time trend.

The alleged conspiracy was a dynamic process, with the Defendants' entering at different times. As the Defendants entered the alleged conspiracy, the effect of the conspiracy on class members' compensation may have changed. Accordingly, the Plaintiffs' expert allowed the effect of the alleged conspiracy to vary over time, as new members joined. These time periods were based on the Plaintiffs' understanding of the record. There were six separate conspiracy control variables that spanned one to two years each.[86] The post-conspiracy benchmark period was 2011-2013.

The results of this regression are presented in Table 1.[87] The result of this analysis was that, in all periods, compensation was suppressed relative to the post-conspiracy benchmark, and this suppression was statistically significant in each period. The magnitude of this estimated compensation suppression varied over time (with the number of Defendants that participated in the alleged conspiracy) and ranged from 5 to 36 log points (5 percent to 31 percent).[88]

---

[86] The conspiracy periods were as follows: Conspiracy 2001-2002 (measures the conspiracy effect limited to Pixar and Lucasfilm, participants in the alleged conspiracy in 2001 and 2002 ); Conspiracy 2003 (Adds DreamWorks); Conspiracy 2004 (Adds Disney and Sony); Conspiracy 2005-2006 (Adds Blue Sky. Because no additional Defendants were alleged to have joined in 2006, the effect is assumed to be the same in 2005 and 2006); Conspiracy 2007-2008 (Adds IMD). Because no additional Defendants were alleged to have joined in 2008, the effect is assumed to be the same in 2007 and 2008); Conspiracy 2009 (The final year of the alleged conspiracy, when DOJ began its investigation into High Tech); Wind Down 2010.

[87] This table is based on Table 7R from the (Redacted) Reply Report of Orley Ashenfelter, April 14, 2016.

[88] *Ibid.* at 56:12-21.

## Table 1: Estimation of Undercompensation of Class Members over the Class Period

| | | |
|---|---:|---:|
| Conspiracy_2001-2002 | -0.367 | -7.28 |
| Conspiracy_2003 | -0.263 | -5.71 |
| Conspiracy_2004 | -0.266 | -6.54 |
| Conspiracy_2005-2006 | -0.097 | -3.43 |
| Conspiracy_2007-2008 | -0.100 | -5.97 |
| Conspiracy_2009 | -0.206 | -8.25 |
| Conspiracy_2010 | -0.051 | -5.36 |
| Log(total annual comp in year t-1) | 0.166 | 6.28 |
| Age^2 | -0.001 | -8.49 |
| Tenure^2 | 0.000 | -0.56 |
| Year (trend) | 0.047 | 3.99 |
| Log(box office revenue) | 0.001 | 6.82 |
| Log(new hires by defendant/total employment by defendant) | 0.007 | 1.70 |
| Log(GDP/GDP in [t-1] | -2.156 | -5.59 |
| Log(total employment by defendant) | -0.091 | -6.34 |
| Log(CPI) | 1.188 | 2.08 |
| Log(share of year employed) | 0.985 | 65.47 |
| Constant | -89.862 | -4.14 |
| | | |
| No of Observations | 40,877 | |
| R^2 | 0.89 | |

**Note:** Total annual compensation includes each individual's base earnings, overtime pay, performance pay (such as bonus), and stock grants and options. Valuations of stock grants are from company annual reports.

**Source:** Redacted Reply Report of Orley Ashenfelter
In Connection With Animation Workers' Antitrust Litigation
April 14, 2016
Table 7R

# REFERENCES

Arnold, David (2020). "Mergers and Acquisitions, Local Labor Market Concentration, and Worker Outcomes." Working Paper. https://ssrn.com/abstract=3476369.

Azar, José, Ioana Marinescu & Marshall Steinbaum (2022). "Labor Market Concentration." *Journal of Human Resources* 57:S167-S199.

Benmelech, Efraim, Nittai K. Bergman & Hyunseob Kim (2022). "Strong Employers and Weak Employees: How Does Employer Concentration Affect Wages?" *Journal of Human Resources* 57:S200-S250.

Persons, Ellen H., Herbert F. Allen & Alexandra G. Brooks. "DOJ Faces Two Strikeouts in First Health Care Wage-Fixing and 'No-Poach' Prosecutions." National Law Review. April 20, 2022. https://www.natlawreview.com/article/doj-faces-two-strikeouts-first-health-care-wage-fixing-and-no-poach-prosecutions.

Prager, Elena & Matt Schmitt (2021). "Employer Consolidation and Wages: Evidence from Hospitals." American Economic Review. 111:12 pp. 397-427.

Rinz, Kevin (2022). "Labor Market Concentration, Earnings, and Inequality." *Journal of Human Resources* 57:S251-S283.

Robert A. Nitsch et al., v. DreamWorks Animation SKG INC., et al., Civil Action No. 14-CV-04062-LHK, *Order Granting-in-Part and Denying-in-Part Plaintiffs' Motion for Class Certification*. United States District Court, Northern District of California, San Jose Division.

United States v. Adobe Systems, Inc., Apple, Inc., Google Inc., Intel Corporation, Intuit, Inc., and Pixar, Civil Action No. 1:10-cv-01629, *Complaint*. United States District Court for the District of Columbia.

United States v. Lucasfilm LTD., Civil Action No. 1:10-CV-02220, *Complaint*. United States District Court for the District of Columbia.

U.S. Department of Justice and the Federal Trade Commission (1996). *Statements of Antitrust Enforcement Policy in Health Care*. https://www.ftc.gov/system/files/attachments/competition-policy-guidance/statements_of_antitrust_enforcement_policy_in_health_care_august_1996.pdf.

U.S. Department of Justice, Antitrust Division and the Federal Trade Commission (2016). *Antitrust Guidance for Human Resources Professionals*. https://www.justice.gov/atr/file/903511/download.

Yeh, Chen, Claudia Macaluso & Brad Hershbein (2022). "Monopsony in the U.S. Labor Market." *American Economic Review* 112:7 2-99-2138.

## CHAPTER 18
# Can Four Traders Fix the Price of Money? The Euro-U.S. Dollar Antitrust Litigation

*By Edward A. Snyder*[1]

## I. INTRODUCTION

Four London-based traders participated in a Bloomberg Chat over the period December 2007 to January 2013: a period of more than 1300 trading days. These lead traders of foreign exchange ("FX") worked for Barclays, Citibank, JPMorgan Chase, and UBS.[2] The bulk of their FX trading involved euros and U.S. dollars. Their daily chats were filled with spritely terms, such as: "building ammo"; "double teaming"; "banging the fix" and "clearing the filth." Each of these phrases corresponded to different trading strategies. Self-described as "the cartel," the traders kept the chat closed to others.

After *Bloomberg News* in June 2013 reported about "the cartel" and their ongoing communications, the four traders were accused of having entered into an illegal agreement to fix the price of money by the United States Department of Justice ("DOJ"), the United States Department of the Treasury ("DOT"), the United Kingdom's Financial Conduct Authority ("FCA"), and other government agencies around the world.[3] The phrase describing the allegations as an attempt to "fix the price of money" is rhetorical, but is not a complete mischaracterization. As the economy become more global in the last century, a wide range of parties began trading currencies in massive volumes every day. In the broad FX market, the world's most important currency pair

---

1 I served as a consulting expert for defendants in the U.S. Department of Justice's criminal cases against individual traders and as a testifying expert for defendants in the civil cases against individual traders brought by the U.S. Department of the Treasury.

2 Christopher Ashton worked for Barclays; Rohan Ramchandani worked for Citibank; Richard Usher worked for JPMorgan; and Matthew Gardiner worked for both Barclays and UBS.

3 The criminal indictments against individual traders were filed on January 10, 2017. Rf. *United States of America v. Richard Usher, Rohan Ramchandani, and Christopher Ashton*, Docket # 09-24-2018, 17 Cr. 19 (RMB) United States District Court, Southern District of New York. I refer to these as the "DOJ Criminal Case." The DOT filed civil claims against Richard Usher and Rohan Ramchandani on January 11, 2017, *In the Matter of Richard Usher*, United States of America, Department of the Treasury, Office of the Comptroller of the Currency. The DOT filed Amended Notice of Charges, OCC AA-EC-2017-3 against Ramchandani and Usher on August 8, 2020. These filings will be referred to as the "DOT Civil Case." As will be explained below, the UK's Serious Fraud Office investigated "the cartel" but decided against proceeding with criminal charges; the UK's Financial Conduct Authority investigated and imposed large fines on the banks.

is euros and dollars. In addition, according to the Bank for International Settlements, the dollar was on one side of 87 percent of all global FX transactions in 2010-2012.[4] The core allegations by governments and other Plaintiffs were that the traders "coordinated their trading by withholding certain bids and offers" and "influenced the EUR/USD trades and the daily reference rates for this currency pair."[5]

This trans-Atlantic litigation is a great medium for learning about core economic concepts that underlie price fixing claims:

i. Were the traders' horizontal competitors or were they in vertical relationships?
ii. Did their daily exchanges of information constitute price fixing?
iii. Did the traders have market power?

Indeed, each of these questions is central to the Plaintiffs' claims and to the Defense arguments. This litigation is also a great medium for learning about FX markets and the institutions that facilitate trading, and why claims that are based on the same allegations can result in starkly different outcomes. With regard to the latter, the actual outcomes in this matter included: (i) banks' paying staggering amounts to settle claims and pleading guilty to criminal charges that were brought against them; but also (ii) outright acquittals of the individual traders who were charged with criminal conduct by the U.S. Department of Justice and an abrupt dismissal of the civil charges against them that were brought by the U.S. Department of Treasury.

This Chapter is organized as follows: Section II provides background that demystifies FX trading and explains what traders actually do. Section III provides details about the claims that were made against the four traders and summarizes information on the outcomes of the litigation. Sections IV and V present the arguments in favor of the Plaintiffs and of the Defendants. Section VI provides my reflections on the litigation and what I learned about the core economic issues identified above.

## II. THE BASICS OF EXCHANGE RATES

Foreign Exchange ("FX") trading – the context in which the price-fixing allegations were made – has some distinctive features: The prices of euros and U.S. dollars are quoted in precise ratios. It takes some getting used to, but the currency in the numerator is the *base currency*. For example, on March 31, 2022, the EUR/USD rate was 1.1007, which means that a single euro could buy $1.1007. The fourth digit to the right of the decimal point is referred to as a "pip": a "price interest point." On the following day, April 1, 2022, the EUR/USD rate rose to 1.1049, which means that the price of euros relative to dollars rose by 42 pips.

Due to fears of a European recession and the toll of the war in Ukraine, the euro lost value in subsequent months and, as of July 2022, the two currencies were near parity: a ratio that is very close to 1. This is in sharp contrast to July 2008 when the EUR/USD peaked at 1.6038. As suggested by these day-to-day and longer-term

---

[4] 2013 Triennial Bank Survey, *Bank for International Settlements*, table 2.
[5] DOT Civil Case, paragraph 22.

changes, the EUR/USD exchange rate responds to changes in supply and demand for the underlying currencies. Just as oceans respond to currents, tides, storms, and weather, trading of euros and dollars responds to global forces that include: macroeconomic developments; changes in global trade and investment; and actions by global businesses.[6] During periods of falling demand for euros, the EUR/USD rate must fall to bring the market into equilibrium.[7]

The daily volumes of FX trading are massive. According to the *Bank of International Settlements*, daily trading volumes on public forums such as the Electronic Broking Services ("EBS") were consistently over $2 trillion in April 2013. That figure does not, however, include trading on bank platforms and large private transactions organized by brokers.[8] According to one testifying expert, the total FX trading reached $5.3 trillion per day during this period.[9] How much of that massive volume was trading of euros and U.S. dollars? A conservative estimate of 25 percent would put the daily total volume of euro-dollar trades well above $1.3 trillion during the time period when the individual traders engaged in their daily chats. There is no doubt, therefore, that the four traders accused of price-fixing were operating in a vast market in which even tiny changes in the EUR/USD exchange rate corresponded to substantial amounts. For example, if $15 billion of euros and dollars were traded during an interval of a few minutes on a given trading day, a one pip difference corresponds to a difference of $1.5 million.

## A. Participants, Trading Venues, and "Fixes"

FX participants include corporations and businesses, central banks, commercial banks, pension funds, asset managers, hedge funds, high frequency traders,[10] and other financial institutions. Corporations frequently buy and sell currencies to finance their operations and investments. A hedge fund may trade currencies based on its assessments of macroeconomic conditions in the EU and U.S. High-frequency traders use sophisticated algorithms to trade almost instantaneously in response to changes in supply and demand, and price.

There is no common or central marketplace for euro-dollar trading. Instead, trades of these two currencies are executed "over the counter" across locations – *e.g.*, London, New York, Hong Kong, Singapore – by a variety of means, including electronic platforms such as Electronic Broking Services ("EBS"), as well as single bank

---

6 For example, during the Greek debt crisis in 2012, demand for euros fluctuated wildly as news regarding the European Union bailout came out. *See, e.g.*, "Eurozone approves new $173B bailout for Greece," *CNN*, February 21, 2012, *available at* https://www.cnn.com/2012/02/20/business/greece-bailout/index.html.

7 The U.S. has allowed the value of the dollar to float against other currencies since 1973.

8 For more detail how FX trading is organized, *see* Rime & Schrimpf, 2013.

9 Testimony of David DeRosa, October 11, 2013, p. 161:21-22 of DOJ criminal case trial transcript.

10 High frequency trading firms, *e.g.*, Jump Trading and Tower Research, use algorithms to speculate and to identify potential arbitrage opportunities. Such algorithmic trading accounted for the majority of trades on the EBS platform during the relevant period.

platforms, multi-bank platforms, private trading that is facilitated by voice communications, and trades that are initiated in chat rooms. At any given point in time during trading days, individual participants can access different trading venues across the globe. However, there are identifiable peak times for trading by location.

Some participants use traders at major banks to find counterparties for their desired trades. In the case of large trades, traders may break up the trade into smaller pieces or offer a slightly better price to attract counterparties. As a result, the spreads between what the parties pay and receive – and what the trader pockets – vary with the characteristics of the trade. Importantly, some participants in FX markets choose to trade at reference prices, known as "fixes." Doing so makes it easy to find parties on the other side and thereby minimizes spreads. Important customers of major banks usually have their trades executed as a complimentary service. Hence, the traders who work for major banks earn no spreads on such trades.

Two independent entities – the European Central Bank ("ECB") and WM/Reuters ("WMR") – post daily reference prices.[11] During the time period in question, the ECB set its fix at 1:15 p.m. London time, and the WMR fix was set at 4 p.m.: the end of the trading day in London.[12] The underlying methodologies that were used by the ECB and WMR to set their reference prices were then, and remain, proprietary. While the ECB approach is more subjective, WMR samples actual trades during the 61 seconds leading up to its 4 p.m. fix. Likely a response to the alleged price fixing, the ECB announced in 2015 that its fixes were for "information-only" and "strongly discouraged" participants from using the reference prices for actual transactions.[13]

## B. Traders' Objectives

The main points of this subsection are that traders who receive flows of large orders constantly seek liquidity and "market color." Liquidity refers to the availability of potential counterparties with whom trades can be made. Market color is information about market developments and how prices are trending. for trades. Each is fundamental to their ability to execute trades without taking on substantial risks and without relying on electronic exchanges such as EBS that are good venues for smaller trades but not for large trades. The usual objective of minimizing risks can give way, however, to traders' taking on risk when they are confident that the EUR/USD is going to move in one direction or the other. Returning to the oceans metaphor, traders occasionally expect a wave and are willing to ride it. A trader who believes that the EUR/USD exchange rate is going to fall for the next two hours can decide to sell euros and buy dollars. If right, holding a net position in favor of dollars will generate profits.

To develop a clear understanding of these points, let us take the point of view of traders at major banks and consider the challenges that they face. These traders

---

11 Expert Testimony of Michael Melvin, PhD, in the DOJ and DOT cases.
12 Amended Notice of Charges – Ramchandani & Usher, paragraph 15.
13 European Central Bank. 2022. "ECB Introduces Changes to Euro Foreign Exchange Reference Rates." https://www.ecb.europa.eu/press/pr/date/2015/html/pr151207.en.html.

receive exogenous flows of large trades from major customers. As orders come in, it is possible that the amount of euros and dollars to be sold will equal the amounts to be bought. In that nirvana, the trader can just match the orders on the order book and then do a deep dive into the latest Premier League news. However, a balanced flow from the bank's order book is a rarity, and net differences in order flows can be large and can change during the trading day.

Given imbalances in orders, a major objective for traders is to end each trading day "flat": They carry no inventory of either euros or dollars into the next trading day. The reason is clear: If a trader has $175 million on the books and the market moves 5 pips against the dollar between the close of trading that day and the opening the next trading day, then the trader has a loss of $75,000. As a result, throughout a given trading day, traders constantly seek *liquidity*, which means identifying parties to take the other side of the trades that they must execute. If various individual traders' imbalances are random as opposed to being part of a systematic market move, then traders experience a version of the nirvana above. By checking with others, individual traders are likely to find matching orders and thereby make progress toward their objective of being flat by the end of the day.

Of course, an individual trader who has a big imbalance in orders does not know whether that imbalance is a random event or part of a systematic move in the market. This fundamental uncertainty underlies the demand by traders for information about market developments and what other potential counterparties are experiencing. If most traders are experiencing systematic price movements – a tide going out as opposed to temporary choppiness – then individual traders need to execute trades to reduce whatever imbalances they have.

For example, if a trader has €5 million to sell and the EUR/USD rate is falling and is expected to continue to fall, selling promptly is likely to be better than hoping that the trend will reverse. As a result, in addition to seeking liquidity, traders also seek information. To obtain "market color," traders and other market participants ask versions of these questions: "Can you buy what I need to sell? Is your order imbalance tilted like mine? Do you see the same shifts in demand and supply for euros and dollars?"

Given their objectives related to liquidity and market color, traders will want to engage in information exchanges with other traders and knowledgeable market participants. Information exchanges also lead to potentially profitable occasions when a trader will want to "ride the wave" and take on more risk for an expected profit. From the individual trader's point of view, however, there are potential dangers with information exchanges: When searching for a counterparty who needs to buy an unusually large volume of dollars, a trader with that imbalance reveals the nature of the imbalance. In this and many situations that involve purchases of financial securities, such revelations might encourage the recipient of the information to "front run" the trade, which in this case would mean buying dollars based on information received.[14] As a result, traders in FX markets may attempt to limit their information exchanges

---

14 Front Running. 2021. *Corporate Finance Institute*. https://corporatefinanceinstitute.com/resources/knowledge/trading-investing/front-running/.

to a small group of participants whom they trust will not take advantage of the private information they receive. Even with others with whom they exchange information regularly, traders may not be completely transparent about the sizes of the net positions that they hold.

## III. A WIDE RANGE OF LITIGATION OUTCOMES FROM SIMILAR ALLEGATIONS

### A. Leading up to the Allegations

The world of FX trading was quite different not that long ago. In 2005 the UK's central bank – the Bank of England ("BoE") – decided that it would sponsor get-togethers for executives from major banks and their top London-based traders.[15] The central bank's lead FX dealer chaired these *Chief Dealer Meetings*, whose attendees included individual traders in "the cartel."[16] According to minutes of their 2006 and 2008 meetings, the group expressed general concerns about how traders could influence the ECB and WMR daily fixes.[17] But the group made no public statements.

Scrutiny of FX trading and the role of reference prices increased dramatically when the financial markets world realized in April 2012 that the most important interest-rate benchmarks in the world – LIBOR – did not reflect actual credit market conditions.[18] The group attending the Chief Dealer Meetings organized by the BoE took note and discussed the need for extra compliance in connection with the EBS and WMR fixes.[19] Attention to euro-dollar trading heightened in June 2013 when *Bloomberg News* reported that London-based traders were using chatrooms to find counterparties, exchange information, and design trading strategies (Vaughan et al., 2013). Termed "banging the fix," one strategy was to break up large orders – *e.g.*, €200 million – into smaller orders for execution during the 61-second window before the WMR fix. That strategy could influence the fix depending on the sampling technique that was used to by the WMR. With rising concerns about the integrity of FX rates and the roles of lead traders at the major banks, the June 2013 Chief Dealer Meeting

---

15 A class action complaint explained that the quarterly gatherings organized by the Bank of England in 2005 included 11 chief traders active in the London FX market and top Bank of England officials. Rf. *In RE Foreign Exchange Benchmark Rates Antitrust Litigation –Consolidated Amended Class Action Complaint*, ECF Case No. 1:13-cv-07789-LGS, United States District Court, SDNY, March 31, 2014.

16 McGeever, Jamie. 2007. "TIMELINE – The Global FX Rigging Scandal," *Reuters*. Referred to subsequently as the "Reuters Timeline." https://www.reuters.com/article/global-currencies-scandal/timeline-the-global-fx-rigging-scandal-idUKL5N1F14VV.

17 Reuters Timeline.

18 LIBOR stands for London Interbank Offered Rate. The LIBOR reference rates were calculated based on the average of a trimmed sample of submissions by 16 banks. During the period 2008-2009, research by major banks concluding that LIBOR rates were often artificially depressed by 40 basis points (0.4 percent). *See* "European Banks: LIBOR-ABILITY – Quantifying the Risk," *Macquarie Equities Research*, July 31, 2012, and "LIBOR Risk Sizing," *Morgan Stanley Research North America*, July 12, 2012.

19 Reuters Timeline.

was the last gathering organized by the BoE.

## B. The Core Allegations Against the Employer Banks and the Four Traders

The core allegations against Barclays, Citibank, JPMorgan, and UBS and their traders were that during the period December 2007 to December 2013, the chatrooms were used by traders to:

>  i. Coordinate their trading in connection with the ECB and WMR benchmarks and thereby influence the daily reference rates;[20]
> 
> ii. Withhold bids so as to allow a trader who had disclosed an open position to buy or sell without interference;[21] and
> 
> iii. Disclose sensitive information about customer orders.[22]

These allegations were the basis for regulatory and legal actions by governments around the world. With respect to the United Kingdom ("UK") and the U.S., the actions included the following:

> i. Based on a referral by the UK's Financial Conduct Authority, the Serious Fraud Office ("SFO") launched an investigation into price fixing of FX rates by major banks;
>
> ii. UK and U.S. banking regulators filed claims against major banks for sponsoring illegal activity by FX traders;[23]
>
> iii. The DOJ brought civil and criminal cases against major banks, including the four banks (Barclays, Citibank, JPMorgan, and UBS) that employed the four traders in "the cartel";
>
> iv. The DOJ brought criminal cases against three of the four traders in "the cartel"; and
>
> v. The U.S. DOT filed a civil case against two traders in "the cartel," alleging that the traders had fixed prices and engaged in other conduct that harmed their employer banks.

## C. Outcomes

The legal and regulatory actions identified above yielded divergent actions: The UK's SFO, which has the ability to bring criminal charges, closed its 18-month investigation into FX trading in May 2016; the SFO stated that the available evidence "would not meet the evidential test required to mount a prosecution."[24] One might take the cynical view that the SFO recognized that if it had proceeded with

---

20 DOT Civil Case, Amended Notice of Charges, paragraph 22.

21 Amended Notice of Charges, paragraph 22.

22 Amended Notice of Charges, paragraph 23.

23 These regulators include the UK's Financial Conduct Authority and the New York State Department of Financial Services.

24 2016. "SFO closes Forex Investigation." Serious Fraud Office. https://www.sfo.gov.uk/2016/03/15/sfo-closes-forex-investigation/.

criminal prosecution, it would likely have to include employees of the BoE, the country's central bank. After all, it was the BoE that organized the Chief Dealer Meetings.[25]

By the end of 2014, UK and U.S. banking regulators imposed over $10 billion in fines on six banks, citing that the banks had failed to prevent their traders from sharing information and attempting to manipulate FX prices. The fine – $1.77 billion – that was imposed by the FCA was the largest fine in its history (Ridley et al., 2014). The criminal and civil cases that were brought by the DOJ led to settlements, which the DOJ characterized as follows: "Five major banks – Citicorp, JPMorgan Chase & Co., Barclays PLC, The Royal Bank of Scotland plc, and UBS AG – have agreed to plead guilty to felony charges. Citicorp, JPMorgan Chase & Co., Barclays PLC, and The Royal Bank of Scotland plc have agreed to plead guilty to conspiring to manipulate the price of U.S. dollars and euros exchanged in the foreign currency exchange ("FX") spot market and the banks have agreed to pay criminal fines totaling more than $2.5 billion."[26] The felony pleas also included commitments by the banks to implement new rules for how traders could acquire information.

Up to this point in the various proceedings, the regulators and enforcers had won without going to trial. That changed with the criminal antitrust cases that were filed by the DOJ against four individual traders in January 2017. Three members of "the cartel" pled not guilty to the price-fixing allegations and thus forced the government to prove its case in court. The fourth trader entered into a plea agreement with the DOJ and testified against the other three. Despite (a) the testimony of the insider, and (b) a ruling that the DOJ could cite the felony pleas of the four employer banks, the two-week trial in October 2018 did not go well for the government. After a short deliberation, the jury returned "not guilty" verdicts for all three traders.[27]

The case that was filed by the DOT in January 2017 was, in effect, a civil analog to the criminal case that was brought by the DOJ, but with a potentially important difference: The *burden of proof* in criminal cases is "beyond a reasonable doubt." Hence, a jury that was hearing criminal charges could be concerned about conduct but not be convinced that the parties entered into an illegal agreement or intended to fix prices. The burden of proof in civil cases is, by contrast, "preponderance of the evidence."[28] Hence, the DOT had a lower burden of proof. Plus, it was also able to cite the previous felony pleas by the employer banks based on the conduct of their traders. Despite these

---

25 In November 2014, the BoE suspended and fired Martin Mallet: the BoE's major dealer and the person who organized the Chief Dealer meetings. Rf. Reuters Timeline.

26 2015. "Five Major Banks Agree to Parent-Level Guilty Pleas." *U.S. Department of Justice: Office of Public Affairs*. https://www.justice.gov/opa/pr/five-major-banks-agree-parent-level-guilty-pleas.

27 Judgment of Acquittal, *United States v. Usher et al.*, No. 17-cr-19 (S.D.N.Y.), October 26, 2018. See also Brendan Pierson, "London forex traders found not guilty in U.S. rigging case," *Reuters*, October 2018.

28 For an explanation, see "Burden of Proof," *Legal Information Institute: Cornell Law School*, June 2017. https://www.law.cornell.edu/wex/burden_of_proof.

advantages, the DOT case faltered as experts filed their reports and provided deposition testimony. The DOT abruptly dismissed the charges in July 2021 "with prejudice": The dismissal is considered to be "an adjudication on the merits."[29]

## IV. THE PLAINTIFFS' ARGUMENTS

The Plaintiffs' arguments began with two observations: First, the major banks that execute trades on behalf of their clients were horizontal competitors. Second, while hundreds of firms traded euros and dollars regularly, a smaller number of banks accounted for a large share of electronic FX trading during the relevant time period and continue to do so. According to research by the Euromoney Institute, the four banks that employed the four lead traders in "the cartel" – Barclays, Citigroup, JPMorgan, and UBS – had a combined share of electronic FX trading in excess of 40 percent.[30] The four lead traders for these banks, therefore, were directly or indirectly responsible for large volumes of trades that were executed on the EBS electronic platform.

While precise data on shares of euro-dollar trading were not available given the multiplicity of venues, volume-based shares could be calculated for trading that was executed on EBS. According to testimony by a government expert, the four traders frequently accounted for high shares of EBS trades during particular time intervals. Among the examples cited, in the five-minute and one-minute intervals leading up to the ECB fix on December 22, 2008, the four traders had, respectively, a combined 47.2 percent and 73.9 percent of trading volumes.[31]

Hence, the four traders had the ability to influence or fix prices – especially given that they were in constant communications. To support that inference, the government expert documented that on many trading days, the EUR/USD rates changed substantially in the 15 minutes that immediately preceded the WMR fix. For example, on January 31, 2008, the EUR/USD rate moved from 1.4835 15 minutes before the fix to 1.4806 at the fix: a decrease of 29 pips. If the four traders had a net "long" position in dollars – say, $200 million – and waited to trade that position at the fix rate rather than at the rate 15 minutes before the fix, then they would have been able to buy an additional €264,060. There is no doubt, therefore, that the traders had a strong financial incentive to engage in price fixing.

Their chat communications on all days during the alleged conspiracy became part of the evidentiary record. Those communications indicated that the traders coordinated their conduct for the purpose of influencing the EUR/USD rates. At certain times, the traders decided to "clear the filth": executing trades with others outside the

---

29 Rf. "With Prejudice," *Legal Information Institute: Cornell Law School*, September 2021. https://www.law.cornell.edu/wex/with_prejudice.

30 2013 and 2022. "Foreign Exchange Survey," *Euromoney Institute*. https://www.euromoney.com/surveys/foreign-exchange-survey#market-share-by-product. These surveys indicate that over time, several high-frequency trading firms – such as XTX Markets, HC Tech, and Jump Trading – collectively accounted for increasingly high volumes of trade and accounted for more than 20 percent of trading in recent years.

31 Expert Report of Jeremy Tilsner in the DOJ criminal case.

chat. According to the Plaintiffs, such actions were intended to enhance the ability of the traders inside the chat to subsequently influence EUR/USD rates. Yet at other times, the traders would "build ammo" so that an individual trader would increase the volume of trades to be executed during a particular time period.

The practice of "double teaming" is a version of the same practices – except that instead of one trader accumulating a net position, more than one of the traders would do so. Another tactic – "banging the fix," whereby the traders concentrated their trading in the time intervals immediately preceding the fixes – was clearly aimed at influencing prices that immediately preceded the WMR fix and potentially exerting influence on the ECB fix.

Last, the government cited instances where traders deferred trades so that others could execute their trades. The DOJ and the DOT developed a compendium of 37 episodes in which the four traders engaged in such tactics.[32] This documentary evidence was supported in detail by specific communications from the chat.

While the effects on EUR/USD rates could not be measured by experts, the bottom-line results on trader profitability were clearly significant. The massive size of daily euro-dollar trading in combination with even small movements in prices translated into big financial rewards to the members of "the cartel." If there was any doubt that the tactics were effective, the evidentiary record also included celebratory statements in the chat by the four traders about the success of their price-fixing schemes. In one exchange, Richard Usher said, "Best day for as long as I can remember," and Rohan Ramchandani responded, "I'm having best week ever too" (Nguyen & Van Voris, 2018). There is no record of the traders' telephone or pub conversations, but it is likely that their commentary would be yet more explicit.

The other component to the Plaintiffs' argument against the four traders was that their employers admitted to the illegality of the conduct. The four banks entered into felony plea agreements following the DOJ's criminal case against them. Moreover, the major banks paid collectively approximately $10.3 billion in fines to regulators and agencies on both sides of the Atlantic.[33]

Why (the Plaintiffs asked) would banks agree to felony charges and pay such massive amounts if their employees had not colluded to fix prices? According to the Plaintiffs, the case against the four traders was straightforward: They should be convicted, sent to prison, pay large financial penalties, and should not have future opportunities to work in the financial industry.

## V. THE DEFENSE ARGUMENTS

The main Defense arguments were that: (i) the traders were not horizontal competitors; (ii) they engaged in information sharing that helped them do their jobs; and (iii) they did not have market power and, therefore, could not have engaged in any

---

32 For details, *see* the DOT's Amended Notice of Charges, OCC AA-EC-2017-3, Ramchandani, Usher. August 8, 2020.
33 Reuters Timeline.

price fixing. Any efforts to fix prices in this fast-moving context that featured multiple venues could never work because the traders could not monitor the actions of others. It followed, according to the defense, that the traders could not alter EUR/USD rates and thereby create a difference between actual rates and what the rates should have been based on market conditions made no sense: Any such *price impacts* would be exploited immediately by sophisticated traders, including the high-frequency traders using algorithms.

The defense acknowledged that the terms that the traders used to describe various trading tactics were colorful, but claimed that the trading behaviors were motivated by individual self-interest and that their trades did not change underlying supply and demand conditions. As to the felony pleas and fines that were paid by their employers, none of the claims against the banks were adjudicated. The defense, therefore, took the approach of portraying them as settlements that reflected standard settle-versus-litigate decisions.[34]

The Defense started with the first point with respect to the difference between horizontal and vertical relationships in antitrust: While the employer banks are horizontal competitors in many dimensions – *e.g.*, competing for corporate clients – individual traders are not and are instead in vertical relationships: They buy and sell to each other. According to the defense, the traders did not, therefore, have aligned interests. To the contrary, when one trader is selling euros and another is buying, the two have divergent interests. The orders that they receive from sales personnel who are employed by their banks could lead to a need to either buy or sell. The questions that they posed to each other concerned what they had to sell, what they had to buy, and at what prices.

The defense emphasized that this lack of aligned incentives is in sharp contrast to the proto-typical price fixing conspiracy where, for example, major manufacturers of microprocessors all would like to see prices increase. Once it is understood that the traders were in vertical relationships, the presumption that certain conduct is *per se* illegal does not apply; and, instead, the conduct with respect to their information exchanges should be evaluated under the *rule of reason*.[35]

The next major line of defense concerned information exchanges: Given that the traders were tasked with executing trades, two of their primary objectives were to find liquidity and gain insights about market conditions: market color. Even the Plaintiff DOT acknowledged that the individual traders and the employer banks

---

34 A robust literature has developed the frameworks that parties use to decide whether to settle or litigate. The key insights are that litigation is a negative-sum game for the litigating parties – because of legal fees – and that even if a party expects to prevail at trial, the incentive to settle exists. *See* Priest & Klein (1984) and Hughes & Snyder (1998).

35 *See* "Antitrust Laws," 2022. *Legal Information Institute: Cornell Law School*. https://www.law.cornell.edu/wex/antitrust_laws.
  "Per se violations of the Sherman Act include price fixing, bid-rigger, horizontal customer allocation, and territorial allocation agreements. A per se violation requires no further inquiry into the practice's actual effect on the market or the intentions of those individuals who engaged in the practice. All other violations will be analyzed under the Rule of Reason."

were at risk in the numerous time periods between when they executed a trade for a customer and when they were able to enter into an offsetting trade.[36] According to the Defense, information exchanges that advance those objectives do not constitute price-fixing. With these arguments, the Defense sought to appeal to Supreme Court precedent that distinguished price-fixing from potentially lawful activity.[37] Indeed, by having information about potential counterparties and market conditions, traders could execute their trades more efficiently, which in turn benefited market participants.

The third point that was advanced by the Defense – with respect to the exercise of market power – was probably the strongest:[38] The argument goes as follows: The four individual traders did not have the ability to restrict output. To the contrary, their job was to execute trades based on the exogenous flow of orders from the sales desks at their banks.[39] Without the ability to restrict output, they could by definition not exercise market power. A related claim was that the underlying supply and demand conditions also made the exercise of market power by virtually any group of traders in euro-dollar trading a non-starter. Both the supply and demand for euros and dollars were (and are) nearly *perfectly elastic*: Market participants can find a large number of buyers and sellers at the market price; but no individual participant (or even four individual participants) have the ability to charge any higher or lower price – because many others are willing to buy and sell at the market price. Other factors – such as the inability of the members of "the cartel" to monitor the trades of others, the existence of high-frequency traders, and low entry barriers – also indicated that conditions in FX trading did not allow for the exercise of market power.

Importantly, even if the Defense's point about the lack of market power is valid, the question of whether "the cartel" could time their trades to influence prices at particular points in time would remain. The Defense's approach on this more sophisticated issue was to critique the empirical analyses that were offered by the government experts with respect to "market shares." According to the Defense, selecting certain times on certain days when the traders executed their trades does not

---

36 In the charges against Mr. Ramchandani and Mr. Usher, the government made these two statements that are relevant to the risk that arises after the customer order is executed and before an offsetting trade can be made:

"Between the time when the customer accepts the bank's quoted bid or offer and when the trader buys or sells in the market, the bank bears the risk that the price of the currency will move in an unfavorable direction (referred to as an 'open risk' or 'at risk' position). A bank will profit on the customer's order if the average rate at which the trader buys or sells in the market is better than the rate at which the bank has agreed to buy or sell to the customer." (Amended Notice of Charges – Ramchandani, ¶ 13).

"A trader must then buy or sell in the interdealer market prior to or during the fix to fill the customer's order. Here, the trader bears the risk that the price of the fix rate will be unfavorable compared to the average rate at which the trader could buy or sell in the market to fill the customer's fix order." (Amended Notice of Charges – Ramchandani, ¶ 17)

37 *See United States v. U.S. Gypsum Co.*, 438 U.S. 422, 441 n. 16 (1978).

38 *See* Kaplow & Shapiro (2007) for an excellent analysis of market power.

39 The DOT made this very point. Rf. Amended Notice of Charges, ¶ 17.

establish that the traders were aware of when they would account for a substantial amount of trading. To preempt the issues related to influencing the fixes, the Defense emphasized that over 140 traders were active participants on EBS in the time intervals that immediately preceded the daily WMR fixes for the years from 2008 through 2012.

The Defense also pointed to the inability of any expert to present a comprehensive analysis of trading across venues. The share data that were presented by the government experts were for only one trading venue and were not, therefore, shares of euro-dollar trading as a whole. Indeed, according to the Bank of International Settlements in 2010, FX trading on EBS accounted for only 26 percent of all trading, as is shown in Figure 1.

**Figure 1: Many Venues Support FX Trading**

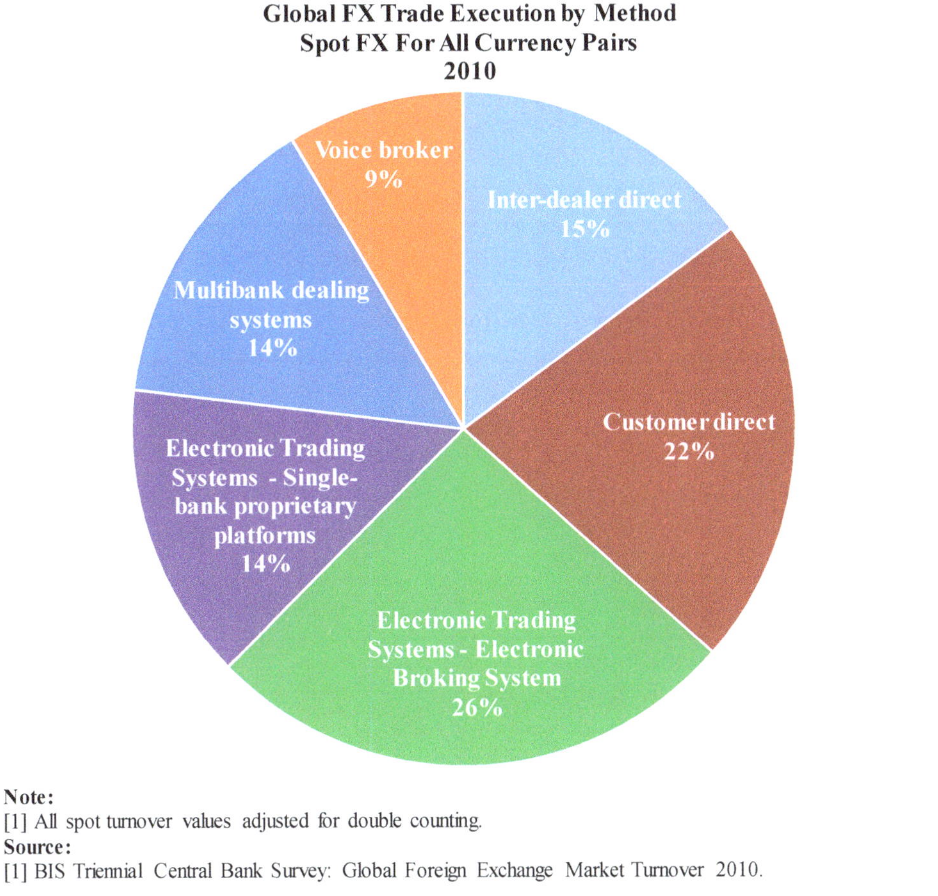

Global FX Trade Execution by Method
Spot FX For All Currency Pairs
2010

- Voice broker 9%
- Inter-dealer direct 15%
- Customer direct 22%
- Electronic Trading Systems - Electronic Broking System 26%
- Electronic Trading Systems - Single-bank proprietary platforms 14%
- Multibank dealing systems 14%

**Note:**
[1] All spot turnover values adjusted for double counting.
**Source:**
[1] BIS Triennial Central Bank Survey: Global Foreign Exchange Market Turnover 2010.

**Source:** Global Foreign Exchange Market Turnover," *Bank of International Settlements Triennial Central Bank Survey*, 2010.

The overarching point for the Defense was that FX participants had an abundance of trading options: across geographies, types of venue, and at different times during trading days. Given the ability of market participants to substitute any these alternatives easily, the four traders did not have market power.

Given the defense arguments, the question of what could be inferred from empirical analyses became central. Despite the availability of second-by-second the trading records on electronic platforms over 1300 trading days, the Plaintiffs did not identify any *price impacts* of the alleged price-fixing, *i.e.*, differences between actual EUR/USD rates and what they should have been or what they would have been if the traders did not participate in their chat.[40] Instead the Government's expert documented 37 "episodes" when FX prices moved and the defendants had high market shares on the EBS platform. The defense argued in response that these did not establish causality and, moreover, they were attempts to: (a) construct a "Catch-22" whereby the traders were accused of wrong-doing no matter what they did; and (b) blame the traders for occasionally trying to make profits by taking on risk. According to the DOJ and the DOT, when traders "cleared the filth" by trading with an external party, they did something wrong. But if they "built ammo" or "double-teamed" – keeping the orders to themselves – they also did something wrong. Hence, according to the government's logic, the traders always did something wrong when they had an imbalance of either euros or dollars.

As to the claims that the traders withheld from trading for short periods of time, those instances actually showed that the four traders in the chat were exchanging valuable information. It is well understood that when parties receive private information, they might engage in "front running": When individual traders in the chat learned that others had large net imbalances, traders could buy or sell ahead of the others based on the expectation that the EUR/USD rate was going to move. But refraining from doing so was not evidence that the traders were acting against their individual interests or somehow illegally coordinating their trading. To the contrary, taking immediate advantage of such information would have risked future information exchanges. Hence, having an understanding that the traders would not front-run increased the future flows of beneficial information.

Last: According to the Defense, the Plaintiffs did not understand the exceptions to the general rule that traders will seek to avoid risk. Based on the market color and liquidity that they receive, traders on occasion develop a view about how EUR/USD rates are likely to move in the immediate term. If we return to the analogy between FX trading and changes in ocean currents: Traders sometimes try to ride the current. When individual traders made such attempts, they were acting in their individual self-interests: They hoped to benefit from market forces and price changes. They were not acting against their self-interest, as would have been true if this had been a collusive agreement.[41] If they made profits from these their attempts and later celebrated them, the correct interpretation should have been that they were realizing returns from their skills and from their efforts to gain useful information.

---

40 Rf. Expert Report of Jeremy Tilsner in the DOJ criminal case.
41 Rf. Carlton & Perloff (2015, Chapter 4).

## VI. CONCLUDING REMARKS

In the early phases of the euro-dollar antitrust litigation, the Plaintiffs succeeded based on a narrow logic: The employer banks were horizontal competitors, and their traders engaged in confidential exchanges of price and volume information. The evidentiary record over 1300 trading days generated a substantial amount of troubling evidence about trader tactics. With this logic and evidence, the Plaintiffs imposed massive fines and secured felony pleas against the banks and one individual trader.

But the DOJ and DOT claims were not grounded in a clear understanding of the relevant economics. The traders were certainly not horizontal competitors in the classic cartel framework. Moreover, the Plaintiffs' arguments did not distinguish between: (i) shifts in supply and demand; and (ii) movements along the supply and demand curves that were caused by the exercise of market power. As students of economics know, both cause price movements; but only the second is price fixing.

This litigation underscores the importance of an ongoing issue in antitrust: the difference between lawful information exchanges and illegal price fixing. When the claims were adjudicated in court, the defense was able to make the point that the traders were in vertical relationships. By explaining their roles, the defense focused on the informational challenges that they faced and their need for liquidity and market color. This exposition put the information exchanges in a different light and was central to the acquittals in the DOJ criminal cases and the dismissal of the DOT civil case. Hence, independent of the legal standard, these two government plaintiffs could not prove their claims.

## REFERENCES

Dagfinn Rime & Andreas Schrimpf (2013). "The anatomy of the global FX market through the lens of the 2013 Triennial Survey." BIS Quarterly Review, p. 27.

Dennis Carlton & Jeffrey Perloff (2015). Modern Industrial Organization. 4th Edition, Global.

James W. Hughes & Edward A. Snyder (1998). "Allocation of Litigation Costs—American and English Rules," The New Palgrave Dictionary of Economics and the Law, ed. Peter Newman, Macmillan Publishers Ltd, vol. 51, pp. 51-56.

Kaplow, Louis, & Carl Shapiro (2007). "Antitrust." in Polinsky, A. Mitchell & Steven Shavell, eds., Handbook of Law and Economics, Vol. 2. Elsevier: New York.

Kirsten Ridley, Joshua Franklin & Aruna Viswanatha (2014). "Regulators fine global banks $4.3 billion in currency investigation," Reuters. https://www.reuters.com/article/us-banks-forex-settlement-cftc/regulators-fine-global-banks-4-3-billion-in-currency-investigation-idUSKCN0IW0E520141112.

Lananh Nguyen & Bob Van Voris (2018). "'I Owe It All to You': Ex-Trader Decodes FX 'Cartel' Tactics," Bloomberg News. https://www.bloomberg.com/news/articles/2018-10-16/-i-owe-it-all-to-you-ex-trader-decodes-fx-cartel-tactics.

Liam Vaughan, Gavin Finch & Ambereen Choudhury (2013). "Traders Said to Rig Currency Rates to Profit Off Clients," Bloomberg News. https://www.bloomberg.com/news/articles/2013-06-12/traders-said-to-rig-currency-rates-to-profit-off-clients.

*United States v. Usher*, 17 Cr. 19 (RMB) (S.D.N.Y. Sep. 24, 2018).

Voigt, Kevin (2012). "Eurozone approves new $173B bailout for Greece." CNN. https://www.cnn.com/2012/02/20/business/greece-bailout/index.html.

Priest, George L & Benjamin Klein. "The Section of Disputes for Litigation," The Journal of Legal Studies, Vol. 13, No.1, January 1984, pp. 1-55.

"Five Major Banks Agree to Parent-Level Guilty Pleas." U.S. Department of Justice: Office of Public Affairs. https://www.justice.gov/opa/pr/five-major-banks-agree-parent-level-guilty-pleas.

2010. Triennial Central Bank Survey. Bank of International Settlements.

2013. "Foreign Exchange Survey," Euromoney Institute.

2017. United States of America, Indictments of Rohan Ramchandani and Richard Usher. United States District Court, Southern District of New York.

2016. "SFO closes Forex Investigation." Serious Fraud Office. https://www.sfo.gov.uk/2016/03/15/sfo-closes-forex-investigation/.

2012. "European Banks: LIBOR-ABILITY – Quantifying the Risk." Macquarie Equities
Research.

2012. "LIBOR Risk Sizing." Morgan Stanley Research North America. http://media.ft.com/cms/d82d6286-cc48-11e1-839a-00144feabdc0.pdf.

2022. "Antitrust Laws." Legal Information Institute: Cornell Law School. https://www.law.cornell.edu/wex/antitrust_laws.

2022. "Foreign Exchange Survey," Euromoney Institute.